Financial Markets and Economic Performance

John E. Silvia

Financial Markets and Economic Performance

A Model for Effective Decision Making

John E. Silvia
Captiva, FL, USA

ISBN 978-3-030-76294-0   ISBN 978-3-030-76295-7 (eBook)
https://doi.org/10.1007/978-3-030-76295-7

© The Editor(s) (if applicable) and The Author(s), under exclusive license to Springer Nature Switzerland AG 2021
This work is subject to copyright. All rights are solely and exclusively licensed by the Publisher, whether the whole or part of the material is concerned, specifically the rights of translation, reprinting, reuse of illustrations, recitation, broadcasting, reproduction on microfilms or in any other physical way, and transmission or information storage and retrieval, electronic adaptation, computer software, or by similar or dissimilar methodology now known or hereafter developed.
The use of general descriptive names, registered names, trademarks, service marks, etc. in this publication does not imply, even in the absence of a specific statement, that such names are exempt from the relevant protective laws and regulations and therefore free for general use.
The publisher, the authors and the editors are safe to assume that the advice and information in this book are believed to be true and accurate at the date of publication. Neither the publisher nor the authors or the editors give a warranty, expressed or implied, with respect to the material contained herein or for any errors or omissions that may have been made. The publisher remains neutral with regard to jurisdictional claims in published maps and institutional affiliations.

This Palgrave Macmillan imprint is published by the registered company Springer Nature Switzerland AG
The registered company address is: Gewerbestrasse 11, 6330 Cham, Switzerland

Dedicated to Tiffani and the four boys (Caesar, Brutus, Diesel and Baron), who were there everyday.

Preface

There are no silos in economics or finance. Yet the segmentation in economic and financial education and, later in post-graduate business and financial markets as well as graduate schools, places decision makers into intellectual silos that produce results without context as the winds of change between silos deliver disastrous results.

This monograph is not a cookbook with a final grand recipe for economic and financial success. The emphasis is on the interactions of each course (chapter) served so that the entire meal (monograph), financial markets and the economy, satisfy a reader's appetite for the appreciation and complexity of the learning experience. Stand-alone recipes, represented by standalone courses such as Macroeconomics, Money and Banking, Econometrics, or Corporate Finance, do not satisfy the appetite.

There is a richness in the capital allocation process directed at economic success. There is also a set of tragedies to accompany success when financial engineering and political actions lead to the misallocation of resources and, ultimately, to economic and financial disaster.

Economics and finance can combine to enhance people's economic lives. But carried too far, the combination can produce tragedy.

The American economy's success through the decades would not have occurred without financial innovation and thoughtful application of economic resources. The nation's growth—and periodic decline—has always been fueled by a combination of (or conflict between) entrepreneurial genius, the creativity of financial engineers and the limits of economic resources.

Progress involves a delicate balance between trends and cycles, excesses, and shortages among the primary markets of goods and financial assets. Disequilibrium, not equilibrium, characterizes economic and financial markets. This monograph examines all these factors and much more.

Understanding the successes and failures of an economy demands a close study of the linkages between real side and market activity. While the real side economy of consumption, investment and government spending is the baseline of undergraduate macroeconomics, finance's central role is often overlooked. Consider, for now, that consumer spending, the C in (C + I + G of undergraduate macroeconomics) is accompanied by credit card, auto and mortgage finance. Business investment, the I, is supplemented by bank loans and corporate bonds. State and federal government spending, the G, is supported by federal debt finance. Coverage of real side activity is often not accompanied by the financial side that supports that activity.

Economic growth moves with credit growth—sometimes ahead, sometimes behind. Despite varying degrees of volatility, business fixed investment and personal consumption move in sync with overall economic growth. Credit spurs growth throughout an economy; lack of credit limits growth. This linkage is even more essential to growth in emerging markets. Patterns of credit allocation and economic activity sometimes operate within different cyclical patterns. Such is the character of the experience.

This monograph focuses on the interactions of four financial markets—those for goods, credit, equity, and foreign exchange and the economic drivers underlying their movements.

Access to finance in each market spurs economic growth. This may appear obvious at first, but the intricacies of the credit and growth linkages provide a fascinating story of trends and cycles and the constant evolution of an economy.

To appreciate the feast set before us, a framework is needed—the interrelationships between the prices of the four markets (equity values, benchmark Treasury rates, corporate profit expectations and equity values, exchange rates) which provides a rationale for the movement of such prices. In addition, the framework highlights the danger of a common approach among many financial and business firms, as well as investors, to analyze markets in isolation—as if each market is its own silo. A focus on private market prices and market fundamentals rests on the logic that these markets reflect these interrelationships and the leading role of prices and price expectations in financial and economic cycles.

In addition, price signals are always moving—markets are in disequilibrium or out of balance. With just four markets, there are many moving parts and prices are constantly adjusting to new information. Economics and finance are dynamics processes—no linear lines here.

Market prices, and their mispricing, provide the disequilibrium/imbalanced forces associated with subsequent economic downdrafts and recoveries. For example, the volatility of commodity (oil, wheat) prices in the 1970s, followed the break in the link between gold and exchange rates in 1971.

The dot-com bubble of 1998–2002 saw a significant mispricing of expected rates of return on equities that brought about an equity market correction and a brief economic recession. In the period leading up to the Great Recession of 2007–2009, mispricing of housing (over counting returns, underpricing risk), drove the boom and then the bust.

An effective model for the demand and supply in any market, such as credit or equity whether by individuals or institutional investors, must reflect a broader set of independent factors. These include: an investor's expectations for economic growth, an interest rate as a discount factor, the wealth of the individual or society (effectively allowing tax policy and inflation in the back door of the model), the expected dollar exchange rate (a benchmark to allow the investor to discern between domestic and foreign opportunities) and, finally, a sense of valuation.

There is no effective alternative to watching the data, following policy turns, and avoiding the anchoring bias that economic values will return to previous benchmarks. This pattern highlights another challenge with market information. Such information reflects a combination of actual economic fundamentals, as well as the expectations of market actors, which can be dashed when future outcomes do not match their expectations. This mismatch is the driver for second-round market pricing and further economic adjustments. Constant action and reaction propels activity and undermines the search for fixed, permanent benchmarks.

In this monograph, I take a broad look at some macro linkages. I review these here simply to show the linkages and the hypotheses underlying such linkages as I consider the baseline patterns of economic growth and inflation, the relative movements in money, and asset prices that provide a perspective on where we are in the economic and credit cycle.Decision-making also requires a disciplined, short list of real and financial indicators. There is no place for single variable explanations. There are no linear patterns of behavior in financial market prices.

Understanding the movement of financial and real goods prices between multiple markets requires an intellectual flexibility that departs from the restrictions imposed by the silos many corporate analysts utilize. Because of such thinking in silos, analysts often fail to notice the movement of prices and their influence between the multiple levels above, below and on the financial, and economic, playing fields of the immediate problem at hand.

Now it is time for a new adventure. What makes markets so fascinating is that we move from one adventure to another. Change is constant and it generates movement in market prices. Commentary must have context. Too much of education is techniques without context. This has been a concern since the time of the scientist and philosopher Francis Bacon. There is precision without purpose—the number of angels on the head of a pin. Too many precise mathematical solutions without a realistic setting of the problem. Often a problem is simply assumed away by excessively restrictive assumptions; this allows a precise but irrelevant result totally devoid of usefulness to decision makers.

Defining signals of change in an economic framework is the next building block for an effective decision-making process. Economic developments reflect movements in both the real economy and financial markets.

Economic and financial decision-making is not just about economic and financial benchmarks. A framework must capture the essence of the story. Thoughtful, economic commentary is based on an initial framework that defines how we see the world and then allows an analyst to incorporate change, make choices, examine the implications of those choices and, if needs be, define a new framework on how the world works. In our first book,[1] we defined this decision-making process because of the frequent practice of defining a framework of price determination but not allowing for possible alterations to that framework. The result is a static, rigid view of the economy without adjusting for change.

This monograph describes two dualities—a duality of the decision-making process and economic and financial market interactions; and a duality in defining the evidence presented and then defining a process to identify change and make choices to alter, or not alter, the framework of price determination in the economy. This is detective work at its best. The nuances and mysteries of the economy and financial markets continue.

Credit has its own cycle, as will be shown in the review of the household, business, and government sectors. Financial markets are interrelated, and the economy and the financial markets are fraternal twins. While so much of current commentary focuses on the economic cycle, it is important to look at the credit cycle and seek hints of possible links between markets.

---

[1] John E. Silvia, Dynamic Economic Decision Making, Wiley, 2011.

Recognizing change in a framework of how the economy works is a foremost challenge to decision makers. There is a tendency to anchor a framework on familiar thought patterns. Yet, in recent years, there have been numerous significant economic and financial changes, which must be incorporated in any framework.

One common strategy in putting together a jigsaw puzzle is to first find the outer pieces that will form a frame for the puzzle and then proceed with putting the inside pieces together following the color and shape clues. For many students of economics and finance, there is a history of learning the theory and gathering the data but leaving the semester without a framework of the subject at hand. The economic clues are all there but what is the framework that ties the theory and data together to solve that mystery? The attack on Pearl Harbor is a case where the clues were there, but nobody put the clues together.

In the following essays, we have provided a framework for examining the data. We focus on stories that puts a picture and an historical context to the data. Not all stories fit perfectly, and some stories do not fit at all. Yet, the cyclical nature of financial markets suggests that stories of the past may provide a framework for decision-making.

Captiva, USA   John E. Silvia

Acknowledgments

From the Movie My Cousin Vinny, 20th Century Fox, 1992

Mona Lisa Vito:	So what's your problem?
Vinny Gambini:	My problem is, I wanted to win my first case without any help from anybody.
Mona Lisa Vito:	Well, I guess that plan's moot.
Vinny Gambini:	Yeah.
Mona Lisa Vito:	You know, this could be a sign of things to come. You win all your cases, but with somebody else's help, right? you win case after case, and then afterwards you have to go up to somebody and you have to say, "thank you."[pause]
Mona Lisa Vito:	Oh my God, what a f*cking nightmare!

Special thanks are due to a long list of long-time friends and colleagues who have contributed to my life-long education in the economy and financial markets. I list here only the usual, and unusual suspects, from many. First thanks to Larry Rothstein and Grace Sauter for their help all along the writing and research process.

For research support, special thanks goes to Brian Lewandowski, Jacob Dubbert, Mariah Coughlin, Ryan Bohren, and Daniel Ortiz. Editorial and research reviews were provided by Matt Burrell, Ken Urbaszewski, Jack Kleinhenz, Carl Weinberg, Chad Morganlander, Brian Belski, Martin Hutchinson, and Ray Stone.

"Inspiration exists, but it has to find you working." Pablo Picasso

The journey behind this book reflects the inspiration of the work of Al Wojnilower, Henry Kaufman, Art Laffer and Rudi Dornbusch, a long-time friend who has passed, as well as the attention given to detail by Steve Slifer, Ray Stone, Ward McCarthy, John Ryding, Mike Lewis, and Maury Harris.

Broader intellectual credit and inspiration remain with Stephen Ambrose, Doris Kearns Goodwin, Jim Grant, Niall Ferguson, Jim Collins, John Steele Gordon, Robert Barro, Richard Neustadt, and Ernest May, and the late Peter Bernstein.

Thanks will always go to my team in the Economics Department at Wells Fargo for their support and insights on the economy.

Final thanks goes to Tula Weis who provided the editorial support to complete this effort.

Contents

1	Why Finance Matters for Economics: The Story of Financing the Railroad	1
2	The Story of the Original Boom and Bust in Western Finance: The Mississippi Bubble	49
3	Price Determination in a Multi-Sector Global Economy	95
4	Credit Allocation and the Role of Interest Rates as the Price of Credit	147
5	Short-Term Credit: Bridging the Next Few Years	183
6	Capital Markets: Financing Business Over the Long Term	215
7	Dynamics of Corporate Finance: What Motivates Change?	251
8	Evolution of Household Finances	275
9	Capital Flows: The Dollar and Global Capital Allocation	307
10	Profits: Rewards and Incentives in an Economic System to Allocate Capital	345
11	Equity Finance: Financing Innovation and Long-Term Household Wealth	371

12	Sovereign Finance: When Economic Growth and Sovereign Debt Are a Mismatch	403
Conclusion		441
Index		445

About the Author

John E. Silvia is currently President of Dynamic Economic Strategy, LLC and focused on financial and economic advisory works, writing a weekly newsletter and presenting economic concepts and commenting on economic issues at several conferences.

Formerly, John was Managing Director and the Chief Economist for Wells Fargo Securities until July 2018. Based in Charlotte, North Carolina, he has held his position since he joined Wachovia, a Wells Fargo predecessor, in 2002 as the company's Chief Economist. John has been a frequent guest on CNBC, Bloomberg (TV and radio), Fox Business and the Nightly Business Report.

John also serves as Economic Advisor to Carolinas Investment Consulting headquartered in Charlotte.

Before his position at Wells, John worked on Capitol Hill as Senior Economist for the U.S. Senate Joint Economic Committee and chief economist for the U.S. Senate Banking, Housing and Urban Affairs Committee. Before that, he was Chief Economist of Kemper Funds and Managing Director of Scudder Kemper Investments, Inc.

John served as the President of the National Association for Business Economics (NABE) in 2015 and was awarded a NABE Fellow Certificate of Recognition in 2011 for outstanding contributions to the business economics profession and leadership among business economists to the nation. He also received several awards for the quality of research in economics.

John holds B.A. and Ph.D. degrees in economics from Northeastern University in Boston and has a master's degree in economics from Brown

University. John's first book, *Dynamic Economic Decision Making*, was published by Wiley in August 2011. His second book, *Economic and Business Forecasting*, was published in 2014, also by Wiley. His third book, *Economic Modeling in the Post Great Recession Era*, was published in 2017 by Wiley.

John is a Certified Business Economist (CBE).

List of Figures

Fig. 1.1	Total credit and economic growth	3
Fig. 1.2	Total credit growth across nations	5
Fig. 1.3	Effective federal funds rate	9
Fig. 1.4	Yen/US dollar exchange rate	10
Fig. 1.5	Earnings-price ratio	11
Fig. 1.6	Real final sales to domestic purchasers	15
Fig. 1.7	Inflation as measured by PCE deflator	16
Fig. 1.8	Ratio of money (M2) to nominal GDP	16
Fig. 1.9	Ratio of NYSE index to nominal GDP	17
Fig. 1.10	Nominal GDP and the US treasury 5 year rate	19
Fig. 1.11	NASDAQ index 2017 to 2021	22
Fig. 2.1	Real final sales to domestic purchasers	56
Fig. 2.2	History of PCE deflator measure of inflation since 1965	57
Fig. 2.3	Financing gap for non-financial corporate business	59
Fig. 2.4	Ratio of corporate debt to nominal GDP	59
Fig. 2.5	High yield option adjusted spreads	61
Fig. 2.6	Net percent of banks tightening credit-real estate	62
Fig. 2.7	Yield curves	63
Fig. 2.8	Ten-year breakeven inflation rate	65
Fig. 2.9	Long term government bond yields	69
Fig. 2.10	Net percent of banks tightening credit-business loans	70
Fig. 2.11	Housing price cycle last thirty years	71
Fig. 2.12	US dollar/British pound exchange rate	78
Fig. 2.13	NYSE equity price index	82
Fig. 2.14	Profit margins	91

Fig. 3.1	Real economic growth and inflation since 1982	97
Fig. 3.2	Real final sales and 2-year Treasury rates	98
Fig. 3.3	Inflation and the yield curve	99
Fig. 3.4	Yen/US dollar exchange rate	101
Fig. 3.5	Five year Treasury rate	102
Fig. 3.6	Global price of copper	103
Fig. 3.7	NYSE equity index	104
Fig. 3.8	Mexican peso/US dollar exchange rate	109
Fig. 3.9	Earnings-price ratio	117
Fig. 3.10	Ted spread	122
Fig. 3.11	US dollar/euro exchange rate	125
Fig. 3.12	Equity index and corporate investment grade rates	126
Fig. 3.13	China: Yuan and share prices	137
Fig. 3.14	Median home sales prices, 1982–2020	138
Fig. 4.1	Long-Term government bond yields	148
Fig. 4.2	Yield curve	149
Fig. 4.3	Term premium on ten-year zero coupon	154
Fig. 4.4	U.S. federal budget balance since 1982	155
Fig. 4.5	Federal Reserve assets since 2004	164
Fig. 4.6	Two-year and Ten-year U.S. Treasury rates post 2012	170
Fig. 4.7	High grade corporate bond rates since 1984	174
Fig. 4.8	History of ten-year and five-year U.S. Treasury rates	174
Fig. 4.9	History of real ten-year and five-year treasury rates	177
Fig. 5.1	Net percent of banks tightening standards on business loans	185
Fig. 5.2	Net percent of banks reporting stronger demand for business loans	186
Fig. 5.3	Bank and non-bank shares of credit supply	187
Fig. 5.4	Credit a nominal GDP growth	188
Fig. 5.5	Ratio of loans to deposits	190
Fig. 5.6	Net percentage of banks increasing spreads on loans	191
Fig. 5.7	Bank loan growth since 1984	195
Fig. 5.8	Bank loans and business equipment spending	196
Fig. 5.9	Net percent of banks tightening standards—CRE loans	198
Fig. 5.10	Net percent of banks reporting stronger demand consumer loans	200
Fig. 5.11	Corporate pre-tax profits as percent of nominal GDP	201
Fig. 5.12	Net interest margins at banks	203
Fig. 5.13	Charge-off rates consumer loans	204
Fig. 5.14	Delinquency rates single-family residences	205
Fig. 5.15	Delinquency rates C&I loans	205
Fig. 6.1	Real Final Sales to Domestic Purchasers	218
Fig. 6.2	Non-financial Corporate Debt as Share of Equity Market Values	223
Fig. 6.3	Ten-Year High Quality Bond Yield	231

Fig. 6.4	Financing Gap: Non-Financial Corporate Business	231
Fig. 6.5	Ratio of Corporate Debt to Nominal GDP	237
Fig. 6.6	Interest Paid as a Share of Operating Surplus	238
Fig. 6.7	Corporate Debt and Fed Funds Rate	239
Fig. 6.8	Unit Labor Costs	243
Fig. 6.9	Manufacturing: Ratio of Short-Term to Long-Term Debt	244
Fig. 7.1	Ratio of corporate debt to nominal GDP	253
Fig. 7.2	Debt as percentage of market value of equity	256
Fig. 7.3	Ten-year high quality corporate bond rate	256
Fig. 7.4	Non-Financial Corporate Debt: Short-term Debt as a Percent of Total Debt	259
Fig. 7.5	Pre-tax corporate profits	260
Fig. 7.6	Tobin's Q	261
Fig. 7.7	Current ratio	263
Fig. 7.8	High yield option adjusted spread	265
Fig. 7.9	Employment cost index	269
Fig. 8.1	Growth of household net worth	277
Fig. 8.2	Consumer credit growth	280
Fig. 8.3	Household assets less liabilities	282
Fig. 8.4	Net percent of banks tighter standards consumer loans	286
Fig. 8.5	Net percent of banks reporting stronger consumer loan demand	287
Fig. 8.6	Loan to value ratio of new car loans	289
Fig. 8.7	Weighted average maturity of car loans	290
Fig. 8.8	New car average finance rate	291
Fig. 8.9	Consumer debt service ratio	292
Fig. 8.10	Financial obligations ratio	293
Fig. 8.11	Charge off rates single family homes	298
Fig. 8.12	Household net worth, income, and the saving rate	298
Fig. 8.13	Delinquency rate—credit cards	303
Fig. 8.14	Delinquency rate—single family homes	304
Fig. 9.1	U.S. Trade balance	311
Fig. 9.2	Exchange and interbank rates	312
Fig. 9.3	Current account	315
Fig. 9.4	Yen/US Dollar exchange rate	320
Fig. 9.5	Export growth-Republic of Korea	320
Fig. 9.6	Swiss franc per US Dollar	322
Fig. 9.7	Foreign direct investment into the U.S.	325
Fig. 10.1	Nominal GDP and pre-tax profits	347
Fig. 10.2	Pre-Tax profits and the corporate AA bond spread	348
Fig. 10.3	Pre-Tax profits as a share of GDP	349
Fig. 10.4	Cost per unit of real GVA	350
Fig. 10.5	Profit per unit of real GVA	351
Fig. 10.6	U.S. exports	354

Fig. 10.7	Trade-Weighted dollar		354
Fig. 10.8	Pre-Tax profit growth		355
Fig. 11.1	Equity indices and nominal GDP		373
Fig. 11.2	Non-financial corporate debt to equity ratio		375
Fig. 11.3	NYSE equity index and real final sales		378
Fig. 11.4	NYSE equity index and high quality bond spot rate		379
Fig. 11.5	Earnings-price ratio		380
Fig. 11.6	Dividend price ratio		381
Fig. 11.7	Profits per unit of GVA		384
Fig. 11.8	Effective corporate income tax rate		385
Fig. 11.9	Unit labor costs		386
Fig. 11.10	Non-financial corporate interest paid		387
Fig. 11.11	Corporate equity market value as a share of net		391
Fig. 11.12	One and five-year ex ante real rates		395
Fig. 12.1	Long-term Euro Government Yields		416
Fig. 12.2	U.S. Federal Budget Surplus/Deficit		424
Fig. 12.3	Yield Curve		425
Fig. 12.4	U.S. 5 Year Treasury Rate and Term Premium		427
Fig. 12.5	Annual Federal Budget Position Since 1984		428
Fig. 12.6	Euro Sovereign Yields 2016 to 2020		433
Fig. 12.7	U.S. Federal Debt Held at Federal Reserve and International Holdings		434
Fig. 12.8	Yen/USD Exchange Rate 2011		435
Fig. 12.9	Three-month Treasury bill yield		436
Fig. 12.10	Five-year Breakeven Inflation		437

List of Tables

Table 4.1	FOMC FFR projections	157
Table 8.1	Shares of household balance sheet	277
Table 8.2	Financial assets by type	280
Table 9.1	Rest of the world buyers of U.S. debt	313
Table 9.2	Rest of the world buyers corporate bonds and equities	314
Table 9.3	Annualized price performance, a in the table (31 December 2013–31 December 2019)	338

1

Why Finance Matters for Economics: The Story of Financing the Railroad

Economics and Finance combine to enhance the economic lives of people. Yet, carried too far, the combination can produce setbacks. Such is the experience of the building of the Transcontinental Railroad.[1]

On the economics, the railroad linked the west coast of the continent, the plains states with their agriculture, and the growing cities and population of the Midwest. Yet the railroad also required a financial vehicle to finance the building of the railroad. Yet, this great achievement and the subsequent expansion of the American economy would not have occurred without financial innovation. The nation's growth—and periodic decline—has always been fueled by a combination (or conflict) of entrepreneurial genius and the creativity of financial engineers. Progress always involves a delicate balance between trends and cycles, excesses, and shortages among the primary markets of goods and financial assets.[2] Disequilibrium, not equilibrium, is the character of the economic and financial markets. This is an examination of all that—and much more. As for setbacks, the problems of the Credit Mobilier became legend.

"For an economic forecast to be relevant it must be combined with a market call.[3]"

---

[1] Nothing Like It in the World, by Stephen E. Ambrose, 2001, Simon & Schuster.
[2] An early introduction of the role of financial assets is found in Karl Brunner and Allan H. Meltzer, "Money, Debt, and Economic Activity," *Journal of Political Economy*, September/October 1972, 80(5).
[3] David Rosenberg, Rules to Guide Research, mimeo.

© The Author(s), under exclusive license to Springer Nature Switzerland AG 2021
J. E. Silvia, *Financial Markets and Economic Performance*,
https://doi.org/10.1007/978-3-030-76295-7_1

Understanding the successes and failures of the economy demands a close examination of the linkages between real-side and market activity. While the real-side economy of consumption, investment, and government spending is the baseline of undergraduate macroeconomics study, the central role of finance is often overlooked. Consider, for now, that consumer spending, the C in (C + I + G of undergraduate economics) is accompanied by credit card, auto, and mortgage finance. Business investment, the I, is supplemented by bank loans and corporate bonds. State and federal government spending, the G, is supported by federal debt finance. Yet the coverage of real-side activity is not accompanied by an examination of the financial side that supports that activity.

The Relationship Between Credit Growth and Economic Growth

Economic growth moves with credit growth—sometimes ahead, sometimes behind. Despite varying degrees of volatility, business fixed investment and personal consumption move in sync with overall economic growth. Credit spurs growth throughout the economy; lack of credit availability limits growth. This linkage is even more essential to growth in emerging markets.

In addition to fueling today's household income and business profits, credit availability allows economic actors to increase their purchasing power. It supports households when they contemplate major spending decisions such as buying an auto or purchasing a home.[4]

Access to credit,[5] therefore, spurs growth in business investment and personal consumption. This may appear obvious, but the intricacies of the credit/growth linkage provide a fascinating story of trends and cycles and the constant evolution of the economy.

Recent policy initiatives by both the Trump, and before that, the Obama administrations have focused on the implementation of fiscal policy to promote economic growth. When looking at the history of real growth, credit growth is also essential to understanding the dynamics of the economy.

---

[4] The role of household balance sheets influencing housing demand specifically is found in Edward C. Prescott, *Effects of Unanticipated Monetary Policies: An Unanticipated Finding*, University of Minnesota mimeo, 1993.

[5] A view on the importance of the credit market appears in James S. Fackler "An Empirical Analysis of the Markets for Goods, Money, and Credit," *Journal of Money and Banking*, February 1985, 17(1).

Growth and Debt Finance

As illustrated in Fig. 1.1, there is a close link between economic growth and domestic nonfinancial debt growth. This pattern reflects an interaction that works both ways. Economic growth prompts creditors and debtors to accept more debt since they expect growth to continue with increased financial rewards to themselves. In turn, credit availability creates opportunities for entrepreneurs to pursue prospects for growth.

During the most recent economic expansion, 2010 to 2019, a very modest pace of debt growth became associated with a period of subpar real economic growth. In part, this pattern may reflect financial regulations that slowed financial risk-taking on new ideas.

Since WWII, growth in nominal Gross Domestic Product (GDP) and nonfinancial credit appear to have followed a similar cyclical trend over a business cycle—particularly noticeable during the 2002 expansion. However, credit growth has never moved into negative territory, even when GDP experienced several quarters of negative growth following the 2008 recession. At

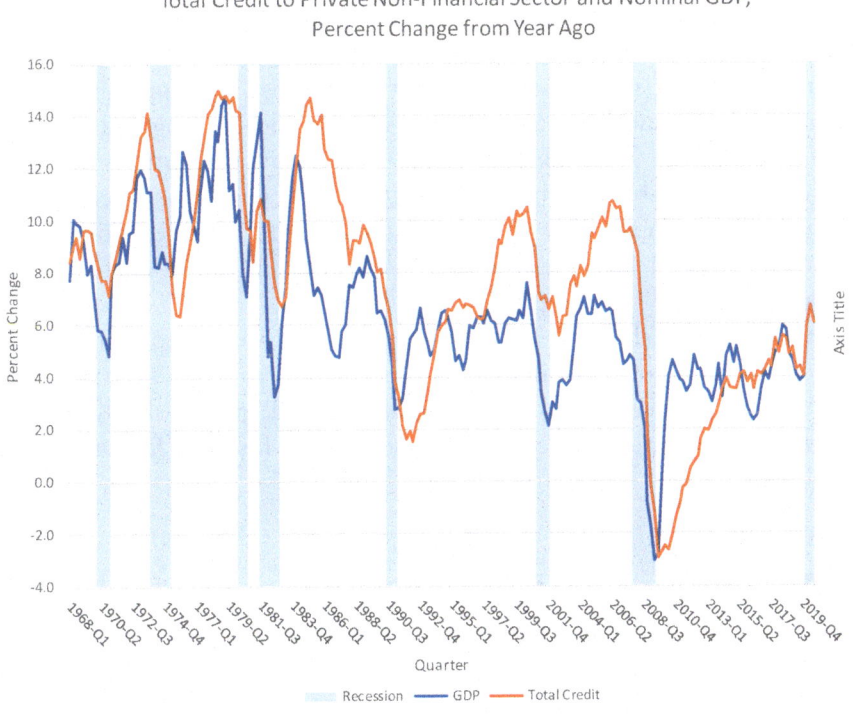

Fig. 1.1 Total credit and economic growth

that time, nominal GDP rose 4.7% in Q1 and 4.5% in Q4 year over year, both slightly below its long-run average of 4.9%. Meanwhile, total credit rose a mere 3.9% on a year-ago basis in Q4. Total credit is further from its long-run average of 6.7%, exemplifying the recent weakness in credit growth.

Credit's tame performance over the 2010–2019 expansion is striking given the relatively low-interest rates of this period. Low-interest rates are normally associated with faster credit growth. Slower credit growth and lower interest rates thus might be contributing factors or the result of a weaker pace of the current expansion. It appears that a credit markets model is much broader in scope than just interest rates and credit aggregates alone.

From a statistical perspective, nominal GDP growth correlates well with credit growth in the US, but growth in credit alone does not stimulate growth in GDP. Theoretically, while these variables are correlated together, causality is a different matter—which we shall see for many economic/financial pairs as we proceed through the book.

The Global Case for Credit and Growth

From an international perspective, credit growth has followed a similarly modest trend over the past several years (Fig. 1.2). In China, for example, credit growth has slowed as the country continues its transition from a production to consumption model of growth. This is occurring as the government of President Xi Jinping attempts to reign in the nation's explosive pace of business debt over the past decade, even as its economic growth has remained steady. In the Eurozone, where the structure of the economy is like that of the United States, credit growth also remains lower relative to the pre-crisis period of 1992 to 2005.

These trends of slower credit growth amid solid overall economic growth support the idea of a similar relationship between credit and economic growth on an international basis. Sustained GDP growth likely requires broader stimulation of the economy beyond simply fostering favorable credit conditions.

Sector Links—The Links of Finance and the Economy at the Sector Level

Three examples illustrate the links between credit and the economy at the sector level. In Chapter 8, real consumer spending is linked to growth in

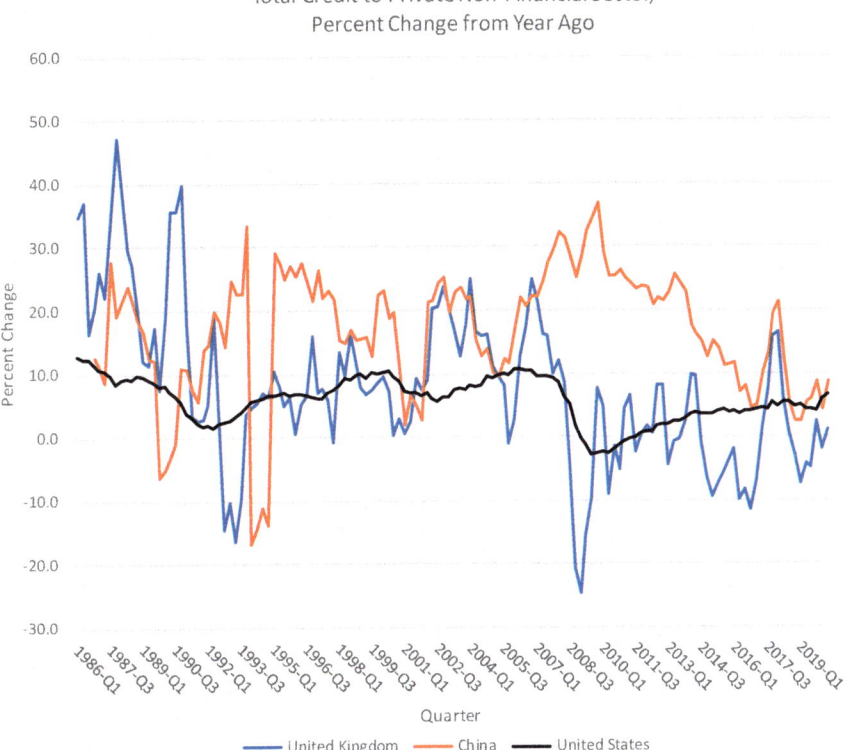

Fig. 1.2 Total credit growth across nations

consumer credit in the forms of credit cards, auto loans, and mortgage credit. Business real investment is related to gains in short-term bank credit and longer-term bond finance in Chapters 5, 6, and 7. Finally, federal government spending is financed, at least in part, by the issuance of federal debt, covered in Chapter 12.

The Specific Issue of Private Credit

During the current economic expansion, the pace of private credit growth to the consumer and business sectors has been particularly weak relative to prior economic expansions—note the modest growth in total credit in the current expansion shown in Fig. 1.1.

Since the business and consumer sectors are major contributors to economic growth and job gains, it is not a surprise that the overall pace of economic growth and job gains have been modest, at best, during the current cycle. This is particularly apparent by the big drag of credit during the first few years of this expansion.

This interaction of private credit and spending imparts a procyclical pattern to both economic activities. If not carefully monitored, this creates an abrupt halt to both when perceptions of risk and economic growth opportunities are altered. This brings into the framework, the role of expectations in setting prices as well as creating volatility in the financial/economic market prices—explored more closely in Chapter 2.

Market Price Framework

> We hear only questions for which we are in a position to find answers.[6]—Nietzsche.

To be in position, we need to have a framework. In our framework, we focus on the interrelationship between four market prices (these relationships are explored in greater detail in Chapter 3). These interrelationships of market prices (equity values, benchmark Treasury rates, corporate profit expectations/equity values, exchange rates) provide the rationale for the movement in market prices and highlight the danger of the common approach among financial firms to an analysis of markets in isolation—as if they are in a silo. The underlying rationale for a focus on private market prices and market fundamentals is that these markets reflect these interrelationships and the leading role of prices and price expectations in financial and economic cycles. Alternatively, a focus on economic indicators, such as GDP, follow, do not lead, the price/market signals.

In addition, price signals are always moving—markets are in disequilibrium/out of balance. With just four markets, there are many moving parts and prices are constantly adjusting to new information.

Market prices, and their mispricing, provide the disequilibrium/imbalanced forces associated with subsequent economic downdrafts and recoveries. The volatility of commodity (oil, wheat) prices in the 1970s, followed by the break of the link between gold and exchange rates in 1971. Subsequently, exchange rate volatility in the 1980s cracked the simpler exchange rate models of prior decades. The dot-com bubble of 1998–2002 saw a significant mispricing of expected rates of return on equities that led

---

[6] Friedrich Nietzche, *The Gay Science, 1882*, Translated from the German by Walter Kaufman, Vintage Books, March 1974.

to an equity market correction and brief economic recession. In the period leading up to the 2007–2009 Great Recession, the mispricing of housing (overcounting returns, underpricing risk), drove the boom and then the bust. Too many people bought houses with an expected rate of return on the house as investment and failed to balance that return with the current and potential cost to finance. But this process was aggravated by banks approving increasingly risky (lower down payments/no income verification) loans and then creating collateralized debt obligations to pass the risk on to investors seeking yield without a lot of due diligence. Once the cost to finance (interest rates) began to rise, the game was over. This pattern of legitimate financial innovation to support economic activity, but then carried too far, we shall see repeated many times in many variations. For researchers, prices act as signals and we follow these prices/anticipate financial market and economic movements.

Price Signals in the Linkages Between Markets

Price signals from the equity and credit markets are easily available due to the pervasive media coverage of equity prices and interest rates. Yet, commodity and exchange rate markets also merit a close review because of their influence upon, and their influence by, changes in the equity and credit markets. The impact of market price changes alters the balance of alternative asset prices. Many investment decision-makers are knocked off balance by the research silos that many financial firms have set up. Client demand for a daily immediate and authoritative assessment of any singular development has driven specialization and expertise that is quickly responsive to numerous financial price developments on any given day.

Yet, an effective model for the demand for equities, or any other asset class, whether by individuals or institutional investors, must reflect a broader set of independent factors. These include an investor's expectations for economic growth, an interest rate as a discount factor, the wealth of the individual or society (effectively allowing tax policy and inflation in the back door of the model), the expected dollar exchange rate (a benchmark to allow the investor to discern between domestic and foreign opportunities) and finally a sense of valuation, e.g., the P/E ratio relative to trend (not the average P/E).

Indeed, a long list, yet a parsimonious list has given the varied potential factors that are cited by some "experts" (sunspots signal a market bottom; if the NFC wins the Super Bowl the market will finish the year higher; if the AFC wins the reverse will occur). Rather than such superstitious connections what is important are the awareness of multiple markets and expectations in influencing the direction and timing of price developments. A call on the equity markets is also a call on the path of expected economic growth, inflation, interest rates, and the dollar exchange rate.

The year 2020 is a testament to the speed at which altered states of expectations deliver altered possible economic outcomes. When the coronavirus was expected to hit only China with some (limited) impact on South Korea/Japan, expectations for global growth were modified. At the same time, there were modest expectations for lower commodity prices due to the expected slowdown in Chinese industrial output. However, the explosion of global Covid-19 outbreaks infecting millions of people and causing widespread deaths leading to the complete shutdown of economies throughout the world altered investor and policymaker expectations.

Shifting Benchmarks: What Is an Investor to Do?

Remember benchmarks shift over time a phenomenon that will be examined more closely in Chapter 2. For now, consider these current pricing issues.

Investors and policymakers may coalesce around a fixed numerical benchmark for some asset price or a valuation benchmark. But in a constantly evolving economy, this is a convenient intellectual crutch but not an effective standard. Economic tides cannot be stopped.

Policy Benchmark: No Single Number But the Result of Many

For many economic and credit cycles, the Federal Reserve's (Fed) federal funds rate served as the benchmark for pricing short-term credit instruments and as a starting point for long-term credit instruments.[7] However, post the high inflation period ending in 1982, which we call here the modern era of modest inflation, the movement in the federal funds rate has reflected a series of structural breaks and a pattern that is not mean reverting (Fig. 1.3). Throughout this book, simple statistical techniques will be applied to numerous financial/economic benchmarks. They will help illustrate the character of each series in terms of its tendency to return to a mean value, its

---

[7] The federal funds rate is the interest rate depository institutions lend reserves to other depository institutions, often overnight, on an uncollateralized basis. The Fed alters the funds rate to achieve its policy goals. The funds rate serves a benchmark to price short-term interest rates in the U.S.

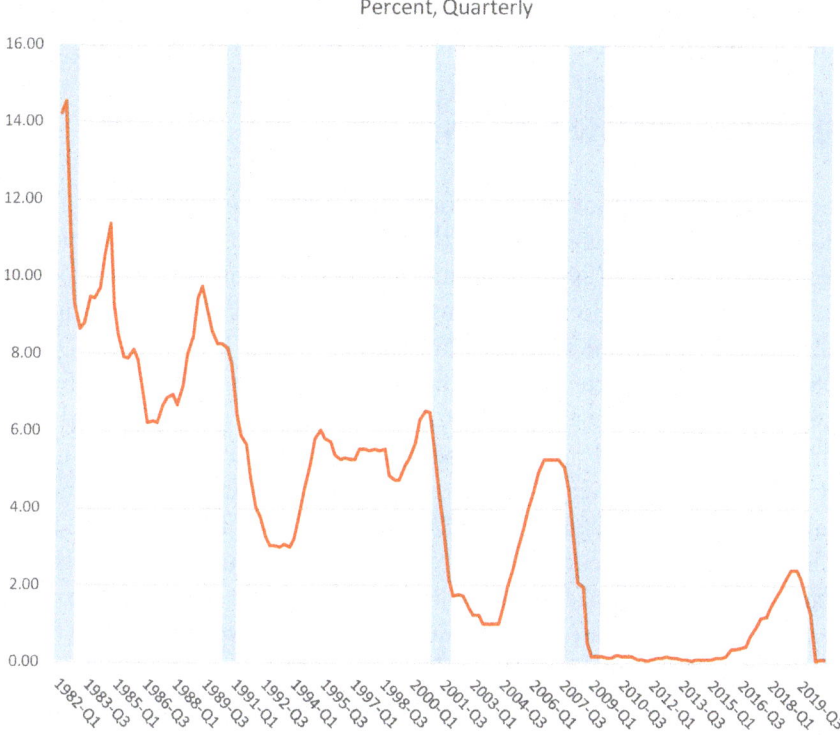

Fig. 1.3 Effective federal funds rate

volatility around that mean and any potential breaks in the values of the series over time. The pattern of the funds rate reflects numerous structural breaks that are familiar to analysts of the history of the Federal Reserve and the associated shift in economic tides that drove such shifts (October 1984, October 1994, December 2008 each represents a structural shift in the behavior of the funds rate). Moreover, since 1982, the federal funds rate has not exhibited mean-reverting behavior and the trend of the funds rate is in a non-linear pattern over that same period. This presents numerous problems in pricing and results in disequilibrium in financial markets over time. This is distinctly different than prior decades when the federal funds rate was treated as the benchmark for financial asset pricing.

For investors and decision-makers, the federal funds rate is a moving benchmark. It responds to the Federal Reserves' evolving policy vision of method and target. As a result, a fixed, numerical funds rate as a benchmark for short-term interest rates is not to be expected. Its influence on other financial markets thus evolves over time.

A Fixed Dollar? How About Not

Another example of a moving benchmark is the trade-weighted dollar. Pursuit of a stable dollar exchange rate faces the same economic reality that confronts all economic benchmarks—the evolution of the economy and, in this case, the evolution of the global economy. The pattern of the dollar, Fig. 1.4, exhibits three significant structural breaks. First, there is a break in October 2008 as would be expected with the onset of a recession at that time. Second, there is a break associated with the Plaza Accord. The Plaza Accord was a joint agreement, signed on September 22, 1985, at the Plaza Hotel in New York City between France, West Germany, Japan, the United States, and the United Kingdom, to depreciate the U.S. dollar in relation to the Japanese yen and the German Deutschemark by intervening in currency markets. Both instances reflect the impact of reality on the pursuit of a fixed dollar exchange rate. Moreover, the dollar exchange rate is not mean reverting and, to further complicate the analysis, the dollar exhibits a non-linear trend. Finally, beginning in the 4Q of 1995 and then peaking in the 3Q of 1998, there was a steady depreciation of the yen associated with the Asian (Thailand) crisis.

Fig. 1.4 Yen/US dollar exchange rate

These results highlight the challenge for investors. Dollar exchange forecasts reflect a myriad of global economic factors and there is no tendency for the dollar exchange rate to return to any specific given benchmark. These factors are further explored in Chapters 3 and 9.

No Simple Benchmarks in a Complex Economic World

There is no effective alternative to watching the data, following policy turns, and avoiding the anchoring bias that economic values will return to previous benchmarks. More recently, there has been a clear break in trend in equity valuation benchmarks, such as the earnings/price ratio, Fig. 1.5, in response to a shift in public policy expectations.

This pattern highlights another challenge with market information. Such information reflects the combination of actual economic fundamentals as well as the expectations of market actors. Expectations can be dashed when future outcomes do not match expectations. This mismatch is the driver for second-round market pricing and thereby further economic adjustments.

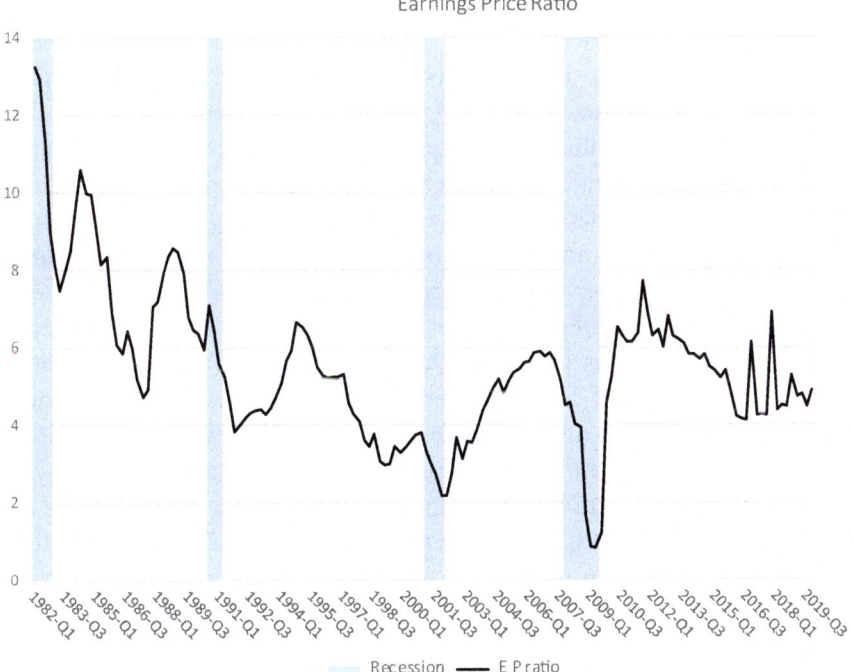

Fig. 1.5 Earnings-price ratio

Constant action/reaction drives activity and undermines the search for fixed, permanent benchmarks.

The Challenge of Anchored Benchmarks and Establishing Market Pricing

Market prices are constantly evolving. Affixing a benchmark value to many prices fails to recognize this evolution and the lack of mean reversion of these prices.

Normalization of Interest Rates?

Although many policymakers and market analysts speculate about a market movement toward normalizing interest rates, no such normalization has taken place. In part, this is the result of a fundamental conflict between market forces and policy intentions on the potential success toward normalizing interest rates. While the Fed could lower its interest rate target to promote faster success of growth to raise inflation to its 2% target, such a move would exacerbate its concerns around leveraged loans and corporate debt in the credit markets, valuation in the equity markets, and the trade-weighted dollar value. As illustrated in Fig. 1.3, the drift lower over time of the effective federal funds rate illustrates the problem of interest rate normalization. A lower federal funds rate was expected to promote economic growth and increase the pace of inflation. But over the last decade growth/inflation did not rise as the federal funds rate fell. In diametrical opposition, was what the media dubbed the "taper tantrum" the 2013 surge in U.S. Treasury yields, which resulted from the Fed's announcement under Fed chair Ben Bernanke of future tapering of its policy of Quantitative Easing (QE)—slowing the pace of its purchases of Treasury bonds, to reduce the amount of money it was feeding into the economy. The ensuing rise in bond yields in reaction to the announcement was the taper tantrum. This occurred again in 2017–2019 in the short-lived attempt by Fed chair Jerome Powell to raise the funds rate. What could account for such asymmetrical responses to changes in the funds rate? Chapter 4 covers in more depth interest rates and credit allocation.

Commodity Prices

On the inflation side of the story, the core Personal Consumption Expenditure (PCE) deflator has indeed been consistently below the Fed's 2% target, within a steady range between 1.5 and 2% for five years. But there is a problem in this market. Other measures of inflation (particularly the Fed-Atlanta sticky price index of a weighted basket of items that change price relatively slowly, had been drifting upward. Moreover, if inflation were considered as being too low, then would not real household income and wealth be perhaps too high? Chapter 3 is devoted to price determination in markets.

Equities

As for equities, even before the coronavirus outbreak, there has been the issue of profitless Initial Public Offerings (IPOS) that are expected to remain profitless for years. In addition, more than one-third of the companies in the widely held Russell 200 K index did not make a profit in 2019. If the economy were to falter further because of the coronavirus, that percentage would likely rise further thereby questioning the valuation in equity prices. In fact, corporate profit growth had already declined in 2019 versus 2018 and even more so given the shutdown impacts of 2020. Finally, on the credit side, the percentage of leveraged loans rated single-B-or-lower by Standard & Poor's (S&P) has been rising over the last five years—perhaps stretching the sensitivity of the loan quality to economic weakness. Profits and equity valuation will be the focus of Chapters 10 and 11.

Foreign Exchange Rates

Exchange rates are often the least analyzed field in most financial and economic reviews. Equity markets get the glamour, credit markets do get some mention, and inflation and commodity prices, especially gold, draw attention at times. However, exchange rates reflect the forces of alterations in expected economic growth and interest rates between nations and that provides a constant impulse toward change. Chapter 9 reviews the importance of these impulses and the consequent alterations in capital flows.

Silos Four Markets: Seeking Out the Linkages

Each one of the four financial markets is not a silo, rather there is a constant set of forces toward interaction of push and pull between markets. This approach defines an effective process to build into decision-making a view of the economic landscape. An economic view should incorporate several economic markets and most of all recognize the interactions in these markets. This is an issue. Many investment firms are staffed with an economist, an interest rate strategist, a foreign exchange strategist, and an equity market strategist. Do these analysts talk to each other on a consistent basis or do they remain in their silos and publish research in their narrow fields? The reality is that they in most cases remain in their silos. Moreover, many economic and market outlooks are static representations of their fields. There should also be a set of signals/possible changes that investors and then public can follow to determine how the economy and investment decisions evolve over time.

In this book, I take a very broad peek at some macro linkages. I review these here simply to show the linkages and the hypotheses underlying such linkages as I consider the baseline patterns of economic growth and inflation, the relative movements in money, M2, and asset prices to provide a perspective on where we are in the economic/credit cycle.

Benchmarking Nominal GDP: Growth and Inflation

The pace of growth in real final sales to domestic purchasers, as illustrated in Fig. 1.6, has been remarkably stable compared to prior economic expansions. To establish a benchmark, the average pace of real final sales was 2.8% since 1982. The period 2016–2017 has been clearly below that average pace with weakness in the pace of real government spending—especially by state and local governments.

Meanwhile, since the establishment of the North American Free Trade Agreement (NAFTA), the PCE deflator, Fig. 1.7, has averaged 1.81% which is slightly below the 2% target set by the Federal Open Market Committee.

Money and Nominal Growth

One persistent concern in financial markets in the 2009–2019 cycle has been the significant increase in the money supply as a potential source of future inflation. As illustrated in Fig. 1.8, M2, as a measure of the money supply, has risen sharply relative to nominal GDP growth with the advent of QE

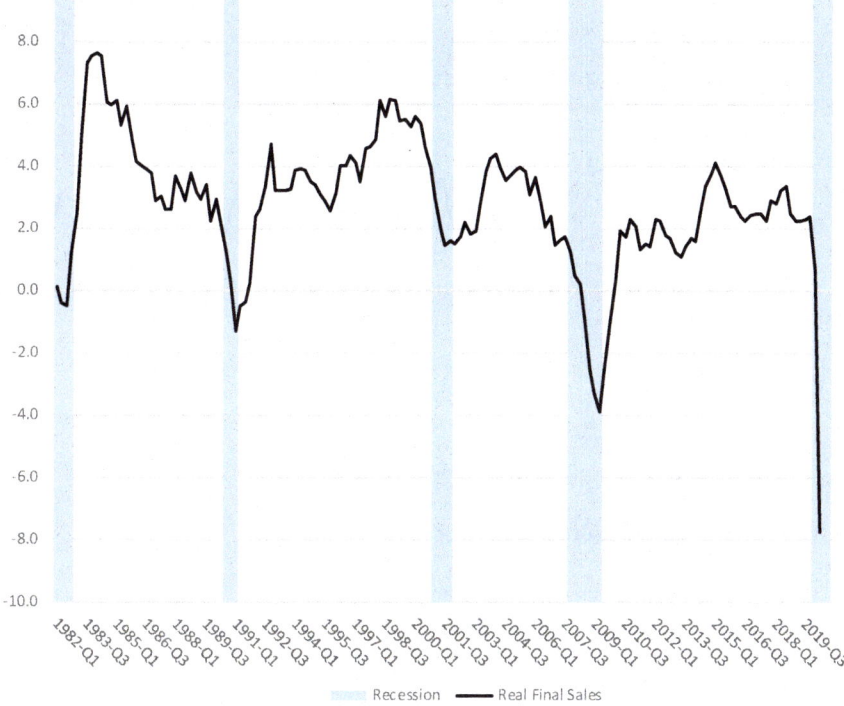

Fig. 1.6 Real final sales to domestic purchasers

policy at the Fed. This increase in the ratio intimates that there is an excess of liquidity in the economic system that has given rise to a decline in the velocity of money. This excess of liquidity is a concern since if that liquidity were put to work then some combination of more rapid economic growth or inflation could result as a solution.

Yet, the pickup of velocity has not yet appeared. Traditionally, velocity would increase as interest rates rise. Interest rates represent the opportunity cost of holding cash and an increase in this opportunity cost will generate an increase in velocity. The opportunity cost represents the cost of what you give up when you make an economic choice. For example, when you hold gold, you give up the rate of return you have on cash. In mid-2020, low and persistently low nominal interest rates provided a rational for rising prices for gold. Going forward, it will be interesting to see how velocity reacts when the FOMC raises interest rates.

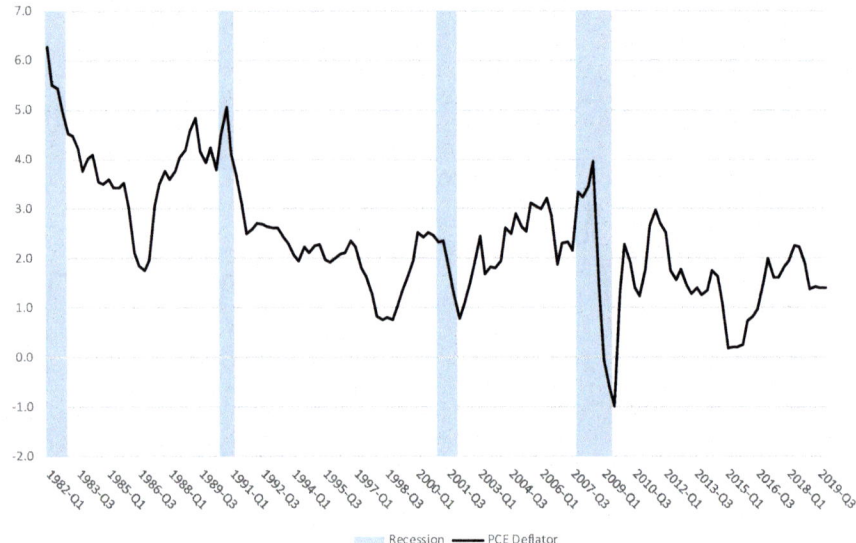

Fig. 1.7 Inflation as measured by PCE deflator

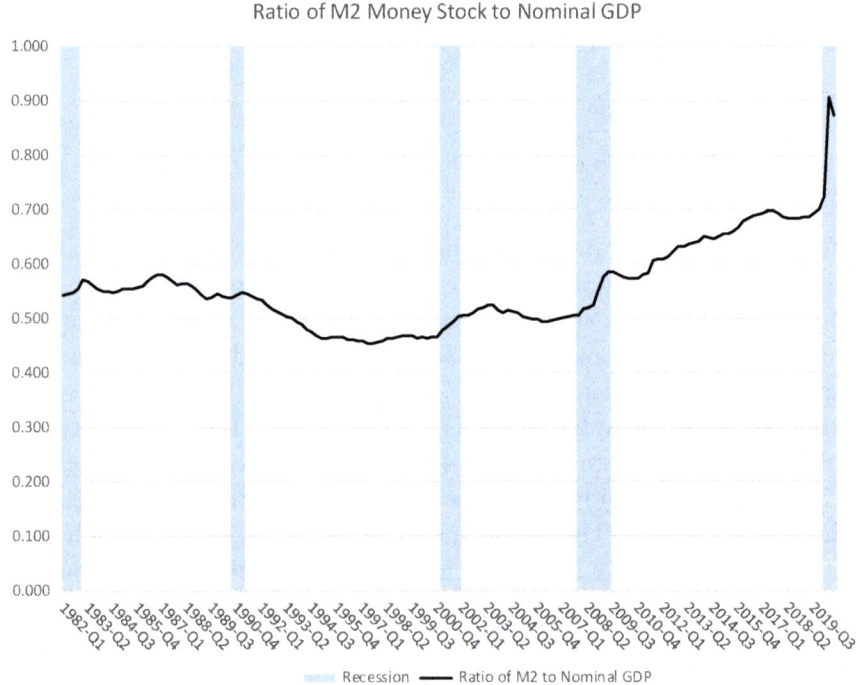

Fig. 1.8 Ratio of money (M2) to nominal GDP

Asset Prices and Nominal GDP

Another concern in the markets is valuation. While the equity market has risen sharply over the last year, the question remains to what extent is the rise in equity valuations out of line with the overall economy. As illustrated in Fig. 1.9, the rise in the NYSE has been sharp since 2010 but not yet as high as the 1998–1999 peak.

Certainly, there is evidence to be cautious since the ratio is higher than the average value over both the 1982 to now period as well as the longer period since 1970. Over the 1982 to now period, both interest rates and inflation expectations declined while a third factor, global trade opportunities, rose dramatically. These three factors would support a rise in equity valuations relative to a domestic measure of nominal GDP. How much of this rise can be justified over time will be tested with changes in interest rates, the trade-weighted dollar, and tax policy in the years ahead.

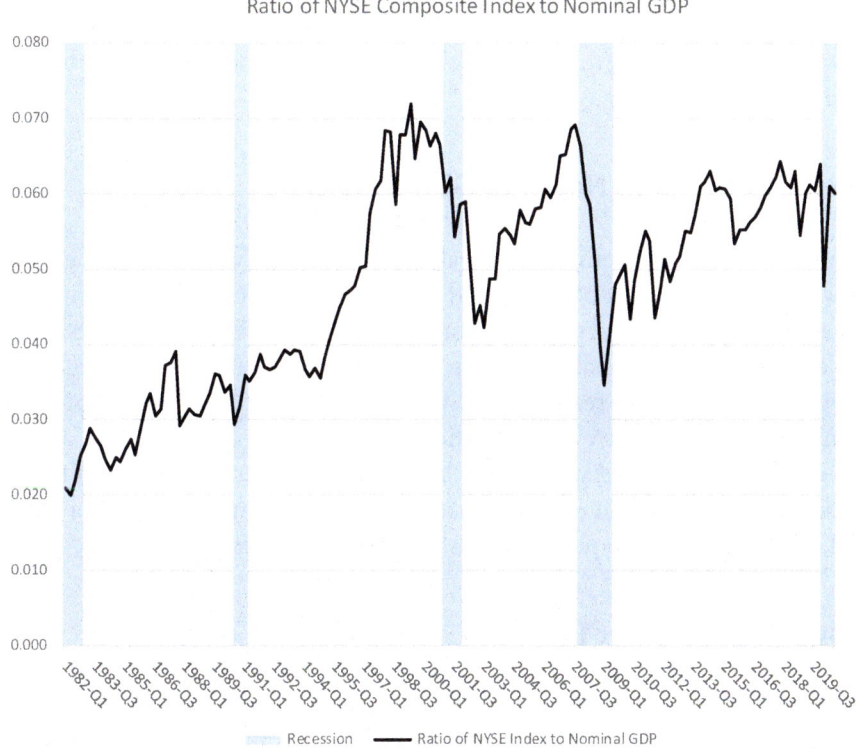

Fig. 1.9 Ratio of NYSE index to nominal GDP

Isolationism Is Not a Viable Approach to Market Interactions

Financial markets interact beyond the typical boundaries of financial analyst assignments. These interactions reflect feedback loops that often surprise and confuse those searching for simple, straight-line explanations. Therefore, a framework for market price determination must reflect these interactions. Examination of markets in isolation does not pass the test for good due diligence. Chapter 4 provides more depth to the discussion but here are some notes to whet the appetite.

Three-Dimensional Chess

As noted already, understanding the movement of financial and real goods prices between multiple markets requires an intellectual flexibility that departs from restrictions imposed by the silos many corporate analysts utilize. Because of this, they fail to notice the movement of prices and their influence between the multiple levels above, below, and on the current playing field of immediate focus.

Interest Rates and Nominal GDP Growth

A traditional starting point for an analyst is the link between nominal growth (real growth plus prices of goods and services) in the economy and intermediate benchmark Treasury interest rates (Fig. 1.10). Nominal interest rates track the path of nominal growth as investors seek to maintain a target real return over time. The search by private investors for real returns provides both an incentive and reward for the allocation of financial capital as well as a rationale for understanding the movement in the economy and financial markets. However, when central banks set short-term interest rates as a policy goal, a side-effect is the potential misallocation of capital.

Moving to Another Level

Moving to another level, we begin with a traditional link between the markets for credit (prices expressed as interest rates) and the market for foreign exchange where prices are expressed as exchange rates. In a world of capital mobility in financial markets, interest rates adjust to differences in current

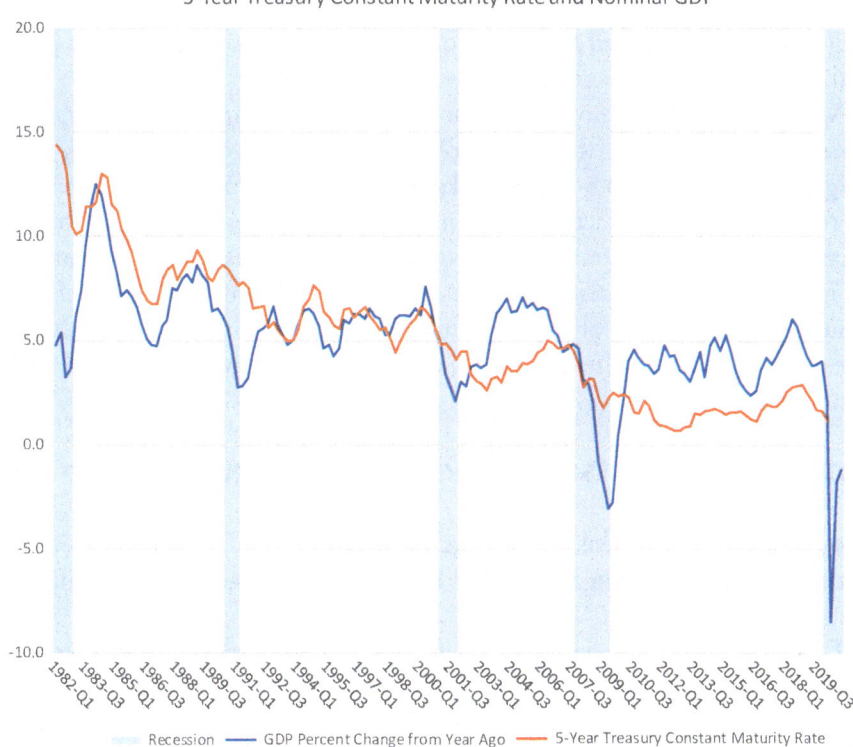

Fig. 1.10 Nominal GDP and the US treasury 5 year rate

and expected exchange rates to move toward equal values once taxes and transaction costs are considered.

This global allocation of capital may result in situations where the attraction of economic gains may lead to an appreciation of the currency. This, in turn, has a feedback effect by diminishing the allure of a nation's exports and influencing the path of trade deficits, which may run counter to a country's policy goals.

The Costs and Benefits of Capital and Growth

Movements in both exchange rates and interest rates alter the cost of capital and the expected earnings from real business investment, thereby feeding back into real and nominal economic growth. As interest rates change, the cost of capital is altered to firms—higher interest rates, holding constant the other elements in the cost of capital calculation—raise the cost of capital and thereby discourage business investment. Moreover, this impact is reinforced as higher interest rates tend to be associated with higher exchange rate values, which lower the expected final sales for exporters and lower the costs of goods sold for importers.

Market prices that move as if part of a game of three/four-dimensional chess is the operational framework of the marketplace even if silos of work assignments persist. One-to-one linkages are not effective. The importance of recognizing other factors that move market prices, ceteris paribus, is paramount. It is important to be aware of what else is changing that may be moving market prices over time that is outside the conventional two-dimensional approach of inflation/interest rates or interest rates/exchange rates that are used so often in financial market commentary.

Financial Markets: The Economy's Fraternal Twin

Growth in both the real and financial sides of the U.S. economy is best understood by examining the linkage between the real economy and financial markets.

Economic and financial analysis are not complete by themselves as each must recognize the behavior of its fraternal twin. Effective due diligence by analysts requires reviewing the signals of economic change on a frequent basis but we are cautious about the effectiveness of several commonly expressed ratios. For example, it is convenient, but terribly misleading, to focus on the ratio of debt to GDP ratios by sector or by nation. The comparison of a stock of debt to a flow of income is common and commonly wrong.

In contrast, we favor the ratio of interest expense to income growth—both flow variables (variables whose value depends on a period, not an instant—not a comparison of stock/flow variables. The comparison of interest expense illuminates the direct impact of changes in interest rates on the numerator and changes in the economic growth rate on the denominator. For the household sector, the focus is on the debt service ratio, in Chapter 8 specifically, as it is seen as a measure of financial pressure. We ignore the debt-to-income ratio commonly cited. The debt service ratio (DSR) (or alternatively the financial obligation ratio) shows that it lies far below the levels of 2000–2007. Moreover, the ratio of household assets to liabilities (stock compared to a stock) has risen since early 2011. The one caution signal for the household sector is the rise in the auto delinquency rate in recent years.

For the nonfinancial business sector (see Chapters 5, 6, and 7), the ratio of short-term debt to long-term debt (both stocks) has declined signifying that nonfinancial firms, on average, are less sensitive to changes in short-term interest rates. Meanwhile, the debt-to-equity ratio has declined in recent years intimating that risk has shifted to equities and away from debt. Finally, the ratio of interest expense to cash flow (both flows) for nonfinancial business firms is remarkably low relative to history—a good sign for corporate debt in general. If there were more micro data available regarding leverage loans, we could discuss the interest expense to cash flow benchmark. The ratio of debt to equity provides a look into the character of corporate leverage from the balance sheet side. On the income side, the ratio of interest expense to corporate cash flow is a benchmark.

On the supply side of the credit markets, bank willingness to make consumer installment loans (see Chapter 8) provides a view from the supply side of credit often overlooked by commentators when viewing household credit markets.[8] The sector detail available from the Fed's Senior Loan Officer Opinion Survey on Bank Lending Practices is invaluable when doing careful analysis. In addition, the survey gives a snapshot of the strength of demand from both the household and business sectors. It provides context to the macro measure of total loans which does not distinguish supply versus demand side pressures.

Two final points. On the equity side, the Price/Earnings (P/E) ratio or as used in this text the earnings-price ratio, E/P, (see Chapter 11), is often seen as a benchmark for value. The issue here, however, is that the E/P ratio is not mean reverting—it is the product of the changes in expectations for growth, interest rates, inflation, and the dollar exchange rate. Markets do not tend toward a given golden mean E/P ratio. Instead, the E/P ratio is a result of market movements in the other three financial markets. Once again, this provides a framework of the interrelationships between markets that is essential for effective due diligence.

The yield curve—the ratio of ten-year to two-year US Treasury yields, has not inverted prior to every recession in the United States since World War II. Moreover, the lead time from an inversion to a recession ranges from 8 to 23 months. When tested, the yield curve inversion does not help predict a recession. The inverted yield curve is a remote factor, a condition that appears before a recession but is not the driving force for a recession. It is not an immediate cause of recession.

Why do we look at the fundamentals for each market? The assumptions and data behind each model set the tone for accuracy. The biases in model building determine the effectiveness of decision-making. What is also

---

[8] One study that looks and bank lending and bank capital is Ben S. Bernanke and Mark Gertler, "Banking and macroeconomic Equilibrium." In *New Approaches to Monetary Economics*, W. Barnett and K. J. Singleton, eds. Cambridge, UK: Cambridge University Press, 1987.

different in our approach is that our focus is on the financial sector and not the macro real side of the economy familiar to most observers.

So, Where Do These Market Observations Take Us?

The purpose of real-side models is to arrive at an equilibrium of the goods and money markets to determine the equilibrium values of output and interest rates. Such a model allows for the assessment of the impact of monetary and fiscal policy but does not address the focus of our work—the workings of financial markets. In the first half of 2020, the hit to global growth expectations showed most clearly in the equity market (Fig. 1.11) and then in the credit markets.

Since the post Great Inflation bubble (ending in 1982), the S&P 500 has been a leading indicator of the alternative paths of growth and recession. Of course, there are periods of over and under valuation in the overall equity market and certainly in select sectors. But valuation issues bring in the real-side indicators and profit growth as indicators. Corporate profits have long

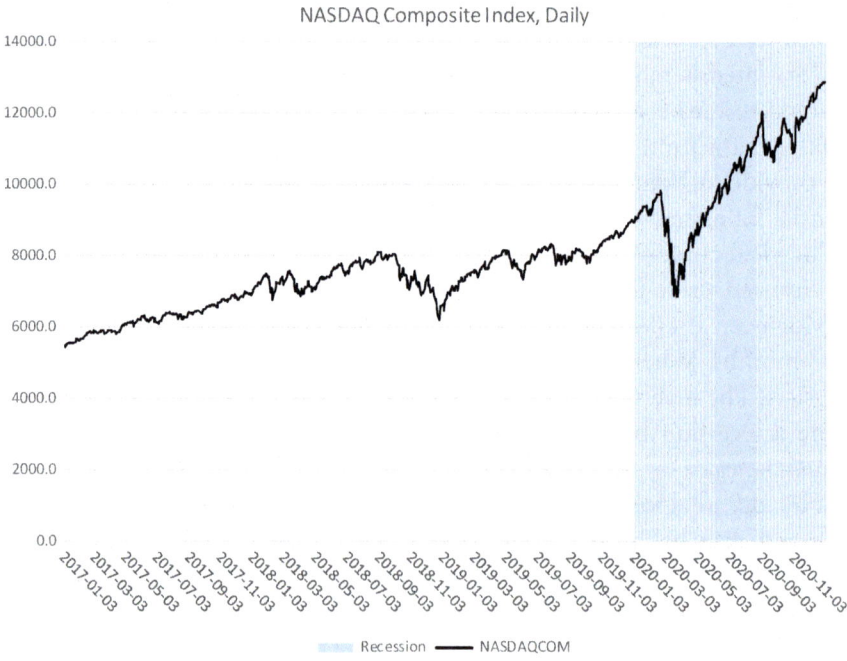

Fig. 1.11 NASDAQ index 2017 to 2021

been a leading indicator. Since they are quarterly numbers, not monthly, they are often overlooked–but they still provide an insight into equity market valuations.

In 2020, equity markets experienced an initial sharp decline in March but then they marched steadily upward as government mandated shutdowns diminished. Historically, the equity market bottomed in September 2001 (recalls the attacks of September 11th) but then registered a subsequent further bottom in February 2003. Expansionary fiscal policy relief in 2001, 2002 and then 2003 finally made a difference in the economic outlook.

Prices and markets reflect the influence of both demand and supply factors. Emphasizing aggregate demand and the two policy tools most associated with manipulating aggregate demand (monetary and fiscal policy) certainly does not address the behavior of markets or prices which is our focus.

The integration of economics and finance is shown by examining the markets for goods, credit, equity, and foreign exchange. The interrelationships between the behavior of individual economic/financial units are multifaceted. For each of these sectors, leading indicators are essential to recognize the appearance of change. We will introduce several indicators of change that have been useful over the years. As expected, no single variable explains financial market prices.

One of the most fascinating challenges to analyzing financial market behavior is the constant interjection of new information. It always shocks the existing status quo and generates regular disequilibrium in the markets.

For interest rates, the lesson learned about single variable explanations is relearned again. A recent commentary asserted that "higher Treasury yields send a hopeful signal to markets.[9]" It cited that ten-year yields fell below one percent. Yet since that time, the ten-year U.S. Treasury note yield has remained far below the one percent level. An economy as diversified as the U.S. economy does not operate off a single indicator. Other factors in model building must be recognized as will be seen in future chapters describing credit market allocation.

Commodity markets are a second financial market that provides insight into the behavior of other markets. The behavior of prices is reviewed later but it is important to note that changes in the West Texas Intermediate crude oil price have predictive ability with respect to general inflation, equity valuations, and interest rates. This is exactly the kind of interrelationships that we track in our framework. We also recognize the shocks that can hit markets as we witnessed with the impact of the Covid-19 shutdowns. Within

---

[9] Barron's March 21, 2020.

our approach, commodity prices do not stand alone. As we shall review in Chapter 3, the interaction of these markets sets the tone for movement in all markets.

As for credit, the ICE (Intercontinental Exchange) BoA High-Yield and High-Grade corporate spreads, widened dramatically in the first quarter of 2020 and provide insight into the state of the overall economy and equity markets as well. These spreads rose in March of 2020 as a signal of the risk-averse behavior of investors in general. Since April, these spreads have declined signaling a more risk-on position of investors. The fundamentals of the private corporate bond market provide insight into the valuation in equity markets and serve as a leading indicator of overall economic growth.

Why a focus on credit spreads? Quality spreads, such as BBB and BB spreads to 5-year Treasury rates, provide insight into risk-taking and risk pricing in the private market. The bond market may not always have it right, but these spreads represent the financial betting of real investors in financial markets with real money on the line. No Monday morning quarterbacks here. Moreover, my experience with traders and portfolio managers is that these bets reflect their interpretation, and yes, their biases, of all the publicly available information at the time.

Exchange rates, particularly the dollar index also act as a barometer of the flight to safety in 2020. At first, the U.S. dollar value rose as investors sought safety in the dollar. Then as problems with Covid-19 persisted in the United States, the dollar's value gradually fell relative to the euro.

In more normal times, the dollar's exchange rate intimates what investors believe about the relative value of the dollar against foreign currencies (i.e., what economies and central banks policies are doing) with particular interest in the dollar/euro and dollar/United Kingdom (UK) sterling rates as the most representative (not perfect) of a free-market exchange rate. How investors interpret and discount the value of relative economic growth and central bank policies will alter the relative attractiveness of alternative country investments and thereby the exchange rate.

Changes in the United States dollar's exchange rate signal what investors believe about the relative value of the dollar against foreign currencies (implicit expectations on economic growth and central bank policy) with particular interest in the dollar/euro and dollar/UK sterling rates as the most representative (not perfect) of a free-market exchange rate. Markets interpret relative economic growth and central bank policies and what influence those policies may have on the relative attractiveness of alternative country investments.

Decision-making requires a disciplined, short list of real and financial indicators. There is no place for single variable explanations.

One lesson of our approach to markets is that no single indicator can serve as a reliable predictor of financial/economic behavior. Moreover, any indicator should be part of a broader framework of economic/financial activity. Mispricing of financial assets is clearly the story today but that was also true even before the virus issue emerged on the current scale in late January.

Moreover, it has become painfully obvious, on the downside, that the interrelationship between prices in different markets accelerated the selloffs in each. Yet, both the disequilibrium and the associated interrelationships produced mispricing of financial assets on the upside. No surprise that energy prices represented a risk to the high-yield market. Profit growth had been slowing for some time and yet equity prices rose. Finally, the sensitivity of equity prices to the Fed's attempted rebalancing of policy in late 2018 was a signal that markets were on a knife's edge of pricing.

Even now, the sensitivity of the dollar to the Fed's recent swap operations suggests that the dollar exchange rate is nowhere near an equilibrium position.

Finally, there is the issue of getting from the current disequilibrium position back to some sense of normal. This must be accomplished while knowing that the pre-virus position of the financial markets, and thereby the real economy, was not an equilibrium position. In part, that is what is making the pricing of financial assets so difficult today. Even more complicated when one market out of balance will generate forces for change in all our other markets. For example, interest rate movements will generate changes in exchange rate and equity market valuations.

Markets in Disequilibrium: Certainly Not Simultaneous Equilibrium in All Four Markets

What would Indiana Jones do? You have the Golden Idol in your hands (low inflation, full employment, and an amazing run of equity market gains—truly a goldilocks position for policymakers). Then you have just placed the right amount (you think) of sand to match the weight of the Idol—but the sand, and your portfolio, start to sink. You then run quickly to save what you can. However, your unfaithful sidekick Satipo convinces you to toss the Golden Idol before you leap across the open well hole. Minutes later you find him impaled by the market. You take the Idol again and run before the crushing ball of market corrections reaches you. You tumble outside the cave only to lose the Golden Idol to your old nemesis, the market.

Now it is time for a new adventure. What makes markets so fascinating is that we, like Indiana Jones, go from one adventure to another. Change is constant and that change generates movement in market prices.

Commentary must have context. In a *Wall Street Journal* article entitled "Some Investors Had Hunch Yields Were About to Fall" on June 9, 2019, the reporters Avantika Chilkoti and Daniel Kruger focused on the recent decline in yields. But for us, the question is why are yields about to fall? If the forecast for lower yields was accompanied by a forecast for recession, then the forecast is of little value for a multi-asset portfolio manager. The article is a good read but does not go far enough in citing the ways that yields may react to different economic scenarios—is the yield falling because of lower growth expectations, lower inflation expectations, easier monetary policy? Where is the why?

Second, one line of thought is that investors should buy equities if the Fed were to lower rates. Again, this one-variable explanation (justification) for buying equities leaves us with the question why? If the Fed is lowering rates (2001, 2007) because of the imminent/coincident collapse of the economy, then the timing to buy equities just as the economy is heading into recession would be unwise. A one-variable framework for decision-making can be very misleading in a multimarket world. Price changes reflect the relative force of supply and demand and recognize the importance of the force of price changes in other markets.

Decision-making requires a disciplined, short list of real and financial indicators. There is no place for single variable explanations.

Gauging Economic Change: Economic Signals

The evolution of the real economy and its influence on financial market prices demands the recognition of a set of leading economic indicators to provide a direction forward. Let us now focus on a limited set of variables that represent exogenous impulses that drive financial markets. We are particularly concerned about the confirmation bias where an advocate for a view searches out a bit of data outside the major indicators to support a view. The thrust of the markets is typically signaled by primary indicators and strategy can be distracted by secondary indicators.

Defining signals of change in an economic framework is the next building block for an effective decision-making process. Economic developments reflect movements in both the real economy and financial markets, however,

For a glimpse of the financials that have served us, we will look at an interview conducted by Barron.[10] Why go to an interview over 30 years ago? First, I am quoted in the interview and second, the financial side of the economy did provide insight for the oncoming recession which was not the consensus view at the time. Moreover, there is too much emphasis on the either/or of boom/bust economies with little reference to financial side leading indicators. Our work emphasizes the cycles of weaker/stronger recoveries as well as a recession.[11]

For the real economy, five signals identify a change in the economic fortunes of the economy. We are not employing these indicators to make a forecast of the trend of the economy—we are interested in cycles around that trend. Initial jobless claims are important as a signal of change in direction for the labor market and thereby a signal of changes in consumer incomes and possibly the unemployment rate as well. Since consumer spending is a large part of the U.S. economy, nearly two-thirds, changes here provide essential information.

Business sentiment (what John Maynard Keynes called animal spirits) is a second signal we follow. The ISM-manufacturing Index series provides insights into the direction of business sentiment. Founded in 1915, the ISM is a composite index that gives equal weighting to new orders, production, employment, supplier deliveries, and inventories. Each factor is seasonally adjusted. This is the first piece of economic news out each month for the prior month. Changes in this manufacturing sector are central to any assessment of the cyclical character of the economy.

Another important piece of monthly information is found in the Factory Orders report from the Census Bureau. This report totals the dollar volume of new orders, shipments, unfilled orders, and inventories reported by domestic manufacturers. These factors provide a signal of tension in the marketplace. Why tension? The balance (more often imbalance) between orders and shipments and signals from unfilled orders allows an assessment of the imbalance among sectors of shipments running ahead or behind orders. The Factory Orders report also provides sector detail that adds to its value as cyclical indicator.

Fourth, for housing, building permits provide a signal of change in this cyclical sector. While home sales are interesting, we focus on the cycle and building permits and pending home sales provide a signal for the future pattern of residential investment. Finally, consumer sentiment (U of MI

---

[10] Are We in Recession? Yes, says John Silvia; Maybe, Says Ed Hyman, Barron's September 3, 1990.
[11] *Is Predicting Recessions Enough?* Co-author with my former colleague Azhar Iqbal and winner of the NABE Contributed Paper Award for 2016.

survey) provides a corroborating piece of information on consumer behavior. Like businesses, consumer can also exhibit animal spirits in their behavior.

For consumer sentiment, information is gathered about consumer attitudes on both their current situation and their expectations for the future. These attitudes will determine their willingness to spend while personal income/employment data would indicate only the ability to spend.

A Historical Context for an Effective Decision-Making Process

Over the last thirty years, I have had the privilege to present the economic outlook, in a lead-off position, for investment conferences inside Kemper/Wells Fargo and outside to clients. My role was to provide a context for decision-makers and investors to view subsequent presentations on business/investment issues. As you probably already surmised, I often stayed after my presentation to appreciate the presentations on foreign exchange, credit, and equities since, in a four-sector framework of market prices, all these sectors are interrelated, no one sector stands alone, and there was much to learn by listening to my colleagues in these other investment fields. Decision-making for investments requires a context that is supplied by examining these four aspects of financial markets.

Decision-making requires a disciplined, short list of real and financial indicators at our investment meeting. There is no place for single variable explanations. Moreover, a framework keeps the analysis on track—it is a discipline.

Decision-making by senior companies or public policy leaders demands that the financial adviser heed the words of Charles Schultze.

> The role of the adviser is to translate economics into language that could be understood by the President rather than spell out the latest refinements of theory and econometrics.[12]

Two recent articles reinforce the importance of retaining a focus on the economic framework and not drifting into confusion or fashion.

"Smattering of Contradictory Data Confounds Economists," *Wall Street Journal*, **February 15, 2019.**

---

[12] Charles Schultze in *"When the President Calls,"* Simon Bowmaker and Minouche Shafik, MIT Press, October 2019, p. 67.

Our framework mandates that we distinguish between leading, coincident, and lagging indicators. Moreover, decision-makers like hockey players must look forward—where the puck is going not where it is. In the above article, the journalist Sharon Nunn cites reports on industrial production, the Purchasing Managers Survey, consumer sentiment, and retail sales as contradictory. Yet, industrial production and retail sales are coincident indicators—they tell us where the puck is today not where it is tomorrow. In my presentations, I have focused on leading indicators to judge the cycle—these include nondefense durable goods orders and consumer sentiment as well as initial jobless claims, for example.

There are numerous economic releases each month and they vary in importance to different benchmarks for different economic activities. Confusion is easy to contract if there is no framework to place these releases in context.

"Worry About Debt? Not So Fast Some Economists Say," *Wall Street Journal*, **February 17, 2019.**

This article by David Harrison and Kate Davidson begins by citing the debt to GDP ratio—a bad sign since we know that comparing a stock of debt to a flow of production (GDP) is incorrect. The focus should be on the growth of the economy (real GDP if you will) to the real interest rate on the debt—both flow variables. This ratio compares the growth of the revenue base of the economy to the growth of the interest rate burden. Too often we find that future growth cannot sustain the debt burdens taken on today (Greece and Italy for example).

The issue is the comparison of future real rates and future real economic growth. Moreover, simply issuing more federal debt begs the question of where the funds will come to buy this debt—more Fed/Chinese/Japanese buying.

One hypothesis is that such fiscal expansion faces no budget constraint and, with interest rates so low, that such a policy can be adjusted based upon some measure of full employment. However, what do we know? Over the last forty years, our benchmark for full employment has continued to change. Moreover, current unemployment rates appear too low for many analysts and, given the policy rule that low levels of the unemployment rate below what is perceived as full employment, would call for fiscal restraint—not ease.

Finally, since 1968, fiscal policy has been burdened by implementation and impact lags, as well as a plethora of special interest provisions that have nothing to do with macro policy. Trying to alter today's fiscal policy based upon today's unemployment rate opens policy to be completely time inconsistent.

A Duality in Frameworks: How We Make Decisions—Not By Economic Numbers Alone

Economic and financial decision-making is not just about economic and financial benchmarks. For both Joe Kenda, a retired Colorado Springs Police Department detective lieutenant who solved 92% of his murder cases and is featured on the television show *Homicide Hunter*, and Sherlock Holmes, evidence is not enough. There must be a framework that captures the essence of the story. First, thoughtful, economic commentary is based on an initial framework that defines how we see the world and then allows an analyst to incorporate change, make choices, examine the implications of those choices and, if needs be, define a new framework on how the world works. In our first book,[13] we defined this decision-making process because the frequent current practice of defining a framework of price determination but not allowing for possible alterations in that framework. The result is a static, rigid view of the economy without allowing for change.

Second, there should be a framework for the economy itself. As observers of my presentations over the years know, I define the economy as a set of interrelated markets. Such an approach views these markets as providing a basis, a first step, in defining the opportunities for investors. The markets are goods (with the quantity and prices representing two defining characteristics), interest rates, exchange rates, and capital (represented by corporate profits). For an example of how we characterize these markets, each one in turn and their link to the other markets.[14]

This duality defines an effective process to build into decision-making a view of the economic landscape. An economic view should incorporate several economic markets and, most of all, recognize the interactions in these markets as we emphasized earlier in this chapter. There should also be a set of signals/possible changes that investors may follow to sense how the economy and investment decisions may change over time.

There is a duality here in defining the evidence presented and then defining a process to identify change and make choices to alter, or not alter, the framework of price determination in the economy. This is detective work at its best. The nuances and mysteries of the economy and financial markets continue.

---

[13] John E. Silvia, *Dynamic Economic Decision Making*, Wiley, 2011.
[14] See my presentation at the AUBER Conference, Salt Lake City, October 14, 2018.

Framing Bias, Risk, and Uncertainty

As an economy evolves, decision makers are constantly challenged to rethink their models of economic and financial behavior. Data is not enough. Our view of the data provides meaning. In astronomy, Tycho Brahe had the data but it took Johannes Kepler to provide meaning to do so; Kepler had to rethink the model of planetary motion.

For him, the first challenge was confirmation bias—looking at the data in a way to confirm the existing beliefs that the planets revolve around the sun in circles. If he had not moved away from this view, he would have never solved the problem because planets travel in elliptical orbits.

"If you can keep your head when all about you are losing theirs," Rudyard Kipling.

In economics and finance there is a tendency to support beliefs by what we know, or think we know about the past, which we term the anchoring bias. In contrast, a recency bias emphasizes recent history as the path to the future. Decision makers fail to recognize change because of the anchoring bias, or they fail to distinguish temporary deviations from trends because of the recency bias. The illusory correlation is most obvious when a graph is drawn with two lines that appear to follow the same path but there is no logical connection between the two. Analysts are also prone to the availability bias—"picking at straws" to find evidence where no reliable support is cited. Finally, the normalization of deviance bias sees the economy remaining the same, e.g., a bull market in equities, when clearly the fundamentals are changing.[15]

In economics and finance, when what we get is not what we expected, then prices move in one sector and then generate further price movement in other sectors. In our review of economic and financial decision making, we will bring in decision making benchmarks/biases to illustrate the problem of actual economic/finance decisions.

---

[15] The normalization of deviance bias is most notably associated with the Challenger disaster. See Diane Vaughn, *The Challenger Launch Decision: Risky Technology, Culture and Deviance at NASA*, University of Chicago Press, Chicago, 1996.

The Anchoring Bias: In the Data and in Policy

"By adherence to a favorite theory, many errors have at times been introduced into general science which have required much labour for their removal,"—Francis Bacon.

As for risk, how we perceive an issue as more risk or more reward reflects our framing bias. Riding the roller coaster is a thrill for many people; for others, it is the uneasy feeling of loss of control and possible, even if unlikely, injury. How we frame an issue is a good indication of the balance between risk and reward. Until early 2020, investors appeared to frame the economy and financial outlook as favoring reward—let us stay fully invested. In early 2020, it appears that investors frame the outlook as more risk/uncertainty than opportunity.

Frank Knight, an economist at the University of Chicago, distinguished between risk and uncertainty in economic activity. For risk, he said there is an historical database of examples that can be drawn upon to provide a sense of the range of possible outcomes. Uncertainty, however, is not accompanied by any historical database. The coronavirus is a good illustration of uncertainty. Until 2020 the medical community had not witnessed an outbreak of this virus before. It had no history of scientific research to estimate the limits of its transmission and how many deaths it might cause. In this case, investors pulled back from exposure to a medical problem for which they could not frame an adequate solution.

Economic Evolution—Cycles and Structural Breaks

Recognizing the change in our framework of how the economy works is a foremost challenge to decision makers. There is a tendency to anchor our framework on familiar thought patterns. Yet, in recent years, we have witnessed numerous significant economic and financial changes.

Fed Balance Sheet—Structural Breaks and an Asymmetric Impact

On the upside, the expansion of the Fed's balance sheet during the Great Recession of 2008–2009, again in 2013/2014 and most recently 2020 was given high marks for its role in financial stabilization. However, something happened along the way. As the Fed shrunk its balance sheet during the period 2017–2019, the impact on mortgage rates and housing appeared to be much greater than anticipated. The expansion of the Fed's balance sheet was given little mention of its impact on housing by analysts, but the shrinking of the balance sheet was considered crucial in the housing slowdown.

There are two issues here. First, the impact of changes in the balance sheet appears to be asymmetric with respect to housing. Second, small changes in mortgage rates had an outsized impact on housing in the context of solid real income gains, wealth gains, and higher consumer confidence. The framework for housing has thus changed relative to what might be expected from historical patterns. It appears that up and down in policy levers may have an asymmetrical impact on economic and financial behavior.

Inflation: The Unreachable Star?

For someone who cut his intellectual teeth on Jimmy Carter's inflation when studying graduate economics in those years, and the additional exciting experience of stagflation brought on Johnson and the Vietnam War as well as Nixon's going off the gold standard—very exciting times—the thought that not enough inflation in today's policy setting is cognitive dissonance in real time. The framework is that economic growth above what we estimate is above its full potential and an unemployment rate below what is estimated as full employment would drive up inflation. Yet, current inflation is far below prior estimates of recent years. The concept of full employment evolved to a point that much lower unemployment rates are not inconsistent with steady to lower inflation rates? It appears the role of the global economy and the dollar dominate. Are we importing deflation today?

Equity Values Rise as Economic and Profit Growth Slows

This is a tough nut to crack. We could argue that the rise in equity values is becoming stretched relative to the ability of companies to deliver those earnings. For example, in recent years, profit growth has slowed. However, interest rates have also declined thereby lowering the discount rate applied to earnings. We could consider this the start of misalignment and mispricing in the market. For our economics framework, the equity values are rising along with a stronger dollar and weaker than expected growth in both Europe and China. This reaffirms the importance of global growth on top-line revenues for U.S. equities—perhaps global, not just domestic, interest rates count as well.

Credit Cycles

Credit has its own cycle, and we shall see this throughout our review of the household, business, and government sectors. Financial markets are interrelated, and the economy and the financial markets are fraternal twins. While so much of current commentary focuses on the economic cycle, it is important to look at the credit cycle and seek hints of possible links between markets.

First the Bad News—Well Not All Bad News—Banking

Bank credit decision making reflects the signals of the marketplace. For example, several traditional benchmarks, credit, and economic activity are coincident. The loan-to-deposit ratio for banks peaks coincidently with the economic cycle. In a reverse twist, charge-off rates clearly peak lagging the onset of recession. Yet, interestingly, charge-off rates do tend to rise prior to the onset of recession—apart from the rise from 1994 to 1997. So perhaps the Asian-led crisis of 1997–1998 was not so much of a surprise. Let us follow the evidence by using the Fed's Senior Loan Officer Survey on Bank Lending Practices. When viewing the index of Banks' Willingness to Make Loans, the Fed reports willingness as an index, there is a clear peak in 1994, then a decline continuing into 1996, again a peak in 1998, another peak in 2006. Interestingly the series breaks below zero prior to the last two recessions. Now the bad news—the survey is reported a month after the survey is taken so its value as a leading indicator of credit quality is reduced. Ah, but all is not lost. As a coincident indicator, the index is closely correlated to peaks in the rate of growth in business equipment spending and peaks in commercial bank lending growth (1989, 1999, 2006).

Consumer Credit: A Threshold Effect?

Turning to consumer credit, the danger is the intellectual bias of anchoring. We sometimes focus on the errors of our parents but end up repeating the errors of our grandparents. Today, much focus is on consumer debt due to the Great Recession. When we look at current data, however, consumer credit is fine for now. First, we return to the Fed's Senior Loan Officer survey. Banks' willingness to make consumer loans fell dramatically from a positive 7.8% in the 2Q of 2007 to minus 6.0% at the start of the recession (4Q 2007) to minus 47.2 in the fourth quarter of 2008. Currently, this indicator stands at a positive 14.0% in the fourth quarter of 2018. Next, looking at another consumer credit series, the Fed's Household Debt Service and Financial Obligations Ratios, the current debt ratio is at 15.0 (1Q 2020), compared to 18.1 in 4Q, 2007 and 17.1 in 1Q 2000, just at the start of the last two recessions.

The linkage between credit and real economy markets provides clues and confirmation of the state of our outlook—still positive.

Monetary Policy, Decision Making, and Cognitive Bias

Analysts and economists all see the same public information. What we do with it is very different. Yet, we know that the decisions of policymakers reflect their prior mental framework although the certitude of that framework may be questioned.

How Long Is Transient?—The View of Inflation in Monetary Policy in 2020

In the early years of World War II, French intelligence identified that German invasions would come through the Ardennes forest. Yet, the focus of the French defense was at the Dyle river which is in central Belgium nearly two hours away. The Germans decided to invade through the Ardennes—same information, different actions.

Two questions must be raised regarding the employment of information within the context of current policy. First, the definition of "transient." How long is transient? This brings up the cognitive bias issue of normalization of deviance made famous by the Challenger O-ring example. On January 28, 1986, the Space Shuttle Challenger exploded 7 seconds after liftoff, killing seven crew members and traumatizing a nation. The cause of the disaster was traced to O-ring, a circular gasket that sealed the right rocket booster. This had failed due to the low temperature (31°F/–0.5°C) at launch time—a risk that several engineers noted, but that NASA management dismissed. NASA's own pre-launch estimates were that there was a 1 in 100,000 chance of shuttle failure for any given launch—and poor statistical reasoning was the key factor the launch went through.

With inflation measures falling below the Fed's target, how long do you stick with the belief that inflation will return to 2% on a sustained basis or accept the fact that something is different? Even more so, can you sustain a belief that the 2% target is symmetric when evidence intimates that all the bias is on the downside of inflation around 2% and not symmetric at all? Moreover, exactly what definition of inflation fits your priors this month—Consumer Price Index (CPI), Personal Consumption Expenditure (PCE), core PCE, trimmed mean CPI—pick what fits. Next month something else. An eagle that chases two fish catches neither.

Modeling Inflation: An Exercise in Ptolemaic Economics?

How many alterations do you make in the Phillips Curve inflation model—named after the economist A. W. Phillips which describes an inverse relationship between rates of unemployment and corresponding rates of rises in wages, before you ask: is the model relevant? Can you torture the data enough to confirm your priors that the model still works (anchoring bias) or does the model really work given the exception of the current period—so ignore recent evidence (recency bias)? How many changes to the model do you make before the model itself morphs into something far more complicated, far too specific, to fit the current period, but likely to produce out-of-sample period forecasts to be totally useless?

Economics research is littered with models that work well in sample but completely fail out-of-sample. For the French, the trench warfare of World War I was their military model but did not fit the out-of-sample experience of World War II. For Germany, the blitzkrieg worked for its invasion of Poland but failed completely as a sustained effort when it attacked the Soviet Union. The Russian winter and the lack of a sustained supply of war material, gasoline, proper clothing, destroyed the simple blitzkrieg approach.

Policymaking as a Source of Financial Market Dynamics

Before any flight, airline pilots put in their current coordinates to provide a starting point for the computer system to calculate a flight path. For policymakers, their expectations provide the basis for how they perceive the policy options going forward.

Public Policy and Private Decision Makers

For both public policy makers, the Fed, and private decision makers, investors and business leaders, the starting point for any decision-making framework begins with their expectations on inflation and the federal funds rate. This difference between expectations and actual outcomes sets in place the forces for change in both the economy and financial markets.

Policymakers and investors face these, the fundamental issues: What is our inflation model and how do we anticipate the path for the federal funds rate in the future? To answer these questions, you must ask: What do I know from experience? The expectations of the Federal Open Market Committee (FOMC) in recent years, and the expectations of many private forecasters, regarding inflation forecasts have been too high. This has also been true of the unemployment rate forecasts. FOMC's long-run expectations for the fed funds rate have regularly declined over the same period. Forecast errors are shared by everyone so this is not an attempt to blame the FOMC.

Administered Versus Market Prices Creates Disequilibrium

A second source of dynamic forces occurs when public policy sets up a price—the federal funds rate for example—or establishes a policy goal of two percent inflation, that may be inconsistent with the workings of the private market. How is credit to be allocated when private return assessments differ from an "administered" public policy rate? There is no inherent reason that a public policy-set funds rate would be consistent with credit allocationin a private economy. Critics of such Fed actions complain about the mispricing of credit/equity markets. But the fundamental issue is the potential disconnect of a policy-set benchmark interest rate and the appropriate, but unknown, interest rate to efficiently allocate financial capital in a society. What if the fed funds rate does not, in fact, match the rates of return on bonds/capital to establish equilibriums in those markets? It is easy to shift a curve on a graph to establish an equilibrium point, but not so easy in real life.

Moving from Points to Process: Where Are We Versus Where We Were

While point estimates are the daily fodder for forecasters and media headlines, the more interesting process is how did we get there. Only by knowing this can an assessment be made of where the economy is going next. In the approach taken here, at least one of the four markets is likely to be in a state of disequilibrium and understanding the forces of that disequilibrium points the direction forward.

Movement from a Focus on Points to Process

Point forecasts distract from an evaluation of processes, cycles, and trends in the markets. Points in time may be of immediate interest; but would it be more interesting to understand the process of motion? Moreover, it is not motion alone that is of interest but the interaction of markets that drive that motion. Ptolemy could describe the motion of the planets but there was that curious pattern of some planets that appeared to reverse course when seen from earth. Of course, Saturn, the planet in question, did not reverse course. But the interaction of planetary motions—like the interaction of markets, provides the incentive to dig deeper than a simple look at points in time.

Four Cases of Persistent Disequilibrium: What Is to Be Learned?

First, the persistence of an inflation benchmark, the core PCE deflator, to rise at a pace below the Fed's 2% target was troubling. This persistence suggested that the model for predicting inflation based upon the concept of a Philips Curve consistently overpredicted inflation as the unemployment rate continued its decline in recent years. Meanwhile, inflation benchmarks published by several Fed Reserve Banks, including Atlanta, portray a path for inflation that exceeds the 2% target.

Second, normalizing interest rates involved a Catch-22. If the Fed lowered rates to boost aggregate demand to spur on inflation, then it would be adding to concerns of speculation excess in equity and corporate bond markets by committing even further to a very low-interest rate regime. Several Fed officials have commented their concerns on leveraged loans for example. Their concerns had justification as the proportion of leveraged loans rated single-B- or-lower by S&P was above 65% in 2019—a steady rise from 53% in 2015 and above the 40% in 2007.

Third, the persistence of managed foreign exchange rates meant that the US pattern of persistent trade deficits would remain and generate continued balance of payments disequilibrium. In the *Wall Street Journal* dated September 10, 2018, the headline stated, "Asian corporates gorge on debt—hard currency bonds." So just before the coronavirus struck and lowered economic growth expectations, and reducing the financial viability of these bonds, corporate borrowers were extending their exposure.

Finally, continued lower interest rates would only exacerbate the problem of equity valuations and profitless IPOs. Each of our four markets/prices was in disequilibrium even before the coronavirus. Thus, when the virus hit, the market reactions were dramatic. Interestingly just over one-third of the Russell 2000 firms generated a loss over the past year and yet the Russell 2000 trades at 38 + times trailing earnings.

Even before the Covid-19 shutdowns of 2020, numerous vulnerabilities existed in pricing and market disequilibrium. Post the initial impact of the coronavirus, with economic expectations reduced, the pricing of financial assets had to adjust to the reality of slower growth/weaker profits.

With markets in disequilibrium, the gap between expected outcomes and actual outcomes will drive economic behavior and therefore pricing. In addition, the issue of notional belief exists where economic agents expect their outcomes, such as personal income, but the economy moves on the discrepancy between these notional demands and what occurs. In 2020, the expected pace of business sales and job gains was clearly disappointed by the actual outcomes associated with state shutdowns. The central role of expectations and desired outcomes relative to actual outcomes motivate change in the economy. For equity markets, the gap between expected and reported earnings moves share prices. The discrepancy between expected and actual monthly job numbers drives both the credit and foreign exchange markets each month.

Constant Disequilibrium and the Discovery of Neptune

With each of the four primary markets we focus upon, there is no expectation that they are all in a state of equilibrium. On the contrary, the state of disequilibrium and the character of feedback loops generate a further change in the asset values of the different markets. Moreover, since the trends/cycles are not synchronized, conflict between markets is a regular, not occasional, event. Prices of credit that were inconsistent with the equilibrium price of goods (housing) generated the housing boom/bust cycle. Equity valuations are out of line with the growth of the economy, or at least one sector of the economy, generated the dot.com bust. Such disequilibrium between sectors gives rise not only to cycles of up/down in sectors but to complete structural breaks in prices (housing, dot.com) generating a new paradigm of valuation in that sector. In fact, we may be seeing mispricing today. Private equity investments in recent IPO start-ups may be mispricing equity valuations despite economic growth expectations in certain sectors that may not support such valuations.

So, what about the seemingly eccentric orbit of the planet Uranus that did not fit the calculations of astronomers? Something was amiss. The orbit of Uranus was not following the predictions of astronomers. Remember Kepler's third law, as well as Newton's universal gravitation? Something was tugging at Uranus—when the math of the missing planet was worked out, then Galle, the astronomer, directed his telescope to the heavens and found Neptune. When distortions appear in market pricing, our challenge is to direct our telescopes for the source of the distortions from our framework and judge whether it is the framework or the market price that requires recalibration.

As planets influence the behavior of each other so do the markets and hence our emphasis on the interaction of the elements of the markets. We are not focused on the motion of a single planet—we want to understand the system. In addition, our four basic markets do not operate at the same stage of expansion/contraction and this sets up the motion of conflict/reconciliation or even failure between markets. For example, British finance (credit) was crucial in the railroad expansion (goods) in the United States. However, the failure of that financial channel later led to the collapse of the railroad boom.

Of course, the failure of many public policy proposals, and later adoptions, come to grief simply because the proposals are considered in a silo without acknowledgment of the interactions of markets. Changes in public policy alter the expectations for growth, inflation, interest rates, and foreign exchange values even as such policies are considered as directed solely to one silo in the economy. Even in an election year, although now it appears every year is an election year, policy proposals move markets even as many proposals will never materialize.

So much for prelims. The four markets begin with the market for goods, whose price is reflected in inflation, and whose drivers include credit, equity capital, and foreign exchange from other markets. Credit, with interest rates as a price, reflects expectations for growth and inflation, and in the short run, the expectations for policy. Equity capital, one price possible is the E/P ratio, reflects the expectations for growth, interest rates, and foreign exchange. This is especially true as changes in foreign exchange rates influence the foreign earnings of private corporations. Foreign exchange rates, as the price of currency exchange and as a proxy for incentives for capital flows, reflect the expectations for growth and credit policies globally.

Interactions and the Role of Expectations

Markets do not stand alone. What makes the subject of economics and the success of investing is the understanding, or at a minimum the recognition, of the interaction of the markets. This recognition begins with the realization that the factors that drive the behavior of one market (for example goods) are also the factors, as well as the central character, prices, that drive the behavior of other markets—for example, credit. To restate a fundamental tenet of good due diligence for investors in a way of another science we can cite the essential insight of Kepler's third law—the orbits of the planets reflected the orbits of the other planets. So, it is in economics and finance, the behavior of one market influences the behavior of other markets.

Moreover, this behavior operates in two distinct ways. First, the movements operate on the upside and the downside of the economic cycle and lead to many mini cycles within the same economic expansion. For example, domestic real final sales were above its trend in 1999–2000, 2004–2006 and again in 2014 while below trend in 2003 and 2013. Second, the interactions are characteristic of a non-recursive model—i.e., feedback loops are prevalent throughout market behavior.

Expectations generate movements in the markets. In fact, the difference of what information is expected versus what is realized, is often the driving factor in many short-term market movements. This is very evident when employment data are released or more recently when trade rumors/commentary is distinctly different from market expectations.

Identifying Change, Evolution, and Regression to the Mean

For decision makers, identifying the evolution of the economy and financial markets is essential for business success.

Throughout our review of financial markets, we will try to characterize the trends, cycles, and structural breaks in the behavior of economic and financial drivers. In addition, we often will address the issue of a "return to normal," when we test for mean reversion and examine the stability ratio of many time series. Many series, for example, interest rates and price-earnings ratios have no tendency to return to some "normal," or more precisely average value. Finally, financial, and economic series will be distinguished by the static stability properties.

Often analysts make anecdotes about a change or break in behavior; however, here we focus on the implementation of state-space techniques to provide a mathematical basis for identifying change. For example, the shift outward in the Beveridge curve provides evidence of a break in the link between job vacancies and the available workers as measured by the unemployment rate. We first identified this break in a paper published in 2006 (Domestic Implications of a Global Labor Market, *Business Economics*, 41(3), July 2006). Identification of the change in the labor market has been critical to understanding the break in the unemployment rate and the inflation rate that is central to many traditional inflation forecast models.

Also, we applied the econometric techniques on the unemployment rates (both U-3 and U-6), and we found that unemployment rate measures are not mean reverting and have a non-linear trend. Basically, our analysis suggests that we should not be looking for a constant equilibrium unemployment rate or expect that the economy will go back to that equilibrium (mean) rate. As economies are evolving over time, so do the mean rates for the different sectors of the economy.

The balance between capital expenditures and internally generated cash flow is not mean reverting, for example. We found structural breaks in both series. A structural break in a series indicates that there is no normal level (no average return) because different periods (sub-samples) have statistically different means and/or deviations from those averages. Often the assumption and expectation of a time series returning to normal is misleading and should be tested in applications. Underlying series should be tested to determine if they are mean reverting.

Evolution of the Economy—And Financial Benchmarks

During the recent economic expansion, a sense developed that the economy continues to evolve over time, but that it also experiences periods of over and under activity. To identify this evolution, we have employed a Hodrick-Prescott filter, which differentiates between a trend and cycles around that trend. Periods of rapid growth in the year-over-year percent change of Gross Domestic Product can be identified. The acceleration in growth was evident from 1998 to 1999 as the actual series stayed above the long-run trend during that time.

As for financial benchmarks, consider how corporations finance their debt. To what extent do they utilize corporate bonds relative to credit market instruments? Is there an average level of corporate debt? The answer is no, once again. Our analysis suggests there is no average level of the ratio of short-term to long-term debt. Moreover, structural breaks in this series indicate that the fundamentals behind the balance sheet management of non-financial companies change over time.

Non-linearity

Another common assumption in the analysis of economic and financial relationships is that there is a linear relationship between two series, i.e., corporations finance debt employing a fixed share of corporate bonds relative to commercial paper, on average. However, both corporate bonds and commercial paper are non-linear and that implies the rate of growth in both series is not constant. Put differently, there are no "fixed" preferences when utilizing corporate bonds or commercial paper for debt finance. Therefore, statistical tests are a must to measure whether underlying series exhibit linear or non-linear behavior, instead of assuming a linear trend.

Regression to the Mean? The Past?

Do economic and/or financial time series revert to some mean (average) value such that when an observation for that series is above (or below) its mean value the series will return to its average value. One figure most often cited as reverting to its mean is the E/P ratio. Yet, the E/P ratio is not statistically mean reverting, as there are several breaks in the series in the 1982–2017 period. Several economic factors, whose values change over time, drive the E/P ratio. The structural breaks in the series are consistent with economic recessions (those of 1991 and 2001). Time series should be tested and evaluated whether a series is mean reverting instead of merely relying on past averages as a guide.

Do Rising Rates Cause (Granger) Recessions?

In a rising interest rates environment, some investors worry about a potential recession soon. A rise in interest rates could drive an increase in interest expenses and may squeeze businesses and consumers and thereby growth. Granger causality tests provide guidance on whether a certain variable does influence the path of another variable. It is defined as the causality of the variable that helps forecast the second variable. Granger causality intimates, for example, that net interest expense does not drive economic growth.

Economies do fall into recessions and a rising rate environment may or may not lead to recessions. Some sort of shock, other than rising interest rates, may cause recessions through a channel other than corporate debt.

Identify Change, Distinguishing Trend and Cycle

For equities and bond markets, debates circle around the question is the market over or under priced relative to value. This opens both public and private decision-makers to confirmation bias—they see what they want to see and find data to support that view. The FOMC and investors may drift toward signals that support the trend view when evidence suggests otherwise. In subsequent chapters, we will employ techniques, such as the Hodrick-Prescott filter, to identify periods where current values deviate from trends.

Inflation: Heading to Success Despite the Evidence

Two percent for the PCE deflator is both the target and the forecast. However, wishing does not make it so—especially considering the history illustrated in the graph, with headline inflation, as measured by the PCE deflator, below 2 percent every month since mid-2012.

This pattern of undershooting the inflation target is also apparent in the history of the European Central Bank and the Bank of Japan. Therefore, there seems to be a broader phenomenon of a ceiling on global inflation that persists despite the growth in the monetary base in the world's major advanced economies. Moreover, the FOMC has consistently overestimated the pace of inflation since 2016. Therefore, caution is advised when incorporating the PCE deflator forecast into decision making. Even now, although we anticipate that inflation will rise toward the FOMC's 2 percent target, the path will be slow and arduous.

Assume the Ideal Outcome in an Imperfect World

For investors, decisions must be made in an imperfect world with periods of high/low volatility and changing risk/reward calculations. In contrast, the pattern of central banks' outlooks is often a linear path, as exemplified by the dot plots on inflation and unemployment provided by the FOMC. While these linear projections are certainly reasonable given the communication constraints at the FOMC, these constraints are annual point estimates which naturally lend themselves to linear paths. Such projections must be viewed as trend projections within the constraint of the expected linear economic projections. However, decision makers invest within economic and credit cycles and the trend does not serve them well as a guideline for the cyclical behavior of markets.

Stories as a Frame, Data as Puzzle Parts

One common strategy in putting together a jigsaw puzzle is to first find the outer pieces that will form a frame for the puzzle and then proceed with putting the inside pieces together following the color/shape clues. For many students of economics and finance, there is a history of learning the theory and gathering the data but leaving the semester without a framework of the subject at hand. For mystery writers, the clues are all there but what is the framework that ties the theory and data together to solve that mystery? The attack on Pearl Harbor is a case where the clues were there, but nobody put the clues together.

In our essays, we have provided a framework for examining the data. We focus on stories that put a picture/historical context to the data. Not all stories fit perfectly, and some stories do not fit at all. Yet, the cyclical nature of financial markets suggests that stories of the past may provide a framework for decision making. I was always intrigued by the television series "*Remington Steele.*" In many episodes, the leads played by Stephanie Zimbalist and Pierce Brosnan would reference a movie that would provide a frame for the current detective case.

Of course, stories can be misleading. In the book "*Thinking in Time: The Use of History for Decision Makers,*[16]" Harvard Professors Richard Neustadt and Ernest R. May provide contrasting stories where decision makers took the wrong lesson from a story in many cases. One section of the book contrasts the response of the Kennedy administration in the Bay of Pigs versus its response during the Cuban missile crisis. In the Cuban missile case, the advice to the president represented opposition views that were debated rather than the view of a single agency. Same administration and yet the decision-making process was very different. Our lesson here is that there is a caution in drawing parallels between different events. Many commentators draw parallels to the coronavirus with other prior virus

---

[16] Richard E. Neustadt and Earnest R. May, *Thinking in Time: The Uses of History for Decision-Makers*, The Free Press, New York, 1986.

problems (MERS, Swine Flu, SARS, and most dramatically the Spanish flu after World War I. But are the parallels accurate?

In Chapter two we will explore the behavior, and excesses, of major significant time series that are the framework for how we view the economic and financial world we live.

* * *

References

Steven Ambrose, *Nothing Like It in the World*, Simon & Schuster 2001. Why a history book on a railroad? We are interested in the dynamic process of choices made and choices changed under changing economic circumstances. One of my twelve must reads when I taught the MBA students at Wake Forest.

W. Barnett and K. J. Singleton, eds. *New Approaches to Monetary Economics*, Cambridge University Press, Cambridge, UK, 1987. A compilation of essays by different authors that offer alternative views of the economic process.

Simon Bowmaker and Minouche Shafik, *When the President Calls*, MIT Press, October 2019. Excellent reviews of U.S. presidential economic advisors since WWII. In some cases, the views are very biased, but others offer excellent insights for all decision makers.

Doris Kearns Goodwin, *Team of Rivals*, Simon & Schuster, 2005. An essential read on effective decision making in very turbulent times. Another history book—yes, because economic and financial analysis must be placed in the context of actual decisions. Another of my twelve must reads.

Grant's Interest Rate Observer, Grantspub, New York, NY. A biweekly publication that takes a cautious view of current financial market developments. In full disclosure, I am a subscriber.

Richard E. Neustadt and Earnest R. May, *Thinking in Time: The Uses of History for Decision-Makers*, The Free Press, New York, 1986. One of my twelve must reads. This book offers a challenge to decision makers and the essay on decisions by President Kennedy is particularly instructive.

Friedrich Nietzsche, *The Gay Science, 1882*, Translated from the German by Walter Kaufman, Vintage Books, March 1974.

Michael A. Roberto, *Know What You Don't Know*, Wharton School Publishing, 2009. A book on thinking before you get into trouble. What are you biases/prejudices? One of my twelve must reads.

John E. Silvia, *Dynamic Economic Decision Making*, Wiley, 2011. Three chapters are essential at this point. Chapter 2 discusses economic benchmarks. Chapter 5 focuses on the use of information and cognitive biases. Chapter 8 focuses in on capital markets. This book reflects some of the lectures I utilized at Wake Forest. One of my twelve must reads. Picking my own book? Yes, because other economics/finance books fail to cover both economics and finance and fail to allow for behavioral finance. Such are the lessons of being in the action on a trading floor.

Thomas Sowell, *Conflict of Visions*, William Morrow, Quill, 1987. An essential read to understand "the other side." To walk a mile in another's moccasins as one might say. Too often discussions are simply two or more people talking across each other—particularly in politics—with little understanding of the other side. One of my twelve must reads.

Diane Vaughn, *The Challenger Launch Decision: Risky Technology, Culture and Deviance at NASA*, University of Chicago Press, Chicago, 1996. The normalization of deviance bias is most notably associated with the Challenger disaster. This is an important lesson for investors who face leadership decisions that continue to justify actions that go off course but are justified as being a temporary deviation.

Wall Street Journal and Barron's. Immediate, real world examples of economic/financial success and failure. Putting your book learning into the real world is enlightened education. In full disclosure, I am a subscriber.

2

The Story of the Original Boom and Bust in Western Finance: The Mississippi Bubble

Story and Motivation 09 20 2020.

> Wisdom lies neither in fixity nor in change but in the dialectic between the two—Octavio Paz

Although investors, business decision makers, and policymakers talk about "the normal" the challenge is to recognize the change in a constantly evolving economic/financial set of markets.

In this chapter, we illustrate several approaches we have utilized in our market experience to identify cycles, trends, structural breaks, and the persistence of disequilibrium in the marketplace. For example, how might we benchmark in statistical terms the comment that "markets are in a correction mode?" What does it mean when we are "returning to normal" or "finding a new normal?".

Forecasts of economic/financial developments are often presented as linear projections but how many time series is linear as opposed to nonlinear? Finally, how often are the basic assumptions of modeling broken? Consider the following two citations.

"The economy—Is There Light at the End of the Tunnel?" *Time* **Sep. 28, 1992**

The cover of Time Magazine on September 28, 1992 when, in fact, the recession was already over.

"So Far, It's not a Crash" *Financial Times* 03 15 1990, Survey of Japanese Financial Markets

The *Financial Times* headline at the time when the Japanese economy, real estate market and financial markets were indeed in free fall. This headline indicates how hard it is to judge the path of the economy and financial markets in real time. The financial/economic decline in Japan had just begun.

The Story of the Original Boom and Bust in Western Finance: The Mississippi Bubble

Although the Tulip Craze in Holland in 1637 is often cited as the first great economic/financial bubble, it had a very limited impact on the Dutch economy. The Dutch remained the preeminent economic power of that age. The country's continued affluence supported the artistic genius of Rembrandt and Johannes Vermeer, among others. Moreover, the bubble bursting had even less impact on the global economy.

The first great example of financial excess is the story of the Mississippi Bubble.

In the early eighteenth century, the economy of France was depressed. Following the death of Louis XIV, the government found itself deeply in debt because of the king's financial excesses. Taxes were very high for the same reason.

France did have one great asset—the colony of Louisiana, a vast settlement in the interior of North America. That was much larger than France. The French knew little about it. But rumor had it that the land was rich in silver and gold, the components of the French currency.

Enter John Law, a tall, handsome, and vain man, born in Edinburgh, Scotland who became a financier. He was a colorful character described as tall, handsome, and vain with a passion for women and gambling.

Law arrived in France in 1714, he renewed his acquaintance with the Duke of Orleans who had become Regent of France after the king's death. The Regent ruled while the heir to the throne was five-year-old Louis XV, a minor. An admirer of Law's ideas, the duke sought John Law's advice in straightening out France's financial problems.

Law was an advocate for paper money and convinced the French government to let him open a bank, the BankGenerale. The bank would issue notes supported by the bank's assets of gold and silver and the notes would circulate as of exchange. Paper money was a new concept for the French. John Law believed paper notes would increase the money in circulation, which, in turn, would increase commerce and revitalize the French economy.

Building on these beliefs, Law organized the Compagnie d'Occident (Company of the West). The French government gave the control of trade between and France and its Louisiana and Canadian colonies to the company. The colony of Louisiana's connection to the Mississippi River gave rise to the company's more popular name, The Mississippi Company.

Law's company had exclusive trading privileges in the territory for twenty-five years; it could appoint its own governor and officers in the colony and make land grants to potential developers. In turn, the company accepted the responsibility of transporting 6,000 settlers and 3,000 slaves to the colony before the expiration of its charter.

Law raised money for the Mississippi Company by selling shares in the company for cash and more importantly, for state bonds. The bonds helped French finances while providing the company with a secure cash flow. The lure of gold and silver brought out many eager investors.

The Mississippi Company was a small part of a much grander financial empire John Law wanted to create. In September 1718, the company acquired the monopoly in tobacco trading in Africa. The next year the French government took over and renamed the BankGenerale the Bank Royale. Law remained in charge and the crown further guaranteed the bank's note issue. In May, Law obtained control of the companies trading with China and the East Indies. He termed his entire business interest the Compaigne des Indies, but most people still called it the Mississippi Company. In effect, Law now controlled all trade with France and the rest of the world outside of Europe.

The company next purchased the right to mint new coins for France, and by October it had purchased the right to collect most French taxes. In January 1720, Law became the Controller General and Superintendent General of Finance. Law was now in charge of all of France's finance and money creation. He also controlled the company that handled all of France's foreign trade and colonial development.

Law paid for these activities and privileges by issuing additional shares in the company. These shares could be paid for with bank notes (from his bank) or with government debt.

The values of shares in the Mississippi Company rose dramatically as Law's empire expanded. Investors from across France and Europe eagerly played in this new market. Shares in the Mississippi Company started at around 500 livres tournois (the French unit of account at the time) per share in January 1719. By December 1719, share prices had reached 10,000 livres, an increase of 1900% in just under a year.

Law's scheme fell apart because of his willingness to issue more bank notes to fund purchases of shares in the company. Stock prices began falling in

January 1720 as some investors sold shares to turn capital gains into gold coin. To stop the sell-off, Law restricted any payment in gold that was more than 100 livres. The paper notes of the Bank Royale were made legal tender, which meant that they could be used to pay taxes and settle most debts. The bank subsequently promised to exchange its notes for shares in the company at the going market price of 10,000 livres. This attempt to turn stock shares into money resulted in a sudden doubling of the money supply in France. Inflation shot up dramatically reaching 3% by January 1720.

Law devalued shares in the company in several stages during 1720 reaching 50% of their face value. By September 1720, the price of shares in the company had fallen to 2,000 livres and to 1,000 livres by December. Law's opponents seized the company by confiscating the shares of investors who could not prove they paid for their shares with real assets rather than credit. This reduced investor shares by two-thirds. By September 1721 share prices had dropped to 500 livres, where they had been at the beginning.

What were the problems that underlay these actions? The private bank set up by John Law had three-quarters of its capital as sovereign debt of the French monarchy (problem Number one, narrow concentration of assets). The company was granted a trade monopoly thereby eliminating competition and competitive pricing that would have provided market discipline to trade and bank finance of the Compaigne. The notes of the bank were guaranteed by the French King (problem number three—a fiat currency backed by a promise to pay from the sovereign—in more paper currency).

As is the tradition of all paper currencies, the bank issued more notes than it could back up with coinage (problem number four). This was repeated by the United States under both Presidents Franklin Roosevelt and Richard Nixon as the fiat currency in circulation exceeded what could be backed by gold. The fiat currency became devalued and inflation rose after Nixon dropped the link to gold and the federal budget/central bank was no longer limited by a link to specie.

Louis XV and his regent failed to reduce spending after the lavish spending and wars of his predecessor Louis XIV. This problem of excessive spending relative to the ability to pay was also a character of the economy of Weimar Germany after World War I. The reparations Germany was forced to pay by the victorious allies were clearly excessive relative to the ability of the German economy to pay those debts. This led the German government to print money which in turn caused hyperinflation. This same pattern has been repeated in many emerging markets since World War II. One might question if the same pattern exists today in the United States following the two trillion dollar bailouts to stabilize the American economy following its shutdowns because of the coronavirus.

John Law exaggerated the investment returns in the Mississippi Company and thereby created expectations of wealth that could not be met by economic reality (problem number six). Exaggerated expectations were repeated in the dot.com era and the housing boom/bust of 2006–2009.[1]

Like many other promoters of financial speculation, Law fled the scene as his properties were seized. He first reappeared in Brussels, then Rome, Copenhagen, and Venice where he continued to gamble. In 1723, Law was granted permission to return to London having received a pardon for four years and then moved to Venice. Contracting pneumonia, he died a poor man in 1729. In the tradition of subsequent promoters of financial speculation, Law never returned to the scene of the financial crime.

Overshooting and Irrational Exuberance—The Excesses on the Up and Down

One takeaway from experience and observation of financial markets is that change/excess in one market motivates change in other markets since prices in our four markets (commodities, credit, equity, and foreign exchange) are mutually dependent. The illustration of these excesses provides light on real-world events.

> One change leaves the way open for the introduction of others. Niccolò Machiavelli

This book's focus is upon the behavior of a selected group of market prices, and their patterns of behavior and interactions, that serve as the focus of daily commentary consumed by investors and decision makers. We look at the cycles[2] and trends for each series while identifying structural breaks in each series that hint at a financial/economic regime change.

We are most familiar with overshooting in the equity markets, but the phenomenon refers to the movement in a market price to a surprise or shock in the short-run that is greater than its long-run response. The initial response to a proposed policy move (easier monetary policy, a fiscal stimulus, or trade initiative) will lead to a jump in market prices, in part because market participants that hold long or short positions in the market must

---

[1] For a perspective on the housing situation early in the crisis see Robert J. Shiller, "Things That Go Boom," *Wall Street Journal*, 2007, 8 (February).

[2] One take on the links between finance and nominal GDP appears in Albert Wojnilower "Finance is the Original Sin," April 12, 2016. Craig Drill Capital Newsletter.

cover those positions. Alternatively, policy announcements, such as The Fed's announcement of their intention to buy corporate debt, will move prices while the long-run buying by the Fed would be more modest than what market participants expected.[3]

Cycles, Trends, and Corrections: Creating a First Impression

Commentary, both economic and financial, is littered with the notice of cycles, trends, and corrections for numerous time series in the economy and the financial markets. But how can you identify a correction and, more importantly, divine its significance? Usually, financial analysts identify a 200-day, or 60-day moving average (ma) of a series and compared that moving average to the current value of that series. If the current value is above the 200-day ma, then things are looking up—if below, well not so good.

However, there is a problem. We can calculate a 200-day ma for any series, yet the ma does not separate the trend from the cycle around that trend. To assess the economy and market prices, we need to know both the trend and deviations from that trend that may signal change. This is currently the core of the debate in 2020 about the trend in the economy (GDP), inflation, and the stock market. To separate trend versus cycle, a time series filter such as the Hodrick-Prescott filter[4] is the first step. A moving average calculation conflates the two. For the analyst separating trend from the cycle is crucial.

What Generates these Cycles Around the Trend?

Innovations/new information tend to generate cycles around a trend that confronts decision makers with the realization that their expectations are not equal to the actual data/observations they are observing. Instead, they need to discern that cycle and keep a perspective to recognize the cycles. Corrections, up or down, move cycles but do not alter trend. Financial analysts at this point talk about underlying value (trend) while economists talk about the

---

[3] Overshooting was initially put forth with the work on exchange rate by Dornbusch. Rudiger Dornbusch, "Expectation and Exchange Rate Dynamics", *Journal of Political Economy*, 1976, 84 (December): 1161–1176.
[4] See John E. Silvia, *Dynamic Economic Decision Making*, Wiley 2011, pp. 361–367 for prior applications for this approach. The original reference to the Hodrick-Prescott filter is found in R. J. Hodrick and E. C. Prescott, "Postwar U.S. Business Cycle: An Empirical Investigation," *Journal of Money, Credit and Banking*, 1997, 29 (1): 1–16.

economy's underlying momentum. For the economy, real domestic final sales were above trend in 1998–1999 and again in 2005–2007. Pre-tax corporate profits were above trend in 2006–2007.

Stability—where trend equals cycle—is the exception. Markets for goods, credit, equity capital are in a constant state of disequilibrium. A movement in one market leads to change in other markets—note the constant back-and-forth influence of interest rates (credit), inflation (goods), and exchange rates (foreign currency) on each other. It is thus imperative to watch all these markets and note the position of their cycle relative to the trend.

There are also issues of friction and imbalance. How far out of line is one market relative to trend and what is the carryover from one market to another (lack of frictions)? Currently, two markets appear considerably out of equilibrium—trade of goods as the United States and China battle each other, and the credit markets as the Fed pursues normalization. A sense of imbalance can be determined by the degree of reaction in equity markets to public commentary on trade with China, and the volatility in credit market spurred by the commentary on possible Fed actions in December 2016, and again in 2019. In both cases, such volatility indicates a high degree of transmission between markets and a high degree of deviation from equilibrium.

None Come to Pass: Expect a Trend, Get a Cycle

What happens when decision makers employ the expected long-run trend as the basis for a short-run forecast? They feel their job is done and there is no need for change—not smart in an evolving economy.

Trend Growth Despite an Up/Down History

Over the course of this expansion, economic growth has fluctuated around the average value of 2.1 percent. Here we focus upon real final sales to domestic purchasers (Fig. 2.1) as a closer benchmark for the pace of spending by domestic economic agents. The series is calculated as a percent change from the previous quarter which provides a time series that is trend-stationary.[5] Signals from this data are not clouded by an underlying economic pattern.[6]

---

[5] Trend-stationarity means that the difference between actual output and a deterministic trend is not explosive.

[6] This unit root problem was identified, and a test developed, by D. Dickey and W. Fuller (1979), "Distribution of the Estimates for Autoregressive Time series with a Unit Root," *Journal of American*

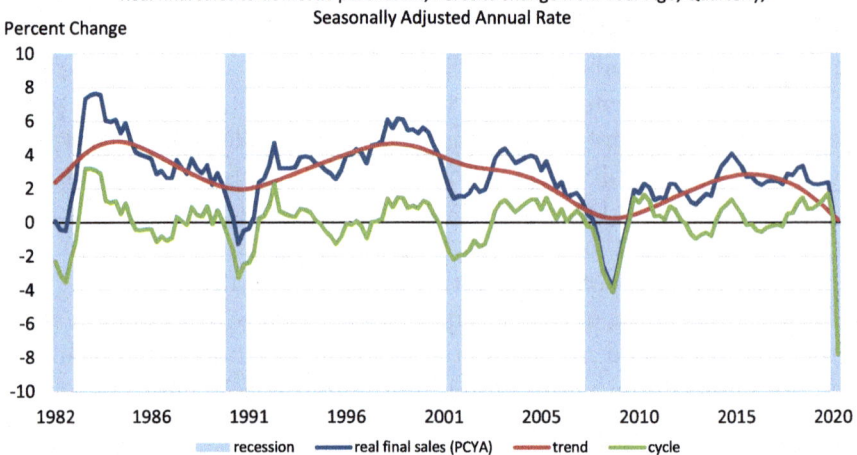

Fig. 2.1 Real final sales to domestic purchasers

Looking back at the economic growth forecasts made over recent years, they often began each year at or above 3%, a pace of growth more reflective of previous recoveries. Each year, however, these forecasts often gradually drifted down to 2.0–2.25%. These numerical forecasts illustrate that cognitive bias, in this case, the anchoring bias that bases current outlooks on the historical pattern, often color the expectations and conclusions economists make about the statistical results. In this example, economists tend to anchor their prior expectations on 3% growth, 2% inflation or a full employment at an unemployment rate at 5% or so. We expect the economy to behave in a way that the results of any change will eventually return to our anchors. A second bias is the normalization of deviance bias where economists see any deviation as just noise and not a signal of change. Third, there is the recency bias—tomorrow looks a lot like the recent past, certainly not the distant past—economists are too quick to judge. This does not allow for factors that may lead to different results, even though the history of economic growth is such that changing fundamentals can lead to breaks with the past.

Finally, this also opens both public and private decision makers to confirmation bias—they see what they want to see and find data to support that view. This creates the risk that the FOMC and investors will follow signals that support the trend view when evidence may suggest otherwise.

Statistical Association, 74: 427–431; D. Dickey and W. Fuller (1981), "Likelihood Ratio Tests for Autoregressive Time Series with a Unit Root," Econometrica 49: 1057–1072. These tests, and their applications, appear in Chapter 4 of *Economic and Business Forecasting*, John E. Silvia et.al., 2014 Wiley.

Inflation: Heading to Success Despite the Evidence

In recent years anchoring bias has been widely seen. Two percent for the headline PCE deflator (Fig. 2.2) is both the target and the forecast. However, wishing does not make it so. As the graph points out, despite 2% inflation as a target, the headline inflation, as measured by the PCE deflator, fell below 2% every month since mid-2012.

For simplicity, consider that the average value of the PCE deflator, measured as percent change a year ago, from the period of 1982–2001, was 2.91% while for the period 2002 to the fourth quarter of 2019 it was 1.78%. Is this difference statistically significant? Yes, and it indicates a 2% inflation target is unlikely to be achieved given the pattern of the last 17 years.

This pattern of undershooting the inflation target is also apparent in the history for the ECB and the Bank of Japan for the last twenty years and even more so for the European Central Bank in more recent years. For this, there seems to be a broader phenomenon of a ceiling on global inflation that persists despite the growth in the monetary base in the world's major advanced economies. In addition, the FOMC has consistently overestimated the pace of inflation in recent years since the Great Recession of 2007–2009. Caution is thereby advised when incorporating the PCE deflator forecast of 2% into decision making to avoid an anchoring bias.

Time series such as the PCE deflator and GDP are characterized by structural breaks in the series. Not surprisingly, breaks appear for the PCE deflator in 1991, 2004, and 2012 which are associated with post-recession periods or

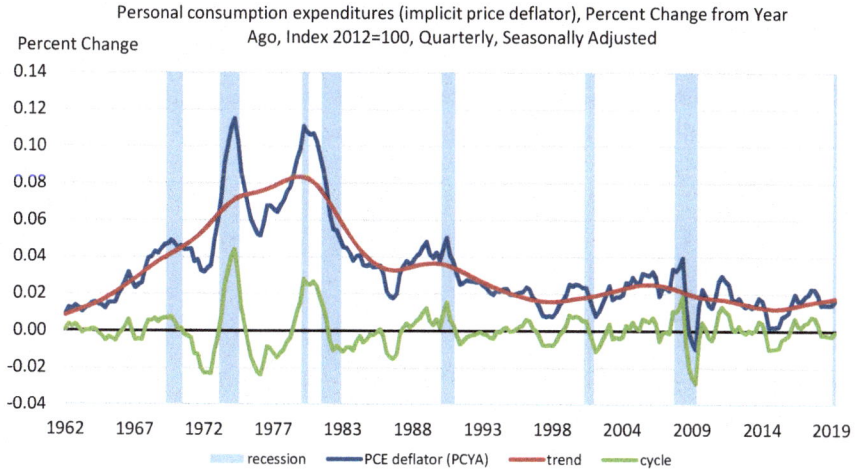

Fig. 2.2 History of PCE deflator measure of inflation since 1965

weak commodity prices. For GDP, breaks are associated with the recession periods of 1990, 2000, and 2008.[7]

Assume the Ideal Outcome in an Imperfect World

For investors, decisions must be made in an imperfect world with periods of high/low volatility and changing risk/reward calculations. In contrast, central bank outlooks are often a linear path, as characterized by the FOMC's fed funds rate projections, which we will cover in detail in Chapter 4. While these linear projections are certainly reasonable given the FOMC's communication constraints, projections must be viewed as trend projections within the constraint of the expected linear economic projections. However, investors calculate risk/rewards within economic and credit cycles and the trend does not serve them well as a guideline for the cyclical behavior of markets.

Expectations of Mean Reversion: Getting Back to Normal

A standard approach for investors/analysts sets expectations of getting back to normal and finding "an average" return on an investment over time. In other words, they believe there is an average return on investments, and deviations from the average are only temporary. Our statistical analysis paints a different picture: there is often no normal level (average). Our analysis suggests that both capital expenditures and internally generated cash flow are not mean reverting, Fig. 2.3. Structural breaks occurred in both series. This indicates that there is no normal level (no average return) because different periods (sub-samples) have statistically different means and/or deviations from those averages. Basically, expectations of getting back to normal are misleading. Statistical techniques are available to test whether underlying series are mean reverting.

Debt Finance

How do corporations finance their debt? To what extent do they utilize corporate bonds relative to credit market instruments and economic growth

---

[7] A state space approach is utilized here. See G. S. Maddala and In-Moo Kim, (1998), *Unit Root, Cointegration and Structural Change*. Cambridge, UK: Cambridge University Press.

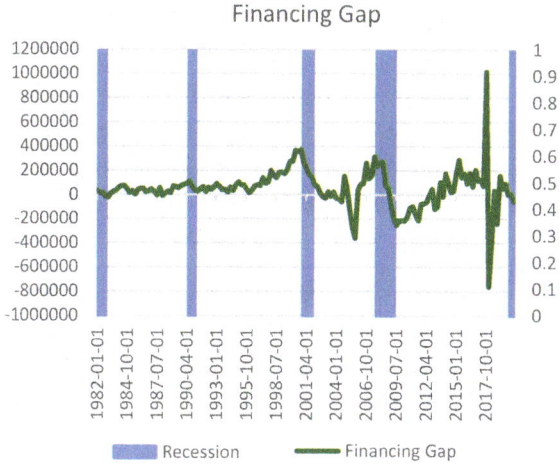

Fig. 2.3 Financing gap for non-financial corporate business

(Fig. 2.4)? Is there an average level of corporate debt? The answer is no—once again. Our analysis suggests there is no average level or ratio of corporate debt finance and nominal GDP. Moreover, we found structural breaks at different intervals for total nonfinancial debt, corporate bonds, and commercial paper at nonfinancial corporations.

Another common assumption is that there is a linear relationship between two series, i.e., corporations finance debt employing a fixed share of corporate

Fig. 2.4 Ratio of corporate debt to nominal GDP

bonds relative to commercial paper, on average. We found that both corporate bonds and commercial paper are non-linear. This implies the rate of growth in both series is not constant. Put differently, there are no "fixed" preferences when utilizing corporate bonds or commercial paper for debt finance. In sum, investors and decision makers need to test whether a time series exhibits linear or non-linear behavior, instead of assuming a linear trend.[8]

If Not Normal, Where Are We in the Cycle? Late

Where are we in the current economic or business cycle is a frequently asked question of analysts. The recoveries from the 2001, 2007–2009 recessions and the 2010 to 2019 expansion are anything but normal. But some patterns provide a heuristic set of signals when the data are distinctly different by cycle and non-linear as well. Searching for statistically perfect "normal rates" may be unproductive. More useful to determining where we are in the credit cycle is knowing that many time series do not return to normal but rather exhibit a distinct cyclical pattern. Over the last twenty years, there has been a constant re-estimation of what policymakers interpret as the natural rate of interest, normal real interest rates, and full employment.[9]

Late Cycle Pricing of High-Yield Credit

As illustrated in Fig. 2.5, the steady rise in the risk premium on high-yield credit can signal credit concerns even before the signs of recession are evident in the real economy. In addition, this risk premium has a distinct cyclical pattern that signals to the analyst where we are in the economic cycle. In the years 2000–2001 and 2007–2008, there was a rise in the risk premium. In contrast, as an economic recovery takes hold, the risk premia tends to decline steadily until just before the next recession.

The pricing of risk in the high-yield bond market is quite sensitive to changes in market perceptions. This pattern is reminiscent of the pattern of corporate profit growth, that we will cover later in Chapter 10, as another

---

[8] Test employed here follows W. A. Brock, Dechert, and J. Schenkman. A Test for independence based on the correlation dimension. Working Paper. University of Wisconsin at Madison, University of Houston, and University of Chicago, 1996.
[9] See for example, 2 Thomas Laubach and John C. Williams, "Measuring the Natural Rate of Interest," *Review of Economics and Statistics*, 2003, 85 (4) (November): 1063–1070. Kathryn Holston, Thomas Laubach, and John C. Williams, "Measuring the Natural Rate of Interest: International Trends and Determinants," *Journal of International Economics*, 2017, 108 (May): S59–S75.

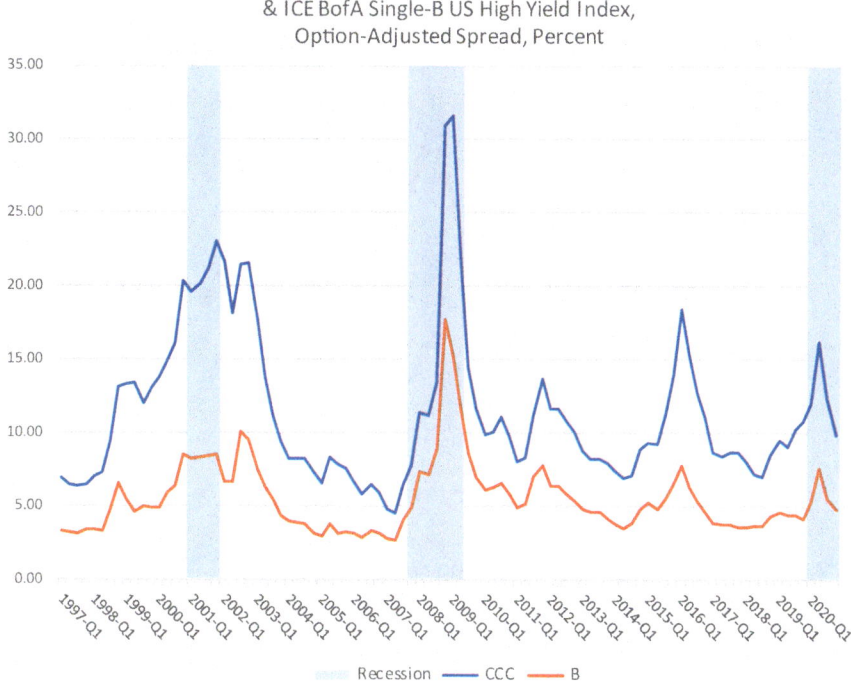

Fig. 2.5 High yield option adjusted spreads

signal of potential economic difficulties. Both indicate that credit premia are rising with the aging of the credit cycle.

Credit Standards: Move to Tighter Standards

Over the economic cycle, banks adjust their lending standards. Unfortunately, the dynamic adjustment of credit standards appears to impart a very procyclical bias to the credit cycle. From Fig. 2.6, the percentage of banks that tighten credit drops dramatically in the early phase of an economic recovery (1992–1994, 2002–2004, 2010–2011) and remains low for most of an economic expansion. The percentage of banks that tighten credit rises sharply just before a recession (1999–2000, 2007–2008). This credit cycle, while certainly rational from an individual bank's point of view, becomes quite procyclical when viewed in the aggregate. A tighter credit phase of this cycle had emerged beginning in 2015 even before the shutdown/COVID recession of 2020.

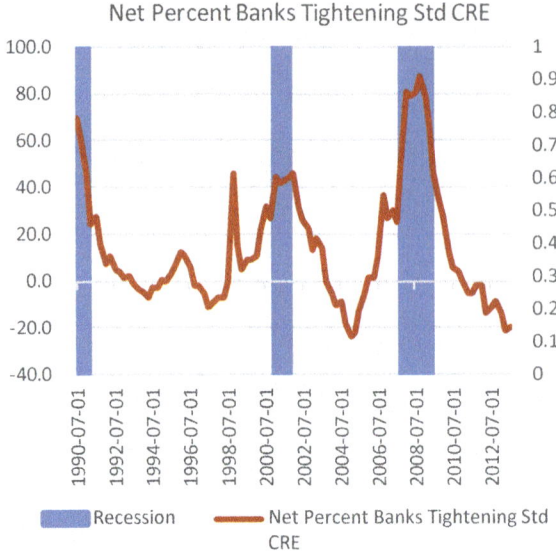

Fig. 2.6 Net percent of banks tightening credit-real estate

For Whatever the Reason: A Flatter Yield Curve

Ever since the taper tantrum in 2013, there have been two distinct moves in the yield curve as illustrated in Fig. 2.7. The long end of the yield curve has exhibited a bullish flattening trade with the decline in the 10-year/two-year spread. This reflects the yield pickup for U.S. Treasury debt relative to what is available for investors in Europe and Japan—also reflecting the incentive of a stronger dollar to attract foreign inflows. Meanwhile, the short end of the yield curve reflects the anticipation of a FOMC increase in rates or at least some form of tighter policy going forward.

Uncertainty in financial markets provides the motivation for two distinct moves. First, investor uncertainty at the global level has prompted a haven move into U.S. Treasury debt. At the same time, uncertainty on the economic outlook limits the extent of Fed tightening of policy as well as the private market discounting of future Fed funds moves.

Sorry but there is no Artificial Intelligence Answer—Actual Thinking is Involved.

Painful indeed—but you knew that. The same economic factors that indicate growth also indicate recessions—or worse. Beyond the economics is an assessment of the ability of the system to adapt. What is the downside and how many deep-pocket investors are there? An open economic system

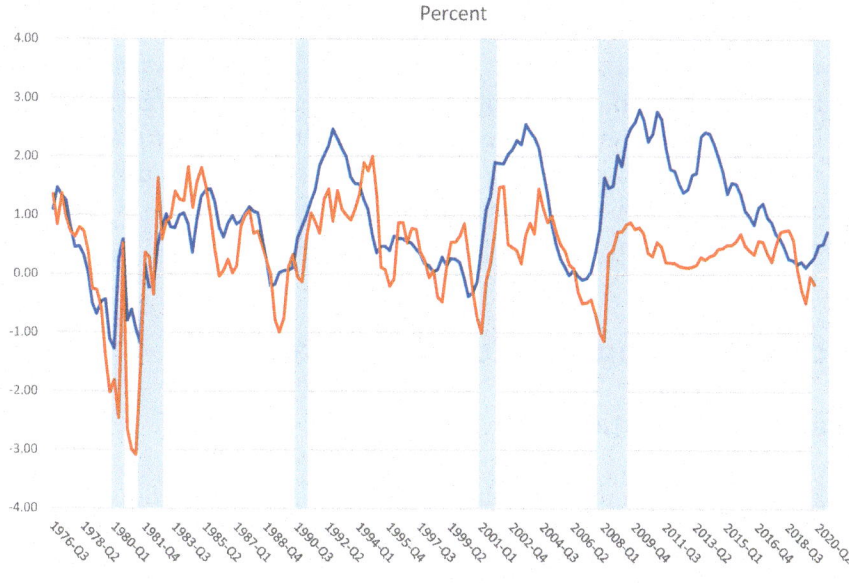

Fig. 2.7 Yield curves

is limited by legal obligations. The ability to meet bank loans (1990[10]), housing mortgages (2007–2009), or even railroad bond payments (nineteenth century) or U.S. Treasury specie payments (FDR and Nixon), the downside may be closer than you think. Second, are you investing or speculating (Mississippi Bubble)? A very tough call in the middle of the action that is debated in the financial markets very day.

In the early phase of an economic expansion, investing is the common motivation where, opportunities abound, and asset prices generally rise. However, then your Excel tables and your recency bias set in. You only recall financial success—memories of past recessions fade away.

The scrolls of financial history are littered with moving average charts that point upward even though there is no there—i.e., valuation. Finally, the anchoring bias, so often apparent in public policy discussions leads to inaccurate answers to such questions as: What should be the correct currency exchange rate to gold (U.K. policy after WWI). What is the neutral fed funds rate (U.S. policy debate of the 2010–2019 period)? Despite the trade

---

[10] The financial stresses of the 1990 period are reviewed in "The Capital Crunch: Neither a Borrower nor a Lender Be," *Journal of Money, Credit, and Banking*, 1995, 27 (3) (August).

issues, the correct price for oil, copper or other commodities such as soybeans (debates for the 2017–2020 period)?

All of this becomes even more fascinating as we recall the interactions between our four market prices. There really is no mean reversion for the P/E ratio for valuation of the equity market. The dollar/yuan/gold exchange rate is as often a matter of policy determination than it is for markets. The Fed sets the short-run policy rate but also directly influences the long-term Treasury rate buy its bond buying. The neutral fed funds rate is subject to constant re-estimation.

Decision Making and Cognitive Biases

Benchmark Evolution

For any investment committee, the fundamental challenge is not to react to point benchmarks, but rather evaluate the relevance of these benchmarks in a constantly evolving economy.

> "Aye, the compass doesn't point North. But we're not trying to find North, are we?"—Mr. Joshamee Gibbs in Pirates of the Caribbean: The Curse of the Black Pearl, 2003, Disney Pictures

For Mr. Gibbs, the pursuit of true north was not the direction to follow. In financial markets, the pursuit of a "true" direction in recent years has been a distraction from correctly observing the evolution of the economy. For example, in an article entitled "What will it take to lift US Inflation?," (*Financial Times*, May 26, 2019) the author Joe Rennison asks what it will take to return to 2% inflation, the stated target of the Federal Reserve. But the accompanying graph illustrates a break in the US break-even inflation rate in October 2018 and then of course in early 2020. Such structural breaks signal a new regime in inflation patterns and make it increasingly unlikely that the Fed can reestablish a 2% inflation rate.[11]

In the rest of the article, Rennison moves from inflation to inflation expectations. That dog doesn't hunt. There is too much shifting between measures of inflation. Finally, the PCE, the personal consumption deflator, is mean reverting but also exhibits a high level of autocorrelation—i.e., it takes a long

---

[11] We shall discuss more on this later with reference to Governor Powell's presentation at Jackson Hole in August 2020.

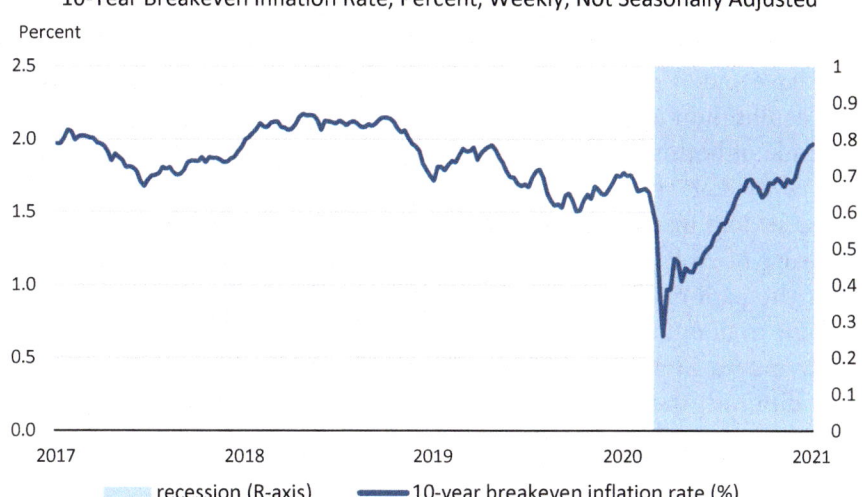

Fig. 2.8 Ten-year breakeven inflation rate

time to return to its mean—which is exactly the behavior we have seen in recent years (Fig. 2.8).

A Man with One Clock Knows What Time It is, a Man with Two Clocks Does not

As Shakespeare's Henry V said, "Once more unto the Breach, dear friends, once more." Again, from the *Financial Times*, (May 23, 2019), another article by Joe Rennison entitled, "Yield Curve inversion keeps investors on their toes." The problem, of course, is that there are two clocks always ticking as investors make decisions. The federal funds rate is the first clock. It is set by public policy actions. Short-term interest rates are priced off that clock. The private market primarily sets the second clock which is the ten-year Treasury interest rate. The public exceptions are the bond rate set by the Bank of Japan and the three-year rate set by the Reserve Bank of Australia. These two different clocks raise a suspicion that the yield curve is not as reliable an indicator of financial stress as it was prior to 2007 given the increase in the Fed's balance sheet through its buying and thereby influence on the slope of the yield curve.

Linkages Between Markets

As we have said, it is not correct to assume that the economy evolves toward a given equilibrium in the market and rarely achieves an equilibrium given the multitude of both supply and demand-side shocks. Rather the economy and financial markets move from one disequilibrium to another. In the markets, there is seldom insufficient time after a given shock for the economy to have the luxury of evolving toward an anticipated end point before another shock moves the path of the economy. Moreover, when we force estimates of the economy to fit our forecasting biases, we fail to see that economic events have already moved in a new direction. Complicating the process, our cognitive biases diminish the importance of new developments since they contradict the success of our initial forecast. We ignore what is different (normalization of deviance) and accept what confirms our priors (confirmation bias).

Price Adjustment

We observe that prices do adjust over time but that our four market prices of primary focus here are characterized by differential speeds of adjustment and that each market incorporates expectations into its price setting.

In the first half of 2020, the rapid easing of monetary policy in the United States was accompanied, in the short run, by a rise in the dollar's value even as interest rates fell. In part, the U.S. dollar, and the benchmark Treasury 10-year rate offered a flight to safety, given global uncertainty of the impact of the COVID virus. Expectations were that the U.S. economy would be more resilient over time than other world economies and that the U.S. dollar/Treasury note represented a safe harbor. From January 2020 to June 2020 the Chinese Yuan depreciated versus the dollar.

But from mid-June to late August the Yuan appreciated versus the dollar. Investor expectations had shifted toward a quicker Chinese recovery and a less pronounced U.S. recovery. America was thrown into a severe shutdown of business due to state-mandated shutdowns resulting in millions of workers losing their jobs or on temporary furlough. Meanwhile, the Federal Reserve sent out signals of persistent easing. The dollar began to decline while U.S. Treasury rates rose modestly.

In each of our four markets, the rate of price adjustment is a function of the difference between current and equilibrium prices as well as the gap in expectations between future values of the current economic benchmarks and their current levels.

Changes in economic policy, when not publicly known or understood (Affordable Care Act), or when quickly reversed (monetary policy 2019), can generate a short-run burst in economic growth and higher inflation/equity values or exchange rates or a short-run turn in interest rates. After the Fed ease in mid-2019, NASDAQ share prices rose steadily until early 2020 and two-year Treasury rates fell for the rest of 2019 as expectations of more Fed easing and lower rates played into market pricing. The break-even 5-year inflation rate fell as the Fed easing altered expectations about the pace of growth and inflation going forward. Once the investing public, expectations will again match ongoing policy. Changes in economic policy impact expectations and therefore aggregate demand/supply relationships.

What changed over time? Investors saw that the expected pace of U.S. growth relative to China was diminished. For them, the longer-run value of the Yuan appreciated relative to the dollar even though in the short run the yuan had depreciated. The Yuan had overshot on the downside in early 2020 and the dollar overshot on the upside.

Markets had also overshot on the downside for benchmark Treasury rates. The low on the benchmark ten-year rate occurred in early March 2020. The rate has risen since although it remains low relative to recent history. In this case, expectations of the long-run value of Treasury debt as a safe harbor have diminished. Spreads on high-yield debt peaked in mid-March and have declined since. Finally, equity values saw its lows in late March and have set new records recently.

What do we take away from here?

- Prices do adjust over time.
- The four market prices are characterized by differential speeds of adjustment.
- Each market incorporates expectations into its price setting.

The speed of adjustment of expectations, rate of convergence depends on the structural parameters/elasticity of each of the factors that determine prices in each of our four market prices.

For the equity markets, modest changes in policy-set interest rates meant a much larger response than for the dollar or for overall aggregate demand in the economy and commodity prices in general. In contrast, housing demand responded sharply to lower rates while business investment demand had a very limited response. Commodity prices rose with expectations of better economic growth but had very little response to lower rates. As expected, the larger the price elasticity of demand (housing), the more the change in actual interest rate will affect demand, even in a period of overall sharp declines in GDP growth. As an aside, what made the first half of 2020 unique was that personal income rose during the recession.

Evolution of Irrationality: Expectations Overwhelm the Fundamentals

The credit cycle, much like the business cycle, is driven by complex economic relationships. Understanding the emotional component in these cycles can equip investors to better identify turning points in the cycle. This is particularly true in situations where expectations overwhelm fundamentals.

Euro Sovereign Debt

> Many liquid assets which are close substitutes for money… [are] only inferior when the actual moment for a payment arrives—Radcliffe Report (1959)

The Report of the Committee on the Working of the Monetary System (commonly known as The Radcliffe Report) was published in 1959 about monetary policy and the workings of the Bank of England. Named after its chairman, Cyril Radcliffe, the report was the result of dissatisfaction with the monetary policy of the 1950s.

For the committee, the growth of credit rises with euphoria. As animal spirits take hold, investors seek out opportunities, producing more credit in the system. The "dot.com" bubble and the subprime housing bubble support the insight that credit availability and risk grow with prosperity.[12] What makes the current (2020) investment scene so challenging is how to value new instruments against the central banks' administered interest rates. Investors know central bank rates are not normalized, but what do they know of the anticipated market returns for new investment opportunities?

As illustrated in Fig. 2.9, when the moment of payment arrived in southern European debt in 2014, liquidity and credit quality became cloudy.[13] The

---

[12] We shall see in Chapter 5 further evidence of the procyclical nature of credit availability.

[13] The importance of illiquidity in financial cycles and crisis is discussed in Jean Tirole, "Illiquidity and All Its Friends," *Journal of Economic Literature*, 2011, 49 (2): 287–325.

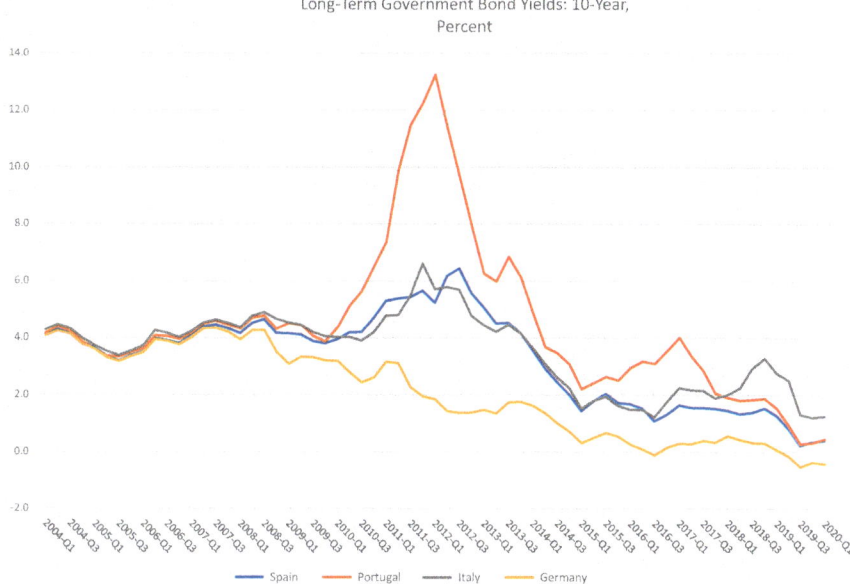

Fig. 2.9 Long term government bond yields

expectations of economic harmony faced the reality of divergent fiscal policies. As a result, bond yield spreads tightened considerably within a very short period until a further regime change was announced by the ECB.

Net Percent of Banks Tightening Credit on Commercial & Industrial (C&I) Loans

Credit quality hurdles differ significantly over the business cycle—to emphasize the issue, these credit benchmarks are very procyclical (Fig. 2.10). Initially, both a creditor and a debtor start the allocation process with an apparently economically legitimate project, where risk/return has a sense of balance. Then, as the first projects demonstrate success, more projects are financed. As credit becomes more available, unfortunately, the expected rates of return diminish at the same time. The low-lying fruit has been picked. An inverse relationship thus exists between demand for C&I loans among firms and the credit standards required by banks to offer loans. Credit agencies are aware of the behavior of investors over the business cycle and try to mitigate credit risk begin tightening standards as demand soars. As illustrated in the figure below, credit standards tighten going into a recession and peak during the recession.

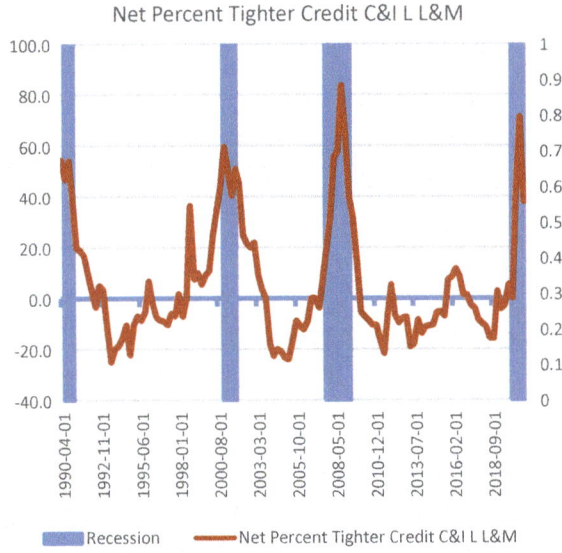

Fig. 2.10 Net percent of banks tightening credit-business loans

Shifting Investor Motivations: From Income to Capital Gains

For J.P. Morgan, the success of the railroads depended on traffic flow. When he looked at the railroad industry, he saw that it was badly overbuilt and consolidated and reorganized railroads—notably the Philadelphia & Reading as well as the Chesapeake & Ohio. But for Jay Cooke, who is credited as being the first major investment banker in the United States, the key to financial success was different from the sale of railroad bonds to European investors with limited knowledge of American geography.

Until 2005, for many American households, the income earned from owning a home had the psychic benefit of safety and place. That year flipping houses and capital gains became the rage. Higher prices lead to expectations of even higher prices—the demand curve sloped upward, and the boom/bust was on. Anchoring home values to fundamentals was gone. The recency bias took off.

Credit Today, Payments Tomorrow

On what basis is credit advanced? At the start of many innovations, credit is advanced in anticipation of an income flow to pay off that credit. The initial investors often get their return based upon actual economic income returns.

As time moves on, credit is advanced to realize capital gains. These gains are less available as the obvious winners are chosen first and then projects with less expected returns follow. This phenomenon is represented in Fig. 2.11, which depicts the run-up in home prices in the mid-2000s. Many individuals believed home prices could not fall and treated the homes as an investment opportunity with little downside. What former Fed chair Alan Greenspan dubbed "Irrational exuberance" became coupled with the decisions of inexperienced investors. This pattern also reflects the cognitive bias of normalization

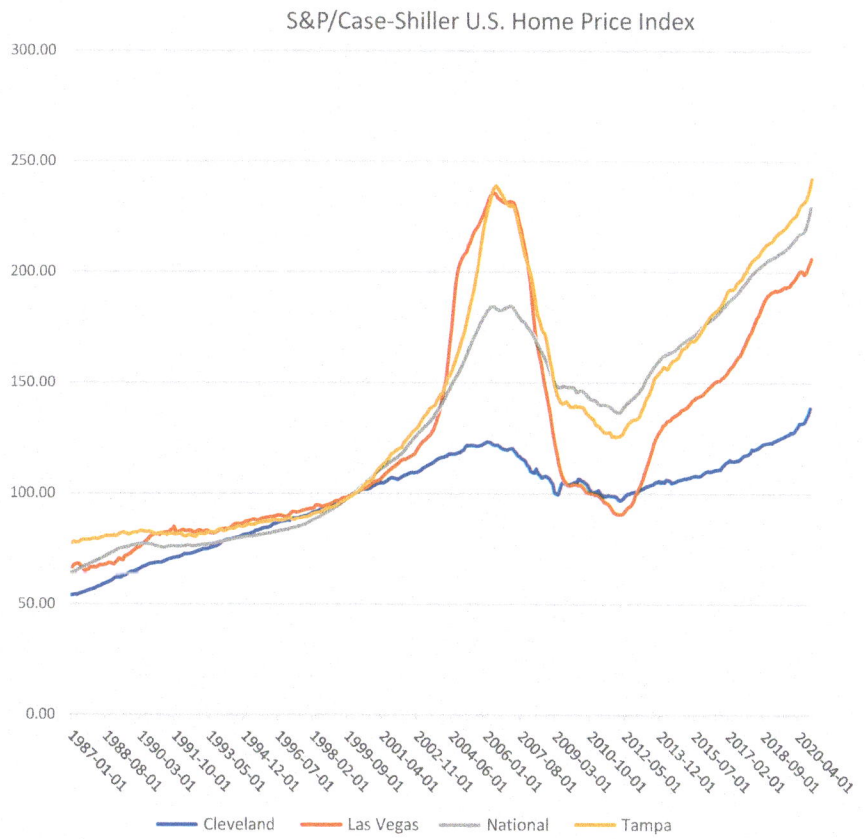

Fig. 2.11 Housing price cycle last thirty years

of deviance where deviations from the normal or average pattern are rationalized as a signal of a new paradigm.[14] The result was the subprime housing collapse, which devastated the global economy. Credit relationships and cycles should not be taken lightly.

These three examples support a dual process of economic/financial analysis along with an awareness of cognitive biases that lead to boom/bust cycles. Many times, graphics or statistical estimates contain hidden thinking traps. How often do we ask why a presenter picked a certain period to illustrate his or her case? Like a trial lawyer, the presenter illustrates evidence in his or her favor. Sometimes a presenter relates data from two periods, sometimes overlapping, as if the same process determines the pattern in both series. These arbitrary periods are particularly prevalent in political ads in an election year such as 2020.

The Interactions Between Expectations and Shocks

Prices reflect expectations. When those expectations are altered prices move. Incorporated into market prices is often the expectation that prices will return to a prior value—positive static stability (as in the design for aircraft). Yet, that is seldom the case as commodity prices as well as other prices, drift, or sometimes jump to a new set of prices that characterize a neutral static stability. Alternatively, home prices soared to what then what appear to be new all-time highs by 2007—but then collapsed. In this case, the argument of a new, higher plateau, a neutral static stability outcome, failed to hold as well. Finally, negative static stability exists when market prices continue to move away and often lead to a collapse of the economy and markets. This is most common in emerging market currency crises. To bring out the old guidance "emerging market currencies don't float, they sink." Consider then exhibit number one Argentina and number two Venezuela. As for inflation, consider then the case of Zimbabwe. In all three cases, fiscal policy excesses were financed by money printing which led to hyperinflation and a collapsing currency.

---

[14] This particularly associated with the Challenger space shuttle disaster. See Diane Vaughan, *The Challenger Launch Decision: Risky Technology, Culture and Deviance at NASA*. Chicago: University of Chicago Press, 1996.

Living Life with Negative Static Stability II

The intellectual journey of economics and financial markets over the last forty years has been fascinating because of the constant movement and learning associated with negative static stability. Economies do not move back to an original equilibrium point nor do they settle on a new equilibrium and sit still. They are journeys of constant motion.

Three types of static stability are common in the pattern of economic data. Positive static stability refers to a pattern in the data where a time series returns to its original value—back to normal—with no structural break in the series. Underlying this positive stability is the assumption that buyers will raise their bids if the excess demand for the product is positive. Sellers will lower their prices if excess demand for the product is negative that is short of what was expected or what would clear the market.

Prices therefore respond to the perceptions of buyers and producers that a situation of excess demand or supply exists in the marketplace. For small price changes in a stable economy, this appears relevant.

But why then do price changes not return to their earlier values? Benchmark Treasury rates have a history of continuous drift lower since the 2000 recession. Most recently, Treasury rates have not returned to pre-Covid values. Meanwhile, equity values in the U.S. such as the S&P 500 have gained ground since the Covid-19 outbreak.

In part, we can identify, a structural break in the pattern of prices which leads us to ask what is different. For exchange rates, the dollar has appreciated relative to the British pound with a structural break identified in 2008. Commodity prices, such as the WTI price of oil, broke lower in 2015. One measure of credit quality, the TED spread, evidences a structural break with a rise in the spread in 1991, 2000, and 2005—all periods associated with a recession or rising credit caution. The Ted spread is the difference between the interest rates on interbank loans and on short-term U.S. government debt (T-bills). TED is an acronym formed from T-bill and ED, the ticker symbol for the Eurodollar futures contract. The TED spread is calculated as the difference between the three-month LIBOR and the three-month T-bill interest rate.

Equities in 2020 offer an interesting lesson and feed into the pattern of booms and busts. Recent commentary has focused on the attraction of momentum investing—higher prices hint at greater values so more money is put into equities with rising prices. In this case, the effective demand curve is not downward sloping but upward sloping giving rise to an unstable marketplace. FOMO—fear of missing out—becomes prevalent. Likewise, the concept of chasing yield in credit markets hints that buyers should pursue higher prices, lower yields, in anticipation of still further lower yields—until they do not.

Disruption is Good, Disruption Without Direction is Chaos

Lewis and Clark had direction—and a good guide, thank you Sacagawea. The Donner party did not. Investors and business decision makers make choices in the face of risk. What direction can they get from the markets? Trade has never been free—never will be. The attempt to alter the trade relations between the United States and its trading partners by the Trump administration upset a false, unstable phony equilibrium—a good idea—but where are we going? The problem for decision makers is not the effort but the perceived lack of direction. Are we friendly competitors talking issues out or is this a chilling relationship that leads to hard decisions and a sense of perpetual negative static stability for trade? Right now, there is no sense of stability in trade. i.e., exports/imports and therefore the dollar exchange value and financial capital flows that, in turn, generate volatility in financial markets.

However, when the dollar exchange rate is unstable, then central bank policies around the globe are altered to suit trade objectives. Even for the benchmark currency, some argue that central bank rates should be cut/remain low to weaken the dollar. But wait—is the weaker dollar a direction the central bank should go? What about inflation and unemployment? Three targets—the dollar, inflation, and unemployment—with one instrument (the funds rate)? This imbalance of targets and instruments (thank you Nickolaas Tinbergen) fails to meet the smell test for the consistency of economic policy. Moreover, there is the question of the effectiveness of an instrument. How effective can a marginal change in an exchange rate be for trade in the face of the overarching uncertainty of trade relations? I am a skeptic. For investors, the issue is the relative importance of policy targets by policymakers. This uncertainty on importance reinforces the tendency of negative static stability.

Signals on the Path to Negative Static Stability: The Race to the Bottom

- Argentine exchange rates
- Brazil exchange rates
- Venezuela inflation

- Zimbabwe inflation
- Euro interest rates

These are all examples of negative static stability. Policy actions lead to altered expectations altered; exchange rate depreciation leads to further expectations for depreciation. A nation's populace comes to understand—fooled in the short run but not the long run. Economic policy objectives by the leadership have changed and thereby the prior combination of interest rates/exchange rates/inflation will be permanently altered.[15]

Assumption of Positive Static Stability Today

Much of recent commentary by the Trump administration officials, some in the media and analysts, claim that the economy and markets will return to their former position—positive static stability.

This is unlikely since the economy evolves and did not return to its prior position after the major recessions of 1982, 2007–2009. Slower global growth, a new trade regime, and a pattern of central banks easing across the globe all suggest a structural break in the ancient regime. Whatever the outcome of trade negotiations, economic growth slowed in 2019 even before the shutdowns, especially industrial production, and are likely to remain lower in 2020/2021 compared to 2018. Higher trade frictions reduce the benefits of trade and will lower economic growth, at least in the short-term horizon. Through interactions in price determination, a trade shock to economic growth will alter the equilibrium values in other markets. Inflation is expected to rise in the short run. Given the perceived reaction function of central banks,[16] slower growth is an issue, slightly higher inflation is not. Therefore, further ease of short-term policy rates is likely. Fed funds stability at the old target of 2.25–2.50 is unlikely to be reestablished any time soon. Slower growth and a lower benchmark policy rate dictate a lower ten-year rate in 2019 and 2020 than in 2018. If not a return to the good old days, then it is a new, stable equilibrium—neutral static stability—but stability, nonetheless.

---

[15] Even more recently, consider the case of Turkey and its policy shift. "In Turkey, Weak Lira Powers Fresh Gold Rush," 09 14 2020 Financial Times.

[16] A central bank reaction function refers to how a central bank will react to changes in its target variables such as inflation and unemployment. This is very evident in Governor Powell's recent comment that the Fed will accept a period of higher inflation above its target of two percent.

Neutral Static Stability: Stay at New Altitude

Both public and private innovations have moved the economy to a new, higher plane. The Kennedy and Reagan tax cuts—shifted upward the rate of growth of the economy and altered expectations on the potential rate of growth and employment for the economy. The change in monetary policy under Paul Volcker to using the fed funds rate to reduce the pace of money growth and lower inflation altered the expectations for inflation going forward and thereby had a distinct impact on the path of interest rates and the U.S. dollar.

Looking through the global lens, German monetary reform in the post-World War II period set the basis for the German miracle period of growth. The opening up in Asia of the Tigers such as Singapore, South Korea, Hong Kong, and Taiwan drove those countries' potential pace of economic growth.

In the U.S. private sector gains in fracking, personal communications and e-commerce have reduced prices, transportation, and communication costs. In addition, the availability of information has lowered the cost of job and home search for example.

Before You Put that 2019 Outlook to Work—Benchmark for Expectations/Actuals, Dynamism/Change

Any economic outlook is a snapshot, yet a good strategy requires a video—a view that captures the momentum of the economy.

An outlook starts with basics on a view of growth, interest rates, inflation, equity valuations, corporate profits, and exchange rates. These views should be consistent. Caution is advised if any of these four elements is provided by different people in different areas of the firm—the silo problem again. Outlooks from different silos are unlikely to be consistent which helps to explain why forecast winners in one area such as economic growth, perform poorly when it comes to interest rates or the dollar.

The benchmark outlook cannot stand alone (the snapshot). We also should see what indicators we need to watch to intimate that the forecast will be changing (the video). What are the leading indicators of change for growth, interest rates, etc.? For most forecasts, this is seldom provided.

Moreover, how is change measured? I am wary of the 200-day moving average because it does not separate cycle from trend and does not give me a view on variance. I prefer some filter for the data to separate cycle and trend such as the Hodrick-Prescott filter.[17]

Even more difficult to glean is the interaction among the key variables. If the growth forecast appears to be off track, what are the implications for the rate or foreign exchange forecast? Recall that a market in disequilibrium will move and that movement will bring changes in other markets. If the Fed is moving short rates to normal then for every asset, (housing, bank loans, equities), prices of those short rates will adjust. No market is an island.

If the outlook is changing, and it always does, then what are your options—your Plan B? There is a duality in decision making. There is a framework for the economy but there is also a framework for making decisions. Change in the outlook means you must make choices and those choices often lead to a new framework. Finally, be very aware of the cognitive biases that may influence your choices. There is a lot to think about when reviewing all those 2019 forecasts.

"Visiting Grandma's House at Thanksgiving": The Price of False Precision

Precise promises in an imprecise world are probably not a good strategy. Too much precision leads to disappointment. Telling Grandma that you will be there at 2 PM on Thanksgiving is not a good strategy. If you do not arrive by 2:30 then Grandma fears you have had an accident. If you arrive at 1:30, she is not ready, and the pillows are not all fluffed. Being too precise on promises is not a good strategy. Grandma will not be happy and if Grandma is not happy no one is happy. Route 128, the real world, has construction sometimes, accidents frequently, traffic always. Far better to indicate flexibility "around 2 PM, maybe 1:30 to 2:30" and better bring the Licor Beirao.[18] Dinner will be around 5 PM. Lesson: Better to be imprecisely right than precisely wrong.

---

[17] This detrending procedure has its own limitations as cited by Timothy Cogley and James M. Nason, "The Effects of the Hodrick-Prescott Filter on Trend and Difference Stationary Time Series: Implications for Business Cycle Research," *Journal of Economic Dynamics and Control 19*, 1955a (January/February): 253–278).

[18] Licor Beirao is a very traditional after dinner Portuguese liquor.

Three ingredients to Watch for Negative Static Stability

What are the witches' brew here that would distinguish neutral versus negative static stability? In both the dot.com period and in the current private equity/IPO tech fascination, we can quickly recognize the inconsistency of financial market expectations with the underlying inability of real-world economies to deliver a path to prosperity. In a similar manner, the prices set by public policy for the Exchange Rate Mechanism (ERM, September 1992, Fig. 2.12), the Sherman Silver Purchase Act, and the housing boom were inconsistent with the underlying economic fundamentals of their times.

Three ingredients created the witches brew for negative static stability (depressions) versus the dot.com (recessions) and possibly the mild case of the positive static stability where private equity/IPO pricing distortions worked themselves out and left the overall economy unharmed.

First, there is the matter of elasticity—are market elasticities able to respond to changes in prices? For the Silver Purchase Act of 1890 and 2005–2007 housing boom, the answer was no. In the 1890s, the demand for specie could not be met by the supply. For housing, collateral values of the homes could not meet financial obligations. The ERM and the resumption of the gold standards in Europe post-World War I were clearly examples of mispricing.

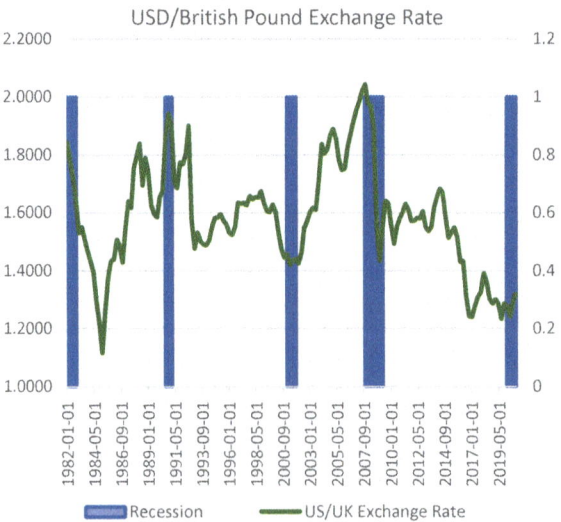

Fig. 2.12 US dollar/British pound exchange rate

Second, there is the shift in motivations—investing or speculation? In several cases, the railroad booms in the United States and in Britain, the initial investors sought income and, in many cases, did make money. As time went on, and this is also the case for the U.S. housing boom, the goal became one of the capital gains for the railroads and flipping houses for profit. In many ways this is the greater fool theory—buy today and sell to a greater fool tomorrow. When the game is speculation—the riches of the South Seas—the result is that any shock cannot be met with sufficient resistance, the market collapses.

Finally, there is the problem of our intellectual biases. Is there an anchoring bias to some past values that simply cannot hold in the current economic scenario? The attempt by both the French and the British post-World War I to resume the gold standard reflects this bias. Second, there is the normalization of deviance. As asset prices rise, these prices make sense given our bias, even though valuation models cannot justify these prices. We hear this discussion in the media all the time during 2020. One commentator says that she cannot justify buying an equity because the valuation is not there. Yet a second commentator says he will buy because the prices reflect future growth opportunities. Can you imagine the discussion at Barings Bank in the late 1880s about the future growth opportunities in Argentina? How about Florida land in the 1920s? How about the growth opportunities of the Nifty-Fifty stocks of top American corporations in the early 1970s? And, of course, the fascinating discussions among investors who were choosing between WorldCom, Cisco, or Amazon during the dot.com era.

Mid-Cycle as Misleading Benchmark for Decision Making

Benchmarking a moving cloud is never easy. Talk about an investment strategy at the mid-cycle of an economic expansion is probably even more difficult. Is there any real content to the phrase? In our view, no, the mid-cycle of an economic/financial cycle is not an identifiable point until after the end of an economic expansion. Moreover, the focus on a single point in time, rather than the behavior of economic/financial signals during the cycle, is misplaced.

There is no fixed amplitude nor length of an economic/financial cycle. Rather they reflect the dynamic interaction of economic, financial, and policy forces. The validity of any investment strategy/economic forecast based upon the assumption of a mid-cycle point of the recovery/expansion is questionable. What is important is the framework for decision making—the start and end of cycles reflect the three forces of the economy, finance, and policy. The whole process of the cycle reflects these three forces rather than a link to a single point in time.

Several approaches might help identify the cyclical process. Frequently, equity strategists compare the moving averages of any time series—often equity prices or Treasury yields for example. Such strategists frequently contrast 30-day and 120-day moving averages. As an illustration, this comparison might be helpful. But the choice of 30 or 120 days, is entirely arbitrary. Picking 120 days is also peculiar since that period covers *more* than a quarter of a year. Many economic series and measures of investment performance are calculated as a quarterly time series.

Another questionable standard is the 200-day moving average, which is more than half a year. This average encompasses different end-of-quarter observations and end-of-year observations (especially important for retail spending). These averages do not adjust for the seasonality of the underlying data nor do they separate cycle and trend components of any time series. On the other hand, moving averages do reflect the dynamic patterns of economic and financial data. They are an improvement over attempts to focus on a particular point, such as the midpoint, of an economic cycle—which is not known until after the fact.

A second approach we have utilized has been the use of filters such as the Hodrick-Prescott/Kalman (it is formally identified as the Hodrick-Prescott filter which incorporates the Kalman) to separate the trend and cycle components of any time series. This approach helps to identify points where a series is above or below trend within an economic expansion. The analysis, however, is historical and static with no predictive power. The results of the filter process change when observations are added over time or when the sample period of the analysis is altered. The filter provides a sense of where we are for the cyclical component of any time series relative to a recent trend, but without a predictive component.

Reality as Unreliable Guide

To illustrate the elusive concept of a mid-cycle, consider the variability of actual results in recent cycles. For the economic cycle that began in 1982, economic growth slowed after the midpoint (known only after the fact) of that cycle. For the economic expansion that began in 1991, economic growth picked up in the second half of that cycle. For the 2001 expansion, growth was relatively unchanged in the second half of the expansion. Finally, for the current expansion, growth picked up in the second half of the 2009–2019 expansion. Knowing the unknowable, the actual midpoint of an ongoing cycle, is not a reliable indicator of the acceleration or deceleration of growth in the second half of the cycle.

For one measure of equity valuation, the E/P ratio, the results are also discouraging. The earnings-price ratio is not a mean-reverting series over the period of 1982 to 2018. There is thus no expectation of a return to a normal level after the hypothesized midpoint of any expansion.

The E/P ratio reflects the ongoing dynamic change in expectations for economic growth/earnings, interest rates, and exchange rates. As a result, there is not a unique movement of E/P values over the cycle to identify a peak. In part, this is because both the price of equities and the earnings of those equities have a cycle of their own. For the 1982 expansion, the early E/P bottom in 1983/1984 was followed by a rise and then a decline to a new low in 1987. This occurred, even though the peak in the equity market, measured by the S&P 500, happened in 1989 before the correction in 1990. In the 1992 expansion, the E/P ratio bottomed early, then rose in 1997 and subsequently declined. Yet, once again the S&P500 indexed peaked later, this time in 2000/2001. In an odd situation, the E/P ratio declined throughout the 2002 expansion. Yet, once again, the S&P 500 index rose until 2007/2008. During the current economic expansion, there was no peak in equity valuations until the shutdowns of 2020.

Introducing Change and Adding Dynamism to Cycles

Midnight Strikes: Cinderella Loses a Shoe, Lives to Dance Another Day?

For the analysts, the economic/financial cycle is driven by actual data that differs from expectations and thereby leads to change in their buying decision and advice. Our old friend the business cycle paid an unwelcome, and unexpected, visit in 2020 as the pandemic interrupted the longest economic expansion in American history. Where was the inverted yield curve? Not there. What makes this cycle intriguing is that the downdraft in our four benchmarks (equity, dollar, credit markets, and commodity markets) was quick to signal problems despite the first quarter's continued good economic data.

Yield Curve: Flatter not Inverted

Good due diligence seldom depends upon a single, all revealing, piece of information that must pass a threshold to be relevant. Two aspects of decision making are important here. First, the movement of a benchmark, such as the yield curve (Fig. 3.3, next chapter) is more important than hitting a threshold value. The direction and extent of the yield curve's movement matter more in a dynamic economy—change over time is central to good decision making. Second, the yield curve does not stand alone—it must fit into the context of a model of financial markets. What else is going on? Do our indicators confirm or conflict with each other?

Ever since the taper tantrum in 2013, there have been two distinct moves in the yield curve. The decline in yields at the long end of the yield curve reflected movements in both the credit and currency markets. This made the interrelationship between markets once again apparent. First, U.S. Treasury debt offers a yield pickup relative to sovereign debt in Europe and Japan. In addition, the flight to safety also reflected the incentive of risk aversion. Finally, the continued pattern of inflation outcomes that fell short of a two percent target in the U.S. reinforced the view of investors to buy U.S. Treasuries to gain a real yield relative to what was available on other global financial assets.

Equity Prices: Enter the Exciting World of False Positives.

Taking equity prices as a leading indicator is certainly a reasonable choice. As observed from Fig. 2.13, the break below zero on the year-over-year change

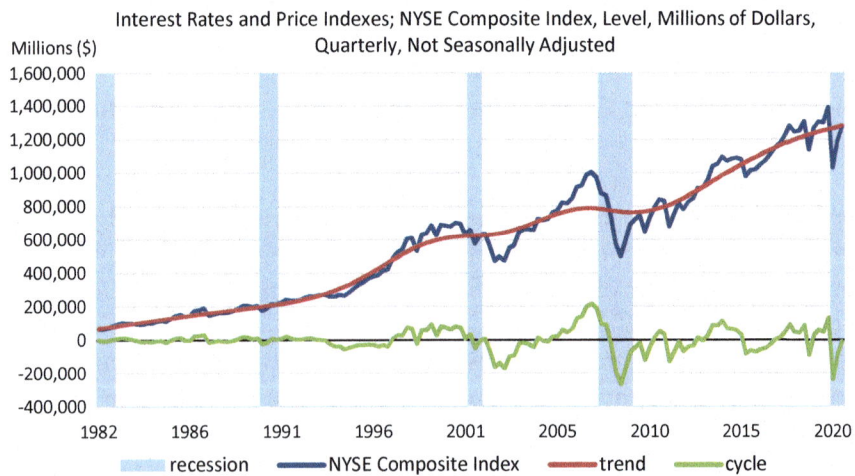

Fig. 2.13 NYSE equity price index

in the New York Stock Exchange (NYSE) composite does precede, or at least is coincident with, the onset of a recession. However, there are times when the index for the NYSE breaks below zero with no subsequent recession (late 1970s, 1984, 1992, twice earlier during the current expansionary period). The principle remains—any financial market should be part of a broader framework of economic/financial activity.

Mispricing of financial assets is a reoccurring reality in any marketplace. But it is the coincidental mispricing in multiple markets that then reflects a broader disequilibrium problem that prompts the downturn in finance and thereby the economy. Indeed, the interrelationship between prices in different markets offers the opportunity to recognize a mispricing that leads to quick and decisive economic change.

Finance and Real Economic Growth: Trends and Cycles

With the determination of the former Fed chairs Paul Volcker and Alan Greenspan to wipe out higher inflation, the link between non-financial credit growth and nominal GDP gains became more apparent. In many ways, the decline in the rate of inflation opened the door to a more efficient allocation of financial capital. Slower credit growth in the 1980s was associated with slower nominal GDP growth. In the 1990s, both credit and nominal GDP growth remained in a 6% range. Faster credit growth was associated with a pickup of nominal GDP growth in the first half of that decade. It was followed by a slowdown in credit growth and nominal GDP at the end of the decade. In the economic expansion that just ended, both credit growth and nominal GDP growth slowed to the 5% range.

When we dig down into the pace of credit growth by type of credit market instrument, since the early 1980s, the share of credit made up of bank loans has steadily declined from 26 to 12%.

In fact, nominal GDP growth leads credit growth not vice versa. You cannot print your way to prosperity. In the economic expansion that just ended, non-financial credit growth has slowed in the United States, the Euro area, and China. For all three countries, credit growth has slowed relative to the pre-global financial crisis era.

Over the Horizon Radar: On the Other Side of the Recession Mountain

What do we think today about tomorrow—once we are on the other side of the mountain? Does recession today lead to recovery tomorrow?

What about the Fed as backstop? Certainly, Fed actions have improved the liquidity and thereby the pricing of U.S. Treasury obligations as well as government-backed mortgages. If the dark cloud of uncertainty still hangs over America (concerns about a reemergence of the virus in the 4th quarter 2020, the lack of an effective vaccine, and the lingering doubt that the economy does not return to its pre-2020 normal in 2021), risk spreads will be wider than pre-crisis. From our view, the pace of economic growth will be subpar, not a V-shaped rebound, in 2021.

The Fed's provisions of the monetary base have been significant. Is it enough or too much? Is it enough to get the economy back to normal (pre-crisis GDP, employment, consumption)? We assume not. There is too much uncertainty out there. Consumers will save more, businesses will hire less, invest less, and build up cash. Certainly, many state and local governments will have to pull in their spending and let employees go when faced with constitutional and other budget constraints. We suspect that the share of government expenditures in the economy will rise. The share of private spending will decline.

Is the Fed's provision of credit too much—i.e., more inflation? Given the recent rush to buy U.S. Treasury debt, an inflation rise on the other side of the mountain to just 3–4% would produce capital losses for recent buyers of U.S. Treasury notes with yields below 1%. When facing the mountain, the Fed and the economy benefit from the reality that both the dollar exchange rate and the benchmark Treasury note are the go-to for risk aversion. However, on the other side of prior recession mountains, inflation does rise, and interest rates follow. For now, we watch our real and financial indicators for signals of sunshine—and—as of now—there is no sunshine. Recession is endured as we plan for the other side of the mountain.

Where We Are is Not Where We Are Going

The current economic scene is not a stable equilibrium point. We are headed somewhere else. As investors, we should continue our search for that new equilibrium realizing that each new discovery leads to more questions.

Recessions and depressions occurred before the establishment of the Federal Reserve and have continued since. In fact, recessions/depressions occurred before the United States existed (South Seas and Mississippi Bubbles). We also know that an inverted yield curve and equity market corrections are not associated one-for-one with an economic recession. In fact, the first Treasury issue was the three-month T-bill in 1929, an auspicious date to be sure, and far after the U.S. financial crises of 1837, 1857, and 1873, and you get the idea, 1893, 1907, etc.

Most intriguing of all, when we write about changes in monetary policy or a change in the yield curve, we are writing about a financial event. Yet a recession is an event in the real economy. How do we get from point A in the financial island to point B in the real economy island—or is it a change in the real economy to the financial sector? We need a bigger boat.

This is a multivariate world with many interactions between the four sectors/prices we have discussed. Imbalances, multiple disequilibrium, are a constant issue and the direction of influence is not always, nor necessarily, from the financial sector to the real sector. While finance may grease the wheels of the economy, the elements of economic speculation on future profits may be the original driving force (railroads, land speculation, capital gains on equities).

Yield curves do not stand in isolation. What is driving that inverted yield curve? What are the implications of that yield curve? What accounts for equity over and under valuations? Linear extrapolation from the yield curve to the economy, which fails to account for the why of the yield curve, infiltrates so much recent commentary. But such speculation provides no real content for thoughtful decision making.

Looking at the Internals of Corporate Finance

Financial pressures in the nonfinancial corporate sector might be a signal regarding the onset of the midpoint of the economic/financial cycle. Alas there is no help here either. One measure we to gauge financial pressures is the financing gap, capital expenditures minus internally generated funds (from the Federal Reserve's Financial Accounts of the United States, FAUS). For the 1982 expansion, the midpoint of the cycle, 1986:3Q, was not associated with any peak in capex relative to internal funds. In fact, capex accelerated after the midpoint and into the 1989/1990 start of the recession. For the 1992 expansion, capex accelerated relative to internal funds after the midpoint of the cycle.

In what maybe a contrary indicator, history hints that the acceleration of capex—relative to internal funds—may be a signal regarding the second half of each expansion. This period in an expansion is characterized by firms expanding capex while internal funds may be providing less support for such financing. Yet the abrupt shift in the financing gap at the end of the 1991, 2007 cycles provided very little lead time to indicate the end of the cycle.

Net, the rise in the financing gap may indeed provide a signal of the midpoint of a cycle but the rise in the gap provides no lead time to signal its own expiration and the end of the economic expansion.

Beyond the internal cycles and trends of any economic expansion, there is the issue of the abrupt end. First, how can we identify a structural change in economic and financial relationships? Second, once we determine these break points, is there a way to identify changes in economic/financial forces that give way to these abrupt changes? Commentary to follow.

Nature of the World Disequilibrium

When the Music is Over, Turn Out the Lights—Part I

The research on recession forecasting indicates that the same factors that are utilized to forecast recessions also are utilized to forecast the pace of economic growth. What is the deal? Economic changes are perennial so to know the economics is not enough. The market structure, expectations and the interaction of credit and economic behavior should also be examined.

Private Markets, Public Policy, Recessions, and Depressions

A recession/recovery cycle is an example of neutral static stability where a shock to the economy leads to a new equilibrium within the economy, while the economic/credit market structure, generally, remains in place. A depression is characterized by a negative static stability situation. Market prices continue to move away from the old equilibrium in the short term, no clear path is evident to a new equilibrium, in the short run, and the existing market structure is altered.

Economic and credit market prices change when expectations no longer match market fundamentals. When this disconnect appears, prices change. But at this point, it is unclear what is the character of static stability in the economy. When market commentators reference the markets trading in a range, then you have a sense they are referring to a state of positive static stability. Changes move market prices, but prices return to or remain around the old equilibrium.

Second, for the dot.com boom/bust era or the Organization of Petroleum Exporting Countries (OPEC) era of the 1970s, expectations for high equity prices for dot.coms or for low energy prices were permanently altered by new economic fundamentals. Dot.com equities could not deliver on growth. Energy-based industrial production was too costly. In both cases, prices moved to a new equilibrium yet, in my view, the overall structure of financial markets and the economy, ex-energy, were not permanently altered. Regional recessions/depressions did occur (Rust Belt in the early 1980s for example but the overall U.S. economy recovered). As I said in Chapter 1, this was true for the Dutch Tulip mania—a shock to financial markets but it did not alter the structure of the Dutch economy. In contrast, the John Law Mississippi Bubble and the American railroad boom/bust in the 1870s did lead to significant changes in the French and U.S. economies. For a time, there was no clear path to a new equilibrium in both countries—a signal of a negative static stability condition.

Despite the political rhetoric of our times that attributes economic troubles to the private sector, not all recessions/depressions are driven by private market actions. In fact, public policy actions underscored, causa remota, both the South Seas bubble[19] and the railroad boom/bust of the 1870s. For the United States, the Panic of 1893 provides an important perspective to the problem of negative static stability. Both the Sherman Silver Purchase Act and the McKinley tariff of 1890 are often associated with the Panic. But the underlying problem was financial—the inability of the U.S. Treasury to meet its obligations to pay in gold and the demand by the public for gold. Silver prices dropped dramatically. In a touch of irony, President Grover Cleveland was forced to borrow from JP Morgan and the Rothschilds to pay investors. The fundamental character of both the economy and the financial system was altered as money/credit expansion became linked to gold and not the printing of paper currency.

Two other examples of the mispricing of markets by public policy were the ERM crisis for the United Kingdom and the post-World War I gold standard benchmarks set by both France and Britain. In the ERM crisis of September

---

[19] In the case of the South Seas Bubble, The British King and Parliament passed the Bubble Act of 1720 which effectively limited other stock issuance in favor of the South Sea promoters and thereby funneled further money into that venture. See John Carswell, *The South Sea Bubble*. London: Cresset Press, 1960.

1992, the British government was forced to withdraw the pound sterling from the European Exchange Rate Mechanism (ERM), after a failed attempt to keep the pound above the lower currency exchange limit mandated by the ERM. In the gold standard crisis, World War I forced countries to go off the gold standard. When Britain and France attempted to reestablish the prewar parity to gold, the limits on the money/credit and capital flows proved unsustainable.[20]

For the United States, public policy incentives to favor housing for low- and moderate-income families created pricing distortions that led to the housing boom/bust of 2007–2009. Public policy provided incentives, through the Department of Housing and Urban Development (HUD), regulatory rules established by the Federal Home Loan Mortgage Corporation (Freddie Mac) and Federal National Mortgage Association (Fannie Mae) to continually increase the percentage of subprime loans distorted market pricing for homes. The percentage of subprime mortgages backed by the Government-Sponsored Enterprises (GSEs) continued to rise. Bottom line, the easing of credit for housing finance outpaced the earnings ability of buyers over time. Equilibrium in the housing market did not match the equilibrium in the financial markets. Credit was too easily available. Similarly, the current economic situation shows that arbitrarily set low-interest rates are employed to sustain an economic expansion. The accompanying growth of credit may, in fact, be promoting speculation, not sustained real investment, over time.[21]

Shock to Market Equilibriums—Generating Negative Static Stability

Overshooting and Irrational Exuberance: Up and Down Excesses

Shocks have their source in both public and private sector choices and especially in the imbalances between markets. Overall, however, the economy and financial markets are driven by the difference between what is expected and what is observed. How can we characterize when the cycles and trends evolve into bubbles—on the upside and bust on the downside? For John Law, irrational exuberance came through an effective marketing scheme.

---

[20] Charles P. Kindleberger, *Manias, Panics and Crashes*, Basic Books, 1978, New York, pp. 135–137.
[21] Too much cash is chasing too few desirable assets, May 5, 2020, *Financial Times*.

This led to irrational exuberance in the growth opportunities in the Mississippi Company, supported, in part, by an irrational expansion in a second sector, money/credit. Working with a four-sector framework, disequilibrium in the growth and money sectors meant disequilibrium in the earnings/equity capital market as well—i.e., earnings expectations too high, joint-stock trading company values too high as well. Printing fiat money destroyed the link of the Franc to gold (the exchange rate).

In 2019, investors considered the issues of equity valuation and trade—often termed as the big risks for the year ahead. Investors are aware that the Federal Reserve wants to return to a "normal" federal funds rate of 2–3% based upon their economic projections. In our terms, this means that the current settings of the credit/interest rate sectors are in disequilibrium. This was the overlooked lesson for equity capital for 2017 and helps explain the "corrections" of 2018 as the Fed continued to raise benchmark interest rates. In addition, estimates of sustainable growth may also have reflected irrational exuberance regarding economic growth. Also reflected was the sustainable pace for the tech stocks as based upon below equilibrium interest rates and the growth of the Fed's balance sheet that provided liquidity to the financial markets. Their equity values are not just a function of economic growth expectations, but of issues of privacy/security which are only now starting to raise investor awareness. As for growth estimates for 2019, consider the Fed's position on full employment in late 2018. If full employment is 4% plus, then an unemployment rate of 3.7% compared to 4.1% a year ago meant that the labor market/growth was in disequilibrium—aggregate demand in the economy was too strong to be consistent with stable inflation. This supported the Fed's case for raising the funds rate in 2018. There were debates on the unemployment rate/wage gains/inflation nexus, but if Fed policymakers act on their beliefs then investors must react to those beliefs. The Fed did raise rates in the 2018–2019 period and housing and equity markets struggled.

Expectations thus create a momentum and possibly an excess/shortage of demand or supply on the upside and the downside. This irrational exuberance/irrational pessimism underlies the extremes of dot.com booms and housing collapses. Consider trade in this context. In recent years, it has been in disequilibrium, especially the trade position of China and the U.S., creating a situation for many firms where the cost of goods sold has been too low and real consumer spending has been excessive relative to the long-run fundamentals. If trade has been in disequilibrium, then the prices of goods have been too low. In addition, equity valuations based upon low import prices and/or ever-expanding foreign markets have also been in disequilibrium. Moreover, discussions about global central banks moving toward a more neutral (read less in disequilibrium) position would support the case that there is less credit/liquidity support for the pace of export/economic growth over recent years.

For the 2021 outlook, these are difficult decision points. It is intellectually hard to look back at recent years and argue that the gains in the economy and equity markets reflected a disequilibrium in the terms of trade and credit markets. But thoughtful decision making insists that we ask the question.

Monitoring the Cycle: Three Rising Pressure Points

By mid-2017, the character of the economic/financial cycle had already started to turn. Three economic fundamentals signaled rising pressures on the sustainability of the economic expansion at recent rates of growth.

Fed's Inflation Target Met

Gains in the PCE deflator and core PCE deflator fell consistently from 2012 to 2016 and remained below the Fed's 2% inflation target. Beginning in mid-2016 and continuing into late 2018, the core deflator rose on a year-over-year basis and eventually exceeded the Fed's two percent target. The Fed, in response, raised the fed funds rate regularly in 2017 and 2018. One factor supporting the rise in the PCE deflator has been the steady increase in labor costs. What we have witnessed, therefore, is that the pattern of wage/price movements has reached the point that the "low-wage growth, low-inflation" framework of decision making of recent years faded away.

Shrinking Margin for Error: A Sign of Imbalance in the Equity Market

For both investors and private businesses, the peak in profit margins (Fig. 2.14) indicates that the combination of rising short-term interest rates and shrinking profit margins provides a smaller margin of error for decision makers in the pre-Covid period of 2014–2017. Looking forward, the rise in unit labor costs, in the face of another year of two percent real growth, meant that the pressure on profit margins was present even before Covid.

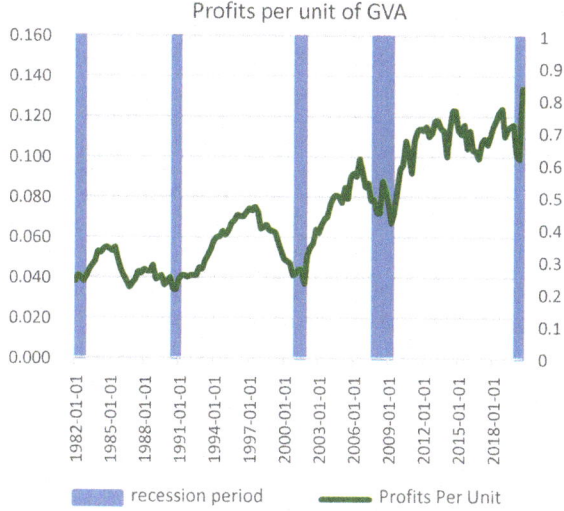

Fig. 2.14 Profit margins

Change Information, Change the Framework of Market Interactions

Changing information displaces old models of behavior with new models. For interest rates, the fundamental drivers of growth and inflation will change behavior leading to a change in the model for rates themselves. For exchange rates, domestic and foreign monetary and fiscal policy shifts can bring drastic changes.

Real Final Sales: Displacement Downshift

In 1907, prior to the establishment of the Federal Reserve, Union Pacific stock, a security widely used as collateral for finance-bill operations, dropped 50 points as concerns rose about the quality of railroad earnings and market liquidity. This event represented an exogenous shock to economic activity at the time and altered the investment horizon, expectations, and profit opportunities for investors. The collapse of Bear Stearns and Lehman Brothers 100 years later was a similar shock to collateral quality and investors' expectations. Information had changed in the market and, therefore, the models had to adjust accordingly. For several economic series, a break in the series was evident in 2008. For real final sales, the series was not a stationary series as there was a clear structural break downward in October 2008. In other words, the series exhibited non-mean-reverting behavior, thus declines in both real final sales and the 10-year Treasury rate since 2008 came as no surprise.

Inflation: PCE Deflator

The FOMC's benchmark for inflation, the PCE deflator, in contrast to real final sales, is a stationary (mean-reverting) series during the sample period of 1982–2017. The process of the series returning to its long-run mean is painfully slow, however. In statistical terms, the PCE is characterized by autocorrelation. This suggests that if the PCE deflator series deviates from the long-run mean, then the series will take an extended period to return to the mean.

Since inflation has an autocorrelation problem it is not surprising that inflation since 2009 has surprised policymakers and financial market participants who stubbornly continue to forecast a return to inflation normality (average inflation rate is only 1.33% for the 2009–2017 period).

Benchmark Treasury Rates

Unlike most inflation metrics, the two-year Treasury rate is a non-stationary, non-mean reverting series with evidence of a structural break downward in November 1987 and again in December 2008. The fundamentals of growth and inflation both exhibit a structural break in the fourth quarter of 2008 and as a result, so does the dependent variable—the 2-year Treasury rate.

As economic drivers, there is a two-way causality relationship between real final sales and the 2-year Treasury rate. That is, real final sales add to the quality of a forecast of 2-year rates. Meanwhile, the 2-year Treasury rate adds to the forecast accuracy for the PCE deflator.

These interactions bring out another characteristic of price movement in financial markets. There are numerous and sometimes complex interactions between prices in various markets for goods, credit, exchange rates, and interest rates—this makes economic analysis even more fun and distinguishes thoughtful analysis from linear extrapolation.

Looking forward to price movements in our four primary markets in Chapter 3, we will characterize the individual price movements and their relationship to prices in other markets.

References

Peter Bernstein, "Against the Gods," Wiley, 1996. A classic read into the history of risky ventures and a reminder that all investments, and economic activity, involves risk. One of my most marked up books and one of the twelve must reads.

John Carswell, *The South Sea Bubble*, London: Cresset Press, 1960. In the case of the South Seas Bubble, The British King and Parliament passed the Bubble Act of 1720 which effectively limited other stock issuance in favor of the South Sea promoters and thereby funneled further money into that venture. This is an important lesson in the actions of government leading to unforeseen financial bubbles.

Rudiger Dornbusch, *Open Economy Macro-Economics*, Basic Books, 1980. A macro text that brings international economic behavior into the core macro curriculum. A book written by a dear friend and mentor who passed away too soon.

D. Dickey and W. Fuller, "Distribution of the Estimates for Autoregressive Time series with a Unit Root," *Journal of American Statistical Association*, 1979 (74): 427–431; D. Dickey and W. Fuller, "Likelihood Ratio Tests for Autoregressive Time Series with a Unit Root," *Econometrica*, 1981 (49): 1057–1072. These tests, and their applications, appear in Chapter 4 of *Economic and Business Forecasting, John E. Silvia et.al.,* 2014 Wiley. Too many economic/financial graphs are used to illustrate patterns when, in fact, these graphs, simply illustrate a trend that needs to be adjusted to allow for causal relationships to be identified between economic series.

Niall Ferguson, "The Ascent of Money," Penguin Press, 2008. A broader history than that of Kindleberger with a writer's flair. Another of my most marked-up books and one of my twelve must reads.

R. J. Hodrick and E. C. Prescott, "Postwar U.S. Business Cycle: An Empirical Investigation," *Journal of Money, Credit and Banking*, 1997, 29 (1): 1–16. A very useful technique to identify deviations from trend that economic and financial analysts will find useful in evaluating over and under valuation in markets.

Thomas Laubach and John C. Williams, "Measuring the Natural Rate of Interest," *Review of Economics and Statistics*, 2003, 85 (4) (November), 1063–1070. Kathryn Holston, Thomas Laubach, and John C. Williams, "Measuring the Natural Rate of Interest: International Trends and Determinants," *Journal of International Economics*, 2017, 108 (May): S59–S75. An essential read into the search for a "natural" rate of interest.

Charles P. Kindleberger, *Manias, Panics and Crashes*, Basic Books, New York, 1978. This is the essential first read on booms and busts—after Thomas Carlyle, of course.

G. S. Maddala and In-Moo Kim, *Unit Root, Cointegration and Structural Change*, Cambridge, UK: Cambridge University Press, 1998. A state space approach is utilized here to identify structural breaks. Much of the economic analysis in this book focuses on the post 1981 period since structural breaks in economic time series as pervasive between the inflationary 1970s and the disinflationary 1980s.

3

Price Determination in a Multi-Sector Global Economy

The Story and Motivation for Price Discovery

The Story of Inflation, Interest Rates and the Dollar in the Administration of Jimmy Carter: Motivation for Price Discovery

For the second half of the 1970s, economy growth was solid from 1976 to 1979 with real GDP rising hovering around more than 5% before dropping to 3.2% and the unemployment rate falling regularly from 1976 until 1979 from 7.7% to 5.8%.

What was distinctive for the period was the interrelationships of market prices in this economy. This period serves as a story, as well as a framework, of how prices can move from one perceived equilibrium period (mid-1970s, good growth and declining unemployment) to a period of disequilibrium (1979–1980 period of high inflation, interest rates, declining U.S. dollar values and declining profits) to a new equilibrium and an eventual long-term recovery in the 1980s.

The below chart indicates the trends of the Carter era:

Carter era	1976	1977	1978	1979	1980
Inflation (%)	4.8	6.8	9.0	13.3	12.4
TW ($)	105.6	103.3	92.4	88.1	87.4
Real GDP	5.4	5.5	4.8	3.2	−0.2

(continued)

(continued)

Carter era	1976	1977	1978	1979	1980
Unemployment	7.7	7.1	6.1	5.8	7.1
UST-3Y	6.77	6.69	8.29	9.72	11.55
UST-10Y	7.61	7.42	8.41	9.44	11.46
After-tax profits	74.3	92.2	102.5	109.2	100.3

As evident from the Carter era, there is a web of interactions in market prices that creates the imperative for a broader analysis of price movements to support effective decision making. The movements in any given market are a function not only of the supply and demand forces in that market but also of the movement in prices in other markets. In preview, simply consider that the PCE price deflator has a Granger Causality link to corporate profit margins, the yield curve, and the TED spread.[1] Profit margins, in turn, have a Granger Causality link to the NYSE Index as well as the high-yield, option adjusted spread.

Price Determination Web of Interactions Between Markets

One of the fascinations of economics and finance is the matrix of interactions among prices. In earlier chapters, we have focused on the interaction of prices for goods, capital, credit, and foreign exchange. In this chapter, we will outline the linkages and driving factors for prices in these core markets prices.

One change leaves the way open for the introduction of others.—Machiavelli

Growth and Goods Inflation: One-Way Link

When we first examine the pattern of goods prices, one driver is the growth of GDP. GDP has a one-way causal link to the PCE deflator (Fig. 3.1). As would be expected in the short run, stronger economic growth tends to raise the rate of inflation, ceteris paribus, as resource utilization increases, thus driving prices higher.

---

[1] C.W.J. Granger, "Investigating Causal Relationships by Econometric Models and Cross-Spectral Methods," *Econometrica*, 1969, 37, no. 3: 424–438. An extensive discussion and application of the causality method is examined in Silvia et. al., *Economic and Business Forecasting*, Wiley, 2014.

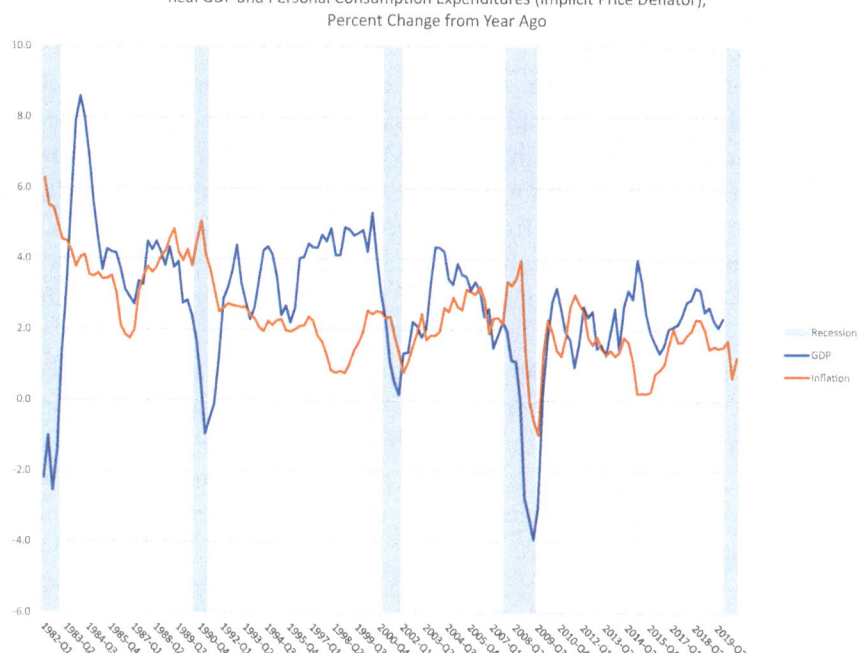

Fig. 3.1 Real economic growth and inflation since 1982

One of the mysteries of the recovery of 2010–2019 for many economists and policymakers was the lack of inflation even though the unemployment rate continued to decline to levels below what was previously considered full employment. This puzzlement might be caused by anchoring estimates of full employment based upon history and not upon the reality of the labor markets of this era. In addition, the PCE deflator is a mean-reverting series with an autocorrelation problem. That is, the process of the series returning to its long-run mean is very slow. This suggests that if the PCE deflator series deviates from the long-run mean, it will take an extended period to return to the mean.[2] Unfortunately, the same conclusion is true for the core PCE deflator series as well. In fact, both series have, to some extent, shifted downward in the last decade. The average for the 2009–2017 period is just 1.3% for the PCE deflator and 1.5% for the core PCE deflator.

---

[2] Inflation inertia and periods of disinflation are associated with periods of below normal output. See Laurence Ball, "What Determines the Sacrifice Ratio?" In *Monetary Policy*, N. Gregory Mankiw, ed. Chicago: University of Chicago Press, 1994, pp. 155–182.

Domestic Demand and the Price of Capital

A second critical price in the economy is the benchmark interest rate, a component of the cost of capital. Consider the relationship described in Fig. 3.2. Here, real final sales have a one-way causality link to the two-year benchmark Treasury rate. This may not be surprising to many because during the period of 2016–2018 the rise in the economy had been accompanied by an increase in the two-year rate. However, this relationship is based upon data over the 1982–2017 period not on a short-term analysis or on the appearance of a one-time phenomenon.

The Real Final Sales of Domestic Product series underwent a downward break in October 2008. The period of "low" interest rates since then is perfectly consistent with the downward shift in its driver—real final sales.

For now, the demand for credit, either in the short-term market from banks (Chapter 5), for example, or from the bond market (more details in Chapter 6) can be expressed as:

$$B^d = f(Y, 1/r, W/P)$$

where Y represents national output, 1/r is the inverse of the interest rate (effectively the price of the bond) and W/P represents real wealth. Bond supply can be expressed in a similar manner. In our framework, copper prices play a role in setting price expectations. The fed funds rate, for example, also plays a role in setting a benchmark rate for pricing the two-year Treasury

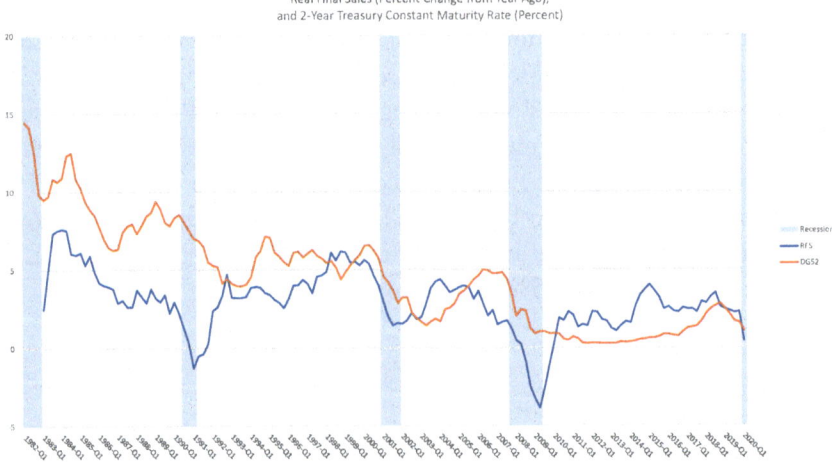

Fig. 3.2 Real final sales and 2-year Treasury rates

note. And the percentage of banks reporting stronger demand provides an indication of the demand for credit.

Completing the Web: Dollar, Interest Rates, and Inflation

Interrelationships between economic and financial factors are fascinating. Consider that both the U.S. dollar (measured as the USD/UK pound over the historical period 1982–2020) and oil prices have one-way causality link to inflation. That is, both influence the behavior of the PCE deflator. In turn, does the PCE measure of inflation help predict the ten-year Treasury rate and the TED spread? There is some influence, but the link is not statistically significant and thereby unreliable in the forecasting sense. A simple equation shows where aggregate demand (AD) is some function of real income (RYD), real interest rates (r), and real net assets (W/P) (Fig. 3.3).

$$AD = F(RYD, r, W/P)$$

In addition, corporate bond spreads and non-financial corporate profit margins influence the NYSE stock composite. The links between the dollar,

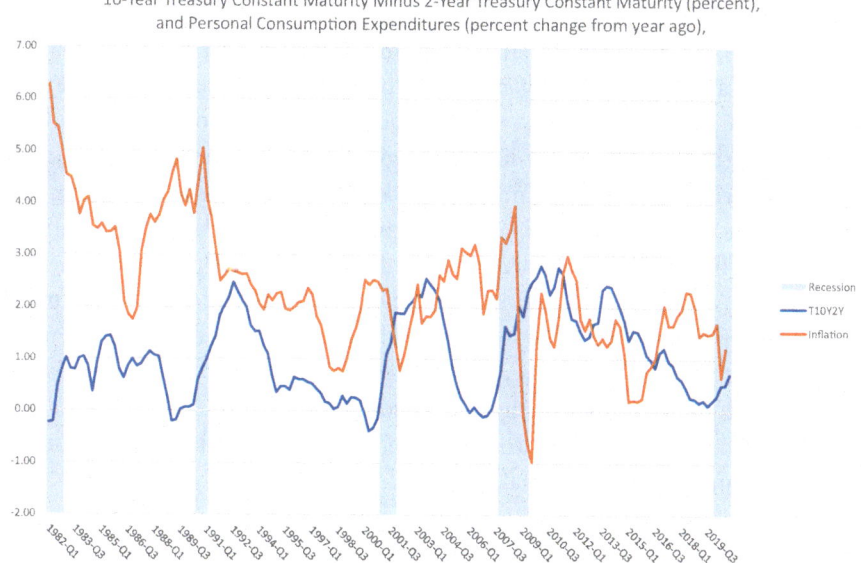

Fig. 3.3 Inflation and the yield curve

Treasury rates, corporate spreads, the NYSE, and inflation reinforce a focus on a broader model of economic behavior than the linear, one-to-one, extrapolations of financial, non-recursive behavior that dominates popular commentary. Moreover, these statistical results remind us to focus on significant links and not be distracted by the myriad of minor economic forces that captivate many commentators and analysts.

* * *

Prices as Signal

Headlines blare stories about booms and recession while overlooking the behavior of critical market prices and their possible contribution to understanding trends, cycles—opportunities to seek profits and to avoid loss.

Our focus is on prices and markets. In contrast, other writers concentrate on GDP and economic growth. Given the large set of numbers and releases involved in GDP forecasting, I believe valuable economic growth forecasts and review of weekly economic indicators can be gleaned each month from many detailed market commentaries from numerous countries such as the Group of Seven (G-7) which includes the United States, Japan, Italy, Canada, Germany, France, and the United Kingdom. Our comparative advantage is a focus on market prices which we believe are the ultimate interest of investment professionals and participants.

Over the last forty years, I have become familiar with the four markets that provide a context for analysis in this book. Experience is a great teacher and, given my many mistakes, I have had multiple opportunities to learn more about the economy and its workings. For any economic outlook, the path must lead to a financial and real market call—commodity prices, credit (interest rates), equity markets, and foreign exchange markets. Second, these markets are linked—they are not isolated lines in GDP accounting. This often happens when lines such as consumer spending, business investment, or government spending (C+I+G) are analyzed and reported by the Bureau of Economic Analysis as if they are independent entities when each sector interacts with the behavior of the other sectors.

For policymakers and investors, Former Treasury Blumenthal's comment is a helpful hint on decision making.

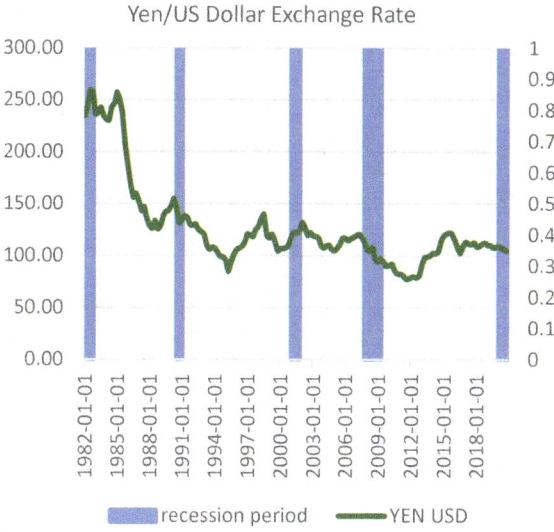

Fig. 3.4 Yen/US dollar exchange rate

There is a basic fallacy in decision making where each person sees the direction of the economy primarily in terms of its impact on himself or herself rather than understanding the much more complex interaction.[3]

In contrast, investment strategy revolves around these four markets. I have learned repeatedly at strategy meetings with my colleagues in equity, bond, and exchange rate markets the importance of these economic areas. Effective due diligence demands consideration of the interactions of these four markets. This approach is distinctly different from what the headline and the accompanying charts of a recent article in the *Financial Times* suggest:

"Commodity producers take currency hits from coronavirus," *Financial Times* **January 29, 2020**

These markets and their prices benefit from two characteristics that contribute to our approach. First, these market prices are not revised monthly as are the entries in GDP and other real economic series such as employment, retail sales, and industrial production. The lack of constantly revised data on equity prices, exchange rates (Fig. 3.4), interest rates (Fig. 3.5), as well as commodity prices, such as Dr. Copper (market lingo for copper as a leading indicator of economic health) and that barbarous relic, gold, eases time-series analysis. Once again, consider this headline between interest rates and equity

---

[3] Michael Blumenthal in "When the President Calls," Simon Bowmaker and Minouche Shafik, MIT Press, October 2019, p. 90.

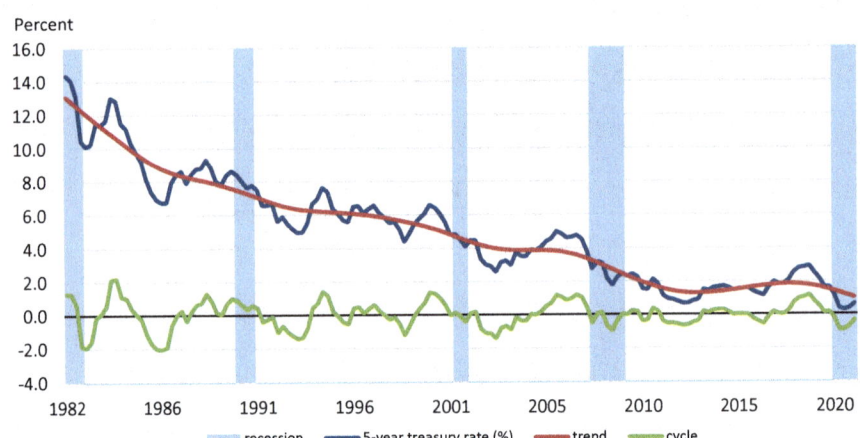

Fig. 3.5 Five year Treasury rate

prices in the *Wall Street Journal*. Gold, however, is also subject to the cognitive bias of illusory correlation where everything appears to be correlated to gold if you torture the data/time period enough.

If we start our analysis from the early 1970s, the yen was considered significantly over valued, there is a structural break in yen valuation in 1978 as evidenced in the graph so its subsequent decline in the late 1980s was not surprising as another shock, 1987, led to another revaluation upward of the yen. Recall the Plaza Accord was in February 1985 so the sharp increase in the yen value (decline in the rate line in the graph) would be consistent with that event. There was a further revaluation upward in 2008.

There are two further interesting observations.

First, the Nikkei index peaked in the early 1990. So, while the yen appreciated against the dollar, the equity value in the Nikkei kept rising in the 1980s.

Second, the ten-year JGB Futures index's benchmark rate peaked in early 1990, consistent with the peak in the Nikkei and the start of a long recession and slow economic growth period in Japan. We start out at disequilibrium and observe a steady appreciation of the currency. Yet since 1990, the yen/dollar rate has remained remarkably steady despite a long period of interest rate declines and subpar economic growth. What is the economic model that would define fair value here?

"Falling Yields Drive Bond Buyers to REIT Stocks," *Wall Street Journal* January 29, 2020

Yes, corporate bond spreads do have a causal link to equity prices. But how helpful is such knowledge? Economists learn about GDP accounting as well as Gross Domestic Income (GDI) accounting in economic principles class. Yet, the GDI approach is quickly put in the rear-view mirror and is seldom discussed in the current economic environment. In a similar way, a focus on GDP accounting is helpful but it ignores the role of markets and prices in setting the tone for assessing economic developments. Once again, benchmark revisions hit both GDP and GDI components while market prices are not revised.

In this way, benchmark revisions make it difficult to judge what data investors and policymakers saw at the time they were making decisions. Thankfully, the Federal Reserve of St. Louis provides some historical data for many series so that analysis of policy actions can be reviewed in the context of what was known at the time in contrast to a review of the revised data which was not available at the time policy decisions were made. Unrevised market data provide the benchmarks that investors and business decision-makers can follow to identify the change in the economy while tracing real side historical data can be very difficult.

When analysts focus on commodity prices (copper, Fig. 3.6, and oil), they skip over the prices of services. This is done on purpose. The problem with many service prices is that the measures are sometimes implicit, not market, prices. Moreover, there is no widespread set of futures prices of these services. I suspect the stability of service prices relative to commodity prices limits the utilization of service prices as signals of the business cycle and changes in

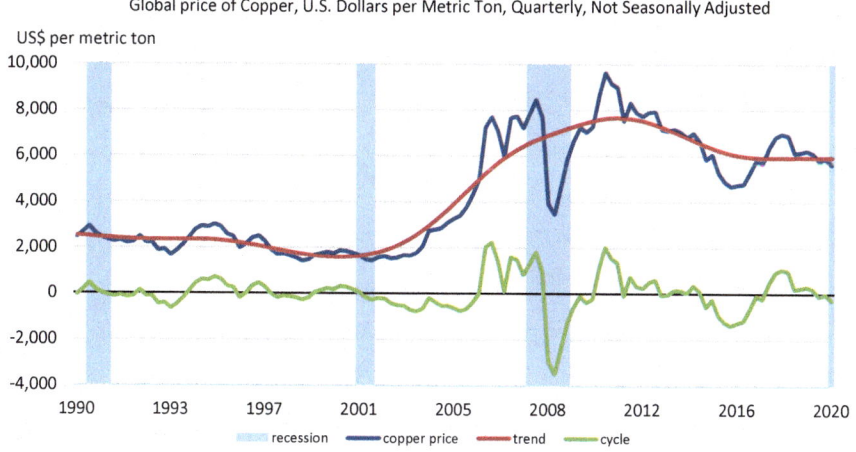

Fig. 3.6 Global price of copper

market sentiment. Copper prices have a causal relationship with the federal funds rate, and, in turn, copper has a causal link to the yield curve.

Time-Series Analysis: Do It Once—With Unrevised Data

The lack of revisions in market price data provides an opportunity to apply time series analysis to the patterns of prices to identify patterns in the data that provide hints that something is changing. For example, the NYSE Index does add value to an explanation of the pattern of copper prices. This is valuable since both series are not distorted by seasonal adjustments and annual revisions. We then can take a closer look at the data and find reasons for any changes in the patterns. Equity prices, Fig. 3.7, present a challenge as the NYSE index, for example, is not mean reverting and presents problems in statistical analysis.

Finally, many of the prices we follow are monitored in futures markets. This allows us a way to gauge market expectations of prices and a view of change over time—a dynamic assessment of market expectations. Changes in market expectations can thus be gauged against economic developments and policy actions.

The path of market prices is a constant winding set of turns over time. In our work, we track a set of indicators that provide signals of future

Fig. 3.7 NYSE equity index

market developments: Granger causality with future developments, or here predictability, of financial prices.

In contrast, reliance on a single indicator can be very misleading. The financial press focuses on a single indicator since that indicator is news but seldom, in our view, does a single indicator provide context. A *Barron's* article (March 20, 2020) asserted that "higher Treasury yields send a hopeful signal to markets."[4] An economy as diversified as the U.S. economy does not operate around a single indicator. The article then talks about the ten-year Treasury yield "soaring" with yields above 1% from a closing yield of 0.57% on March 9th. Soaring is plainly hyperbole. The author (Randall Forsyth) then compares this current yield with the ten-year yield rising post-October 1987 and in October 1998 (which were periods of rising rates but without a recession). But these yields Mr. Forsyth referred to were occurring during the 2020 recession caused by the Covid-19 shutdown. Mr. Forsyth provided another example that happened after the dot-com crash of 2000—the ten-year yield reached a bottom on October 9, 2002. Fine, but that recession ended in November 2001. The author, in my opinion, failed to make the case for employing the ten-year yield as an independent benchmark signaling the all-clear in markets.

A more reliable approach is to review the market prices of the four markets and the interaction of these markets. Let us start with the actual data for a commodity price, WTI oil, and a corporate bond spread, the High-Yield Index for the fascinating last two economic cycles. The WTI Index tracks the economic recovery from 2001 to 2008 with its price reacting sharply downward to the 2007 recession and the shutdown of 2020. This series is cyclical in character and is clearly a non-linear series. Finally, there is the break in oil prices in 2015 that appears independent of any economic weakness.

As for credit, the ICE (Intercontinental Exchange) BoA (Bank of America) High-Yield Index spread rose dramatically to 9.04% from 3.56% on January 2, 2020 to 5.06% on February 29th. This risk off position indicates that investors were unwilling to take the risk given the uncertainty of the economic outlook. The leading indicator character of this series is intriguing. High-yield spreads began to rise in spring 1998, before the March 2001 recession and hit an interim peak in October 2001, declined, and then a subsequent peak in October 2002. In a similar way, high-yield spreads rose in early 2007 before the recession began in December 2007.

As for exchange rates, the dollar index hit 101.95 in late March 2020, up 5.8% year to date at that time. This signaled a strong flight to safety

---

[4] "Higher Treasury Yields Send a Hopeful Signal to Markets," *Barron's* March 20, 2020.

and a mood of caution. During a prior recession and recovery period, the dollar and British pound exchange rate peaked at 1.40 in June 2001 and then deteriorated continuously to the 4Q 2007.

Finally, for the equity market, the S&P 500 Index (SPX) closed at 2304.92 in late March 2020, down 28.7% year to date. For both the S&P 500 and NASDAQ indices in a prior recession period, there was an initial bottom in September 2001 (recall the attacks of September 11, 2001) and then a subsequent bottom in February 2003. Expansionary fiscal policy relief in 2001, 2002, and 2003 appeared to have made a difference in the economic outlook.

No single indicator can serve as a reliable predictor of economic behavior or of other market prices. Any indicator should be part of a broader framework of economic and financial activity.

* * *

A Framework for Prices in Four Markets

We can specify the framework in the goods market as aggregate demand as a function of income, Y, interest rates, r, and wealth W/P as determinants of consumption while business investment demand is a function of expected final sales, subsumed in Y, interest rates and cash on hand, subsumed in W/P. Finally, exports reflect global demand and the terms of trade, eP*/P where e is the exchange rate, P* as the price of goods abroad, and P the dollar price of goods. There is also the autonomous, A, impact of fiscal and monetary policy.

$$\text{Aggregate demand} = A + bY - cr + W/P + eP*/P$$

Aggregate supply is a function of technology, T, the real wage bill, W/P, and the gap between current and potential output, Y − YPOT.

For the bond/credit markets we have the equation

$$B^d = B^s = f(Y, 1/r, W/P)$$

Foreign exchange markets are reflected in the balance of payments model where the balance of payments reflects net exports and net capital outflows. Net exports reflect the influence of U.S. prices, P, and the exchange rate, e as well as incomes abroad, YROW, and through e the transformation of foreign goods prices into U.S. prices. Net capital flows are a function of relative interest rates, r*.

$$NX = f(eP*/P, YROW, r*)$$

Unsurprisingly, German ten-year yields do have a causal link to U.S. corporate bond yields and the TED spread.

For the equity market, we begin with the demand for equity capital which depends on the return it yields relative to the returns on alternative assets as well as the income and wealth of the household or investor.

$$EQ^d = f\left(r_{eq}, r_b, Y, W/P\right)$$

Here the returns on both equity and bonds are uncertain going forward. The allocation of financial capital between equity and bonds varies with the business cycle and, as we shall see, evolves over the long run (more details in Chapter 11). Bond returns, for example, have a Granger causal link to the NYSE Index.

In future chapters, we identify a set of variables that serves as either (1) forward-looking indicators of price change or (2) explanatory variables in a framework of price movements over time. For decision makers, parsimony is essential. Given the evolution of the economy and its complexity, the focus should be on a reliable, limited set of market prices that can serve as benchmarks for decision-making.

Price Determination over Both the Short and Long-Run

We approach the examination of market prices from two perspectives. First, the behavior of prices in the short run often differs from the price in the long run. Isolated shocks to the economy, such as Covid-19 in 2020, provide a vivid example. Other examples of shocks that led to sharp declines in the Dow Jones Index but were subsequently totally reversed two months later included the 1963 assassination of President John F. Kennedy (political uncertainty), the Hunt brothers attempt to corner the silver market and subsequent crash in 1980 (commodities), the Financial Panic of 1987 (asset valuations) and England's withdrawal from the European Exchange Rate Mechanism (ERM) because of a crisis in the pound sterling in 1992 (exchange rate).

Second, as mentioned earlier, there are financial silos. At investment meetings, strategic discussions bring together professionals from different disciplines (economics, equity, fixed income, and currencies). How to integrate these areas into one intellectually consistent strategy? Price determination reflects the activity in both a partial and a general equilibrium framework.

We start with the traditional downward-sloping demand curve in a market. The demand curve represents combinations of price and output that clears our output/credit/equity/foreign exchange markets. In a fully employed economy, the long-run aggregate supply curve is vertical such that full employment is given. We expect that the markets, in general, will move to the point where the combinations of labor, capital, technology, and entrepreneurship set the base for full employment. Changes in aggregate demand will be reflected in changes in prices but not the level of output.

What about the short-run supply curve? The answer depends on how quickly prices and price expectations adjust to the perceived change in economic circumstances. Here we recognize the specific behavioral relationships of our four markets. For example, corporate bond spreads and equity prices tend to be leading indicators; consumer goods prices are prone to lag changes in the economy. Production and employment decisions in a market such as autos depend on the price level but must be made before the price level is known. This is familiar to investors with respect to the initial price offering.[5]

Expectations about prices play a central role in setting the short-run aggregate supply curve and the responsiveness of prices to a change in expected output. Any deviation between the actual and expected price level—an unanticipated price change such that the reactions of economic agents will add to the dynamics of the price system. Actual and expected price changes can and do evolve over time. When actual prices do not equal expectations, output deviates from the natural rate and agents revise price expectations. The equity investor sees this in earnings reports that exceed or fall short of expectations. In the foreign exchange market, the impact of Brexit, England's political decision to leave the European Union, can be seen on the British pound exchange rate to the U.S. dollar. On June 20, 2016, the dollar traded 1.46 to the pound; on July 7th, the dollar traded at 1.29 to the pound; by August 18, 2020, the dollar traded at 1.32 to the pound. The London Gold Fix for the pound was 874 on June 20th. It rose to 1046 on July 7th and rose again to 1517 on August 18th. This pattern illustrates static stability because the dollar and pound exchange rates, once shocked, did not return to its original level. In neutral static stability, the values of the dollar and pound exchange rates do shift and, in this case, to a new lower plateau. For exchange rates, we can also examine the case for the Mexican peso Fig. 3.8 which does not appear to exhibit any tendency to a new plateau and would be considered a

---

[5] For example, "During Covid-19 Pandemic, Biotech IPOs Already Surpass Record," *Wall Street Journal,* August 10, 2020 and "WeWork/Luckin Coffee: When the Tide Goes Out," *Financial Times* April 3, 2020.

3 Price Determination in a Multi-Sector Global Economy

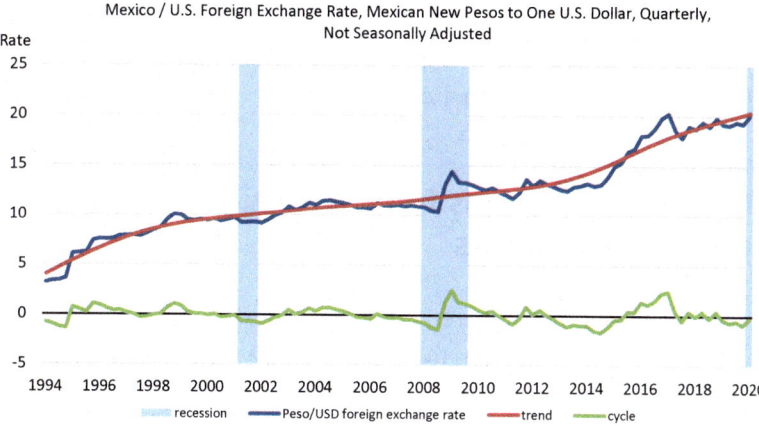

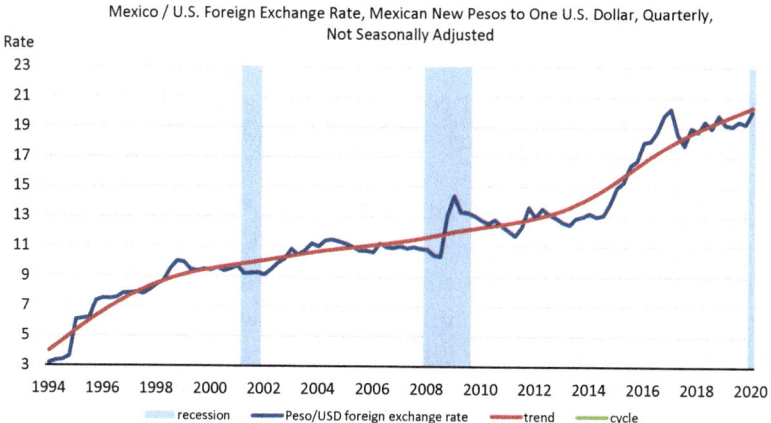

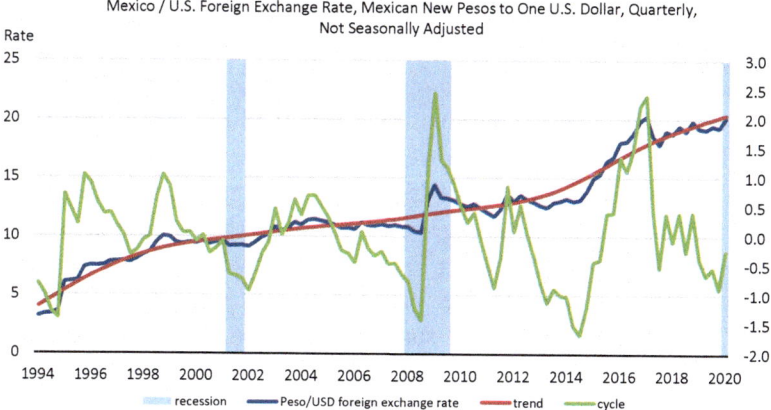

Fig. 3.8 Mexican peso/US dollar exchange rate

case of negative static stability. The Mexican peso/U.S. dollar exchange rate exhibits a structural break in 2008. The TED spread and the Mexican peso exchange rate have a bidirectional causality link.

Intellectual Challenges to Conventional Views of Market Interactions

Static stability is significant here. Prices can move in three different ways in a manner inconsistent with the concept of a move to an equilibrium and certainly not a return to "normal" that market participants recognize as normal.

For any given change in a market price, there are three different scenarios. In the first case, the price change is expected to persist in the future at a new plateau.

Consider the investment and economic implications if this scenario was applied to the future of oil markets during the pandemic. The market adjusts to new information (less global and domestic travel) that gives credence to the new, lower WTI price. The emergence of fracking in recent years altered global oil prices to a lower level than was had been projected as well as changing the balance of polictical power in the global oil market. On February 21, 2020, in the first quarter, WTI traded at $53.38. The price plateau was again altered by the OPEC/Russia agreement in March 2020 to lower prices. This once more threatens the financial viability of many fracking producers. Oil prices fell throughout March and went negative for a short time in later April. From July to August, the WTI price remained in the low $40 range. Going forward, it is now uncertain if the OPEC/Russia agreement will lead to only a short-run change in oil prices or to a more sustained lower oil price. WTI prices are a neutral static stability outcome as prices have stabilized at a new, in this case, lower, plateau.

For investors, the conventional assumption of a return to "normal" is out. Instead, the intellectual challenge is to consider the impact of a cognitive bias in projecting oil prices going forward. The anchoring bias would signal a return to the prior $50 plus per barrel price that was prevalent in the first quarter. The recency bias would suggest a price in the low $40 per barrel. The intellectual challenge in modeling this market is to discriminate between these two biases.

In financial markets, a "correction" is a short-run move in prices that disappears over time. In modeling, this suggests a return to prior values. The series is characterized as mean reverting. Many series, such as the benchmark ten-year rate or the NYSE Composite Index are not mean reverting when expressed in level form. Yet, it is this level form that is exactly the most common way such benchmarks are cited in the media and by strategists. Intellectually then, there is a challenge to analyze series similar to these in a way to remove that bias in the data.

What can be learned from a "correction?" Some analysts claim the price change is not warranted and that the future price will be closer to the original price level than the current price level. For the equity investor, the price change may represent an overbought (too high) or oversold (too low) condition. As cited earlier, market sell offs in response to singular events are examples of an oversold condition.

Finally, there is the price change that leads to a greater change in expectations of future prices. When shutdowns began to hit the United States as a response to coronavirus, analysts and media commentators predicted another Great Depression. There were also predictions of a deflationary spiral. In both cases, the initial economic shock led not only to weakenss in the economy but also expectations of further weakness would lead to a depression and deflation, along with U.S. interest rates falling into negative territory.

This pattern of interlocked expectations occurs on the equity side. Analysts act together after they see a surprise jump in a company's earnings report. This leads to expectations of even better earnings and higher prices in the future. In turn, this futher boosts earnings expectations and analysts boost their price targets. In this case, the overshooting is characteristic of booms and busts in financial markets.

The Challenge of Interest Rate Parity

Interest rate parity is a no-arbitrage condition representing an equilibrium state under which investors will be indifferent to interest rates available on financial assets in different countries.

Central to interest rate parity is the assumption of perfect substitutability of domestic and foreign assets. This is seldom true for any two assets and the degree of substitutability varies over time. In a four-sector framework of financial market prices, this degree of substitutability between asset classes is paramount to price determination.

In the spring of 2020, as the pandemic gathered steam, investors were risk averse and thus favored benchmark bond rates relative to equities or commodities. Risk aversion also changes over time for currencies as evidenced in the behavior of the British pound with variations in sentiment on Brexit negotiations.

Once again, the role of expectations is central to price discovery. Yet, these expectations change over time, presenting a continuing challenge to analysts—ceteris paribus never stays the same.

Anchoring Bias for Inflation Target: When Actual and Policy Targets Diverge

> If a man will begin with certainties, he shall end in doubts; but if he will be content to begin with doubts, he shall end in certainties.—Francis Bacon

For much of the 2015–2020 period, Fed monetary policy was anchored to a 2% inflation target, yet we have not been there for a while. Policy is anchored to reaching 3% GDP but since 2015 we have averaged 2.4% and in no year did growth reach 3%. Policy is anchored to some concept of the neutral interest rate and the full unemployment rate that continues to drift over time. Such drifting got the Pilgrims to Massachusetts and not Virginia—more on this later.

For Investors Let's Start at Naught

We shall take reality as it is—inflation a bit below 2%, GDP growth at 2.4 percent (still above the Congressional Budget Office's estimate for potential) and accept that the current unemployment rate is below estimates of full employment. We will leave the definition of the true neutral interest rate to the philosophy department—they oversee truth. Indiana Jones says to his class: "Archaeology is the search for fact, not truth. If it is truth you are looking for, Dr. Tyree's philosophy class is right down the hall."[6]

There Are No Prompter Screens at Investment Meetings

So what are we doing? Are public policymakers pursuing a bridge too far that will and does, in fact, distort market pricing? It appears so. How is it that consumer equity stocks that do not make a profit—and some have no clear path to profitability in the short term—merit such high valuations as some

---

[6] *Indiana Jones and the Raiders of the Lost Arc,* Lucasfilms and Paramount Pictures, 1981.

commentators are anticipating a recession in one or two years? If you can't make a profit at 2.4% GDP how will you make a profit in a recession?

These were legitimate questions before the pandemic hit and even more so after it shattered normalcy and upended the economy. As we question equity valuations in some cases, we also need to ask about bonds—equities half-brother. Are the same growth, inflation, and interest rates assumptions that underlie equities also influencing bond investors around the strategy table? For the analyst, the problem is that when one market appears in a state of disequilibrium, it intimates that other markets are also out of balance.

If bond rates are too low, then are equity prices too high? If bond and mortgage rates are too low, then are housing prices too high?

* * *

Works in Theory, Works in Practice

Employment releases by the Bureau of Labor Statistics provide an excellent practical example of the importance of maintaining a broad framework of economic interactions. Although an up or down surprise may begin in the labor market and employment reports, the subsequent market movements reverberate in credit, equity, and foreign exchange markets.

Markets move based on the difference between what we get and what we expected. No clearer example is the market movements subsequent to the employment release.

Stronger or weaker than expected job gains alter expectations about monetary policy and thereby interest rates. Expectations also revolve around the Federal Reserve policy meetings as well. In July 2020, a further easing was still the majority expectation of analysts. But the lack of action by the Fed led to a reduction in the market probabilities for a second and third easing. In July, the Fed funds futures market (which are financial contracts that represent the market opinion of where the daily official federal funds rate will be at the time of the contract expires) downshifted expectations of a 50-basis point cut in July from near 30% to less than 10%. Disequilibrium characterizes the credit markets. Set in motion was the search for a new set of equilibrium interest rates in the credit markets. Both two-year and ten-year benchmark U.S. Treasury rates rose given the shock that the Fed was not going to cut rates so soon. Both current and expected future interest rates were altered based upon the outcome of the Fed meetings.

This pattern of reacting to Fed policy actions is often repeated giving credence to the belief that policy actions will alter not only market prices today but expectations of future prices. A disequilibrium in market prices today is followed by disequilibrium adjustments tomorrow. A sequence of policy rate increases from March 2017 to December 2019 put in motion a repricing of credit instruments as well as expectations for future economic growth. In May 2013, Chairman Ben Bernanke simply mentioned the possibility for reducing the Fed's balance sheet as part of its Quantitative Easing (QE) which had been initiated to deal with the Great Recession of 2008–2009. This set off a period of rising benchmark Treasury rates: 2% in May which peaked at 3% by the end of the year. The trade-weighted dollar also rose over the same period. The dollar exchange rate rose in response to the altered expectations of monetary policy and thereby the future path of credit market rates. Less aggressive Fed easing also raised the attractiveness of the dollar relative to foreign currencies.

Market interactions are pervasive—changes in interest rate policy at the Fed alter the credit market as well as the dollar exchange market.

* * *

Price Shock from the Supply Side

During the *1973* Arab–Israeli War, Arab members of the Organization of Petroleum Exporting Countries (OPEC) imposed an embargo against the United States in retaliation for the United States' decision to re-supply the Israeli military and to gain leverage in the postwar peace negotiations. The oil embargo led to a significant change in the terms of trade and aggravated an already rising U.S. inflation trend. This supply shock was followed by a decline in economic growth in 1974 and, as expected, a drop in manufacturing and transportation profits in 1974. Equity valuations declined. The rising inflation trend fed into interest rates as yields on three-month T-bills, 3–5-year Treasury notes, and Federal Housing Administration (FHA) mortgage rates rose. With the higher oil import bill, America's current account deficit—the value of the goods and services the U.S. imports exceeds the value of the products it exports—rose in 1974 and the dollar exchange value declined in the first half of 1974. Since the dollar is a relative value, the exchange rate rose versus, for example, the French and Japanese currencies as their trade positions were even further impacted by the oil embargo than for the United States.

Exchange Rate Surprise: The Plaza Accord

The foreign exchange market can also be a source of disequilibrium in other financial markets. However, attempts to alter nominal exchange rates face the reality of the underlying economy and politics. As mentioned earlier, the Plaza Accord of February 1985 aimed at reducing the exchange value of the dollar by reinforcing the expansionary impact of the lower fed funds rate policy of mid-1984. As expected, the growth slowdown in GDP from 1984 to 1985 was halted and growth rates stabilized for 1986 and 1987. In turn, adjusted corporate profits rose in both 1986 and 1987. The S&P 500 Index rose in both 1986 and 1987 until Oct. 1987. The slowdown in core inflation from 1984 to 1985 stabilized at 4% for 1986 to 1987.

"It's the Lure of Easy Money, It's Gotta a Very Strong Appeal"—Smuggler's Blues, Glenn Frey, and Jack Tempchin

For decision makers, the dot.com boom provides an example of where price gains fed a mentality of expectations for further price gains. For investors, this idea is captured in the concept of momentum investing and expressed in the comparison of 30-day and 120-day moving averages of a particular price series. However, in a time series that has a unit root, statistically, a time series that has a unit root contains an underlying trend in the data.[7] This unit root, if not corrected, would lead to misleading standard significance tests. A calculation of a moving average would simply pick up that trend regardless of the underlying "value" of the series, here equities, is involved. Yes, the NASDAQ Index does have a unit root so calculations of the index (such as the moving average) will reflect the bias in the underlying data.

Equity valuations can thus create their own disequilibrium. Equity valuations should reflect discounted future earnings—not price momentum. NASDAQ (National Association of Securities Dealers Automated Quotations) valuations peaked in March 2000; the S&P 500 peaked a month later. Adjusted corporate profits peaked in the third quarter along with business investment in equipment and software. Real GDP growth slowed sharply in the same quarter and growth remained low into the decline of the third quarter of 2001 (caused by the attacks on September 11th). Consumer price inflation slowed from 2000 to 2001. The fed funds rate peaked in July. Markets are interrelated.

---

[7] See William H. Greene, *Econometric Analysis*, Sixth Edition, Pearson, Prentice-Hall, 2008, Chapter 22.

No man stands alone, no market stands alone. Ted Williams and Ernie Banks were great hitters—neither won a World Series. One future hall of fame player alone does not make for a championship in a team sport.

* * *

A Focus on Price Cycles: Not Busts

For decision makers, too much focus is spent on trying to predict when the next recession will hit while overlooking the behavior of critical prices over and between financial cycles.

The Benchmark 10-Year Treasury Rate

For the benchmark ten-year Treasury rate, the behavior of the series does not exhibit mean-reverting behavior over time. Our analysis found that the 10-year series is non-stationary with multiple structural breaks suggesting there is no past average to which the 10-year Treasury yield would revert. Put differently, if an analyst expects the current yield to revert back to a certain benchmark rate, then that thesis is misleading from an econometric perspective. Another critical observation from the figure, is that the 10-year series has a declining trend over time, suggesting that, on average, every business cycle has a lower 10-year yield compared to that of the previous cycle since 1982. This trend demonstrates that the 10-year Treasury yield is not mean reverting. There is evidence of structural break points in the ten-year rate in 1979, 1987, and 2002.

Evolution of Prices: When Slow-And-Steady May Not Win the Race

As illustrated in Fig. 3.12, the pace of inflation, as measured by the benchmark PCE deflator, has exhibited two distinct long-term trends. In the period leading up to the 1980s, inflation rose steadily. Along with the change in monetary policy, the market shock of the Hunt Brothers Silver Crisis in early 1980,[8] signaled a change in the inflation model. However, beginning in 1982, we found the PCE deflator declines and becomes mean reverting since

---

[8] Jerry W. Markham, *A Financial History of the United States: From the Age of Derivatives into the New Millennium: (1970–2001)*, volume 3, M.E. Sharpe, 2002.

1982. The process of the series returning to its long-run mean is painfully slow—in technical terms, the PCE deflator is characterized by autocorrelation. That suggests if the PCE series deviates from the long-run mean at a point in time, then the PCE deflator will take an extended period of time to get back to the mean. For example, the PCE deflator has been below its 2% target since May 2012 (except for January–February 2017) as the core (excluding food and energy) PCE deflator rose from 1.2% in the 4Q 2015 to 2.0% in the 2Q 2018. Decision makers need to consider that the PCE deflator's deviation from the mean may persist for some time even though it is a mean-reverting series.

The Equity Earnings/Price Ratio: Another Complex Pattern

Commentators frequently argue that equity earnings/price ratios are either above or below some average value and that this difference indicates the equity market is under or overvalued. However, as illustrated in Fig. 3.9, an average value can be calculated for any time series, but that does not indicate that the behavior of that series will return to some average value. Mean-reverting behavior for a series cannot simply be assumed—it must be tested and supported by econometric evidence.

Fig. 3.9 Earnings-price ratio

In fact, the E/P ratio is not mean reverting. Significant shifts in the series can be seen such as in October 1987 (downward) and October 1991 (upward) and then down again in July 2002. The E/P ratio is dependent on the behavior of several economic fundamentals such as expected nominal growth and interest rate polices, as well as regulatory changes and exogenous shocks that alter the risk/reward calculus. The E/P ratio is not independent of but instead is a product of the many forces of the economic cycle.

Prices and the Economy; The 2020 Experience

Prices Lead the Economy: February 20th A Day that Will Go Down in…

One similar observation that many commentators made in the early weeks of the pandemic was that the markets reacted to certain developments while many economic indicators (Institute of Supply Management (ISM) Manufacturing Index, jobless claims, building permits, for example) continued to suggest steady economic growth and indicated very little reaction to breakdown caused by the coronavirus and the drop in OPEC prices.

This is not surprising. In this book, we do not focus on GDP and select real-side indicators, in part, because many of these numbers are coincident—not leading indicators. Many are reported with a significant time lag. Instead, we focus on market prices that send signals for future economic and financial activity. Let us review the 2020 experience.

"Not Paid for the Risk," *Time* February 21, 2020

The Atlanta and New York Fed offered excellent reviews in the spring of 2020[9] of the current state of the economy; in contrast, market prices discounted the future. Why this disconnect? Currently, the typical approach in many commentaries was to examine supply and demand fundamentals to determine a market price for equities or corporate debt. But let's reverse the process by treating price as a signal and not the solution. For example, equity price commentary normally focuses on a fair value—that is the result of the fundamental and technical factors considered by a strategist. Yet, equity prices are a leading indicator and looked over the valley of economic weakness associated with the Covid-19 shutdowns.

Unfortunately, selected equity markets entered the Covid-19 shutdown in an overvalued position. On February 20th, the Russell 2000 of small-cap

---

[9] "Small Businesses Feel Pressure from COVID-19 Pandemic, Fed Research Shows," June 12, 2020, Federal Reserve Bank of Atlanta and New-York-Fed-Staff-Nowcast, various issues, Federal Reserve Bank of New York.

companies, a series I highlighted in my Atlanta Fed presentation of February 27th,[10] peaked at 1696. By March 12th it had fallen to 1122. At the time, more than 20% of the Russell 2000 companies did not earn a profit. Yes, you could argue—and some analysts did—that small caps remained the place to be due to their long-run historical performance. Yet the index fell continuously despite this optimism. Consider this disconnect. The Composite Index of Leading Indicators aka the Leading Economic Index (LEI) for January, released on February 20th (how is that for irony?), was up 0.8% based upon a broad improvement in several indicators. Meanwhile, the New York Fed Nowcast, intended to inform the public as to where the economy is at this moment, indicated growth in the first quarter of 2020 at 2.01, In a February 28th update, growth was put at 2.14%. By March 6, the NY Fed Nowcast assessed first-quarter GDP at 1.71%. The Fed's Nowcast tells us where we are now. Unfortunately, many commentators focused on economic indicators that were indicative of the current economy while price movements were signaling problems in the future.

Tracing Through COVID with Market Prices: Exercise in Price Adjustment

For the second quarter of 2020, the New York Fed Nowcast signaled a downshift in growth expectations. On June 6th, the outlook was for 1.3% growth in the second quarter. By March 13th, the outlook was further downgraded to 1.08%. By June 19th, it reached −19.03%. By the second quarter, the Bureau of Economic Analysis announced that GDP was −31.7%. Yet, the New York Fed Nowcast signaled a dramatic turn in growth ahead.

Equity prices are a leading indicator. The S&P 500 Index stood at 3373.23 on February 20th, then fell to 2304.92 as of March 20th. When the first release of GDP for the second quarter came out on July 30th, the S&P 500 Index had rallied to 3246.22 while, on the same day, the second-quarter GDP was reported by the BEA, in contrast to the Nowcast at the Federal Reserve Bank of New York, at −37.9%. Equity prices have a Granger causality link to both real final sales and the personal consumption deflator.

What about commodity prices? What is particularly telling was that the ICE Brent Crude Futures contract was $53.78 on February 20th and, except for a one-day collapse on April 20th, the bottom was $12.48 on April 28th. The WTI rose steadily, if slowly, to $43.04 on August 27th. It peaked at

---

[10] "Economic Outlook: A Perspective from the Markets and Prices," John E. Silvia, presentation at the Banking Outlook Conference, Federal Reserve Bank of Atlanta, February 27, 2020.

$59.31, you guessed it, on February 20th and sat at $34.97 on March 13th. The economic message of recovery was positive even though, on March 9th, the *Financial Times* headline read "Saudi Arabia launches oil price war after Russia deal collapse." Commodity prices were signaling recovery despite the headline. Important to note that the WTI has a Granger causality link to the personal consumption deflator signaling price stability ahead despite economic weakness.[11]

As for credit, the ICE BoA High-Yield Index spread declined from 3.95% on January 30th, 2020 to 3.57% on February 19th. By February 24th, the spread had widened out to 4.03%. The index peaked at 10.87% on March 23rd and then steadily declined, helped by the Federal Reserve's announcement of an intention to buy corporate debt. By August 27th, the yield stood at 4.98%. Corporate spreads have a Granger causality link to real final sales.

As for exchange rates, the yen/dollar rose steadily from August 12, 2019 at 105.38 to a peak of 111.86 on, wait for it, February 20th and then fell quickly to 108.12 by February 28th and steadily appreciated to 105.88 as of August 21. Interesting that the appreciation of the yen began before the Fed ease and while the New York Fed was raising their 1Q GDP forecast. This suggests that expectations of change, before the actual change, are an essential ingredient to explain market price movements. The yen/dollar exchange rate has a Granger causality link to both the benchmark two-year Treasury yield and the U.S. Treasury yield curve.

On the global outlook, consider that the iShares IMSCI (Morgan Stanley Capital International) Emerging Market ETF peaked on January 17th at 46.23, hit 43.54 on February 20th and stood at 33.71 on March 12th. Another price signal of global economic weakness before many global economic forecasts was downshifted.

Prices and Economic Data—What Is the Point?

Time inconsistency is a perennial problem in economic and financial analysis. Commentary often focuses on current indicators such as employment and consumer spending. But these are coincident, not leading indicators, and even then, the latest economic releases of these indicators are reporting data for last month, not next month. In contrast, financial market prices

---

[11] Price adjustments can occur due to several economic factors. See Andrew Caplin and Daniel Spulber, "Menu Coats and the Neutrality of Money," *Quarterly Journal of Economics*, 1987, 102 (November): 703–725.

are forward looking—equity prices discount future earnings. Yield spreads discount the relative future risk of alternative corporate investments.

All of this may seem obvious but consider communications problems. Number one is the conflation of leading, coincident, and lagging indicators. Just recently on March 6, 2020, the Bureau of Labor Statistics released employment (coincident) and the unemployment rate (lagging) indicators, and both were cited by commentators as signals of economic strength going forward. Unemployment claims, released the day before by the Department of Labor, are the real leading economic indicator but get far less play than employment or the unemployment rate.

Another communication problem arises when multiple economic releases come out the same week but cover alternative time periods. On the week of February 10, 2020 retail sales along with existing home sales were released. In the same week, housing starts' data for January were announced. In public commentary, all three series were treated as important data points but seldom mentioned the different coverage periods. Coverage focused as usual on housing starts, while true leading indicator—building permits—scarcely got a mention.

Finally, we run into our old friend the confirmation bias. Whenever prices move, we hear commentary that tends to find data and anecdotes that confirm the bias of the speaker. One old saw is that "the price action confirms…" This suggests that prices are the result of movements elsewhere rather than as a signal on their own.

Price Determination: Cycles, Trends and Playing from a Different Playbook

Despite the simple assertion that interest rates and exchange rates are directly linked embodied in the hypothesis of interest rate parity, the last thirty to forty years have brought into focus the importance of recognizing that we are starting at disequilibrium and exogenous factors (ceteris paribus). Analysts seek to define fair value as if a single number defines the golden mean of some economic or financial series. Unfortunately, equity analysts are burdened by this search for "fair value" often benchmarked as a target price-earnings ratio.

"Prescient or Pollyannaish? Explaining the Market's Rally," *Wall Street Journal* **April 18, 2020**

Equity analysts are not alone in this search for "fair value". Submitted for your approval is the case of the TED spread, a measure of risk (Fig. 3.10),

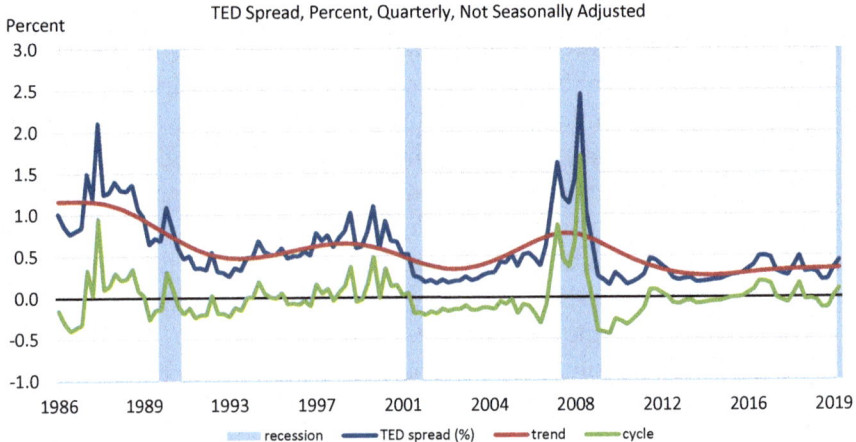

Fig. 3.10 Ted spread

whose behavior illustrates to the thoughtful analyst, and to a fictional character named Max Phillips, an insight into life that should not be forgotten. I saw recently a rerun of a classic *Twilight Zone* episode entitled "In Praise of Pip." Rod Sterling introduced the show with his usual dour, clipped cadence intoning that: "…This to be a gift of love to a son named Pip. Mr. Max Phillips, homo sapiens, who is soon to discover that man is not as wise as he thinks. Said lesson to be learned in the Twilight Zone."

The problem we often face as analysts is that we do not start at square one but rather we start at a point of disequilibrium.

In the case of the ten-year United Kingdom benchmark yield, the rise and fall of inflation and its impact on yields are very apparent. Once again, we face the challenge of defining fair value since the series is clearly not mean reverting. In addition, when we examine the pattern of the U.S. dollar/sterling exchange rate, there are periods of dollar depreciation (late 1980s, 2001–2009) and dollar appreciation (2010 to now) that appear independent of the pattern of British interest rates. Our challenge, of course, in finding fair value is realizing the pattern of exchange and interest rates represent a world of relative changes within the context of what is happening to economic growth in each country.

"Why the Japanese yen is not the haven asset it once was," *Financial Times* January 13, 2020

As illustrated in this headline, the value of selected currencies as haven assets has changed over time. Once, some believed the euro could become an alternative to the U.S. dollar but that has not happened. So, beyond the economics, the risk/reward trade-off is key to currency selection. Yet, once again, the view of the yen as haven asset, as hinted at in the above headline, does not appear. The fluctuations of the yen/dollar since the mid-1990s are limited compared to what you might expect if the yen is an in and out haven asset.

"**Bank of England holds rates but cuts growth forecast,**" *Financial Times* **January 30, 2020**

Meanwhile, consider the intellectual break implied in the context of this headline from the *Financial Times*. Benchmark interest rates remain the same, but the Bank of England cuts its growth forecast. Interesting that sterling rose in value versus the dollar despite the slower growth outlook and a weaker economic outlook before Brexit negotiations began in full swing. Moreover, longer-term U.K. gilt yields rose while the policy benchmark remains unchanged, growth expectations declined, and the sterling appreciated.

* * *

Price Discovery: Cycles, Trends in Three Interlinked Markets Part II

Second-quarter 2020 provided several examples of the interactions of market prices that bolster the case for a market framework that focuses on the prices of commodities, credit, equity, and foreign exchange and not individual market silos. Consider then the following headline.

"**Oil Crash Accelerates, Rippling to Currencies and Stocks**" *Wall Street Journal* **April 21, 2020**

The authors Dylan Moriarty and Vivian Ngo first made a link between government policy and oil demand: "The convulsions in oil markets underlined the huge hit that government-imposed lockdowns designed to stall the spread of the coronavirus have dealt to oil demand." Beginning with the shutdowns, it would be expected that the pace of economic activity going forward would decline. It would not be surprising that equity valuations would decline as a direct effect. Yet, that direct effect brings out an interesting path of study. Lower oil and gas prices traditionally signal higher personal income for consumers and increased spending. But the shutdowns also meant a substantial increase in unemployment and a significant decline in consumer confidence. In addition, the decline in expected economic growth, including the possibility of a recession (which became a reality) hit equity values, and thereby household wealth—another negative for consumer spending.

What is intriguing is the pattern of ten-year TIPS in recent years. TIPS is a Treasury bond that is indexed to an inflationary gauge to protect investors from the decline in the purchasing power of their money. The principal value of TIPS rises as inflation rises while the interest payment varies with the adjusted principal value of the bond. There is a clear cycle of up and down in 2015 and in the first half of 2016 and then a steady rise from 2016 to 2019. Beginning in January 2019 a clear decline in the TIPS value begins eventually becoming negative on a regular basis starting in January 2020. Yet, WTI prices did not decline in 2019. So as an indicator of deflationary pressures, lower oil prices did not factor in the decline in the TIPS yield. Meanwhile, at the end of 2019, the three-month Consumer Price Index inflation rate was 3.4% for the last three months of the year and 2.3% for the next twelve months. No signal of inflation deceleration here. So, for the next ten years, investors were betting on a decline in inflation even before oil prices broke down. This suggests that longer-term TIPS are being driven, at least in part, by Federal Reserve purchases. What about currencies? Well, let us look. The influence of the Fed on market prices extends to other areas of the market as we shall see.

Dollar/Euro Value: Long Cycle or a Downtrend?

Does the pattern of dollar/euro values, illustrated in Fig. 3.11, signal a long cycle or a more recent downtrend? A lower Russian ruble relative to the dollar is not a surprising outcome of the recent decline in the oil prices, as Russia is a major exporter of oil and thereby its export revenues would decline.

Yet, the U.S, dollar's decline since early 2018 occurred much earlier than any concern about a recession. What was behind the sustained decline? The U.S. Dollar Index (DXY), is a measure of the value of the United States dollar relative to a basket of foreign currencies. The dollar value reflects the expectations of growth and interest rates going forward. While economic growth in the United States accelerated after the 2016 election, growth slowed in 2018 consistent with the lower values of the U.S. dollar. This relationship between growth and the dollar was repeated in 2020 as the DXY declined from 102.82 on March 20, 2020 to 100.29 on April 24, 2020.

There is also a broader issue of perception. In my view, history offers no support for the comment that "There is little precedent of an advanced

3 Price Determination in a Multi-Sector Global Economy

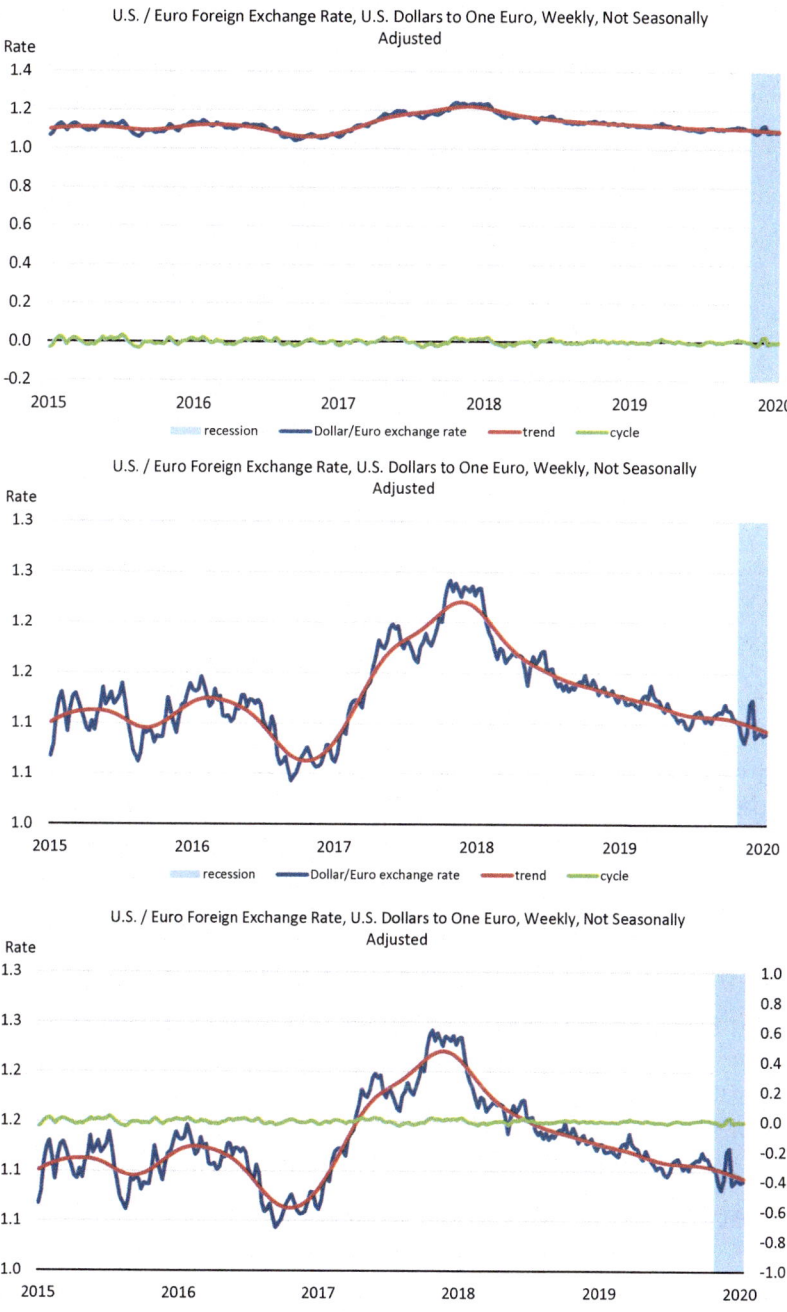

Fig. 3.11 US dollar/euro exchange rate

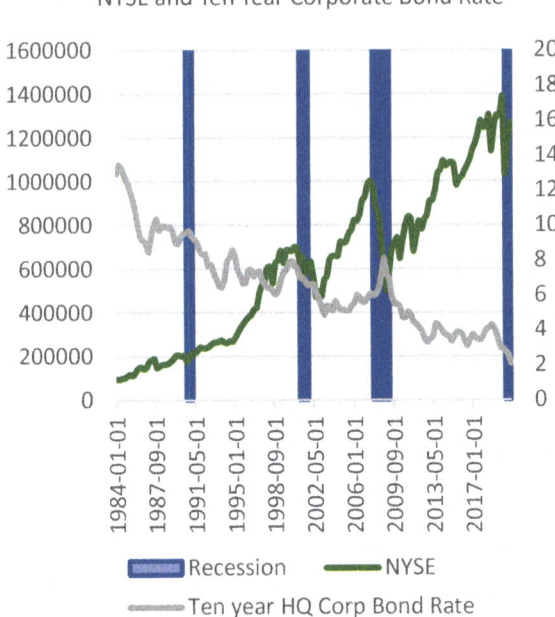

Fig. 3.12 Equity index and corporate investment grade rates

economy that controls its own currency being unable to borrow."[12] (Simply recall the case of the United Kingdom having to go to the International Monetary Fund (IMF) in 1976.) That year the Labour government of James Callaghan had to borrow $3.9 billion from the IMF to stabilize the value of the pound. The loan was also accompanied with conditions to cut public spending and raise interest rates. Moreover, debt rising today does not mean that risks are not increasing—they simply have not appeared yet. This is particularly true of inflation. The problem is one of a sudden drop in economic growth prospects in the future that render the debt undertaken in the past unable to be funded. This is what happened in Argentina in 1999 and in Mexico in 1982.

Rate Setting in Global Capital Markets

Traditionally, analysis starts with the domestic and then moves internationally. Let us reverse the process. As illustrated in Fig. 3.11, there appears to be a link between the EUR/USD exchange rate and the 90 days US less Euro

---

[12] Greg Ip, "The Debt Is Soaring; Debt Risks Are Not," *Wall Street Journal*, April 24, 2020.

spread. If there is a relationship, the next natural question is whether that relationship is statistically significant? Before we jump to test for a statistical relationship, we must make sure both series are mean reverting (stationary and no structural breaks). Put simply, if both series are mean reverting and have a statistically significant relationship then we can forecast a path for the EUR/USD using the interest rate spread. However, if both series are non-stationary and suffer breaks during the 2000–2017 period, they are not mean reverting. Two points, result from the analysis. Causality runs from the euro/dollar exchange rate to interbank rates in Europe. Second, the inflation rate in the U.S. has a causal link to the euro/dollar exchange rate. No wonder opinions can differ given the different views of underlying economic factors.

Of course, the United States is in an enviable position in that the country issues its benchmark sovereign debt in the benchmark global currency. This was also true of the United Kingdom during the first half of the twentieth century. Moreover, many commentators focus on extreme outcomes. The question is not that the United States would default in the near future, but the possibility of a default could occur slowly by a thousand cuts—a bit more inflation, bit higher real interest rates, and a bit weaker exchange rate. It is useful to recall the President Franklin Delano Roosevelt effectively defaulted on U.S. debt to be paid to foreigners when he delinked the U.S. dollar to gold.

Context matters here. Issuing the benchmark sovereign debt during a global recession would be expected to meet a friendly market. The problem is what happens when the pace of U.S. economic growth going forward disappoints relative to the rest of the world? Alternatively, the pace of real economic growth could fall below the real interest rate on the debt. Both outcomes are possible. Timing is important. Today may not be a problem—but tomorrow could be.

"Mind the gap between the markets and the real economy," *Financial Times* April 17, 2020

While the financial markets, especially the S&P 500, are a leading indicator, economic measures of GDP, employment, and personal income are coincident indicators. As we have discussed before, there is an apparent conflict when some economic indicators, for example, home sales in recent months (coincident indicator) are reported along with jobless claims or consumer sentiment (leading indicators). Yet, the media usually gives them equal coverage.

The gap between the information value of markets and the economy reflects the gap in timing. Financial markets are forward looking. The economic numbers are split—some forward, some coincident, and some lagging. This is not an area for casual commentary blindly stepping forward but for careful inspection of the economic minefield.

Price Determination, Policy Indetermination

In the rush to determine prices on credit (interest rate) equity capital and goods (inflation), the fundamentals of how and when prices move are overlooked. There is too much emphasis on news and much less on the inner workings of markets.

First, prices may adjust in the short run. But the question is: have the fundamentals changed such that the long-run equilibrium price is altered as well? This the natural rate problem. Do short-run changes in monetary policy alter the natural rate of unemployment or the real interest rate? If not, then any short-run change will give way to a second move toward the natural rate. This second move may be in the opposite direction of the initial short-run move. If the long-run equilibrium rate is set by technology and the structure of the labor market, then the natural rate of unemployment will not change. A shift in short-run interest rates will not be sustained.

Second, consider the uncertainty associated with a lack of any accurate framework of the economy, labor market, or credit markets. Estimates of the natural/equilibrium rates appear to constantly change. Decision makers are left with a high degree of uncertainty as evidenced by the regular changes in the assessments whether interest rates are close to neutral.[13] Of course, that does not address whether long rates on Treasury debt or corporate debt are close to neutral.

Third, look at the trade problem. Investors view it as a major risk or alternatively as an opportunity. Why does this matter for prices? Our first problem is that the financial markets are clearly not at equilibrium—especially when viewed by policy makers. Neither the price of imports and exports nor the exchange rate is considered equilibrium. What about the recent trade "truce" between China and the United States? Let us look at the deal's details. Since the truce was a happy surprise to many investors, it was an unexpected policy action that promised to alter the terms of trade. In this case, export prices/regulations exporting to China were changed. There were no

---

[13] John M. Roberts, "An Estimate of the Long-Term Neutral Rate of Interest," FEDS Notes Washington: Board of Governors of the Federal Reserve System, September 5, 2018, https://doi.org/10.17016/2380-7172.2227.

increases in tariffs on goods from China which lowered price expectations. There were more farm exports to China which drove higher price expectations on farm goods that were exported. There were increased exports of energy and industrial goods to China which pushed price expectations. Finally, if the truce results in a reduced bilateral trade deficit, a change in the yuan/dollar exchange rate may occur. All these short-run changes in price expectations may be dashed if China and the United States do not follow through on their promises. Short-run expectations may not meet long-run reality.

Decision makers need to monitor exogenous factors that may shift demand (monetary policy, credit, trade policy, net exports) and shifts in business and consumer confidence. The trade truce may alter short-run outcomes leading to higher equity prices. But will these factors be sustained in the long run? This adds a dynamic to any assessment of the economy and to policymaking. Is there a sense of a stable, predictable, economic policy now or will the views of the natural unemployment rate, exchange rate, and inflation target signal more changes ahead?

Benchmarking the Light at the End of the Tunnel

No single indicator can serve as a reliable predictor of economic behavior. Moreover, any indicator should be part of a broader framework of economic and financial activity. Mispricing of financial assets is clearly the story today but that was also true even before the virus emerged in late January 2020. As cited, Russell 2000 had moved up significantly despite many of those equities being unprofitable.

On the downside, the interrelationship between prices in different markets accelerated the selloffs in each market while the disequilibrium and the associated interrelationships produced mispricing of financial assets on the upside. It was no surprise that energy prices represented a risk to the high-yield market. Profit growth had been slowing for some time and yet equity prices rose. Finally, the sensitivity of equity prices to the Fed's attempted rebalancing of policy in late 2018 was a signal that markets were on a knife's edge of pricing.

Even now, the sensitivity of the dollar to the Fed's recent swap operations suggests that the dollar exchange rate is nowhere near an equilibrium position.

Finally, there is the issue of getting from the current disequilibrium position back to some normal, pre-virus position of the financial markets, and thereby the real economy, was not in an equilibrium position. In part, that is what is making the pricing of financial assets so difficult today.

The Disequilibrium World for Price Determination

Prices are seldom at equilibrium and even more so with a view of the interactions of financial markets. In addition, price movements may exhibit a short-run cycle around a longer-run trend. The concept of mean reversion is considered in this recognition.

In part, adjustment costs exist on both the demand and supply side of the scissors that determine the pace of movement to a price equilibrium.[14] The movement from a short-run supply situation to a long-run position has been amply demonstrated in the Covid-19 shutdown of 2020—too few medical supplies and too many brick and mortar retail outlets. Hospitals beds were in short supply in some areas. Restaurant seats went empty.

For the U.S. labor market, there was both an excess supply of leisure and hospitality workers and a shortage of health care workers. In the short run, there was an excess supply of equity shares, oil barrels, and corporate bonds. Over time, these imbalances were eliminated, although the evidence of structural breaks may signal a new long-run equilibrium in bonds prices and inflation in the future.[15]

Vladimir and Estragon Search for the Perfect Price

There are many aspects of price determination and, like Vladimir and Estragon of Samuel Beckett's play *Waiting for Godot*, we are constantly in search mode for the perfect price. Consider the most recent market experience for the price that would satisfy both original private equity investors and public market investors in IPOs—unfortunately, and perhaps to be expected, the perfect price to satisfy everyone simply did not appear.

For exchange rates, the perfect price did not appear after the Plaza nor the Louvre accords. In the fall of 2018, the Federal Reserve raised the fed funds rate only to lower the rate in 2019—the perfect fed funds rate remains elusive. How about OPEC's pursuit of the perfect price for a barrel of oil? No luck here either.

---

[14] Alfred Marshall employed the allusion of the scissors to illustrate the effect of both demand and supply cutting to an equilibrium value in the market.

[15] For a more complete treatment of this topic see "Adjustment Costs and the Theory of Supply," *Journal of Political Economy*, 1967 (August), Lucas.

Isolated Actors in Interdependent Markets

For analysts, the obvious problem is that isolated actors, such as investment bankers, the Fed, or OPEC, act in one market and, as a first approximation, estimate a partial equilibrium solution. Yet markets are interdependent. Prices will change in other markets in response to the price set in an individual market. The most familiar example is that of the response of equity and dollar exchange markets to changes in the federal funds rate.

Second, prices, such as the WTI price for oil (October 2008) or the five-year Treasury rate (November 1987, and again, January 2008) are subject to structural breaks in the series such that the link of economic activity in other markets no longer have the same relationship to the price of oil or intermediate Treasury rates.

Structural Break

Decision makers also need to recognize the difference between the short-run and the long-run behavior of each price in each sector. No matter what price is set in the short run, economic agents will react and estimate the excess demand or supply conditions in that market as well as the implications for pricing in other markets. The importance of expectations is very apparent. Recently, two examples of policy changes that alter incentives in the short and long run became evident. On the fiscal policy side, short-run changes in the tax deductibility of state and local taxes created the incentive for workers to move to lower tax states. Over the long run, we will watch how policymakers in higher tax states react. The recent experience of the Fed is also illustrative. Although the Fed in the short run, the fall of 2018, raised the fed funds rate, the implication for markets in the long run, reflected in a dot-plot, was that the funds rate was also going to rise over time. Interestingly, the FOMC's administered short-run price set shared the spotlight with expected future rate moves.

The Fed also provides an estimate of the future path of the fed funds rate. For example, in December 2018, the FOMC indicated that the end-of-year funds rate, 2.4% in 2018, would rise to 2.9% in 2019 and then 3.1% in 2020. The FOMC's estimate of the long-run median fed funds rate was 2.8%. Note the disconnect. Whatever the short-run equilibrium value of the federal funds rate in December 2018, its long-run value was significantly different. Markets move to where the puck is going and so reacted to the expected future path of the funds rate. Every day there is a similar pattern in the equity market. A firm announces its current quarter results, but it is the guidance on future earnings that often dictates the actual pattern of equity prices.

For decision makers, the challenge is: whether the current, short run, price set in an individual market is consistent with the short-run fundamentals in its own market, as well as the fundamentals in other markets and the perceived, long-run equilibrium price in both the individual and general markets. Consider again the Plaza Accord. From 1980 to 1985, the U.S. dollar appreciated. This led to a larger U.S. current account deficit, slowing the pace of the economic recovery, and creating trade problems for many U.S. industries, including autos. The Plaza Accord aimed to weaken the dollar, which it did. The weakness, however, exceeded expectations. The Louvre Accord (formally, the Statement of the G6 Finance Ministers and Central Bank Governors) aimed to stabilize international currency markets and halt the continued depreciation of the U.S. dollar. The Louvre Accord was signed by three principal countries—United States, West Germany, and Japan in 1987.

For investors and business decision makers, the pursuit of the perfect price for the dollar resulted in a cycle of ups and downs in the dollar exchange rate.

Decide Today—Discover the Price Tomorrow

One problem facing decision makers is that decisions, such as that for production of goods or the private equity pricing for an IPO, must be done before that actual price level is known that will clear the market. As a result, it is not surprising that producers/bankers will often miss the perfect market price.

Consider the following example:

WeWork to Raise Billions Selling Debt Ahead of IPO.

Workspace company is raising cash that could help it dodge issues that plagued Lyft and Uber debuts, *Wall Street Journal* July 7, 2019

The huge capital raised even before the IPO reflects the skepticism surrounding well-known companies such as Lyft Inc. and Uber Technologies Inc. that have racked up steep losses and gone public with much fanfare but without much trading success in 2019. Both Lyft's and Uber's stock prices are below where they went public, and even further below lofty pre-IPO expectations of how high they could trade. To quote the *Wall Street Journal*, "WeWork, which lost $1.9 billion last year, has been dogged by comparisons to Uber and Lyft and haunted by a huge, planned investment from SoftBank Group Corp. that fell apart after some key investors balked at the plan."

Then in a follow-up article, a *Wall Street Journal* (November 19, 2019) headline and subhead read:

"WeWork effect hits IPOs as investors hold out for better deal
A series of high-profile flops have tempered underwriters' ambitions"

The article itself explained: "WeWork, the office space provider, scrapped plans to list entirely in September after investors balked at the company's steep price tag and questionable governance structures.

The aborted WeWork deal signaled that the high valuations companies have built up in private ownership will not necessarily stand up to the scrutiny of public markets. WeWorks's valuation has tumbled from a high point of $47bn set in its last round of private fundraising, January 2019, to about $8bn, according to the terms of a rescue package hammered out last month[16] by SoftBank, its largest shareholder."

We are also familiar with what happens when public policymakers set prices in other markets. For exchange rates, there is the experience of the Exchange Rate Mechanism for the United Kingdom, as well as the Plaza and Louvre Accords for the U.S. dollar exchange rate. When policymakers set prices that are inconsistent with market fundamentals, price fixing inevitably fails when faced with reality.

One additional issue is that the speed of adjustment differs between markets. The Phillips Curve argues that workers respond late to a change in inflation, and this generates a cycle in real wages and thereby employment. What gives the financial markets an advantage as leading indicators is their quick response to economic and financial events.

Yet, at the portfolio management level, there is a lagged adjustment process both for equity and bonds. Despite any given economic or financial news, portfolio managers are limited to how much of their portfolio they can sell on any day without taking a significant hit to their pricing (liquidity has its limits). In some situations, segments of their portfolio are locked in. They must sell what they can. For example, if the quality of the portfolio is in question, portfolio managers may find that they can only sell high-grade bonds, even at a modest loss, relative to the significant hits on high-yield positions. The liquidity of many portfolios is examined by their investment managers every week by gauging the size of the portfolio versus the daily trading volume of assets in that portfolio. Intellectual biases also influence trading and price

---

[16] Rescue package October 23, 2019 reported in *Financial Times* that day.

discovery. The aversion to taking losses can lock an investor into a position such that there is a delay in the marketplace in finding the perfect price.

The Element of Surprise: New Information in One Market Alters Price Expectations in Another Market

To reemphasize the interdependence of markets, both the real economy and financial markets offer up some detours on the road to the perfect price. For investors, the most obvious case is that of the monthly jobs report. A stronger than expected jobs report alters expectations for economic growth and future Fed activity—both of which have implications for the dollar exchange rate. It is often common to see a surprise employment number on Friday lead to asset price volatility the following week after the investment committee has met and decided on a new portfolio allocation. This is illustrated by the following headline and subhead:

"U.S. Unemployment Rate Fell to 11.1% in June," *Wall Street Journal* July 2, 2020

U.S. stocks rose as the employment figures brought reassurance that the economic recovery was continuing.

On the Exchange Rate Front

Brexit has certainly generated its own level of uncertainty and set of surprises. The initial vote to leave the European Union in 2016 generated furious price action as did the 2020 decision by Parliament to ask for more time after recently elected Prime Minister Boris Johnson appeared to have an agreement outline. Since the initial Brexit vote, the British pound has declined versus the U.S. dollar and the euro. British economic growth has been below the pace of Eurozone growth. On the equity front, the FTSE 100 has risen less than U.S. and Euro equity benchmarks. This pattern can be seen in the below headline:

"Investors Bet Against Pound as Focus Returns to Brexit," *Wall Street Journal* June 24, 2020.

On the Trade Front

China's growth expectations and news on the U.S. China trade talks have altered market expectations for economic growth, the yuan/dollar exchange rate, and market short-term interest rates.

"Chinese Yuan Skids to 2019 Low as Trump Ramps Up Trade Conflict," *Wall Street Journal* August 2, 2019

On the Monetary Policy Front

Fed policy pronouncements by the FOMC and the economic projections reflect the reality of ongoing fluctuations in the economy that generate, quite reasonably, fluctuations in the numbers published as central tendencies by the FOMC. This can be seen in the following headline:

"Markets in rally mode after latest Fed package to support economy," *Financial Times* March 24, 2020

Searching for the Perfect Price: Life in an Action-Adventure Movie

Multiple markets, multiple players, problems of timing and a constant flow of new information are all the elements of an action-adventure movie—what more could an investor want? Current and market prices reflect all these factors—and nothing less.

* * *

Silos Fall in a Financial Windstorm: Reality TV for Investors

Decision making for investors does not proceed in a static world. Yet every day, our news is presented in silos—equity indices, credit and rates, economics, and foreign currency. The financial markets know no such silos. Case in point—midyear 2015.

Cross-Silo Lessons from the FOMC's Non-move

Market volatility reflects the gap between expected and actual—a regular occurrence in 2018–2019. When the FOMC decided not to raise the funds rate, the impact was felt across multiple markets including the NYSE which rose in all four quarters in 2019. Equity prices reacted to the surprise move of no action by the Fed in contrast to the continual raising of the fed funds rate in 2018. Equity markets rallied on inaction—interest rates were unchanged relative to market expectations, and Fed's earlier guidance that it would raise the benchmark rate. The difference between what was expected (higher rates) and the actual lack of change in rates generated an equity market rally.

First, of course, the paths of short- and long-term rates were altered. Any adjustment in the market for Fed funds and short-term Treasury debt dictates an adjustment in several crucial areas. The equity markets (Fig. 3.12) reflected two opposing forces. Does the FOMC inaction suggest a weaker economy and thereby weaker earnings growth ahead? Certainly, the emphasis on "global developments" reinforces investor concerns about growth in Asia, particularly China, and thereby the earnings outlook for companies doing business in that nation. In opposition, the lower level of short-term interest rates would suggest a lower discount factor for future corporate earnings and is a plus for equity valuations. After a short dip in the two-year rate in August 2020, the rate returned to its pre-August level. In contrast, the NYSE Index did not—global earnings expectations downshift may be the key factor.

Lessons from the Chinese Devaluation—2015

Two opposing winds were in play during 2015 that caused investors to contemplate the following situations: Does the devaluation indicate current economic weakness in China and, thereby, an attempt by Chinese policy-makers to offset that weakness? Or, alternatively, is it just an adjustment to open the foreign exchange market for future maturation and open trading for the yuan? Note the timing—since the devaluation of the yuan occurred before the dip in the Shanghai index (Fig. 3.13), perhaps the devaluation was a signal that lowered equity investor expectations.

Lessons from Disappointing Growth

Downshifting economic growth expectations by FOMC members during the 2014–2016 period may have influenced their level of caution in the conduct of monetary policy. Moreover, this downshift in expectations may have spilled into equity market expectations of future earnings and, thereby, equity valuations. Both channels were reinforced by the perceived weakness in Asian economies relative to prior growth expectations, which, in turn, was reinforced by the Chinese devaluation. Timing indicates that equity values did not decline in line with lower FOMC GDP projections until the August

Fig. 3.13 China: Yuan and share prices

2015 break. Once again this suggests that the break reflected factors other than domestic economic expectations or the two-year rate (see above).

Price Discovery—Our Never-Ending Journey

Our economic and financial markets are in a state of constant price discovery. In many presentations, I find it useful to ask my audience several questions each based upon the search for the right price.

Housing—Both Cyclical and Secular Forces

House prices change and their variation over the economic cycle is readily apparent (Fig. 3.13). Over the long term, the level of home prices continues

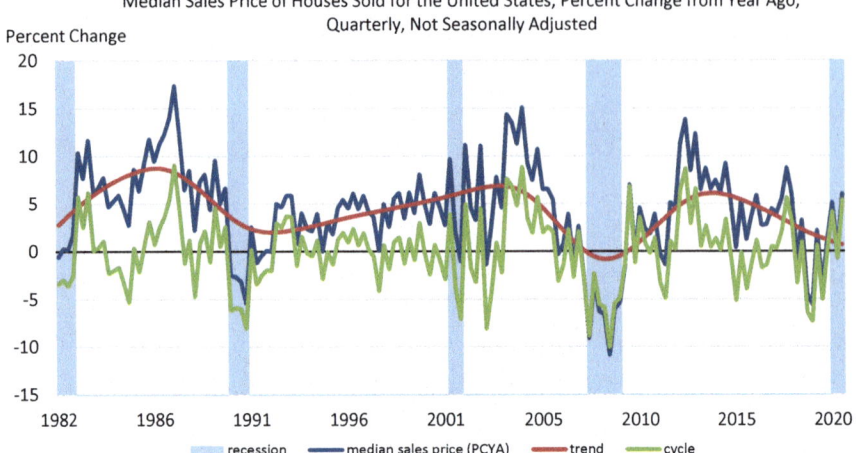

Fig. 3.14 Median home sales prices, 1982–2020

to rise reflecting the population and growth of wealth in America. How to judge that change is the difficult part. On the cyclical side, the increase in mortgage rates from mid-2017 to late 2018 is typical of a traditional economic expansion. Meanwhile, the reduction in unemployment rates and the rise in jobs and real incomes is also typical. Just on cyclical grounds, the "right" price will evolve over the cycle. Meanwhile, secular forces of population movements, land availability and the relative growth of metropolitan areas will also help determine the "right" price. All of this appears obvious. Yet so little of this price discovery process is considered in most, yes most, of the commentary on house prices. Why are house prices so expensive in some areas, so cheap in others? Too many people with good jobs and incomes want to live in areas with too many people already there and significant land and building restrictions to boot. Real Final Sales and equity prices (NYSE index) have a causal relationship to median home prices (Fig. 3.14).

That Risk-Free Rate—A Benchmark for Investors

While casual commentators cite too much debt, in the matter of price discovery, the problem is the lack of market pricing. The growth of the U.S. federal debt over the last ten years accompanied by very low-interest expense for the federal government is an obvious example. This situation can only exist in an environment where policy-administered rates are set below what one might consider free-market rates. In our past textbooks, we note that market rates on debt are priced off the risk-free short-term rate, the

3 month T-bill rate, but that rate is distorted by current federal economic policy. That policy provides the incentive to issue and buy that debt as well as non-financial corporate debt. Markets operate off incentives and prices. Set prices low, you get more.

Another lesson here that administered prices interfere with market adjustment. They create persistent surpluses and shortages resulting in continual disequilibrium in prices. This is especially prevalent in financial markets when central banks dictate benchmark interest rates and central government set exchange rates.

Wages, Productivity and Inflation: Linkage of Factor and Output Markets

Wages, the nominal cost of labor, reflects the patterns of productivity and output inflation. This is basic first-semester economics. Too many superficial commentaries on "low" wage growth skip over this fundamental economic principle. What is interesting is that in 2019 wage growth has risen as productivity has risen while the ten-year break-even inflation rate has declined from 4Q 2018 to 4Q 2019. Wage growth reflects the patterns of productivity growth and inflation expectations. Complaints about "low" wages do not reflect the fundamentals of price discovery in a low-inflation environment.

Multiple Markets, Multiple Surprises: A Bumpy Road Ahead?

Our emphasis on a multimarket economy focuses on the linkages between sectors and markets. Evaluating the behavior of a particular series is essential for decision makers as they design and implement policy.

Irrational Prices as a Challenge to an Economic Framework

> Markets can stay irrational longer than you can stay solvent.—John Maynard Keynes

Central to all market commentary that we read or listen to is the context of our discussions on prices—commodity prices, exchange rates and interest rates. Such commentary focuses on news, not analysis and not context.

Markets are left with short-term volatility with little change in the underlying fundamentals.

Short-Run Movements Around a Longer-Run Trend: Would the Real Long-Term Value Stand Up? (A Tell the Truth reference)

> By adherence to a favorite theory, many errors have at times been introduced into general science which have required much labour for their removal.—Francis Bacon

Consider three cases of short-run movements in search of long-run fundamentals. First, is the challenge around goods prices since 1982. As cited earlier in this chapter (Fig. 3.12, which covers the late 1970s), a break in the pattern of inflation occurred around 1980. Since then, even when we eliminate the unit root in prices, the short-run movements around trend are apparent. Investment managers have two problems to consider. First, why has the consensus view of a link from the overall unemployment rate to wages (the Phillips Curve) clearly broken down[17]? Unlike America's 1970s period of high inflation, high wage growth and low economic growth relative to potential, the country now has low inflation, and low-wage growth in an environment of above potential (as defined by the Fed) growth. Consider that the Employment Cost Index held remarkably steady at 2% from 2010 to 2015 but then broke upward from 1.8% in the 1Q 2016 to 3% by the 4Q 2018. Where is the long-run equilibrium? Too much market commentary is focused on the irrational short-term and not on the possibility that the long-run equilibrium has truly changed. Oil prices have a causal link to the PCE deflator while the PCE deflator has a causal link to the yield curve and the Ted Spread.

Second, there is a break in the trade consensus. There is too much discussion about free trade when we have never had free trade and will never have free trade. Trade is in constant disequilibrium as tariffs, quotas, and sanctions proliferate. Traded goods prices and exchange rates will also deviate but sometimes exhibit long periods of up/down. Many commentators anticipated an upturn as rates approached 3% but the benchmark Treasury rate has remained

---

[17] Lawrence Katz and Alan Krueger, 1999 "The High-Pressure U.S. Labor Market of the 1990s," Brookings Papers on Economic Activity, no. 1, 1–87. This article provides an argument for a lower natural rate of unemployment.

below that target for some time. What are the long-run equilibrium values when current values for each appear irrational?

Irrational Prices and an Uncertain Framework: Equities

"I Believe in Mean Reversion" An oft-cited commentary

Ok, but mean reversion of what? The statement on mean reversion is made frequently but the problem is that since World War II there has been no mean reversion of the most frequently discussed equity indices—the P/E ratio. For our equity framework, the P/E ratio, for example, is not mean reverting. Simply because the current P/E ratio is below some average indicates little. Averages can be calculated for any series, for any time period. So the statistical evidence does not show that the P/E ratio will move to that average over some unspecified period in the future. Earnings, moreover, are quite cyclical and, like the economy, they are irregular in both amplitude and length. Finally, the P/E ratio, as for interest rates, exchange rates, and inflation, are all determined within an economic system and are not determined outside that system unless set by government fiat.

Melt Up, Melt Down—How do you want your melted cheese sandwich?

There is little meaning to the phrase melt up or melt down when discussing equity prices. Instead, let's explore this idea through the issue of the static stability of prices and price expectations. For any given change in an equity price, there are three different scenarios.

First, if the price change is expected to persist in the future, this is positive static stability. Something fundamental has moved and equity prices have adjusted accordingly. The market has adjusted to new information that gives credence to the new price.

Second, the price change is not warranted and the future price will be less than the original price change. Commentators often refer to this as a correction but more precisely it is neutral static stability—although the equity price moves in the short run, prices will return to their original value.

Finally, there is the price change that leads to a greater change in expectations of future prices—the melt up. Sometimes a new paradigm of pricing delivers an equity valuation far outside the bounds of the prior set of fundamentals. All three outcomes can be seen by the response of certain sectors to the Covid-19 shutdown shocks. Communication technology, health care, and internet security equities rallied and energy and entertainment sector equity valuations declined.

For investors, the challenge is what are the fundamentals that will justify the melt up or melt down? Will there be new information? Or was the current information set not appreciated by the market and future price moves would be justified based upon already existing information? That is, to what extent is the market acting rationally? Asserting there is a melt up or melt down is not enough. Decision makers want to know what information is not being discounted in the marketplace to justify a change in price expectations.

Administered prices, those set by a public policy maker, are unlikely to be consistent with any market-determined price. Such prices set up a persistent disequilibrium in the marketplace. For as long as these prices exist, the original market price is unlikely to be recovered. Instead, we are in a world of negative static stability. The problem here is that an administered price in one market (fixed exchange rates, central bank administered benchmark rates, or price controls on commodity prices) may be inconsistent with prices in other markets or with the long-run equilibrium of that market.

Distracting Dilemma: No trade-off for two forces—deal with both, may have opposing impacts

Trade or the Fed? In early 2020, the question at many investment meetings and published forum articles was whether trade or the Fed had the biggest impact on equity markets. This question was of no use to investors. Shocks, from anywhere, alter market prices and both trade talks and the Fed were having significant impacts on the markets in the first quarter of 2020. A shock from trade initially impacts the real side of the economy: supply chains, import and export prices and exchange of goods. A shock from the Fed initially impacts the financial side of the economy: interest rates, cost of capital, and equity valuations. For investors, trade has its primary impact on industrials, materials, and technology, while the Fed influences patterns in housing and equity valuations. There is no dilemma—both trade and Fed are essential considerations for investors.

What if No Price Is the Right Price?

If a company cannot make a profit in the current economic framework (above trend economic growth over the past two years, solid consumer gains in income/confidence/wealth, low-interest rates and liquid capital markets) then when? If the current business model does not generate a profit, then why should an investor believe profits will rain down when a new business model is adopted? Why invest now? Why not just wait for the new business model? What if no price generates a profit for the current business model?

What the Covid-19 shutdown experience revealed is that certain business models had no price at which they could make money. However, this was not the first, and probably not the last, time this will happen.

During the World War I period, the federal government decided to build its own armor plate for warships since it thought it was being overcharged by the steel companies. The government estimated that it could produce armor plate for 70% of what the steel companies charged. You know what is coming. The plant was completed three years after World War I, millions over budget with a price for steel twice what the steel companies charged. The plant produced one batch and shut down. There was no price that justified the production.

There are true believers, speculators and then investors. For true believers, any price is the right price. They believe in the dream/the guru/the fascination of the new. For speculators, today's price is the price of getting in early on the hope that at one point in the future profits will flow. This is speculation by people with deep pockets and that is okay. Yes, there are successes—but also many failures (recall the dot.coms). Then there is investing—the far less romantic act of putting money to work to improve wealth over time. Finally, if companies cannot make money today what happens to hope when the economy slows or enters recession? Hope is not an investment strategy.

Economy at Non-market Prices

When making a forecast and an investment decision, judgment is needed on where in the spectrum of disequilibrium, we are in the four sectors. Observers of the economic and financial markets take a major risk when they believe current market prices represent trading signals in a free-market economy. Instead, the persistent excess supply of goods and labor hint that the pressure on prices is still downward once the federal stimulus programs of 2020 end. A significant share of current household income and spending reflects federal subsidies such as the direct supplementary payments to the unemployed and the impacts of lower interest rates and greater liquidity provided by the Federal Reserve. The excess supply of restaurants and entertainment venues, and their workers, is clear enough as consumer preferences have shifted to greater degrees of safety than in the past.

In financial markets, the Fed has generated an excess supply of credit as bank loans are retained under forbearance guidelines and corporate debt spreads are arbitrarily low given the Fed's purchase of corporate debt ETFs in 2020. Nominal interest rates on sovereign debt are below the pace of inflation thus delivering negative real rates even before taxes reduce returns even further. Moreover, the growth of the real stock of government debt grows faster than the economy and, as the demand for such debt is limited in the private markets, the debt is being financed essentially by effectively printing money as stated by Fed Chairman Jerome Powell[18] and thereby threatening dollar depreciation and inflation over the long run. The excess supply of credit can be found by observing the very low TED spread (0.17% as of August 17, 2020) which is below the average of the 1986–2020 period even though America is in a recession environment. The current high-yield bond spread (4.98% as of August 27, 2020) is also below the average of 1997–2020 period. Since both are stationary series, the current assessment of risk spreads has not normalized and remains low given the current outlook for credit delinquencies and bankruptcies in the marketplace.

The current matrix of yield spreads reflects the role of public policy—particularly that of the Federal Reserve. The Fed is mandated to do what it takes to sustain economic recovery which it achieves, in part, through its announcements on the economy and such direct actions as its massive purchases of corporate debt. A rough guide of the scope to its efforts can be traced by the growth in the Fed's balance sheet from $4.2 trillion on March 4, 2020 to $7 trillion by August 19, 2020.

The Bank of England and the European Central Bank (ECB) have also expanded their balance sheet thereby lowering the price of both sovereign and corporate debt. In the United Kingdom, the benchmark ten-year rate declined from 0.744% in the 4Q 2019 to 0.2514% in the 3Q of 2020. For Germany, the benchmark ten-year rate fell from −0.37% to −0.52% over the same period.

We are left with two issues. Benchmark interest rates are lower than they would be otherwise. No true free-market set of rates or spreads exists that represent a true risk and reward trade-off.

And there is no clear indication of how quickly the Fed or other central banks will allow free-market pricing of corporate risk. For decision makers and investors today, the excess supply of credit by central banks, especially the Federal Reserve and the ECB, indicates that Treasury bonds, mortgage-backed securities, and asset-backed securities are all trading at below free-market price levels.

Such non-market pricing of risk indicates that the excess supply of credit is artificially propping up housing and corporate financing and therefore, both the real market pricing and issuance of credit are shrouded by the veil of federal intervention.

---

[18] Chairman Jerome Powell, *60 Minutes* interview May 18, 2020.

"Fed Backstop Fueled Corporate Bond Surge," *Wall Street Journal* June 30, 2020

"Eurozone borrowing costs drop to pre-crisis levels, ECB intervention sparks recovery in bond prices," *Financial Times* July 8, 2020

As these headlines indicate, from a credit allocation point of view, the Federal Reserve acts as a policeman who remains on one street corner and witnesses no crime and yet wherever the policeman is absent, crime continues.[19]

Non-market pricing creates problems for any Fed and ECB exit strategy as well as for investors who bought bonds and lenders who made loans under an interest rate suppression regime. This was seen before in the "taper tantrum" period of 2013. As we saw before with Chairman Powell in 2017 and 2019, a Fed exit strategy would not just be an increase in the funds rate but also, given Quantitative Easing, a stabilization or reduction in the Fed's balance sheet via corporate, agency, and Treasury debt.

Both central bank options—a stable balance sheet or a continued increase in the balance sheet—have implications for the path of market prices. The most obvious impact is on interest rates and equity markets. But there are effects for commodity prices as the Fed's 2% inflation target remains in place. Finally, a policy of continued easing and no preemptive rate increases in anticipation of a rise of inflation, suggests the bias in the dollar exchange rate is downward, ceteris paribus.

* * *

References

Robert Barro and Herschel Grossman, *Money, Employment and Inflation*, Cambridge University Press, 1976. A view of macroeconomics from the vantage point of addressing disequilibrium in the markets and how economic actors adjust to supply/income/credit constraints. A text I was privilege of studying with drafts from my professors.

William Branson, *Macroeconomic Theory and Policy*, Harper & Row, 1972. One of three essential macroeconomic texts that provide a framework for analysis. Branson brings in several chapters on international economics.

---

[19] See our commentary "The Evolution of the Economy, Credit and Economic Policy," Conference at the Federal Reserve Bank of Atlanta, Debate of Atlanta, Debate and Confirm: 2009 Banking Industry Outlook, February 19, 2009.

Robert Crouch, *Macroeconomics*, Harcourt Brace, 1972. A second macroeconomic text that provides a framework for analysis. In this text, the authors provides a framework to link commodity, money and bond markets and price determination between markets.

C.W.J. Granger, "Investigating Causal Relationships by Econometric Models and Cross-Spectral Methods," *Econometrica*, 1969, 37, no. 3: 424–438. An extensive discussion and application of the causality method is examined in Silvia et al., *Economic and Business Forecasting*, Wiley, 2014.

William H. Greene, *Econometric Analysis*, Sixth Edition, Pearson, Prentice-Hall, 2008. A essential econometric text for advanced research.

Robert Lucas, "Adjustment Costs and the Theory of Supply," *Journal of Political Economy*, 1967 (August). An excellent read on the adjustment costs of an economy in disequilibrium.

Jerry W. Markham, *A Financial History of the United States*, M.E. Sharpe. 2002. An excellent review of the financial history of the United States.

John M. Roberts, "An Estimate of the Long-Term Neutral Rate of Interest," FEDS Notes. Board of Governors of the Federal Reserve System, Washington, September 5, 2018, https://doi.org/10.17016/2380-7172.2227.

David Romer, *Advanced Macroeconomics*, Third edition, McGraw-Hill, Irwin, 2006. A third macroeconomics text that provides a framework for analysis. The sections on dynamic adjustment, imperfect information, partial adjustment and profits/risks are essential reads.

John E Silvia, "The Evolution of the Economy, Credit and Economic Policy," Conference at the Federal Reserve Bank of Atlanta, Debate of Atlanta, Debate and Confirm: 2009 Banking Industry Outlook, February 19, 2009. A look at the economy as signals of economic recovery began to appear.

John E Silvia, "Economic Outlook: A Perspective from the Markets and Prices," Presentation at the Banking Outlook Conference, Federal Reserve Bank of Atlanta, February 27, 2020. A view of the U.S. economy just before the COVID breakout and shutdowns.

4

Credit Allocation and the Role of Interest Rates as the Price of Credit

Interest rates are the price of credit determined in the financial marketplace not just a policy tool for a central bank. While commentary focuses almost exclusively on the Federal Reserve altering benchmark interest rates to change the path of the macroeconomy, at the micro level changes in interest rates impact the distribution of financial resources across the economy. Credit allocationis a journey across time (the yield curve) and space (between companies and countries). Let us go there.

Credit Allocation and the Role of the Price of Credit: Housing 2005, Corporate Debt 2020

> John Bull Can Stand Many Things, but He Cannot Stand Two Percent—Walter Bagehot

For John Stuart Mill, the problem was that "of a low rate of profit and interest, which makes the capitalists dissatisfied with the ordinary course of safe mercantile gains.[1]" That is, capitalists push the envelope of risk to achieve higher returns commensurate with their perceived target or normal rates of return. The pursuit of yield has taken investors to a very broad range of asset

---

[1] John Stuart Mill, *Principles of Political Economy, with some of Their Applications to Social Philosophy* (1848; 7th ed., reprint ed.,) Longmans, Green, London, 1929, p. 709.

classes where the accurate measure of risk and return has been altered by the low administered interest rates set by central banks.

In recent years, the era of administered rates provided little guidance on what should be the proper level of interest rates to price financial capital and thereby judge the viability of real-world activity. As illustrated in Fig. 4.1 sovereign yields in European debt spiked in the period from 2011 to 2012 but then have declined and were for some time below U.S. Treasury yields.

Did the decline in Euro yields coincide with improving economic fundamentals or were they the product of public policy, including the direct purchase of those bonds by the European Central Bank? Ten-year spreads for Portugal, for instance, exhibit structural breaks in 2010 and 2014 consistent with shifts in ECB policy.

Our view is that these low yields reflect the policy of the ECB in buying both sovereign and corporate debt. But here is the rub. When the ECB normalizes interest rates, what happens to business finance, real growth, and the euro exchange rate? Even more intriguing, if the ECB does not normalize rates what is the longer-run impact on capital flows out of Europe and potentially higher inflation as the ECB continues to increase the size of its balance sheet? What are the economic and financial impacts of moving from an era of administered rates to an era of market rates or perhaps less administered rates?

Arbitrarily low policy-determined interest rates are an incentive to private markets to misprice credit. In a traditional macro model, low-interest

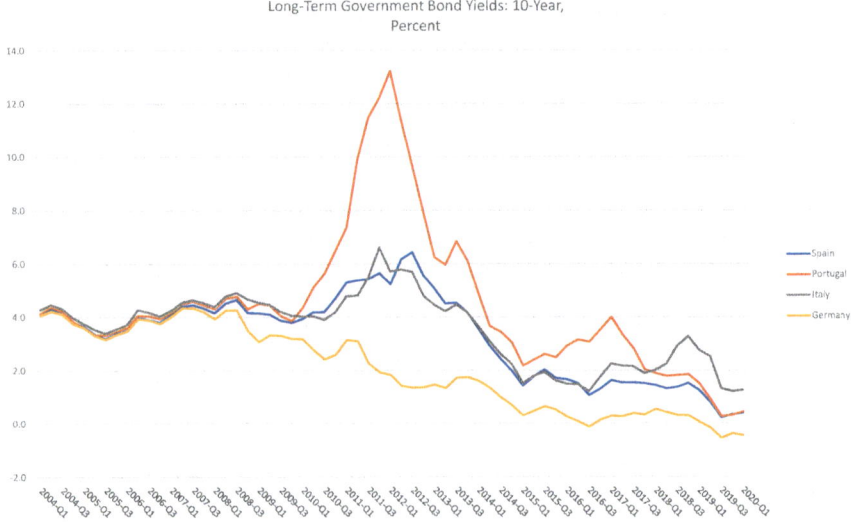

Fig. 4.1 Long-Term government bond yields

4 Credit Allocation and the Role of Interest Rates as the Price of Credit

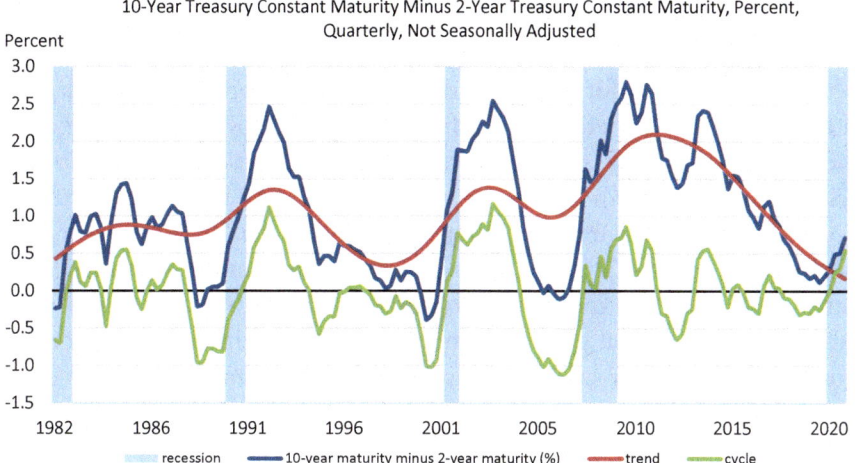

Fig. 4.2 Yield curve

rates prompt increased consumer spending and business investment thereby promoting economic growth. However, the case of the housing bubble and bust of 2008 indicates that low-interest rates, in a broader financial context, will lead to a misallocation of both financial and real capital in the economy.

In February 2005 Federal Reserve Chairman Alan Greenspan commented that the 10-year Treasury yields failed to rise despite a 150-basis point increase in the federal funds rate. Financial market participants considered this a "conundrum" since the term structure of interest rates dictates that longer-term rates should react to changes in short-term rates (Fig. 4.2).[2] However, the connection between the 10-year Treasury yields and the federal funds rate was severed years before as evidenced by structural breaks in 4Q of 1994 and again in the 2Q of 2000. Greenspan's observation emphasizes the role of structural breaks in financial relationships when public policy benchmarks are changed. Reflecting another structural break in the link of interest rates and the economy, Governor Powell and the Federal Open Market Committee altered its use of the federal funds rate.[3]

---

[2] Research from the late 1970s supported the expectation that changes in short-term rates would impact long-term rates. See Timothy Cook and Thomas Hahn, "The Effect of Changes in the Federal Funds Rate Target on Market Interest Rates in the 1970s," *Journal of Monetary Economics*, 1989, 24 (November): 331–351.

[3] "Fed's New Strategy Confronts Old Questions on Financial Trade-offs," September 30, 2020, *Wall Street Journal*.

A Framework for Credit Allocation

What sets the context for the demand for credit in the private marketplace? As with many markets, there are three fundamentals—growth, price, and assets. The demand for credit is first a function of the current and expected pace of real final sales (RFS) for any business. For households, current and expected income, Y, are the driving forces. The link between final sales and income to the demand for credit is a direct one. As a firm perceives the economy getting better, it will demand more credit to finance increases in production or the purchase of new capital goods. For households, better income prospects may prompt a demand for credit to buy a new car and improve or buy a new home.

The price of credit is represented by the interest rate, r, charged for the use of the credit. Finally, an increase in real wealth (W/P), on the part of the household for example, typically accompanies a rise in the demand for credit. For most households, income growth is associated with increased demand for a second car, a bigger home, or the desire to start a business. We can simply express the demand for credit as

$$D^c = f\,(RFS \text{ or } Y,\ r,\ W/P)$$

The Granger causality test supports the link of causality from real final sales, high-yield bond spreads and the NYSE Index, as a measure of wealth, to the percent of banks reporting stronger demand(based on the Fed's Senior Loan Officer Opinion Survey).

The supply of credit is reflected by the same three variables but from a different viewpoint. Banks and other lenders of credit will lend more based upon the pace of expected economic growth and profitability of a business or expected income of a household. A higher interest rate, for a given level of risk, will be associated with an increase in the supply of credit. Finally, the liquidity and reserves of the lender will also influence the willingness of the lender to promote credit growth.

$$S^c = f\,(RFS \text{ or } Y,\ r,\ W/P)$$

For given levels of real income, Y, price level P, real net assets, wealth, W/P then we get demand and supply of credit that will determine a level of interest rates for a given level of risk. An increase in income and income expectations will increase both the supply and demand for credit, and depending on risk preferences, leave the level of interest rates the same.

Income and profitability is also an expectation. Real wealth depends upon the pace of inflation. Bank liquidity reflects the influence of central bank policy and the setting of the benchmark policy rate as a base to price the lending rate. All of this presents a cyclical pattern to credit and changes in central bank monetary and regulatory policy represent a structural break in the supply of credit.

For households, a shift toward liquidity preference, as was evident during the housing bust of 2008–2009, when the personal saving rate rose from 3.1% in November 2007 to 8.2% in May 2009. Household demand for credit, especially credit cards and home equity loans, fell even as policy-determined interest rates went lower.

In 2020, demand for credit (in this case bonds) and the supply of credit both rose as interest rates declined. Federal Reserve and the European Central Bank entered the bond market to buy bonds to provide liquidity into the market, as well as set a lower benchmark rate on longer-term debt.

What are our takeaways? The market for credit with credit demand and credit supply provides a starting point in the determination of the price of credit. Our task is to take that framework and examine the cyclical and secular patterns of interest rates and the yield curve. An additional challenge is recognizing changes in financial regulation and central bank policies that will alter the expected pattern in interest rate changes. Ceteris paribus has never been so popular.

Credit supply and demand is not solely dependent on interest rate. There are feedback effects from other markets as interest rates will impact the demand for commodities (lumber, steel, and cement for housing starts and remodeling for instance), the attractiveness of alternative currency rates, and equity valuations (particularly in 2020 when the concept of TINA (there is no alternative) has prompted a rise in equity prices.

Recognition of feedback effects emphasizes the Walras principal (named after the economist Leon Walras in 1874[4] that when considering any market, if all other markets in an economy are in equilibrium, then that specific market must also be in equilibrium). We thus cannot ignore any other market (e.g., equities) when examining the price behavior of a given market. Interest rates are simultaneously determined by mutual interaction of all of the system's variables.

A critical link also exists between the financial cost of credit and the real sector cost of capital. Firms will acquire physical capital until the real rental price of a unit of capital is equal to the value of the marginal productivity

---

[4] Leon Walras, *Elements of Pure Economics*, 1874, published 1954 by Routledge, Abingdon, UK.

of that capital. The price of capital services is directly related to the rate of interest, so the optimal stock of capital is inversely related to the rate of interest. When interest rate rises, the price of capital services rises and the optimum stock of capital falls.

There is also the time preference—the optimal consumption balance between present and future goods. This brings into focus the problem of the current monetary Federal Reserve policy. When it attempts to affect long-term interest rates and thereby alter the yield curve, are they in conflict with the private market pricing of time preference?

As policy rates change, a new optimal capital stock calculation comes into being. But is that optimal capital stock in line with the long-run viability of a business? In 2020, many bonds were sold, and deals were financed where the economic viability of the assets (such as malls and commercial office space) remained in question.

The Interest elasticity of the demand for real capital will influence the demand for machines and capital goods in response to interest rates, The change in economic activity in response to any exogenous policy change in interest rates brings us to the role of policy.

Price Determination, Policy Indetermination

In the rush to determine prices on credit (interest rate), equity capital, and goods (inflation), the fundamentals of how and when prices move are often overlooked by commentators who emphasize news and not the inner workings of markets.

For example, consider that prices may adjust in the short run but have the fundamentals changed such that the long-run equilibrium price is altered as well? This the natural rate problem. Do short-run changes in monetary policy alter the natural rate of unemployment or the real interest rate? If not, then any short-run change will give way to a second move toward the natural rate which may be in the opposite direction of the initial short run move. If the long-run equilibrium rate is set by technology and the structure of the labor market, then the natural rate of unemployment will not change. A shift in short-run interest rates will not be sustained.[5]

Next, consider the uncertainty associated with a lack of any accurate model of the economy, labor market, or credit markets. Estimates of the natural or

---

[5] The difficulties of determining a natural rate of unemployment and long-run projections in growth and inflation are highlighted in Jerome Powell's speech at Jackson Hole, "New Economic Challenges and the Fed's Monetary Policy Review," August 27, 2020 and published on the Federal Reserve's website, https://www.federalreserve.gov/newsevents/speech/powell20200827a.htm.

equilibrium rates appear to constantly be changing leaving decision-makers with a high degree of uncertainty.[6] Of course, considerations of a neutral fed funds rate do not address whether long rates on Treasury debt or corporate debt are close to neutral. Economists Holston, Laubach, and Williams highlight the importance of international factors, such as expected global interest rates and capital flows, in setting the benchmark funds rate.

In addition, consider the international trade and capital flows problem. Investors cite this as a major risk (or perhaps, alternatively, as an opportunity). Why does this matter for prices? Persistent trade deficits signal that the economy is clearly not at an equilibrium, especially when viewed by policymakers. This disequilibrium impacts both the price of imports and exports and the exchange rate.

What about a possible trade "truce" between the United States and China or between the United Kingdom and the Eurozone? Any sustained truce would be indeed a happy surprise to many investors. This unexpected policy action would alter the terms of trade. In this case, export and import prices would fluctuate and thus alter capital flows and the trade-weighted dollar. Without an impending increase in tariffs on goods from abroad, this reality would lower price expectations over time. In recent years, the ups and downs of trade negotiations have affected both short-run and long-run expectations for exchange rates and, in turn, capital flows and relative interest rates.

For decision-makers, monitoring exogenous factors such as trade negotiations may prompt a shift in aggregate demand (monetary policy, credit, trade policy, and net exports), and business and consumer confidence, (relief from the trade truce). And it may alter short-run outcomes—higher equity prices. But will adjustments in trade be sustained in the long run? Since 2017, U.S. equity prices have moved up and down with the perception of trade progress.

The tension between short-run and long-run movements in independent factors in determining interest rates adds a dynamic to our assessment of the economy credit allocation. Is there a sense of a stable, predictable, economic policy now or will the views of the natural unemployment rate, exchange rate, and inflation target signal more changes ahead? Given the sentiment expressed by Chairman Powell at Jackson Hole in 2020, the outlook is one of continued disequilibrium in financial markets and an uncertain outlook for the real economy.

---

[6] See Holston, Kathryn, Thomas Laubach, and John C. Williams, "Measuring the Natural Rate of Interest: International Trends and Determinant," *Journal of International Economics*, 2017, 108 (May, S1): S59–75.

Tension in the Yield Curve and the Allocation of Capital Over Time

Yields on long-term bonds are generally greater than yields on short-term bonds. This term premium, Fig. 4.3, reflects the amount investors expect to be compensated for lending for longer periods. For the period from 1990 to 2019, the term premium declined at an irregular pace. In fact, there are structural breaks in the series in 1995, when the Fed altered policy, and then again in 2004, 2011, and 2016.

Under conditions of uncertainty, the yield curve, in contrast, reflects the expectations of private market participants of future short-term interest rates and the term premium. Given the importance of central bank policy, changes in short-term rates and expectations about future short-term rates will impact the slope of the yield curve. There is also the link between current short-term rates and the central banks expected long-run equilibrium policy rate.

Interactions between inflation, interest rates, and Fed policy provide a laboratory for the behavior of the yield curve. From October 2016 to December 2016 the yield curve rose even though the Fed did not alter short-term rates. What did change was the rise in the core PCE deflator over the period December 2015 to February 2017. The private markets were discounting a rise in inflation but also anticipated a Fed move to offset a rise in inflation.

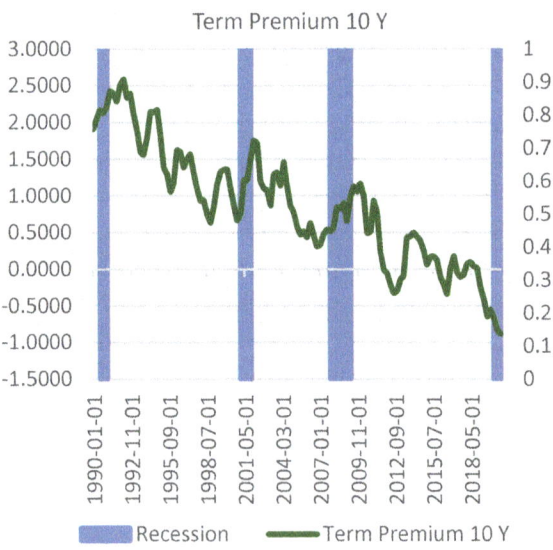

Fig. 4.3 Term premium on ten-year zero coupon

4 Credit Allocation and the Role of Interest Rates as the Price of Credit

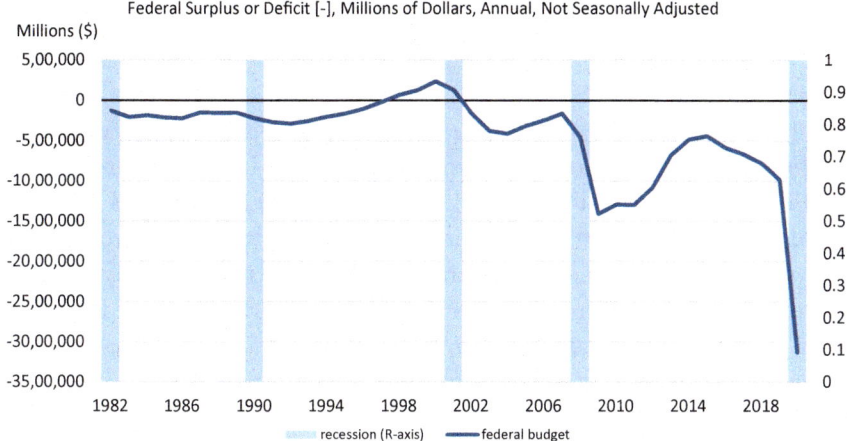

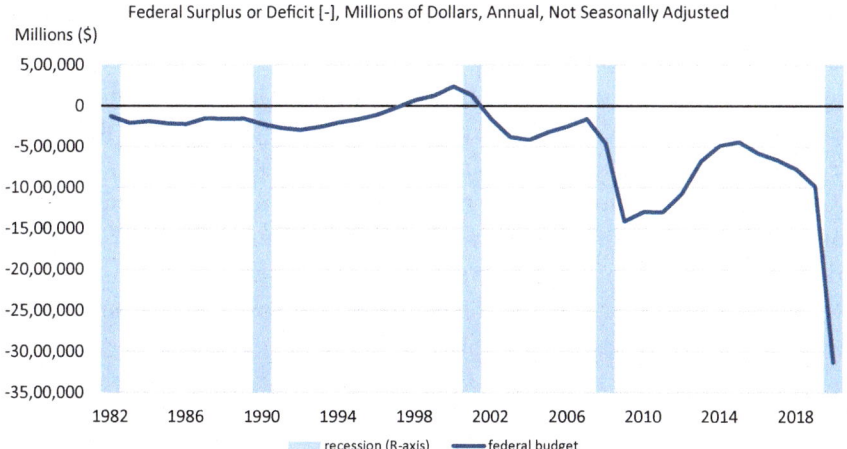

Fig. 4.4 U.S. federal budget balance since 1982

In December 2016, the Fed began a series of increases in the policy rate that continued to December 2018. The core PCE deflator also rose from mid-2017 to mid-2018. During that time, the yield curve declined as the two-year rate rose in line with increases in the funds rate. From mid-2018 to early 2019, the core PCE deflator declined. In July 2019, the Fed began a series of policy rate cuts that continued into the first half of 2020 as the Corona-19 virus triggered a recession.

Movements in the yield curve allocate spending in the real economy over time. For households, the yield curve signifies the credit cost of financing short- or long-term expenditures. It is particularly associated with households taking on flexible or fixed mortgage rates as well as refinancing opportunities for an outstanding mortgage. Low interest rates and reduced qualification standards led to a rapid increase in housing finance from 2004 to 2008 especially in the face of the high "expected" returns of home ownership during that period.

As for businesses, the yield curve represents a series of alternative maturities along which to take on short-term bank debt or issue longer-term bonds of different maturities. These options will be explored more in Chapters 5, 6, and 7 but for now it is important to link the rates along to the yield curve to the character and pace of investment in the real economy. A steeper yield curve will prompt more short-term investment with a more immediate payoff. A flatter yield curve, as in 2020, would promote more long-term financing associated with longer-term business development.

This link between market interest rates and the real economy was addressed initially in a framework associated with the Swedish economist Knut Wicksell.[7] He compared the marginal, natural, product of capital (real economy) with the cost of borrowing money (interest rate). If the rate of interest were below the natural rate of return on capital, business leaders would borrow at the money rate to buy capital. If interest rates were greater than the natural rate of return on capital, then business leaders would not invest.

Of course, the natural rate is not observable and the interest rate that prompts action will differ between households and many types of businesses and their time horizon. Calculations of the natural rate of return on capital will vary over time. Yet, the link between real economic activity and market interest rates is there and the incentive to act is there as well.

Interdependent Markets

Credit Allocation: The Story Behind the Curtain

While many words can and are written on the allocation of credit in a society, our focus here is the story behind the curtain. What is the framework that allows us to understand the path of interest rates as the price of credit and the pitfalls of looking for the perfect price of credit in a world of interdependent markets that are often (always?) in disequilibrium. Our focus is purposely narrow to highlight a framework that is built over time.[8]

---

[7] "The Influence of the Rate of Interest on Commodity Prices," 1898 reprinted in Erik Lindahl, ed., *Selected papers on Economic theory* by Knut Wicksell, 1958.

[8] For a broader review of resource misallocation in a society see Diego Restuccia and Richard Rogerson, "The Causes and Costs of Misallocation," *Journal of Economic Perspectives*, 2017, 31 (3).

"Big Money poll: Why Wall Street Is Scared of Washington," *Barron's* October 26, 2019

The importance of credit allocationand interest rates in a society is easily apparent in the above headline. Even before the establishment of the Federal Reserve, and ever since, the problem of the cost of credit and the role of public policymakers, not markets, in setting benchmark interest rates has faced private market decision-makers.

Interdependent Markets as Framework to Examine Credit Allocation

Both the supply and demand for credit shows the influence of multiple factors from outside the market for credit alone. In part, this reflects the terminology of technical versus fundamental factors that drive interest rates. Moreover, a framework for credit indicates the non-recursive nature of all prices-interest rates, inflation, and exchange rates. Actual and expected changes in interest rates will alter the price of equity capital.

As a start, a review of the actual time series for interest rates is a useful step. As illustrated in the graph below, the history of the ten-year Treasury benchmark interest rate, is clearly nonlinear and is not mean reverting since 1982. There were structural breaks in the ten-year benchmark rate occurred in 1987, 1992, 2000, and 2008 all associated with financial shocks/recession periods. Finally, real final sales have a causal link to the ten-year yield. Meanwhile, fluctuations in short-term interest rates would be expected given the movement of the FOMC's target funds rate (Table 4.1). In both cases, there is a clear hint of a downtrend in rates.

There are several patterns worth noting. First, the FOMC projections each year anticipated rising federal funds rates for the period ahead. Yet, there

Table 4.1 FOMC FFR projections

FOMC FFR projections										
	EOY									
	2016	2017	2018	2019	2020	2021	long run	5Y FWD	BE	Baa Spread
Mar-16	1.4	2.4	3.3				3.5	1.69	1.41	4.77
Mar-17		1.4	2.1	2.9			3	2.16	1.84	3.9
Mar-18			2.1	2.7	3.1		2.8	2.16	2.02	3.14
Mar-19				2.9	3.1	3.1	2.8	2.01	1.82	2.43

is a clear downward movement in the FOMC's expectations for the long-run funds rate. The FOMC's expectations were not out of character with the actions in the private marketplace—note that the five-year forward (5Y FWD) inflation and the 5-year breakeven (BE) inflation rates in March of 2016, 2017, and 2018 were higher (or at least equal to) the FOMC's projection for the funds rate at the end of the year. Only in 2019, was the FOMC's projection out of line with the March values of the inflation benchmarks.

Finally, the funds rate has a causal link to the BAA-fed funds rate spread. Therefore, the continued decline in the spread suggested the spread was discounting a reduced risk of recession/inflation relative to the prior values of the spread.

Over the last thirty years, the evolution of the supply of credit has been a fascinating development. Historically, the role of British and German finance in the nineteenth- century railroad expansion, especially the Illinois Central in the United States, is well documented.[9] A majority of railroad stock was held abroad from the 1850s to the 1890s. Shortly before assuming chairmanship of the Fed, Ben Bernanke spoke of a global savings glut.[10] His view was that global savings exceeded real investment and that the excess savings help explain the decline in interest rates. The Fed's balance sheet, Granger causality, leads to changes in both the 5-year Treasury and 10-year Treasury benchmark interest rates at the 10% and 1% significance levels, respectively.

For investors, central bank activity alters market interest rates and influences the allocation of credit as well as real economic resources. Central banks activities for both business and investors affect the allocation of resources. The issue is, then, whether these resources are being distorted in a negative way (the recent IPO experience for example). With credit flowing to U.S. Treasury debt, perhaps the real cost of treasury debt is being suppressed, but, as a follow-on, private corporate and mortgage debt is also mispriced.

On the demand side, the cost of credit is balanced against the expected rate of return on real economic capital. In turn, this reflects private market expectations on the economic return of a given real investment and, therefore, the influence of real economic growth expectations. In part, these expectations

---

[9] Charles Kindleberger, *Manias, Panics, and Crashes*, Basic Books, New York, 1978. p. 132 and A Stylized Outline of Financial Crises at the end of the text at what I will term p. 253 although the pages are not numbered for the Outline. Ross Robertson, "History of the American Economy," Second Edition, Harcourt, Brace & World, Inc., 1964, pp. 138–140.

[10] Ben Bernanke, "Global Savings Glut and the U.S. Current Account Deficit," *Virginia Association of Economists*, March 10, 2005.

4 Credit Allocation and the Role of Interest Rates as the Price of Credit 159

also incorporate expectations on exchange rates which will impact the cost of goods sold (imports) and the competitiveness of exports.

Firms, for example, will add to real capital when they expect real final sales to grow and the cost of capital is perceived to be low relative to the returns on real capital. In addition, there are adjustment costs to the stock of capital to be considered. These types of considerations will be reviewed in Chapter 7.

Timing Issues: Interest Rates as a Video Not a Snapshot

Three timing issues make the analysis of interest rate patterns a bit more complex than prices in other sectors. These timing issues provide insights to the behavior of the credit as well as other markets.

First, the yield curve, Fig. 4.2 above, represents the price of credit over time. The basic argument is the short-term interest rates are priced off the fed funds rate and that yields along the yield curve reflect expected future sequential short-term interest rates. Intriguingly, in late 2004 and early 2005, the upward move in short-term rates by the FOMC, led by Chairman Greenspan, did not result in a rise in long-term rates. This unusual behavior in long rates that did not follow the upward movement in short rates was a signal that credit market allocation has changed. In research, often the unusual (think Alexander Fleming, molds, and penicillin here) provide clues to understanding. When longer-term interest rates did not respond to the rise in short-term rates, then some information was in the markets that kept expectations of future economic growth and inflation muted relative to the concerns of the FOMC.

The timing of interest rate changes may precede policy moves and, in some ways, obviate the need for policy adjustments. For example, in 2013 Chairman Bernanke hinted at future tapering of the then current easy Fed policy. Private markets reacted as both the 5-year Treasury and 2-year Treasury rates rose relative to the funds rate even before there was any change in the Fed's benchmark rate. Subsequently, longer-term U.S. Treasury interest rates declined, and, for some commentators, this reduced the likelihood of further Fed easing. The private market did the easing for the Fed.

Finally, there is the issue that credit borrowed today at any interest rate and for any period takes place before the actual returns on the real investment are known. This is very apparent in speculative periods such as the nineteenth-century railroad boom, the twentieth-century dot.com boom, and the twenty-first century housing boom. As a result, the credit markets, especially when demand exceeds supply, create their own economic cycles, an ongoing, evolutionary view of the economy, where the pursuit of credit on the upside creates its own revulsion on the downside.

The Thankless Job for Private Investors and Central Banks

Financial markets and the Fed spend their lives in constant disequilibrium where changes today have their impact on the future. These changes play out the context of other multimarket changes that may offset or reinforce the intentions of private investors and policymakers.

Interest Rates: Income and Substitution Effects

For both households and businesses, there is a curious substitution effect that impacts the responsiveness to interest rates. For households, a higher interest rate would first be expected to reduce current household consumption and increase the desire to save more for the future. However, a higher interest rate increases the return on household assets that earn an adjustable rate of interest thereby increasing household income and boosting income for households that are net creditors.

There is also a wealth effect. A rise in interest rates reduces the market value of financial assets, such as bonds purchased in the past. If such assets need to be sold, a household could experience a capital loss, leading to reduced current and future consumption. As a result, a change in interest rates cannot dictate, a priori, the impact on consumption ahead of time. The net outcome depends on whether the household sector is a net borrower or lender and the types of assets owned. We will examine this more in Chapter 8.

As for businesses, the demand to buy and hold capital depends on the return it yields relative to the returns available on alternative assets (capital, bonds) and on the income, balance sheet, and cash of the firm. We will cover more of this in Chapters 6 and 7. For now, what needs to be realized is that the interaction between changes in interest rates and credit allocationis more complex, and far more interesting, than the linear tie of rates to credit supply and demand.

Evolving Framework, Fed Balance Sheet, Forces for Inflation

What Did We Learn about Our Evolving Framework?

For an investor, the perceptions of the policy goals of the Federal Reserve are a central input to strategy. After the experience of 2016–2019, markets came to view Fed actions to shrink the Fed's balance sheet as having a significant impact on mortgage rates and housing. Beginning in December 2017, the Fed provided hints of limiting its balance sheet reduction, as well as limiting any fed funds rate increases in 2019. Financial and housing markets quickly discounted such hints. Mortgage rates declined and existing home sales rose sharply. More recently, Chairman Powell's comments at Jackson Hole[11] further reinforced market expectations that the FOMC was unlikely to raise the fed funds rate in 2020 and that inflation is well within target.

Our decision-making framework has indeed changed. First, the impact of changes in the balance sheet is viewed as asymmetric with respect to housing. A bigger balance sheet may not prompt buyers to act but a shrinking balance sheet is associated with an increase in interest rates and a quick housing slowdown. Second, small changes in mortgage rates had an outsized impact on housing in the context of solid real income and wealth gains, as well as higher consumer confidence.

Inflation: What to Say at Our Next Strategy Meeting?

How are we to estimate inflation pressures? For the Fed not enough inflation appears to be a problem. For someone who cut his intellectual teeth on Jimmy Carter's inflation, the thought that not enough inflation is cognitive dissonance in real time. For policy decision-makers, their view had been that the economic growth above what they estimate as potential, and an unemployment rate below what they anticipated as full employment, would drive up inflation. What inflation did occur during the 2016–2019 period as unemployment continuously fell below prior estimates of full employment was far less than policymakers anticipated.

Central banks, such as the Fed and ECB, appear to believe that the link of growth and unemployment to inflation is less reliable than in prior days—again reinforced by Chairman Powell's Jackson Hole comments in August 2020. So central banks have not raised rates as anticipated. The role of the

---

[11] Jerome Powell, August 2020.

global economy and the dollar is central to the inflation and interest rate outlook. Global economic growth has been disappointing. Global competition for market shares for goods and services, by price cuts, has lowered the pace of inflation. Meanwhile, U.S. dollar strength from mid-2018 to early 2020 helped to lower the price of imported goods.

Introduce Change: When Actuals Do Not Equal Expectations

For credit allocationthrough the interest rate, one factor stands above all others—change. Benchmark U.S. Treasury yields are constantly changing with the economic cycle. After a jump in the benchmark two-year Treasury yield in late 2016, the yield continued to rise from the middle of 2017 to late 2018.

Changing fundamentals were central to understanding the move in the two-year rate. In late 2016, the Fed began to raise the federal funds rate and continued to raise the funds rate until December 2018. Meanwhile, the PCE deflator rose from a low in early 2016 to peak a bit over 2% in early 2018. Credit market participants could easily see why the two-year note rose given the rising pace of inflation and the increase in the policy rate set by the Fed. In addition, the yen/US dollar exchange rate exhibited a gentle uptrend from 2013 to 2018. Both the fed funds rate and the Yen/USD have a Granger causal link to the two-year Treasury note. The Yen/USD also has a causal link to the yield curve. In addition, the pace of pre-tax corporate profits has a causal link to the two-year Treasury rate. In this example of one benchmark Treasury rate, the links between the commodity (PCE), foreign exchange market (Yen/USD), and corporate profits can be seen with an additional dose of public policy (fed funds rate).

A Comparative Look

By early 2018, looking ahead, the expectation from the Blue Chip Economic Indicators Survey was 3.3% for 2019 for Treasury yields and a CPI at 2.2%. The actual outcome was 1.8% for the CPI and 2.14% for the ten-year Treasury note. The expected pace of Fed moves, illustrated in Table I, earlier in this chapter, the projected CPI at the time and yen/dollar exchange rate all influence the path of benchmark Treasury rates. The concept of Appropriate Pace of Policy Firming would have led the market to expect higher policy rates in both 2018 and 2019 relative to the December 2017 policy statement.

From the Federal Reserve's point of view, the Appropriate Pace reflected their expectations of the path of the Federal Funds rate that is consistent with achieving their targets of inflation stability and full employment. In October, the 10-year yield did briefly break above 3% and as both the three-month Treasury-bill yield and fed funds rate rose steadily throughout 2018.

Interest Rates and Federal Finance: Role on Non-Price sensitive Buyers

This has been a perennial debate given the difficulty of identifying the individual impact of fiscal finance among the other influences on interest rates. In today's environment, the large pace of purchases of U.S. federal debt by central banks, such as the Fed, the Bank of Japan, and the People's Bank of China, has added a non-price sensitive set of buyers to the Treasury market and have minimized the market impact of increased Treasury supply on market interest rates.

Many unknowns still exist regarding Treasury net issuance in the years ahead. According to the CBO's "An Update to the Budget Outlook, 2020 to 2030," fiscal deficits are estimated to be $6.5 Trillion over the 2021–2025 period,[12] all of which have implications on shifts in the yield curve. The balance between an interest rate insensitive issuer, The Treasury, and interest rate insensitive buyers such as the Fed, the Bank of Japan, and the People's Bank of China, is an interesting prospect to ponder.

A New Player Enters the Credit Market: Fed Balance Sheet, and Benchmark Treasury Rates

Fed's Balance Sheet Drives Benchmark Treasury Rates

Does the size and change in the balance sheet alter benchmark U.S. Treasury rates? As the Fed has increased its balance sheet, rates change—we shall see what happens on the downside as we live in an evolving world.

---

[12] An Update to the Budget Outlook, 2020 to 2030. Congressional Budget Office, September 2020.

Yes, the Size of the Balance Sheet Drives the Ten-year Treasury

At least on the way up and we shall see on the way down. To test a statistical relationship between the Fed balance sheet and interest rates (5 and 10-year Treasury yields) we employ the Granger causality test. This test helps determine whether changes in the balance sheet are useful to predict interest rates movements. Our results suggest that there is a one-way causality from the level of the Fed's balance sheet, Fig. 4.5, and benchmark 5 and 10-year Treasury rates. One-way causality means that the size of the Fed's balance sheet drives 5 and 10-year Treasury rates.

However, is it possible that the relationship will not hold as the balance sheet shrinks rather than grows? Would a reduction of the size of the balance sheet lead to an increase in the benchmark 5 and 10-year Treasury rate? A priori, there would appear to be no reason why if all other factors are held constant. In the first part of this cycle, the Fed was increasing the balance sheet size as the economy was recovering from the Great Recession (and a slower economic recovery compared to historical standards). Meanwhile, the fed funds rate was near zero. In addition, expectations were for an accommodative monetary policy for an extended period under the condition that the Fed balance sheet did move rates.

During the period from 2016 to 2018, the Fed balance sheet did indeed shrink modestly, and the 2-year Treasury rate did in fact increase. Therefore, in a period of modest economic growth (real GDP grew 2.5% over the mid-2015 to 2018 period) and low inflation (PCE deflator was rising from 1 to

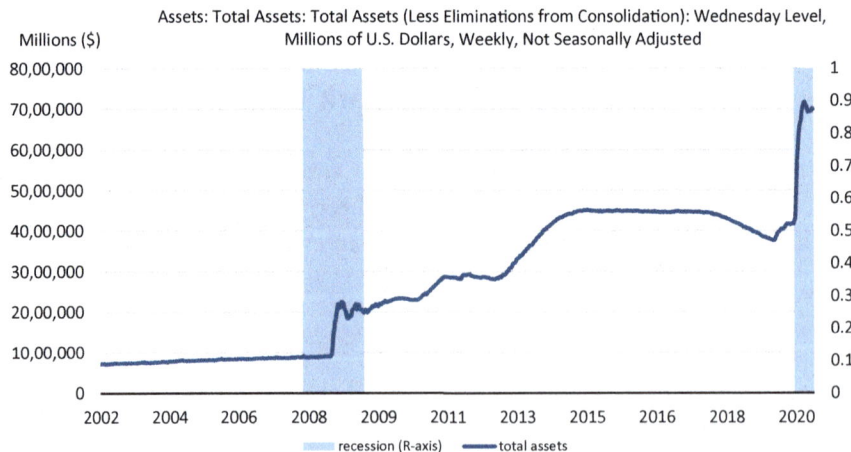

Fig. 4.5 Federal Reserve assets since 2004

4 Credit Allocation and the Role of Interest Rates as the Price of Credit

2% over that period), there indeed was a reverse relationship between the Fed balance sheet and short-term interest rates. During 2020, the conditions of growth and inflation and household, business, and banking liquidity preferences were altered dramatically. Much of the increase in the Fed's balance sheet went to bank reserves and cash and did not translate into real economic activity.

The current environment, and expectations about the state of the economy and monetary policy stance, will affect the relationship between changes in the balance sheet and interest rates.

Does the Composition of the Balance Sheet Matter?

Yes, but the causality is reversed. When we consider causality, the size of the Treasury holdings in the Fed's balance sheet is driven by the 5 and 10-year benchmark Treasury rates. Why could this be possible? This result intimates that the Fed's balance sheet reacts to the level of rates. This would be true if the level of rates is a signal to the Fed to increase its balance sheet. This follows the approach of the Fed lowering (twisting) the yield curve by altering the balance sheet to lower long-term rates. Treasury rates are not the result of policy actions but the driver of balance sheet adjustment.

Political Outcomes, Expectations, and Long-Term Benchmark Yields

In the aftermath of the 2016 U.S. presidential election, markets priced in the likelihood of higher inflation, chiefly on the expectation of the incoming Trump's administration intent on expansionary fiscal policy. However, the upward momentum in long-term yields (from 1.5% in July to 2.5% by March 2017) was largely reversed with yields on a downward trend to September 2017. Legislative obstacles quickly lessened the likelihood that the Republican party's agenda would be passed in its campaign-trail form. Likewise, the timeline for corporate and individual tax reform was pushed back while the administration's spending outlook was also scaled back, which weighed on inflation expectations. In response, longer-term benchmark Treasury rates declined. Political expectations, as well as inflation expectations, define the path of benchmark rates.[13]

Expectations of greater government spending and higher consumer spending, as a reflection of tax cuts legislation, resulted in a pick-up in expected inflation, especially given that the economy was close to full employment. Ten-year breakeven rates rose from 1.47% in July 2016 to 2.02% by February 2017. Subsequently, the ten-year breakeven rate fell to 1.73% by June 2017.

Multi-factor Determinants of the Yield Curve

The first decade of the twenty-first century provides a real-world exercise in the multifactor determination of the yield curve. First, growth expectations, not simply inflation or central bank policy expectations, alter its patterns. From the start of the economic recovery in 2002, real GDP growth accelerated to a peak of 4.32% in the 4Q of 2003. This acceleration should lead to a steeper yield curve which did indeed occur up to August 2003. Meanwhile, the pace of the PCE deflator rose from less than 1% in the 1Q 2002 to 3.2% in the 2Q of 2006. This would also support a steeper yield curve over that period.

The Fed began to raise the federal funds rate in mid-2004 and from then on, the funds rate rose to a peak in mid-2006. Interestingly, the 10-year and the 2-year yield curve peaked in August 2003 even before the Fed began to raise the funds rate. The impact of slower economic growth or the markets sense of the economic slowdown played a key role in shaping the yield curve.

The experience of the 2002 to 2006 period highlights the multifactor character determination of many economic series and, in this case the yield curve, is readily apparent.

This multifaceted determination of the yield curve emphasizes that challenge for analysts with the complications involved with the problem of administered rates (the federal funds rate) and the purposeful change in the pricing of credit by the central bank policy. Traditionally, changes in central bank policy are considered a positive move in the correct direction to moderate growth and inflation trends. There is no obvious truth that whatever the central bank policy rate is, it is indeed the correct rate for real

---

[13] An early exposition of the role of inflationary expectations is discussed by William E. Gibson "Interest Rates and Inflationary Expectations: New Evidence," *American Economic Review*, 1972, 62: 845–865.

long-term growth in the economy. The frequent alterations in central bank benchmarks provide a hint that such policy settings do reallocate capital in a very uncertain economic environment (even more obvious in the resetting of growth, inflation, and unemployment in the Fed's set of economic projections) The impact of central banks in our four price sectors is further illustrated by the experience of major central banks, such as the ECB, as well as numerous emerging markets in the twenty-first csentury. The "conundrum" cited by Chairman Alan Greenspan about the yield curve hints at the limits of our expertise.

Lessons of 2019: Optimism on Rates, Expectations, and Outcomes

The experience of 2019 provides an understanding price of determination, especially in credit markets, by assessing what is expected, then what we get, and finally, how the difference generates change in financial markets. This can be seen on the first Friday, generally of each month, as the Bureau of Labor Statistics (BLS) releases employment data. Gains in the employment number greater than expected will increase expectations for better economic growth, inflation, and central bank tightening, or in some cases, less ease in Fed policy.

On March 8, 2019, the BLS released its employment report for February and the outcome was disappointing. The 10-year Treasury yield fell from 2.72% before the report to 2.64% on Monday after the report. In contrast, on July 5, the June jobs report was strong, and the 10-year yield rose. Consistent with the 10-year note, the 10-year breakeven inflation rate fell after the February jobs report and then rose after the July report.

Over the past three years, the path of the ten-year Treasury rate followed the policy mix of expansionary fiscal policy and tighter monetary policy. Historically, this has been associated with a stronger dollar and higher Treasury benchmark rates.[14] In both 2017 and 2018, the ten-year Treasury rate did rise as the Fed increased interest rates. But in late 2018, the breakeven Treasury rate broke lower in the third quarter even before the benchmark Treasury rate peaked in the fourth quarter.

Although better economic growth and/or expansionary fiscal policy continued into 2019, Treasury note yields fell. Expectations changed in late 2018 and into 2019 and yields followed. In contrast, recall the taper tantrum

---

[14] Robert A. Mundell, "Capital Mobility and Stabilization Policy Under Fixed and Flexible Exchange Rates," *Canadian Journal of Economic and Political Science*, 1963, 29 (4): 475–485.

of 2013, when rates rose on expectation of a Fed reduction in the balance sheet although the Fed did not follow through. Expectations are a key driver of market prices.

Inflation: What You Get, What You Expected—Betting on Economic Policy

Post-election 2016 provides another perspective on the impact of expectations, this time for economic policy actions on the fiscal side and on interest rates. Benchmark 10-year Treasury rates rose from 1.97% on November 4, 2016 to 2.37% on January 5th. Breakeven 10-year rates rose from 1.68% to 1.95% over the same period. Were these adjustments just a catch-up to the past or a projection of further growth and inflation premiums In the future? These increases reflect the forces of expectations particularly for an expansionary fiscal policy.

Core PCE inflation did rise in 2016 and peaked in February 2017. Meanwhile, the Fed continued to raise the benchmark funds rate throughout 2017 and into 2018. Expected fiscal stimulus combined with actual monetary policy tightening delivered rate increases in late 2016 and early 2017 until the peak of inflation in early 2017.

The perceived trade-off of stronger economic growth and higher inflation began to seriously breakdown in 2019 and by early 2020, pre-Covid-19, the perception grew that inflation could remain at a more moderate pace, despite the decline in the unemployment rate. Seller competition on a global scale, dollar appreciation, and/or more modest energy price increases lowered inflation expectations. The view on FOMC policy was that it would not need to be as aggressive in raising the funds rate going forward as in the past in response to expected inflation trends. CBO estimates of the natural unemployment rate declined steadily over the last three years. Meanwhile, estimates of the natural rate of interest also declined since the recession of 2007–2009.[15]

---

[15] Measuring the Natural Rate of Interest, Holston, Laubach and Williams, December 15, 2016, Federal Reserve Bank of San Francisco.

Nature of the world disequilibrium credit allocation

Interest Rates as the Price of Credit: Altered Fundamentals

At his Jackson Hole speech in 2020, Chairman Powell altered the perspective of monetary policy. Previously, policy had been conducted in a proactive manner as the Fed anticipated change in the economy and in inflation and adjusted interest rates to lean against the wind. Effectively, the Fed had adjusted interest rates to fit its vision of the proper level of rates to achieve policy goals. In contrast, Powell indicated a new policy role for the Fed—it would now react to economic developments

Back to Normalization: Administered Rates to Market Rates

Credit allocationhas been distorted in recent years as the Federal Reserve attempted to spur the real economy. While from a public policy view these distortions have a positive economic goal, for investors alterations of market prices, whether in credit or product or exchange markets, creates a tension, an observable disequilibrium between policy-set prices and market-determined prices that must be resolved over time. In the 1970s, wage-price controls created the disequilibrium. In the early 1990s, the tension in the Exchange Rate Mechanism led to a large, sharp adjustment in exchange rates. Throughout the post-World War II period, central banks have set benchmark policy rates in a way to move economic activity. Effectively this meant setting a rate that was not consistent with current economic fundamentals but reflected what a central bank thought would be best to achieve economic goals over the long term.

In recent years, an era of administered rates has created a credit disequilibrium. There is thus little guidance on what should be the proper level of interest rates to price financial capital and to judge the viability of real-world activity. As illustrated in Fig. 4.6, America has moved to a new economic environment since the fall of 2017 searching for a new equilibrium in interest rates, inflation, exchange rates and real economic growth. The challenge for central bank authorities is that the setting of a fixed, administered interest rate, in a constantly changing economic environment, will create constant disequilibrium in the markets. As illustrated in Fig. 4.8, the ten and two-year

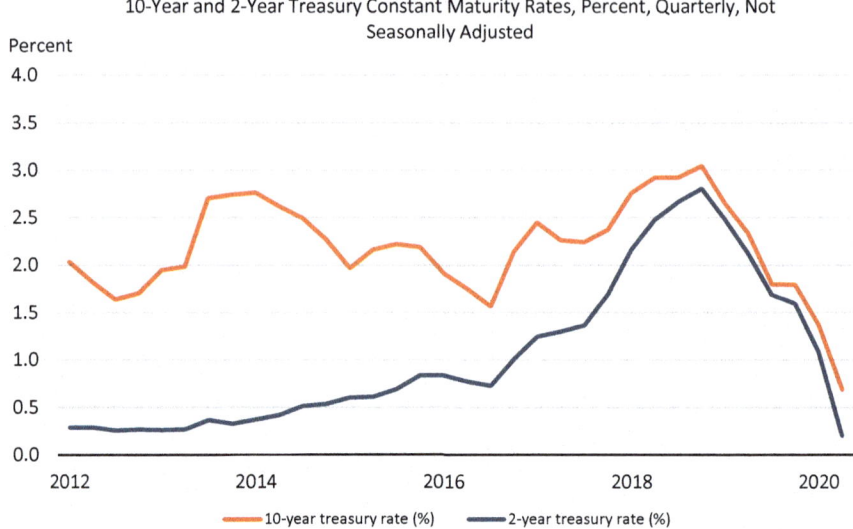

Fig. 4.6 Two-year and Ten-year U.S. Treasury rates post 2012

yields rose in alignment with the increase in the funds rate over the same period.

Altered Fundamentals: Altered Market Prices

Since November 2017, there has been a distinct shift in the fundamentals underlying the search for equilibrium in credit markets. Expectations for economic growth, inflation, and exchange rates have moved, so why not market interest rates? Expectations for growth and inflation expectations rose from November 2017 to February 2018. Expectations were also for a decline in the dollar's value over the same period. The net outcome has been a rise in interest rates. Altered expectations of growth and inflation have moved investor expectations of monetary policy actions. The probability of Fed action in March 2018 went from 65% in January to 99% in February. In March, the Fed did indeed raise the funds rate target.

Interest Rates: Setting the "Normal" Benchmark

The Great Recession of 2008–2009 has "added fun" to interest rate modeling. The most widely utilized estimation method is Ordinary Least Squares, (OLS) regression. One major assumption of OLS is that the underlying data is stationary and has no structural breaks. However, if the data is non-stationary and/or has structural breaks then OLS estimates are not reliable.

Many major macroeconomic variables, including interest rates, experienced structural breaks during the Great Recession. Both the 10-year and 2-year series have non-linear (declining) trends since the 1980s. Interest rates and the growth rate of the economy, which is also a declining rate, are thus not constant overtime.

Another major hurdle for modeling interest rates is the fed funds rate's behavior since 2008. The fed funds rate hit the 0–0.25% range in December 2008 and stayed there until December 2015. Unusual fed funds rate behavior, along with structural breaks in interest rates, pose great challenges for modeling. Add factors are the adjustments made to equation-based projections over a forecasting period are the best friends of analysts since the Great Recession and it does not seem likely to change soon. The challenge in setting policy rates at the Fed can be seen by the debate surrounding the Taylor rule.[16] Proposed by the Stanford University economics Prof. John B. Taylor in 1992, it is a central bank technique to stabilize economic activity by setting an interest rate. The Taylor rule is based on three main indicators: the federal funds rate, the price level, and the changes in real income. Questions of the reliability of the independent variables in the Taylor rule and the structural breaks in the economic series are a significant challenge to policymakers since structural breaks alter the relationship between economic series and thereby invalidate any estimates coming from the Taylor rule. Finally, the rule is based upon deviations of inflation and economic growth. The recessions of 1990 and 2007–2009 were financial events so real-side economic factors did not provide the central bank with reliable leading signals of problems.

Central Banks, Administered Rates, and the Purposeful Mispricing of Credit

The essence of monetary policy is to set an interest rate distinct from current market rates. This will alter the current economic landscape to help it move toward an economic status more consistent with what the Fed views as sustainable with its policy objectives. These objectives, mandated by law, are associated with stable, low inflation, and full employment.

In this way, the markets are frequently in disequilibrium and the Fed is often "fine-tuning" current policy to reach a longer-run, desired economic

---

[16] John B. Taylor, Discretion versus Policy Rules in Practice (1993), Stanford University, Stanford, CA.

scenario. This discussion on fine-tuning picks up in the debate between the British Currency and the British Banking Schools in the early nineteenth century proving once again that everything old is new again. The Banking School argued for the need to expand credit to stimulate economic growth, a view frequently heard in mid-to-late 2020. On the other hand, the Currency School proposed that credit expansion be limited to covering actual commercial transactions to curtail speculation. Of course, policymakers find it very hard to declare a stopping place. Expectations of financial returns, and the willingness to offer credit, both tend to be very procyclical.

Monetary and credit expansion is systematic and endogenous, as evidenced by policies of the Fed and the ECB, rather than random and exogenous. Speculative manias gather speed through expansion of money and credit—from the history of John Law and the South Seas Bubble to British railroads in the nineteenth century to housing speculation in the United States during 2005–2009.

Market Interactions in 2018–2019; Principles Matter

Essay Interrupted; Principles Continue to Matter

Global financial markets are interrelated, and asset prices must reflect the influence of at least the four sectors we consider—credit, equities, foreign exchange, and real sector commodity and service prices. If any one market is overvalued or undervalued, then the other three markets are also mispriced. During the recent period, investors chased yield to drive down both the level of interest rates and the spreads along the yield curve and between private bond issues and sovereign debt. Is this narrowing of spreads consistent with the behavior in other markets?

In the commodity markets, core PCE peaked in mid-2018 at 2% and then declined in January 2019 and remained in a range of 1.6%-1.9% for the second half of 2019. In the foreign exchange market, the yen depreciated against the dollar for all of 2018. Finally, the NASDAQ Index, along with the PCE and yen has a causal link to the yield curve. Lower inflation and an appreciating currency will attract domestic and foreign investors seeking yield and benefitting from the decline in 10-year rates beginning in the fourth quarter of 2018. The principles of market interactions provide guideposts to asset prices.

For equity markets, the decline in the high-grade bond spread was a positive for equity values and non-financial corporate profit margins rose throughout all of 2017, declined in 2018 but remained above the levels of the fourth quarter of 2016.

TINA: There Is No Alternative

Turning to 2020, what if growth expectations are too high for those analysts who are making the case for a V-shaped recovery with continued low-interest rates? In recent months, the dollar has depreciated against the yen thereby diminishing the reward for foreign investors in U.S. financial assets. Financial markets continue to be in a state of disequilibrium as equity prices appear to be high relative to expectations for growth and a weaker currency. In addition, the core PCE deflator has risen in recent months reducing the real returns on Treasury instruments and, perhaps, prompting even further buying of equities. The prevailing view among investors is that there is no alternative (TINA) to equities. The interactions among markets ensure that the price of assets in any one market is a function of prices and fundamental forces in all four markets.

Tipping the Bond Market Equilibrium in the Corporate Sector

As illustrated in Fig. 4.7, the 10-year high-quality market corporate bonds spot rate exhibits periods of above and below trend values and is seldom at an equilibrium given the obvious longer-term downward trend. Movements in high quality, AA, spreads have a causal link to real final sales, equities (NYSE index) and the term premium on the ten year.

In 2020, these ups and downs were amplified by the emergence of the Fed as a buyer of high-grade corporate debt. When the Fed in early March 2020 announced that it was planning on buying corporate debt, it immediately led to a decline in corporate spreads over Treasury debt and a rapid increase in long-term debt sold by nonfinancial corporations. The Fed's policy drift into the world of administered rates entered the realm of corporate bonds.

This leaves investors with the valuation problem. As the Fed lowers corporate bond rates through its buying, the question remains—what is the real economic value of these bonds? Corporate profit growth for all non-financial companies declined in 2019 relative to 2018 even before the Covid-19 shutdown. Profit growth will be negative in 2020. What is the value of these

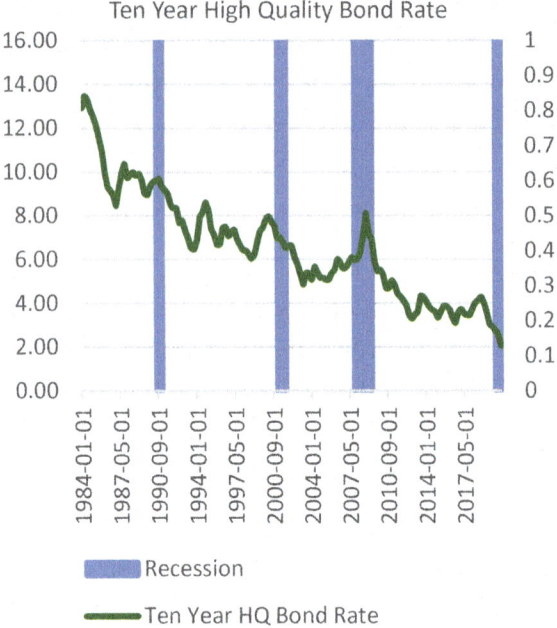

Fig. 4.7 High grade corporate bond rates since 1984

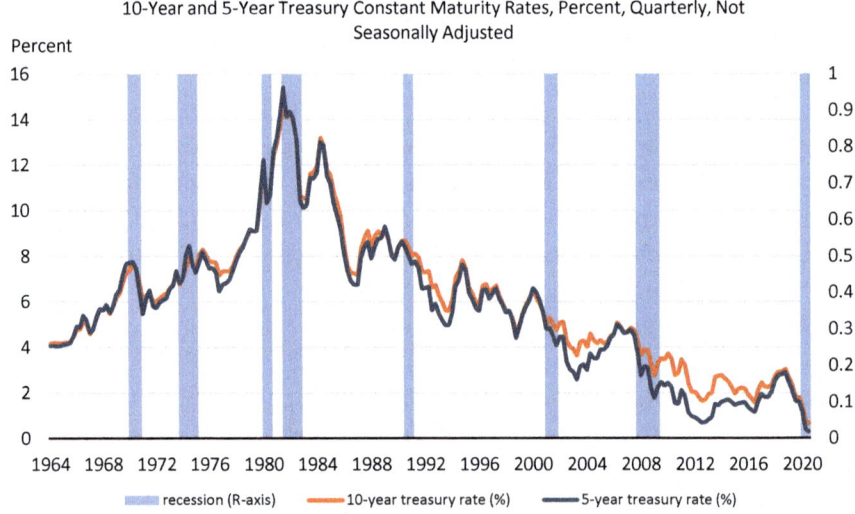

Fig. 4.8 History of ten-year and five-year U.S. Treasury rates

bonds? For many companies that do not earn a profit and have no clear path to profitability over the next two years, there is no pretense of a balance between real and financial values given the outlook for significant corporate restructuring in the years ahead.

Disequilibrium—Fed Can Be Patient but Markets Are Always Moving

While it is perfectly reasonable for the Fed to declare a policy of patience in 2019–2020, the financial markets are always moving. Decision-makers and investors must focus on the dynamic character of the economy and anticipate where the puck is going. As evidenced in Fig. 4.2, shown above, the yield curve in mid-2020 steepened even as the Fed policy was to stay with low policy rates and a stable balance sheet.

Interest rates are not simply a linear function of Fed policy. Interactions between inflation, interest rates, exchange rates, and Fed policy provide a laboratory for the behavior of the yield curve. The yield curve rose in the fall of 2010 without a move from the Fed. The yield curve also rose in the second half of 2013 again without any Fed move. From October 2016 to December 2016 the yield curve rose even though the Fed did not alter short-term rates. What did change was the rise in the core PCE deflator over the period December 2015 to February 2017.

What happened in 2020? The breakeven ten-year inflation rate is a market-based measure of expected inflation and is the difference between the yield on the 10-year nominal bond and an inflation-linked bond of the same maturity. Breakeven inflation rates rose from less than 0.8% in early 2020 to 1.8% in August 2020. Inflation may be low while breakeven inflation rates may be low but rising. From the economist perspective, the level is far less important than the change in direction.

Meanwhile, there is the matter of the exchange rate. The yen/dollar exchange rate has a Granger causality link to the yield curve. In 2020, the appreciation of the yen relative to the dollar has been significant. For international investors, this is important because the total return on a bond for a foreign investor is reduced by the depreciation of the dollar relative to their home currency. Year-to-date, the DXY is down 3.4%. At the margin, where all investors live, this is central to the story of total return.

Markets interact as decision-makers and investors weigh opportunities across the spectrum even when the Fed is on hold. We cannot have an output market in disequilibrium (too much growth, too low unemployment as in 2019) and not anticipate change in our other markets. If we anticipate that the economy will move to its long-run position from its position in 2019, then inflation is likely to decline—but that is further away from the Fed's target.

Declining real economic growth and lower inflation would call for further Fed easing, favor a greater sovereign debt position and, moreover, would question the allocation for corporate and household private debt. Slower growth would also suggest further downward pressure on profit margins altering expectations for equity returns. Weaker growth and lower fed funds rates would suggest downward pressure on the dollar.

Markets do not stand in isolation. If there is a disequilibrium in the output market, then adjustments must be made in other markets and in investment and business decisions. In 2019, growth was perceived to be above potential and yet inflation remained low. With the 2020 recession, growth is perceived to be below potential and would remain there for 2020–2021. Meanwhile, the Fed is on hold, but markets are moving, and decision-makers must adjust.

Overcoming Obstacles in Developing an Investment Strategy

History can be a poor guide to effective investment strategy. Portfolio managers in the early post-World War II period did not foresee the rapid rise of inflation in the late 1960s and 1970s that resulted in negative real returns on bonds. In the early 1980s, decision-makers, guided in part by the prior two decades, continued to over forecast inflation and unemployment rates and under forecast gains in real economic growth. These patterns reflect the anchoring bias that hinders investment performance.

Anchoring our expectations for the future based upon some history is susceptible to the problem that the future may be quite different. We can test this by looking for structural breaks. Consider then that both the 5-year and 10-year Treasury benchmark yields rose steadily from 1968 to 1979 and then moved in a distinct downtrend after that (Fig. 4.8). These two distinct patterns indicate that neither the 5-year nor the 10-year Treasury rates over this period is mean reverting and treating either rate as a consistent series is not the correct approach. The structural break in both series (identified as 4Q 1982) is associated with the regime change in monetary policy under Fed Chairmen Paul Volcker and Alan Greenspan.

Since Treasury rates serve as the benchmark for pricing corporate debt, corporate Aa and Baa rates also exhibited a structural break in the 4Q of 1982. Given the shift in nominal rates what might be happening with real

4 Credit Allocation and the Role of Interest Rates as the Price of Credit

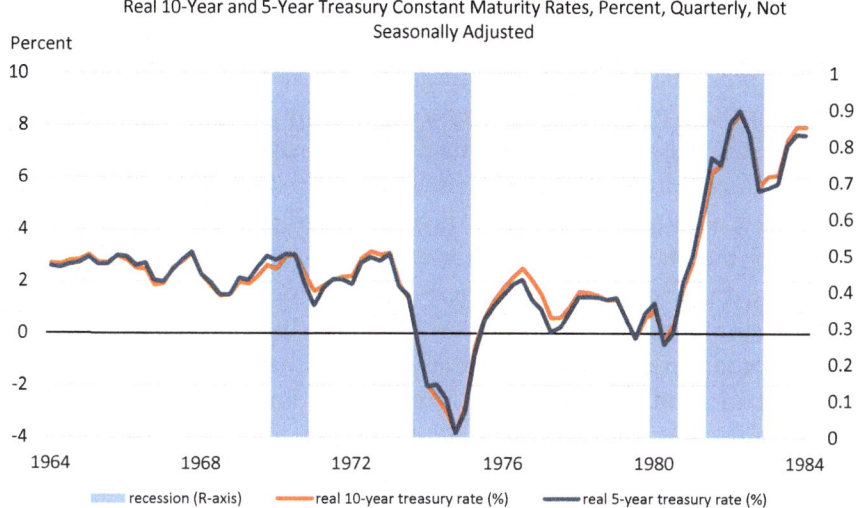

Fig. 4.9 History of real ten-year and five-year treasury rates

rates? Negative real rates in the late 1970s gave way to significant positive real rates in the 1980s (Fig. 4.9). The real ten-year rate exhibits structural breaks in 1987, 1992, 2002, and 2007- all periods associated with financial shocks and/or recessions.

Incomplete and Imperfect Information: Another Aspect of Credit Allocation in the Real Economy

When economic agents have incomplete information, they may delay decisions or make different decisions than they would have been made if perfect information is available. This was very evident in the aftermath of the Dodd-Frank Act (which reformed the U.S. banking system), the Affordable Care Act (which reformed the U.S. healthcare system), and Basel III (which reformed the international banking system). For each initiative, several years passed as the details and regulations continued to be rolled out.

For each initiative, there are costs of adjustment for private agents and certainly very high costs to adjustments that later limited the growth of bank credit in the post-2010 period. These costs lead to a distributed lag process where the short-run price and output moves were not likely to be the long-run equilibrium level of each. Incomplete information also leads to a bias in thinking termed the hindsight bias. Sometimes called the "I-knew-it-all-along" thinking, the hindsight bias is the tendency to see past events as being predictable at the time those events happened. In the global context, incomplete information was the context for investors on the true status of sovereign debt, and policymaker intentions in Europe, and certainly not the sensitivity of Euro finances to the Great Recession. In a similar vein, as tax revenues plummeted because of the shutdowns caused by Covid-19, the true weakness of U.S. state and local budgets was revealed.

Imperfect information appears where the pricing of financial assets does not reflect the reality of market forces.[17] We witness this in the case of administered interest rates. Here there are issues of adverse selection (when sellers have information that buyers do not have, or vice versa, about some aspect of product quality), moral hazard (the risk that a party has not entered a contract in good faith or has provided misleading information about its assets, liabilities, or credit capacity), and questions about the quality of bank lending, and corporate, state, and local balance sheets. Moreover, monetary policy differences between central banks alter the valuation of relative investment opportunities across borders. As illustrated by MIT economics Prof. Robert Townsend, there is a significant cost to verification which will impact economic activity.[18]

One obvious area of disconnect between market fundamentals and pricing is the European sovereign debt markets where slow growth and high debt levels are combined with very low sovereign interest rates. Is the future in Europe one of perpetual ECB buying of sovereign debt? Or is there a possibility that the ECB will limit its buying and interest rates may rise more than currently discounted in the marketplace?

Domestic Yields in the Global Context

U.S. interest rates reflect not only domestic forces but also the global allocation of financial capital. We are familiar with the management of global bond portfolios where the selection of the assets in the portfolio is a choice across boundaries. A structural downshift in global yields (G-6 yields which exclude the United States) occurred in the 4Q of 2008. We also had two-way causality, which is statistically significant, between G-6 and U.S. yields over the 1982 to 2017 period. Finally, the root-mean-squared error of a model

---

[17] This has been a long-term debate not just for the current 2020 corporate markets. See Richard Fisher, "Fed's Fisher Concerned Credit Spreads Have Narrowed too Much," *Reuters*, June 30, 2014.
[18] Robert Townsend, "Optimal Contracts and Competitive Markets with Costly State Verification," *Journal of Economic Theory*, 1979, 21 (October): 265–293.

used in global yields to predict the benchmark 10-year U.S. yield is lower than a model without such a yield.

Exiting Financial Repression Era-Correcting Mispricing No Easy Matter

After years of financial repression from central banks, the path to equilibrium means backtracking through the minefields of mispriced real and financial assets based upon administered rates. After the "taper tantrum" of 2013 and the aborted "normalization of 2017–2018," the path back to normal rates would be considered a period of upsetting administered, below market, interest rates and thereby rising more market-determined interest rates which feed into the real growth of household spending and business investment.

In this difficult context, as central bankers move away from an environment of administered prices (interest rates and bond prices) other financial markets must adjust. Financial markets are moving from one disequilibrium point with interest rates held below market values (and below inflation) to generate growth, to another nexus of interest rates, growth and inflation that remains undefined given the uncertainty about the equilibrium level of real interest rates, the potential growth rate of GDP and the Fed's commitment to a 2% inflation target. Finally, as the years 2020/2021 unfold, is the Fed committed to market-setting interest rates? Or are we simply moving from an era of close-to-zero interest rates to an era of slightly higher rates, while still being administered by the central bank?

As we shall see in the next chapter, the pricing of credit at the short end of the curve through bank and non-bank lending is both a cyclical and secular story of constant change. The pattern of current market pricing reflects both change in the nominal and in the real component of interest rates. Over the last two years, there have been significant shifts in both the demand and supply of credit.

References

Ben Bernanke, "Global Savings Glut and the U.S. Current Account Deficit," *Virginia Association of Economists*, March 10, 2005. A view on the global imbalance of saving and investment.

Jim Collins, "Good to Great," *Harper Business*, 2001. An examination of the proper allocation and misallocation of credit in many real-world cases. One of my twelve must reads.

Congressional Budget Office, "An Update to the Budget Outlook, 2020 to 2030," September 2020. This annual update is an essential starting point for both the economic and financial market outlook for the intermediate and long-term.

Timothy Cook and Thomas Hahn, "The Effect of Changes in the Federal Funds Rate Target on Market Interest Rates in the 1970s." *Journal of Monetary Economics*, 1989, 24 (November): 331–351. Research from the late 1970s that supported the expectation that changes in short-term rates would impact long-term rates.

William E. Gibson, "Interest Rates and Inflationary Expectations: New Evidence," *American Economic Review*, 1972, 62: 845–865. An early exposition of the role of inflationary expectations.

James Grant, "Bagehot," W.W. Norton, 2019. A biography, and a view, of the role of central banking in England during the Victorian period.

Holston, Kathryn, Thomas Laubach, and John C. Williams, "Measuring the Natural Rate of Interest: International Trends and Determinant," *Journal of International Economics*, 2017, 108 (May, S1): S59–75.

Erik Lindahl, ed., *Selected papers on Economic theory* by Knut Wicksell, 1958. "The Influence of the Rate of Interest on Commodity Prices," 1898. Wicksell's work is often cited but the original idea is worth the read.

John Stuart Mill, *Principles of Political Economy, with some of Their Applications to Social Philosophy* (1848; 7th ed., reprint ed.,) Longmans, Green, London, 1929. One of the economic classics that provides a framework for decision making.

Robert A. Mundell, "Capital Mobility and Stabilization Policy Under Fixed and Flexible Exchange Rates," *Canadian Journal of Economic and Political Science*, 1963, 29 (4): 475–485. An essential read into the role of global capital flows and financial markets.

Jerome Powell, Speech at Jackson Hole. "New Economic Challenges and the Fed's Monetary Policy Review," August 27, 2020 and published on the Federal Reserve's website, https://www.federalreserve.gov/newsevents/speech/powell20200827a.htm.

Diego Restuccia and Richard Rogerson, "The Causes and Costs of Misallocation," *Journal of Economic Perspectives*, 2017, 31 (3). A broader review of resource misallocation in a society. Unfortunately, misallocation is too common an occurrence.

Ross Robertson, "History of the American Economy," Second Edition, Harcourt, Brace & World, Inc.,1964, pp. 138–140. A primary read on economic history which sadly is not taught in many American universities anymore.

John B. Taylor, Discretion versus policy rules in practice (1993), Stanford University, Stanford, CA. A statement of the Taylor rule that is often cited in both academic and business writings.

Robert Townsend, "Optimal Contracts and Competitive Markets with Costly State Verification," *Journal of Economic Theory*, 1979, 21 (October): 265–293. Information is not free and often very difficult to verify—as we have increasingly experienced in recent years with social media.

4 Credit Allocation and the Role of Interest Rates as the Price of Credit

Leon Walras, *Elements of Pure Economics*, 1874, published 1954 by Routledge, Abingdon, UK. A focus on the linkages between markets and how price movements in one market depend upon movements in other markets.

5

Short-Term Credit: Bridging the Next Few Years

Story and Motivation

Why Am I Reading This?

Short-term credit (3–5 years is the focus) through the banking system acts as a primary channel for central bank policymakers to influence economic activity and the focus of this chapter and yet, non-bank lending has grown increasingly in importance. The banking system has also been the traditional saving vehicle for households and small businesses which, the bank, in turn, creates the credit available to other households and small businesses. For households, credit cards, short-term installment, home equity, and auto loans have been a traditional way to borrow through the banks. For small businesses, inventory finance and small capital purchases are frequently made with bank credit. Both residential and small commercial lending travels via the bank channel.

Barings Bank and the Louisiana Purchase[1] Credit Availability on the Upside

In a pattern we shall see repeated in twentieth- century finance, bridge financing, short-term credit was provided by a bank to complete a long-term deal. The role of Barings Bank of London and the Hope Bank, another merchant bank,[2] of Amsterdam in the Louisiana Purchase illustrates the role of intermediary finance that continues to characterize the actual financing that continues today and thereby emphasizes the importance of liquidity in credit markets. This lesson has just recently been reinforced by the illiquidity in the Treasury/repo market in the 2019–2020 period.

Jefferson disliked the idea: purchasing Louisiana from France would imply that France had a right to be in Louisiana. Napoleon needed money. The finance of the purchase involved the Barings Bank, which took 60% of the deal, along with Henry Hope that took 40% of the deal. The United States purchased Louisiana from the Barings Brothers and Hope & Co.

Credit quality matters. Napoleon trusted Baring's paper over that of the United States (not an unreasonable view given the creditworthiness of the nascent republic at that time[3]). Napoleon bought Louisiana from Barings and Hope and then Barings turned the title over to the United States in exchange for $11.25 Million in bonds at 6%.

One final note is of interest. Although it is commonly believed that the United States paid $15 million for Louisiana, the reality is that Barings/Hope bought the U.S. bonds from Napoleon at a discount of 87 1/2 per each $100. As a result, Napoleon received only $8,831,250 in cash for Louisiana. Such is the price to Napoleon of his immediate need for cash—emergency funding in other terms.

Credit Shortage on the Downside: 1990–1991

Credit standards set at commercial banks provide an insight into the patterns of credit supply in the short-term credit market (Fig. 5.1). There is a strong cyclical pattern to credit standards, as witnessed by the tight in standards

---

[1] "We Banked on Them," in *The Business of America, John Steele Gordon*, Walker & Co, New York, 2001.

[2] Merchant banks at the time provided underwriting and fund-raising services for large enterprises and did not provide banking services to the public.

[3] You would consider the U.S. as an emerging country. New issue government bond rates were 7.34% compared to British new issue rates of 4.41%. Sidney Homer, "A History of Interest Rates," *Rutgers*, 1963.

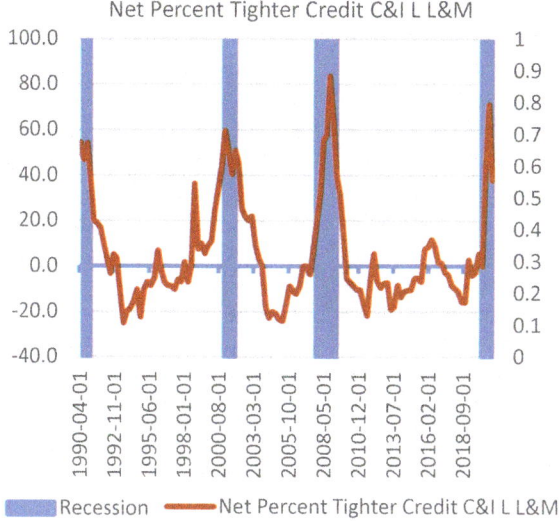

Fig. 5.1 Net percent of banks tightening standards on business loans

in the 1990 recession[4] and then again, the tighter standards going into the 2001 and 2007–2009 recessions. The regional character of the New England and Texas bank shutdowns makes the most recent crisis interesting in that with larger banks more geographically diversified, bank crisis has been less damaging in some specific regions while being nasty for the entire financial system/country. The onset of the 2020 recession came so abruptly, however, that credit standards tightened coincident with the recession.

From the lenders point of view, slower economic growth, rising unemployment, and declining consumer confidence provide the basis to reduce lending. Bank lending is also constrained by the financial conditions of the bank—stricter regulation following 1990 and 2007–2009 as well as the goals of bank management to maintain credit quality and limit delinquencies/charge-offs. Financial conditions of banks as an industry and individual matter. Interesting to note that pre-tax corporate profits has a causal, leading, relationship to tighter standards as would be consistent with the signal of weaker/stronger profits lead banks to alter credit standards.

From the demand side, (Fig. 5.2), there is a clear pattern of weak demand associated with the recession periods as well as a decline in the percentage of small firms looking to borrow before the recession hit. This decline is particularly noticeable prior to the 2002 shutdowns/recession. In contrast, there are

---

[4] The 1990 financial bank crisis/recession was particularly harsh in New England while Texas banks were hard hit in the oil price slump of the 1990s.

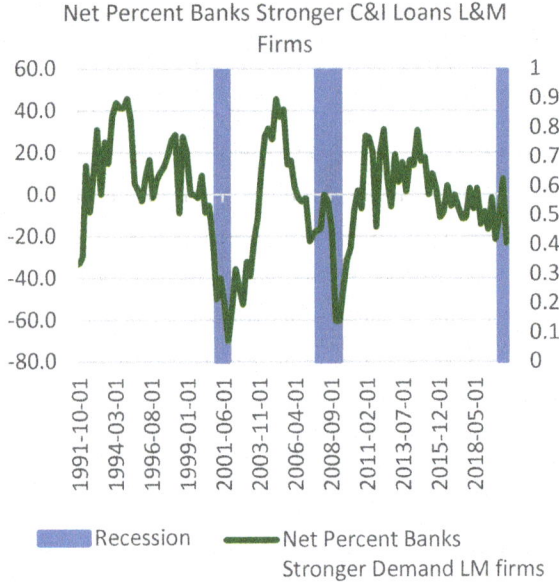

Fig. 5.2 Net percent of banks reporting stronger demand for business loans

structural breaks in the series in 1999 on the downside at the time of recession and then an upward move in 2003 at the start of an economic expansion. As consistent with the linkage between sectors, real final sales have a causal link to C&I loan demand from large- and medium-sized firms.

Beyond the simple cyclical patterns of credit supply and demand, there is a longer-term secular change in the availability of credit from non-bank sources—the "so called' shadow banking industry (Fig. 5.3). The flow of funds to the private, nonfinancial sector reflects the growing influence of non-bank institutions in the financial system. Life Insurance companies and pension funds increased the supply of credit during the 1990, 2001, and 2007–2009 periods. These institutions sought higher yield and shorter maturities than those provided in their traditional long-term investments. Investors seeking exposure to commercial bank loans and their attractive returns—including commercial and multifamily loans (CMBS), residential mortgages (RMBS), credit card loans, and auto loans—have funded special financing vehicles. These vehicles funnel funds from investors to borrowers—traditionally the role of a commercial bank.[5]

---

[5] Even in a recession, there are financial vehicles to deal with distress "Public Real-Estate Companies Are the New Way to Buy Distress," *Wall Street Journal*, June 24, 2020.

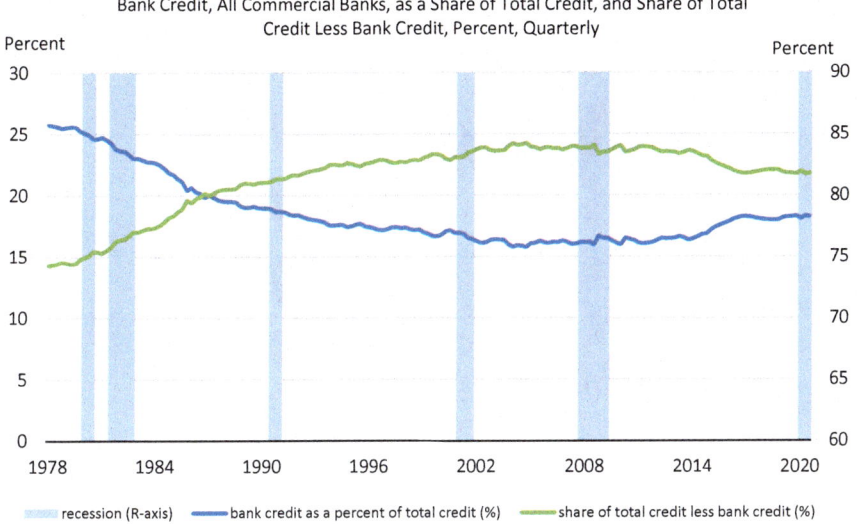

Fig. 5.3 Bank and non-bank shares of credit supply

Consider then the following headline from the Financial Times August 17, 2020. In the latest recession new forms of non-bank lending are appearing to fill in the gaps on bank lending.

"Online loans defy fears of mass delinquencies" FT August 17, 2020.

Yet, surprisingly, the share of credit offered through banks has risen since 2010. Banks remain the minority supplier of credit but their share has risen in recent years.

Supply and Demand for Short-Term Credit

Credit growth, including short-term credit, whether household credit cards, bank loans, bank acceptances, or commercial paper, is highly correlated to growth in the economy (Fig. 5.4). This is the liquidity that keeps the economy moving in the short term.

Demand for short-term credit from a bank, can be expressed in a traditional demand format with demand a function of a measure of output/income, the price of credit where the price is the interest rate as the price of credit, the price of an alternative to bank credit, (for example, commercial paper) and, finally, the wealth or cash position/balance sheet of the borrower.

For simplicity, we can say that households utilize credit cards for daily expenses and take auto loans. For business firms, there is the need to finance

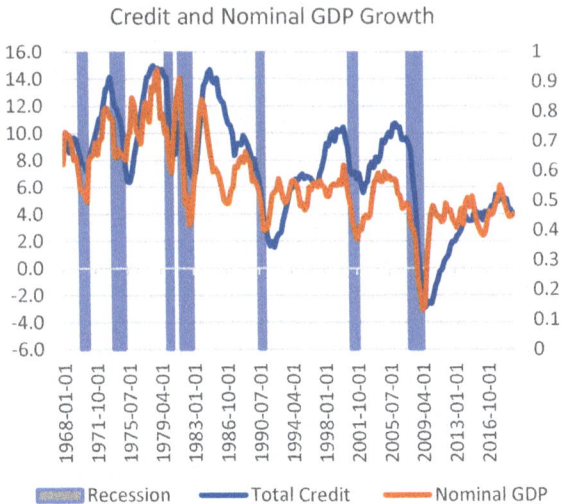

Fig. 5.4 Credit a nominal GDP growth

sort-term assets such as inventories, business equipment, and global letters of credit. In these cases, there is a link between the real economy and the financial sector, each with their own cyclical and secular character. These cyclical and secular patterns are not captured in the traditional comparative static views of comparisons of loan volume or interest rates between two points in time. Global trade relies upon letters of credit.

Between the Lip and the Cup: The Evolution of Credit Demand

At once, we distinguish between the demand for credit from small and medium/large firms. Small firms are more likely to be dependent on bank credit since the cost of alternative financing is likely to be greater and the quality of their balance sheet not as deep as it would be for medium/large firms. Small firms are the dominant form of the firm in the land development/construction business so we expect the impact of credit pricing would be more significant here than for medium/large firms. Fed data shows that the "small" U.S. banks (all banks not in the top 25) hold > 40% of loans in CRE of one form or another. This is partly due to their location—they know the local developers and conditions better than the large banks. In addition, they calculate that many forms of consumer loans have become too expensive for them to offer profitably due to the scale required.

Small firms are likely to have less access to non-bank external capital markets available to the larger banks and are perceived to be more bank-dependent borrowers than large firms.

There is also an issue of asymmetric information, especially for smaller firms, that would not be as well followed/analyzed by market participants. An individual small firm would be better informed of its prospects and internal finance than an outside lender. Therefore, banks and other lenders will specialize in acquiring and processing such information although there remains an information gap. This is also present in the case of individuals whose credit card, installment credit, or auto loans would represent an asymmetric information disadvantage to the bank issuing the credit card, installment credit, or auto loan.[6] This asymmetric information raises the cost of external finance and thereby discourages investment. In the post housing bust period, the once burned lending institutions certainly were more cautious in lending and this was apparent in the slow economic recovery from that period.

For medium/large firms, the pursuit of bridge financing, for M&A purposes for example, would be more prevalent than it is for small firms. The availability of commercial paper as an alternative to a bank loan would be more available to large/medium firms than it would be to small firms (at least until 2007).

Over the last thirty years there has been a growing use of loan commitments—agreement between borrower and lender that allows the borrower to draw down a line of credit at the borrower's discretion assuming the borrower consistently meets certain financial requirements set by the lender. In such cases, both the borrower and lender benefit: the former from the certainty of knowing it can quickly access financing when needed, and the bank from the small fee for providing the quasi-guaranty of funding upon request. This emergence of loan commitments would suggest a smaller response, in the short run, in any additional loan demand, outside of the commitments, to any given change in bank loan rates than otherwise.

We can distinguish the behavior of small as opposed to medium/large firms demand for bank credit by examining the series released in the Fed's Senior Loan Officer Opinion Survey.

In Fig. 5.2, we can view the patterns of changes in the net percent of large/medium firms and that of small firms that are reporting stronger demand for credit.

---

[6] Douglas W. Diamond, "Financial Intermediation and Delegated Monitoring," *Review of Economic Studies*, 51 (July): 393–414.

Supply of short-term credit also follows the fundamentals of all supply curves. Supply is some function of perceived output/income prospects, the interest rate, the cost of alternative financing, and the quality of the borrower. There is one more condition—the quality of the lender. As evidenced since 1990, the quality of the lender and its capital constraints has put a limit on the bank's supply of credit. Over the economic factors listed above is the regulatory caution present which is also a cyclical factor.

Between the Lip and the Cup: The Evolution of Credit Supply

On the supply side, the emergence of the non-banking (shadow) sector, as illustrated earlier in Fig. 5.3, has been a significant factor in the provision of credit as banking regulations have increasingly limited the ability of banks to provide credit in an economic expansion. In fact, this emergence has been even more significant since the 2009 financial constraints placed on banks. Within the banking sector, the structural break in the loan/deposit ratio (Fig. 5.5) provides a long-term, dynamic, perspective to the analysis of short-term lending. Given the downshift in the loan/deposit ratio, any change in policy rates/central bank provision of reserves to banks, is likely to have less of an expansionary impact of credit availability than in the past. Moreover,

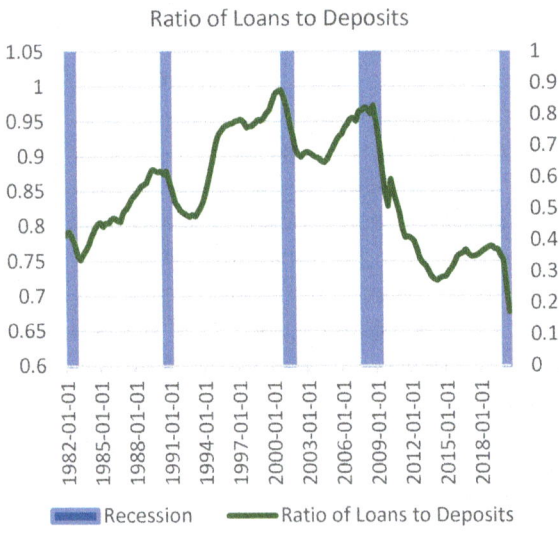

Fig. 5.5 Ratio of loans to deposits

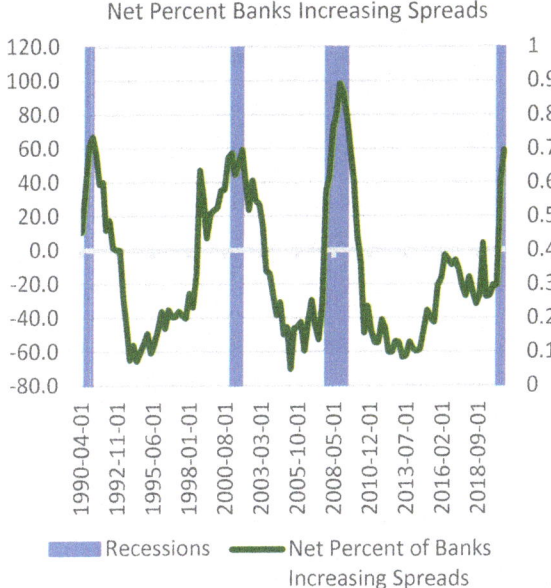

Fig. 5.6 Net percentage of banks increasing spreads on loans

the loan/deposit ratio of the largest U.S. banks and the small U.S. banks has diverged meaningfully since 2009.

A second distinction on the supply side is that the cost of information on lending to small versus medium/large firms will be significantly different including access to obtaining independent credit ratings which tend to focus on larger companies seeking access to the capital markets. Therefore, the higher cost of lending would likely be witnessed in a move to tighter lending standards especially in a period of economic weakness.

Finally, medium/larger firms would have more financing options, and this may lead to lower lending costs to medium/large firms given the competitive pressures on bank pricing.

Under what conditions does the supply of credit change during the economic cycle? How do we look at both the price (interest rate) and credit standards as a signal of changing credit availability? First, the actual interest rate charged on nearly all bank loans is a base rate (prime, Fed funds, LIBOR, SOFR[7]) plus a spread. The banks cannot do much about the base rate, but they obviously have great control over the spread Fig. 5.6. As evident in the Figure, there is a strong procyclical pattern to the spread—increasing sharply

---

[7] SOFR, the Secured Overnight Financing Rate, has its own issues as discussed in "The Fed's Libor Replacement Would Shackle Small Banks," *Wall Street Journal*, December 18, 2019.

just before and into a recession and then declining with the economic expansion. Credit standards do vary over the economic cycle, along with the price of credit, and the availability of credit reflects the size of the firm.

There is the fascinating pattern of commercial banks altering the spread on loans versus the cost of funds. The spread has a strong cyclical pattern thereby amplifying the procyclical pattern of bank credit in the financial system. Moreover, there is an association of wider spreads in 1994–1995, 1999–2000, and again most recently in 2016–2018 with an increase in the federal funds rate.

In contrast, the spikes in the spread (1990–1991, 2001, 2007–2009, and of course 2020) are associated with recessions but also a possible behavioral pattern at commercial banks where spreads represent an attempt to retain some bank margins and limit new credit given the deterioration of loan quality associated with a recession. High yield and AA corporate spreads have a causal link to increasing bank lending spreads as would be consistent with an increasingly cautious approach to offering credit by both commercial banks and creditors in general.

Short-Term Credit: Just in Time Finance

Trend and cycle are characteristic of the demand for, and provision of, credit over the economic cycle. Within the context of the economy, and the interaction between the real and financial sides of the economy, growth in the economy tends to drive growth in the demand for credit. There is a procyclical bias in the demand for credit as illustrated in Fig. 5.2. Moreover, changes in the willingness and ability of banks to extend credit have implications for economic growth.

To reinforce the procyclical bias, there is also a tendency for the loan/deposit ratio of banks (Fig. 5.5) to rise with an economic expansion as depositors employed their deposits for investing in growth opportunities, and borrowers seek loans for the same reasons. Even more so, credit standards, as evidence by the Federal Reserve's Senior Loan Office Survey, tend to ease as the economy improves and tighten as the economy weakens as banks seek to improve profitability in "good times" and limit profit declines in "bad times." Indeed, the procyclical pattern for credit is apparent on both the supply and demand side of the credit market.

Secular, not just cyclical, characteristics appear in the behavior of the loan-deposit ratio at commercial banks. Over the 1980s and 1990s economic cycles, loans expanded relative to deposits as banks employed a more intensive application of their funds to lending in an expanding economy. For the

1990–1991 recession, the decline in bank capital reduced the ability of banks to lend. Banks themselves were dependent on external finance, thereby raising their opportunity cost of funds and thereby made banks less willing to lend.[8] When recession hits, there is a retrenchment in bank lending.

Up until the 2010–2019 expansion, the intensive use of loans relative to deposits rose in the prior three cycles. Then, it stopped. During the 2010–2019 cycle, there is no cyclical uptrend. The heavy bank regulation imposed by Dodd-Frank legislation lead to the structural change in the cyclical pattern of the loan/deposit ratio.

Bank lending has become more cautious, and this helps explain the recent modest economic growth.

The loan–deposit ratio also reveals several structural breaks in the series at key points where recessions were followed by more restrictive financial regulation and subsequent new legislation altered the risk/reward ratio for bank lending, as evidenced in 1990 (Financial Institutions Reform, Recovery, and Enforcement Act of 1989, also known as FIRREA), 2000 (Sarbanes Oxley, 2002) and 2008/2009. The latest being the Dodd-Frank Act. The cyclical upswings in the loan/deposit ratio ended abruptly, as regulatory reaction to the perceived excesses of the expansion came to produce a recessionary period. Regulation directly constrains the ability of banks to make new loans based on their models before each recession. Lending continues but how it is done, and its standards, evolve.

Lending is far more restrictive post-2009 indicating more bank caution but also a more restrictive regulatory regime. In part, this also helps explain the slower pace of overall economic growth post-2007 since we know that the pace of credit growth is linked to the overall pace of economic growth and vice versa. There is also the issue of limited liability/risk aversion since home mortgage borrowers did not bear the full cost of home price collapse—many just walked away. Given the incentive to flip homes in many cases, home buying was more risky (adverse selection) than in the traditional home buying to live in approach.[9] Going forward, lenders would be more cautious and likely charge a premium to lend via fees, interest rates and higher down payments. Banks were not the only lenders in the 2002–2007 era, though the system that grew during that time did mean the banks didn't need to be as risk-averse in credit selection because they were not the ultimate holder of

---

[8] Ben Bernanke and Cara Lown, "The Credit Crunch," *Brookings Papers on Economic Activity*, 1991, no. 2: 205–247.
[9] Adverse selection is associated with the paper "The Market for Lemons: Quality Uncertainty and the Market Mechanism" by George Akerlof, *Quarterly Journal of Economics*, 1970, 84, no. 3 (August): 488–500.

the loan. Of course, there were many culprits: borrowers, investors, ratings agencies, and federal/state regulators.

Credit cycles also reinforce the importance of recognizing cognitive biases in our thinking. Principles of prudence appear to be forgotten when money is involved. When both the demand and supply of short-term credit are procyclical and credit standards are loosened, there is an apparent, not real, demand and supply for economic activity (home purchases, auto loans, business inventories) that cannot be justified by the longer-run outlook for sustainable real economic activity. Too many homes are built, too many autos are bought, too much inventory is carried. That is to say, the cycle of credit availability exceeded the underlying trend growth of the economy. This is observed clearly in Fig. 5.4[10] for the period from 2002 to 2007.

Evolution of Short-Term Credit Markets

Beyond the basic supply/demand framework, numerous developments have added several slips from the cup. First, the emergence of loan commitments and their growth since the late 1970s has weakened the link between changes in Fed policy and the alteration of lending rates and restrictions on credit demand. This creates two classes of borrowers—restrictive policy actions do impact business borrowers without a loan commitment (most likely smaller banks). Second, meanwhile larger banks have been more affected by policy changes given the changes in capital requirements and limited dividend distributions. Finally, for policy, the lag between policy changes and business borrowing can be variable and longer given the numerous regulatory guidance requirements in implementing any law.

Second, the emergence of nonbank credit sources, especially for consumer and real estate loans, has provided competitive pressures on banks and thereby limited their pricing/covenant power over time. Second, there is the non-banking credit market. While regulators have squeezed the banking sector, the real action and innovation, remains in the non-banking arena. Many commentators will mention that bank lending has been modest this economic expansion. However, the Federal Reserve's data reveals that most of the short-term credit growth has occurred in the non-banking arena[11]—see WSJ references on this. Squeeze the credit balloon here, the air goes somewhere

---

[10] An Asian proverb meaning that even when things seem certain, something can go wrong. The task may seem simple, like drinking from a **cup**, but a lot can still go wrong.

[11] "Apollo Launches Platform to Make Big Loans," *Wall Street Journal*, July 6, 2020; also, "Fintech Can Come Out of the Shadows," *Wall Street Journal*, September 10, 2020.

else. The growth of shadow banking system has, in many ways, made banks far less important in the transmission of credit and lending than in the past.

Introduce Change: Dynamism as the True Character of Credit Markets—Not a Move from One Equilibrium to Another

Cyclical Pattern of Bank Lending

Short-Term Credit: Both a Supply and Demand Story

Credit is both a short-term and intermediate-term story—as well as both a supply- and demand-side story. Moreover, much commentary cites credit data as if it is a demand phenomenon, whereas the credit numbers we see are the result of both sides of the scissors. Finally, short-term credit has both cyclical and secular patterns. All this means is that the analyst must stay on watch as the markets continue to turn. Measuring the growth of loans is not the same as measuring demand and we would be well served to recognize both demand and supply forces.

Total Loans at commercial banks exhibit a cyclical character associated with changes in Fed policy as well as recessions (Fig. 5.7). This would be expected since real final sales, the NYSE index, and the PCE deflator have causal links to total loans of commercial banks—an example of the extensive

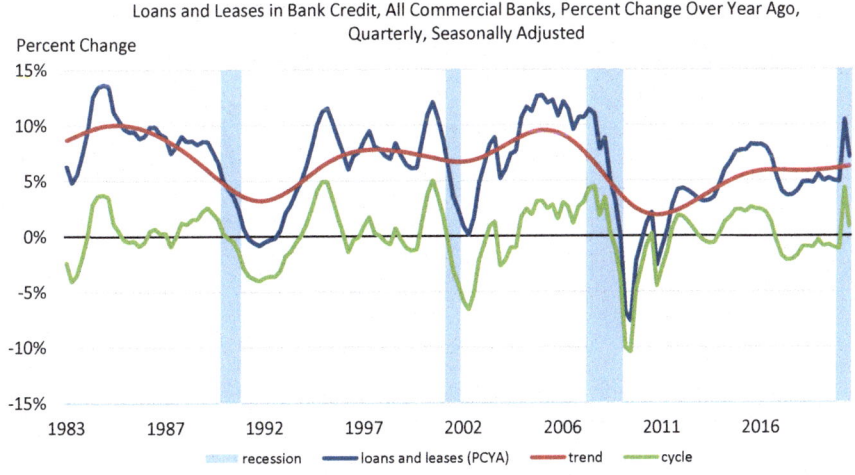

Fig. 5.7 Bank loan growth since 1984

link between real and financial sectors in the economy. Therefore, there are at least two factors influencing the pace of loan growth which we can see evidenced.

Focusing on Commercial & Industrial Loans as Cyclical Barometer

Commercial and industrial lending by banks has a strong procyclical character to its behavior, as illustrated in Fig. 5.7. Everyone is to blame here. On the demand side, business firms retrench sharply as recession nears (2000–2001) or at the start of the recession (2007–2008). Business borrowing reflects the fundamentals of expected final sales, interest rates, and cash on hand as an alternative to external finance at banks. Without a positive view of economic growth, firms will not borrow no matter what the interest rate.

One interaction between the real economy and the credit market is reflected in the pattern of movements between real business investment and commercial and industrial (C&I) loans (Fig. 5.8). Unfortunately, both series are highly volatile, highly cyclical, and therefore, their timing of mutual interests is unsatisfied. Equipment spending picks up quickly early in the economic recovery (e.g., 1983–1984, 1992–1994) but bank lending lags as evident in the 1990 and 2000 economic recovery. This pattern is even more obvious in the 2010 expansion. Increased regulation for banks limited the

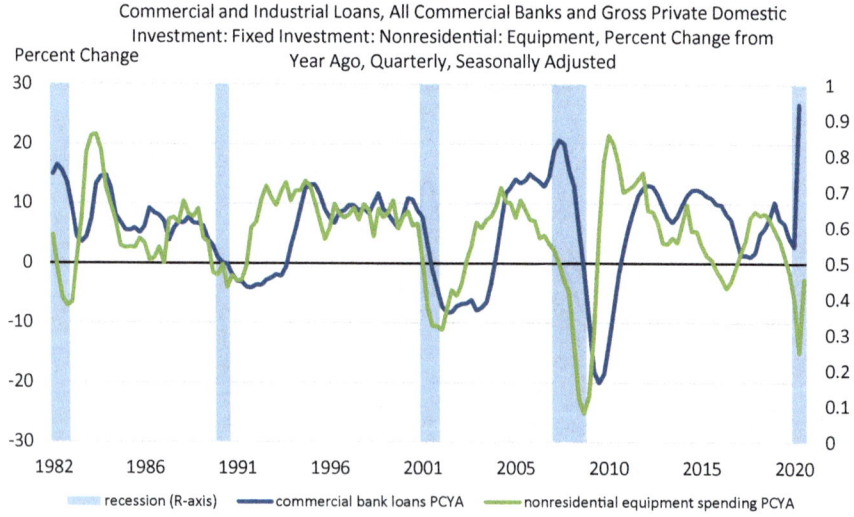

Fig. 5.8 Bank loans and business equipment spending

recovery of bank credit, and, even today, the pace of bank lending significantly lags the pace of earlier expansions. This opened the door wider for suppliers of non-bank credit. Bank lending on the credit side, therefore, has a clear link to the real side of the economy. This link reinforces the lesson that the slow growth in credit post-2010 was a significant explanatory factor in slower business investment in the 2010–2019 expansion.

Commercial and industrial lending has a strong procyclical element in its behavior. On the demand side, firms are likely to retrench at times of recession (shaded areas) and economic weakness/uncertainty (1985, 1998) for example. Without a clear, positive, vision of the strength of the economy, firms will remain cautious on going to the borrowing window. Meanwhile, on the supply side, banks will be cautious to lend in a recession period and periods of economic uncertainty. Moreover, the depth of the decline during the 2008/2009 period reflects the influence of the extent for financial regulation.

To emphasize the structural shift in bank/non-bank lending, note how bank lending slowed in 2014–2016 despite the strength of equipment spending.

The Bank Credit Cycle: Mean-Reverting but the Credit Cycle Remains

The Federal Reserve reports a bank's willingness to make loans on a quarterly basis as part of the Senior Loan Officer Opinion Survey. Such a qualitative measure is telling of lender expectations and is often consulted to predict the coming credit conditions in the market. A bank's willingness to make loans is a stationary series, which contains no structural breaks. That is, the series acts in a predictable nature, allowing one to refer to it as a benchmark to assess lending practices over a business cycle. At the beginning of an expansionary period, as banks are very willing to extend credit, the series rises. Once reaching its peak, a bank's willingness gradually decreases until turning negative during a recessionary period.

Yet, bank standards did not react in a uniform, timely manner with respect to recoveries and recessions. For example, the net percent of banks tightening credit on mortgage loans in 2000 barely rose at all, but the tightening on both small and large/medium firms for C&I loans was significant. In the 2007–2009 period, credit standards were tightened significantly more for mortgages and credit cards than non-CRE commercial loans. Changes in lending standards are not a "one-size-fits-all" decision –they are often different across loan categories.

When we examine the history of bank standards in recent economic expansions, there is a clear cyclical pattern, and surprising to some, there is a clear pattern of banks tightening credit for commercial real estate before the recession. Bank credit standards tightened in 1999–2000 and before the 2001 recession (Fig. 5.9). Again, bank standards tightened beginning in 2005 before the 2007 recession. One can claim that standards were not tightened sooner or enough to avoid a recession. However, two points are critical here. One, bank lending standards are clearly procyclical. Standards ease early in recoveries and then tighten later in the economic expansion. Second, tighter standards do accompany economic slowdowns. The cause and effect here run both ways. The results illustrate the highly cyclical pattern of credit standards in the 1990 to 2010 period.

Changes in the credit markets are not simply a result of recessionary shocks. The Federal Reserve's April 2017 Senior Loan Officer Opinion Survey (SLOOS), which roughly corresponds to Q1 2017, points to a general slowdown in loan demand for businesses and consumers. Reports of tightening lending standards varied across loan categories, however.

Large and small businesses demand for loans has been moderating since the start of 2016. Domestic and foreign banks reported weaker loan demand on net over the first quarter. Notably, the slowdown in commercial & industrial (C&I) loan growth does not appear to be due to stricter lending standards alone as banks reported no significant net tightening. Reduced demand and higher loan pricing were also factors, as both demand and supply sides of

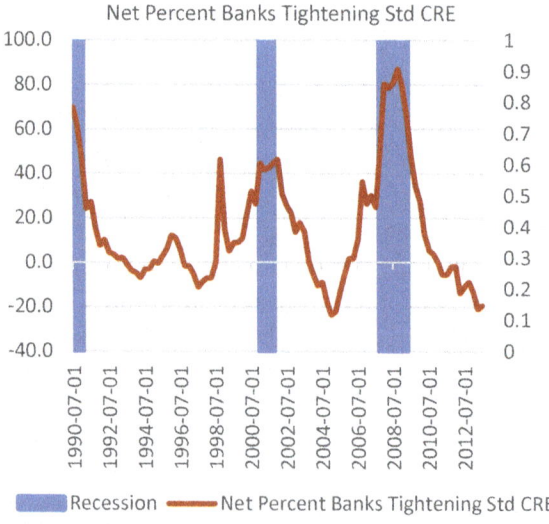

Fig. 5.9 Net percent of banks tightening standards—CRE loans

the credit market determine the pace of loan growth. The survey showed a modest net easing for C&I loans by domestic banks, but a slight tightening by foreign banks. Cycles matter in the credit markets and not all cycles lead to recessions—or booms. In the current expansion, the net percent of banks tightening standards on commercial real estate for nonfarm, nonresidential structures evidenced a modest tightening in 2016, as oil prices declined from mid-2014 to early 2016 and growth in real final sales slowed in 2015 and 2016, then a very muted pattern until 2020.

The tone of bank regulatory authorities and the regulations themselves both have an impact on bank capital and the pace of bank lending. Moreover, if there is a greater expectation for domestic economic growth, then both bank and non-bank credit will expand. Significant liquidity in the banking system will also allow for the increase in the supply of credit. As a result, interest rates may not rise as much or as quickly as some analysts would project. There is a certain degree of flexibility in the bank credit process depending on the willingness of banks to lend and regulators to allow an expansion of lending.

The Cyclical Character of Credit Remains After 2009

We have another way to cut at the character of both the demand and supply of credit over the business cycle. The Fed's Senior Loan Officer Opinion Survey offers us a view of the cyclical patterns for both the demand and supply side of the bank credit/loan market.[12] For example, the net percentage of banks reporting stronger consumer loan demand (Fig. 5.10) rose consistently from 2011 to 2014 as would be consistent with the economic recovery. However, on the business side, beginning at the end of 2015 and throughout 2016, there was a distinct slowdown in business equipment spending and structures that would be consistent with the decline in banks reporting stronger demand for C&I loans. Two points are essential to our understanding. The slowdown in the percentage of banks reporting strong demand corroborates the real economy slowdown for investment. Second, the slowdown in both real spending and credit demand reemphasizes the importance of looking beyond a single market to understand the linkages between sectors such as products/growth and credit.

For both financial regulators and credit market participants, the evolution of the economy has been accompanied by the evolution of financial markets.

---

[12] For an earlier take on these cycles see John A. Weinberg, "Cycles in Lending Standards?" *Federal Reserve Bank of Richmond Economic Quarterly*, 1995, 81, no. 3 (Summer).

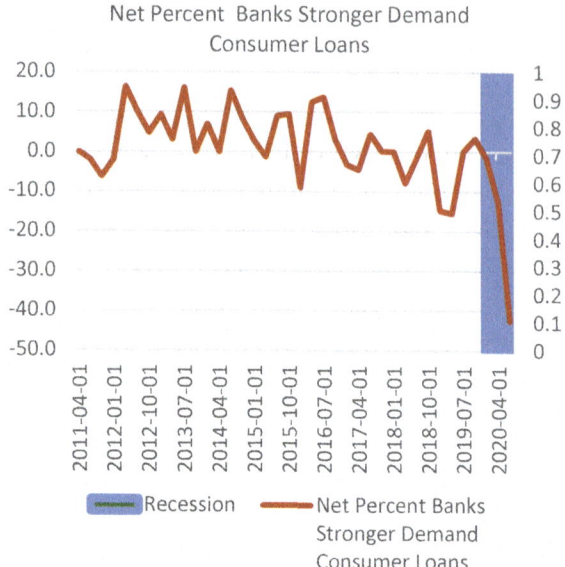

Fig. 5.10 Net percent of banks reporting stronger demand consumer loans

While legislation and rules today may appear to "fix" the financial system, the evolution of an evolutionary economic reality will dictate new methods to finance new economic initiatives in the future.

Profits: Actual and Expected Part of Cyclical Demand

Corporate profits as a share of GDP (Fig. 5.11) appear to follow a cyclical pattern in which they gradually increase, peaking late in an expansionary period, before steadily declining during a recession. However, pre-tax corporate profits are non-stationary, and thereby are a less predictable series. Although profit growth as a percent of GDP appears to follow a traditional peak to trough trend, there have also been various structural breaks within the series leading to highly irregular and quite misleading judgments based on prior trends. Although this might not be very surprising, the larger decline being in the 2001 recessionary period seems unusual. The greatest decline in corporate profits would be assumed to have occurred during the Great Recession, as we saw dramatic movements in a bank's willingness to lend as well as households acquiring record amounts of debt. That is, one might suspect a similar case of dramatics in the decline of profits during the Great Recession; however, the drop was more significant in 2001.

Fig. 5.11 Corporate pre-tax profits as percent of nominal GDP

Profit expectations are essential factors for both the demand and supply of credit. On the demand for credit, it is the expectation of profits that prompts a firm or entrepreneur to seek credit. On the supply side, it is the expectation of profits in an enterprise that prompts a bank to extend credit. Pre-tax corporate profits have a causal link to real estate and commercial loan standards as well as an intriguing link to residential mortgage delinquency rates. There is also the causal link to the net interest margin at banks.

Credit Per-Covid Shutdowns: How Did It Look?

A More Resilient Financial System—The Fed

In late 2018 Vice Chairman Quarles provided testimony to the *Supervision and Regulation Report House Financial Services Committee*. At that time, he stated that "the banking sector remains in strong condition, in line with strong U.S. economic *performance, with lending growth, fewer nonperforming loans, and strong overall profitability.*

Large institutions are well capitalized and liquid, and their capital planning and liquidity-risk-management processes are improving. Ninety-nine percent of regional and community banks are currently well capitalized, and supervisory recommendations made to smaller firms during the financial crisis have largely been closed."

This report is a twice-a-year snapshot. For decision-makers, how can we make a dynamic, ongoing assessment of credit quality using publicly available information? We have used three sources in the past to provide a more dynamic ongoing video of credit quality thereby avoiding a reliance on the semiannual snapshot.

Senior Loan Office Opinion Survey—Demand and Supply Sides of the Credit Market

In summary, there are two sides of the credit transaction—a buyer/borrower on the demand side and a lender, banks, and nonbanks, on the supply side. Unfortunately, movements in credit measures are frequently referred to as movements in credit demand—that is incorrect—reported credit measures are the intersection of supply and demand sides of the credit market. Tighter credit standards provide a benchmark for the supply side. On the demand side, banks report on the demand for consumer and residential loans as well as construction/multifamily loans. We have reviewed this survey earlier. Shadow banking has taken on growing importance although the creativity of shadow banking developments limits the quantitative assessment, the qualitative importance grows over time with rising concerns about an old nemesis—leverage.[13]

FDIC: Quality Standards for the Banking System Itself

On a quarterly schedule, the Federal Deposit Insurance Corporation (FDIC) issues a report (Quarterly Banking Profile) that provides several benchmarks to directly assess the quality of the banking system, based on the financial performance and the condition of the regulated institutions. The FDIC report indicated that net operating income and net income for banks had improved and net interest margins (Fig. 5.12) had also risen into early 2019. Higher net interest income helps lift bank earnings. However, as evidenced in Fig. 5.12 there are both a secular and cyclical pattern to net interest margins. Net interest margin is the difference between the interest income generated by banks and the amount of interest paid out to their lenders, relative to the amount of interest earning assets.

---

[13] "Private Equity Owners Pile on Leverage to Pay Themselves Dividends," *Financial Times*, September 17, 2020.

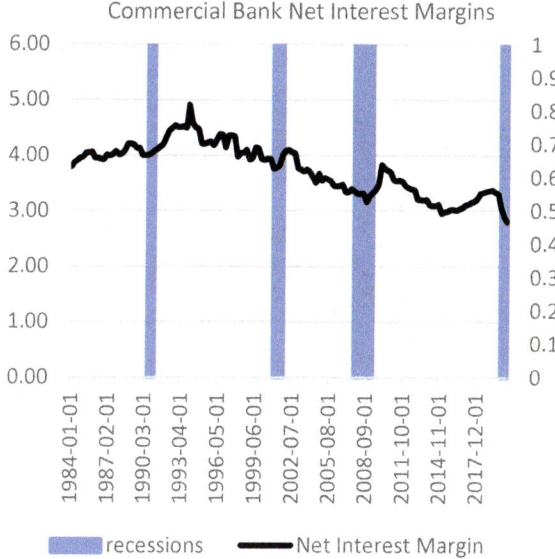

Fig. 5.12 Net interest margins at banks

Net interest margins have a causal link to credit standards and total loans as would be expected given that margins are an incentive to lend and impact the setting of credit standards.

The Federal Reserve had been gradually tightening monetary policy since December 2015, raising the federal funds rate to 1.50 from 0.25% over that period. As a result, the net interest margin at banks had improved helping boost revenues and earnings—until the COVID pandemic hit when interest rates fell quickly and materially reduced the net interest margin for the industry—probably for a while. Yet, this mid-cycle increase in margins is facing the secular winds of lower margins as bank competition from non-banking institutions reduces the pricing power for banks on the lending side. Meanwhile, competitors have risen to compete for bank deposits, especially since the early 1980s, in the form of money market funds.

Charge-off rates, Fig. 5.13, rise with the economic expansion and peak shortly after the recovery/expansion begins. What is distinctive is that the erosion of credit quality came about gradually prior to the 1991 and 2001 peaks but very rapidly, and dramatically, prior to the 2009–2010 peak. There was, until the 2009/2010 period both a secular rise in charge-off rates as well as cyclical peaks as the recession ended.

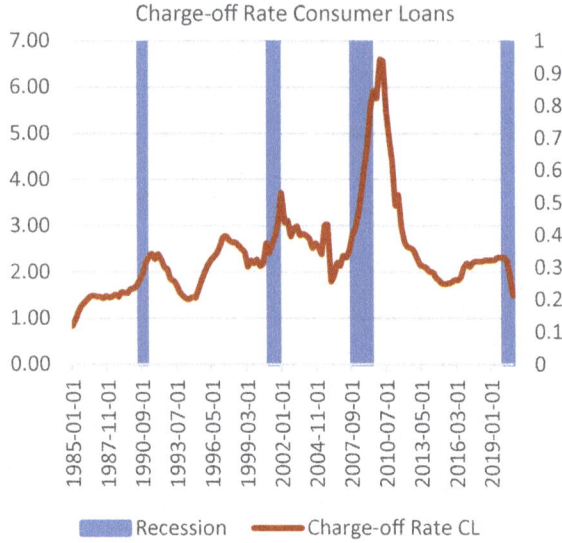

Fig. 5.13 Charge-off rates consumer loans

Delinquencies on the Decline: Welcome Sign

The delinquency data on bank balance sheets are one of the more useful segments of the report and provides insight into potential risks in financial markets. Single Family Residential delinquency rates (Fig. 5.14) rose dramatically in late 2007 and then peaked in 2010 and have gradually returned to pre-housing bust levels.

C &I loan delinquency rates rise just before the recession starts (Fig. 5.15) although the extent of the increase is not enough, except in 2000, to give analysts enough time to identify a recession on the horizon. Delinquencies peak after the recovery/expansion is underway. As anticipated, real final sales, as well as the equity index NYSE) have a causal link to commercial loan delinquency rates.

On the consumer stage, credit card delinquencies evidenced the most significant spike in 2007–2008 in its history since the data started in 1991. Delinquency rates for commercial real estate hardly moved during the 2000 recession but rose dramatically during 2007–2009.

A less accommodative stance on monetary policy, and thus higher interest rates, have far reaching economic implications. While certain market participants such as banks may see an uptick in earnings on the back of a higher net interest margin, consumers who finance purchases with credit may start to feel the squeeze.

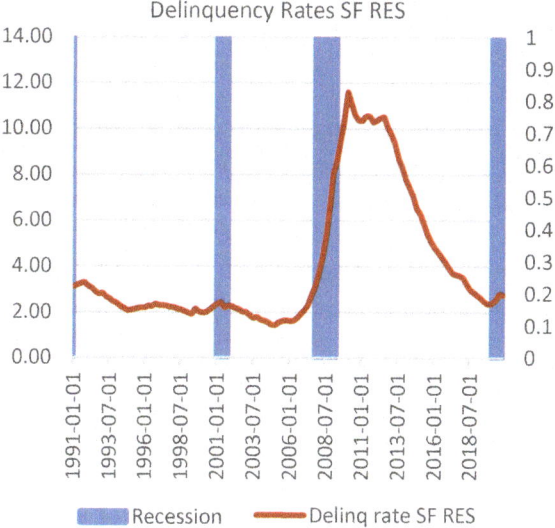

Fig. 5.14 Delinquency rates single-family residences

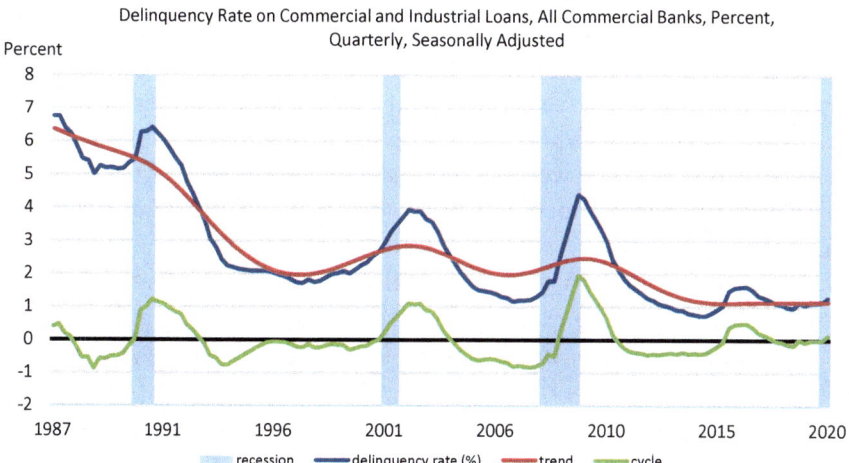

Fig. 5.15 Delinquency rates C&I loans

Delinquency rates for C&I loans (Fig. 5.15) had consistently declined in each of the economic expansions since 1982. Delinquency rates for consumer loans and consumer credit loans also show a cyclical pattern with the highest peaks since 1988 during the 2007–2009 period for both types of loans.

The reserve coverage ratio (loan loss reserves relative to total noncurrent loan balances) had evidenced a similar cyclical pattern. The Federal Deposit Insurance Corporation (FDIC) also offers data for different geographic regions of the United States so there is some interesting regional data. The FDIC Quarterly Banking profile showed total loans and leases grew steadily to the end of 2019.

Cycles within the economic expansion and across regions can be quite varied. Noncurrent C&I loan rates rose from Q1-2015 to Q1-2017, even though the pace of real growth in the economy remained positive and improved noticeably from 2016 to 2017. Yet, there was little improvement in noncurrent loan rates as well as significant variation between FDIC administrative regions. For example, the Dallas region continued to have problems due to low oil prices while urban regions such as Chicago and San Francisco showed improvement. Within the national economic expansion, there exists both improvement and deterioration across regions. Our lesson is that credit performance on loans requires a view of both national and regional developments, reflecting an earlier note on regional bank failures and prior regional recessions (New England, 1990–1991 and Texas, mid-1980s).

Short-Term Credit: Aftermath

Two problems confound our assessment of short-term credit. First, credit is provided today but the payback for credit cards, autos, business loans occurs in the future—a future whose economic tenor may be, and often is, quite different than today. The worst of loans is made in the best of times. All the loans have been made, lenders and borrowers reach an agreement. Now what? What is the aftermath?

Quality in credit, as in wine, is revealed only with the passage of time. Loans are made with the expectations, we assume, moral hazard aside, that the loan is paid off over time. Yet, we know that the quality of the loan will reflect the behavior of the economy, interest rates, and corporate profits. When expectations do not meet actual outcomes then the fun begins. As of January 1, 2020, banks are now required to reserve for every loan its estimated lifetime loss upfront. Prior to 2020 reserving was done as needed (essentially assuming all loans are good until proven otherwise). This could have a dampening effect on loans with high loss content (credit cards, riskier commercial real estate) or long maturities (mortgages). This is a material change on how the cost of credit is handled going forward versus the past.

Over time, net interest margin at commercial banks have declined. For banks, the steady decline in the net interest margin since 1996 has reinforced the importance of credit quality in the portfolio as a lower net interest margin represents a low margin for error in loan origination. On average most banks generate 65–70% of revenue from net interest income. Largest banks are close to 55–60% due to having greater sources of non-interest revenue (fees, capital markets, asset management, etc.).

Noncurrent Loan Rates: Paint It Black

Noncurrent loan rates have a strong cyclical pattern. This is certainly true for the four major loan types: real estate, C&I, credit cards, and other loans to individuals. This pattern is most obvious for all four types in the latest recession period, but there was a noticeably short, practically none in real time, lead time to highlight a potential economic downturn. Historically, credit quality would be considered a lagging indicator but noncurrent loan rates for C&I loans rose before the 2001 recession and were concurrent with the 2007–2009 recession. Note in this latter case, unfortunately, noncurrent loan rates for real estate gave no warning of the devastation to come in 2007–2009—indeed the pattern here gives credence to the view that the bubble did burst—no slow letting air out of the balloon. As the latest twist, note how noncurrent loan rates rose tracking the slowdown in the economy from 2015 to 2017. Recognition of the interaction between economic growth and credit quality is an essential aspect of good due diligence.

Charge-Off Rates—High & Dry

Unfortunately, at some point, some of the noncurrent loan brethren fall by the wayside into the charge-off bin (Fig. 5.13). Here we can observe two phenomena. First, there is a tendency for charge-off rates to rise going into/during a recession (1990–1991, 2001, 2008–2010) or in a period of economic slowdown (1996–1997). The pattern of charge-off rates reflects the influence of economic forces of growth and policy actions. The interaction of credit quality, noncurrent loans, and charge-offs, with the cyclical character of economic growth, is intriguing as there is no simple link. Sometimes credit quality leads, sometimes it is coincident.

Second, what is also intriguing is the link between interest rates and credit quality. The rise in charge-off rates in 1989–1990 followed a rise in the federal funds rate in early 1989 as well as the lower oil prices hurting Texas borrowers, and a deep recession in New England. The rise in charge-off rates in the mid-1990s followed the rise in the federal funds rate in 1994 and early 1995. This pattern repeats in 1999, 2006, and even in 2015–2017.

Distinguishing expected versus actual is essential in economics and money management—no different for bank lending. Changes in credit quality follow periods where the pace of economic growth disappoints relative to expectations while the rise in the federal funds rate exceeds expectations. The difference between expected and actual outcomes remains a driver of economic and financial activity and provides a dynamic character to both.

The Special Situations File: Banking and the 1990 Recession

The recession of July 1990 to March 1991 was a particularly interesting case of the interaction of bank credit and economic growth.[14] Commercial bank loan growth slowed in the second half of 1990. There were issues at the time of loan quality, capital constraints, and stricter regulation. Already by late 1989, banks had begun to tighten credit standards due to a deteriorating loan performance. This period reinforced our observation that financial conditions and the state of the economy are strongly linked.

But this period also exhibited a shift to non-depository intermediation— a shift to offset the effects of reduced bank lending, that gave rise to a phenomenon of shadow banking, where lending sources broadened to Life Insurance Companies and Pension Funds, for example, and then began to include investor-financed funds sponsored by asset manager or hedge funds. The emergence of shadow banking became more obvious in the pre-2007 period of housing finance and, since the 2007–2009 recession, the emergence of nonbank finance has become essential to supporting the economic expansion.

Decision-Making as an Essential Ingredient: Evidence of Intellectual Bias in the Credit Cycle

A review of both noncurrent loan rates and charge-off behavior intimate that regulators, borrowers, and lenders react to recent events, a recency bias, out of line with the longer-term trend of the economy and credit risk. As for regulators, they appear to always fight the last war. They regulate the area that just caused a crisis, sowing the seeds for the next crisis in some other area. For example, having regulated the banking system so tightly, the

---

[14] See "Loan Quality and How It Reflects the Overall Economy," Remarks by Governor Olson, February 28, 2005 at the Government Affairs Conference of the Credit Union National Association.

area of shadow banking has now become a major concern.[15] For example, charge-off rates react very quickly to a rise of interest rates and weakness in the economy. Consumer charge-off rates tend to be highly correlated to changes in the unemployment rate—specifically non-mortgage consumer credit. While the economic fundamentals, in turn, would indicate a stronger economy in 1994–1997 and again 2003–2006, the speed of reduction in charge-offs indicates that banks responded very quickly to the improvement in the economy by reducing charge-offs. However, in addition, the loss rate quickly declined, due, in part, to quick changes in underwriting standards. This speed of response on both the up and downside would reinforce the procyclical patterns of credit availability. Interesting to observe the interaction of frameworks for both decision-making and economic activity.

Normalization of deviance was very evident in the housing boom/bust cycle. Delinquency rates on adjustable rate mortgages were already moving up in 2006 relative to 2005 and up again in 2007.[16] Yet, the pace of home buying and the rising price of homes kept the boom going even though the boom reflected massive credit leniency and not economic fundamentals related to affordability over the long run.

Even earlier, November 2006, the signals of excess were already in place and documented.[17] As reported at that time, delinquent ARM loan balances were up in the United States, California, Nevada, Florida for both prime and subprime borrowers as of the second quarter of each year. Meanwhile, the excess availability of credit was apparent as the net percent of banks increasing spreads to small firms was at a negative 45% in early 2006 implying lenders were highly accommodative for such loans. Not to be outdone, the CDS investment grade less Corporate Investment Grade Index basis had declined to less than 10 from 25% a year earlier implying investors also believed credit losses would remain at benign levels into the future. High yield BBB CLOs spreads had declined to less than 150 basis points in mid-2006 from over 300 basis points in early 2003. Across the markets, there was little room for error, never mind a housing bust.

Also, the framing bias comes into play in the credit process. When a decision-maker anticipates problems, that frame makes them cautious. When

---

[15] "Fed's Quarles Says Market Turmoil Triggered by Covid-19 Revealed Fragile Non-Bank System," *Wall Street Journal*, October 21, 2020.
[16] John E. Silvia, "Economic Outlook: The Role of Finance," February 26, 2007, FRB-Atlanta Banking Industry Outlook.
[17] John E. Silvia, "Supervisory Challenges at the Mid-Cycle of the Economic Expansion," November 6, 2006, presented at the Interagency Bank Supervision Conference, November 6–7 at the William Seidman Center, Arlington, VA.

a decision-maker sees opportunity, that allows for more risk-taking. This framing bias also adds to the procyclical character of credit.

5a. Aftershock

Cyclical and structural change illustrate the evolution of this lending from both the demand and supply side. The evidence of the Senior Loan Officer Opinion Survey provides an interesting cyclical perspective for both demand and supply of credit.

Stimulus to Action: Whatever the Intentions, Action, and Inaction, Have Their Impacts

The essence of monetary policy is to set an interest rate, distinct from current market rates, to alter the current economic landscape to move toward an economic status more consistent with what the central bank views as sustainable with its policy objectives. These objectives are associated with stable, low inflation, and full employment. No matter what the honorable intentions of the central bank, the impact is to create a disequilibrium and thereby lead to market price adjustments in several markets. Central bank policy purposely alters the allocation of credit in an economy to slow or speed up economic activity to what the central bank perceives as sustainable over time. Policies that alter credit allocation will alter market prices, whether in credit, equity, product, or exchange rate markets.

> Investors should not ignore the supportive role played by suppressed government bond yields, and how they will shape the performance of equity and credit from here. 08 21 2020 FT

Over an exceptionally long period, the secular climb in benchmark rates from 1968 to 1980 altered the relative returns between bonds, equities, and real assets. From the peak in 1981 to 2020, the process was reversed. In recent years, the era of administered rates, especially suppressed short-term two-year rates, has created a new set of financial incentives to alter asset prices. Treasury benchmark rates have a causal link to bank credit standards and thereby provide a link between benchmark rates and the availability of bank credit.

Thereby markets are searching for a new equilibrium in interest rates, exchange rates, and real product markets. The challenge for central bank authorities is that the setting of a fixed, administered interest rate, in a constantly changing economic environment, will create constant disequilibrium in the markets. There is an observable disequilibrium between policy-set and market-determined prices that must be resolved over time.

Yes, the Size of the Balance Sheet Drives the Ten-Year and Alters Credit Allocations

At least on the way up—we shall see on the way down. To test a statistical relationship between the Fed balance sheet and interest rates (5 and 10-year Treasury yields, we employ the Granger causality test. This test helps determine whether changes in the balance sheet are useful to predict interest rate movements. Our results suggest that there is a one-way causality from the level of the Fed's balance sheet, graph below, and benchmark 5 and 10-year Treasury rates. One-way causality means that the size of the Fed's balance sheet drives 5 and 10-year Treasury rates.

However, is it possible that the relationship will not hold as the balance sheet shrinks rather than grows? Would a reduction of the size of the balance sheet lead to an increase in the benchmark 5 and 10-year Treasury rate? A priori, there would appear to be no reason why if all other factors are held constant. In the first part of the 2002 expansion, the Fed was increasing the balance sheet size as the economy was recovering from the Great Recession (and a slower economic recovery compared to historical standards). Meanwhile, the fed funds rate was near zero. In addition, expectations were for an accommodative monetary policy for an extended period under the condition that the Fed balance sheet did move rates.

During the period from 2016 to 2018, The Fed balance sheet did indeed shrink modestly, and the two-year Treasury rate did in fact increase. Therefore, in a period of modest economic growth (real GDP grew 2.5% over the mid-2015 to 2018 period) and low inflation (PCE deflator was rising from one to 2% over that period), there indeed is a reverse relationship between the Fed balance sheet and short-term interest rates. Ceteris paribus is essential to provide context.

Fed's Dual Mandate and Credit Allocation

From the period of 2016 to the shutdowns of 2020, the traditional tools of monetary policy and their impact on inflation and unemployment were not as straightforward as suggested by economic theory. This view was reinforced recently by Chairman Powell's presentation at the Jackson Hole conference.

The Federal Open Market Committee (FOMC) sets the stance of U.S. monetary policy and has a dual mandate to maintain price stability and foster maximum employment. Our research has raised questions about the relationship between the fed funds rate, inflation rate and unemployment rate, particularly which variables are leading and which are lagging.[18] For example, does the fed funds rate react to realized inflation or proactively move in advance of it? Has one side of the mandate played a bigger role in driving policy changes? Economic theory, such as Taylor-type rules, proposes a relationship between the fed funds, inflation, and unemployment rates. However, economic relationships evolve over time. Therefore, we statistically reexamine the relationship between these three variables.

The Great Recession and the Fed Funds Rate's Effectiveness

We utilize the Granger causality test to inspect the statistical relationship between the three variables. This causality test is a way to identify statistical-causality, i.e., which variable is leading, and which one is lagging. To be thorough, it is best to utilize several different sample periods for the analysis. Different conclusions from different sample periods would pose challenges as the cause–effect relationship would not always be consistent. The results show different results for different sample periods and reveal that the relationship between the variables has evolved over time.

Yes, This Time Is Different for the Fed Funds Rate

Different results in different periods indicate possible structural breaks in one or more variables. The fed funds rate hit the zero bound in December 2008 and stayed there until December 2015, and inflation has stayed below the 2% target for several years for the first time in history. Over the 1982 to 2081 period, economic series such as the unemployment rate, the fed funds rate and inflation rate have experienced structural breaks.

The statistical results suggest that for the complete period, there is a relationship between the three variables. However, there is no lead/lag relationship between the fed funds rate and inflation since 1990. The unemployment rate seems to grab the FOMC's attention as we found a statistical relationship between the fed funds and unemployment.

---

[18] John E. Silvia, "Is the Fed Funds Target Rate Effective?" March 6, 2014.

Decision-makers should exercise caution on relying on historical relationships between the fed funds rates, inflation, and unemployment rate, as the interaction between them evolves over time.

Credit Allocation

However, a persistent disequilibrium in the policy goals and realizations creates an imbalance on other markets. With the federal funds rate set at 0.0–0.25% for the foreseeable future, then short-term credit market prices, based on the funds rate, will also be persistently low. As a result, despite the 2020 shutdowns, the housing market is strong. In addition, as expectations of continued easy monetary policy/low short-term rates persist, then the dollar continues to depreciate against the Japanese yen, the euro, and the Chinese yuan. Equity prices have rallied through the recession.

The problem here is that an administered price in one market (short-term credit/fed funds rate) has implications and will be inconsistent with prices in other markets or with the long-run equilibrium of those market as well as the short-term credit market itself. These implications, and their feedback impact on short-term credit, will be reflected in Chapters 6 and 7 as we review the corporate bond market.

References

George Akerlof, "The Market for Lemons: Quality Uncertainty and the Market Mechanism," *Quarterly Journal of Economics*, 1970, 84, no. 3 (August): 488–500. The reality of adverse selection in decision making is associated with this paper.

Douglas W. Diamond, "Financial Intermediation and Delegated Monitoring," *Review of Economic Studies*, 51 (July): 393–414. Asymmetric information is the message and a message that characterizes most financial and economic transactions.

Ben Bernanke and Cara Lown, "The Credit Crunch," *Brookings Papers on Economic Activity*, 1991, no. 2, 205–247. The linkage between credit and the economy is highlighted.

John Steele Gordon, "We Banked on Them," in *The Business of America*, New York: Walker & Co., 2001. This paper highlights the importance of Barings Bank and the Hope Company to complete the U.S. purchase of Louisiana. The reality is that finance is a crucial element in any business deal. This book offers several essays of interest to understanding the economy and decision making. The book is one of my twelve must reads.

Sidney Homer, "A History of Interest Rates," *Rutgers*, 1963. The title exactly covers the material. A fascinating account of interest rates over time and among countries.

Governor Olson, Federal Reserve, "Loan Quality and How It Reflects the Overall Economy," Remarks by Governor Olson, February 28, 2005 at the Government Affairs Conference of the Credit Union National Association.

John E. Silvia, "Supervisory Challenges at the Mid-Cycle of the Economic Expansion," November 6, 2006, presented at the Interagency Bank Supervision Conference, November 6–7 at the William Seidman Center, Arlington, VA. By November 2006, the signals of excess in the housing market were already in place and documented. Contrary to many assertions by others, not all economists missed the developing housing bust.

John E. Silvia, "Economic Outlook: The Role of Finance," February 26, 2007, FRB-Atlanta Banking Industry Outlook. Normalization of deviance was very evident in the housing boom/bust cycle. Delinquency rates on adjustable-rate mortgages were already moving up in 2006 relative to 2005 and up again in 2007.

John A. Weinberg, "Cycles in Lending Standards?" *Federal Reserve Bank of Richmond Economic Quarterly*, 1995, 81, no. 3 (Summer). An early review of the cyclical character of credit.

6

Capital Markets: Financing Business Over the Long Term

The Story of Boom, Bust, and Redemption in Credit Innovations:

Capital markets are a travelogue of ups and downs, trends, cycles, and occasional changes in financial regimes. It is also a story of constant innovation with many successes but a few dead ends. In this chapter, we focus on the corporate bond market as an example of one of these roads traveled.

Today's high-yield bond[1] market is a regular feature on the financial pages and serves as a reliable means of finance for many corporations with household names. Yet this market has undergone several transformations over the decades. Beginning as a market for fallen angel companies whose debt was downgraded to junk status due to a deteriorating financial position, high-yield bonds became a means to finance mergers, acquisitions, and leveraged buyouts.[2] Yet financial innovation, as in many other times and markets, was carried far beyond the economic fundamentals. By the late 1980s, the economic viability of many deals just was not there. But that was not the first time—nor was it the last.

Financial success is the balance between innovation that succeeds in a supportive economic context—read that as economic growth enough to sustain the payments on the debt. After the Civil War and the success of

---

[1] A high yield bond today is a non-investment grade bond which has a higher risk of default due to adverse credit events (poor earnings over the economic cycle for example) and offer higher interest rate returns than investment grade bonds as compensation for risk.

[2] The leveraged buyout is the case where the acquiring firm issues below investment grade debt to help pay for an acquisition and then use the target's cash flow to help pay the debt over time.

© The Author(s), under exclusive license to Springer Nature Switzerland AG 2021
J. E. Silvia, *Financial Markets and Economic Performance*,
https://doi.org/10.1007/978-3-030-76295-7_6

the Transcontinental Railroad, a railroad boom occurred, helped by subsidies and grants from the Federal government—a precursor to the subsidies and special regulations that supported the housing boom of 2004–2007.

But the balance of a supportive economy was about to give way. Railroads are a heavy fixed investment industry where costs are primarily in track, locomotives, rolling stock, stations, and terminals. While railroads were expanding rapidly in the American west, the German government reduced the use of silver coin which, in turn, lowered demand for silver in western mines. The U.S. government compounded the problem with the Coinage Act of 1873. The act abolished the right of holders of silver bullion to have their metal struck into fully legal tender dollar coins, thus ending bimetallism in the United States, and leading to a de facto gold standard. This reduced the money supply and drove up interest rates.[3] Higher rates lowered bond prices which caused a shift away from long-term bonds. Jay Cooke, the first recognized investment banker, was unable to market his Northern Pacific Bonds at a reasonable price and did not receive a government loan—in contrast to the oft-seen behavior of many firms seeking government subsidies for projects that may or may not pass muster in the private marketplace. Cooke's firm declared bankruptcy in late 1873. The Panic of 1873, which rolled on until 1879 and was known as the Great Depression, followed. In its wake, J.P. Morgan began the reorganization and consolidation of many railroads including the Philadelphia & Reading.

There is a distinct cycle of financial innovation, excess, and destruction. New financial instruments emerge, are tested, appear dead only to reappear in a more sustainable form. In truth, there is an underlying rationale for those instruments in the right economic setting. Railroad bonds, such as the Chicago & Northwest, reemerged as benchmarks for financial quality.[4] Finance evolves with the economy.

---

[3] Commercial paper rates rose from 8.28% in 1872 to 10.27% in 1873. They fell to 5.98% in the first complete year, 1874, of the Depression of 1873–1879, "A History of Interest Rates," Sidney Homer, Rutgers State University, 1963. p. 319.

[4] Sidney Homer, A History of Interest Rates, Rutgers University Press, 1963, pp. 314–316. As a benchmark for the financial markets, the Dow Jones Transportation Index was created in 1884, before the Dow Jones Industrial Index. The transportation index had 9 railroads, including the Chicago & North Western, Union Pacific and the New York Central as some of the 11 components.

Financing the Credit Cycle—What's Behind the Demand and Supply of Bonds

It is too easy to cite the booms and busts of any financial market, including bonds, without any real understanding of the fundamentals behind the curtain. In recent years, reports on bond market behavior are primarily about personalities not economics. There are reasons for the credit cycles. We just need to ask why.

To restate the thesis of financial innovation, history in corporate credit has been characterized by a pattern of first, the emergence of new financial instruments (commercial paper, railroad bonds, high-yield bonds[5]), then a test by fire (defaults and financial recession), followed by a shunning, no-touch, period and then finally the reemergence, in a new more sustainable form consistent with economic growth opportunities.

A Framework for the Market for Long-term Finance: Supply and Demand

Bond demand reflects an investor's expectations for a risk-adjusted yield that would appear attractive relative to other available financial assets. As such, the independent variables that drive investor demand are expectations for growth that is capable to pay the interest on the bond, expectations of interest rates, and the wealth position of the buyer. In addition, the attempt to match the duration of assets and liabilities has been an incentive to increase the demand for longer maturities.[6]

We can express this simply as

$$B^d = B^d(Y, r, W/P)$$

Bond demand is positively linked to expected economic growth. Expectations for better growth imply an increase in bond demand as growth indicates an ability to make interest payments. If expectations for growth decline, then

---

[5] High yield spreads rose quickly after the 1987 stock market crash from 12.59 in September to 14.31 in November 1987 and then again in 1990 on the onset of the recession, from 15.04% in August to 18.78 percent in November. Salomon Brothers mimeo.

[6] Life Insurance companies are one example specifically cited as matching duration in "Long-Duration Bond Funds Thrive Amid Market Carnage" March 16, 2020 *Wall Street Journal*.

Fig. 6.1 Real Final Sales to Domestic Purchasers

so will the demand for bonds.[7] While simple, this observation immediately gives bond demand a cyclical character and helps explain the rush into and climb back out of bonds as expectations for the economy change. To confirm this point, the evidence supports the case that real final sales causes, in the Granger sense, credit markets, measured as the high-quality bond index and the equity market, as proxied by the market value of equity. and the operating surplus, in turn, is a driver of pre-tax corporate profits and AA corporate rates,—the source of repayment on bond obligations (see Fig. 6.1).

We identify movement in the price of bonds as the inverse of the interest rates. A higher interest rate is associated with a lower bond price—a phrase employed in market articles in the commonly read financial press such as the *Wall Street Journal*. To the extent that bond investors anticipate a rise in market interest rates, then the demand for bonds will decline.

In addition, an increase in real net financial assets is positively associated with a rise in the demand for bonds. Household increases in real wealth are associated with greater holdings of all three portions of their portfolios—equities, bonds, and cash.

Inflation enters in these relationships in two ways now. First, a faster pace of inflation is associated with a rise in interest rates and a reduced demand

---

[7] For an example of this, see the initial approach to COVID shutdowns and their impact on investor expectations in "Asset Managers rocked by Record Bond Fund Outflows", March 20, 2020, *Financial Times*.

for bonds, leading to lower bond prices. Second, higher inflation is also associated with a decline in the value of real net financial assets. In both cases, higher inflation is associated with a reduction in the demand for bonds.

In the late 1970s, inflation rose and, as interest rates increased in response, money market funds escalated as a share of household wealth and bonds declined. In the early 1980s as interest rates fell, the reverse took place. As evidenced by behavior in 2020, not much has changed as investors sought price protection in money market funds.[8] In both cases. A flatter yield curve also reduced the demand for longer-term corporate credit.

Of course, one thing has changed—a new elephant in the room. Now the demand for bonds reflects the willingness of central banks such as the Federal Reserve the European Central Bank, and the Bank of Japan to buy corporate bonds and place them in their portfolio.[9] The Fed has even acted as a broker in the purchase of corporate debt during 2020.

Supply of Bonds

What makes a firm willing to issue debt to the market? In its simplest form, the same fundamentals will apply, in a slightly different form.[10] The supply of bonds can be expressed as

$$B^S = B^s(Y, r, W/P).$$

The supply of bonds will be positively related to the expected future path of economic activity. Increases in real economic growth would indicate a case for greater issuance of corporate bonds. In addition, a company-specific incentive is also present as some firms are driven by the desire to increase a firm's capital. From the view of the private markets, consider then the experience of net monthly average bond issuance[11] during the recovery from the 1982 recession and then the increase in policy rates in 1984.

---

[8] "Investors spooked by outbreak seek safety [price protection] in money market funds," March 27, 2020 *Financial Times*.

[9] "Bond ETFs Climb as the Fed Kicks Off Historic Purchase Program," May/13, 2020 *Wall Street Journal*.

[10] As in an earlier chapter, the issues of adverse selection and asymmetric information will also apply here. The experience of WeWork and the skepticism of its business model is reflected in "As WeWork Grew, Wall Street Lent It Money and Credibility," November 8, 2019 *Wall Street Journal*.

[11] Comments on Credit, various issues, Salomon Brothers.

	1981	1982	1983	1984	1985
Net Issuance ($B)	$15.1	$9.1	$8.3	$3.6	$5.8

Once again, we can identify a cyclical bias to the supply of bonds. As expectations for economic growth improve, the supply of corporate debt rises as we have witnessed from the demand side, investors are willing to buy more bonds. The bonds have found a receptive market.

As for interest rates, the experience of 2020 is very illustrative.[12] As interest rates fell, corporate bond supply rose. Real bond supply increases when interest rates fall (bond price increases). Firms have found a less expensive means to issue debt.

The issuance of bonds reflects a corporate leadership's assessment of the user cost of capital. Initially, when a firm finances the purchase of capital by borrowing, the interest cost is considered the basic measure of the user cost of capital. Setting aside taxes, the depreciation of capital is a second component of the user cost of capital. Therefore, the user cost of capital is the sum of the interest rate and the rate of depreciation on capital equipment minus the price of capital.[13]

From earlier chapters, we know that expectations matter. The expected real interest rate will determine the pace of business investment. For a firm willing to issue debt, the expected pace of inflation will influence its calculation of the expected real interest rate. Higher expected inflation will mean a reduction in the real interest rate paid on any bond issued.

A firm can also trade-off the issuance of debt with the issuance of equities or the use of its cash. Therefore, the price of equity issuance will influence its decision to issue debt. The use of cash to finance operations, as an alternative to bonds, would also be considered. Over the period 2019–2020, an interesting twist developed where companies with plenty of cash find that issuing debt is far more attractive and they found willing buyers for the debt.[14] Twitter sold convertible bonds in December 2019 while their cash and short-term instruments were bigger than their outstanding debt. Instead of using all that cash, they issued bonds instead. The financial markets assessed that the cash flow into Twitter reduced the risk on the bonds.[15]

---

[12] "U.S. companies near 2019 bond-issuance total with coronavirus binge," June 16, 2020 *Financial Times*.

[13] David Romer, "Advanced Macroeconomics," pp. 387–388, McGraw Hill Irwin, their edition, 2006.

[14] Mark Gertler and Simon Gilchrist note that due to imperfect capital markets, small firms are likely to face larger barriers to outside finance than small firms. See "Monetary Policy, Business Cycles, and the Behavior of Small Manufacturing Firms," Quarterly Journal of Economics 109 (May 1994): 309–340.

[15] "Twitter Sells Bonds at Low Rate", December 06, 2019. *Wall Street Journal*.

The demand and supply of corporate debt reflects the interaction among short-term credit markets (and thereby central bank policy), expectations for economic growth, inflation, and the fundamentals behind equity valuations.

The period 2019–2020 has also witnessed the importance of exogenous shocks to a growing economy. The obvious shock was the Covid-19 pandemic and the ensuing business shutdowns because of public health reasons. But let us take a careful look at the economy before these crises occurred. Trade policy lead by President Trump's America First approach and subsequent imposing of tariffs on various nations, particularly China, was impacting the U.S. economy as real net exports declined in the 3Q 2019. In that same quarter, pre-tax corporate profits declined. Domestic final sales had declined in the second and third quarters of 2019 from the first quarter. Finally, the U.S. ten-year Treasury rate had dropped below 2 percent in the second half of 2019. There was talk, once again, of Japanification of the U.S. economy with both low inflation and low-interest rates.

For the bond market, the drop in domestic final sales suggested a retrenchment in both bond demand and bond supply. Lower corporate profits suggested weaker income growth to support bond repayment. Finally, the lower ten-year Treasury yield, as we mentioned above, is a signal of weakness, not strength, in the economy, ceteris paribus, and is consistent with the low inflation and the drop in domestic final sales.

Then Covid-19 and business shutdowns hit. The motivation of flight to safety drove Treasury bond yields lower as investors sought safety in Treasury yields. High yield spreads spiked from 3.66% on February 21 to 10.87% on March 23 and then settled at 6.43% on June 1, 2020.

Why did the spike peak in late March? Another exogenous shock came forward—Fed intervention.[16]

Federal Reserve Unveils Major Expansion of Market Supports, 3/23/2020 WSJ.

Longer-Term Fixed Income Credit: Framework for Analysis

Patterns of corporate debt finance are a mixture of cyclical and secular patterns with a few structural breaks thrown in for good measure.

---

[16] An interesting paper that predates the 2020 intervention and offers some insight on the Fed, liquidity and corporate finance is found in Guillaume Rocheteau, Randall Wright, and Cathy Zhang, "Corporate Finance and Monetary policy," American Economic Review, 2018, 108 (4–5): 1147–1186.

"Corporate Bonds Give Reassuring Signals Amid Market Jitters," so reads the headlines of a recent article in the *Wall Street Journal* (June 17, 2019).

In contrast, "Corporate debt dangers still lurk even if Fed eases" so reads the *Financial Times* only three days earlier.

What to make of all this hash?

To establish a baseline, the principle starting point is the view that longer-term corporate debt follows the patterns of the cyclical and secular movements much as we saw earlier with respect to short-term credit. Moreover, the principle remains from earlier notes that we compare the stock of debt to the stock of assets and not fall for the fallacy of comparing stocks and flows for the corporate sector.

Short-Term Debt and Interest Rates: Linking Quantity and Price

For some time, we have utilized the ratio of short-term debt to long-term debt (see *Barron's* September 3, 1990[17]) or short-term debt to total debt to provide a signal of the state of corporate finance. Since the early 1980s, short-term corporate financing has steadily declined as a percentage of total credit market debt. The secular pattern is clear.

Interestingly over the same period, the AA corporate bond yield has also declined. The two series are linked but which drives which? As it turns out, corporate decision-making follows the interest rate. Corporations appear to have followed a lower AA yield by issuing more long-term debt to "term out" their debt i.e., a transfer of debt internally by capitalizing short-term debt to long-term debt on its balance sheet. Causality runs from AA yields to the Debt to market value of equity as well as an impact on the equity market as measured by the NYSE index.

In turn, the pace of inflation, as measured by the PCE deflator has an impact on the corporate AA rate in the credit market as well as the operating corporate surplus which reflects an impact on the equity market.

The decision to term out lending reflects the cyclical pattern of corporate bond yields. The behavior of the spread between the Baa corporate bond rate and the fed funds rate has a distinct cycle and trend. For the cycle, our priors are confirmed that the bond spread rose before the recessions of 1990, 2000, and 2007 intimating that the spread does indeed serve as a leading indicator of economic problems ahead. Meanwhile, the trend component shows

---

[17] "Are We in Recession? Yes, Says John Silvia; Maybe, Says Ed Hyman," September 3, 1990 *Barron's*.

a modest uptrend from 1990 to 2011 but then a sharp drop off after that. Interesting that pre-virus, the trend did not signal a leveling off (up to the 4Q 2019) but rather a period of decline leaving us with no clear guidance on what is the post-virus equilibrium value.

Two points follow. First, nonfinancial corporations today are less sensitive to changes in interest rates since the lower percentage of short-term debt intimates that the service cost of the debt will be less affected by changes in short-term rates, by a central bank, for example. Second, this reduced sensitivity to short-term rate changes has continued since the early 1980s. Interest changes are thus having less of an impact on the interest expense faced by corporations in the short run.

Corporate Leverage: Debt-to-Equity Ratio

Leverage in the corporate sector is sometimes judged by the ratio of debt to equity as illustrated in Fig. 6.2. First, the series is non-stationary and thereby is not mean reverting. While many commentators would like to envision an optimum ratio, the markets do not allow for such a result.

Second, there are several statistically significant breaks in the series. There are two examples of upward shifts—October 1987 and October 2008—both associated with large declines in the equity market. Finally, there is the nonlinear character of the series that one can observe from the graph. There

Fig. 6.2 Non-financial Corporate Debt as Share of Equity Market Values

are distinct peaks in the series at or near a recession as the equity market tends to sell off as earnings disappointments increase.

Debt and Equity: Trends, Spikes, and the Leverage Issue

As a measure of corporate leverage, the ratio of debt to equity, Fig. 6.2, has declined since the early 1980s. So, despite the constant assertions of the over-leverage of the corporate sector,[18] debt has declined relative to equity over the period 1991 to 2018. The spikes associated with this series appear in periods of sharp economic weakness and resulting equity price declines.[19]

When examining the evidence of corporate balance sheets, however, there is a distinct structural break in the ratio of corporate debt to equity. Contrary to the priors some analysts might have, the structural break occurs with the 1990 recession not the recession of 2007–2009. Since 2000, there has been little change in the trend of the market value of debt relative to corporate equity values. Also, in this case, the cyclical component appears to follow, not lead, the economic cycle as peaks in the ratio appear to be consistent with drops in corporate equity values associated with recessions. In this case, there is an argument to be made of a return to a stable ratio of debt-to-equity values after recessions.

Finally, another measure of corporate finance that helps to assess leverage is the interest coverage ratio.[20] This measure shows how easily a firm can cover its interest expense from current cash flow generated by current operations.

When net interest expense to operating surplus is compared (note a flow compared to a flow, thereby maintaining our principle of not comparing a stock versus a flow), interest expense is consistent with the mid-cycle lows of the 1990s and 2000s expansions. Federal Reserve Chairman Powell reinforced the importance of this comparison when he commented that the most basic measure of riskiness is not growth in absolute debt levels but rather the proportion of cash flow to interest expense (*Wall Street Journal* May 21, 2019).

---

[18] "Investors fret as leveraged loan market gets junkier," June 8, 2020 Financial Times.

[19] Phelan examines the leverage and risk in the banking sector and emphasizes the dynamic nature of leverage and intermediation there. Gregory Phelan "Financial Intermediation, Leverage and Macroeconomic Instability," American Economic Journal, 2016, 8(4): 199–224.

[20] The interest coverage ratio was cited in my Barron's interview, September 3, 1990 as a signal of a possible forthcoming recession—which in fact did occur. "Are We in Recession? Yes, says John Silvia, Maybe says Ed Hyman," *Barron's* September 3, 1990.

Back to Basics Once More: Supply and Demand in the Bond Market as Engines for a Procyclical Behavior of Bonds: Recent Evidence

While we can examine the bond market as a static balance between supply and demand forces, the reality is that the bond market is a very procyclical force. It is viewed, as is all markets in our framework, as the result of the demand and supply of bonds reflecting the expectations of market agents. The supply of bonds needed for capital is related to a firm's expectations for growth and the level of interest rates relative to its expectations for future interest rates. Corporate bond issuance increases with increases in real income for the economy. Firms experiencing an increase in economic activity and expecting that activity to continue and or grow, would be more willing to sell bonds in the marketplace. This provides a procyclical bias to the supply of bonds.

A decline in interest rates relative to a firm's expectations for future interest rates provides the incentive to issue more long-term debt which was apparent in 2020. The real supply of bonds increases when interest rates fall (bond price increases) therefore the outstanding bond supply rises when the price of bonds increases, a positive slope to the supply curve as expected. In a recent article "Signs Point to Increase in Corporate Bond Sales," (*Wall Street Journal* October 11, 2019), the link between bond sales and lower interest rates is given prominence.

On the demand side, the factors of expected economic growth, expected interest rates, and wealth and cash are prominent. The stronger the expected economic growth, the greater the demand for financial assets, such as bonds and equities, relative to cash. The choice between bonds and equities is a subject for another time but it follows, as expected, investor anticipation of relative future returns. The lower the interest rate (higher price per bond) the lower the demand for bonds.

These principles have been very evident in recent years where the expected returns on equities have outpaced the expected returns on bonds. Financial investors have thus gravitated toward equities rather than bonds.

Finally, increases in wealth tend to be associated with increases in the demand for bonds. Individuals and institutional investors need to put money to work to maintain a desired cash/bond/equity/alternative assets allocation in their portfolio. Yet, here too, there is a procyclical pattern to household wealth and thereby a procyclical pattern to bond ownership.

Linkages and the Bond Market: Pretzel Logic

For policymakers and some financial market participants, the bond market may appear to be a separate entity. The bond market is more often an over-the-counter or electronically traded marketplace without the glamour of a physically imposing Greek revival building that houses the New York Stock Exchange. Yet, like any market, the bond market influences the activities of other markets and is itself influenced by other markets. The linkages are everywhere.

In private financial markets, Monday morning investment meetings begin with a quick economic overview to analyze and discuss the patterns of the economy. These patterns of the economy and inflation set the tone for both the equity and bond markets and, as we have reviewed, economic expectations are essential to making a call on the outlook for both bond and equity markets. Both the supply and demand for bonds are moved by changes in the expectations for economic growth. Meanwhile, changes in the expectations for inflation will alter the expected real return on bonds. Changes in growth and inflation expectations will change perceptions of monetary policy going forward.

Revisions in growth and inflation expectations will alter the preferred allocation of financial assets between bonds, equities, and cash. As for the market for foreign exchange, these same expectations will influence the supply and demand for any currency. Linkages matter.

Sometimes, logic would appear at first glance to be pretzel logic. Consider this headline from the *Wall Street Journal* (November 10, 2019) "Rising [government] Yields Quiet Bond Market's Key Recession Alarm." In this article, rising interest rates are interpreted as an economic positive. In contrast, consider the negative signal sent off when the ten-year Treasury rate fell below 2% in the second half of 2019.[21] On the other hand, rising interest rates could signal an increase in the demand for credit. and thereby could be interpreted as optimism and expectations for better growth ahead (Independent of any Fed action to raise rates).

Procyclical Patterns Open the Door to Disappointment When Expectations are not met.

The worst loans are made in the best of times. There is a procyclical pattern to both the supply and demand for bonds but when an economic shock happens, the viability of many bonds disappears.

---

[21] "Investors Rush into Havens as Growth Fears Persist," August 9, 2019 Wall Street Journal.

Entering late 2019, what were some of the cyclical patterns that we could watch for clues about the sustainability of economic growth and functioning bond markets? As cited in the Barron's article of 1990, the interest coverage ratio (earnings before interest and taxes relative to net interest expense) had fallen from a small peak in 1989 to 1990. Ominously, we saw this same pattern with a peak in 1998 leading into the 2000 recession and again in 2007 leading into the 2007–2009 recession. In much of economics, the concept of low or high can be very misleading.[22] As for a signal of improving or deteriorating conditions, we are always concerned about the marginal change in the series. Declines in the interest coverage ratio translates into greater sensitivity to exogenous shocks in the economic system. In addition, the rise and decline of the ratio is also a signal of what is happening beneath the surface. In essence, a rising ratio signals that earnings are improving relative to interest expense—a particularly good situation. However, when the ratio is declining, then earnings are no longer keeping up with interest expense and there is a problem afoot. The interest coverage ratio peaked in 2015–2016 and had been steadily declining into 2019 which was before the Covid-19 shutdowns.

Return on assets, net income as a percent of total assets, is a second indicator of cyclical patterns for corporate credit quality. We can recognize the peaks in this series in 1989, 1997, 2007, and again in 2013. The principles remain the same, the continued decline in the return on assets creates a sensitivity to shocks. High or low is not a relevant benchmark. Direction dictates risk. In both these series, there is an underlying behavioral framework that explains what is going on and why this behavior can create or ameliorate problems.

Finance for the Long Term: The Multiple Forces in Corporate Bond Markets

Financing private, long-term corporate activity through the bond market is a fascinating subject to study due to the multiple actors and multiple factors in the marketplace. For actors, there are plenty of diverse agents on the supply and demand side of the market. On the supply side, corporations, for example, are eager to issue debt when they perceive that the funds raised will offer a return on invested capital, such as a new plant or equipment, more than the cost of debt finance. On the demand side, investors will offer

---

[22] Consider the following headline for perspective "US corporate debt is high but not yet dangerous," Financial *Times* April 11, 2019.

to buy the debt when they perceive the return on the debt exceeds the return on alternative investments, such as Treasury debt, when adjusted for risk.

For individual firms, the challenge is making endogenous calculations that compare the risk and reward balance of the expected rate of return on any project relative to the cost to finance—here considered the bond market. On the exogenous side, we examine our faithful companions in our intellectual journey—growth, inflation, interest rates, the dollar exchange rate, and the path of profits—which are factors driving any investment and financing decision. When commentators complain about too much corporate debt we ask: Too much relative to what? Your expectations for future growth? Future interest rates? Future profits? There must be a market context for any answer. Yet seldom, if ever, do we get the underlying assumptions of the pro and con commentators. Commentary without context is not useful.

There is also a critical time inconsistency. Bonds are bought and sold today based upon expectations of economic activity in the future. Finance today is paid back tomorrow. This brings in an interesting aging and calculation problem. How does one measure default rates? Default rates should be compared to the cohort issuance of the bond. Comparing defaults today to issuance today would not provide an accurate assessment of the quality of the market pricing. Moreover, a bond issued in 2014 has had four years of economic growth to work out the kinks. A bond issued today may face a recession on the immediate horizon.

Die Another Day[23]

There is also a lesson in the rhetoric around financial assets and liabilities such as commercial paper, high-yield bonds, home equity loans, and leveraged loans in mid-2020. In the three prior cases, commercial paper, high-yield bonds and home equity loans, the underlying logic of the financial instrument outlived the short-run crisis. In each case, the application of the instrument was pushed too far in economic circumstances (the exogenous factors) that would not support the financial viability of the instrument over time. Yet, each instrument lived to finance another day. So, it would appear to be so in current commentary regarding leveraged loans.[24] Rather, commentators should ask: What are the economic assumptions that would challenge the leveraged loan market and what are the economic factors that would support

---

[23] United Artists, 2002.
[24] "Leveraged loans: the unbearable liteness of covenants," Oct. 21, 2020, Financial Times.

the continued expansion of that market? Once again, to simply criticize the use of a financial instrument without context is not useful to an investor.

Finally, there is the very intriguing interplay between the ex ante (based on forecasts rather than actual results). and ex post (based on actual results rather than forecasts) movement of interest rates and the evaluation of bonds. Ex ante, both the buyer and seller of the corporate bond assess that the bond price and rate is a good deal. But in the long history of rates since 1982, the decline in rates was a surprise to both buyers and sellers. Ex post, the buyers did well. Bond suppliers rushed to refinance older, more expensive debt.

Yet, there is also an interesting perspective on the yield curve. A steep yield curve would be an incentive to finance short-term ex ante. But if the level of rates were to rise in the future, refinancing that short-term debt would be more expensive. Both the slope of the yield curve and the level of rates matter. Unanticipated, or worse, unconsidered, changes in interest rates matter.

Expectations and Cognitive Biases: Rebounds in Credit

All of which again brings us another lesson in the distinction between ex ante and ex post returns and the important role of expectations and cognitive biases such as anchoring and recency biases. Ex ante and ex post yields for U.S. Treasury benchmark ten-year notes are clearly different. Yet, the anchoring bias for some analysts creates the attitude that short-term interest rates (the Fed's persistent 2% federal funds rate projection along with ten-year Treasury yields at 2.5%) should be consistent with a sense of normal, pre-virus, 2010–2019, financial market pricing.

This is doubtful. In the short run, the International Monetary Funds' outlook in mid-2020, noted in the *Financial Times*,[25] sent a message to financial markets that there was evidence of a recession in the core Euro areas of Germany, France, and the United Kingdom. as well as the broader global economy. Meanwhile, slower growth in China also hints that emerging market gains in Asia will be more moderate than in the past. Interesting that an exogenous shock weakens the U.S. economy but strengthens the attractiveness of U.S. markets on a relative basis due to the flight-to-safety incentive.

Financial market bond prices followed the changes in the economic outlook. The high-yield option adjusted spread was 3.62% on February 20th

---

[25] "IMF downgrades are a warning to the world," *Financial Times* June 25, 2020.

but then hit a peak at 10.09% on March 20th, just before the Fed's announcement to purchase corporate debt, and by late September the spread had declined to 5.47%. High-grade bonds had a similar spread issue. The AA spread was 0.57% on February 20th, rose to 2.76% on March 20th and in late September was 0.87%. The U.S. economy was in recession during the second quarter of 2020, but the bond market had turned in late March/early April anticipating Fed action would lead to economic recovery as illustrated by the following headline from the Wall Street Journal.

Fed Moves Spark Corporate Bond Rally *Wall Street Journal* **April 10, 2020.**

"September Busiest Month Ever for Corporate Bond Issuance," *Financial Times* **October 1, 2019.**

On September 30, 2019 came this news story from the *Financial Times*.

Ok, but why the issuance? In the article, the author Joe Pennison cites low costs to finance (a supply-side incentive) and search for yield (demand side). For an economist, anytime a journalist cites supply and demand factors is an exciting time. So, let us dig deeper into the dynamics behind the bond market and seek an understanding of the cyclical and secular trends of corporate bond issuance.

Low Costs to Finance

As perceived through the lens of high-quality corporate bond rates, the period of late 2019 was indeed a period of low costs to finance Fig. 6.3. Moreover, for the entire post financial crisis of 2007–2009, the AA yield spread was the lowest for the entire period.

Incentive to Finance: Capital Spending Plans Out Run Internal Funds

Financing costs impart a dynamic, cyclical character to the role of desired capital spending and debt/bond issuance. As illustrated in Fig. 6.4, the financing gap is highly cyclical. A firm's demand for real capital investment depends on expectations of real economic growth and the cost of capital. Increases in expected real final sales will prompt a desire to invest. The balance between the demand for funds to finance capital expenditures and the internal funds available are seldom, actually, in balance thus imparting a cyclical character to the demand for physical capital as well as external

6 Capital Markets: Financing Business Over the Long Term 231

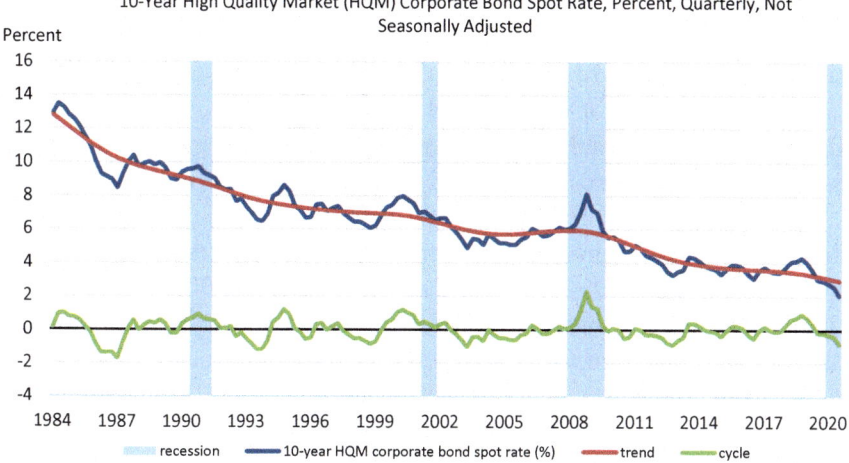

Fig. 6.3 Ten-Year High Quality Bond Yield

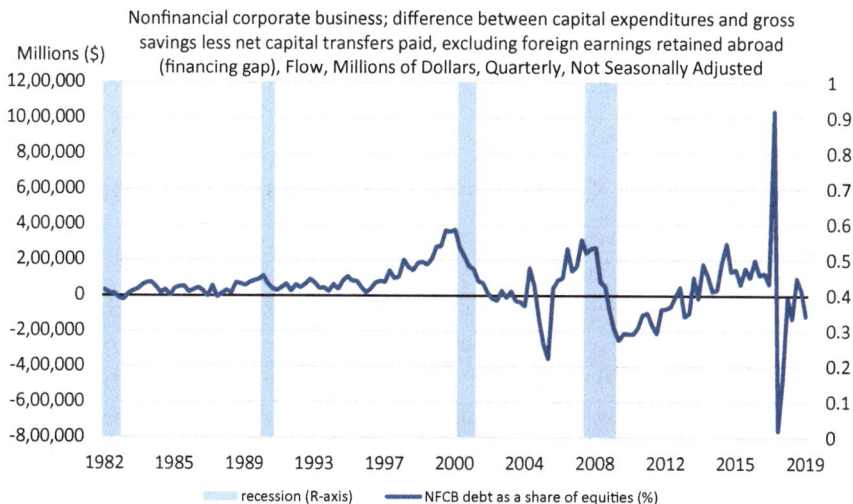

Fig. 6.4 Financing Gap: Non-Financial Corporate Business

finance. As firms feel more comfortable with expected future sales, the desire, and actual, pace of capex, tends to rise as the cycle matures (1997–2000, 2007–2008, 2014 to 2019) compared to early cycle periods such as 1992–1996.

In the expansion that began in 2010, the financing gap remained negative until early 2014 but then moved definitively into positive territory by mid-2015. This was an encouraging signal for the economy as firms, up to then, had been reluctant to make capital investments. Increased capital investments reflect an improved outlook for the economy. Meanwhile, internal cash flow was weaker due to slower export demand, a stronger dollar, and weaker pricing power for businesses. This feeds back into the use of external sources of financial capital, such as bonds, to facilitate the growth of real business investment. One positive result of this process of bond finance was the decline in short-term corporate debt relative to long-term debt. There was a reduced sensitivity to any possible increase in interest rates going forward as we witnessed in mid-1994–1994 and again in 2006 to 2008.

In the 2009–2019 cycle, the National Federation of Independent Business (NFIB) survey jumped upward, and capital goods orders rose in 2016 after Donald Trump was elected president. Both the NFIB and orders data reflected an optimism on a rise in real final sales—all of this is true to form. Equipment spending followed a traditional "accelerator" principle when business investment intentions accelerate to meet the higher expected pace of final sales going forward. Unfortunately, in recent months a slowdown in economic growth reflecting trade uncertainties and slower growth in both Europe and China has emerged hinting at lower expected final sales and thereby less external finance as the industrialized economies entered 2020.

Business Loans, Cash, Debt, and Equity: Financial Options

Financing business spending primarily is characterized by four basic options—bank loans (reviewed in Chapter 5), retained earnings (to be covered in Chapter 10), corporate debt, and equity issuance (Chapter 11). Our focus here is on what information we can glean from movements in each of these series. In so doing, we get a sense of the trade-offs in debt and equity finance by reviewing the behavior of the debt-to-equity ratio.

We return for a moment to the ratio of debt to equity as the series is frequently cited as a benchmark for leverage in the nonfinancial sector. However, conclusions based upon this ratio, without context, are sketchy at best. Here we focus on the statistical character of the debt-to-equity ratio.[26]

Our problem begins that the series is non-stationary and thereby is not mean reverting—there is no "golden mean." There is no perfect price as we

---

[26] The ratio itself has been a subject of study and the proposition that the value of the firm is independent of the debt/equity ratio is well known. For a note on this see Merton H. Miller, "The Modigliani–Miller Propositions After Thirty Years," Journal of Economic Perspectives V. 2 No. 4 Fall 1988 pp. 99–120.

have witnessed in many financial benchmarks in Chapter 3. Many financial commentators imply that there is an optimum ratio, that is, one that is above or below some idealized number. However, the actual data do not admit of such a result.[27]

Beyond the secular pattern of the debt-to-equity ratio, moreover, there are several statistically significant breaks in the debt-to-equity ratio time series. There are two examples of upward shifts—October 1987 and October 2008—both associated with large declines in the denominator (equity values). Finally, there is the nonlinear character of the series which makes a linear projection of the series off base. There are distinct peaks in the series at or near recession periods as the equity market tends to sell off as earnings disappointments increase.

All of this is symptomatic of financial benchmarks that are part of a greater financial and economic model. Debt and equity decisions are not made independent of growth, inflation, exchange rate, and interest rate expectations. These decisions are co-determined by the movements in other economic and credit markets.

A Look Back at the Early 1990s and the Channels of Influence

For the first half of the 1990s, the ratio of debt to equity represented a sharp break with the prior decade and that break continued throughout that decade. During the early 1990s, corporations refinanced their 1980s debt as AA corporate rates declined from 1990 through to 1994. The implications of such refinancing were pervasive in the economy. Realizing that several other factors were at work, as companies saved on interest payments, nonfinancial corporations reported higher net income (pre-tax corporate profits rose from 1992 to 1994) thereby providing an upward bias to equity valuations (S&P 500 also rose from 1992 to 1994) and a possible boost for dividend payments to shareholders (personal dividends increased those same years). Higher net income will lead to some increase in federal tax payments and will reduce the Treasury demand for finance in the bond market. Gains in corporate income would allow for greater spending on business investment in plant and equipment (that spending also surged from 1992 to 1994) and structures (as would be expected, structures spending lagged the cycle and only began to climb in

---

[27] The substitution of debt for equity in many deals, independent of the outlook for the economy or interest rates, has led to financial stress in the corporate bond market. "More Companies Stumble Under Debt Load." *Barron's* March 18, 2018.

1994). This process illustrates the interrelationship of financial markets and their implications for real investment spending.

Domestic nonfinancial borrowing rose from 1992 to 1994 for mortgages, bank loans, and commercial paper. Interestingly, the exception was corporate bonds, which rose in 1993 but reacted negatively to the increase in the federal funds rate by the Fed in 1994.

Who's Buying? "Corporate Pension Funds Pile into Bonds" *Wall Street Journal* **April 13, 2015 and John Bull's 2% Warning Again.**

On the demand side, net purchases of U.S. corporate bonds climbed for many sectors since 2014. Compared to 2016, purchases by life insurance, property, and casualty companies as well as pension funds all rose by 2019, although a dip occurred in 2018 for some sectors. Purchases by foreign residents, mutual funds, and ETFs also surged from 2016 to 2019. For pension funds, the incentive to meet long-term obligations is obvious.

Feedback into the real economy is intriguing. The demand for long-term corporate debt provides an incentive to firms to sell such debt to raise capital for real business investment as well as to meet pension obligations. The conventional channel of lower interest rates (corporate bond spreads from 2012 to 2018) did lead to greater business investment. On the demand side, at the same time, the pursuit of yield by pension funds and insurance companies provided a willing buyer to support the decline in corporate rates over the same period.[28]

Too Much of a Good Thing?

Economists debate whether exceptionally low-interest rates provided too much of an incentive to issue debt to finance investments in the real economy that do not, in fact, yield any real returns over time. In the 1800s, famed British economist and philosopher John Stuart Mill proposed that interest rates could be so low that they could distort the allocation of resources in an economy. This occurred in the early 1920s around the Florida real estate boom and then around equities in the late 1920s. Decades later in 1994, this concern could be seen in the issue of emerging market debt, particularly regarding Mexico. Most recently, the housing bubble of the 2000s represented a misallocation of capital when the credit cost of buying a house was too low relative to the actual risk of price declines. By the end of 2019, the issue again arose as investors debated the merits of the issuance of too many bond issues

---

[28] One look at credit spreads and business cycles is Hui Chen "Macroeconomic Conditions and the Puzzles of Credit Spreads and Capital Structure," Journal of Finance, Vol. LXV, No. 6, December 2010.

given slower economic growth and stagnating corporate profits during the 2019 period.[29]

Creating Disequilibrium: Cycles, Trends, and Structural Breaks in Credit Pricing and Availability

When examining the behavior of corporate debt markets and the underlying change in corporate balance sheets, distinct patterns emerge that provide clues to when change is coming. In addition, how do we interpret the interaction of the real and financial sectors of the economy to project the movement of the real economy and financial markets going forward?

Interaction of the Real Economy and Finance

Real investment demand (e.g., equipment spending) is a major focus of economic policy because investment is a crucial element in defining long-run potential economic growth and a society's standard of living. Fundamentals dictate that the demand for investment capital depends on expectations for real final sales and the cost of capital. Increases in expected real final sales will lead to an increase in business investment.

Yet, we have witnessed, with the financing gap, the balance between the demand for funds to finance real capital spending capex and the internal funds available is seldom in balance. Capital spending tends to pick up momentum as the economy expands, usually putting upward pressure on interest rates from the demand side. In contrast, in the expansion from 2010 to 2019, the cost to finance debt steadily declined.

By the latter half of 2019, the combination of rising capital spending financed by increasingly less expensive bond finance had appeared. This once again gave support to the suspicion that the expansion of capacity to deliver products and services was excessive relative to the sustainability of demand. Then the Covid-19 shutdowns hit revealing the excesses. Only through the 2020 workouts did we see the cutbacks in retail stores and restaurants in 2020 that some analysts had identified as excessive in 2019.

By the benchmark, Commercial Property Price index, retail space had the smallest price rise since 2006 compared to the other three commercial property types: office, industrial, and apartments.[30] Asking rents for retail peaked

---

[29] "Money pours into US corporate debt despite warnings," *Financial Times* November 21, 2019.
[30] [30] Real Capital Analytics, CoStar and Wells Fargo Economics, October 2019.

in 2017 and had declined in both 2018 and 2019 on a year-over-year percent change basis. Finally, asking rents declined in markets such as New York City and Boston.

Demand for Credit: ProCyclical

How do we monitor the procyclical character of the corporate bond market to identify the change in the credit and economic cycle? In recent economic expansions, corporate bond issuance rises with the economic expansion (1985–1988, 1993–1998) and most vividly, and not yet restrained, in the 2010–2019 expansion.

However, there is a noticeable reaction of bond issuance to an increase, even modest, in interest rates (AA yield). Late in the 1980s, 1990s, and certainly in 2006–2008 noticeable declines occurred in bond issuance even though the extent of the interest rate increase appeared modest, see Fig. 6.2.

Suppliers for Credit: Who is Buying?

Meanwhile, on the supply side, there was a noticeable procyclical pattern of increasing supply of credit for corporate debt in the 1980 and 1990 expansions. However, this behavior ended abruptly between mid-2004 and mid-2005. The recovery of 2009–2019 reflected the search for yield by many life insurance companies.

The pattern of net purchases, by life insurance companies, for example, follows the pattern of gross and net issuance for the corporate bond market. The spike of purchases in Q3-2016 reflected a surge in issuance for several one-time factors. The net result is that the supply of corporate debt will find a home—but at what price?

Benchmarking Corporate Benchmarks and Corporate Leverage

What are the statistical properties of the most familiar corporate financial benchmarks? Once estimated, what do these statistical numbers indicate about actual corporate activity? One comment that pervades discussions during economic expansions is that corporate debt is high and low relative to the size of the economy. This series is illustrated in Fig. 6.5 and

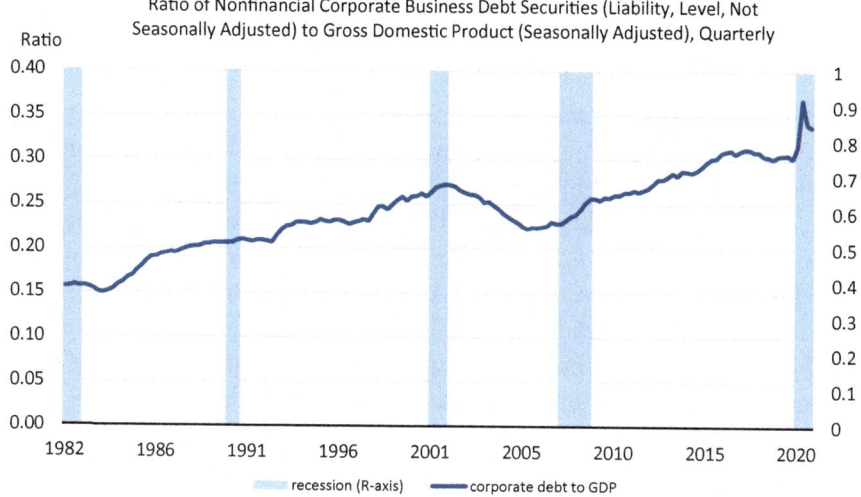

Fig. 6.5 Ratio of Corporate Debt to Nominal GDP

exhibits several interesting properties. First, the series is not mean reverting and provides evidence of two structural breaks since 1982. One suspects the series is not mean reverting, even without the Dickey-Fuller test, by simply looking at the Figure and noticing that the series appears to drift up over time. In this sense, corporate debt is more leveraged today than in prior periods. However, the graph compares a stock of debt versus and a flow, Gross Domestic Product, in the economy and is therefore misleading.

There are two structural breaks in the series. First, in October 1985 there is a shift upward that appears reasonable given the downshift in market rates at the time that would have led to greater issuance of corporate debt. Second, there is a downshift in the series in October 2009 which is also reasonable in response to the 2008–2009 recession. Finally, the series is nonlinear as would be expected by viewing the graph. This makes linear projections of the corporate debt-GDP ratio immediately inaccurate.

Instead, the interest expense as a share of corporate operating surplus provides a flow-to-flow benchmark for the state of the corporate income statement. This ratio, Fig. 6.7, is lower today than in most periods in the past 30 years indicating no excessive leverage, given the current state of economic growth, inflation, and interest rates.

Interest Coverage: Cyclical Patterns Subject to Exogenous Shocks

A better approach is to compare interest expense as a share of the corporate operating surplus cash flow. By that measure the corporate sector, in general, is less levered today than most periods in the past 30 years.

Interest coverage, as benchmarked by the interest expense to corporate operating surplus, (Fig. 6.6) provides a distinct pattern over the business cycle, but it is also subject to sharp downdrafts due to exogenous shocks. Interest coverage rose steadily in the late 1990s and then fell continuously into the 2001 recession. Interest coverage again rose steadily until 2007 when another shock drove the ratio down until the end of the 2007–2009 recession. In the recovery after 2010, the ratio increased only modestly as nominal GDP gains were below the pace of the prior three expansions. The interest coverage ratio is not mean reverting and so there is no value in the concept of low and high values. Moreover, the series is nonlinear since the ratio is a derivative of the behavior of other business cycle fundamentals (economic growth, profitability, and interest rates).

The numerator of interest coverage reflects retained earnings and, as such, has its own cyclical pattern. Earnings increased sharply from 1991 and maintained solid growth with nominal GDP gains of 5% on average. Earnings

Fig. 6.6 Interest Paid as a Share of Operating Surplus

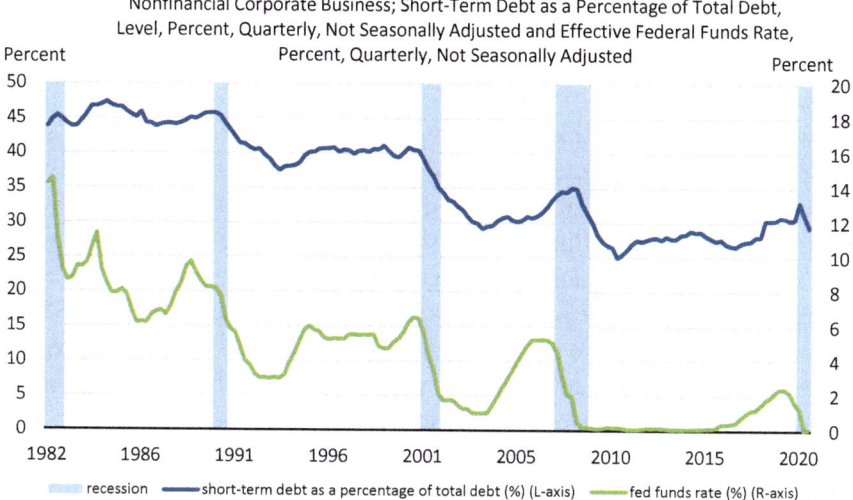

Fig. 6.7 Corporate Debt and Fed Funds Rate

and nominal GDP rose again sharply from 2002 to 2006 and then improved modestly with nominal GDP from 2010 to 2014.[31]

Interest rates are a second factor in the pattern in interest coverage. During the late 1990s, the Fed raised the funds rate in both 1999 and 2000. It also raised the funds rate from 2004 to 2006 but it was not until the economy slowed in 2007 that the interest coverage ratio fell. The Fed raised the funds rate during the years 2016 to 2018 and the interest coverage rate declined.

Finally, the issuance of nonfinancial corporate debt illustrates the procyclical character of debt issuance and further complicates the balance between interest coverage and earnings. For example, debt issuance rose in the late 1990s while the Fed raised the funds rate. From 2004 to 2006 the Fed raised the funds rate and debt issuance rose. Finally, the Fed increased the funds rate in 2016–2018 and issuance rose. The procyclical pattern of debt issuance indicates that the cost of carrying the debt was met by rising earnings. However, when earnings were hit with a slowing economy, the interest coverage became a problem. As in most debt cycles, the increase in debt continues until it stops.

---

[31] Even within an economic expansion, changes in the fortunes of different sectors can bring forth financial stress. See "Wave of Financial Stress Hits Low-Rated Companies," *Wall Street Journal* October 22, 2019.

Short-Term Versus Long-Term Debt and the Funds Rate

Our work always emphasizes the link between markets. For the ratio of short-term to total debt finance, as illustrated in Fig. 6.7, the interesting observation is that causality runs from the federal funds rate to interest paid as would be expected but also influences the share that bonds and other long-term debt, such as mortgages, take as a percent of corporate liabilities. This would certainly help explain the long downward slope of this series since 1982 that has corresponded with the long-term decline in the funds rate. It also explains the decline in long-term rates and the willingness of both companies to issue long-term debt and of investors to search for yield in corporate debt.

This series has a linear trend which opens the possibility that we can estimate the effect over time of the funds rate on this ratio. It also raises the possibility that a rising fed funds rate scenario going forward would be associated with a rising short-term and total debt ratio—quite a change for the markets going forward (perhaps—a subject for future research for sure).

Dealing with Disequilibrium: The Age Before 2020

Cautionary tones before the 2020 shock bring back lessons on the importance of financial signals in a prior expansion, that of the 1980s, and illustrate the secular and cyclical trends in financial ratios in a different era.

The ratio of the broader aggregate, domestic, nonfinancial debt to GDP, had risen sharply in the period from 1982 to 1986, (refer to Fig. 6.5), after a remarkably steady period from 1960 to 1979.

Nonfinancial corporate liabilities to GNP had risen steadily from 1955 to 1975, leveled off from 1975 to 1980, and then spiked sharply upward in the 1982–1985 period. Spikes in this series appear in the recession periods of 1957, 1960, 1969–1970, 1973–1975, and again in 1980–1982. The ratio of debt to net worth also broke above its trend line in the mid-1980s, consistent at the time with the rise in mergers and acquisitions.

Another trend of interest during the period from 1955 to the mid-1980s was the rise in the ratio of short-term debt to total liabilities from 0.3% to 0.5% by 1985. During the period of the early 1960s when commercial paper became commonly issued, rates on three-month paper rose from 3% in 1961 to 10% by 1973 and then 16% in 1981. Meanwhile, corporate AA paper was 3% in 1955, then 8% in 1969, and then on to 14% in 1981 with a spread over Treasuries of 245 basis points in 1981. The increasing cost of issuing long-term debt encouraged the issuance on short-term debt.[32] Yet this dependence on short-term instruments did raise the interest rate sensitivity of corporate finance during that period. A steeper yield curve did impact corporate finance.

As the yield curve flattened and interest rates declined in the 1980s, corporate debt became an increasing share of corporate finance. Corporate bonds rose from 36 to 56% of total outstanding corporate financial debt by 2003 while bank loans fell from 28 to 16%.[33]

Financial markets and the economy are of course intertwined. The ratio of corporate cash flow to debt service declined from a ratio of 7 in the mid-1950s to below 3% by 1985. Yet there were downward spikes in the series associated with recessions in 1957–58, 1960–1961, 1969–1970, 1980 to 1982. Meanwhile, the ratio of financial assets to short-term liabilities (the quick ratio) declined from the period of 1955 to 1980. The interaction of secular change in the pre-1982 era and the economic cycle is a fascinating journey through the same fundamentals that move markets that we consider today.

Linkages from Balance Sheet to Real Economic Activity

The economic expansion since 2009 provides another example of the linkage of finance to real economic activity. The nonfinancial sector continues to borrow on net, which has been the case for much of the current recovery yet, unlike past periods, the use of the funds appears more directed to capital investment rather than the mergers and acquisitions of the 1980s.

Putting the Financing Gap to Work

The financing gap narrowed rapidly during the period from 2010 to 2014 and then turned positive when it jumped to 1.3% of GDP in the second quarter of 2015. The financing gap represents capital expenditures less internally generated funds and the difference between the two represents the external financing required to fund the capital expenditures. This is an

---

[32] Analytical Record of Yields and Yield Spreads, March 1990, Salomon Brothers.
[33] Ned Davis Quarterly Data release June 2003.

encouraging sign for the economy as the demand for capital will turn the financing gap positive.

For much of the recovery and expansion period, firms have been reluctant to make capital investments, with many firms preferring to reduce their leverage During the mid-phase of the 2010–2019 cycle, the sharp gains in equity valuations outpaced the growth of liabilities. Increased capital investment reflected an improving outlook for the economy and would support the case for growth in the supply side of the economy.

One caution on the capital investment story is an associated weakness on the financial side. While capital expenditures increased during 2014–2015, there has also been a moderation in internally generated cash flow. Slower demand from abroad, a stronger dollar, and a lack of pricing power weighed on internally generated cash flows. If capital expenditures remain at a high level despite the decline in internally generated funds, it would bode well for the productive capacity of our economy and reflect improved confidence from the nonfinancial corporate sector. But on the financial side, there is increasing strain as demand outpaces supply. That said, this would imply a sustained increase in the financing gap and would also require firms to have continued access to capital.

One Last Driving Factor of Corporate Finance: From the Inside

Unit labor costs, Fig. 6.8, has a pervasive impact on corporate balance sheets and income statements. Unit labor costs have a causal link to pre-tax corporate profits which, in turn, impacts credit markets, through bond rates, and equity markets as well. As highlighted later in Chapter 10, corporate profits are a fundamental element influencing household wealth and business finance as well as attracting foreign capital, Chapter 9.

Interest Rates and Corporate Financing

Nonfinancial corporates are relatively less exposed to rising interest rates but the pervasive impact of credit markets, benchmarked by the five-year Treasury rate, is readily apparent through its impact on corporate AA rates, corporate interest expense, and the corporate debt to the market value of equity. Short-term financing has accounted for a much smaller share of financing during this expansion than in previous cycles. This may in part reflect firms

Fig. 6.8 Unit Labor Costs

attempting to "lock-in" low borrowing costs in the extremely low-interest rate environment over the past several years.[34] In fact, a longer time series shows that the trend toward longer-term financing tracks interest rates relatively closely. The maturation of U.S. capital markets over the past several decades also likely increased the attractiveness of corporate bonds as a means of financing, which is often longer term.

Market Incentives and the Sources of Corporate Funds

Popular commentary regularly cites the role of disruption in the economy. Yet, disruption has been a common theme in the financial markets, especially in the context of corporate finance.

Short-term, Long-term Debt: Secular Change for the Manufacturing Sector

Manufacturing, along with construction, is more representative of the economic cycles than the steady pace of consumer spending. Recently these two sectors have altered the patterns of sources of funds in response to market

---

[34] Corporate incentives to borrowing is reviewed in Stewart C. Myers, Determinants of Corporate Borrowing," Journal of Financial Economics, 1977. V. 5 pp. 147–175.

incentives—especially in response to expected interest rates and bond market liquidity. On the demand side, liquidity in the bond market has become more global and more liquid in the range of corporate debt offered to the investor. On the supply side, the character of corporate debt has also become more flexible in structure.

This behavior is illustrated in Fig. 6.9. The ratio of short-term debt (due in less than one year) to long-term debt exhibits a secular decline in recent economic expansions. The result is that nonfinancial corporations have reduced sensitivity to a change in short-term interest rates. Post the 2001 recession, manufacturing firms did reduce their short-term debt relative to long-term debt. However, with the rise in the federal funds rate during 2004–2006, these firms employed more short-term debt to avoid locking in longer-term higher rates as Corporate AA rates rose from 3.48 percent in 2004 to 5.83 percent by June of 2006. The dramatic decline in rates during and after the 2007–2009 recession prompted manufacturing firms to reduce their exposure to the risk of short-term volatility and issue more long-term debt.

This ratio of short-term debt to long-term debt has a pervasive impact on the broad economy as the ratio has an impact on Libor and two-year rates with a follow-on impact on corporate interest expense and corporate net worth.

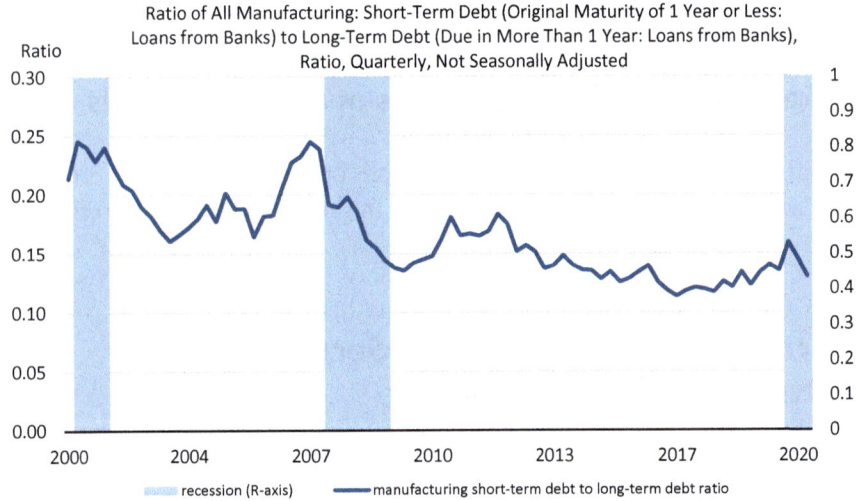

Fig. 6.9 Manufacturing: Ratio of Short-Term to Long-Term Debt

Interest Coverage Ratio and GDP: Who is in Charge? Growth

By mid-2018, several commentators raised the concern that higher corporate interest expense and debt could lead to a weaker economy in the year ahead. As illustrated in Fig. 6.5, there would appear to be a relationship between the two series. However, the relationship runs from economic growth to net interest expense and not the other way around. A high level of net interest expense does not lead to economic weakness but, rather, economic weakness does drive a higher level of net interest expense as a percent of operating surplus.

Often, the causal appearance of a relationship between economic activity and financial benchmarks can be taken as fact. Unfortunately, the appearance of causality can be misleading. It is essential to examine the variables and determine whether one consistently is leading or lagging the other. Causation cannot always be derived from this practice, but often the behavior of the variables can be forecasted with more directional certainty.

Distinguishing Trend and Cycle in Nonfinancial Corporate Finance

Recent patterns of corporate finance over the last two decades provide a valuable context to understand the current financial picture. Over longer-term periods, the patterns of trend and cycle also prove instructive. Three patterns of long-term secular behavior in the nonfinancial corporate finance world provide a context to judging the character of the current credit cycle. There is merit in splitting the cyclical and trend components of corporate credit benchmarks to provide a cautionary signal when bonds are rich or at bargain prices relative to trend. As in the bank loans market, the worst bonds are bought at the best times. There is a procyclical pattern to both the supply and demand for bonds—and bond prices. When times are good, both buyers and sellers want more. But when an economic shock happens, the viability and willingness to buy and issue bonds disappears. Bond prices decline and interest rate spreads rise.

Falling Share of Short-Term Debt

Anchoring bias tends to fix many commentators on linking short term, mostly bank credit, with the ability of firms to finance their activity. However, as we reviewed in a prior chapter, the role of bank credit has diminished over time due to federal regulations, the emergence of non-bank credit, and the increasing role of longer-term finance options. Along with the long-term drop-in private market interest rates has been the expected decline in short-term debt as a share of total credit market debt, as illustrated earlier in Fig. 6.7.

Terming out debt (replacing short-term with longer-term debt) makes sense when long-term rates are expected to rise in the future. Firms avoid rolling over short-term debt at increasingly higher interest rates and lock in cheaper, over the long run, long-term debt. In addition, since the interest is deductible, this substitution helps lower a firm's effective tax rate. Current tax policy has implemented some limits on the interest rate deduction on high-yield debt. Future tax policy options play a greater role here. Any further reduction of the interest rate deduction would significantly increase the cost of debt capital and would discourage debt finance at the margin, offsetting some of the effects of a lower rate.

Corporate Bonds Rise as AA Rates Decline

Corporate bonds have increased their role in the total liabilities of the nonfinancial corporations from about 16% in 1984 to 28.8% as of the fourth quarter of 2016. The secular rise on corporate bond finance as a share of total liabilities mirrors the long-term decline in AA corporate rates since 1982. Once again, there is a strategic decision for business leaders. For example, in 2016 after the presidential election, they had to determine if they should offer long-term debt given the outlook for corporate tax reform, changes in interest deductibility, and gradually tighter monetary policy which would lead to higher short-term interest rates.

Bank Loans as Debt Finance: Smaller Share Since 1980s

As we saw in Chapter 5, bank loans (both high grade and high yield) as a share of credit market financing, have declined since the early 1980s and this evolution has two parts of the corporate credit story that bear watching. First, the lower cost of long-term finance has encouraged firms to term out their financing since the early 1980s. Second, alternative non-bank financing options have grown. In some cases, the term shadow banking is utilized, but this has a negative connotation. Non-bank financing is expected to continue to grow as firms seek flexibility to an increasingly uncertain economic global outlook.

Today, corporate tax reform and bank regulation and deregulation provide two influences on the pattern of credit financing going forward. Economic activity and credit finance will continue to grow. Yet how that finance is conducted—either through banks or bank-like conduits or in other more "shadow-like" channels—will reflect a decision based upon tax and regulatory policies. Secular trends over the last thirty years have indicated a pattern of lower interest rates and financial innovation. The make-up of these factors is certainly likely to change going forward.

Shocks: The Perennial Change in Public Policy

No matter what the country, a new national administration means change for financial markets—even more so when international policy impacts domestic finance.[35]

Early in the Civil War, the Confederacy relied mostly on tariffs on imports and taxes on exports to raise revenues. However, with the fall of New Orleans in 1862 to Admiral David Farragut of the Union Navy, the South was forced to shift financial strategies.[36]

Southern financing moved to employing cotton as collateral for a cotton-backed bond. The bonds were issued in London and Amsterdam, denominated in British sterling, and convertible to cotton in the pre-war price of six pence a pound. The price of the bonds rose with the price of cotton between 1862 and 1864 but then fell with the destruction of Atlanta by General William Tecumseh Sherman. Moreover, the Union naval blockade made it increasingly difficult for investors to access the cotton. Eventually, the South simply printed money and the North pledged not to honor the debts of the South. Meanwhile, the price of the Dutch-issued loans fell throughout the war and the South selectively defaulted on these.[37]

In the coronavirus shutdown periods of the first half of 2020, the pivot in the attractiveness of high-yield debt during the crisis reflects the initial shock and then subsequent policy response. Like the cotton bonds, high-yield debt reflected the changing winds of economic forces.

---

[35] "Argentina's 'Preposterous' Century Bond Never Got Chance to Grow Old," *Wall Street Journal* September. 1, 2020.
[36] Niall Ferguson, "The Ascent of Money," The Penguin Press, 2008. Pp. 92–97.
[37] Marc Weidenmier, "Money and Finance in the Confederate States of America", EH.Net Encyclopedia.

"Investors, Fearing Defaults, Rush Out of Junk Bonds," *Wall Street Journal* **March 26, 2020**
And yet, just a few weeks later
"Coronavirus latest: U.S. junk bonds rally most since 2009 after Fed intervention, "*Financial Times* **April 10, 2020**

Shocks can also appear in pairs. Structural patterns and breaks are superimposed on the trend and cyclical patterns. This pattern gives rise to the sentiment that what hit the bond market was a liquidity not solvency issue. For example, the energy sector faced a shock in early 2020 when the impact of the Russia and OPEC actions in 2020 set a much lower bar for oil prices.[38] The West Texas Intermediate (WTI) crude price on April 13th was at $23.71 a barrel compared to$58.23 a barrel in January 14th. Here is the evidence of a structural break in the pricing of WTI and it would be expected to lead to a revaluation of the viability of high-yield bonds in the oil sector.[39] Clearly, the expectation of sustained energy independence for the United States at 50 dollar plus ran against the foreign policy, political, and economic aspirations of OPEC and Russia. Hence the oil price breakdown.

The fallout in other markets (dollar exchange rate and benchmark Treasury yields) hinted at a secular gain in the economic role for the United States in other markets. What may be a cyclical weakness in an economy may also be perceived as a gain in secular strength. Again, for due diligence it is imperative to distinguish between the cyclical weakness evidenced in the equity market, compared to relative global gain in foreign exchange and credit markets.

The Trade-Weighted U.S. Dollar index published by the Federal Reserve rose from an index value of 117.29 on February 20th to a peak on March 23rd of 126.47 and by early September 2020 had fallen back to mid-February values.

The equity market, as measured by the NASDAQ index, registered at 7772 in March and rose to 11,212 for August 2020.

Meanwhile, expectations of a return to normal (perceived by some as above 1%) for the benchmark 10-year Treasury rate remain dashed. In February, the ten-year Treasury note yielded 1.50% and for August the yield fell to 0.65%.

---

[38] "Oil industry faces biggest crisis in 100 years", *Financial Times* March 26, 2020,
[39] "US shale industry braces for wave of bankruptcies", *Financial Times* May 26, 2020.

What About Bond Rating Agencies and Credit Default Derivatives?

Bond rating agencies publish ratings on high-grade and high-yield bonds that are employed by investors to assess the likelihood of default on a given bond. This field has become very controversial since the housing bust in 2007–2009. The concern remains on conflicts of interest. In response to the 2010 Dodd-Frank overhaul, the Securities Exchange Commission (SEC)s did study alternative business models. The SEC completed its study in 2012 but never implemented a new business model. The controversy remains on the housing boom-bust if AAA bonds, Mortgage-Backed Securities (MBS) and Collateralized Debt Obligations (CDO) tranches were not as prevalent as they were at the time would there have been an economic collapse. In addition, Credit Default Derivatives (CDD) were another influence of corporate bond prices and trading. These are fields of considerable controversy and remain touchpoints in the financial markets.

In our next chapter, we will look at the financial fundamentals behind nonfinancial corporate finance and the time-series character of those fundamentals.

* * *

References

Barron's, "Are We in Recession? Yes, Says John Silvia; Maybe, Says Ed Hyman," September 3, 1990 Barron's.
Richard A. Brealey and Stewart C. Myers, "Principles of Corporate Finance," Third Edition, 1988, McGraw-Hill, Inc. New York. My basic text on corporate finance.
Hui Chen "Macroeconomic Conditions and the Puzzles of Credit Spreads and Capital Structure," Journal of Finance, Vol. LXV, No. 6, December 2010. This note is one look at credit spreads and business cycles.
Niall Ferguson, "The Ascent of Money," The Penguin Press, 2008. Pp. 92–97. An interesting note on the shift in Confederate finance during the U.S. Civil War.
Sidney Homer, A History of Interest Rates, Rutgers University Press, 1963.
Mark Gertler and Simon Gilchrist note that due to imperfect capital markets, small firms are likely to face larger barriers to outside finance than small firms. See "Monetary Policy, Business Cycles, and the Behavior of Small Manufacturing Firms, "Quarterly Journal of Economics 109 (May 1994): 309–340.
Merton H. Miller, "The Modigliani-Miller Propositions After Thirty Years," Journal of Economic Perspectives V. 2 No. 4 Fall 1988 pp. 99–120. The debt/equity ratio

itself has been a subject of study and the proposition that the value of the firm is independent of the debt/equity ratio is well known.

Stewart C. Myers, Determinants of Corporate Borrowing," Journal of Financial Economics, 1977. V. 5 pp. 147–175. A review of corporate incentives to borrow.

Guillaume Rocheteau, Randall Wright, and Cathy Zhang, "Corporate Finance and Monetary policy," American Economic Review, 2018, 108 (4–5): 1147–1186. An interesting paper that predates the 2020 intervention and offers some insight on the Fed, liquidity, and corporate finance.

David Romer, "Advanced Macroeconomics," pp. 387–388, McGraw Hill Irwin, third edition, 2006. A fundamental review, and reminder of the user cost of capital.

Analytical Record of Yields and Yield Spreads, March 1990, Salomon Brothers.

Marc Weidenmier, "Money and Finance in the Confederate States of America", EH.Net Encyclopedia. A view of financial flexibility during turbulent times.

7

Dynamics of Corporate Finance: What Motivates Change?

Finance and Economics Linkage: The Case of the Transcontinental Railroad in the United States.

Celebrated in portraits, photographs, movies, and by a postage stamp, the completion of the Transcontinental Railroad in 1869 provides an excellent example of the interaction of corporate finance and economic activity. The railroad boosted the settlement and economy of the northern states involved in the construction. Even more important for our framework, this story illustrates the tension between finance today and economic results tomorrow. To finance the railroad, state and federal governments sold bonds and the railroads—the Central Pacific Railroad Company of California and the Union Pacific Railroad—sold mortgage bonds to finance construction. The federal government paid the railroads by the track mileage laid. The financial realities were more complex, however. The railroads made money on the construction, not on the operation of the railroad. As is typical of many large transportation infrastructure projects, the profits accrue to the builders since the high fixed costs of a project are significantly larger than the revenues from the operation of the railroad in this case.

Economic growth requires finance. This interaction provides a basis for both the economic growth and the financing activity.

Lessons from a Prior Cycle

"But in retrospect, the growth of debt and leverage was out of line with subsequent economic expansion and asset appreciation." Chairman Alan Greenspan, *Monetary Policy Report to Congress* February 1992.

In his report to Congress, Chairman Greenspan made two major points: he saw a link between economic activity and finance; and he argued that the leverage (an investment strategy of using various financial instruments to increase the potential return of an investment) and the debt of today must be paid out of earnings from a project sometime in the future.

The 1990s are generally considered a period of economic prosperity. But even then, the balance of economic growth and financial activity was misaligned. For Chairman Greenspan, the problem was, in part, the lingering inflation psychology from the 1970s that still existed in the minds of decision-makers. They issued debt but a decline of inflation resulted in a rise in the real value and burden of the debt, as well as a real higher carrying cost of the debt.

An outsized accumulation of certain kinds of real assets and an even more rapid growth of debt and leverage was reflected in an appreciation of the price of real assets. This pattern of behavior was repeated in the housing bubble of the 2000s.

Credit today and payback tomorrow reflects a future imperfect—expectations of growth, inflation, interest rates and corporate profits, ex ante, may not prove out over time. Even in Chairman Greenspan's testimony, he cites that, in some parts of the country, buying new homes "seemed to be motivated more by speculative considerations than by fundamental needs."

For the business sector, there was also an increase in desired leverage. Deals were predicated on overly optimistic assumptions about what the economy could deliver without setback and that asset prices would always rise. There was a surge in debt-financed commercial real estate construction. Bank credit grew more than nominal income growth. The inevitable correction appeared as economic growth slowed to potential growth rates. Asset values declined as debt servicing burdens rose.

For Chairman Greenspan, despite his growing concern, there were signals of stress and then improvement in the financial sectors that supported a recovery—debt to equity at book value, lower interest rates, and the increased issuance of equity. We now turn to look at the internal dynamics of corporate finance and their position relative to the economic developments.

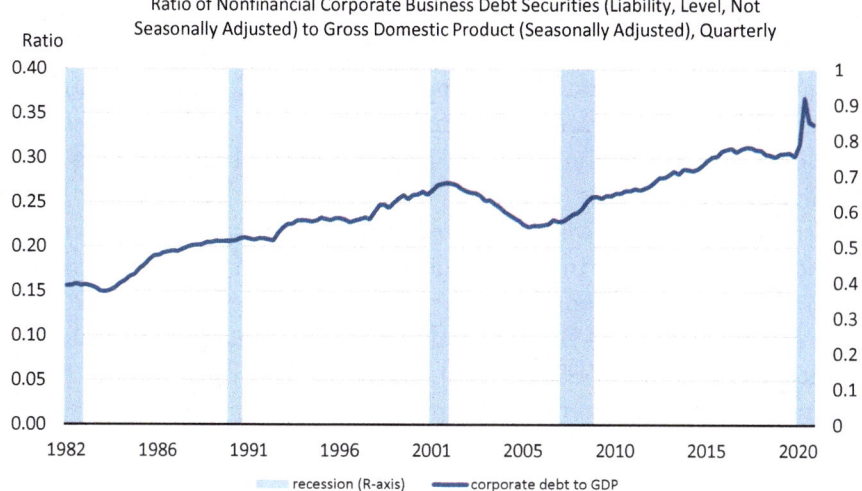

Fig. 7.1 Ratio of corporate debt to nominal GDP

Putting Corporate Debt into Perspective

Nonfinancial corporate debt, relative to GDP, has risen during the 2010 to 20,119 expansion (Fig. 7.1) which is like the peak of the previous 2000s expansion. Low-interest rates and longer payment periods have kept corporate debt cheap, but these trends are beginning to reverse.

Corporate debt growth turned positive in 2011 and has averaged 5.8% a year since, propelled higher by low-interest rates and robust investor appetite for fixed income securities. Interestingly, nonfinancial corporate debt has a causal link to both real final sales and the core PCE deflator.

The overall U.S. economy has become less indebted since the recession of 2007–2009, with domestic debt outstanding as a percent of gross domestic product (GDP) falling to 33% in Q1 from more than 370% at the start of 2009. Shrinking debt relative to GDP is mainly due to deleveraging in the household and financial sectors, while debt has grown faster than GDP for government and nonfinancial business. One caution, comparisons of a stock of debt to a flow of income is quite common.[1] We use it here simply as an example of a comparison found in many financial commentaries.[2]

---

[1] Bade and Parkin, *Macroeconomics*, 8th edition, Pearson, p. 495.
[2] "The Precarious Global Debt Picture," *Financial Times*, October 28, 2020.

Internal Dynamics of Corporate Finance

For an analyst, it is critical to distinguish stocks and flows in examining the behavior of corporations. After-tax profits provide a basis for assessing the ability of a corporation to invest, pay its labor, and make good on debt obligations.

There is also a critical role for external finance—equity, bonds, mortgages, bank loans, and short-term finance such as commercial paper. For example, in 2019, the increase in nonfinancial corporate liabilities totaled $1.26 T. of which bonds were $247.4 B., loans and mortgages totaled $304 B. and equity issuance was a negative $699 B. Internal and external funds are not perfect substitutes and there is an information asymmetry about these funds (covered in Chapter 6). There is also a premium to external finance relative to the cost of internal funds.

Several financial ratios illustrate the behavior of corporate finance over the cycle and the long run. Before becoming Fed chairman Benjamin Bernanke[3] cited in a research paper the behavior of the debt to market value of equity as one measure of corporate leverage. This reflected a comparison between the stock of debt to the stock of equity and benchmarked the extent to which corporations rely on debt rather than equity to fund operations. The ratio of debt to total assets at historical costs tends to rise. But when with market value for equity as the denominator, this ratio declined as equity market valuations improved.

In his paper, Bernanke also cited the flow concept of interest expense relative to cash flow (coverage ratio). This reflects the number of times cash flow could meet the existing interest burden of the debt. This interest coverage ratio exhibited peaks in 1997, 2006, and 2015 and signaled a change in the wind for the economy.

Again, to quote a respected financial source Mr. Joshamee Gibbs in the *Pirates of the Caribbean:* "Leverage says you. I feel a change in the wind says I."

The popular preoccupation[4] with the total amount of corporate debt and its ratio to GDP is a comparison of a stock of debt to a flow of income. This ratio provides little insight into what is going on behind the reality of corporate finance. Patterns in net interest expense relative to operating surplus, current assets to current liabilities, the quick ratio, and the financing gap provide cyclical patterns to corporate finance. These patterns illustrate

---

[3] Ben Bernanke, John Y. Campbell and Toni Whited, "U.S. Corporate Leverage: Developments in 1987 and 1988," *Brookings Papers on Economic Activity*, 1990, 1.
[4] Is There Too Much Business Debt? *Anna Kovner and Brandon Zborowski 05 29 2019 FRB NY.*

the sensitivity of corporate balance sheets to economic change in the credit markets (interest rates) and the pace of economic growth. Like Bernanke, we keep our ratios, for the most part, where data allows, on stock/stock and flow/flow comparisons.

A broad credit channel for monetary policy exists—especially in the era of Covid-19 shutdowns.[5] With the direct buying of U.S. Treasury debt, mortgage debt, and corporate bonds, the central banks, such as the Fed, European Central Bank, and the Bank of Japan, are directly influencing capital markets and the pricing of debt.

The quick ratio (the ratio of current assets less inventories to short-term liabilities). This ratio was particularly useful before the 2000–2001 and again the 2007–2008 downturns. This ratio was also useful in signaling caution for the 1990-1991 recession as sharp declines in the ratio from 1987 to 1999 gave a heads-up to the oncoming credit squeeze (see my interview, "Are We in Recession" in Barron's September 3, 1990).[6]

Looking Behind the Veil of Corporate Debt

The stock of corporate debt is a snapshot of one side of the nonfinancial sector's balance sheet—certainly, an inadequate benchmark for serious investors. Both sides of the balance sheet are important such as the ratio of debt to the market value of equity cited by Bernanke et al. and reviewed in Chapter 6. Different time dimensions are important such as current assets to current liabilities and the ratio of short-term debt to long-term debt. The income side of the firm is important as evidenced in the net interest expense to cash flow. Finally, the balance between a firm's cash flow and its capital spending is another benchmark. Perceptions of value matter as exemplified by the Tobin Q ratio (The Q ratio equals the market value of a company divided by its assets' replacement cost).

Changes in interest rates and inflation provide a link to the ratio of debt to market value, Fig. 7.2, and the economy. The federal funds rate, a policy rate set by the Federal Reserve, has a causal link to the corporate AA rate, Fig. 7.3, as well as interest expense for nonfinancial corporations as well as influencing the ratio of short-term debt to long-term debt for these same corporations. A

---

[5] Stephen D. Oliner and Glenn D. Rudebusch argue in favor of this channel for small firms long before 2020. See "Is There a Broad Credit Channel for Monetary Policy," *Federal Reserve Bank of San Francisco Economic Review*, 1996, no. 1.

[6] The commentary in Barron's reflect my long-time interest and prior research on the link between economic growth and the interest burden of corporate debt. See John E. Silvia "Corporate Debt: The Interest Burden in the Next Recession," Paper presented at the Eastern Economic Association Conference, Baltimore, March 4, 1989.

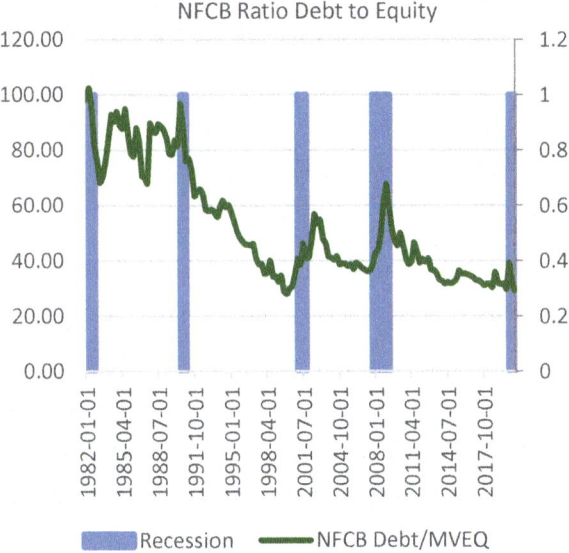

Fig. 7.2 Debt as percentage of market value of equity

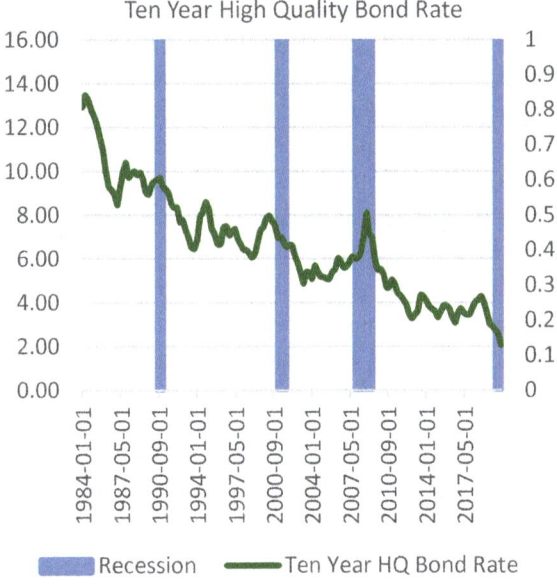

Fig. 7.3 Ten-year high quality corporate bond rate

rise in nominal rates, accompanied by a rise in inflation, would cause the real value of depreciation and inventory deductions to fall (for firms using FIFO). The drop in the value of these deductions would imply an increase in the use of debt during the time FIFO (first in, first out) was a standard procedure.

The short-term debt to long-term debt ratio provides an interesting perspective. Since 2001, firms have termed out their debt as evidenced by the secular decline in short-term debt as a percent of long-term debt. Incentives are the driving force: interest rates and bond market liquidity. Lower interest rates (higher bond prices) provide an incentive to term out debt by issuing more long-term debt. This terming out reduces the sensitivity of the balance sheet to changes in interest rates. On the demand side, global liquidity, and lower bond returns in Europe, have meant an increase in the marketplace for U.S. corporate debt as investors seek yield.

This series of short-term to long-term debt has a linear trend which opens the possibility that we can estimate the effect over time of the fed funds rate on this ratio. Also, a possibility is that a rising (falling) fed funds rate scenario going forward would be associated with a rising (falling) short-term and long-term debt ratio—quite a change for the markets going forward.

In fact, causality runs from the fed funds rate to this ratio and not from this ratio to the fed funds rate. This would certainly help explain the long downward slope of this series since 1982 that has corresponded with the long-term decline in the funds rate.

While the secular trend in the ratio of short-term to long-term debt has declined since 2001, there is also a cyclical pattern where short-term debt rises in the early phase of an economic recovery (2004–2006, 2010–2012) and then resumes its secular downward pattern. The period of 2004–2006 saw a rise in the U.S. fed funds rate. The rise in the ratio intimates that perhaps corporations decided to finance short term. They may have perceived that the rise in rates was also short term and they anticipated that long-term rates would come down soon enough. Speculation to be sure but it turned out to be a particularly good guess.

The rise in short-term debt in 2010–2012 is not associated with a rise in the fed funds rate but the period of 2010–2012 was associated with a sharp rise in Euro sovereign yields. This would indicate an incentive for U.S. firms (and for Euro investors as well) to avoid long-term debt as a means of risk avoidance. Another sign of global capital markets in action.

Unexpected changes, meanwhile, in interest rates and inflation would affect the total value of the firm. Increases in the real after-tax discount rate would reduce the value of the firm. For a given inflation, it would raise the debt-value ratio. A rise in the inflation rate, given nominal interest rates, (thereby a decline in the real rate) would lower the debt-value ratio.[7]

Each of these series carries an underlying pattern of behavior that varies over the economic cycle and travels a special path over time. The pioneering economist Irving Fisher emphasized as far back as the 1930s that debt is a complex phenomenon.[8] Beyond just the dollar amount, there is the issue of the maturity structure of the debt. The concept of indebtedness is a relative concept that depends on wealth, income, and the availability of liquid assets.

The high levels of debt relative to equity in the 1980s reflect a high level of corporate leverage during the period. During this period, interest expense ran at 21% of corporate cash flow—an extremely high percentage compared to the mid-1950s to mid-1970s average of 40–50%. Over time, there was a loss of corporate flexibility. External financing was the outcome as retained earnings fell relative to interest expense from 1980 to 1988.

For the real economy, leverage reduced business' ability to respond to changing circumstances setting a limit on the growth of real business fixed investment. Moreover, the first half of the 1980s was a period of relatively high-interest rates and an overvalued dollar before the Plaza Accord. These factors incentivized business to restructure. Credit was needed to finance change and restructuring. Reorganization required financing and long-term financing is a two-edged sword—it finances competitiveness today, but it risks restricting corporate flexibility in the future.

Patterns of short-term to total corporate debt (Fig. 7.4) have both a cyclical and secular character and were cited, along with several other benchmarks, such as the interest coverage ratio in a Barron's interview.[9] During the periods of 2004–2006 and again in 2010–2012, short-term debt rose but over the entire 2002–2017 period, the ratio of short-term to long-term debt declined. On net, nonfinancial corporations have reduced their sensitivity to changes in short-term interest rates and, perhaps, the vagaries of the pace of economic growth over the short term. The ratio of short-term to total debt impacts both the real side of the economy, real final sales, and the credit markets through the high-yield spread over Treasury rates.

---

[7] Joao Gomes, Urban Jermann, and Lukas Schmid, "Sticky Leverage," *American Economic Review*, 2016, 106, no. 12: 3800–3828 and Roger H. Gordon, "Interest Rates, Inflation, and Corporate Financial Policy," *Brookings Papers on Economic Activity*, 1982, 2.

[8] Irving Fisher, "The Debt-Deflation Theory of Great Depression," *Econometrica*, 1933, 1, no. 4 (October).

[9] This ratio of short-term to long-term debt was cited by me in the Barron's article "Are We in Recession?" Barron's September 3, 1990. At that time, I argued for the affirmative.

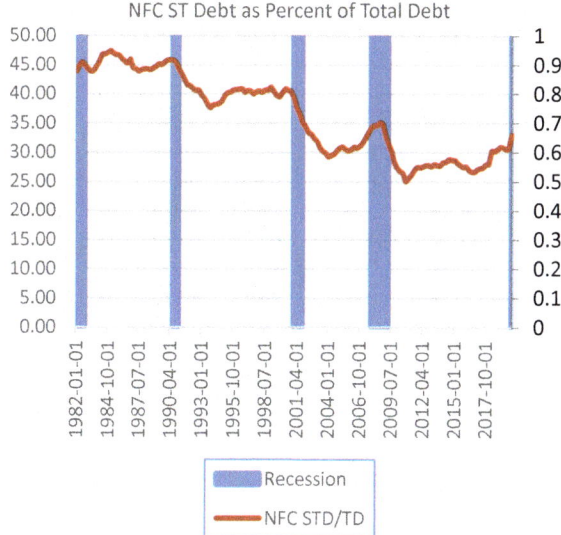

Fig. 7.4 Non-Financial Corporate Debt: Short-term Debt as a Percent of Total Debt

However, there could be a catch. If firms are committed to a series of long-term interest payments that would be excessive if the pace of economic growth were to significantly slow over time, then the burden of that long-term interest commitment (relative to a slower pace of earnings to pay that debt) would create financial stress.

Corporate financial leverage varies over the business cycle. It therefore provides a cyclical character to the sensitivity of corporate credit quality to changes in interest rates and the pace of economic growth. It will be interesting to observe what value these ratios play in tracking the cycle itself. Over time, there are significant breakpoints in 1965, 1981, 1991, 2002, 2009. The last four are associated with recession eras where the lack of economic growth led to a downshift in short-term debt as interest rates fell and firms could term out their financing. Corporate bond spreads and the PCE deflator measure of inflation have causal links to the ratio of short-term to long-term debt.

In a similar vein, corporate profits, Fig. 7.5, has both a cyclical and secular pattern.[10] Since the dawn of the modern, post-inflation spike/Paul Volcker Fed financial era began in 1982, net interest expense has steadily declined along with nominal GDP. Of course, except—there is always an exception—during the rapid declines in nominal GDP associated with economic weakness and recessions—1989–1990, 2000–2002, 2007–2010. The balance

---

[10] This series on interest coverage was also cited as a reason to argue that we were in recession in 1990 as quoted in *Barron's* September 3, 1990.

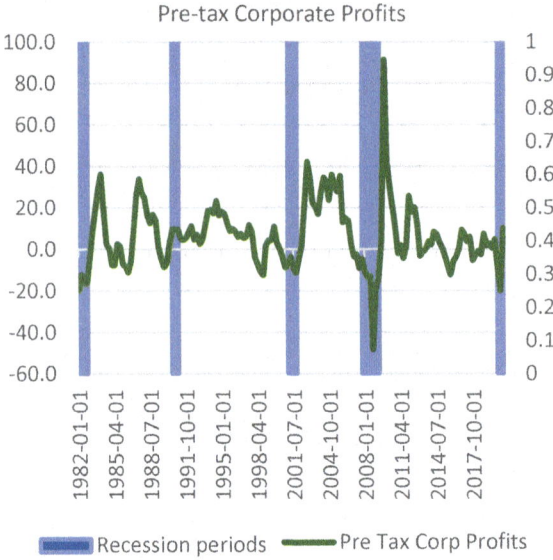

Fig. 7.5 Pre-tax corporate profits

between expected economic growth and the future interest burden of the debt is subject to considerable variability. The interest expense ratio highlights the cyclical sensitivity of the economy, for example in the late 1980s, in late 1990s, and in the 2004–2006 period. This became painfully obvious again in 2020. Credit quality is far from static. It is the product of expectations for both interest rates and economic growth and of a rising net interest expense ratio highlights a growing sensitivity of the corporate balance sheet to shocks in the economy.

Interest Coverage Ratio and GDP: Who is in Charge? Growth

The linkage between interest expense and economic growth has led to speculation that higher corporate interest expense and debt could lead to a weaker economy. There would appear to be a relationship between the two series. However, the relationship runs from economic growth to net interest expense and not the other way around. A high level of net interest expense does not lead to economic weakness but, rather, economic weakness does drive a higher level of net interest expense as a percent of operating surplus. The ability of a corporation to pay interest reflects the forces of changes in corporate profits (often linked closely to the pace of economic growth) and changes

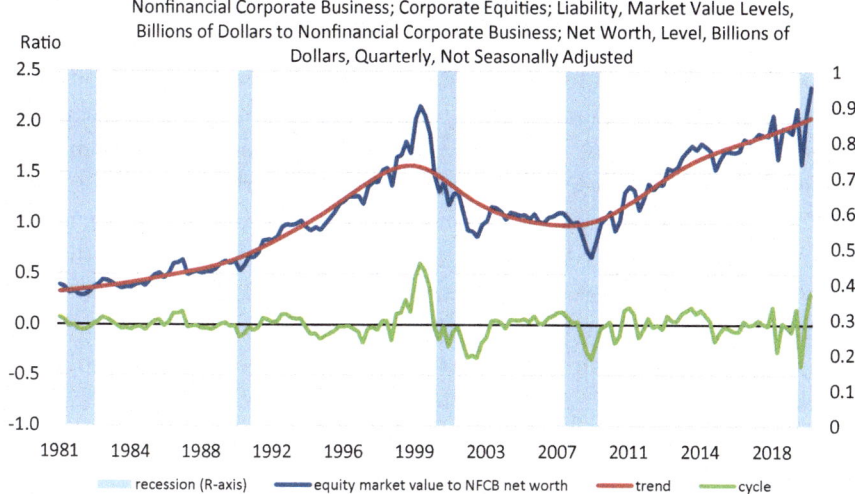

Fig. 7.6 Tobin's Q

in market interest rates. Periods of rising interest expense are associated with rising interest rates (1988–1989, 1994–early 1995, and then again 2004–2006) and with a peak in the ratio of interest expense to corporate earnings just before a recession. Interest coverage is indeed cyclical.

Often, the causal appearance of a relationship between economic activity and financial benchmarks can be taken as fact. Unfortunately, the appearance of causality can be misleading. It is essential to examine the variables and then determine whether one consistently is leading or lagging the other. Causation cannot always be derived from this practice, but often the variables' behavior can be forecasted with more directional certainty.

A static (today), one variable (total corporate debt) view fails to allow for change in the financial framework, as well as an appreciation of the underlying economic incentives that make that framework viable. Today's corporate debt must be repaid out of future corporate earnings which creates a dynamic process of financial opportunities and risks.

Tobin's Q as Benchmark for Value: **"More what you'd call 'guidelines' than actual rules.**[11]**"—Captain Hector Barbossa**

Tobin's Q (illustrated in Fig. 7.6) provides a rough gauge of the balance between the market value of equities and the replacement cost of existing assets. (Tobin's Q is defined as the market value of equities outstanding relative to the net worth of nonfinancial companies) The ratio equals 1.0 when

---

[11] Captain Hector Barbossa in *Pirates of the Caribbean: The Curse of the Black Pearl*, Walt Disney Pictures, 2003.

market values reflect the replacement values. When Tobin's Q is above 1.0, then market values are relatively high, providing an incentive for a company to issue equity capital and invest in real assets. In contrast, when Tobin's Q is below 1.0, market values are low relative to the replacement costs. The market may be thus undervaluing the book value of the real assets of the company.

This ratio provides a very rough gauge of equity market value and suggests a link between financial market activity and the real economy. At the current Tobin Q reading, just a bit above 1.0, the market may be slightly overvaluing real capital. suggesting that firms have an incentive to issue equity, but investors need to watch valuations.

Finally, Tobin's Q exhibits an interesting pattern. From 1982 until 1999, the market value of equities steadily rose (consistent perhaps with the steady decline in interest rates) but then broke sharply below 1.0. Since 2009, there has been a steady rise in the ratio again.

The Tobin Q was devised by economist Nicholas Kaldor and popularized by Noble Prize-winning economist James Tobin for whom it is named. It is a guideline for the balance of valuations between the real physical value of a company and the financial market assessment of that value. We are interested here in what the ratio may indicate about the broader economy (market for goods and services) and the financial economy (market for financial capital). Tobin's Q is only a guideline since the calculation does not include a measure of market hype and the intellectual capital of the firm—both highly visible in the tech era of investing since 2002.

Since 2013, this ratio has been above 1.0, providing a firm with the incentive to issue equity capital. Unfortunately, current values may be creating too much of an incentive to issue equity capital given the public market performance of recent IPOs. The Tobin Q ratio has a causal link to both the ten- and two-year Treasury rate as well as real final sales and the core PCE deflator.

Many economic series are often more of a guideline rather than a rule in decision-making and this hints at a more reliable use of Tobin's Q. For example, the Q-ratio collapsed in the 1970s and yet business fixed investment rose. Tobin's Q provides a rough gauge of the balance between the replacement costs of real assets and the market value of equities. It will be interesting to observe the link of this ratio to other financial and economic benchmarks. Blanchard, Rhee, and Summers argue that fundamentals are better related to real business investment than Tobin's Q.[12] In their study, profits play a central role in determining real business investment. This is another example of the importance of linkages between economic and financial sectors.

---

[12] O. Blanchard, C. Rhee and L. Summers, "The Stock Market, Profit, and Investment," *Quarterly Journal of Economics*, 1993, 108, no. 1: 115–136.

"September Busiest Month Ever for Corporate Bond Issuance," *Financial Times* October 1, 2019

Corporate financial leverage varies over the business cycle which provides a cyclical character to the sensitivity of corporate credit quality to changes in interest rates and the pace of economic growth. Concerns about corporate leverage are a recurring theme in every economic cycle. One interesting aspect of the balance sheet for nonfinancial corporations is their ratio of current assets to current liabilities, Fig. 7.7. There are two distinct patterns in this series. During the 2000s expansion, this ratio rose with the economic expansion as assets rose relative to liabilities.

However, since 2010, leverage in the manufacturing sector has risen as current assets have declined relative to current liabilities. The ratio of current assets to current liabilities does impact the debt to market value of equity.

Since 2000, this ratio exhibits long trends consistent with an economic expansion and then a change in direction with a recession. This series has clearly not behaved as if it is mean reverting to any single value in a way. Manufacturing and nonfinancial corporations have insulated themselves more and more over time away from the impact of higher interest rates as the ratio of short-term to long-term debt has declined.

It is not the simple increase in liabilities that appears to be an issue. Rather, it is the proliferation of such liabilities into a marketplace that cannot support that issuance due to the cyclical nature of the economy and market-determined interest rates. While the willingness to seek credit may be

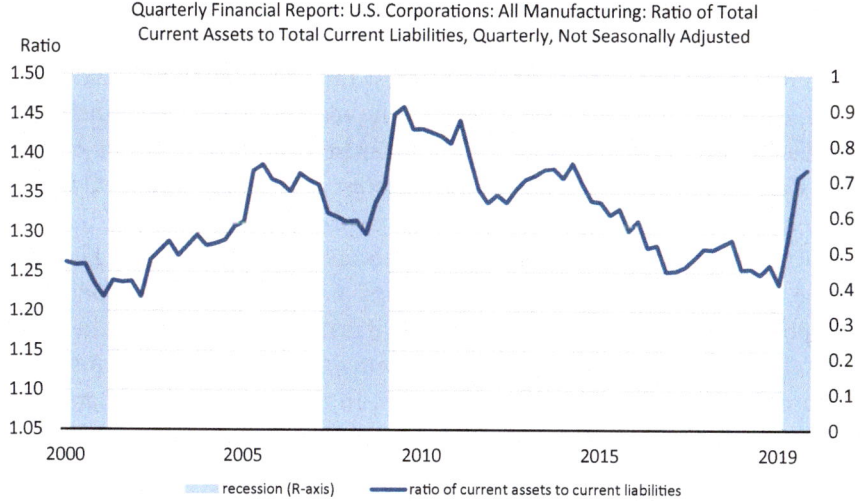

Fig. 7.7 Current ratio

unlimited, there is a limit to the willingness of suppliers of credit to accept that credit at given interest rates and credit standards.

Causality: From Equity Markets to Credit Markets

Corporate finance reflects the impact of equity markets, as benchmarked by the NASDAQ or NYSE, stock indices. Movements in equity market benchmarks impact corporate net worth of corporations but also provide predictive value for nominal GDP and high-quality corporate rates—both of which impact business leaders expectations as well as hiring and business investment decisions.

Corporate Leverage: A Note on the Influence of Changes in Corporate Benchmark Yields

Since the early 1980s, short-term financing as a share of total credit market debt for nonfinancial corporations has steadily declined along with the AA corporate bond yield. This ratio provides a perspective on the degree to which nonfinancial corporations are dependent on short-term debt and therefore changes in interest rate expense. Statistically, this ratio is not mean reverting and is nonlinear so there is no path to a "normal" rate. Corporations appear to have followed the AA yield down with less and less short-term financing and adding on more long-term debt to term out their interest burden. Indeed, causality does run from AA yields to the ratio of short-term debt. This result reinforces the expectations that the debt burden on nonfinancial corporations would be less sensitive to changes in interest rates than in prior decades.

The early 1980s is a cautionary tale of the real burden of debt when inflation declines faster than expected.[13] Economist Jerome Fons points out that when disinflation is unanticipated, real interest rates rise and the real burden of interest payments rises. In the 1970s, there was an upswing in the share of short-term debt relative to long-term debt as interest rates rose. The rapid decline in the AA corporate rate in the first half of the 1980s should have prompted an increase in long-term debt issuance to term out debt repayments. Short-term debt finance, however, remained high as many firms lacked the liquidity to refinance at favorable terms. In contrast, note the sharp move to term out debt in response to the 1990 recession period. As an indicator of

---

[13] Jerome S. Fons, "Debt-Deflation and Corporate Finance," *Economic Commentary*, Federal Reserve Bank of Cleveland, March 15, 1987.

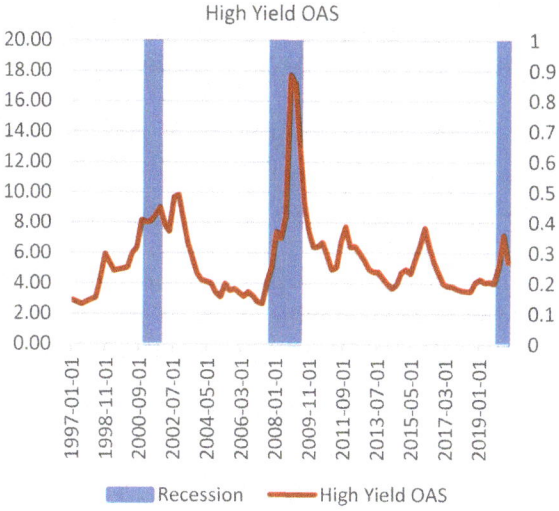

Fig. 7.8 High yield option adjusted spread

the lack of liquidity and cash flow squeeze, the net interest payments of nonfinancial corporations as a percent of cash flow rose rapidly in 1984–1988 and approached the recessionary periods of 1974–1975 and 1982–1983 while exceeding the peaks in the recessions of 1970–1971 and 1980. In their review, Merrill Lynch cited the issue of "a potential loss of corporate flexibility" due to the burden of this high ratio.[14]

Introducing Change: The Role of Inflation and High Yield Spreads

The core PCE has an impact on the rate of growth for unit labor costs which, in turn, impacts pre-tax corporate profits. This causal linkage provides an important link from monetary policy directed at an inflation target to unit labor costs and thereby corporate profits.

Meanwhile high-yield bond spreads, Fig. 7.8, have a pervasive impact on the debt/equity ratio for nonfinancial corporations as well as corporate interest expense and thereby their operating surplus. The long downtrend in high-yield spreads since 2010 has bolstered corporate balance sheets and reduced, but not eliminated, the risk of credit shocks to nonfinancial corporations and the overall economy.

---

[14] Merrill Lynch, "Weekly Economic and Financial Commentary," March 28, 1988.

Forged in Fire: Indicators of Tensile Strength in the Nonfinancial Corporate Asset Market

Fear and closing one eye are the natural reaction, at least for me, of watching one of the three judges on the History Channel's *Forged in Fire* bend a sword blade to test the sword's ability to come back to true. If you catch an episode when they do this, the experiment is intriguing. Examining the corporate balance sheet and income statement is an experiment in bending the financial cutting edge to find the breaking point.

"Deals were predicated on overly optimistic assumptions about what the economy could deliver without setback and that asset prices would always rise." Alan Greenspan, Congressional Testimony, February. 19, 1992.

"The logic of an investment is never so clear and compelling as at the top of the market." Jim Grant, *Wall Street Journal*, October 25, 1988.

Given the cyclical behavior of the manufacturing sector, a closer look at the manufacturing sector is worth the peek. The ratio of operating income to interest expense for the manufacturing sector is a cyclical series that improves as corporate profits recover after a recession but can drop quickly as profits collapse during a recession (2008–2009). What is unusual is that since 2015, interest coverage has declined even though the economy has continued to grow. Manufacturing firms have failed to take advantage of the decline in corporate financing rates and this raised their financial sensitivity going into the year 2020.

There are two issues here. First, top-line operating income has been impacted by the decline in profit growth since 2014 and profit growth became negative on a year-over-year basis. Moreover, nonfinancial domestic corporate profit margins peaked in early 2014 and have declined over the past two years.

Second, The FOMC had been raising the benchmark fed funds rate since the end of 2015 to the end of 2018 and this has been associated with a rise in net interest expense over the same period. In 2017 and 2018 the FOMC anticipated that further upward inflation pressures going forward in 2017 and 2018 would justify higher fed funds rates. For nonfinancial corporations, this would raise interest expense and weaken interest coverage. The interest coverage ratio provides a glimpse into the trends and cyclical behavior of financial ratios over the credit cycle.

Two other ratios also offer some insight. The return on assets, net income as a percent of total assets, provides another guideline as peaks in 1998, 2007, and most recently 2013 supply a note of caution on the financial character of corporate finance. As we have cited in an earlier note, the equity market, like Wile E. Coyote, can levitate longer than the support of the ground below it. We are cautious, but not entirely skeptical, on utilizing the S&P 500 index alone as a signal of credit issues.

Once Again, the Importance of Cognitive Bias Recognition Not Just Number Following

There is not a single indicator of emerging credit problems or strength in the nonfinancial corporate credit sector. Moreover, there remains a clear cycle of credit spreads over U.S. Treasury yields that appear, in retrospect, inconsistent with the evolution of the data (the image of Wile E. Coyote is useful here as well). The laws of crowd psychology have not been repealed. First, there is the demonstration problem. As innovation succeeds in reaping profits, imitators tend to follow as was true of the 1830s British railroad bubble. Initial success led imitators to invest and stretch the boundaries of economic possibility and, for some, to ruin. In the United States, many imitators of the Erie Canal were also brought to failure. Several generations later, history brought another example in the railroad bust of the 1879s.

In other examples, the initial instrument for success—commercial paper, high-yield bonds, CDOs—when carried too far led to failure although the instrument itself was sound. Unfortunately, the conditions of its issue (covenants, financial strength of the issue) fell prey to the evolving conditions of the economy. It is no surprise that securities issued in the early phase of an economic expansion default at a much lower rate than those that are issued in the latter stages of the economic expansion. Once again, we witness the integration of economics and finance. Companies and credit instruments do not stand alone. The conditions of the economy are paramount to judging credit quality. The price today is not a benchmark for value in the future. Like our discussion on bank lending, we lend today but the quality of a loan is determined by the economic and financial conditions in the future.

"September busiest month of corporate bond issuance," *Financial Times* October 1, 2019.

Establishing a baseline for corporate finance is essential to developing a perspective on current issues. How might we characterize the corporate bond market in the period before the 2020 recession and compare that to the longer-run history of critical financial benchmarks that are familiar to us?

In recent years, low-interest rates relative to the perceived rate of return on real investment or refinancing of past more expensive bond issuance has led to an increase in bonds as a share of corporate liabilities (Chapter 6). Credit standards for Commercial and Industrial (C&I) loans have also eased (especially in 2016–2018, Chapter 5) and credit spreads narrowed in the period of 2015–2018.[15] Were these spreads enough to compensate for the risk of weaker economic growth and higher interest rates? Changes in LIBOR, as a measure of short-term rates, and the pace of inflation, as measured by the PCE deflator, have a causal link to the high-yield spread. There are breakpoints in the series associated with recessions in 2000 and 2007 as would be consistent with the expectation that recession would lead to a retrenchment in risk taking and thereby an increase in spreads. The high-yield spread has a causal link to nonfinancial corporate interest expense and operating surplus.

The case against high-yield debt in the late 1980s was not against the instrument itself. Rather the concern centered on the proliferation of debt in the face of crowd psychology where the rush into high yield, both on the demand and credit side, was reminiscent of the rush into many new opportunities a la the California and Alaska Gold Rushes. Prosperity should make borrowers and lenders guarded as bad times always follow good. The credit cycle has not been repealed. Securities issued late in the 1920s defaulted at a significantly higher rate than those issued in the early 1920s. The first gold miners made the money while very few of the followers ever made it rich. As financial innovation succeeds, for example, high-yield bonds, imitators follow. Under the press of competition, lending standards invariably slip.

Calculating the growth of debt by itself is not useful nor is the ratio of corporate debt (a stock) to GDP (a flow) is useful. We need to take a closer look at the underlying fundamentals that drive the macro numbers of debt and GDP.

For interest rates, we can trace the patterns of the three-month LIBOR rate as a benchmark for the user cost of capital. This rate has both significant secular and cyclical trend characteristics. This rate drifted up throughout 2016–2018 as the Fed raised its funds rate. This would signal rising financing costs for nonfinancial companies. As reviewed above, LIBOR has a causal impact on both high-yield and high-quality spreads as well as nonfinancial interest expense, the yield curve, and the benchmark ten-year rate. The impact of changes in LIBOR is pervasive.

---

[15] Interestingly, Geoffrey Moore identified both relaxation of credit standards and a reduction of risk premiums as two of several factors in credit cycles. Geoffrey H. Moore, "The Quality of Credit in Booms and Depressions," *Journal of Finance*, May 1956.

The Character of Manufacturing Finance Leading Into 2018

Manufacturing profits sat at a relatively high level compared to previous expansions in 2018. Though firms have been taking on more debt, equity relative to debt also remained in a better position than in the prior cycle.

Manufacturing after-tax profits per dollar of sales have hovered around nine cents through much of this expansion. These margins are higher than in the prior two economic recoveries. Profits fell in Q4 2018 to around seven cents per dollar against the backdrop of significant changes to the tax code but remain near the upper end of historic norms. With corporate tax rates falling to 21% from 35% as of January 1st, firms may have shifted earnings and expenses between late 2017 and early 2018 to reduce tax liabilities. Therefore, the recent drop in profits is likely noise.

Profits, Growth, and the Economic Cycle

One possible reason for the higher after-tax profits as a percent of sales is the apparent downshift in the Employment Cost index for private workers in the manufacturing sector (Fig. 7.9).

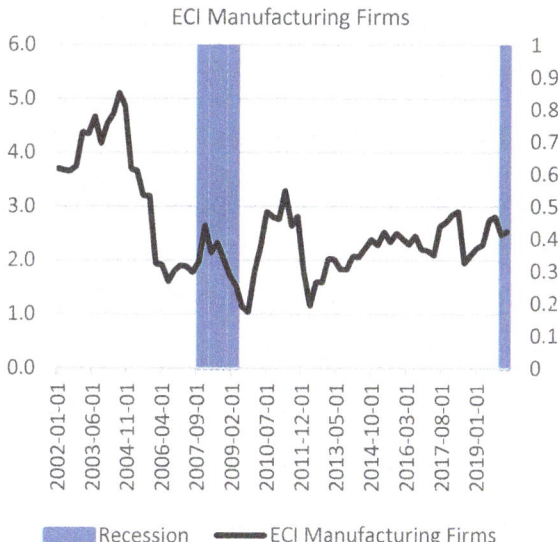

Fig. 7.9 Employment cost index

Relatively high margins should help manufacturing firms maintain their current advantageous financial position. However, downturns in manufacturers' profit margins are sharp and swift (2001, 2007–2008). They come with little warning (see below). Assurances of credit quality today may quickly turn into warnings tomorrow. As a principle of action, the manufacturing sector remains cyclical and its movements in response to downswings and upswings in profit margins are more extreme than for the economy overall.

Sector Linkages

The period of the 1970s to 2006 provides several observations of the linkage of inflation and disinflation to financial ratios along with the additional impacts of changes in the dollar exchange rates and equity valuations. Following the Crash of 1929, economist Irving Fisher commented that debt was not one-dimensional. Debt can be characterized as both a total in dollars and by the maturity structure of debt. The over indebtedness of a firm depends on national wealth, income, and the availability of liquid assets.

Major downturns for Fisher were associated with over indebtedness and a deflation of the value of the assets. Deflation also meant an increase in the real interest rate associated with the debt. This over indebtedness would lead to distress, selling at fire sale prices, a loss of business confidence, and general retrenchment in business spending.

There is an absence of new opportunities to invest at above-normal prospective profits. As Fisher asserted,[16] there is a need to offset deflationary forces by creating more liquidity (his examples were 1837, 1873, 1893, 1929). Today we can see central bank actions during 2007–2009 and again in 2020 in the same light. These same sentiments of monetary actions to offset deflationary forces were asserted by Walter Bagehot in Lombard Street.[17]

Evolution of Growth and Interest Coverage

A popular commentary[18] regularly cites the role of disruption in the economy. Yet, disruption has been a common theme in the financial markets, especially in the context of corporate finance (1991, 2002, and 2011) and represent

---

[16] Irving Fisher, "The Debt-Deflation Theory of Great Depression," *Econometrica*, 1933, 1, no. 4, October.
[17] Walter Bagehot, Lombard Street, Scribner, Armstrong & Co. 1874, pp. 51–52.
[18] "We Need Some 'Creative Destruction' to Address Today's Challenges," *Financial Times*, April 6, 2020.

structural breaks in the high-grade bond market. Over recent credit cycles, nonfinancial corporations have gradually altered the patterns of sources of funds in response to market incentives—especially in response to expected interest rates and bond market liquidity. On the demand side, liquidity in the bond market has become more global and more liquid in the range of corporate debt demanded by the global investor. On the supply side, the character of corporate debt has also become more flexible in structure.

Recognizing Evolution in Financial Benchmarks

In addition to the evolution of interest expense over the credit cycle, other financial ratios provide illustrations of both a cyclical and secular character to the patterns of corporate finance. These illustrations are the result of a choice of a deeper corporate decision-making process that signals the impact of and upon the broader economy.

The financial gap benchmark provides an insight into the interest in business to invest and their allocation and availability of internal funds to do so.

Also limiting the corporate debt burden is a shift toward more long-term debt, reviewed above, which means lower principal payments due in each period, given the downtrend in long-term financing rates. Short-term debt (due in less than one year) represented 9.4% of debt held by manufacturing and retail corporations in Q1 2018. This compares to over 13% at the end of the previous expansion.

First Half of 2018: Prelude to Covid Shutdowns and Recession

What was the character of corporate bond markets in 2018? This was a period of rising fed funds rates but what was perceived to be exceptionally low corporate yields. Economic growth in 2017 was considered trend growth of 2.2%, benchmark inflation, measured as the core PCE deflator was 1.6%. This was below the Fed's 2% target. The trade-weighted dollar had declined slightly in 2017 below the end of 2016 level.

At the time, businesses appear to be taking the recent series of rate hikes by the Fed, and subsequent rise in the cost of credit, in stride with total nonfinancial corporate business credit rising 5.2% in Q1 2018 year over year. Beyond a few wiggles in the data, short-term financing as a share of total financing remained below its pre-recession peak, at roughly 28% of total debt in Q1. Long-term financing has surpassed its pre-recession peak to reach almost 72% of total credit market debt in Q1.

The financing gap (previous Chapter Fig. 6.4) measured as the difference between capital expenditures and internally generated funds, had also moved into negative territory in Q1, reversing the more than $200 billion increase seen in Q4 on a four-quarter moving sum basis. Firms appear to have become a bit cautious due, perhaps, to higher financing costs.

Consistent with the higher share of debt financing going into the long-term market, businesses continued to rely on debt issuance to support financing needs in this expansion. Corporate bonds remained the largest component of debt financing, comprising roughly 60% of total credit market instruments on balance sheets in Q1, 2019. This is occurring in part due to long-term corporate bond yields reaching historic lows up to that point.

On net, businesses look to be satisfying financing needs for the time being. However, if interest rates continue to rise across the curve, businesses may soon face a higher cost of credit for both short-term and longer-term debt. We expect that the ramp up in business investment is likely behind us as the corporate sector adjusts to a tighter credit market.[19]

For the period up to 2018, the links between inflation, interest rates, and financial ratios provide insight into the behavior of the economic cycle. There is a constant disequilibrium between finance today and economic outcomes in the future, which provides both cyclical and secular characteristics to corporate finance.

Interest rates and inflation are both linked to the composition of corporate debt. In addition, there is a net tax advantage to debt by borrowing to replace equity. However, there is also a risk of bankruptcy.[20] Without taxes and bankruptcy-related costs—firms are indifferent as argued by economists Franco Modigliani and Merton Miller, under very restrictive conditions such as no taxes, no agency costs, no bankruptcy costs, and no asymmetric information—all issues we must recognize in the trading of markets today.[21]

Unexpected changes in the path of monetary policy, fiscal policy, inflation, and interest rates will have an impact on observed financial ratios such as the debt-value ratio. Unexpected changes impact both the market value of the firm and the market value of the firm's liabilities.

---

[19] Business investment is also with adjustment costs. It is costly for a firm to adjust its capital stock. Moreover, the marginal adjustment cost increases with the size of the adjustment. There is also an asymmetry in capital stock adjustment—easier to increase the capital stock than to decrease it. We set this aside to focus on the external financial incentives for adjustment.

[20] "Is There Too Much Business Debt?" Federal Reserve Bank of New York, May 29, 2019.

[21] Franco Modigliani and Miller H. Merton, "The Cost of Capital, Corporation Finance and the Theory of Investment," *American Economic Review*, 1958, 48 (June): 261–297.

In the patterns of each economic and credit cycle we can see several steps in the evolution of credit. First, a rapid increase in the quantity of credit accompanies the initial stages of the economic recovery. Second, there is an increase in the prices of real assets that are bought on credit—for example housing in the 2004–2007 period. Third, aggressive competition becomes the norm among lenders for new business with the resultant relaxation of lending standards as we have reviewed in Chapter 5. These relaxed standards are accompanied by a reduction in risk premiums required by the lenders as we have witnessed with the narrower spreads on corporate bonds we reviewed in this chapter. Then, a shock appears in the form of disappointing returns to an overleveraged investment. Credit revulsion takes hold, and a recession ensues. The cycle begins again as public policy acts to restore economic and credit growth.

We will see this process played out in the next chapter on household finances.

References

Bade and Parkin, *Macroeconomics*, 8th edition, Pearson, p. 495. One caution to analysts is the comparisons of a stock of debt to a flow of income. While useful as a teaching tool, for analysis of the dynamics of the U.S. economy the comparison is misleading.

Walter Bagehot, Lombard Street, Scribner, Armstrong & Co. 1874. This is the oft quoted commentary on the implementation of monetary actions to offset deflationary forces.

Ben Bernanke, John Y. Campbell and Toni Whited, "U.S. Corporate Leverage: Developments in 1987 and 1988," *Brookings Papers on Economic Activity*, 1990, 1. An essay that focuses on corporate leverage in the mid-1980s.

O. Blanchard, C. Rhee and L. Summers, "The Stock Market, Profit, and INVESTMENT," *Quarterly Journal of Economics*, 1993, 108, 1: 115–136. The authors argue that economic fundamentals are better related to real business investment that Tobin's Q.

Irving Fisher, "The Debt-Deflation Theory of Great Depression," *Econometrica*, 1933, 1, no. 4 (October). The original statement of the impact on the real burden of debt due to deflation.

Jerome S. Fons, "Debt-Deflation and Corporate Finance," *Economic Commentary*, Federal Reserve Bank of Cleveland, March 15, 1987. The early 1980s is a cautionary tale of the real burden of debt when inflation declines faster than expected. We will see this again in Chapter 12 when we examine sovereign debt.

Joao Gomes, Urban Jermann and Lukas Schmid, "Sticky Leverage," *American Economic Review*, 2016, 106, no. 12: 3800–3828, and Roger H. Gordon,

"Interest Rates, Inflation, and Corporate Financial Policy," *Brookings Papers on Economic Activity*, 1982, 2. This article examines the importance of unexpected changes, in interest rates and inflation, that would affect the total value of the firm.

Alan Greenspan, *Monetary Policy Report to Congress*, February 1992. An assessment by the Chairman that the growth of debt and leverage was out of line with subsequent economic expansion and asset appreciation.

Anna Kovner and Brandon Zborowski, "Is There Too Much Business Debt?" May 29, 2019, Federal Reserve Bank of New York. An interesting assessment of corporate debt on the eve of the 2020 recession.

Franco Modigliani and H. Merton Miller, "The Cost of Capital, Corporation Finance and the Theory of Investment," *American Economic Review*, 1958, 48 (June): 261–297. Without taxes and bankruptcy related costs, the firm would be indifferent, under very restrictive conditions such as no taxes, no agency costs, no bankruptcy costs and no asymmetric information between debt and equity. Yet all these assumptions are very real issues in the financial markets.

Geoffrey Moore, "The Quality of Credit in Booms and Depressions," *Journal of Finance*, 1956 (May). Moore identifies both the relaxation of credit standards and a reduction of risk premiums as two of several factors in credit cycles.

Stephen D. Oliner and Glenn D. Rudebusch, "Is There a Broad Credit Channel for Monetary Policy," *Federal Reserve Bank of San Francisco Economic Review*, 1996. The authors argue the case in favor of a credit channel emphasizing the role of small firms.

John E. Silvia, "Corporate Debt: The Interest Burden in the Next Recession," Paper presented at the Eastern Economic Association Conference, Baltimore, March 4, 1989. This commentary reflected an early interest and prior research on the link between economic growth and the interest burden of corporate debt.

8

Evolution of Household Finances

On the Road to Irrationality: Housing Finance in the 2000s

Both the supply and demand for household credit, associated with the housing crisis of 2007–2010, reflect public policy incentives and private sector reactions to such policies. These incentives and reactions were matched by the influences of cognitive biases, such as the recency bias, that drives both borrower and lender expectations. All this simply repeats the cycles of discovery, excess, and credit revulsion described in Chapter 2 as exemplified by the railroad boom of the 1870s, and the Florida land and stock market booms of the 1920s.

Credit and financial deregulation are procyclical and may be well intentioned, but its impact, when carried too far, can become disastrous. In 1992, Congress enacted "affordable housing goals" for two Government-Sponsored Enterprises (GSEs)—the Federal National Mortgage Association (Fannie Mae) and the Federal Home Loan Mortgage Corporation (Freddie Mac). These GSEs were designed by Congress to provide liquidity in the housing market by conducting secondary market operations i.e., they purchased mortgages from banks and other lenders and these purchases provided cash to the lenders and fostered further mortgage lending.

Over time, these GSEs' share of the housing mortgage market grew steadily, enabling them to set underwriting standards for the entire market.

Problems set in when the Department of Housing and Urban Development (HUD) expanded the quota of low to moderate income loans to over 50% in 2001 while lowering down payment requirements. There were also requirements to support loans in underserved areas. By 2000, Fannie Mae and Freddie Mac were buying loans with zero down payments thus motivating buyers to purchase a home also with zero down payments. Since banks could sell these mortgages to Fannie Mae and Freddie Mac, they were incentivized to generate those mortgages with little oversight on the true quality of these mortgages (there was serious underreporting on the documentation as the incentives were focused on generating fees and meeting affordable housing guidelines as well as the reality that many of these mortgages were not retained but packaged and sold off to investors, the game was afoot. Credit is a procyclical marketplace. When momentum in prices is in place for homes, especially as credit standards fell, buyers only remember that prices have recently increased (the recency bias) and forget the history of credit and economic cycles.

Well-intended, but poorly proscribed, federal housing incentives and financial deregulation offered a field of experimentation that follows the historical experience of earlier financial innovations—innovation carried to excess ending in ruin.

Two Sides to the Household Balance Sheet

Although subject to scare headlines, increases in household debt, alone, tells us little about the actual financial state of a household. A better approach is to compare assets and liabilities—the concept of household net worth (Fig. 8.1).

On the financial asset side, cash, bonds, and equities would be typical of a financial portfolio. As for real capital, autos, and housing represent the household's position. A breakout of the financial assets for Households and Nonprofit Organizations comes from the Federal Reserve's Financial Accounts of the U.S. Z.1 report.

Shares of wealth held in each asset form on the asset side of the balance sheet, Table 8.1, depend on the expected income and rate of return on that asset. In recent years, the portfolio share of equity has risen as the expectation rose that there is no alternative (TINA).

Finally, it is important to note the dynamics of asset markets: If two markets (cash and bonds for example) are in equilibrium, then a third market

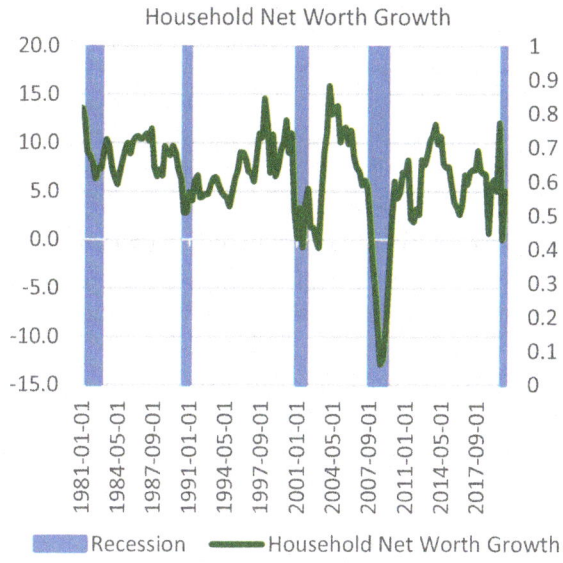

Fig. 8.1 Growth of household net worth

Table 8.1 Shares of household balance sheet

Household and nonprofit organizations Z1. September 2020 ($B)			
Total financial assets		Total liabilities	
Deposits	12,185.8	Residential mortgages	9914. 4
Debt securities		Consumer credit	3813.0
US treasury	1132.4	Other	1662.1
Agencies	451.9		
Municipal	1892.5		
Corporate and foreign bonds	990.8		
Loans	903.0		
Equities	18,278.2		
Mutual fund shares	8654.8		
Pension entitlements	25,900.2		
Life insurance reserves	1626.6		
Equity in noncorporate business	11,089.8		
Other financial assets	1448.4		

(equities) is in equilibrium. Equilibrium is established when the actual holdings of assets equal desired holdings at current market prices. Given the price movements of markets over time, equilibrium is a rare event.

On the liability side, the relative attractiveness of financing consumption depends on the income, wealth, expected inflation, and relative prices of alternative financing options. With the change in the tax laws in 1986, the tax deduction for consumer credit was eliminated but the tax deduction paid on interest expense for a home-equity loan remained. There was a dramatic shift away from consumer credit to home equity loans as households took advantage of the shift in the deductibility of home mortgage credit but not credit cards. Why the shift? Up until 2007–2009, home values stood as collateral against home mortgages and home equity loans and thereby were considered more secure than credit card/auto loans. A rise in inflation, for a given set of nominal interest rates, lowers the real cost of a home mortgage. So, it is not surprising that home financing demand rises with a decline in real interest rates.

Liquidity constraints, even if not currently in place, may also impact consumption and saving decisions. Constraints may limit current consumption and increase savings to provide insurance against future falling income.[1] There is a further complication. When the federal government borrows and future tax liabilities by households increase, lenders to households anticipate that the chances of being repaid on any loan have been reduced. In this case, future lending will be constrained.[2]

We can express household assets as a function of expectations for economic growth, inflation, wealth, and interest rates. As in prior models, the difference between expectations and actual outcomes generates the dynamics we see in the marketplace. For example, in the housing crunch prior to 2007, the expected pace of housing appreciation started to decline and yet the financing costs rose relative to earlier teaser (below market, temporary) rates. Therefore, the actual refinancing cost of many mortgages was greater than lenders and buyers anticipated while the actual appreciation in the real estate was less than expected. This shock led to the housing bust. This bust was amplified by the creation of CDOs (collateralized debt obligations[3]) and Credit Default Swaps that had lead to increasing speculation on subprime mortgages and the rise of "shadow" banking which also fueled the 2008–2009 economic collapse. Cordell et.al. comment that the risks of the CDOs were greatly underestimated.

The stock of housing held exceeded the desired holding given the lack of price appreciation. Meanwhile, the stock of mortgages held exceeded the

---

[1] Stephen Zeldes, "Consumption and Liquidity Constraints: An Empirical Investigation," *Journal of Political Economy*, 1989, 97 (April): 305–346.

[2] Fumio Hayashi, "Tests for Liquidity Constraints: A Critical Survey and Some New Observations." In *Advances in Econometrics*, Truman F. Bewley, ed. Cambridge: Cambridge University Press, 1987, Vol. 2, pp. 91–120.

[3] Larry Cordell, Yilin Huang, and Meredith Williams, "Collateral Damage: Sizing and Assessing the Subprime CDO Crisis," No. 11–30 Working Paper, Federal Reserve Bank of Philadelphia, May 2012.

desired amount given the nonperformance on existing mortgages. The price of homes fell along with the value of mortgages.

Demand for an asset is a function income, inflation, wealth, and the expected rates of return on an asset and its close substitutes. An increase in household income would generate an increase in the demand for cash, bonds, and equities in a balanced portfolio. An increase in the expected rate of return on any asset would lead to a desire to own more of that asset and less of others. Since 2010, the rise in the expected returns on equities relative to bonds and cash has led many investors to shift toward owning more equities and less cash and fewer bonds.

In recent years, the expected price appreciation of homes has prompted many buyers to step into the housing market. When the expected return on a capital asset, such as a home, rises buyers reallocate their assets to reduce cash and increase real asset holdings.

Evolution of the Balance Sheet

The evolution of household financial behavior is such that historical averages cannot be relied upon to predict future behavior. As apparent in the graphs below, each series is not mean reverting and is instead a function of the various independent variables specified above for the demand and supply of credit. We will examine these dynamics and implication for public and private decision-makers.

Importance in Understanding Household Behavior

Private consumption is an important economic driver and the largest part of GDP. Public and private decision-makers thus need to understand the behavior of this sector and the makeup of household balance sheets as they work to understand and then forecast consumer financial trends.

Evolution of Both Sides of the Balance Sheet

For households, our statistical analysis shows that assets and liabilities are non-stationary and non-mean reverting. That is, prior trends and historical averages should not be used by decision-makers to predict future consumer behavior. Table 8.2 indicates that corporate equities' share of financial assets is relatively volatile and reflects the fluctuations of the fundamentals (interest rate and growth expectations). Corporate equities ranged from around 10%

Table 8.2 Financial assets by type

	Percent of all financial assets		
	1982	2000	2020
Equity	12	28	22
Deposits	22	10	12
Mutual Funds	2	8	11
U.S. Treasury Debt	4	3	2
Corp and Fgn Bonds	1	3	2

These are financial assets outside of less liquid assets such as pension funds
Source Federal Reserve Board

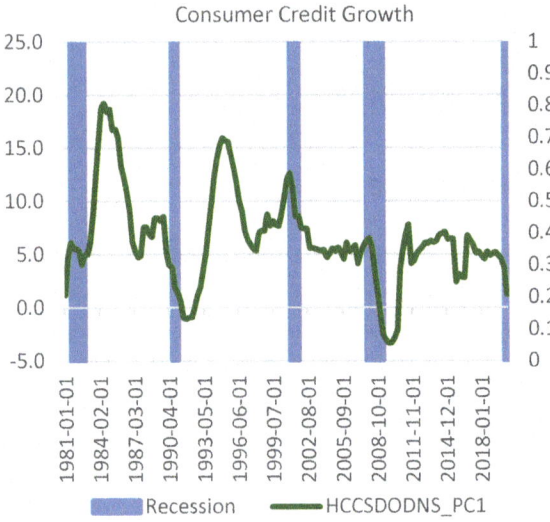

Fig. 8.2 Consumer credit growth

to more than 20% of total financial assets over the past 10 years, while there is clearly a more consistent trend in household allocations to credit market and mutual fund holdings (Table 8.2).

Liabilities: Growth Rates also Change

The composition of household balance sheets varies over different time periods. Employing past benchmarks in certain assets and liabilities series to predict future outcomes is therefore misleading. Note in Fig. 8.2 the evolution of the growth rate of consumer credit.

In the case of consumer credit, there is a clear slowdown in the growth of consumer credit over time as tax laws have changed as well as the preference for using consumer credit has changed as well.

On the mortgage front, households were highly leveraged in terms of housing debt in prior cycles (the run-up in the 2004–2007 period up to the most recent financial crisis) but the shock of 2007–2009 has altered the willingness to take on mortgage debt in current or future cycles in a similar way. In fact, the subdued housing recovery during the 2010 expansion reflects, in part, the caution of households in taking on home mortgage debt. Home mortgage liabilities show the slowest year-over-year growth, at just 3% in Q4, 2018. Meanwhile, the net percentage of banks tightening standards on prime mortgage loans rose sharply between the 3Q of 2007 and the 3Q of 2008.

Net Result: Trends and Structural Breaks—Not Constant

Since the 1960s, the expansion of credit availability to households has accompanied a secular (long-term) decline in household assets to liabilities. This would be expected as households sought financial means to raise their standard of living as real assets, such as single-family homes, rose in value. This secular trend reflects both economic factors as well as changes in consumer perceptions of debt over time.

Consumer behavior is not consistent with the theme of a return to "normal." That is, the assets-to-liabilities ratio is non-stationary, and the rate of growth of assets relative to liabilities varies significantly over the economic cycle, Fig. 8.3, which indicates that the growth of assets less liabilities and illustrates how households accumulate wealth will be different over different time periods. This reflects the ongoing evolution in the economy and financial market regulation. Decision-makers need to note this dynamic as they attempt to understand future consumer trends. During the period of 1978–1990, there were significant changes in banking structure, innovation etc., that, in turn, altered returns on savings, types of mortgages (Adjustable Rate Mortgages (ARMs) and their permutations) and the increasing utilization of credit cards as direct payment as a substitute for cash.

For example, stricter financial regulation and consumer caution certainly help explain lower home mortgage liabilities in the current cycle, while the upswing in equity valuations has boosted assets. On net, the upswing in the assets-to-liabilities ratio reflects the evolution of economic fundamentals. In

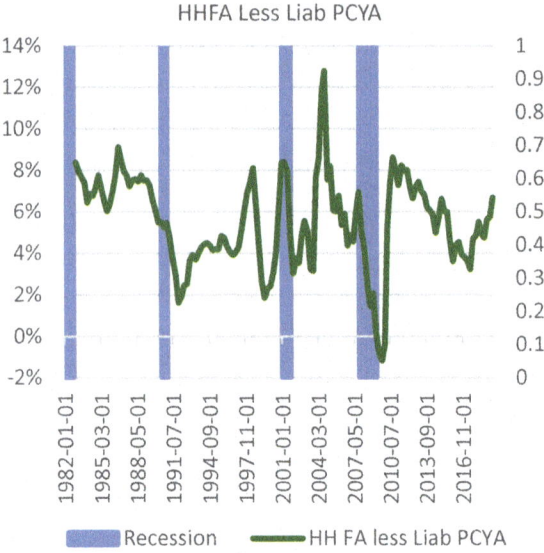

Fig. 8.3 Household assets less liabilities

part 2 of this chapter, we will examine the tensions and statistical relationships between the assets and liabilities series and what they mean for future household wealth.

Assets/Liabilities and Structural Breaks

One of the most significant post World War II innovations that continues to influence economic activity today is the development of household credit instruments that allow households to access real goods (autos, homes), services (meals, rental cars), and even the seed corn or the start-up capital to launch) to start a small business. The link between goods and credit markets has increased over time. Policymakers have lost some of the appreciation for these financial innovations in the United States and instead only focus on the downside risks when such innovations are stretched too far. The innovations themselves are an economic good, such as an automobile, it is the drunk driving that creates the problem. In recent years, the microfinance in many developing nations has made a big difference in many small venues, especially for water quality, and has promoted economic growth.

True to form, consumer credit has both a trend and cyclical character that fits within the framework of a multimarket view of goods, credit, equity, and real economic growth. For much of the post-World War II period, household assets to liabilities have followed a downward path—until 2008. The asset-liability series is non-stationary, that is it does not return to a single mean value thereby providing a dynamic character to the evolution of the household balance sheet. There is a distinct structural break in 2008.

Why the change since 2008? One of the great factors that caused an abrupt shift in the trend is a change in psychology. For financial asset investors, the history is clear. At first, investors have a sense of the income and dividends that they can receive from an investment—think Graham and Dodd.[4] However, unlike Johnny Cash, who proclaimed in *I Walk the Line*— "I keep a close watch on this heart of mine"—discipline and valuation drift away and investors wander into investing and speculating for capital gains. For the 1970s there was the nifty-fifty (fifty large cap stocks sold on the New York Stock Exchange), for the 1990s there was the dot.com craze and in the mid-2000s, house buying became the vogue. A home which had historically meant shelter, psychic income, and a place to rest became a vehicle for speculation on capital gains and flipping houses. The aftermath is evident in the ratio of assets to liabilities.

Since 2008, the gains in assets have been mostly in equities and mutual funds. On the liabilities side, the drop has been in the decline in consumer credit and home mortgages. It took until 2014 when the negative equity gap in owner's equity (mortgage debt exceeded the owner's equity) was eliminated. In 2008 there was a clear break in the willingness to seek and supply credit on the part of households and lending institutions.

Households: Both a Consumption/Saving and Portfolio Decision

The evolution since World War II in the usage of credit to purchase real goods highlights that household decisions carry both a consumption/saving and portfolio decision. These decisions are not independent of each other. Consumer spending rises with increases in income and wealth but is negatively impacted by rising interest rates. However, the story does not end there. When households cut back on spending, then a decision must also be made on what asset the household wishes to hold if saving is increased.

For households, an asset, either financial or real (such as a car, house) is considered as a long-lived commodity that can be purchased for a certain

---

[4] Benjamin Graham and David Dodd, *Security Analysis*, Whittlesey House, McGraw-Hill Book Co., 1934.

price and that yields a stream of income or services over several years. In deciding how to allocate financial resources among the financial and real options, a household considers both the price and the expected yield on the asset. The internal rate of return on an asset reflects the average rate of return over its lifetime.

The period since 2007–2009 has evidenced a distinct shift in household expectations in these future return calculations. Since 2009, households have clearly upgraded their expected future returns in corporate equities as hinted at by the rise in corporate equities as a share of total financial assets. In contrast, deposits have trended sideways beginning in 2012. Credit market instruments (bonds for example) have declined sharply since 2010, although since 2014, there has been an increase in U.S. Treasury debt holdings.

On the liabilities side, the sharp drop in home mortgages since 2007 suggests that household interest in housing debt finance has diminished relative to the past. Until recently, housing starts have been below the peak prior to the housing bust. In fact, the allocation to equities has exceeded the allocation to real estate since late 2013. Overall, the biggest gain in liabilities since the recession has been in student loan debt, then followed by auto loans. As expected, home equity loans have steadily declined from 2010 to the 4Q of 2020.

Life Cycle Behavior—More Than Just a Cyclical Pattern

Demographics adds another element to the usage of credit—especially in the post-World War II era. Debt is often taken on in the early stages of life when current income is low, but consumption needs are relatively large. This was especially true for families headed by veterans after World War II who desired to reestablish a lifestyle that went along with a period of rising economic growth and aspirations. The baby-boom generation repeated this pattern. As each generation aged, their earnings improved, and they gradually paid down debt. Eventually they built up wealth for retirement as well as sufficient funds to make a bequest to support the next generation. This age-earnings profile meant that demographics would influence the debt-to-income ratio that appeared. Prof. Alain Enthoven[5] of Stanford University made this observation as early as 1957. He argued that the long-run age-earnings profile

---

[5] Alain Enthoven, "The Growth of Installment Credit and the Future of Prosperity," *American Economic Review*, 1957, 47 (December).

reduced the concern about the potential burden on consumer spending at a time of the rapid rise in consumer installment debt.

Within the stylized model of age-earnings there are many factors including the rate of time preference and the strength of the bequest motive. Among the economic factors that we examine there is the elasticity of substitution on the credit side and then the change in real interest rate and real income growth. The role of the real interest rate was revealed in the real-life experiment of the 1960–1990 period. For much of the early part of that period, the real interest rate declined, and consumer spending rose and there was less interest in financial assets. With the 1980s, real interest rates turned positive as inflation declined and investment in financial assets increased. We emphasize the interest expense to income ratios since aggregate debt-to-income ratios are sensitive to changes in the real interest rates, the rate of economic growth but especially the influence of demographics. In addition, it is our tradition to avoid debt (stock) to income (flow) comparisions where possible.

Credit Cycle: Short-Term View

Demand and Supply of Credit Over the Economic Cycle

The Federal Reserve Board report, termed the Senior Loan Officer Opinion Survey, is one of a very few places that the researcher can get a view of both the demand and supply side of the bank credit market.

On the supply side, a bank's willingness to make consumer loans on a quarterly basis is a qualitative measure of a lender's inclination to make loans and offers insight into credit conditions in the loan market. A bank's willingness to make consumer loans is a stationary series, which contains no structural breaks. That is, the series acts in a predictable nature, allowing one to refer to it as a benchmark to assess lending practices over a business cycle (Fig. 8.4). Meanwhile, bank supervision and regulatory changes can alter the criteria for making real estate loans. After the global financial crisis (2007–2009), banks introduced an added element of caution in the face of heightened bank supervision. From the Federal Reserve Board surveys, the willingness of banks to lend may reflect an altered benchmark measuring stick compared to the past. Minimum down payment, debt-to-income ratios and FICOS scores may alter the benchmark for measuring a shift in bank willingness to lend.

Banks willingness to make consumer loans shows a distinct tendency to tighten credit before the 2001 and 2007–2009 recessions. In procyclical fashion, the net percent tightening credit declined from 1997 to 2000 and again from 2002 to 2006. Bank consumer credit is indeed procyclical.

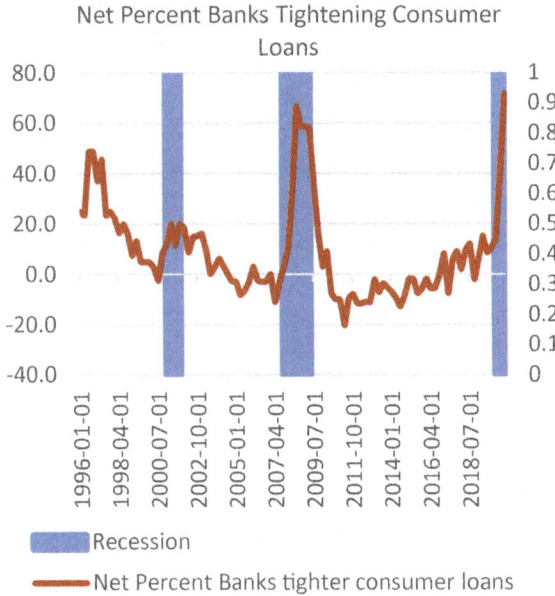

Fig. 8.4 Net percent of banks tighter standards consumer loans

During the sample period from 1990 to 2011, the series' secular characteristic is stationary (no trend over time) and exhibits no structural breaks. For our business cycle analysis, this series is a far more reliable indicator than other series that exhibit a trend over time. This allows us to refer to the series as a benchmark to assess lending practices during an economic expansion and between cycles.

At the beginning of an expansionary period, as banks are very willing to extend credit, the series rises. Once reaching its peak, banks willingness to lend gradually decreases until turning negative during a recessionary period. That said, the willingness to make loans has peaked in the 2009–2019 expansion, which is in line with our assessment of the business cycle being in its late stage.

Consumer Short-Term Credit: Another Exercise in Pro-Cyclical Behavior

Consumer spending on durable goods, such as autos, requires credit. As with business credit, we can monitor both the demand for credit and the changing standards of lenders on the supply side.

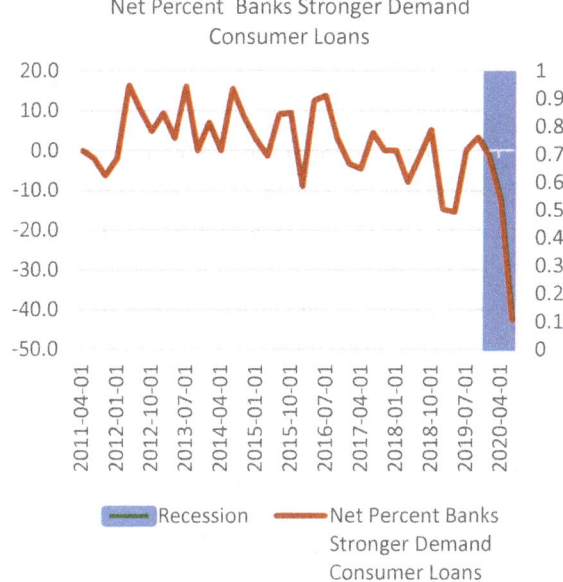

Fig. 8.5 Net percent of banks reporting stronger consumer loan demand

Demand for consumer loans during the 1991 to 2011 period is shown in Fig. 8.5.[6] Three recessions occur, first in 2001 and then again in 2007–2009 and again in 2020. Three observations are worth noticing. First, the net percent of banks reporting stronger demand drops significantly prior to recessions. Second, the net percent reporting stronger demand does not deviate far from zero over the entire period of expansions. Finally, the net percent reporting stronger demand drops sharply, not shown here, when the Fed raised the funds rate in 1994, 1999–2000, and again 2004–2005.

A Closer Look: Cycles in Credit, Economics, and Auto Finance

Business cycle trends differ across major sectors; while some series are mean reverting, others are shifting over time. Careful analysis leads to a better understanding of "normalcy." Let us look at the link between credit and auto

---

[6] The Federal Reserve's survey of consumer demand and tightening standards was altered in 2011 so we use the earlier period to give us a better sense of the cyclical character of these series.

finance. Auto purchases, as a durable good, are very cyclical. Banks willingness to make loans and the demand for those loans indicate phases of the economic cycle.

For the period 2001 to 2016, bank lending standards remained easy for auto loans. Then beginning in mid-2016, those standards tightened modestly until 2018 when the Fed raised interest rates. Those standards remained in neutral territory into early 2020 when banks tightened standards significantly.

On the demand side, the strength of auto loan demand continued to ease from 2011 to 2017 and then fell off sharply in early 2020 and bottomed in the third quarter of 2020. Most recently, auto demand has returned to neutral.

Unfortunately, these series on auto loans are very short term but longer time series provide some insight into patterns over a longer horizon and several economic cycles. The loan-to-value ratio on new car loans, Fig. 8.6 shows a cyclical character as loan-to-value ratios fall in recession periods (1981–1982, 1989–1992 for example) and rise in periods of economic expansion (1985–1989, 1993–1996). In fact, the observation for September 2006 exceeded 100—an optimistic month! The time series ends in 2010 but there was a noticeable decline in the loan-to-value ratio in August 2008, a brief rise in 2009 and then a definite decline in the ratio through 2010 and early 2011.

Secular change in the auto loan market is evident in the continued rise in the weighted average maturity of auto loans shown in Fig. 8.7. In the 1970s, the weighted average maturity was three years or less and then in 1977 it rose to 40 months plus. In the mid-1980s the maturity increased to 50 months and then to 60 months in 2003. Effectively, the spreading out the payments reflected the significant rise in the price of autos as dealers reduced payments to fit the budgets of a larger customer base. Auto leasing has been around for a long time but the real rise in popularity began in the mid-1980s with the rise in auto prices.

The impact of rising auto prices and the need to spread out the payments is also interesting in the context of the steady decline in auto finance rates over time (Fig. 8.8).

Monitoring the Cyclical Patterns of Ratios: Debt Service and Financial Obligations

Over the economic cycle, financial stress on households is a product of changes in household income and interest expense. The Federal Reserve Board of Governors provides two summary measures of this stress. One benchmark for household financial stress is the debt service ratio. A second is

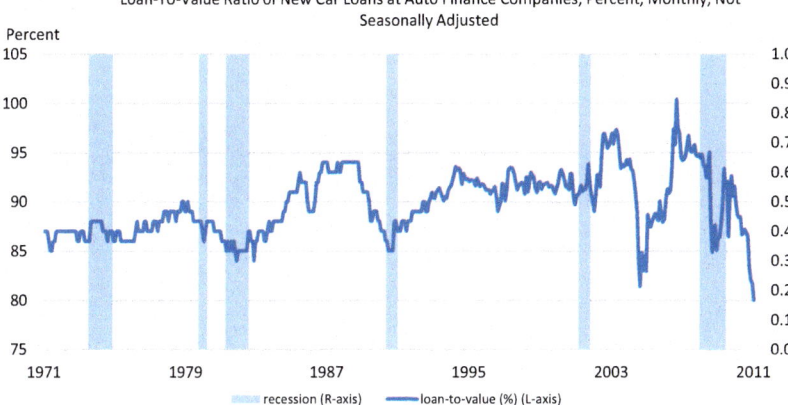
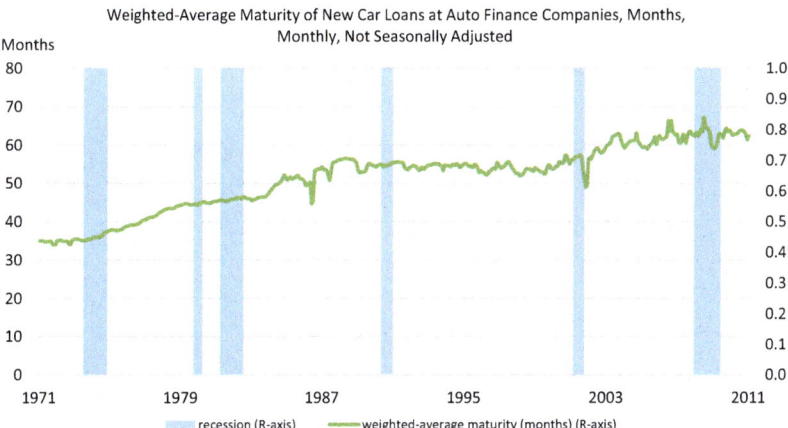
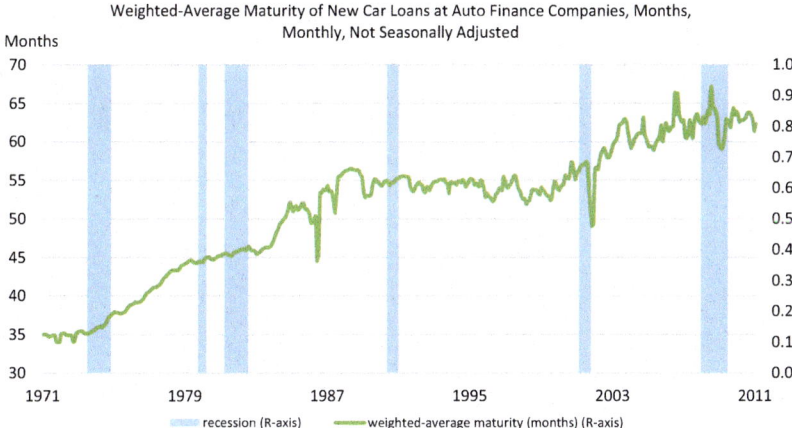

Fig. 8.6 Loan to value ratio of new car loans

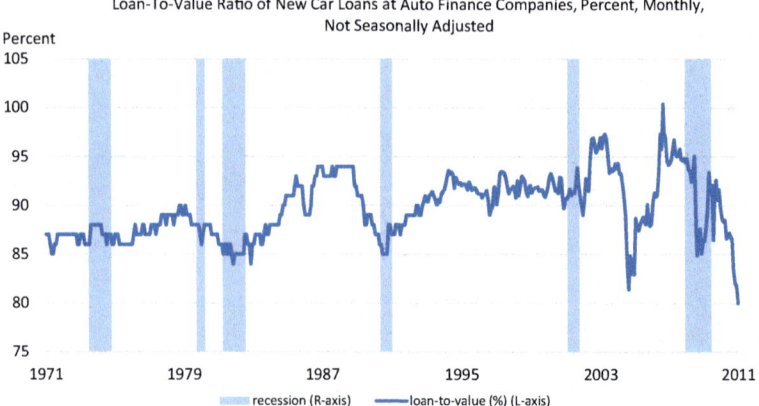
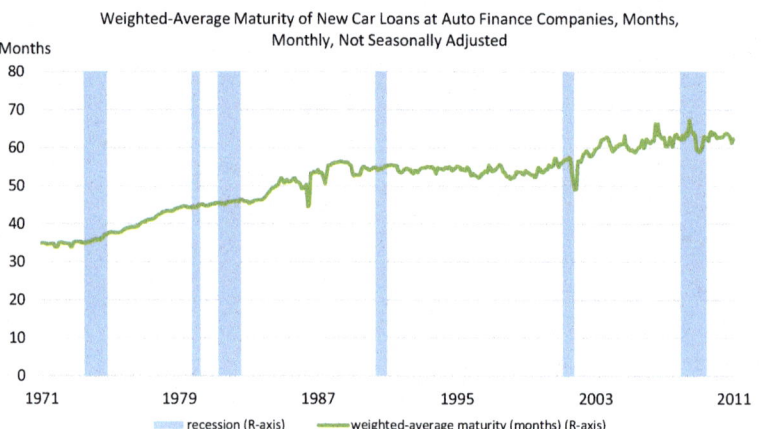
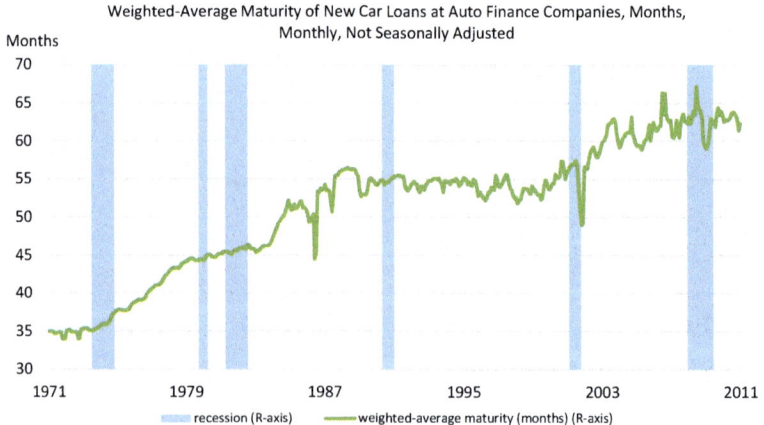

Fig. 8.7 Weighted average maturity of car loans

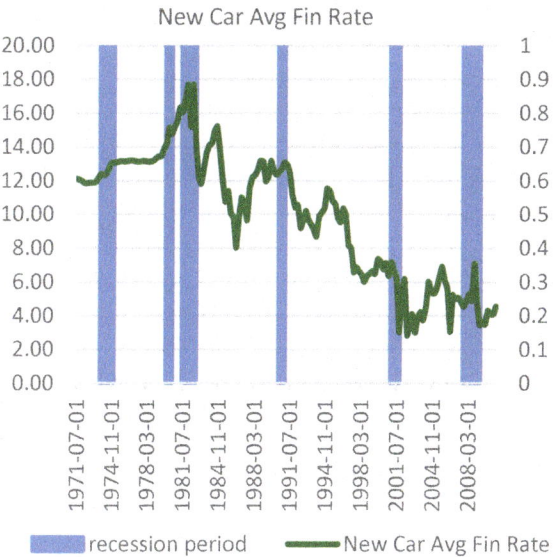

Fig. 8.8 New car average finance rate

the financial obligations ratio. These two series provides a cyclical character to credit quality, but the series' structural breaks offers a reassessment of the outlook associated with recessions.

The debt service ratio includes regular mortgage payments and consumer debt payments. These payments vary in size relative to each other depending upon the variability of mortgage interest rates. In the 4Q of 2019, mortgage payments and consumer debt payments made up 4.09 and 5.61% respectively of disposable personal income.

Similarly, the financial obligations ratio is the ratio of household debt payments to total disposable income and measures how much household income is being spent on repaying debts and other financial obligations. It includes rent payments on tenant-occupied property, auto lease payments, homeowners' insurance, and property tax payments and represents a larger share of disposable personal income (15.12% in the 4Q of 2019) than debt service.

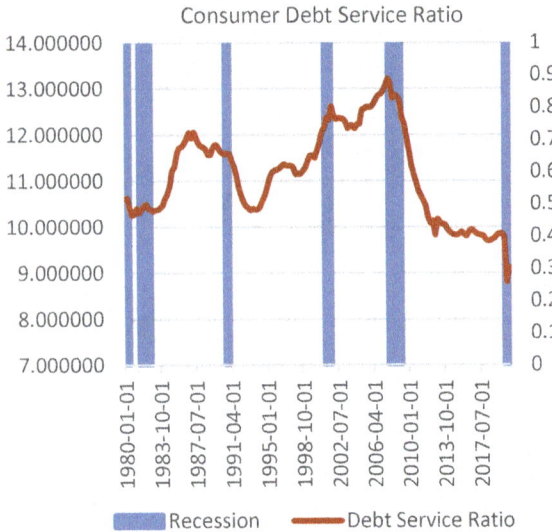

Fig. 8.9 Consumer debt service ratio

From the Income Statement: Debt Service Ratio

Household interest expense is properly compared to disposable personal income. In contrast, a measure frequently quoted,[7] but is misleading, is total household debt or sometimes the debt-to-income ratio. This latter measure compares a stock of debt to a flow of income and is not a precise measure of the consumer debt burden since the interest expense on the debt is not considered. Moreover, the availability bias—use what is convenient, not what is precise—is evident when the debt-to-income ratio is employed by so many commentators.

For the household debt service ratio, there is a cyclical pattern but also a secular change as well (Fig. 8.9) indicates a better economy leads to higher debt payments as a share of income. Moreover, from 1992 to 2008 there was also an upward trend which ended in 2008.

Debt service as a percent of disposable personal income has declined significantly since recession of 2008. Many households cut back their credit use given the crunch on many household balance sheets and the weakening consumer sentiment caused by the recession. The flow of debt payments declined versus a flow of income. Hence, the sharp drop in the debt service ratio was abrupt and unanticipated.

---

[7] "Credit-Card Debt in U.S. Rises to Record $930 Billion," *Wall Street Journal*, February 12, 2020.

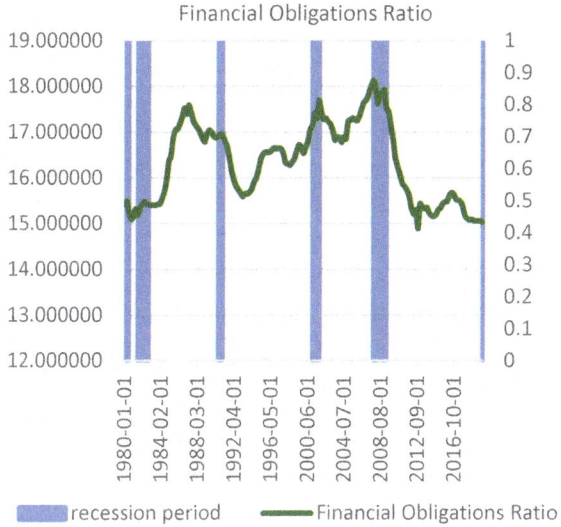

Fig. 8.10 Financial obligations ratio

Financial Obligations Ratio

The financial obligations ratio (Fig. 8.10) has a distinct cyclical pattern. This ratio rises in the early to mid-phases of an economic expansion (1980s, 1990s, 2000s). But then in 2010 there is a distinct structural break in the series with no mid-cycle recovery in the 2012–2017 period.

As of the 2Q 2019, both the debt service ratio and the financial obligations ratio are currently at their lowest values since the early 1980s. As of the 1Q of 2020, the debt service ratio remains low—subject to the whims of, you guessed it, job growth, interest rates, and credit availability.

The Consumer Debt Issue Post WWII and into the 1980s: Interplay of Markets

Household Balance Sheet 1970s

Prior to 2007–2009, the recession of 1973–1975 represented one of the most severe economic contractions in the postwar era. A significant portion of household assets traditionally was held in residential real estate. That was the sector most overvalued and subject to the greatest financial correction during this period. This contraction offers some insights to the household financial condition beyond the more narrowly focused housing crunch of later years.

The NYSE index peaked in the 4Q of 1972 and then fell to a low and bottomed in the 4Q 1974. The S&P 500 index peaked in 1973 and did not regain that peak until 1976. This represented a reduction in household net worth while savings also dropped from 1973 to 1974. Net investment in consumer durables and non-corporate business also slid but both remained positive.[8] Consumer durable spending had a positive link to the value of financial assets and a negative link to liabilities.

All these events reveal that balance sheet changes have powerful effects on consumer durable spending. A deterioration of the value of household net worth, declines both in savings and equity values, had a depressing impact on consumer spending since households perceived that lifetime financial resources have diminished. This principle harkens back to the view that household spending is linked to a household's perception of their lifetime income. In addition, the wealth effect[9] on consumption estimated by studies shows that for every $1 of permanent wealth there is 2–5 cents of spending associated with this gain. For recessions, and especially 2007–2009 recession, the reverse was also true.

As the recession played out, these financial hits were indeed followed by a decline in real consumer spending from 1973 to 1975 with a sharp drop in consumer durable spending that helped initiate the recession starting in the 4Q 1973. Slower consumer spending is consistent with the life cycle hypothesis of economists Modigliani and Brumberg[10] in that consumers consider their lifetime resources in making consumption decisions. The 1973–1975 equity market decline was the worst bear market since the Great Depression.

Into the 1980s, rising consumer debt relative to personal disposable income was a concern on the part of some commentators.[11] Details matter, however. First, as we reviewed earlier, the use of the ratio of debt to income is misleading as debt is a stock and income a flow. Second, several factors—deregulation, the end of formal credit controls and the 1986 Tax Act—permanently altered the household's calculation of the utilization of debt. Third, the willingness to take on debt is endogenous to the economic cycle. Increases in wealth and income that typically accompany the economic

---

[8] Economic Report of the President, 1977.
[9] Michael R. Darby, "Wealth Effect," The New Palgrave Dictionary of Economics, 1987, pp. 883–884.
[10] Franco Modigliani and Richard Brumberg, "Utility Analysis and the Consumption Function: An Interpretations of Cross-Section Data." In *Post-Keynesian Economics*, Kenneth K. Kurihara, ed. New Brunswick, NJ: Rutgers University Press, 1954, pp. 388–436.
[11] The Council of Economic Advisers urged the enactment of legislation re-establishing war time standby controls on consumer credit. Economic Report of the President, January 1956, pp. 93–94, 138 and S. E. Harris, "The Economics of Eisenhower: A Symposium," p. 358 in the Review of Economics and Statistics November 1956, XXXVIII.

expansion led to increases in household utilization of debt. As in the short-term business credit case, both the supply and demand of consumer credit is procyclical.

The end of credit controls and usury ceilings[12] during this period opened the use of debt and credit cards as a substitute for cash. It also gave consumer installment credit a convenient use that fit into the more mobile lifestyle of the baby-boom generation. In addition, many financial institutions, as a means of competition, lengthened the maturities of most types of consumer credit such as new car financing reviewed earlier. Higher limits were added for average monthly payments.

What were the economics behind all this? Debt, per se, is neither good nor bad. To evaluate debt, we must identify the purpose to which the funds were used and the ability of the borrower to repay. Here, then, is the central core of the change in thinking in consumer credit that began to take place after World War II.

The maximum amount of debt a consumer can incur without going bankrupt is limited by the discounted present value of his future income plus current net worth. Actual or expected changes in income or current asset values affect debt capacity. A consumer's debt capacity is also determined, in part, by market conditions. Creditors, in the presence of adverse changes (recessions are the most common example) in interest rates and expectations about the creditor's future income and loan losses will alter the lending limits to reduce consumer bankruptcy risks. Again, we see the procyclical character of lending as in the short-term business case.

Debt to current income, the common way analysts portray the consumer debt issue, focuses on the absolute level of current income in the belief that consumption follows current income during a lifetime. However, households tend to pursue a consumption pattern quite different from current income alone. We consume more than our income when we are young and setting up households, hence the jump in the 1980s for the baby-boom generation, and in later years we repay earlier debt and provide for retirement. The relevant income constraint is not current income but the present value of the expected income stream over a lifetime. Consumption is proportional to lifetime income.

---

[12] In 1978, The U.S. Supreme Court held that the National Banking Act of 1863 allowed nationally chartered banks to charge the legal rate of interest in their state regardless of the borrower's state of residence (Marquette National Bank of Minneapolis v. First Omaha Service Corp).

In 1980, Congress passed the Depository Institutions Deregulation and Monetary Control Act. Among the Act's provisions were that it exempted federally chartered savings banks, installment plan sellers and chartered loan companies from state usury limits. Combined with the *Marquette* decision that applied to national banks, this effectively overrode all state and local usury laws.

Declining real interest rates in the 1980s raises the present value of real household wealth. Household net worth grew steadily in the mid-1980s (Fig. 8.1). In addition, declining inflation reinforced the increase in the real value of financial assets as evidence by the rising equity market in the 1980s. Permanent consumption and real net assets would rise even without a rise in measured income. The decline in inflation and interest rates in the 1980s resulted in a tremendous increase in the real value of bonds and a five-year bull market in equities. Household net worth rose regularly during that decade. Household net worth has a Granger causality link to real consumption and real GNP. The traditional debt to income ratio has no Granger causality impact on either real consumption or real GNP.[13]

As a result, the increase in current debt to current income is a misleading tool for forecasting consumption. Alain Enthoven focused his 1957 article on the dynamic aspects of the lifecycle model and that the relative frequency of indebtedness declines steadily with increasing age. Enthoven concluded that the growth of installment debt facilitated the channeling of the savings of older people to finance the deficits of the younger group.

Exogenous shocks, such as federal legislation, can alter the patterns of consumer credit in the economy. The Tax Reform Act of 1986 eliminated the interest cost deduction for consumer installment debt and investment properties—and thereby reduced the ability to expense instalment credit interest—but retained the deduction for home mortgage interest as home mortgage debt was the primarily liability of many American households. As a result, home equity loans became the debtor's choice to finance continued spending.

Exogenous Shock: Home Prices Can Decline

When does the evolution of household finances during the economic expansion begin to evidence signs of a break down? Three signals provide clues—housing leverage, the debt service ratio, and the saving rate. They are pressure points that could signal a break in consumer finance patterns.

Volatility Is the Character of the Housing Market

To say that housing is cyclical is to restate a cliché. Real insight comes from identifying a structural break in the housing market in the post-World War II period. Housing values and mortgage burdens illustrate both volatility

---

[13] John E. Silvia, *Borrowed Prosperity*, Economic Study published by Laffer Associates, September 1988.

and structural breaks that characterize the asset side (owner's equity) and the liability side (mortgages) of the housing finance market, as well as the variability of household saving rates. Given this volatility, our statistical analysis demonstrates that the assets and liabilities side of the housing finance market are not mean reverting. This diminishes the prospect of finding a reliable forecasting method for either series. Moreover, the structural breaks in both series intimate that changes in housing finances were abrupt and were likely to be unanticipated—indeed as evidenced by the widespread financial failures. While the conditions for identifying housing corrections may exist, the precise timing to reliably forecast such a correction remains elusive. Going forward, further research and analysis will be required to establish a reliable interest rate and housing starts relationship given the constant evolution of housing finance.

Evaluating Credit Pressures Amid Unpredictability

Since selected financial assets and liabilities are non-stationary, we cannot evaluate the series in terms of causality. We do not know which series leads the other in creating a trend. It would be misleading to attempt to argue one way or the other. Series such as the household debt service ratio (DSR), reviewed earlier as Fig. 8.12, illustrate the problem of abrupt and unanticipated change. The DSR declined 34% between its peak in Q4-2007 and its trough in Q4-2012 yet has risen only 4% since that time. The steady gains in personal income coupled with flat interest rates, despite an economic recovery, indicate a change in traditional economic growth and interest rates links.

Time inconsistency is a problem for credit. Auto and mortgage loans are made over a significant period. Auto loans today, for example, extend out five to seven years. Yet, credit decisions today to take on a loan are made midway through an economic expansion (1984–1985, 1994–1996, and 2004–2006) and often precede a rise in the DSR and a commensurate period of pressure on consumer finances. For the loans made in 1985, 1996, and 2006, they were all made within five years, or less, of a recession. Delinquencies are sure to follow.

As illustrated in Fig. 8.11, the charge-off rates on single-family homes had historically been extremely low with a small spike in the recession of 2001. The charge-off rates of 2008–2010 represented a significant structural break in the series. Lenders recognized a new paradigm existed and they became more cautious regarding credit criteria going forward.

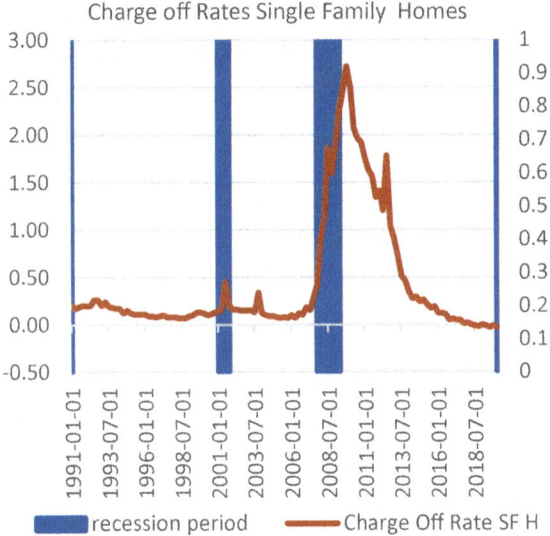

Fig. 8.11 Charge off rates single family homes

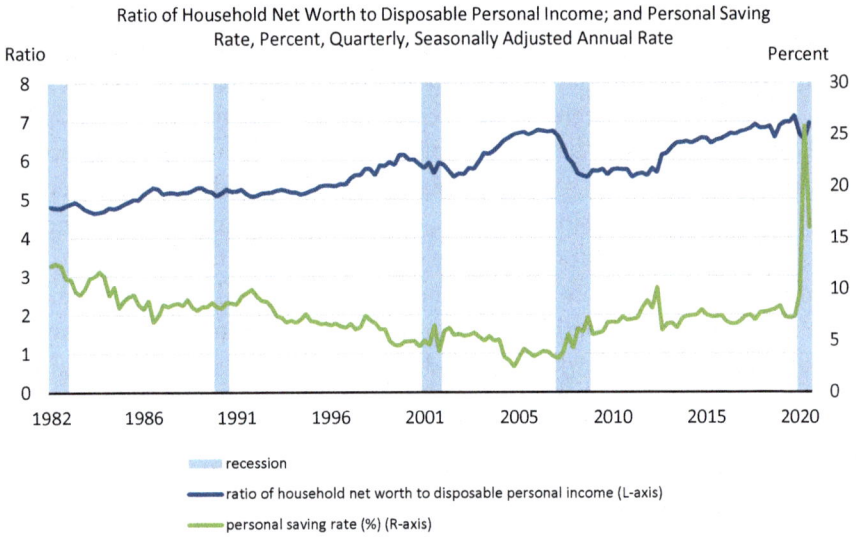

Fig. 8.12 Household net worth, income, and the saving rate

Animal Spirits and Economic Cycles: Explaining Abrupt Behavior

As an economic recovery and expansion evolves, as evidenced in Fig. 8.12, incomes tend to improve. Households become more optimistic as their net worth rises, and tend to reduce their saving rate (1992–2000, 2005–2006, and 2014–2018) Household net worth increases over the cycle as equity in housing improves and equity gains in the NYSE emerge. This relationship, however, can go the other way as consumers can pull back their spending when they are less optimistic. This occurred in early 2020 as households increased their savings rate despite gains in net worth and personal income. Such vigilance, brought on by the threat of the corona virus, meant that those gains did not have to be spent. The savings rate increases were conceptually consistent with increased caution and rising personal income and wealth.

The Household Balance Sheet—not a Partial Score

"U.S. Economy Fuels Boom in Consumer Debt," *Wall Street Journal*, December 28, 2018

Of course, the headline from the *Wall Street Journal* misrepresents the consumer financial situation by violating two principles. First, there is no balance between a view on debt and a view on financial assets as well as no historical perspective. Second, there is no sense of the income side of the consumer financial situation.

Focus on the Household Balance Sheet—Not Just Debt

"While consumer debt (liabilities) has risen during the current recovery, consumer assets have risen even faster, thereby preventing the emergence of consumer retrenchment." from "There is no Consumer Debt Problem," by John Silvia, *Wall Street Journal* April 13, 1987.

When we examine the household balance sheet there has been a rise in the ratio of assets to liabilities, as there was in the 1980s referred to above, during the economic expansion prior to early 2020. This is a clear break from the trend over the last fifty years, although there have been periods when asset gains outperformed liability growth (early 1980s, late 1990s). The long-term downtrend in the assets-to-liabilities ratio is clearly non-stationary indicating there is no mean reversion—no golden mean. In addition, the make-up of assets and liabilities has changed over time especially since 2007–2009. On the asset side, corporate equities and, to a lesser extent mutual funds, have gained favor with households. Credit market instruments have lost attraction. On the liabilities side, home mortgages dropped significantly relative to the pre 2007–2009 recession period.

2019 Before 2020 Shutdowns: Looking at the Balance Sheet

From the period 2016–2019[14] median family income rose and along with economic growth, so did house and corporate equity prices. On balance, median and mean family net worth rose as did homeownership rates as well.

Credit costs rose. Rates on consumer loans (mortgages, new vehicles, credit cards) rose, typical of the economic cycle, while debt payment to income ratios increased slightly from 2016 to 2019.

Survey results indicated the expected outcomes in some fields. Median income increases with education. Median net worth rises with age to 66–74 and with education. During the 2016–2019 period, transaction deposits were the most common component of household assets followed by retirement accounts. For nonfinancial assets, vehicles were the most common asset followed by a primary residence. One new development was that the percent of respondents holding credit cards exceeded the percent owning a primary residence for the first time.

Mean student debt was $23.9K which is interestingly far below the mean income of $87.4K. Mean net worth was $193K. The payment to income ratio median was 15.3% and 7.4% of respondents had payment to income ratios greater than 40%.

Household Credit: Another Look at the Supply and Demand

Just knowing the amount of consumer debt tells us nothing about the dynamics of supply and demand for consumer credit. The reported outstanding amount of consumer debt is the result of the supply and demand by the credit lenders and the consumer, respectively, and is not driven by either force alone.

Consumer Credit: The Federal Reserve Bank of New York—Quarterly Survey

The New York Fed provides detail on the consumer credit experience in its quarterly report entitled *Household Debt and Credit*. The survey results provide a pattern over time of household credit. We glean the following from the 4Q of 2018 report. By mid-2018, aggregate household debt balances were

---

[14] The Federal Reserve publishes its Survey of Consumer Finances every three years. The 2019 survey provides an excellent perspective on the consumer situation just before the shutdowns of 2020.

above their prior peak in the 3Q of 2018 and aggregate debt was up to 18 consecutive quarters—again confirming the observation that credit operates in a procyclical pattern. Credit card balances retouched their 2008 peak. In contrast, home equity loans continued their secular declines since 2009.

Aggregate delinquency rates remained steady in the 4Q 2018 as 4.7% of outstanding debt was in some stage of delinquency. The flow into 90+ day delinquency for credit cards had been rising since 2017. For autos, the flow into 90+ day delinquency had been slowly trending upward since 2012.

For student loans, the percent of loans 90+ days delinquent were the highest for all liabilities. Credit cards were the next highest. As for the trend in delinquencies, since 2016 there was an upward trend in 90+ delinquent loans for both student loans and credit cards. The percent of balances that were 90+ days delinquent were up for credit cards since 2017 and for auto loans since 2014. For mortgages, the percent of balances had declined over recent years. Of course, delinquency rates may be understated, especially in 2020, since many are in deferment, grace periods, or forbearance and therefore not in the repayment cycle.

By the time we examine the 4Q 2019, the Federal Reserve Bank of New York Survey estimates 11% of student loan debt is 90+ days delinquent or in default.[15] In terms of age, the 18–29 cohort represents the highest percentage of serious delinquent credits for both auto and credit cards—a not surprising result. By state, the top two most indebted states are California and New Jersey. After student loans and credit cards, the percentage of auto loans delinquent 90+ days has drifted upward and now approaches 5%.

By age, the 18–29 cohort had the highest transition percentage into serious delinquency (90+ days) for any group with the 30–49 age cohort next. These rankings by cohort were also true for the individual categories of auto and credit cards. There was a sharp jump up in the transition into serious delinquency for the 18–29 cohort starting in 2014.

There is also some state detail that is interesting. Total debt balances per capita were highest in California at $70K plus. New Jersey was next at around $60K. The California balances showed a drift upward since 2015. In California, as in all the states in the Fed survey, mortgage debt was the major form of debt. The delinquency status of debt balance per capita ranked California as the highest.

---

[15] Federal Reserve Bank of New York, Household Debt and Credit, 4Q, 2019, February 2020 release.

Secular Change in Household Debt

Results from the New York Fed Survey provide hints on the evolution of household debt in recent years. First, a warning that debt alone does not determine the fragility of consumer spending nor the growth of the economy. Therefore, concerns about household debt at all-time highs are off the mark. Debt must be balanced by an assessment of assets and debt service placed within the context of personal income. Also, there is a focus on the shifting of the types and ages of debtors that should be considered. As highlighted in the New York Fed Survey, the focus on rising serious delinquency rates for student loans and credit cards, in an economy with growing income and lower unemployment rates, is a concern.

If the value of financial assets, income, and broader economy rise, then debt would not appear to be a problem, but it is the balance between debt payments and income that remains the dividing force between credit expansion and credit revulsion.

Since 2010, the fastest growing liability for households is the growth of consumer credit, while home mortgages have grown at a more moderate pace. Mortgage and auto lending is interesting in that the biggest gain in lending in recent years has been to the highest credit quality (FICO scores above 760) group.[16] Post-2007, the biggest significant development has been the continued low-interest rates of the period. The surprise has been that interest rates have hardly risen as they usually do during an economic expansion. A driving force behind the pattern of debt service payments is the movement of the federal funds rate. This signals another structural change in the link between interest rates, the economy, and consumer interest expense. The early and mid-cycle periods of a rising federal funds rate (1982, 1994, 1999–2000, and 2005–2006) are correlated to the rise of debt service payments. This suggests that household debts are given in the short run and therefore when the funds rate is raised, debt service payments rise on a stable level of debt. Debt service payments also have a procyclical pattern as debt service increases with the aging of the economic cycle. This makes sense since households would take their prosperity today as a signal of prosperity ahead. With rising income and wealth, taking on debt appeared reasonable.

---

[16] FICO scores reflect the output of the Fair Isaac Corporation. Scores between 670 and 739 range indicate "good" credit history. Credit quality also reflects household income, job history and type of credit requested.

What to Watch for—Delinquency Rates in the Covid-19 Shutdown Era

Delinquency rates provide another time series to monitor the progress of the credit markets. Delinquency rates remain highest for student loans and then for credit cards. However, although the delinquency rates for student loans is the highest it is not getting worse and has, in fact, been steady since 2013 (perhaps a byproduct of a better labor market). Meanwhile, 90+ days delinquency rates for credit cards have declined significantly since peaking in 2010 and are below the rate of 2007—a surprise!

In the Senior Loan Officer Opinion Survey of October 2019, auto loan delinquencies were rising. Going forward we may observe a changing credit dynamic emerging. Since 2014, there has been an increase in serious delinquency for 18–29-year-old borrowers. Delinquencies for borrowers with low origination FICO scores have also risen. When we examine the delinquency rate on credit cards, there was already an uptrend in these rates starting in 2015 (Fig. 8.13) although the extent of the increase was very modest.

When we examine the delinquency rates for single-family residential mortgages (Fig. 8.14), we do not see any tendency for delinquency rates to rise. However, there are two cautionary issues. First, home prices have steadily risen in recent years so home buyers have been in the black. Second, even

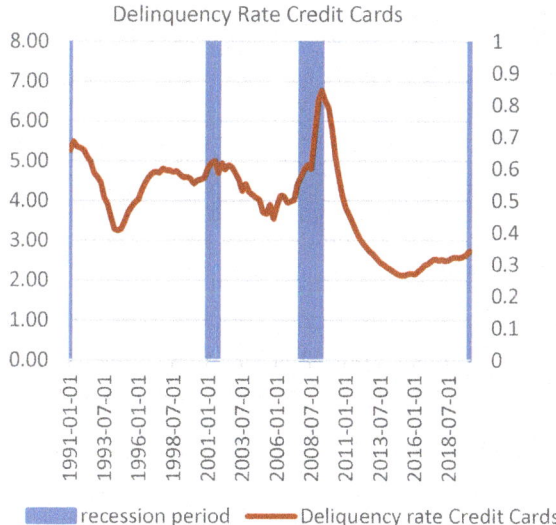

Fig. 8.13 Delinquency rate—credit cards

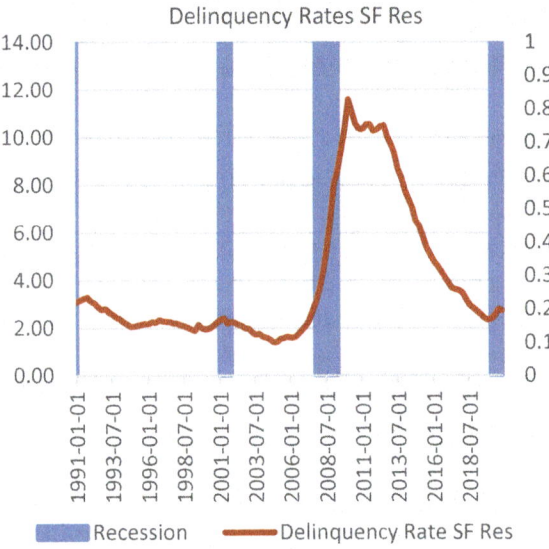

Fig. 8.14 Delinquency rate—single family homes

in the 2006–2008 period, the increase in delinquencies was not enough to signal a true breakdown.

Delinquencies on consumer credit exhibits characteristics of both cyclical and secular elements. There are strong cyclical patterns of delinquencies in mortgages, HELOCs (home equity loans of credit), and credit cards. One interesting note is that both mortgage and HELOC delinquencies rose sharply prior to the onset of the 2008 recession. Meanwhile, credit card delinquencies increased sharply halfway through the recession. In contrast, student loan delinquencies exhibited a secular trend upward from 2003 through 2008, then dipped before resuming the uptrend over 2013–2020:1Q period.[17] Despite the improvement in jobs and income over 2013–2020:1Q period, there was no improvement evidenced in student loan delinquencies. Finally, there is a disappointing gradual rise in auto loan delinquencies prior to the 2020 downturn. This may be a signal that credit has been extended too far into a lower quality credit pool. According to the Federal Reserve of New York Household Debt and Credit report, there was a steady rise in auto loan origination for those buyers with FICO scores below 620 and between 620 and 659.

---

[17] Household Debt and Credit, 2020 3Q, November 2020 release, Federal Reserve Bank of New York.

Consumer Finance: An Evolving Economic State

Consumer debt, as a percentage of GDP, is a poor indicator of the state of household finances. The imperative for analysts is to gauge the stock of debt and assets, the flow of interest expense, and income.

Increases in household debt, alone, tells us little about the actual financial state of the household. Over time, the expansion of credit availability to households and the changing demographics of households also provides contrasting perspectives on the state of household finance.

Since the financial crisis of 2007–2009, the household debt service ratio has remained at a level below that of early 1980s. This structural break in the series commands a new framework for both the supply and demand for household credit. Once again, this brings us back into the underlying cyclical and structural changes in both bank willingness and household demand for consumer credit. Looking forward, we are likely to see another break in the credit and economic linkages with the 2020 shutdowns.

We shall see in Chapter 9, how the global capital flows may also change with the post-2020 economy.

References

Larry Cordell, Yilin Huang, and Meredith Williams, "Collateral Damage: Sizing and Assessing the Subprime CDO Crisis," No. 11–30 Working Paper, Federal Reserve Bank of Philadelphia, May 2012. One of three essays dealing with household financial constraints.

Michael R. Darby, "Wealth Effect," The New Palgrave Dictionary of Economics, 1987, pp. 883–884. A discussion of the importance of the wealth effect on consumer spending.

Alain Enthoven, "The Growth of Installment Credit and the Future of Prosperity," American Economic Review, 1957, 47 (December). Alain Enthoven makes the case that demographics would influence the debt-to-income ratio for households.

Benjamin Graham and David Dodd, Security Analysis, Whittlesey House, McGraw-Hill Book Co., 1934. The classic book on investing.

The Council of Economic Advisers. Economic Report of the President, January 1956. The Council urged the enactment of legislation re-establishing war time standby controls on consumer credit.

The Federal Reserve, Survey of Consumer Finances. Published every three years, the 2019 survey provides an excellent perspective on the consumer situation just before the shutdowns of 2020.

Federal Reserve Bank of New York, Household Debt and Credit, 4Q, 2019, February 2020 release. A quarterly note that provides essential data and insight to household credit behavior.

S. E. Harris, "The Economics of Eisenhower: A Symposium," p. 358 in the Review of Economics and Statistics Nov. 1956, XXXVIII. A review of economic thinking, particularly about the household, during the 1950s.

Fumio Hayashi, "Tests for Liquidity Constraints: A Critical Survey and Some New Observations." In *Advances in Econometrics*, Truman F. Bewley, ed. Cambridge: Cambridge University Press, 1987, Vol. 2, pp. 91–120. A second essay dealing with household financial constraints.

Franco Modigliani and Richard Brumberg, "Utility Analysis and the Consumption Function: An Interpretations of Cross-Section Data." In *Post-Keynesian Economics*, Kenneth K. Kurihara, ed. New Brunswick, NJ: Rutgers University Press, 1954, pp. 388–436.

Brian Motley, Money, Income and Wealth, D.C. Heath, and Company, 1977. Motley provides an assessment of the linkages between the real economy and financial markets.

John E. Silvia, *Borrowed Prosperity*, Economic Study published by Laffer Associates, September 1988. In this paper, I show that household net worth has a Granger causality link to real consumption and real GNP. The traditional debt to income ratio has no Granger causality impact on either real consumption or real GNP.

Stephen Zeldes, "Consumption and Liquidity Constraints: An Empirical Investigation," *Journal of Political Economy*, 1989, 97 (April): 305–346. Third essay dealing with household financial constraints.

9

Capital Flows: The Dollar and Global Capital Allocation

Exchange rates are a fourth price in our assessment of market activity. They serve the purpose of driving and being driven by global capital flows in search of credit and real economy resource allocation. These flows follow investor expectations. Expectations of profitability—those of the early American colonies—when correct lead to long-run gains in trade and economic growth in both the capital exporting and importing nations. However, expectations can also be spectacularly wrong as in the Darien scheme by Scottish investors.[1]

This was an unsuccessful attempt to gain wealth and by establishing *New Caledonia*, a colony located on the Gulf of Darien. The plan was for the colony to manage an overland route to connect the Pacific and Atlantic oceans. The undertaking was beset by poor planning and provisioning; by divided leadership; by a lack of demand for traded goods; and by devastating epidemics, among other reasons. It was finally abandoned in March 1700 after a siege by Spanish forces. Since the scheme was backed by approximately 20% of all the money circulating in Scotland, its failure left the entire Lowlands in substantial financial ruin.

Often success and failure can be associated with the same event, as British investment in U.S. railroads in the nineteenth century were an initial success but then carried too far led to overbuilding and financial ruin for many.

---

[1] John Prebble, *The Darien Disaster*, Holt, Rinehart and Winston, New York, 1968.

This chapter presents linkages between economic and financial sectors. This chapter also provides some historical episodes to illustrate the challenges in following the many impacts of various economic/financial sectors have on each other and why the economic and financial professionals have such difficulty in forecasting exchange rates.

The story of the Mississippi Bubble is a prime example of this pattern. Expectations of profits generated capital flows that initially met with success but then, when pushed too far, led to ruin. At the outset, the expectations for profit and growth from the beaver trade in French North America was the economic rationale for the Compagnie d'Occident. Both profits and the liquidity associated with the company stock were limited but the issuance of paper currency was not. The excess paper currency issuance eventually led to the currency becoming worthless. This pattern has been repeated many times. The framework for capital flows is that such flows depend upon expectations of economic growth (and thereby profits), and a stable exchange rate (thereby limited inflation). If these expectations are initially met with financial success, and then dashed by failure, a disequilibrium is created and a rapid adjustment in market prices occurs that includes the equity valuations of investments, interest rates, exchange rates, and inflation.

Global Capital Flows: Credit Allocation Across Borders and the Associated Exchange Rates

Financial market prices proceed within a framework of expectations for growth, inflation, profits, and interest rates—all consistent with a set of exchange rates and a transfer of economic impacts from one currency into another.

Optimism on the Dollar: An Economic Driver and Rider Both

Dollar strength over the period 2018 to 1Q 2020 reflected financial market confidence that expansionary fiscal policy and deregulation efforts had prompted gains in real economic growth.

Economics is a study of interrelationships between markets, and the value of the dollar reflects the confluence of exchange rates, the prices of goods and services, and credit markets. The value of the dollar is both a driver and a rider in economic activity.

Financial markets discount a combination of easier fiscal and tighter monetary policy within an economy with a floating exchange rate and open capital markets, as associated with the Mundell–Fleming model.[2] In this approach, an easier fiscal policy and tighter monetary mix would typically be associated with a stronger dollar. The easier fiscal policy would be expected to promote economic growth and stimulate capital inflows which, in turn, would drive up demand for the dollar. Conversely, a tighter monetary policy would raise interest rates and stimulate capital inflows which would drive up the value of the dollar. This pattern adheres to a traditional economic framework. Yet, little of recent experience is anything like traditional.

The Mundell–Fleming model builds upon the traditional IS–LM model that focuses on the domestic, closed, economy.[3] The IS–LM stands for "investment-savings" (IS) and "liquidity preference-money supply." It shows how the market for economic goods (IS) interacts with the loanable funds market (LM) or money market. The focus in the Mundell–Fleming model is on the short-run linkages between economic growth, interest rates, and monetary and fiscal policy under conditions of fixed versus flexible exchange rates and different degrees of capital flows. The impacts of monetary and/or fiscal policy are dependent than on the exchange rate regimes and the degree of freedom of capital flows. For purposes of this manuscript, we will see the implications of the model throughout this chapter. A review of the Mundell–Fleming model can be found in Mankiw[4] as well as Rudiger Dornbusch.[5]

The character of the 2010–2019 expansion, with a given economic policy along with low inflation and moderate economic growth, created a path of moderate appreciation of the U.S. dollar. This path did not harshly limit growth in exports and GDP while it also kept a lid on inflation through import prices. Concerns linking the trade deficit to the exchange rate were overstated. Growth, both here and abroad, played a larger role than the dollar in determining trade deficits (Fig. 9.1). The elasticity of import growth with respect to growth in domestic demand was much higher than the elasticity of import growth with respect to changes in the exchange rate—the same holds for export growth during the expansion. Given the policy focus on boosting U.S. economic growth, a wider trade deficit would be expected to follow.

---

[2] Robert Mundell, "The Appropriate Use of Monetary and Fiscal Policy under Fixed Exchange Rates," International. Monetary Fund Staff Papers, March 1962.
[3] For example, see N. Gregory Mankiw, *Macroeconomics*, Seventh Edition, Worth, pp. 287–308.
[4] N. Gregory Mankiw, *Macroeconomics*, Seventh Edition, Worth, pp. 339–370.
[5] Rudiger Dornbusch, *Open Economy Economics*, Basic Books, 1980, Chapter 11.

The Linkages Between the Four Economic Sectors

Economics is a science of interrelationships between markets. The value of the dollar reflects the confluence of exchange rate, goods and services, and credit markets. The value of the dollar is both a driver and a rider in economic activity.

Financial markets have discounted a combination of easier fiscal and tighter monetary policy during the 2015–10′8 time frame. In an economy with a floating exchange rate and open capital markets, an easier fiscal policy and tighter monetary mix would typically be associated with a stronger dollar. This follows from the prior comment that capital inflows will increase, driving up the U.S. dollar exchange value as expectations for economic growth and interest rates increases become widespread. This pattern adheres to a traditional economic framework. Yet, little of recent experience is anything like typical.

For the 2010–2015 period expansion, economic policy was characterized by easier monetary and fiscal policy in an economy with free capital flows. The easier monetary policy lowered market interest rates lead to greater business investment and economic growth. The easier fiscal policy spurred further increases in aggregate demand via government spending and, with lower tax rates, increased household and business investment while also putting upward pressure on credit demand and interest rates. The offsetting interest rate impacts from monetary and fiscal policy kept rates range bound. As for economic growth, both policies promoted growth. Because of excess capacity in the economy after the 2007–2009 recession, inflation remained low relative to the two percent inflation goal of the Federal Reserve. This kept monetary policy easy for the first half of the past decade.

Going forward, economic policy and the character of this expansion can create a path for the dollar of moderate appreciation. This path would not too harshly limit growth in exports and GDP while also helping keep a lid on inflation through import prices. Concerns linking the trade deficit to the exchange rate may be overstated as growth, both here and abroad, plays a larger role than the dollar in determining trade balances Fig. 9.1. The elasticity of import growth with respect to growth in domestic demand is much higher than the elasticity of import growth with respect to changes in the exchange rate—the same holds for export growth. Given the policy focus on boosting U.S. economic growth, expectations for a wider trade deficit follow. The Canadian and Euro exchange rates, as well as the PCE deflator, do have a causal link to the trade balance.

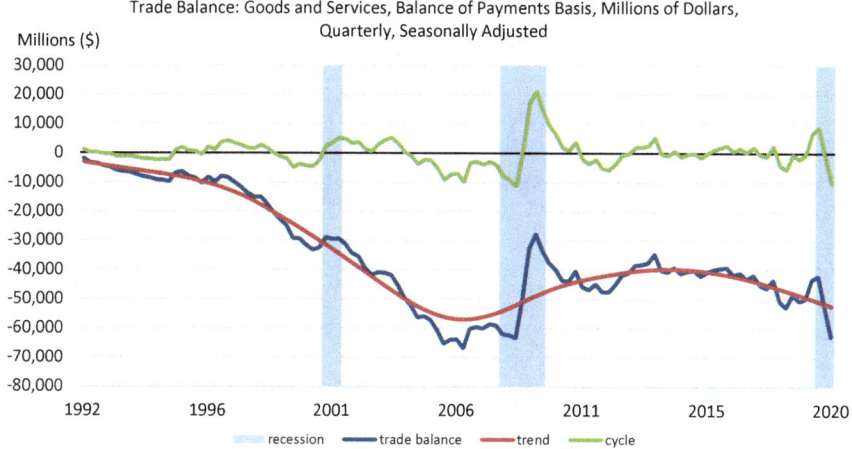

Fig. 9.1 U.S. Trade balance

After Accounting for Growth: Dollar and Interest Rates

Divergence among global short-term rates has been a persistent phenomenon for some time. On the U.S. side, the Fed raised rates in 2015 and increased the benchmark fed funds rate again in December 2016. With the labor market continuing to tighten and with inflation expected to rise, the Fed increased the benchmark federal funds rate multiple times in 2017 and 2018. Meanwhile, other major central banks, such as the Bank of Japan, Bank of England, and the European Central Bank, were aggressively easing via accelerated asset purchases, rate cuts, and unlimited liquidity offers. As illustrated in Fig. 9.2, periods of a rising interbank rates of U.S. rates relative to Canadian rates would appear to be associated with the depreciation of the Canadian dollar against the U.S. dollar (early 1990s for example). However, there is no causality between interbank rate differences and the Canadian dollar over the 1982–2020 period. Instead, changes in the corporate AA spread (credit markets) and the NYSE (equity market) have a causal link to the Canadian and U.S. dollar. The lack of the interest rate and exchange rate link is also apparent in the yen and dollar relationship.

Stronger Growth Drives Multiple Factors

A policy to pursue stronger growth also brings with it the prospect of drawing in capital from abroad that can finance economic growth as well as limit the rise in interest rates. Fiscal and monetary policymakers, however, will have

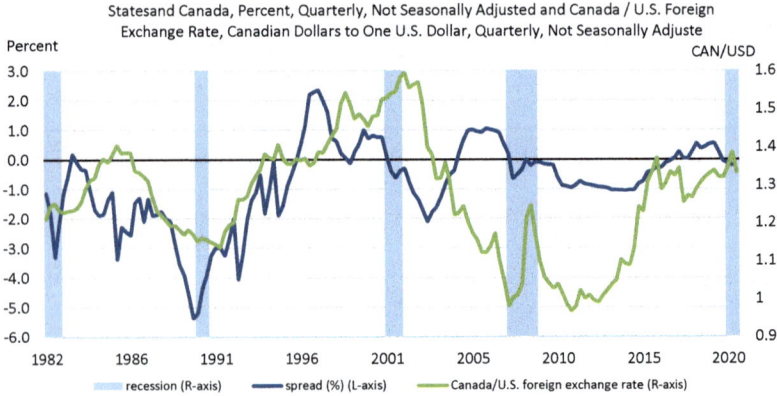

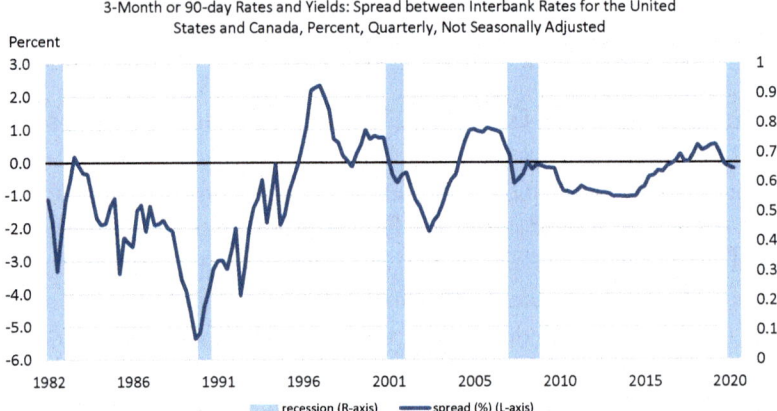

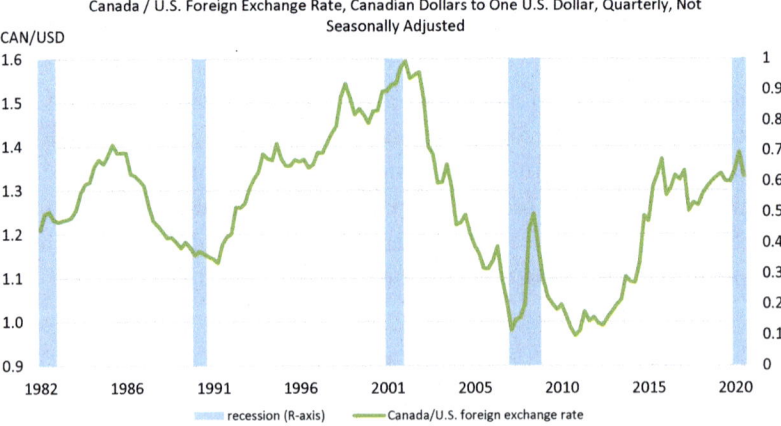

Fig. 9.2 Exchange and interbank rates

to walk a fine line. Too much dollar appreciation would inhibit exports and boost imports, exerting a drag on economic growth. A depreciation of the dollar, however, would lead to higher import prices and potentially losing hold of the inflation target. Economics is also a science of trade-offs; a fact policymakers need to bear in mind moving forward.

Finally, the role of capital flows is critical to determining the allocation of credit between sectors. A policy to pursue stronger economic growth also brings it with the prospect of drawing in capital from abroad that can finance economic growth as well as limit the rise in interest rates. Fiscal and monetary policymakers, however, will have to walk another fine line.

Foreign private purchases of U.S. credit securities present many patterns reflecting numerous influences of economic factors (Table 9.1). During 2017–2019, the Treasury market benefitted from continuous capital inflows. This had the follow-on impact of lower benchmark interest rates than otherwise. As an aside, China and Japan remained the top two foreign holders of U.S. Treasury debt. Moreover, there has also been a decent demand for agency debt in the United States, sometimes at the pace nearly that of the prerecession period of 2005–2007. Finally, foreign private purchases of corporate debt recovered beginning in 2015, reviewed below in Table 9.2. This also contributes to sustained gains in domestic bond issuance in support for equity buybacks, dividend payments, and capex (capital expenditures) and employment gains. There has been a significant interaction between capital inflows and interest rates which supported continued real economic growth in the United States.

* * *

Table 9.1 Rest of the world buyers of U.S. debt

	ROW buyers ($B)			
	Treasury debt	Agency debt	5Y yield	TW$
2019	225.7	56.1	1.95	115.7
2018	120.2	95.7	2.75	112
2017	308.2	22	1.91	112.8
2016	−107.8	79	1.33	113.1
2015	42.7	24.7	1.53	108.2
2014	374.2	−8.1	1.64	95.6
2013	423.2	−83.3	1.57	92.8

Table 9.2 Rest of the world buyers corporate bonds and equities

	ROW buyers ($B)			
	Corp bonds	Corp equities	Baa rate	NYSE
2019	153.1	−207.7	4.37	1316.6
2018	−62.2	110.9	4.8	1235.3
2017	321.5	116.9	4.44	1206.8
2016	326.3	−186.3	4.71	1061.9
2015	334.9	−191.4	5	1041.2
2014	209.6	114.3	4.85	1076.2
2013	210.3	−54.9	5.1	956

For Decision Makers: Getting Beyond the Headlines

Exchange rates are central to the allocation of resources as well as signals of trends on other markets such as relative interest rates, capital flows, inflation, and expectations for growth and inflation. Yet exchange rates are often treated as a financial stepchild. The equity market grabs the headlines, credit is second and if there is any space left on page one, the dollar gets a mention. Corporate profits, considered evil by some, are relegated to the financial pages, Section C of the newspaper.

Good due diligence in foreign investment reflects a careful balance of risk and reward. Yet in so many cases, the South Seas Bubble being one of the earliest examples, investors put lots of money in without a proper perspective of the expected returns and the risk involved. What is exotic may be wonderful for vacation but could be disastrous for investors.

The lesson from the South Seas Bubble? As we reviewed in Chapter 2, the South Seas Company was founded as a public–private partnership. It sold stock on the expectations of the growth of trade in the Caribbean (the South Seas) and South America. Despite a grant of monopoly by the British crown, the company did not earn a profit and went bankrupt. Capital flows follow the expectations of a profit and when no profit is realized, the capital flows, and the value of the underlying securities, disappears.[6]

As is often the case, considerations when evaluating any effort to source financial capital globally must reflect objectives for the investors in terms of time and expected returns versus the viability of the project itself.

International balance of payments reflects two major accounts. First, there is the current account for goods and services. It is reflected in the balance

---

[6] John Carswell, *The South Sea Bubble*, Cresset Press, London, 1960.

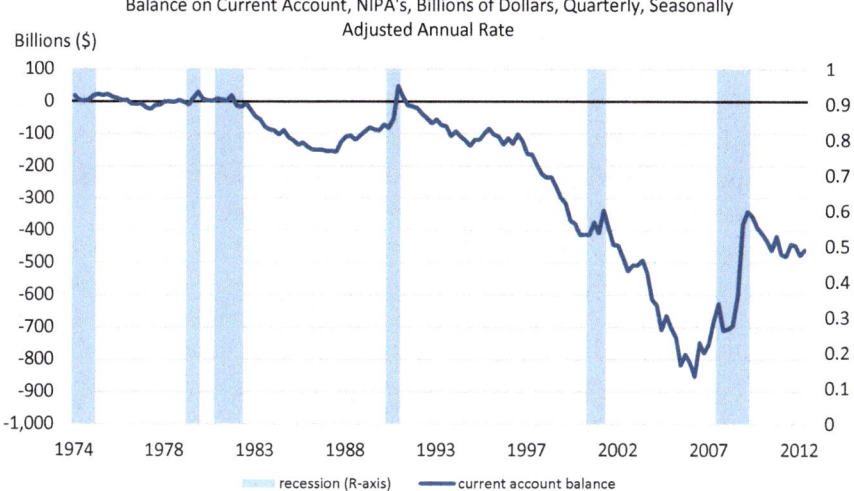

Fig. 9.3 Current account

of net exports as well as net transfers, interest payments and wage remittances, and profits of international corporations (Fig. 9.3). As illustrated in this figure, the balance has continued to deteriorate over time while also registering a modest narrowing of the deficit in recession periods as imports decline. Real final sales and the PCE deflator indeed have a causal link to the current account.

The second major account is the capital account which measures the flow of funds from and to the United States from foreign purchases of financial assets. The balance on capital account measures the net outflow of funds to purchase assets abroad.

We can express that the official settlements balance is equal to the change in foreign exchange reserves and errors and omissions which are frequently unrecorded capital flight.

To identify the linkages in our financial markets, we measure net exports less the net private capital outflow, CF, less net transfers to foreigners, TR. The balance of payments is always zero. Here BP is the "official settlements balance," and it is equal to the change FX reserves and errors and omissions, again which are frequently unrecorded capital flight.

$$BP = (X - M) - CF - TR$$

Real exports, x, will depend on the U.S. price level, P, and the exchange rate er

$$x = x(P, er)$$

Real imports, m, will depend upon the U.S. level of income, y, the exchange rate, er, and the price of competing U.S. goods, P.

$$m = m(y, P, er)$$

Our focus in this chapter is on the capital flows that result from the purchase and sale of real and financial assets. For any given set of interest rates, a foreign and domestic investor will allocate holdings between foreign and domestic assets depending on the level of interest rates at home and abroad. This allocation also reflects the expected pace of economic growth and inflation between domestic and foreign opportunities.

$$CF = CF(r, y, P)$$

As U.S. interest rates rise, ceteris paribus, it is expected that net capital outflows declines but there is scant evidence to support this linkage. Instead, changes in expected, relative economic growth and expected, relative inflation changes appear to dominate capital flows.[7] Interest rates, such as the AA corporate rate have a causal impact on the balance of payments as well as U.S. real final sales and PCE inflation.

Capital Flows, Interest Rates, and Asset Prices

Interactions between capital flows, asset prices, and economic factors (economic growth and inflation) are critical to understanding the process of price determination. The allocation of capital around the globe both drives and is driven by capital flows.

Yet, foreign exchange rates also face government intervention. Moreover, any attempt to target an exchange rate opens markets to spillover and repercussion effects which again alters equilibrium values in other markets. Spillover effects are the second order effects of a change in one country's economic circumstances and policy which has an economic impact on the

---

[7] "Booming Demand for Chinese Assets Boosts Renminbi's Global Role," *Financial Times*, October 8, 2020.

economy in a second country. This is most often witnessed when emerging market economies respond to changes in expected developed country growth or in U.S. monetary policy.[8] Repercussion effects refer to the third order impact that changes in emerging markets now feed back into financial markets in developed countries.[9]

During the 2010–2019 economic recovery, foreign private investors were consistent buyers of Treasury debt, helping to lower average interest rates over this period (Table 9.1).

In addition to Treasuries, there has been healthy demand for both agency and corporate debt since 2014. This has allowed U.S. issuers to place that debt at reasonable interest rates and limit the extent of the rise in interest rates during the recovery.

On the global scale, this has meant a significant allocation of credit toward the United States supporting the continued growth of the economy. This interaction of capital flows, interest rates, and economic growth reinforces our emphasis on a multimarket approach to thoughtful analysis.

Capital Flows and Equity Markets

The incentives of economic expectations on capital flows and asset prices are very evident in the foreign purchases of U.S. equities (Table 9.2). Capital flows influence and are influenced by expectations of economic growth and policy actions. Whatever the politics, equity capital inflows picked up noticeably with the 2016 election run-up and followed through with further gains in 2017 and 2018 as the NYSE index continued to gain. This would intimate that foreign private investors bet on pro-growth policy initiatives that would stimulate the U.S. economy and corporate profits. Yet, 2019 evidenced a decline in rest-of-the-world buying of equities despite a rise in the NYSE and continued growth expectations.

Meanwhile corporate bond buying has a clear inverse relationship to the changes in the Baa yield. Declines in the yield are associated with strong buying while the only rise in the yield (2017–2018) was associated with a decline in bond buying.

---

[8] "Emerging-Market Bond Funds Face Reckoning," *Wall Street Journal*, September 4, 2020.
[9] "Economists See U.S.-China Trade War as Biggest Threat in 2019," *Wall Street Journal*, December 18, 2018.

Top Holders of U.S. Treasuries: Finance Asian Style

As exemplified by the British finance of American railroads in the nineteenth century, U.S. economic growth has historically benefitted from the inflow of foreign capital from Europe, especially England. However, in the twenty-first century, the particulars of U.S. Treasury finance have taken on an Asian tone (Table 9.1).

Current foreign ownership of U.S. Treasury debt is distinctly concentrated in China and Japan, which creates some intriguing questions. First, will currency interventions and the conduct of monetary policy in China and Japan alter the incentives of both public and private buyers to purchase Treasury debt? Second, if investors perceive better economic prospects in both foreign countries, then will the risk-on trade dominate and thereby reduce the appeal of Treasury debt? Third, with the Fed maintaining its easy policy stance and other major central banks continuing with their easy policy settings, in which direction will the yield-hungry investors send their capital in the context of continued low short-term policy-determined interest rates?

For decision makers, the shift from European finance to Asian finance carries both economic and political changes in information gathering. The global financial markets evolve, and our analysis must evolve with them.

Capital Flows: A Brief History of Variability

European finance was critical in the finance of railroad expansion, especially the Illinois Central, in both the pre-and post-Civil War periods[10] but when several railroads, including the Northern Pacific, were unable to sell bonds for construction that had already begun several major banking houses failed.

For Argentina, along with other nations in Latin America, the opportunity to export commodities in the World War I period brought prosperity. But the expansion of production led to oversupply after the war as European production gained momentum. This period is also a lesson on the linkages between sectors. The fall in commodity prices, such as wheat, coffee, and cotton, meant imbalances in trade. For Latin America, as well as Britain, France, and Germany, poorly fixed exchange rates generated significant redirection of capital flows. Exchange rates depreciated for these countries. Meanwhile, when U.S. policymakers lowered interest rates to support the British pound in 1927, the U.S. stock market rose sharply, and capital flows were redirected

---

[10] Ross Robertson, *History of the American Economy*, Second Edition, Harcourt, Brace and World, New York (?), 1964, Chapters 5, 12.

to the United States and away from Germany for example. This illustrates our earlier point that the interest rate impact on exchange rates is often dominated by changes in growth expectations. Yet, lower interest rates in the United States did signal greater economic and financial opportunities in the equity markets and led to greater capital inflows into U.S. markets. Germany deflated its economy to address its balance of payments deficit. Political uncertainty rose after the 1930 National Socialist gains in Germany. The interactions between markets, and the speed of the interactions, illustrate the usefulness of a broader model of market prices.[11]

* * *

Capital Flows and Market Prices

For much of the post-World War II period, both fiscal and monetary policy have been used to stimulate aggregate demand to generate faster economic growth. In our framework, an expansionary fiscal policy should increase aggregate demand and economic growth. Gains in the relative pace of U.S. growth would imply an increase in capital inflows to the United States, higher interest rates and a stronger currency, for a given monetary policy. From its initial position, the trade balance would be expected to deteriorate as imports increase.

The expansionary fiscal policy of the early 1980s (lower taxes and increased spending) in the United States resulted in a faster pace of economic growth and a rise in real interest rates relative to the late 1970s. The shift in the yen/dollar exchange rate was very apparent from 1974 to 1994 (Fig. 9.4). Interestingly, the yen/dollar exchange rate has a causal link to CC corporate spreads, the two-year Treasury rates, and the ten-year less two-year yield curve.

Export led growth is characteristic of the Asian Tigers (Hong Kong, Singapore, South Korea, and Taiwan) between 1960 and 1980 as illustrated by Korea in Fig. 9.5. Export led growth increases the aggregate demand for goods and services, promotes domestic economic growth and employment while generating a trade surplus. In this export system, there are often governmental subsidies and better access to the local markets where labor costs are often suppressed, and the currency is often undervalued.

---

[11] Charles P. Kindleberger, *The World in Depression, 1929–1939*, Berkley University of California Press, 1973.

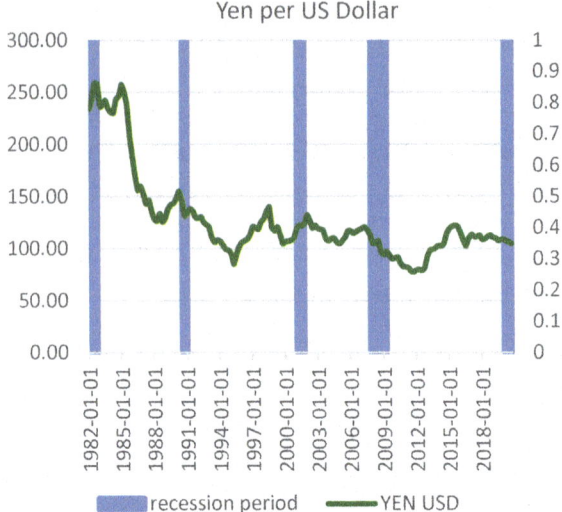

Fig. 9.4 Yen/US Dollar exchange rate

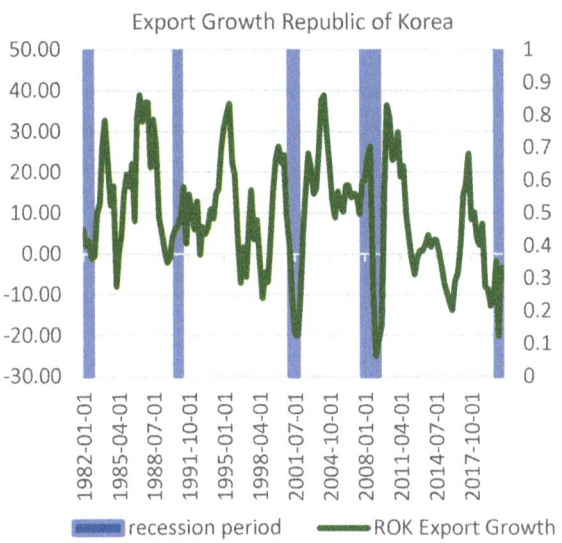

Fig. 9.5 Export growth-Republic of Korea

Interdependence, Spillover, and Repercussion Effects

As in most fields of economics, changes for international economies bring forth further changes in both the home and foreign economies. Increases in economic growth in one country, such as the United States, have spillover effects for the exports of Canada, Mexico, and Germany. Post-World War II Japan and Germany benefitted from favorable trade terms and the rapid U.S. expansion from the 1940s to the early 1970s. The Euro community today benefits from the growth in Germany and Southeast Asian countries benefit from the economic gains in China.

For each country, the size of the spillover impact reflects the size of the country. Growth in the U.S. economy would have a larger spillover effect on Canada and Mexico's growth than vice versa. Openness to trade is also very important. The more open the economy, the more the important a spillover effect. Finally, some countries have a higher propensity to import than other countries so the spillover effect would also be larger.

For our purposes, the spillover effect is not simply limited to goods and services. Interest rates, credit flows, exchange rate policies, and equity markets all have their spillover effects. For benchmark central bank policy rates, the Federal Reserve sets the standard. Changes at the Fed have global implications—especially for countries that import financial capital.[12] In the bond market, Chinese debt is finding a new home.[13] Finally, there is the link between growth expectations, equity valuations, and the U.S. dollar.[14] Spillover effects are transmitted via many channels.

Within the simple balance of payments expression, we can anticipate the impacts of shocks in one country on another country's economy. An economic slowdown in China has implications for exports for Asian economies. Higher policy rates in the United States put financial strains on emerging markets as their capital inflows slow. Increases in domestic prices in one country reduces the attractiveness of their goods exports thus worsening the trade balance. When equity market values in the U.S. decline, the perceived cost of financial capital rises and slows economic growth.

The balance of payments, which is zero, reflects the influence of net exports, (NX) and capital flows, which, in turn, reflect the current and expected pace of interest rates, r and r^e, and economic growth, y, y^e.

$$BP = NX + CF(r, r^e, y, y^e)$$

Repercussion effects reflect the influence and feedback effect of changes in one country leading to changes in a second country which feedback to

---

[12] "Emerging Market Debt: A Case for Concern?" *Financial Times*, January 10, 2020.
[13] "Beijing's First Bond Offer to US Investors Draws Record Demand," *Financial Times*, October 15, 2020.
[14] "The Allure of U.S. Stocks Could Keep Dollar Steady, Defying Gloomy Forecasts," *Barron's*, October 13, 2020.

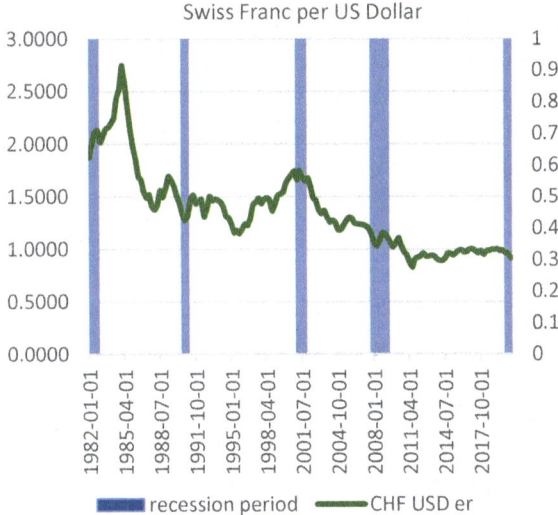

Fig. 9.6 Swiss franc per US Dollar

the first country. On the positive side, repercussion effects were positive for Canada, Mexico, and the United States with the passage of NAFTA. In general, a fiscal expansion in one country will raise income in the home country and the second country in a two-country model.[15] In a similar manner, credit easing on one country will lower interest rates and increase income in both countries.[16]

From mid-2011 to mid-2019, one of the more fascinating spillover effects is the appreciation of the Swiss franc (Fig. 9.6). The Swiss franc is viewed as a safe haven asset which will rally as investors become risk averse. The strength of the Swiss franc has promoted one policy action and perhaps will avert another. On the Swiss side, Swiss officials have regularly intervened to limit the appreciation of the franc. On the aversion side, Swiss officials are expected to avert any policy actions by the United States. The U.S. Policy makers can declare Switzerland a currency manipulator and thereby these policy makers could impose tariffs and other punitive actions. Interbank spreads do not have a causal link to the Swiss franc. Interestingly, the Swiss franc exchange rate does have a causal link to the two-year U.S. Treasury rate.

---

[15] Rudiger Dornbusch, *Open Economy Macroeconomics*, Basic Books, New York, 1980, pp. 199–202.

[16] The spillover effects from the Federal Reserve to emerging markets were apparent during the Fed's tightening policy period of 2017–2018.

In stark contrast, in the fall of 2020 the Turkish lira fell to an all-time low versus the dollar. Expectations for Turkish economic growth were downgraded and the decline in the exchange rate meant a rise in inflation and an increase in the burden of debt for Turkish companies. To add to these problems, there were the political tensions between Turkey, the EU, and the United States. The linkages between growth expectations, inflation, and political uncertainty produced a downward spiral in the Turkish lira exchange rates at that time.

Linkages

Exchange rates, as is true for prices of goods, equity valuations, and credit (interest rates), reflect the conditions of the marketplace, although those conditions are framed quite distinctly from the conditions of the credit market for example. The U.S. dollar exchange rate for any other currency is a price, in fact a relative price. We are therefore dealing with a non-recursive model, meaning that it contains one or more "feedback loops" or "reciprocal" effects. Any exchange rate today reflects expectations for growth, interest rates, and equity returns if the returns to investors are intended to be a profitable return.

The value of any currency reflects the variety of connections through commodity markets (oil prices being the most obvious for oil importers such as Japan and Germany). Connections exist through short-term capital movements, such as capital flight. In 2019, the focus for investors was China's ability to prevent capital outflows.[17] Yet, the reality was that China was using its reserves to invest in new relations with new emerging market partners, not losing its reserves.

Depreciation in the yuan above the 7-to-the dollar level had prompted the U.S. Treasury to label China as a currency manipulator which led to escalating trade tensions between the two nations. For many reasons, including many noneconomic ones, China has had difficulty controlling capital outflows. The weaker currency creates problems for many corporate borrowers who earn profits in yuan but pay international borrowings in dollars. For Chinese authorities, capital controls are a tool to control capital flight.

In an interesting turnaround, since mid-2020 the Chinese yuan has appreciated relative to the dollar. This reflects the change in fundamentals as

---

[17] "Weaker Yuan Tests China's Ability to Prevent Capital Flight," *Wall Street Journal*, August 11, 2019.

Chinese economic growth has picked up relative to expectations of U.S. economic growth as well as political uncertainties in the United States. If we adopt a longer-term perspective, demand for yuan is rising as the yuan-denominated so-called "Silk Route" trade expands. Potentially this would offer China the opportunity to build its own monetary system.

Evolution of Capital Flows and Exchange Rates

Since 2019, the Chinese and U.S. interactions reflect the continued evolution of capital flows and exchange rates that are characteristic of financial markets.

Sourcing Capital on a Global Scale

Colonel to General: "We are surrounded." General replies: "Good, we can attack in any direction."

Such is the foreign exchange market—influences that drive the market arrive from all directions—and the impact of changes in exchange markets radiate out in all directions. Such pathways lead sometimes to chaos and wonderful economic lessons always.

Sourcing Capital on the Global Scale

For the United States, as well as almost every other country, capital flows (in and out) are a major source of the financial capital needed for economic growth and employment as well as major drivers of the value of a nation's currency. In recent years, capital flow constraints have become a significant foreign policy weapon. As illustrated above in Table 9.1, China, Japan, the OPEC nations, and, to some extent, financial firms operating in the Caribbean have become major holders of U.S. Treasury debt. In part, the purchase of U.S. financial assets accompanies a purchase of U.S. dollars. In this way, the capital flows and exchange rate adjustments fit into our assessment of the balance of payments.

U.S. economic growth has benefitted historically from foreign capital inflows exemplified by British financing of American railroads in the nineteenth century. Now capital inflows in the credit markets have taken on an Asian tone. Policy actions in China and Japan may introduce a noneconomic set of forces that will alter the prices of foreign exchange and credit.

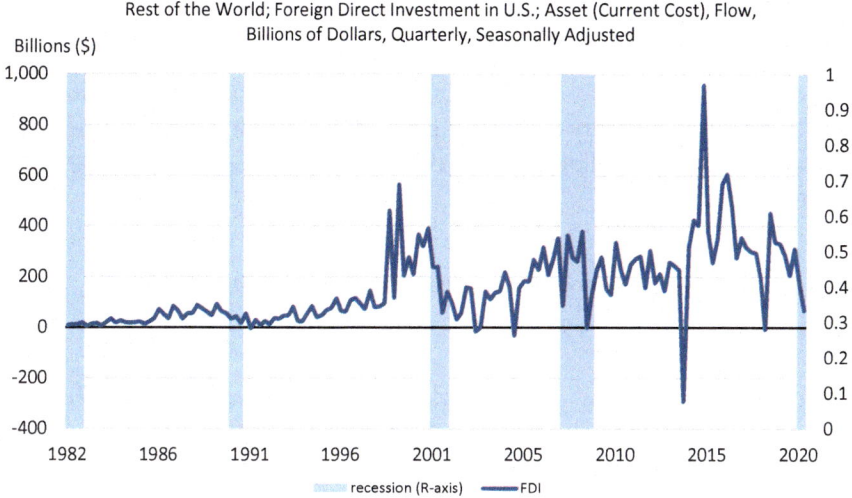

Fig. 9.7 Foreign direct investment into the U.S.

On the foreign direct investment side, Fig. 9.7, the pattern of foreign, private, direct investment indicates both a long-term secular increase for direct investment and a distinct cyclical pattern. The direct investment reflects the expectations for economic growth (real economy and profits) and credit markets (interest rates) but is complicated by current and anticipated policy actions. To confirm that view, the yield curve has a causal link to foreign direct investment.

Three Sources of Disturbance in a Market in Constant Disequilibrium

Igniting the Fire on the Domestic Front

Increased domestic demand in the United States in the early 1980s provides an example of an exogenous, policy-driven, change in the demand for goods and services that led to an increase in domestic growth and income with follow-on increases in interest rates and dollar valuation. An expansionary fiscal policy and a tighter monetary policy drove increases in both interest rates and the U.S. dollar. Net exports declined because of these moves. In

1985 the Plaza Agreement[18] depreciated the dollar to address the perceived excess valuation of the dollar at that time.

These economic price movements reflect the importance of price flexibility and capital mobility—how are prices set. Price flexibility is a necessary element in the proper allocation of economic resources and the achievement of economic goals.

Exogenous Increase in Export Demand: A War-Time Tradition

One of the main forces that moved the U.S. economy out of the Great Depression and created the basis for the U.S. industrial strength post-World War II was the surge in industrial production to arm our allies even before the America officially entered the war. The Lend-Lease program approved by Congress on March 1, 1941 gave President Franklin D. Roosevelt virtually unlimited authority to direct material aid such as ammunition, tanks, airplanes, trucks, and food to the war effort in Europe without violating the nation's official position of neutrality. Such goods flowed mainly to the United Kingdom and the Soviet Union. This meant an outward shift in aggregate demand as foreign demand for the U.S. produced capital goods went up with lend-lease, increasing overall aggregate demand for the U.S. economy. Increased aggregate demand resulted in a rise in domestic incomes as well as the demand for the dollar which caused dollar appreciation. This occurred while there were limitations on domestic spending—in part due to household caution due to Great Depression memories and later rationing when America entered the war. The rise in output for export demand boosted U.S. economic growth. At the same time, because the nation was still under a gold standard, there was an increase in gold holdings in the United States. This allowed for an expansion in the money supply. But the expansion was limited by policy and by the caution of both lenders and borrowers given the recent end of the Great Depression.

During the 2010–2019 economic recovery and expansion, bond markets benefitted from the continuous capital inflows into U.S. Treasury notes and bonds. Foreign investors sought opportunities due to perceived better economic growth opportunities and a higher nominal demand for real goods and financial assets. Increased external demand can arise from the real side (goods) as well as the financial side (bonds and equities). Beyond the demand

---

[18] Yōichi Funabashi, *Managing the Dollar: From the Plaza to the Louvre*, Peterson Institute, Washington, DC, 1989, pp. 261–271.

for sovereign debt, foreign private purchases of corporate debt recovered beginning in 2015. This also contributed to sustained gains in domestic bond issuance in support for equity buybacks, dividend payments, and capex and employment gains. There has been a significant interaction between capital inflows and interest rates which has helped support continued real economic growth in the United States.

Shifting Preferences: Buy local—The Patriotic Pocketbook

Moral suasion by public policymakers focuses on altering consumer preferences to buy domestic goods and away from foreign goods. In terms of an economic framework, this approach shifts aggregate demand to domestic production and reduces imports. Referring to our balance of payments equation, the net result is that the trade balance will improve as well as there will be an increase in domestic income. As for prices, the dollar exchange rate and interest rates are likely to rise in this situation. In recent years, this approach of moral suasion is exemplified by the Trump administration.

Thinking Beyond Step One

During election years, many economic policy proposals fail to reach implementation. Serious investors instead must address interdependence, spillover, and repercussion effects. Interdependence income determination exists between the U.S. and Chinese economies. U.S. economic growth bolsters Chinese exports while Chinese growth increases the growth profiles of many Asian nations and U.S. exports. Spillover effects signify that investors must gauge U.S. growth while estimating gains in China and emerging markets as well. Repercussion effects refer to the additional effect on U.S. growth and income caused by the reaction of a foreign country's income to the initial increase in aggregate demand in the United States.

Spillover and repercussion effects are particularly important for investors in European and emerging markets. Here reaction to the U.S. and China growth expectations and their exchange rate alterations will be significant.[19]

---

[19] Multicountry models began development in the 1970s. Two notable efforts were Project Link, 1977 by Lawrence Klein and Guy Stevens, Richard Berner, Peter Clark, Enrique Hernandez-Cata, Howard Howe, and Sung Kwack, "The U.S. Economy in and Interdependent World: A Multicountry Model," published by the Board of Governors of the Federal Reserve (??), 1984. See also John A. Sawyer, *Modelling the International Transmission Mechanism*, North-Holland Publishing, Amsterdam, Netherlands, 1979.

Dollar as a Price: Global Allocation of Resources

The dollar, often the stepchild in media coverage as we have expressed before and reemphasize here, plays a central role in the allocation of global resources. The dollar exchange rate reflects the supply and demand conditions of the marketplace. But since the dollar is expressed as a relative price, the exchange rate is a two-step process—appreciation of one currency against another—and may reflect the improvement of one currency's prospects versus the deterioration of another currency. If the U.S. dollar appreciates against the euro, for example, have U.S. dollar prospects improved or has the euro outlook depreciated?

Failure at a Distance: The Many Linkages in Exchange Rates

In 1979, the second oil shock doubled the price of oil (a commodity) but not just for the United States although Americans tend to focus solely on our economy. For Brazil, the value of its exports (particularly coffee) declined relative to its imports (oil), therefore there was a deterioration in its terms of trade (the ratio of an index of a country's export prices to an index of its import prices). Moreover, the rise in market interest rates (price of credit) increased Brazil's balance of payments problem adding to the downward pressure on Brazil's exchange rate.

For the United States, the linkage between the trade balance and the Canadian dollar and U.S. dollar exchange rate in recent years has been an interesting path for change. The trade balance reflects the influence of several factors including exchange rates (euro, Canadian dollar, British pound), interest rates (high yield and AA spreads), and inflation, as measured by the PCE deflator and equities (NASDAQ).

U.S. buyers of imported goods (elasticity) are greater than the willingness of foreign buyers of our exports in response to change in GDP. Stronger GDP growth in 1997–2000 and again from 2002 to 2006 led to a deterioration of our trade position. Meanwhile, the real dollar major currencies index rose from 1996 to 2000—consistent with the deterioration of America's trade position. In contrast, a weaker dollar accompanied trade deterioration from 2001 to 2006—no single variable explanations here—once again revealing that tracking several markets is essential to understand the economy. As would be expected, during recessionary periods, (periods of weak economic growth and slower import growth) the trade balance improved in both 2001 and again in 2008–2009. Yet, outside a good recession, there is no statistically significant linkage between economic growth and the trade balance.

Balance of Payments: Growth, the Exchange Rate, and Interest Rates

Recognition of interactions between real and financial markets is the hallmark of thoughtful investor due diligence. The balance of payments provides a concise summary of these interactions between the forces of several sectors, although at the end the balance of payments is always zero.

Net exports reflect the real economic impact of both domestic and foreign growth on exports and imports. Of course, the dollar exchange rate also enters here as a relative price of exports and imports. The second part of the balance of payments, capital flows (often overlooked) reflects expectations of relative economic growth, as well as relative interest rates. The roles played by expectations and relative interest rates are essential and make assessment of capital flows tricky.

Increases in real economic growth in the United States, relative to growth abroad, should, ceteris paribus, generate an increase in U.S. imports and a decline in net exports. An exogenous change in the dollar exchange rate, for example an appreciation of the dollar, would lead to more imports but lower exports, all else held constant. Yet an exchange rate devaluation does not necessarily lead to an improvement in the trade balance, and vice versa for appreciation.

Finally, expectations of faster economic growth and/or higher interest rates in the United States relative to abroad, would lead to greater capital inflows. All this is straightforward.

What is not straightforward is anticipating changes down the road. Think of it as an economic chess game. The first move is never the last and any move must be thought of as part of a sequence—the good analyst must anticipate the sequence.

In the early 1980s, an expansionary economic policy in the United States led to faster than expected economic growth, appreciation of the dollar, and higher than expected real interest rates. As part of the sequence, capital inflows followed as the U.S. balance of payments deteriorated. As a counter move, this resulted in the coordinated government intervention known as the Plaza Accord of September 1985 to depreciate the dollar relative to the Japanese yen and West German Deutschemark. Yet, the Plaza Accord was followed only two years later by the Louvre Accord which attempted to moderate the dollar decline.

> "Wisdom lies neither in fixity nor in change, but in the dialectic between the two."—Octavio Paz

Domestic policies can also significantly alter capital flows with major economic and political consequences. The Fordney-McCumber Tariff Act of 1922 raised tariffs above those set in 1913. One unintended consequence of the act was that it made it more difficult for European nations to export to the United States and earn the dollars needed to service their war debts. Not having the dollar earnings from exports significantly limited these countries from servicing their foreign debts.

Interventions can have unanticipated consequences when prices do not match what is required for clearing markets. The expansion of economic production outside of Europe during World War I and post-war was not sustainable at World War I prices for commodity items such as Argentine, Canadian, Australian, or U.S. wheat. With the Great Depression, the collapse in wheat prices further negatively impacted capital flows.

Finally, U.S. monetary policy in the 1920s lowered U.S. interest rates to weaken the dollar and bolster the British pound. However, this tended to prop up U.S. equity prices in the late 1920s. Capital flows increased into the United States making German war reparations more difficult to finance. U.S. capital inflows diverted investors from projects and investments in Germany. Keynes described this process of capital flows as "a great circular flow of paper" across the Atlantic.[20]

Failure at a Distance—Again

What is to be learned regarding capital flows? None of the above is definitive in leading to the Great Depression or the other numerous economic political problems of the 1930s. However, the lesson is that arbitrarily set prices and including exchange rates create distortions in markets and have impacts far afield and long after the original policy action.

Lower wheat prices created balance of payments problems for Argentina which then led to a currency depreciation and economic recession. Lower wheat prices in the United States persisted throughout the 1930s. The lower rates to prop up the British pound aggravated the mispricing of equities in

---

[20] Liaquat Ahamed, *Lords of Finance*, Penguin Press, New York, 2009, pp. 215–216.

the United States and contributed to the eventual sharp (inevitable?) equity correction. Finally, tariffs and capital flows changes impacted the ability of Germany to repay war reparations with the subsequent obvious long-term political impacts for Germany and the world.

* * *

Linkages in a Non-Recursive Economy

"… the anticipated effects of these interconnections…"

In 2019, Federal Reserve Chairman Powell spoke in Paris about the importance of the global dimension of domestic policy—for investors, the effects of these interconnections work both ways as global policies, such as the Plaza and Louvre Accords, have significant domestic impacts.[21]

Decision Making in a Non-Recursive Global Economy

We are familiar with U.S. domestic monetary policy creating ripples on emerging markets, for example, in mid-2018. Yet, Powell's global dimension is not a one-way track from Fed policy to the globe. Changes in the economic outlook after the Asia flu (starting July 1997) led to a sell-off in U.S. equities and a decline in consumer spending and confidence. The Fed lowered the funds rate three times in 1998.

Domestic Policy in a Global Capital Market

For both investors and private business leaders, global capital markets create feedback loops for any change in fiscal and monetary policy in any country. The lowering of the U.S. corporate tax rate altered the incentive to move capital to the U.S. Higher capital inflows reduced the cost of capital and promoted economic growth. Meanwhile, a tighter monetary policy in 2018 created problems for emerging markets' finance as cited above.

A reduction in European and Japanese central bank interest rates created the incentive for investors to move capital to America, a higher economic growth economy. This had the effect of boosting U.S. growth, lowering the

---

[21] Jerome Powell, "Monetary Policy in a Post-Crisis Era," July 16, 2019, at "Bretton Woods: 75 Years Later—Thinking About the Next 75," a conference organized by the Banque de France and the French Ministry for the Economy and Finance, Paris, France.

cost of capital, and, ironically, reducing the credit finance pool for growth in the European and Japanese economies.

Lower interest rates abroad, in response to their economic weakness, did not prompt stronger economic growth there. Instead, it appeared to confirm to global investors that their economic subpar growth would continue, prompting investors to seek opportunities elsewhere. Policy easing abroad did not alter growth expectations upward but reinforced expectations of weakness.

What About Fed Easing in an Era of Perceived Economic Strength?

Here is an interesting contrast to the European and Japanese case. The state of policy debate in mid-2019, at the time of Governor Powell's presentation in Paris, was that the U.S. economy is doing quite well (low unemployment, low inflation, trend plus growth) so what would be accomplished by another 25 basis points of easing? Well, we return to our framework. If the economic energy of easing adds little to economic growth, then the impact must fall elsewhere (thank you Lord Kelvin) in a manner of higher asset prices and a lower dollar exchange rate. What remains to be seen is to what extent a lower short-term interest rate would reinforce economic growth expectations for asset prices and offset those same expectations on the dollar.

"… the anticipated effects of these interconnections…"

In July 2019, there was also the issue of whether another central bank, the ECB, could do enough to make a difference. For the analyst, the focus is on doing what with another round of easing. Nominally, the case for the ECB and Fed easing is that such a cut would increase the probability of the ECB avoiding deflation and the Fed achieving its 2% inflation target. The argument appears to be that a lower interest rate on short-term credit would boost business investment and consumer spending thereby increasing aggregate demand.

This brings us to the problem of a liquidity trap, i.e., where lower market interest rates do not elicit an increase in business investment since the expected future pace of real final sales does not merit new investment. In other words, the returns to investment are outweighed by the risk, In the 2010–2019 expansion period, financial intermediaries sat on excess reserves rather than lend them out because they are constrained by capital adequacy or because they see real investment as too risky.

But There Is a Bigger World Out There

Business investment is primarily a function of expected final sales and not interest rates. What do we know of expected final sales? The IMF outlook in mid-2019 was for slower growth.[22] Meanwhile, consumer spending was already very strong due to solid real income and wealth gains and high consumer confidence.

In the case of the Euro area, an interest rate cut was unlikely to have much impact. Moreover, a tiering process by the ECB for bank deposits was unlikely to offset weaker German industrial output and employment. The ECB, in mid-2019, adopted a two-tier system of reserve deposit remuneration.[23]

What Difference Would Monetary Easing Make—Let Us Ask Lord Kelvin

Central banks do what they do. Our job is not to tell them what to do since there are plenty of commentators such as the print[24] and TV media who are willing to tell them. As advisors, our task is to anticipate the financial implications of their actions. Monetary easing must go somewhere. If not real aggregate demand, then impacts should be found in the foreign exchange, bond, and equity markets.

Easier Fed policies and ECB actions are likely to continue to support the dollar given expected real economic growth that favors the United States. ECB and Fed actions are likely to lean toward lower bond yields, particularly if the ECB extends bond buying by raising its issuer limits which would help southern European bond issuers.[25] Finally, equity markets would benefit by lowering the discount rate on future earnings.

Unfortunately, for investors, easing would further make asset valuation more difficult. Pricing of both bonds and equities has been distorted by monetary easing to the point we have to ask whether there is any meaning to the concept of a risk-free (default risk that is) interest rate.

For investors, central bank fears of a doom-loop, i.e., a negative spiral that can occur when banks hold sovereign bonds and governments with weak

---

[22] "IMF Cuts Global GDP Forecast for 2019, Citing Fallout from Trade Tensions", *Wall Street Journal*, July 23, 2019.

[23] The ECB exempted from negative rates an amount of each EA bank's excess reserves equivalent to 6 times (the "exempt tier multiplier") the minimum required reserves (MRR). The exempt tier will earn 0% instead of -50bps. However, the multiplier is set to be a function of excess liquidity.

[24] For Example, "The Fiscal Federal Reserve," *Wall Street Journal*, October 7, 2020 and The ECB buys time for a more important task, *Financial Times*, June 8, 2020.

[25] For 2021, Euro Bonds, a new asset class for 2021, came into being without any limits.

public finances bail out such banks appears to be transforming into becoming a boom loop. Here valuations are increasingly stretched as future earnings on bonds and equities become increasingly valuable as the discount factor increasingly disappears. Lord Kelvin anticipates a imbalance in the flow of heat—not in the economy, but in financial markets.

Disequilibrium in the Four Sectors of the Market Prices: Exchange Rates, Interest Rates, and the Expected Return on Capital

The relationship between interest rate expectations and exchange rates has become harder to quantify, largely due to the unique nature of the current economic cycle. This changing dynamic ultimately affects capital flows.

What About Expectations?

Capital flows respond to relative interest rate and exchange rate dynamics across borders. We now turn to the effect of expectations on our three variables. Expectations have played an increasingly important role in market participants' reactions to global events. For example, Italian political uncertainty in 2018[26] led the euro to decline against the dollar, while Italian bond yields rose more than 100 bps.[27] While it is too soon to determine the impact, these political tensions could have on capital flows, expectations play a role in short-term exchange rate and interest rate dynamics. In the long run, these dynamics affect capital flows.

Expectations of central bank actions have also caused unpredictable swings in foreign exchange rates and interest rates. Rate hikes from the Fed do not appear to be supportive of the U.S. dollar exchange rate as there is no causal link between Fed rate moves the dollar exchange rate. In contrast, tightening on the part of foreign central banks has been more supportive of foreign currencies. Throughout much of 2017, short-term rate expectations moved in favor of the U.S. dollar, but the dollar declined. This is likely due, in part, because the FOMC was further along its tightening path relative to other major central banks. At that time, the ECB and Bank of Japan were pursuing Quantitative Easing and negative interest rates. Financial market participants

---

[26] Italy's Salvini ramps up rhetoric as bonds face new pressure, *Financial Times*, October 8, 2018.
[27] "Yields on Italian Bonda Hit 4 ½ year High on Budget Concerns," *Wall Street Journal*, October. 8, 2018.

were also pricing in future rate hikes by the Fed. During the 2016–2018 period, market-implied probabilities of a rate hike rose but market participants also anticipated that the FOMC had only so many rate hikes left before reaching its terminal rate. This meant the potential for rate hike "surprises" was much lower. So, perhaps, market expectations limited any dollar appreciation in response to any interest rate increase.

In turn, the effect of interest rate expectations on exchange rates has been harder to quantify. The dollar exchange rate started to rise in 2014. As the Fed began to tighten policy in 2015–2016, one could identify a more direct relationship between the probability of a Fed rate hike and its effect on the dollar as the trade-weighted dollar rose over the period of 2015–2017. However, as global central banks have since engaged in unconventional monetary policy measures, the focus has turned toward perceived policy stances through actions such as Quantitative Easing, rather than a pure reaction to actual rate hikes.

Reviewing Past Cycles: All Else Is not Equal for Capital Flows

The evolving relationship between interest rate expectations and exchange rates confirms why this cycle is unique. We have found that country-specific characteristics lead to volatility in capital flows, and similarly influence expectations. In the United States for example, prior cycles may have had a rising rate environment but lacked a fiscal stimulus. This difference is compounded by unconventional global monetary policy and a deteriorating fiscal outlook during one of the longest economic expansions in recent history (see Chaper 12). These differences influence investors' relative allocation of capital. Decision makers would do well to pay attention to the unique outcomes that stem from differing market expectations.

Spillover Effects and the Canadian Experience: Exogenous Increase in Export Demand

Canada is an economy most likely to benefit—and suffer—from its close links to the U.S. economy as exemplified by spillover effects. As the U.S. economy began its recovery in the second half of 2009, we would expect that export gains in Canada to the United States would start to appear and indeed that did happen. Canadian exports rose from C$107B in the second quarter of 2009 to C$143B by the fourth quarter of 2011.

In turn, Canadian economic growth picked up from the negative 4% in the third quarter of 2009 to the 2.5% range from 2010 to 2012. Increases in foreign demand from the United States accompanied a rise in Canadian exports and overall economic growth. Over that same period, ten-year benchmark interest rates in both the United States and Canada declined but the decline in Canadian rates was less. The spread of U.S. rates over Canadian ten-year rates fell from 26 basis points at the start of 2010 to just 4 basis points by the start of 2013. Given the near perfect capital mobility between the two countries, it is not surprising yield spreads would decline as the economic risks of investing in Canada declined over time. Finally, the Canadian dollar did appreciate from 2010 to 2012.

The economic recovery in the United States during this time generated a spillover effect and created a disequilibrium situation in the markets. U.S. economic growth led to a gain in Canadian exports driving up their economic growth. Better growth caused a narrowing of interest rate spreads and an appreciation of the Canadian currency in the short run. The linkages between markets remain a central part of understanding the economy.

The United States: Endogenous Increase in Fiscal Expansion and Dollar Appreciation

For the United States in the post-1981–1982 recession period, a significant fiscal expansion, accompanied by tighter monetary policy, led to a rise in aggregate demand and economic growth, with real GDP going from −1.8% in 1982 to 4% plus in 1983, 1984, and 1985. This growth in aggregate demand, along with restrictive monetary policy, prompted a rise in market real interest rates. As a result, the yen/dollar exchange rate remained above 220 yen per dollar and was perceived to be undervalued which led to the Plaza Accord and the sharp appreciation of the yen in 1985. Between 1982 and 1985, the balance on current accounts for the United States went from negative $8B to negative $107B in 1985.[28] Imports from Western Europe rose from $52.9B in 1982 to $72B in 1984 and from Japan from $37B in 1982 to $60.2B in 1985. The net international investment position of the United States fell from $147B in 1982 to $28B in 1984. Dollar appreciation was associated with a deterioration in the current account position.

---

[28] Data cited here are taken from *Economic Report of the President*, February 1986.

Trade deficits rose. The linkages between markets remain a central part of understanding the economy.

The United States: Endogenous Increase in Monetary Policy Restraint

In the fall of 2016, the Federal Reserve hinted at a normalization of interest rates. By December 2017, the Federal Reserve began a series of eight policy rate increases. Under a flexible exchange rate regime, as the relationships between sectors would suggest, the trade-weighted dollar rose in the Fall of 2017, then declined. Then it began a sustained rise in the second quarter of 2018 that continued for the rest of that year. The U.S. net export position first dropped in the 2Q of 2018 and bottomed in the 4Q of that year. Real GDP growth slowed steadily from the 2Q of 2018 and into the next four quarters. The PCE deflator slowed from 2.2% in the 2Q of 2018 to 1.44% in the 1Q of 2019.

The NYSE peaked in the 3Q of 2018 and returned to that level by the 2Q of 2019. The biggest problem for the financial markets at the time was that emerging markets were put under stress as higher financing rates and slower export growth meant problems for debt finance as the following quote at the time illustrates.[29]

> **"Fresh Stress Grips Weakest Emerging-Market Currencies"**
> "The Argentine peso hit a record low and the Turkish lira resumed its slide, dramatizing the strains faced by emerging markets most vulnerable to a rising dollar.
> While Argentina and Turkey are in particular trouble, many developing countries are being squeezed as the Federal Reserve raises interest rates, boosting the U.S. currency. The central bank's actions are felt globally but it has no particular responsibility for international financial conditions, unless they feed back into problems at home."[30]

---

[29] See Paul R. Krugman and Maurice Obstfeld, *International Economics*, Second Edition, Harper Collins, New York, 1991, pp. 647–652 for a more focused discussion on the 1980s developing economies crisis and on Mexico, 1982.

[30] "Fresh Stress Grips Weakest Emerging-Market Currencies," *Wall Street Journal*, August 30, 2018,

Table 9.3 Annualized price performance, a in the table (31 December 2013–31 December 2019)

	CAGR (USD)ª (%)	CAGR (local) (%)
STOXX Europe 50	−0.9	2.6
MSCI Europe	0.2	3.7
S&P 500	9.8	9.8

The U.S. Experience in 2014–2019: Above Average Global Growth and Interest Rates

During much of mid-to-late 2014–2019, the United States was characterized as an economy with growth above the world economic pace and interest rates above the world average. Relatively higher interest rates and growth would encourage capital inflows and dollar appreciation. With relatively strong output gains, the U.S. economy experienced faster employment gains and declines in the unemployment rate. Declines in the unemployment rate were associated with price increases as the PCE deflator rose from 0.2% (year over year) in the 4Q of 2015 to 2.3% by the 2Q of 2018. Dollar appreciation led to a decline in the import price index from plus 4.2% in the 2Q of 2018 to minus 2% by the 3Q of 2019. Net exports declined sharply in the second half of 2018 and remained low in 2019.

Disequilibrium in Europe: The Case of Below Global Growth and Rates

What about Europe where growth was below the global pace and interest rates were low? In this case, lower interest rates would intimate euro depreciation. Below average economic growth suggested greater underemployment and lower wage and price gains. The number of prime age (25–54) employed in the Euro Zone declined steadily from 2009 to 2014 and remains below the peak of 2008. Meanwhile, euro inflation has remained below the 2% since 2013. As a result, German benchmark interest rates have declined steadily and are negative—in an economic environment of low inflation and slow growth. Over that same period, the Euro equity market, Table 9.3 underperformed the U.S. equity market.[31]

---

[31] Data kindly provided by BMO Capital Markets.

When the Tide Goes Out

Current thinking on capital flows and exchange rates focuses on China, Switzerland, and several emerging markets where capital flows into China and out of emerging markets highlight the implications for exchange rates, interest rates, and domestic growth. There is also discussion of the capital flows and their impact on the value of the Swiss franc. The historical experience of capital flows, their sudden stop, and impact on exchange rates is amply demonstrated with the Asian financial crisis in 1997. Even in crisis situations the framework remains centered on the set of interrelated markets and prices. For the investment community that I worked with for many years, these markets provided a basis, a first step, in defining the opportunities for investors. The markets are goods (with the quantity and prices representing two defining characteristics), interest rates, exchange rates, and capital (represented by corporate profits).

Capital, whether foreign or domestic, seeks an acceptable risk and reward balance. International capital flows influence and are influenced by incentives (expected profits) and risks (economic and political). While the history of speculation (the South Sea Bubble) is fascinating, our focus is on capital flows that reflected a reasonable assessment of economic opportunity and the result of the diminished expectations as circumstances changed (our decision-making framework examines economic change that leads to choices and how those choices lead to a drying up of capital flows).

Cotton Bonds: Gone with the Wind

Investors will easily conjure up a vision of the Southern cotton industry and the importance of those exports to Britain in the days before the Civil War (the goods market). But what happened when the Confederate currency was no longer considered convertible (failure of the foreign exchange market)? In short, cotton bonds. Bonds issued in five European cities were redeemable for Confederate cotton. In effect, the bonds acted as currency that could be traded for real goods. One interesting fact is that one provision of the 14th Amendment to the U.S. constitution forbade the payment of these bonds. Money for nothing shall we say.

The Euro: If at First You Do Not Succeed—Quit[32]

The Plaza Accord, the Louvre Accord, the Exchange Rate Mechanism, the Euro are more recent examples of fiat exchange rates that were created in a disequilibrium situation to provide a basis for an equilibrium situation. Instead, they created further distortions. We applaud the attempts, but for investors and decision makers, we must recognize that fiat exchange rates aggravate already existing imbalances for credit and interest rate markets, equity markets, and economic growth overall which were already in disequilibrium.

The 1987 Black Monday episode which saw the stock market fall 20% is often cited as the result of program trading (the romantic explanation, blame the instrument,). In fact, we can call upon our more prosaic problem of disequilibrium exchange rate and interest rate policies (focus on market imbalances) to provide the real reason for the dramatic slide. Investors see these disequilibrium situations as opportunities. Administered exchange rates, in the face of growth and interest rate disequilibrium, simply will not work.

Shocks in the Commodity Markets: A Long and Dismal History—Brazilian Coffee

Although the focus of commentary on the Great Depression of the 1930s is on the United States and Germany, the experience of Brazil, and other commodity exporting nations is instructive.[33] Export world demand, for coffee for example, declined sharply caused by the global decline associated with the Great Depression. At the same time, production capacity for coffee had expanded during the prior decade of the 1920s. Export prices of coffee fell sharply, and Brazil's terms of trade deteriorated significantly. The Brazilian currency experienced successive depreciations. Inflation rose for consumers. In a play presaging the Mexican crisis of the 1980s, a loss of foreign earnings and a large foreign debt led to the suspension of a portion of the country's debt payments and eventually to imposition of exchange controls. A domestic Brazilian program to support coffee prices went bankrupt in 1930.

---

[32] The Euro Zone may be described as a monetary union. Unfortunately, this union was formed from a grab bag of economies that were not converged in the economic cycle or policy introduced stresses on adjustment mechanisms. In this case, the euro would not be considered a fiat currency regime: The euro trades freely and with liquidity on open global markets.

[33] For more detail in Brazil see Celso Furtado "Diagnosis of the Brazilian Crisis," Editora Fundo de Cultura S. A. 1964. A later English Edition was published by the Regents of the University of California, 1965.

In contrast, there are significant implications when an imported commodity rises in price. In 1979, a second oil shock nearly doubled the price of imported oil to Brazil and lowered the terms of trade. The rise in world interest rates sharply increased Brazil's balance of payments problem and the size of the foreign debt. As a result, real GDP declined in Brazil.

The (Latin American (LATAM) debt crisis of the 1980s reflected the twin pincers of super-high Fed Chair Paul Volcker's U.S interest rates and a crash in oil and commodity prices that drove dozens of emerging economies into a liquidity crunch. Their subsequently impaired debt service capability threatened to bankrupt the advanced economies banking systems. The strong and rising dollar in this period—there was massive devaluation of LATAM currencies as the economies failed and hyperinflation reigned—complicated the problem by raising the domestic currency cost of debt service more than they raised export revenues in a depressed world economy.

Oil shocks of the 1970s created huge current account surpluses in OPEC countries and huge deficits in oi importing countries. This dollar "glut," financed by U.S. current account deficits, drove the price of the dollar lower. This led to innovations in capital markets including extensive use of Euromarkets and new Euromarket credit instruments. And it drove the growth of cross-border banking and added sovereign lending to banks portfolios and Euromarket bonds.

Commodity Shocks, Corn Laws, and Post-Napoleonic Europe

Postwar dislocations also have a long history of economic impact. Both the Napoleonic wars and World War I saw a boost to the economic fortunes of agricultural interests in Britain, during the Napoleonic era and in Argentina during World War I. After the wars, agricultural production returned on the European continent and agricultural prices declined creating an excess capacity of production and, if let be, lower commodity prices.

The Corn Laws were introduced in Britain between 1815 and 1846 as tariffs on imported food and grain ("corn"). In the short run, the Corn Laws sustained the profits, political power, and lifestyles of the great British estates.[34] The laws redistributed income by reducing the real disposable income of many households and limited the growth of manufacturing to the

---

[34] For an interesting examination of one lifestyle supported by the Corn Laws see Niall Ferguson, *The Ascent of Money*, Penguin Press, New York, 2008, Chapter 5, pp. 234–241.

benefit of agricultural interests. In 1846, Prime Minister Robert Peel helped repeal the Corn Laws.[35]

Shocks in the World of Imperfect Capital Mobility

In all the cases we have reviewed the inability to adjust quickly to economic shocks represents evidence in the favor of imperfect capital mobility. In the case of 1980s U.S. economic policy, a fiscal expansion gave rise to faster economic growth and higher interest rates domestically and a rise in the exchange rate. The increase in the exchange rate resulted in an increase in the capital inflow and a deterioration in the current account. For the U.S. experience, higher interest rates and a higher trade deficit did not offset the fiscal expansion and thereby income rose. The voice of experience conveys several unique observations derived from the vantage point of being there at the time.

The result in the U.S. case was that the United States retained an interest rate differential, not entirely offset by capital flows, an increase in the capital account, and the current account for the trade of goods and services, remained out of balance.

For the United Kingdom, an easing of the Bank of England policy rate from 1989 to 1997 was accompanied by a decline in the current account deficit. Lower interest rates led to a capital outflow offset by current account improvement. Real GDP growth did improve from minus 1.1% in 1991 to 2–4% over the period 1993–2002. With imperfect capital mobility, an expansionary monetary policy is effective in increasing the pace of growth. The 1980s and 1990s in the United Kingdom was also a period of deregulation and privatization of state-owned companies (as well as council housing) that also assisted in promoting economic growth.[36]

With imperfect capital mobility, both monetary and fiscal policy are effective. The extent of the improvement in economic growth and income depends upon the extent to which changes in interest rate differentials affect capital flows.[37] For the United States, the interest equalization tax of the 1960s and early 1970s was an attempt to discourage American investors

---

[35] The role of economic philosophy is debated in the motivation to repeal the Corn Laws. See Douglas Irwin, "Political Economy and Peel's Repeal of the Corn Laws, *Economics and Politics*, 1989, 1, 1 (March).

[36] Niall Ferguson, *The Ascent of Money*, Chapter 5 Safe as Houses, pp. 252, 267.

[37] The existence of a home bias also limits the adjustment of portfolios to changes in expected rates of return between countries. See Kenneth French and James Poterba, "Investor Diversification and International Equity Markets," *American Economic Review*, 81 (May): 222–226.

from putting money abroad. The tax was aimed at reducing the balance of payments deficit. Capital controls were common for Japan from 1970 to 1990 and for China in recent decades.

Free capital movements can destabilize the monetary system of a less developed economy when the flows exceed the ability of a central bank to sterilize their impacts on the money supply and banking system. Perfect capital mobility is often not the right answer for emerging economies. The Asia crisis is another perfect example of why. It started in Thailand in July *1997* and spread across East Asia, wreaking havoc on economies in the region and leading to spillover effects in Latin America and Eastern Europe in 1998.

Exogenous exchange rate adjustments, in a world of imperfect asset substitution, create a risk premium on domestic assets when the stock of domestic government bonds available to the public rises and falls as the central bank's domestic assets increase. Private investors become more vulnerable to changes in the home currency as the stock of government debt they hold rises.[38] This will be covered more extensively in Chapter 12 but first, we review the economics behind corporate profits and the equity market in the next two chapters.

References

Liaquat Ahamed, *Lords of Finance*, Penguin Press, New York, 2009, pp. 215–216. A view of central banking in an overlooked era and the importance of personalities, not models, that set the economic and financial tone of the 1920s and 1930s.

Barron's "The Allure of U.S. Stocks Could Keep Dollar Steady, Defying Gloomy Forecasts," *Barron's*, October 13, 2020. An interesting view on the linkage from equity values to the dollar exchange rate.

John Carswell, *The South Sea Bubble*, Cresset Press, London, 1960. The classic review of the South Seas Bubble and the international movement of capital in search of profit.

Rudiger Dornbusch, *Open Economy Economics*, Basic Books, 1980, Chapter 11. A review of the Mundell-Fleming model can be found in Dornbusch.

Kenneth French and James Poterba, "Investor Diversification and International Equity Markets," *American Economic Review*, 81 (May): 222–226. The existence of a home bias also limits the adjustment of portfolios to changes in expected rates of return between countries.

---

[38] See Paul Krugman and Maurice Obstfeld, *International Economics*, Second Edition, Harper Collins, 1991, pp. 487–488.

Yōichi Funabashi, *Managing the Dollar: From the Plaza to the Louvre*, Peterson Institute, Washington, DC, 1989, pp. 261–271. Dollar management is a fascination for national policy makers.

Celso Furtado, "Diagnosis of the Brazilian Crisis," Editora Fundo de Cultura S. A. 1964. A later English Edition was published by the Regents of the University of California, 1965. A detailed economic rundown of the Brazilian economy.

Douglas Irwin, "Political Economy and Peel's Repeal of the Corn Laws, *Economics and Politics*, 1989, 1, (1) (March). The role of economic philosophy is debated in the motivation to repeal the Corn Laws.

Charles P. Kindleberger, *The World in Depression, 1929–1939*, Berkley University of California Press, 1973. An interesting read given the later publication by Ahmed.

Lawrence Klein and Guy Stevens, Richard Berner, Peter Clark, Enrique Hernandez-Cata, Howard Howe, and Sung Kwack, "The U.S. Economy in an Interdependent World: A Multi-country Model," Published by the Board of Governors of the Federal Reserve, 1984. Multi-country models began development in the 1970s.

Paul R. Krugman and Maurice Obstfeld, *International Economics*, Harper Collins, New York, 1991, 2nd ed., pp. 647–652. A more focused discussion on the 1980s developing economies crisis and Mexico, 1982.

N. Gregory Mankiw, *Macroeconomics*, Seventh Edition, Worth, pp. 287–308. A review of the Mundell-Fleming model can be found in Mankiw.

Robert Mundell, "The Appropriate Use of Monetary and Fiscal Policy under Fixed Exchange Rates," International. Monetary Fund Staff Papers, March 1962. A primary source for the argument that economic policy, capital flows and exchange rates have numerous linkages in determining free market prices.

Jerome Powell, "Monetary Policy in a Post-Crisis Era," July 16, 2019, at "Bretton Woods: 75 Years Later—Thinking About the Next 75," a conference organized by the Banque de France and the French Ministry for the Economy and Finance, Paris, France. A view of monetary policy and flexible/fixed exchange rates.

John Prebble, *The Darien Disaster*, Holt, Rinehart, and Winston, New York, 1968. A story of speculative investment in the new world.

Ross Robertson, *History of the American Economy*, Second Edition, Harcourt, Brace and World, New York, 1964, Chapters 5, 12. The story of global finance for U.S. railroads.

John A. Sawyer, *Modelling the International Transmission Mechanism*, North-Holland Publishing, Amsterdam, Netherlands, 1979. Another early model of multi-country economic linkages.

10

Profits: Rewards and Incentives in an Economic System to Allocate Capital

The Story of Profits in the Wilderness: the Colonies Get Their Start

Profit-seeking, not just religious freedom, was a major motive that spurred the settlement of New England and ultimately America. In fact, the search for profit prompted many a voyage (Portuguese, Spanish, British, and Dutch) to explore the unknown and to establish colonies throughout the world.[1]

Both the Massachusetts Bay Colony (the Puritans) and the Plymouth Colony (Pilgrims) were organized as joint-stock companies—they were out to make a profit.,[2] In good capitalist fashion, the Massachusetts Bay and Plymouth colonies merged in 1691—the economics of the Plymouth Colony being somewhat disappointing.

Profits, like interest rates, are both an incentive (the establishment of the American colonies as joint-stock companies) and a reward (economic success for the Puritans led to an expansion of territory beyond Boston with accompanying greater prosperity.)

---

[1] John Frederick Martin, *Profits in the Wilderness: Entrepreneurship and the Founding of New England Towns in the Seventeenth Century*, University of North Carolina Press, Chapel Hill, NC, 1991.
[2] John Frederick Martin, *Profits in the Wilderness: Entrepreneurship and the Founding of New England Towns in the Seventeenth Century*, University of North Carolina Press, Chapel Hill, NC, 1991.

As the journalist and historian John Steel Gordon wrote: "The settling of New England was the work of a breed of men so new they would not even have a name for two centuries: entrepreneurs.[3]"

The pursuit of profits prompts entrepreneurs, in any field, to take risks, to foster innovation, and to generate new visions. The lack of profits signals entrepreneurs that they need to rethink the viability of their visions. Profits provide the funds to seek capital investment and to expand employment. And they are income to owners and shareholders. The growth of profits reflects the growth of the economy, fluctuations in both interest rates and exchange rates and the influence of prices and price flexibility.

Profits: Engine of Enterprise

For the engine which drives enterprise is not thrift but profits.—John Maynard Keynes

Profits central role in financing economic growth, employment, and household wealth is often misunderstood, misrepresented, and even denigrated by many politicians who benefit from these same profits in their pensions, retirement funds, and saving accounts.

Corporate profits are a major player in economic cycles. Nonfinancial profits reflect and are influenced by the cycles of growth, inflation, interest rates, and exchange rates—all of which adds to the volatility of profits and leads, naturally, to the reason why profits are so difficult to forecast. (a nod to my equity and credit analyst friends).

Additionally, greater profit growth, and sometimes just the anticipation of profits, provided alternative financing options to seeking bank and credit finance for the acquisition of capital and for the hiring of labor. For larger corporations, profits offer an alternative to equity and bond finance. For smaller firms, profits substitute for bank loans, friendly uncle financing, or credit card finance.

Profits, Growth, and Their Symbiotic Relationship

As illustrated in Fig. 10.1, there is a clear link between growth in profits and nominal GDP—in this case, causality runs both ways, nominal GDP drives

---

[3] John Steel Gordon, *The Business of America: Tales from the Marketplace*, Walker Books, New York, 2002.

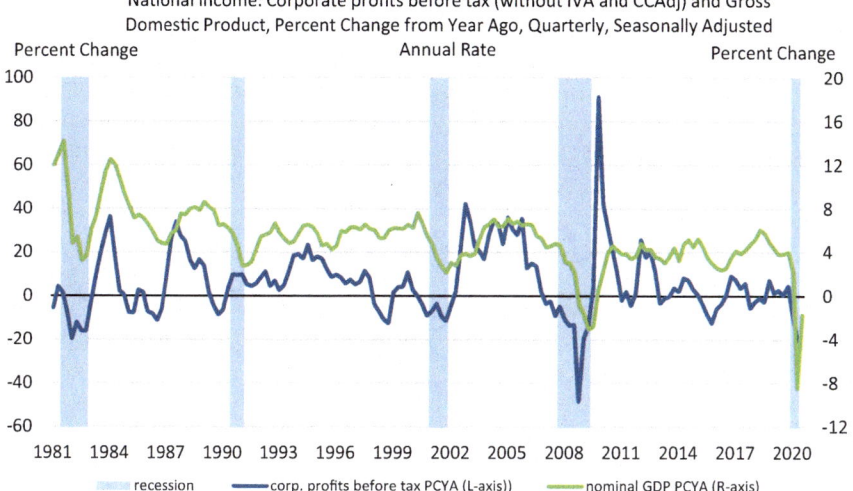

Fig. 10.1 Nominal GDP and pre-tax profits

profits, profits drive nominal GDP. Profits have a dual character. Stronger nominal GDP growth creates greater corporate top-line revenue. In turn, this allows for greater corporate pricing power that provides the incentive to invest in both people and equipment. Alternatively, greater profit growth creates alternatives to credit finance for corporations and small businesses. The interactions between economic growth, profits, credit markets and interest rates are essential elements of the U.S. economy.

For profit growth, there is an interesting pattern in the data: profit growth is mean reverting over the 1982 to 2017 period. Profit growth is very cyclical but there is no secular trend upward. Unfortunately for analysts, the average profit growth is less than its own standard deviation. This indicates that the deviations from average profit growth exceed that of average profit growth itself. Thereby we have an outsized measure of volatility (stability ratio) helping to explain the difficulty of forecasting profits and the salaries of better-than-average equity analysts.

Profits: Overlooked Contribution to Growth and Lower Rates

Profits serve as a source of funds that accomplish two important functions. First, profits are a source of funds to support real economic growth. Second, profits provide an alternative to credit demand.

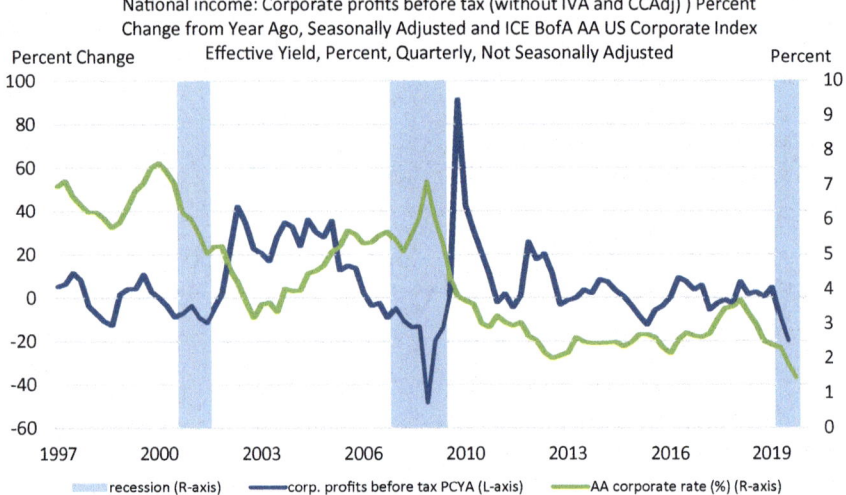

Fig. 10.2 Pre-Tax profits and the corporate AA bond spread

Profits and Raising Capital Funds: One Input to the Economic System

Profits offer an alternative way to raise capital to reduce the demand for credit and thus put some downward pressure on interest rates. As evidenced in Fig. 10.2, there is a link between economic profit growth and the AA corporate bond rate. In this case causality runs both ways. In addition, profit growth leads earnings per share (EPS) growth over the 1983–2017 period which is a very important benchmark for equity market valuation.

Investors can thus anticipate that an improvement in profit growth will lead to a movement in the AA corporate rate for example. Better profits feed into alternative paths for financing growth as profit growth has a causal link to one and five-year real interest rates. An improvement in profits also signals downward pressure on interest rates going forward. In this case, profit gains offer a different view on the outlook for both equity and credit finance. Profit growth and interest rates are indeed interrelated.

Exposure to Global Economy: Linkages as Another Part of the System

Two drivers of profits that reflect the global economy are the dollar exchange rate and economic growth. The importance of global growth is illustrated by the fact that over 30% of S&P revenues are earned abroad. This percentage is even higher for four sectors: energy, health care, materials, and information technology.

These revenues are the product of income and relative price pressures. For income, the improvement of global growth has been a plus. Growth in both the Eurozone and Canada has improved over the 2017 to 2019 period. Chinese economic growth has remained steady despite market expectations. Brazil and Russia have evidenced growth in 2017–2019 from their respective 2016 recessions.

* * *

Linkages

Pre-tax profits, as a share of GNP (Fig. 10.3), have strong cyclical, but nonlinear pattern. Profit shares gradually increase over the cycle, tend to peak mid-expansion before tapering off and falling throughout the latter stages of the economic expansion and dropping sharply in a recession. This pattern reflects the rebound in final sales (revenues) consistent with a rebound in economic growth (goods market, prices).

However, pre-tax corporate profits are non-stationary, and thereby are a less predictable series than a stationary series which returns to an average

Fig. 10.3 Pre-Tax profits as a share of GDP

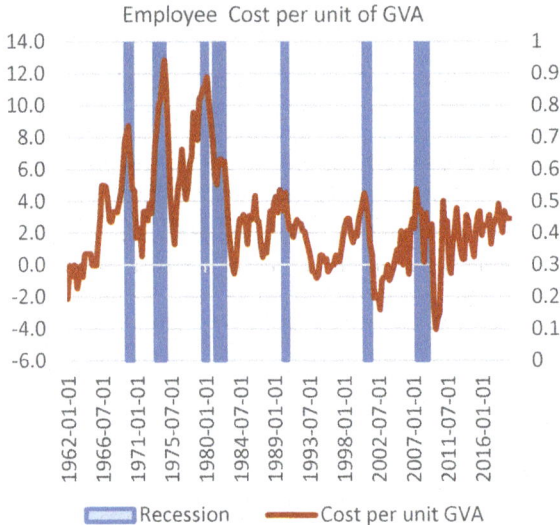

Fig. 10.4 Cost per unit of real GVA

value. Although profit growth as a percent of GDP appears to follow a traditional peak to trough trend, various structural breaks within the series lead to highly irregular and quite misleading judgments based on prior trends. Although this might not be very surprising, the larger decline being in the 2001 recessionary period appears unusual. The greatest decline in corporate profits would be assumed to have occurred during the Great Recession but that is not true. There were dramatic movements in a bank's willingness to lend, as well as households acquiring record amounts of debt. That is, one might suspect a similar case of dramatics in the decline of profits during the Great Recession; however, the drop was more significant in 2001.

The internal cyclical patterns of productivity and labor costs further complicate the behavior of profits. The cyclical pattern of underlying costs per unit of real gross value added for nonfinancial corporate business (Fig. 10.4) reflects the gains in productivity in the early stages of the economic expansion. Then when productivity weakens, simultaneously, costs per unit of value-added rise thereby putting the squeeze on profit margins.

Profit Margins: Top-Line Growth and a Mid-Cycle Peak

Shrinking Margin for Error

Profit margins, as illustrated in Fig. 10.5, have a clear cyclical pattern, and are characterized by mid-cycle peaks—hence the 2010 expansion is no exception.

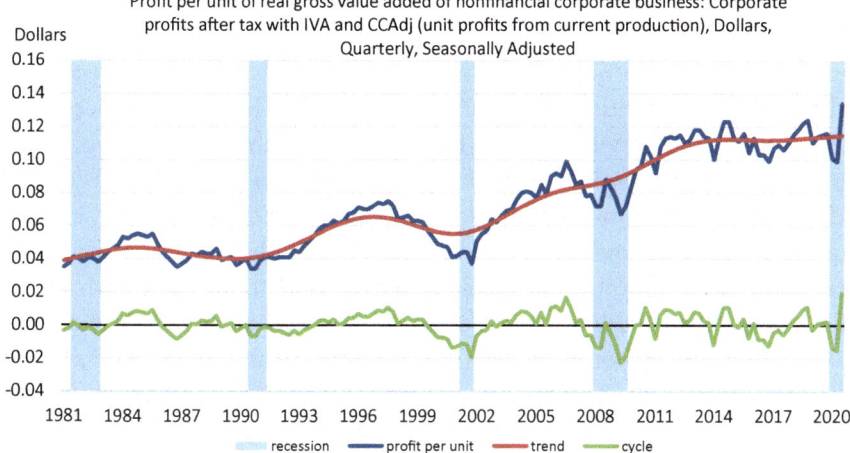

Fig. 10.5 Profit per unit of real GVA

The dynamic character of the demand and supply set of interactions provides a context for judging the outlook for profits in a cycle of ups and downs in the economy.

Profit margins are not mean reverting over time. Profit margins were higher after the 2007–2009 recession than in the prior expansion. In fact, profit margins were higher after the 2007–2009 period than in any period since the Korean War. Among other factors, the lower labor costs, faster rates of economic growth and low-interest rates tended to boost profit margins. Adding to the challenge of monitoring profit cycles is the reality that profit cycles differ across major sectors—while some series are mean reverting, others are shifting over time.

Domestic nonfinancial profits are calculated as a share of Gross Value Added of nonfinancial corporations. Corporate profits are not compared to GDP but rather, more properly, corporate profits are compared to the output of corporations associated with the generation of those profits. The common usage of GDP is misleading. Interesting to observe that profit shares tend to rise with an economic expansion and then peak at what appears to be mid-cycle (judging after the fact) and then decline gradually into the recession.

Although profit margins do have a mid-cycle peak it is not possible to determine that until after the fact. Profit shares (margins) are very cyclical, and, as evidenced in the graph, do not continue to rise uniformly over time. Talk about an economic series at the mid-cycle of an economic expansion is common among journalists, but is there any real content to the phrase?

In our view, no. The mid-cycle of an economic and financial cycle is not an identifiable point until after the end of an economic expansion. Moreover, the focus on a single point in time, rather than the behavior of economic and financial signals during the cycle, is misplaced.[4] Experience since all this mid-cycle commentary has proven this commentary has been wrong.

As we already know, there is no fixed amplitude nor length of an economic and financial cycle. In contrast, cycles reflect the dynamic interaction of economic, financial, and policy forces. We question the validity of any investment strategy and economic forecast based upon the assumption that an economy is at the mid-cycle point. The framework for decision making is what is important—not a point in time. The start and end of cycles reflect the forces of the economy, finance, and policy. The whole process of the cycle consists of these three forces rather than a link to a single point in time.

In the prior economic expansion of 2010 to 2019, for both investors and private businesses, the rise in inflation and unit labor costs signaled a possible decline in profit margins in 2016, which occurred. With the additional pressure of rising interest rates, the peak in profit margins indicates that the combination of rising short-term interest rates and shrinking profit margins provides a smaller margin of error for decision makers both as investors and business stewards. Higher interest rates and rising unit labor costs indicated the pressure on profit margins, and those margins did not recover until the 3Q of 2018.

"Investors Brace for Hit to Profits as Costs Rise," *Wall Street Journal*, April 3, 2019

In 2019, we witnessed a demonstration of the role of productivity and labor costs in profit determination. Wages alone do not explain the cycle nor any other single factor. It is more interesting than that. At the start of each economic expansion, the output gains proceed faster than the rise in the cost of labor inputs. The result—the rise in productivity in 2001–2004 and again in 2010 and 2011 (Fig. 10.4). At the same time, profit margins rise (Fig. 10.5). However, as the expansion continues, firms add labor at a faster pace than output gains and productivity declines on a cyclical basis. In addition, as the economic cycle matures, attracting more workers requires higher pay and benefits at the margin. The net result is that unit labor costs rise and, profit shares slowly take on their cyclical character.[5]

---

[4] CNBC discussion July 9, 2018 and Fed Chair Jerome Powell mid-cycle adjustment, July 31, 2019.

[5] It may be argued that the initial tax cuts of 2017–2018 did boost profits and profit margins but this one-off impact has since been overwhelmed by the perennial cyclical forces of slower productivity gains and rising unit labor costs.

The Globalization of Opportunity: Profits Earned Abroad

North American Free Trade Agreement (NAFTA) and the emergence of the World Trade Organization have certainly hurt some U.S. businesses. Despite this reality, both the agreement and the organization broadened the number of global markets available for many other U.S. firms. For example. About one-third of S&P companies earned their revenues abroad. This percentage is higher for energy, health care, materials, and information technology. Slower global growth translates into slower earnings growth while faster global growth translates into faster earnings growth. Interestingly, perceptions among investors was for faster economic growth for the years after trade agreements appeared (NAFTA mid-1990s and China WTO 2001). Equity values rose in anticipation of better growth and earnings on the global scale.

Patterns in global growth, and fluctuations in the dollar exchange rate, influence future business revenue estimates. Revenues are the product of economic growth and income gains abroad. Cyclical patterns of global growth impart a cyclical pattern to overseas earnings. However, the overall opening up of markets has provided a secular push to these revenues. Markets continued to open over the last 30 years allowing firms to enter these markets and increase their output. Opening markets also introduced the possibility of greater price competition. This may explain the slower pace of inflation for industrialized countries in recent years.

Exchange rates represent the influence of relative prices on the flows of exports and imports and the measure of profits adjusted for exchange rate moves. Movements in the value of the U.S. dollar alter the value of foreign earnings and reinforce the gains and losses in foreign earnings of U.S. corporations. When profit gains exist, this result further lowers the pressure on credit financing and interest rates in the United States.

Exchange rates influence both the competitiveness of exports and the price of imports and this has become apparent in the debate on the trade arrangements between the United States and China trade link. Beginning in the 1990s, the shift in relative exchange rates has had a profound impact on trade flows and on the relative profitability of private enterprises both here and abroad.

From 1982 to now the growth of U.S. exports, Fig. 10.6, has opened many opportunities for both workers and companies to participate in the global economy.

Global growth is simply one factor that drives export gains. Another factor is the value of the trade-weighted dollar, Fig. 10.7, that influences the relative prices of U.S. exports and imports. In addition, dollar movements influence

Fig. 10.6 U.S. exports

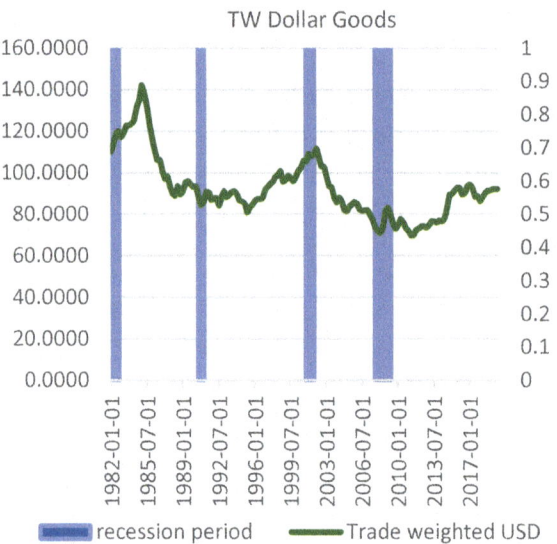

Fig. 10.7 Trade-Weighted dollar

the value of foreign earnings by U.S. companies. Increases in the value of the trade-weighted U.S. dollar reduces the value of foreign earnings when those earnings are brought back into the United States.

Fluctuations in exchange rates provide a level of uncertainty on the value of future profits when returned to the United States and make it more difficult to predict profits. Exchange rates influence the relative prices of the flows of exports and imports and the measure of profits adjusted for exchange rate

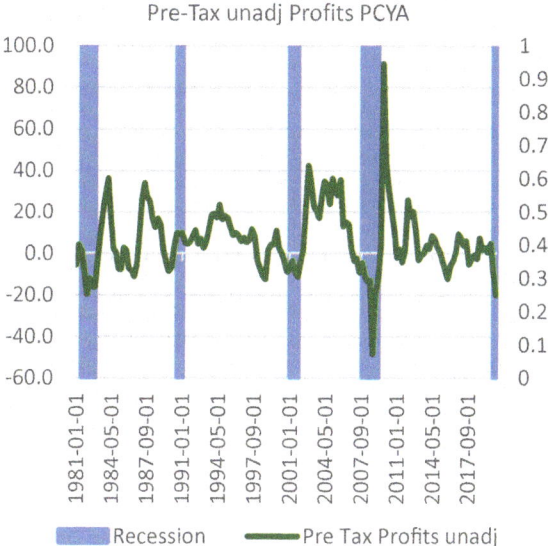

Fig. 10.8 Pre-Tax profit growth

moves. Declines in the value of the dollar improve the value of foreign earnings and reinforce the gains in foreign earnings of corporations. This result further reduces the pressure on credit financing and interest rates in the United States. In contrast, a rise in the dollar exchange value lowers the value of foreign earnings and may diminish the value of a firm's cash flow. In turn, this reduces its internal cash flow and, if needed, may motivate the firm to seek greater domestic credit and thereby push up domestic interest rates.

Is There Value in the "Profits Recession?" More Guidelines, Not Rules

The linkage between profits, equities, and economic recessions has a quite varied history.[6] First, let us define the term profits recession in a manner like an economic recession—an outright decline in the growth rate of corporate profits and let us set the bar, at least initially, at two quarters in a row of profit declines (Fig. 10.8). Since 1982, pre-tax profit growth has declined in the mid-1980s, again in the late 1990s and in the middle of the last decade at a time independent of overall economic recession periods. Yet profits do retain their leading indicator character as evidenced in late 1980s, late 1999/2000

---

[6] "Stocks and Recessions: Assessing Recent History", *Wall Street Journal*, July 26, 2020.

and again in 2007–2008. It just appears that profits do give some false positive signals over economic cycles.

In the post-inflation spike era,[7] we start with our most precise example. Profits first declined in the second quarter of 1980. In a similar manner, EPS fell in the 2Q as well as GDP. Here, profits and economic recessions line up. This example, unfortunately, is the outlier. This perfect line up of profits recession, EPS and GDP did not repeat again since the 1980 experience.

The profits recession of 4Q 1981 through 1Q 1983 did accompany a drop in GDP beginning in the 4Q of 1981 but EPS peaked in the 2Q of 1981, then dropped, and then peaked again in the 4Q 1981. Profits recessions of 1985, 1986, 1989, 1998, 2000 were not accompanied by a decline in GDP.

In 1989, EPS peaked in the 1Q, however, profits started to decline in the 3Q 1989, and GDP did not decline until the 4Q 1990. In our latest economic adventure into a house of horrors, a profits recession beginning in 1Q 2007 preceded the EPS peak in 2Q 2007 and then an initial GDP decline in the 4Q 2007.

Consistent with much of our approach, guidelines are useful, but rules are misleading. There are few, if any, one variable explanation for the behavior of GDP, EPS, and corporate profits. All three are actors in motion—sometime preceding, sometimes lagging, each other—as they appear on the economic stage. And, although as a quarterly series profits are a leading economic indicator, they are not included in the leading indicators index.

Incentives provided by the pursuit of economic profit encourage an entrepreneur to innovate and to increase business efficiency. We witness this in our daily efforts when we seek a return to our work.

Yet, the pursuit of profit may also lead an entrepreneur to underprice risk and misallocate capital to projects with subpar economic returns.[8] We shall return to this shortly.

Role of Profits in a Four Sector Economic Framework

How do profits fit into the framework for the economy? Profits act as a source of funds both to corporations and households. For firms, profits are an alternative to both bank credit and bond finance to finance future growth. An improved profit outlook lowers a firm's cost of capital and profit growth is linked to economic growth. Profits are a return to invested capital and

---

[7] We examine this era as a post inflation spike era, given the significant changes in both fiscal and monetary policy during 1979–1982 and the empirical fact that many series are characterized by structural breaks during that time.
[8] "Darien: The Scottish Dream of Empire," John Prebble, Edinburgh, Birlinn, 2000.

entrepreneurship. The real sector, the economy, interacts with measures of economic profit in a two-way relationship. Stronger economic growth is associated with better profit growth. An improvement in expected profit growth motivates firms to hire and invest, which promotes further economic growth. Gains in profit growth impact the credit markets. They function as both a reward for taking risk and an incentive and return for innovation.

As an internal source of funds, profits relieve the pressures of having to search for external funds and lowers interest rates by providing an alternative to bond and bank finance. Profit growth is also a signal of credit quality in the corporate bond sector creating downward pressure on risk premiums.

Gains in corporate profits domestically provide an incentive for foreign investors to seek opportunities in the United States. As a result, capital inflows to America provide an upward push to the U.S. dollar. There is also the link between inflation and profits. Greater than expected inflation in the 1970s was associated with a decline in profits as a percent of GDP. In contrast, the decline of inflation in the 1980s was associated with a rise in profits as a percent of GDP.

Unfortunately, the level of profits presents a forecasting problem since they are a residual between top-line revenue and bottom-line operating costs. Profits are the leftovers and the most cyclical form of income compared to wage or dividend income for example. Whereas top-line (an increase in gross sales or revenue) GDP growth would boost profits, the bottom-line (net income) cost structure can offset that top-line growth. For example, stronger economic growth tends to be associated with better revenues in the airline industry and yet, better growth is also associated with rising energy prices and the increasing cost of airline fuel.

Profits are also a source of dividend payments and, associated with a growing economy and capital gains on assets, lead to gains in household income. Profits feed into the Individual Retirement Accounts (IRAs), pension plans, and employer sponsored 401(k) plans of middle-income Americans.

We can characterize corporate profit growth as a nonlinear series. Thus, the attempts by much of the media to estimate profit and earnings improvements using a linear procedure are doomed. And to reemphasize an earlier point, the standard deviation of profit growth is greater than the average pace of growth since 1973. It is impractical to simply cite the average value over some period as a benchmark of value without also citing the volatility of the series over the same period. One means of tracking the over and under in the pace of profit growth is with the Hodrick-Prescott filter (despite its shortcomings). We will cover this later.

Profits as Return to Entrepreneurs and Risk-takers

Profits are an incentive to take risks. They are both a signal of economic success and failure. Returning to the American colonies, consider the experience of the Virginia colonies.

The Virginia Company of London was the first joint-stock company to travel to the new world. After hearing stories of the Spanish finding gold in South America, Virginia Company investors thought it would be easy to find gold if they too started a new settlement. They named it Jamestown after King James I, who granted the charter.

Landing in Virginia in 1607, 13 years before the Pilgrims arrived in Massachusetts, the 104 Englishmen found that prospecting for gold turned out to be much more difficult than planned. They were unprepared to handle harsh winters and malaria. More than that, the first colonists were wealthy gentlemen unused to manual labor. Much of their energy was wasted and their pursuit of gold was in vain.

The true gold for Virginia turned out to be in tobacco. Shown how to use the plant by Native Americans and given the region's rich soil, tobacco became Virginia's cash crop. In 1639, Jamestown exported 750 tons of tobacco. Unfortunately, it also meant the expansion of slavery given the enormous physical effort to plant and harvest the crop.

As the Virginians learned, profits are not guaranteed. Current profits are a signaling device. Profits signal the possibility of future profits and encourage entry into a business. Losses signal exit. However, it is the expected future profits that give rise to hiring and real capital investment.

Expected profits provide the dynamic character to economic activity simply because expectations can be disappointed on the downside or surprised on the upside. As in much of economics, it is the difference between expected and actual outcomes that move economic prices, equity values for example. When you listen to commentaries by analysts and portfolio managers, it is this difference that generates the flow of capital into and out of any sector. Consider the recent experience of the unicorn IPOs (Docusign, PagerDuty, Zoom) which have been very successful compared to the notable failures of Quibi, Zynga, and Powa Technologies when expectations of future profits dramatically declined. Once the investing public doubted their path to profitability, equity valuations plummeted. Interestingly although investor expectations changed, the management and business model of some of these firms did not. Interest rates also did not change. In fact, they were lower in recent months than they were while valuations ran up last year. Timing, and expectations, are indeed everything (almost).

Role of Profits in the Economy

Profit growth is both a product of economic factors as well as an input to many economic activities. Profits, like interest rates, goods prices, and exchange rates are at the center of many real-side economic activities.

On the business income side, they reflect the pattern of real final sales, as a proxy for nominal GDP (current prices without adjusting for inflation), for the domestic economy. Meanwhile, export growth offers a proxy for international sales. The importance of both domestic sales and exports brings in the role of prices such as the PCE deflator and the trade-weighted dollar.

On the cost side, we have discussed the importance of the Employment Cost index as a benchmark for measuring labor wage costs. Interest expense is also a factor and that is reflected in market interest rates.

For investors, profits set the tone for retained earnings (the amount of net income left over for a business after it has paid out dividends to its shareholder) which have an impact on equity valuations. Retained earnings can be volatile since they are a residual of real final sales and costs of production. Retained earnings reflect the impact of tax changes which generates structural breaks in the after-tax series. Meanwhile, a portion of profits enters dividends which feed into personal income. Both dividends and equity valuations are inputs to pension fund valuations and household net worth. Profits are income to someone. In terms of volatility, these dividends are more volatile than wages and salaries as inputs to personal income.

In equity and debt markets, valuations today reflect the ex ante, or forecasted, estimate for profits. Ex post is the result, the after the fact. As in all economic activity, the difference between ex ante and ex post is a driver for economic and financial decisions. Profits always act as a signaling device—where to invest and where to pull back.

Statistical Character of Corporate Profit Growth[9]

Corporate profit growth is a complex time series that is a challenge to forecast. In part this is because it is a residual between corporate earnings and input costs. Both series, in turn, reflect other exogenous forces. The rate of growth of profits is mean reverting over the entire 1982 to 2017 period—that is, its growth tends to return to an average over time.

---

[9] For an earlier review of these issues see John Silvia and Azhar Iqbal, "Three Simple Techniques to Analyze a Complex Economic Phenomenon: The Case of Profits," *Business Economics*, 45 (2).

We can characterize profit growth by asking three questions: Is profit growth mean reverting? How volatile is profit growth and does this volatility obscure the message of average profit growth for decision makers? Can we identify the trend and cycle for profit growth and determine whether current profit gains are above or below trend profit growth?

Specification of the form of the independent and dependent variables is important since the use of a nonstationary series will result in spurious regression results. To test whether a series is stationary we employ a Dickey-Fuller test.[10] Spurious results are evident when a regression with time-series variables produces a very high R^2 even though there is no meaningful relationship between the variables. In forecasting, when levels are employed, the forecast band, the upper and lower limits of the confidence interval, will be narrower than the stationary series band. This is because the ordinary least squares (OLS) regression model assumes that the forecast variance is constant over time, when in fact, this is not true for a nonstationary series.[11]

Pre-tax corporate profits, as for many series expressed in level forms such as GDP or employment, is not a stationary series. It must be transformed into a series that would be useful for analysis. When doing so, profit growth is a stationary series and exhibits no structural break points over the 1982 to 2019 period. Profits grow over time, as does nominal GDP, but the rate of profit growth exhibits no tendency to accelerate, or decelerate, over long periods. The profit growth does vary over the economic cycle but the stationarity of profit growth over time allows for the statistical analysis of results without concern for spurious statistical results.

Corporate profit growth is volatile as its average, mean, value is less than its standard deviation over the 1982 to 2019 period making some observations outside the bounds of a normal range of error. Moreover, the average rate of profit growth and its standard deviation vary between economic cycles. The stability ratio, standard deviation as a percent of its mean, is greater than one in most cycles tested. This volatility is not surprising given that profits are a residual between revenue and costs as in most residuals (budget or trade balances for example) the series is characterized by volatility.

---

[10] D. Dickey and W. Fuller, "Distribution of the Estimators for Autoregressive Time Series with a Unit Root," *Journal of the American Statistical Association*, 1979, 74: 427–431 and D. Dickey and W. Fuller "Likelihood Ratio Tests for Autoregressive Time Series with a Unit Root," *Econometrica*, 1981, 49: 1057–1072.

[11] C.W. Granger and P. Newbold "Spurious Regressions in Econometrics," *Journal of Econometrics*, 1974, 73:111–120.

Separating out trend and cycle periods of profit growth, utilizing the H-P filter[12] as a first approach, identifies periods of over and undervaluation of earnings potential. Identifying when profit growth is above or below trend is done with the help of the Hodrick–Prescott filter. At any point in time, we can test whether a time series is moving above or below trend which may be characterized in equity market terms as above or below trend profit growth. Profit growth was above the long-run trend during the early recovery periods of 1982–1983, 2002–2003, and 2010–2011 as a clear signal of above average profit prosperity. In contrast, profit growth slows and becomes negative in the years prior to a recession—1989–90, 1999–2000, and 2007–2008.

Decision makers can employ the H–P filter on any time series of interest and identify whether a series is above or below trend and then investigate what might be driving that behavior.

Examining the Behavior of Profit Fundamentals in the 2010 expansion

Equity values, proxied by the NYSE index, bottomed in the 1Q of 2009, just before the recession ended in the 2Q of 2009. This trend continued upward until mid-2015. Are there any fundamentals behind this move?

First, the Federal Reserve had lowered the federal funds rate throughout the 2007 and 2008 period of recession and ended their easing at a funds rate of 0–0.25% in December of 2008 the lowest rate since the 1950s. Meanwhile the two-year Treasury rate was 1.13% in July 2009 and declined steadily and stayed below 0.5% until November 2014. The Corporate AA rate declined steadily from 2009 to mid-2013 and remained below the levels of the prior economic cycle from 2014 to 2018.

Thus, the discount factor, the interest rate, applied to future earnings declined sharply over the 2009 to 2014 period. What about earnings? Pre-tax corporate profits rose steadily from 2009 to 2014 although the years 2011 and 2013 exhibited flat profit growth. Unit labor costs, on a percent change, declined from 3Q 2009 to 3Q 2012 except for a brief rise in cost in the first half of 2010. Profit margins improved steadily over the 2009 to peak in 2015 with short dips at the end of 2010 and 2013. Wider profit margins are consistent with improvements in prior expansions.

Trends in profits, bond yields, and unit labor costs suggested that the equity market was following the fundamentals. Equity, interest rate, and real

---

[12] Hodrick, Robert and Prescott, Edward C., "Postwar U.S. Business Cycles: An Empirical Investigation," *Journal of Money, Credit, and Banking*, 1997, 29 (1): 1–16.

sectors appear to be working. The decline in AA corporate spreads from 2.03% in July 2009 to a low of 0.64% in July 2014 further supported the case for equities as an asset class and for a favorable outlook for the economy. Except for brief periods in 2011 and 2012, the implicit price deflator remained below the Fed's 2% target and thereby gave no signal of a change in financial prospects.

The Why and How of Cyclical Variation for Profits

Profits are a residual between two moving forces—revenues and costs—making them quite volatile in the short run. There is an interplay here between expectations and results, product, and labor markets with the additional twist of dynamic adjustment in markets over time. Output and price fluctuations contribute to the change in top-line revenues. Revenues rise with increases in output driven by increases in real final sales (demand) in the economy. Yet we know that real final sales growth varies over the cycle. Early recovery sectors such as housing pick up quickly at the start of the cycle while other sectors such as construction pick up the pace later in the economic expansion.

In the early phase of an economic expansion, increases in real final sales are initially met by caution. Firms that will decrease inventories and then carefully increase output as revenues improve. Then they add labor and eventually new capital to expand capacity. As the outlook for sustained real final sales becomes more probable, output prices tend to rise. They are generally slow to respond to increases in real final sales tending to lag the pickup in real economic growth.[13]

This process illustrates the dynamic, partial, adjustment character of firm behavior. In addition, it shows the importance of information—the view on the sustainability of a gain in real final sales—to a firm. Since the process of acceleration and slowdowns in real final sales is not frictionless, so profit modeling should reflect this dynamic.

On the supply side of the process, the structure of the response of supply to changes in demand is critical. In the short run, the aggregate supply curve is upward sloping. That reflects that some factors of production are fixed (business capital and structures being a good example) in the short run.

Labor inputs are variable and are characterized by diminishing returns in terms of output per unit of labor. In the short run, the aggregate supply

---

[13] For further reading on this dynamic process see N. Gregory Mankiw, *Macroeconomics*. Ninth Edition, Worth Publishers, Chapters 9, 13, 14.

curve is upward sloping as the marginal product of additional labor units applied to the fixed capital of the firm will be met with diminishing marginal product and higher per unit costs. In the early phase of an economic recovery, an increase output will be accompanied by modest price increases but even more modest increases in marginal costs. The margin between selling price and marginal costs widens in the early phase of the recovery increasing profit margins. Wider margins are possible in the short run since output prices are less subject to friction in adjustments than labor markets.

This dynamic does not last long. As the economic recovery persists, labor costs increase as marginal productivity slows and labor compensation rises. This rise outpaces the one in selling prices and profit margins shrink. In addition, while output prices outpace unit labor costs in the early phase of an economic expansion, the reverse is true in the latter phases of an expansion.[14] The process, in summary, is that in the short run, increases in aggregate demand, measured as real final sales, are not fulfilled entirely by increase in output. Supply responds but with an increase in marginal costs. In the short run, the aggregate supply curve is upward sloping, with some capital factors fixed, labor subject to diminishing returns and thereby marginal costs increase with output.

In contrast, in a perfectly competitive economy, labor markets are perfectly flexible so a rise in employment does not mean a rise in marginal costs. Firm-specific skills are one factor that prevents the perfectly flexible labor market. As a firm begins to hire workers the firm is hiring untrained workers for that firms' specific needs.

The Cyclical Character of Corporate Profits Opens Up the Opportunity to Identify Three Pressure Points in the Cycle

Three Rising Pressure Points for Investors

Movements in the economic expansion provide key signals of increasing pressures on the sustainability of the economic expansion and the pattern of corporate profits.

---

[14] "Investors Brace for Hit to Profits as Costs Rise," *Wall Street Journal*, April 3, 2019.

Fed's Inflation Target and Expectations for Market Interest Rates

Twin fundamentals of inflation and interest rates play a central role in the behavior of profits over the economic cycle. Increases in the PCE deflator met the Fed's inflation target in the first quarter of 2017. Both the overall PCE and the core PCE rose during the previous six months. The outlook had been that the PCE deflator would hit 2% in the first quarter of 2017, with the core deflator reaching the 2% mark later this year and this was coming to pass.

One factor supporting the rise in the PCE deflator was the steady increase in labor costs. Wages accelerated during the 2016–2017 period along with average hourly earnings. Unit labor costs rose from 0.6% in the 4Q of 2016 to 3.0% in the 4Q 2017. Clearly the pattern of wage and price movements reached the point that the "low-wage growth, low-inflation" framework of decision making of prior years faded away.

For the markets, the increasing pace of inflation was accompanied by a spike in the federal funds rate as the Fed raised it in December 2016 and again in March and June of 2017. Meanwhile, real final sales also have a causal link to corporate profits.

Room to Move

Experience for investors was that increases in measured inflation was associated with an increase in the Fed funds policy rate. This experience was repeated during 2017–2018 as inflation data showed signs of moving toward the 2% policy threshold. From the Federal Reserve's point of view it was catch-up time. The Fed's policy moves and the rise in measured inflation resulted in the two-year U.S. Treasury rate climbing from 1.01% in the 4Q of 2016 to 1.69% in the fourth quarter of 2017 and eventually peaking at 2.80% in the 4Q of 2018. There was still plenty of room for the FOMC to move to achieve a target zero percent real funds rate.

Cyclical Dynamic: Economic Accelerator and Financial Outcomes

The accelerator effect has traditionally been employed to explain how faster than expected growth in aggregate demand will lead to increased business spending. In addition, faster than expected growth would also signal an improvement in profit expectations. Acceleration and deceleration in the profit cycle reflect fluctuations in the economy but in a more pronounced way. Relative to real factors such as economic growth, employment, inflation, wages, or even interest rates, profits are far more variable.

In economics, the accelerator effect[15] is a concept that informs our thinking about how business investment decisions are made in the context of the overall growth in the economy. First noted by Noble Prize winner Paul Samuelson in the late 1930s, the accelerator effect tells us that as the economy improves, corporate profits rise, as does the utilization of spare capacity. The accelerator effect is the propensity of businesses to increase capital investment in equipment and structures to create additional capacity and thereby further support profit growth.

The stock of capital in a firm depends upon the level of output. The flow of investment, net investment, occurs when output is expanding. A pickup in the pace of growth signals a need for net investment to meet new profitable opportunities. In contrast, a slower pace of growth leads to a retrenchment in opportunities. A faster pace of growth, for example, above trend, is associated with a faster pace of business investment and hiring labor. A slower pace of growth, even if still growth, suggests a slowdown in net investment and expectations for profit.

On the upside of an economic expansion, an increase in the pace of growth, above trend for example, would give rise to an acceleration in business investment and an acceleration of expectations for profit. However, a deceleration of growth would result in a deceleration in net investment and a deceleration for profit expectations.

Acceleration in real economic growth relative to trend tends to happen, although not always, at the start of an economic expansion. For example, the acceleration in economic growth from the 4Q of 1982 to the 1Q of 1984 did accompany an acceleration in the rate of business investment from the 1Q of 1983 to the 2Q of 1984. As expected, the pickup in economic growth leads to business investment. For our purposes, the acceleration in profit growth from the 4Q of 1982 to the 1Q of 1984 suggests that profit growth accelerates at the start of the economic cycle. In addition, it is consistent with the acceleration of real final sales and the lagged response in unit labor costs as the economic expansion matures.

This same pattern was repeated at the start of the 3Q 1991 expansion, the 4Q 2001 expansion, and the 3Q 2009 expansion. The process works as well in reverse. The economic slowdowns in 1Q 1986 and 1Q 2015 were

---

[15] Paul A. Samuelson, "Interaction Between the Multiplier Analysis and the Principle of Acceleration," *Review of Economics and Statistics*, 1939, 21 (May): 75–78.

accompanied by profit slowdowns. The exception was the 4Q 2003 economic deceleration which was met by an acceleration in profit growth.

Finally, periods of rapid profit growth acceleration are surprisingly, or perhaps not, short-lived. Acceleration of profit growth far above trend occurred in 1983–1984, 1986–1988 (a mid-cycle acceleration), 1994–1995, another mid-cycle boom, 2002–2005, and 4Q 2009–3Q 2010. These periods are very short. They thus intimate that a short-run supply curve allows for accelerated profit growth but lags in productivity gains are short-lived and the rise in wages and unit labor costs are quick to follow.

Profit Growth: What about Late in the Economic Expansion?

Profit growth can sometimes be strongest as the economy recovers from recession and slows as the economic recovery matures. For profit margins, nonfinancial profits as a percent of Gross Value Added, the peaks tend to occur in mid-cycle—1985, 1996–1997, 2006, and 2014. What else was going on to prompt a peak in profit margins at the mid-cycle of economic recoveries?

The acceleration in profit margins in 1996–1997 and again in 2014 were associated with an acceleration of real economic growth to a pace above the trend of the economy at the time. This fits the historical pattern of a pickup in profit margins along with the acceleration of economic growth. For 1985 and 2006, the peak in profit margins followed a sharp decline or long period of below trend growth in unit labor costs.

Fiscal and regulatory policy can provide a basis for faster economic growth and an acceleration in profits. The tax cuts of 1986 were followed by an acceleration in economic growth in 1987 and above trend growth from 1987 to 1989. Profit margins improved from the 4Q of 1986 to the 4Q Q of 1988. Personal income tax cuts in 2001 were followed by an acceleration of economic growth and improving profits from 2001 to 2006.

Tension on the Profit Margin Front: Current Policy Proposals

Profit margins tend to peak mid-cycle and then gradually decline until the next recession. In the early phase of the business expansion, productivity growth tends to be high and labor cost growth modest.

At first glance, policy proposals appear to improve profits and profit margins. First, policy proposals to stimulate aggregate demand could improve top-line revenues and allow an increase in margins following increased sales. Second, a lower corporate tax rate could increase after-tax earnings. Finally, reductions in business regulation could reduce operating costs, increasing margins.

The effectiveness of such policy initiatives could be impacted by the stage of the economic cycle and the behavior of monetary policy. Policy actions without context do not lead to clear outcomes. Success via expansionary fiscal policy to stimulate aggregate demand and increase profits faces a constraint from the supply side on costs. The optimistic case for higher profits, business investment, and employment rest on input costs remaining tame enough to maintain margins amid stronger revenue growth. However, as an economic expansion ages, the reality of continued low input costs runs against the tide of typical economic cycles. This is amplified in an era where raising trade barriers and tariffs are a policy option that may work to increase imported goods prices and thereby lower profit expectations.[16]

Profit Margins and Public Policy: The Equity Market Correction in 1999

By the autumn of 1999 and early 2000 something was amiss between equity market valuations and profit margins and monetary policy. The NYSE index had moved up regularly from a low in the 4Q of 1994 to the 4Q of 1999 and then peaked in the 4Q of 2000. By The fourth quarter of 1999, the Federal Reserve had raised their benchmark federal funds rate three times and were on a path to up the funds rate three more times in the first half of 2000.

Questions were raised about the viability of profit margins and growth in this period. Profit margins had peaked in the 3Q of 1997 and had declined into 2000 and would bottom only later in 2002. Unit labor costs had exhibited a favorable decline from the 3Q of 1998 to the 3Q of 1999 but then rose sharply in late 1999–early 2000. Growth in pre-tax corporate profits peaked in the 4Q of 1999 and then declined steadily as growth fell the next three quarters. The rise in unit labor costs along with higher interest rates signaled that the cost side of business had deteriorated. This showed up first in the decline in profit margins and then in the overall pace of profit growth.

---

[16] "Trade Tensions and Global Slowdown Weigh on US Company Profits," *Financial Times* March 13, 2019.

Higher costs and dwindling profit margins made the case for an overbought equity market.

Yet, the replay of the disconnect between the ability of companies to deliver profits and the expectations of investors to reap these same profits appears every economic cycle. Wishing does not make it so. This connect reflects the time inconsistency of investing today for profits in the future where, in between, the forces of the economy can alter the best laid plans.

Change in Investor Behavior: Expectations: From Income to Capital Gains Again

One interesting twist in recent years has been the willingness of investors to invest in capital gains rather than income. This was most evident in the housing boom-and-bust where flipping homes for capital gains was the motivation to invest rather than the psychic income of homeownership. This pattern was not original as evidenced by the experience of the Dutch Tulip Bulb bubble.

In our next chapter, we take the concept and behavior of corporate profits and link that behavior to the financial market and economic benchmarks.

* * *

Author's Note At first glance, the brief listing on a chapter on profits may appear odd. However, when you review both macroeconomics and money & banking texts, references to profits are even more scarce. Moreover, in finance texts, there is little discussion of the economic process that generates such profits. These observations were one factor in prompting the inclusion of this chapter and the next.

References

D. Dickey and W. Fuller, "Distribution of the Estimators for Autoregressive Time Series with a Unit Root," *Journal of the American Statistical Association*, 1979, 74: 427–431 and D. Dickey and W. Fuller "Likelihood Ratio Tests for Autoregressive Time Series with a Unit Root," *Econometrica* 1981, 49: 1057–1072. When dealing with macro level data, such as profits, removing trend is essential to effective decision making. The level of profits, as in output and employment, rises over time so to analyze movements, the data must be detrended.

John Steel Gordon, *The Business of America: Tales from the Marketplace*, Walker Books, New York, 2002. A review of enterprise and the pursuit of profit that leads to economic growth and employment.

C.W. Granger and P. Newbold "Spurious Regressions in Econometrics," *Journal of Econometrics,* 1974, 73:111–120. This article emphasizes the importance of testing for causality as often simple correlations/regressions run between variables offers no real explanatory power.

Hodrick, Robert and Prescott, Edward C., "Postwar U.S. Business Cycles: An Empirical Investigation," *Journal of Money, Credit, and Banking*, 1997, 29 (1): 1–16. Separating trend from cycle in any time series is an important component of analysis.

N. Gregory Mankiw, *Macroeconomics*, Ninth Edition, Worth Publishers, Chapter 9, 13, 14. Economic activity is a dynamic process and the interaction between profits and real final sales is important to understanding cycles.

John Frederick Martin, *Profits in the Wilderness: Entrepreneurship and the Founding of New England Towns in the Seventeenth Century*, University of North Carolina Press, Chapel Hill, NC, 1991. Profits as a motivating factor in the establishment of the colonies.

John Prebble, "Darien: The Scottish Dream of Empire," Edinburgh, Birlinn, 2000. The story of the pursuit of profit with little due diligence.

Paul A. Samuelson, "Interaction Between the Multiplier Analysis and the Principle of Acceleration," *Review of Economics and Statistics*, 1939, 21 (May): 75–78. A simple principle that provides complex interactions in economic cycles

John Silvia and Azhar Iqbal, "Three Simple Techniques to Analyze a Complex Economic Phenomenon: The Case of Profits," *Business Economics*, 45 (2). An approach to identifying the underlying patterns in profit growth.

11

Equity Finance: Financing Innovation and Long-Term Household Wealth

Dutch Joint Stock Company: A Combination of Funds to Promote Trade

Beginning in the 1400s and continuing through the 1600s was an era described by historians as the Age of Exploration (also called the Age of Discovery). It was a period when European nations traveled the world discovering new routes to India, much of the Far East, and the Americas.

Incentives matter and the attractive business opportunities brought on by the Portuguese discovery of the sea route to the East Indies via the Cape of Good Hope, prompted an Age of Exploration.[1] The Portuguese discovery of the sea route to India was under the command of Portuguese explorer Vasco da Gama during 1495–1499. It is considered one of the most remarkable voyages of the Age of Discovery.

The expected rate of return of such voyages appeared attractive. However, before economic activity can be conducted efficiently money capital must be raised and risk minimized. Now enters the Dutch East Indies Company.

Trading voyages were possibly very lucrative, but the risks were high given the long voyage and the calamities that could be caused by pirates and the weather. For entrepreneurs, and the Dutch government, the best way to deal with this reality was to combine resources into a single company, the United East India Company chartered in 1602. As a joint-stock company, they were

---

[1] Niall Ferguson, *The Ascent of Money*, New York: Penguin Press, 2008. p. 127.

a private entity guaranteed a trade monopoly in exchange for rights paid to the Dutch government.

To raise the capital needed for such an enterprise, the company sold shares to all residents of the Dutch Provinces and there was no limit on the number of shares available. The company was the biggest enterprise of the era outpacing the more famous British East Indian Company (mentioned in *Pirates of the Caribbean*. It was famous before the movie).

The profit model for trade was set. Companies could raise lots of financial capital to engage in activities that might generate a healthy rate of return. Although not an immediate success, trading in company shares gave rise to the growth of the Amsterdam stock market, founded in 1602, as the oldest stock market in the world. The original design to end the shares and company in ten years gave way to the realization that the company could be successful over time.

This pattern of an initial offering of shares to support the economic efforts of a company is the same framework used today.

Of course, this process can create unanticipated consequences. Speculation in the South Sea Company in the early eighteenth century gave way to the Bubble Act of 1720 which forbade further joint-stock companies without explicit approval of Parliament.[2] Our purpose here is to note the unintended consequence of this action as cited by author John Carswell.[3] The Bubble Act, intentionally or not, supported the company since Parliament sought to repress rival bubbles that might divert capital subscriptions in cash needed by promoters of the South Sea Company. When all investors must travel through the same door, the price of admission rises—as did the price of South Seas Company stock.

Equity offerings are a means to raise financial capital and reduce the risk to individual companies through its limited liability provisions. This model persists to this day, yet few students of economics are exposed to the role of equity markets as an allocator of capital in most undergraduate economics courses, as well as many graduate programs, and the raising of capital to support capital spending and employment in a growing economy. At the same time, economists are often asked their view by the financial press to forecast trends in equity markets although most economists never teach or conduct research in equity market valuations.

Equity markets provide a channel for financing innovation as well as the long-term value of household wealth in so many retirement plans and pension systems. They serve several functions in an economic system: they raise

---

[2] For a more complete recitation of the South Seas affair see Charles P. Kindleberger, *Manias, Panics, and Crashes*, New York: Basic books, 1978.
[3] John Carswell, *The South Seas Bubble*, London: Cresset Press, 1960, p. 161.

capital, allocate capital, and parcel out the gains to investors and particularly households over time.

The Equity Market—And Its CoConspirators

Equity markets do not stand alone. Every equity market forecast rests upon a series of assumptions, often unstated, about inflation, interest rates, and the dollar—as well as politics. Each market performs its function in the allocation of capital and, as the history of the last forty years reveals, the interactions are obvious but often overlooked.

So, Galileo What Do You See?

We often observe that the pattern of equity prices is frequently compared to the pattern of the economy over time as illustrated in Fig. 11.1. The initial hypothesis for many strategists is that equity prices (financial values) should reflect the activity in the economy. Indeed, that should be approximately correct—but only approximately. Better economic activity should represent better returns to the owners of financial capital (shareholders) over time. Between 1982 and 2019, real final sales to domestic purchasers has grown, on average, a bit over 2.5%. Inflation, measured as the PCE deflator, has

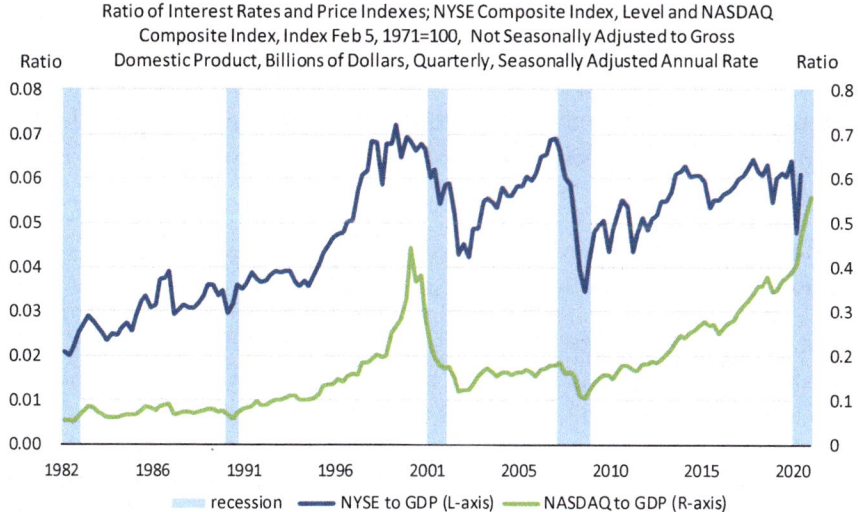

Fig. 11.1 Equity indices and nominal GDP

averaged a bit less than the Fed's 2% target. Since the earnings of American companies are global, the performance of the equity market has been helped by the gains in global trade post-NAFTA. On a cyclical basis, the NYSE index rises with an economic expansion. But what explains the variation in the ratio of the NYSE to nominal GDP over time?

A casual review of Fig. 11.1, especially the periods of the 1990s and the recent economic expansion, suggests that the decline in U.S. Treasury rates, a financial competitor to equities, supports the upward swings of the NYSE relative to nominal GDP for both the 1990s and the 2010s expansions. Equity prices are a function of expected economic growth, expected future interest rates, expected inflation, and the exchange rate. Moreover, since interest rates act as a discounting mechanism for earnings, the value of expected earnings rises as interest rates fall. The decline in the ten-year rate since the early 1980s was greater than expected. So, equity prices also benefitted from the surprise premium where interest rates rose less than expected in each period. Rise? In fact, interest rates fell while the consensus expectation among economists and analysts was that rates would rise during the 1990 and 2002 expansion periods—a sharp disparity of expected and actual outcomes—always a driver of economic and financial activity.

Money, Interest Rates, and the Missing Invited Guests

As illustrated in Fig. 11.2, the pattern of the debt-to-equity ratio for nonfinancial corporations has a pervasive causal impact on nominal GDP, real final sales, and high yield bond spreads. All three of which have follow-on impacts on equity markets. Since the early 1980s, the general decline in the debt-to-equity ratio has been associated with economic growth and lower bond yields and thereby higher equity valuations.

> "Stocks and Recessions: Assessing Recent History" *Wall Street Journal*, July 27, 2020

For analysts, the failure of inflation, and thereby interest rates, to return to prior historical levels is intriguing as it represents two distinct models of market expectations in the 1990s and then during the recent recovery.

During the 1990s, many economists and financial analysts worried about a repeat of rising inflation. Further, many thought a decline in money growth would spur interest rates to rise as liquidity and credit was being tightened in the financial markets (Fig. 11.2). Yet, as we witnessed in the 1990s, the

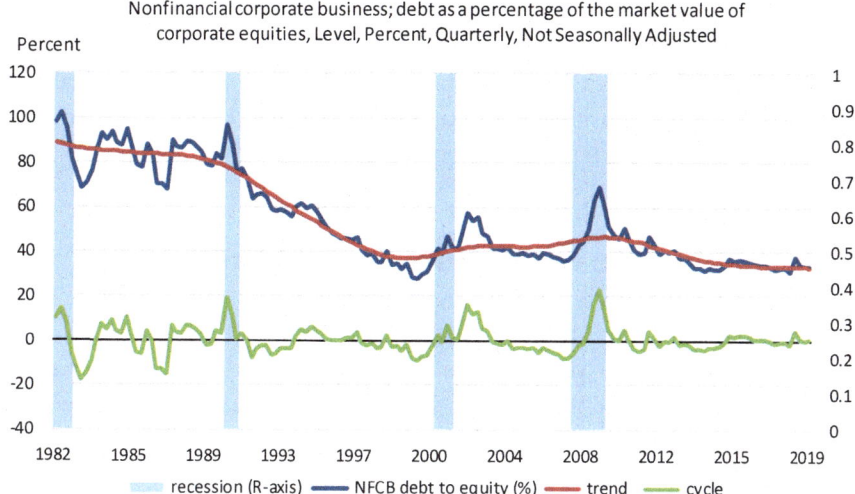

Fig. 11.2 Non-financial corporate debt to equity ratio

PCE deflator's decline exceeded expectations (in fact, expectations were that inflation would rise along with the economic expansion), such that the failure of our inflation guest to appear left more food and drink at the party for equity investors.

Flipping the coin on its other side, the rapid expansion of Fed easing during the 2010 recovery, both with lower rates and a bigger balance sheet, gave rise to expectations that inflation would rise. Yet, once again, the inflation guest failed to arrive and, as a result, its partner, interest rates, also failed to appear at the party. Once again, more food for the equity investor.

Intriguing that alternative views of the link between the money supply and product/credit markets failed to produce the expected result of higher inflation and interest rates. As a result, we get the following headline from Barron's.

"Falling Bond Yields Make Equities Hard to Ignore," *Barron's*, **August 13, 2019.**

OK Mr. Kepler, with These Observations What Are Your Laws?

Johannes Kepler benefitted from the accumulation of observations of the planets by Dutch nobleman and astronomer Tycho Brahe much as economists benefit from the data gathering of the United States Census

Bureau, the United States Department of Commerce, and the Bureau of Labor Statistics (BLS). Kepler put Brahe's observations to work and concluded that the planets traveled around the sun in an elliptical, not circular orbit (the assumption of Copernicus). Kepler went on to add two more laws based upon the observations. But why did these laws work?

Yet, There is One Final Twist to the Story

Adding intrigue to Fig. 11.1, is that during the 2010 expansion, was the pattern of the value of the U.S. dollar. The rise in the NYSE relative to nominal GDP was accompanied by an increase in the U.S. trade-weighted dollar.

NAFTA in the mid-1990s and China and the World Trade Organization (WTO) in the early 2000s opened trade and profit possibilities for U.S. companies. This income effect of large markets abroad for equities was so positive that it outweighed any negative relative price effect from a stronger dollar during the second half of the 1990s. There were also expectations for lower input costs that would also boost equity valuations. Evidence indicates that corporate bond purchases picked up in 2015 while foreign private equity purchases grew in 2016–2017. This supported the inflow of financial capital and the stronger dollar during recent years.

Galileo, Kepler, and Isaac Newton

For Galileo, his observations were like our figures: they Illustrate the phenomenon but do not explain why. For Kepler, his three laws of planetary motion treated each planet, in isolation, in its travels around the sun. Kepler took the observations and provided a mathematical law to relate the observations to the orbits of the planet. But why? It was left to Newton to introduce the laws of motion and universal gravitation to explain the motions described by Kepler. His work explained that every planet in the universe pulls on every other planet as is evident especially in the tides we see every day here on earth.

We can observe equity prices in the same manner as did Galileo. We can provide rules and models (dividend discount models, for example) for equity prices, as did Kepler. Yet, like Newton, we must recognize that the actual path of equity prices reflects the broader pull of inflation, interest rate, exchange rate, and public policy forces in our economy. No market stands alone. What is interesting is the dynamic character of equity prices. While the impact of expected economic growth and profits, as well as the expected future interest rates and dollar values may be familiar to readers, it is expected, not actual, values that are reviewed. In addition, the influence of wealth and the existing capital relative to the anticipated need for capital that provides a dynamic character to equity markets.

* * *

Equity Markets and Their Role in an Economy: The Efficient Allocation of Capital

Unfortunately, the study of equity markets in economic courses is minimal, if at all. (Why?) From my view, the basis of most post-WWII macroeconomics texts reflects the focus on GDP determination and the role of the consumer, business real investment, and government spending. The impact of monetary policy and the money supply, exchange rates, international trade, and capital flows as well as the equity markets on capital allocation were not discussed in a meaningful way. This disconnect is also apparent in the study of the broader credit market and the economy in finance courses. Even more apparent each day is the short shrift given by the media (both general and business media) for the fundamentals behind the role of the equity market in the economy. Market prices run along with the bottom banner of the TV screen, but little explanation is offered on the fundamentals for so many companies beyond the hot stock, in terms of price movements, of the day. Yet, the equity market is, along with the credit market, a critical market for the efficient allocation of financial capital in producing real economic growth. They are a bridge between separate, but increasingly interrelated, international capital markets.

Equity Allocation

"**The End: The Era that Defined Wall Street is Finally, Officially Over,**" *National Business News,* **January 2, 2009.**

Equity Market: The Returns and Cost of Capital

Despite the glamour, or opprobrium, attached to the equity market, this market is simply one arena where firms can attract financial capital and that investors can allocate their financial capital to achieve real economic results. We begin our analysis by examining the estimate a firm must make about its expected returns and its cost of capital. Estimated marginal benefit (marginal revenue product) and marginal cost (rental price) of any economic activity serve as the basis for good decision making.

As a starting point, let us examine the real final sales of domestic product (Fig. 11.3) and immediately grasp the cyclical character of the series. As a proxy for the expected return for real investment, real final sales provide a gauge for the expected rates of return on equity capital over the business cycle, and ceteris paribus, what might be the cyclical character of equity market prices. Also, intriguing is the apparent secular decline in the growth of real final sales from 1982 to 2018. The series does not exhibit any structural breaks over this period. Real final sales are indeed cyclical but act within a framework that did not change over the sample period. Finally, real final sales have a causal link to the NYSE index—values of real final sales help predict future values of the NYSE. This provides a linkage from the real sector to the financial sector via equity prices.

On the right side of our market equation we must consider the cost of capital. To keep the analysis simple, and mercifully short for now, its financial cost (again to be brief we ignore deprecation and a change in the price of the actual real capital good) reflects the interest rate return a firm will get if the

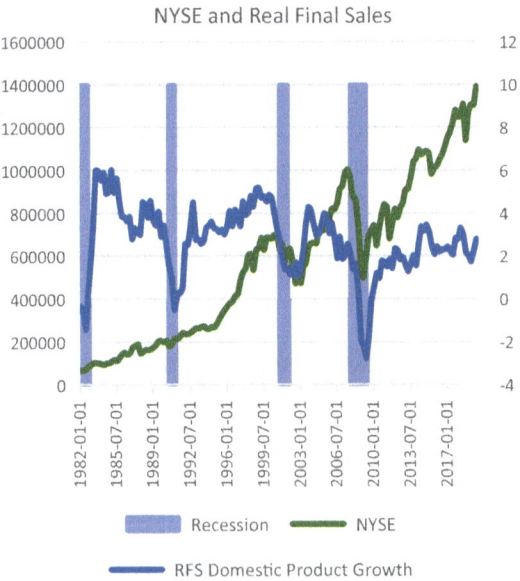

Fig. 11.3 NYSE equity index and real final sales

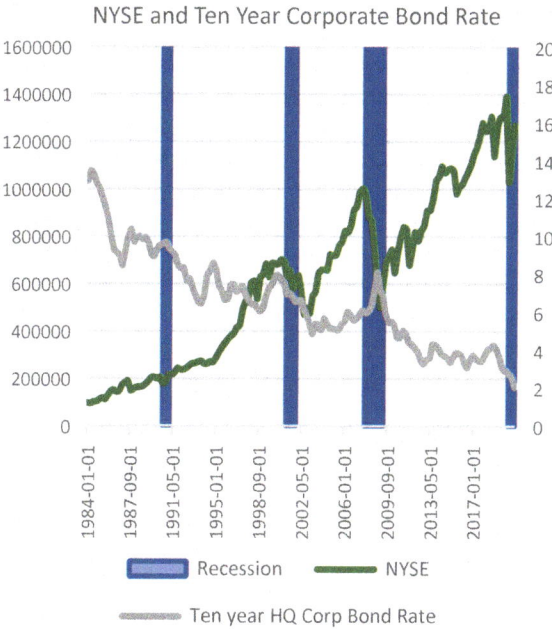

Fig. 11.4 NYSE equity index and high quality bond spot rate

firm lends out its cash. A higher interest rate makes real investment more expensive in terms of its opportunity cost. In terms of the credit market, a higher interest rate diminishes a firm's willingness to issue debt. Here we use the AA corporate bond rate as a cost of capital for a firm, Fig. 11.4, which has a distinct nonlinear and procyclical pattern—values of the AA rate help predict values for the NYSE. This provides a linkage from the credit and interest rate sector to the equity market sector.

Where do market prices for goods and services enter the picture? The Personal consumption deflator, PCE, has a causal link to the high-quality bond index and thereby influences the path of equity prices.

The Equity Island—With Bridges Attached

The equity market is simply one of several interrelated markets. This helps explain the circular firing squads of discussion when two equity strategists argue. Where is the credit market in these discussions? How about the foreign exchange market in these discussions? Finally, what about inflation and the product market in these discussions? Without a complete assessment of the factors driving equity prices, speculation on price and valuation is just speculation. Good due diligence requires an assessment of behavior in these other markets and must be represented at the table—perhaps an oblong, not circular, table to boot.

Let us return to the E/P ratio and the dividend and price ratio as signals of market interactions. As illustrated in Figs. 11.5 and 11.6, respectively, there are a cyclical and secular pattern to the earnings-price (E/P) ratio. This ratio fell from 1982 to 2000. The E/P ratio then peaks at different times during the recent cycles—mid-cycle 1995, late cycle 2007. The ratio tends to rise sharply early in the cycle, (1983–1985, 1992–1995, 2010–2012). Looking at all the evidence, the economic cycle alone is not enough to explain the patterns of the E/P ratio. As in many economic and financial series, there are numerous interrelationships between sectors that determine the behavior of a series such as the E/P ratio. Fundamental factors, such as rising interest rates (credit market), equity market overvaluation and tensions on the issues of trade (foreign exchange market) and budget deficits (future interest rate expectations) sustain the longer drop in the E/P ratio over time. For example, the trade-weighted dollar declined sharply from its 1985 peak to the time of the equity market crash of 1987. Core consumer prices had risen sharply in 1987 over 1986. Future inflation concerns were on the rise. These other factors have a role in determining the movement of the E/P ratio over time.

"Dividends can tell You a Lot About a Sector's Strength," April 5, 2019 Barron's.

Fig. 11.5 Earnings-price ratio

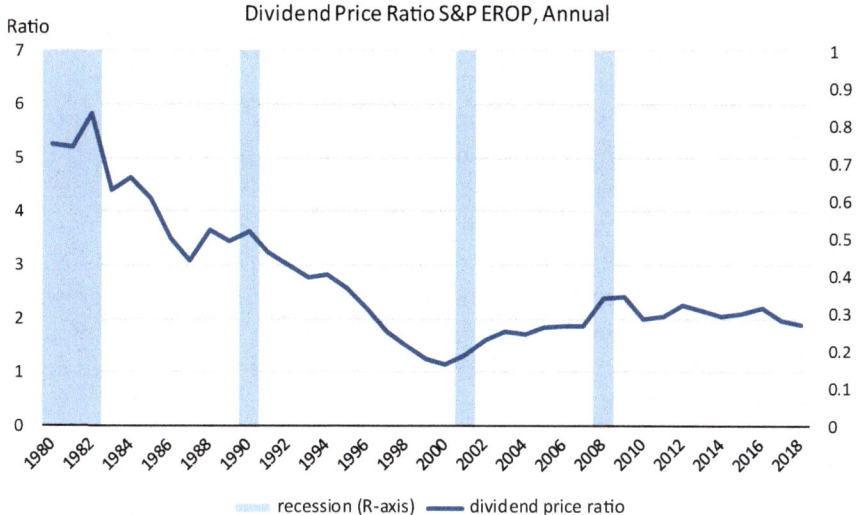

Fig. 11.6 Dividend price ratio

In general, firms try to maintain a long-run dividend payout ratio. Changes in dividends follow shifts in long-run sustainable earnings.[4] Dividends then are a weighted average of current and past earnings with an eye to the future. Figure 11.6 illustrates the ratio of current dividends to equity values (NYSE).

The extent of equity price movements comes back to expectations of the sustainability of movements in the real economy either up or down. For many corporations, the annual change in profits tends to be greater than the changes in dividends as corporations prize steady dividends.

The 2019 period was not the first where equity prices rose in an environment of slower profit growth. Moreover, equity valuations are a central holding for household wealth. The reliability of that wealth for retirement needs may be questioned if rising equity prices, in an environment of slower profit growth, was a signal of market excess.

Profits act as a signaling device for greater economic growth, opportunity, profits, and a reduction in credit risk and bank lending. Profits are a signal about the viability of repayment to the lender. Profit growth in 1993–1994, 2002–2004, and again in 2012 was associated with growth in bank loans. On the fixed-income side, profit growth was associated with declines in corporate credit spreads. For example, in 1988, 1994–1996, 2004–2006, 2009–2011, profit growth was associated with decline in the Baa over the 10-Year spread.

---

[4] Terry A. Marsh and Robert C. Merton, "Dividend Behavior for the Aggregate Stock Market," *Journal of Business*, 1987, 60 (January): 1–40.

Here, profits tend to lead dividend increases as seen in 1988–1991, 1994–2000, 2002–2007, 2009–2019. These dividends, along with equity price gains, increase household wealth measures.

Today's equity values reflect expectations of future dividend receipts plus the proceeds from selling equity at an expected higher price. Dividends reflect a company's future prosperity but also a company's policy to pay those dividends. Firms leaders take economic prospects into account when setting the payment of dividends. The cost of equity finance for a nonfinancial corporation is the expected dividend yield plus expected nominal growth of dividends. The gains in profits provide the basis for dividend growth and lower the cost of equity finance. Profit growth tends to lead credit finance activity.

Earnings per share reflects the rate of return on capital. Earnings can be split into retained earnings and dividends. Increased dividend payments will reduce retained earnings, ceteris paribus. Lower dividends will increase the capital backing each share thereby increasing the expected EPS in the future. This was evident in the reduction in bank dividends during the Covid-19 shutdowns of 2020.[5]

Retained earnings benefit shareholders if the return on the company's marginal investments exceeds that could have been obtained by shareholders elsewhere. If not, then the corporation is misallocating capital on projects that yield less than would be obtained otherwise.

The P/E ratio, that is commonly assessed by others, reflects their perceived required rate of return on capital invested and the proportion of earnings distributed to shareholders as dividends. Ceteris paribus, the lower the required rate of return, the greater the growth of earnings, or the greater the ratio of dividends to earnings, the greater is the price shareholders are willing to pay per dollar of earnings. An increase in the P/E ratio reflects an increase in the rate of return on investment relative to the rate of growth on returns for other profitable opportunities. During 2018–2019, the expected returns on business investment in a growing economy would be greater than the return on cash or bonds in a low-interest rate environment.

Appreciation in equity prices should match the expected appreciation of earnings and dividends over time. If there is a positive outlook for the economy, then any short-run decline in equity prices, the first half of 2020 for example, will be less than the drop in expectations for earnings and dividend growth over time. This equity price decline will be met by a correction in the market to restore the link between equity prices and profit margins. The

---

[5] "Bank Dividends Face Manageable Stresses, But There Are Some Wild Cards," *Barron's*, June 28, 2020.

equity market will decline less than earnings in a bad year (first half of 2020). Alternatively, if the bad outlook persists than equity prices will decline more than earnings over time. By mid-2020, equity price expectations had turned upward.

What Are the Details Behind the CAPE Ratio[6]?

Simply, the CAPE ratio (Cyclically Adjusted Price-to-Earnings) is not mean reverting, as was true of the basic P/E ratio and is true of many financial benchmarks since these measures are all part of a broader economic and financial framework. Both ratios (CAPE and P/E) reflect the influence of the evolutionary values for other economic and financial factors. The CAPE ratio is another measure to benchmark the pattern of equity finance costs relative to a recent history of the stage of the business cycle. For example, the CAPE ratio rose with the 1990s economic expansion and again in 2000s. The CAPE ratio, as well as the P/E ratio, is subject to many exogenous forces that result in a pattern of behavior that reflects economic, political, and regulatory influences.

Since the CAPE ratio is not mean reverting, no single number that serves as a standard of value. The CAPE ratio is also subject to several shocks, as well as the evolutionary changes in economic and financial values, that alter the behavior of the series (September 2001, October 2008) and that provide statistically significant evidence of a structural break in the series. Therefore, there is limited, if any, ability to judge the cost of equity finance relative to the recent past due to the structural shifts in the CAPE series. Once again, due diligence requires a degree of caution on comparisons of equity values over long periods (since World War II for example) that are common but misleading. The economy has evolved and so has the cost of equity capital.

Three Factors Driving Corporate Profit Growth and Equity Prices

Profit Margins

As reviewed in Chapter 10, profit margins, Fig. 11.7, have a strong cyclical character which in turn reflects the cyclical character of unit labor costs and interest rates. First, we will examine the role of corporate income taxes.

---

[6] John Y. Campbell and Robert J. Shiller, "Stock Prices, Earnings and Expected Dividends," Journal of Finance, 1987, 43 (3) (December).

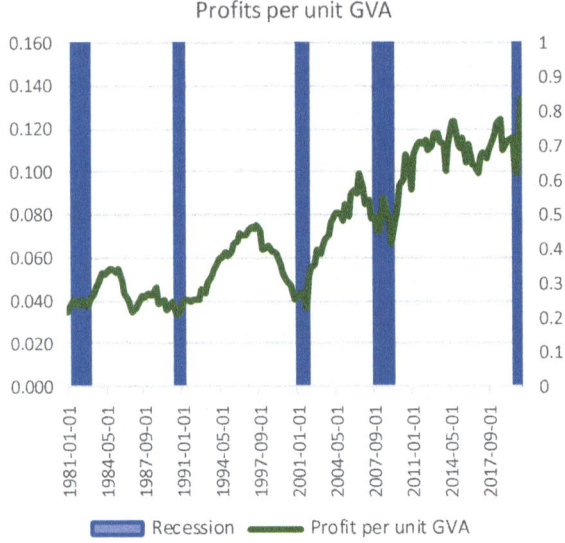

Fig. 11.7 Profits per unit of GVA

Corporate Taxes and Capital Spending: Not So Clear a Story

Over the past 25 years, there has been a modest down swing in the effective corporate tax rate (Fig. 11.8). At late stages of an economic expansion, the effective rate has risen. In both cases, there is very limited gain in cash flow due to lower tax rates and thereby little incentive for private corporations to add to the capital stock. There is also the result that the corporate income tax reduces overall economic activity.[7] Finally, the burden of the corporate income tax falls on the shareholders, workers, and customers of the corporation. How much each pays remains a debate.[8]

Despite all the discussion surrounding the importance of lower taxes, there is a nuance that we should recognize. To start, a firm will seek to equalize, at the margin, the after-tax marginal product of capital with the after-tax user cost of capital to maximize profits. Lower taxes would be associated with higher after-tax profits and more investment.

---

[7] Austin Goolsbee, "The Impact and Efficiency of the Corporate Income Tax: Evidence from State Organizational Form Datal," Working paper No. 9141. Cambridge, MA: National Bureau of Economic Research, September 2002.

[8] Victor Fuchs, Alan Krueger and James Poterba, "Why Do Economists Disagree About Policy? The Roles of Beliefs about Parameters and Values," Mimeo Stanford, CA: Stanford University, August 1997.

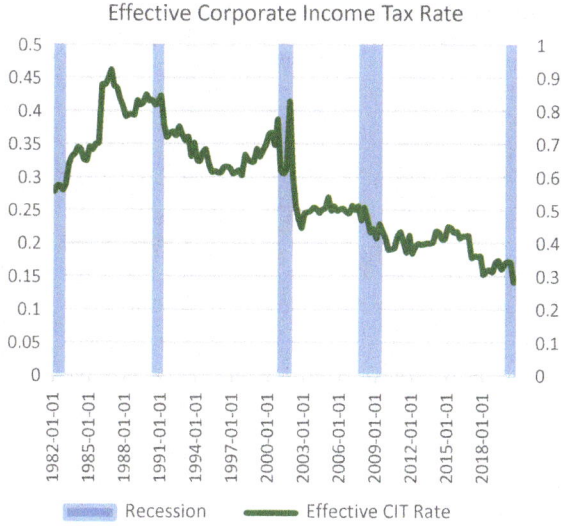

Fig. 11.8 Effective corporate income tax rate

When we examine the effective corporate tax rate, Fig. 11.8, the series has a downward trend since 1990 but is also very irregular with numerous ups and downs. When we focus on just the dips, they appear strongly related to economic recessions in the 2000–2002 period and again from 2008 to 2010.

Yet, apart from the business cycle, why is it so hard to identify a clear link between taxes and economic activity, such as adding capital? First, a firm seeks to equalize, at the margin, the after-tax marginal product of capital with the after-tax user cost of capital to maximize profits. This is a very fundamental economic behavior. Lower taxes would, therefore, be associated with higher after-tax profits and greater real investment.

However, interest costs are treated as a deduction from revenues in the calculation of corporate taxes. A lower tax rate would lower the value of the tax deduction on interest. The boost to capital spending would not be as large as the static estimate of the first impact on what the corporate tax rate cut alone would indicate.

Alternatively, a lowering (raising) of the corporate tax rate would also signal the intentions of any administration's fiscal policy. A lower tax rate would indicate an expansionary fiscal policy that would promote business investment. In this sense. it is difficult to separate the individual response of equity prices to a specific cut in the corporate tax rate. There is a need to control

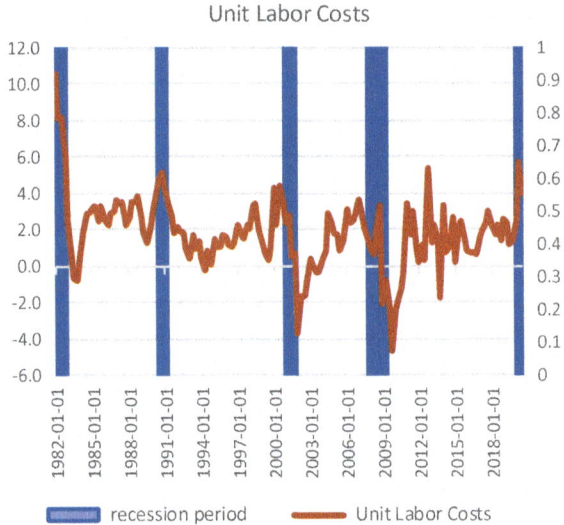

Fig. 11.9 Unit labor costs

for the change in investor attitudes toward future growth that would accompany such a move, as well as the possible accompanying easier monetary and regulatory regime and/or accompanying expansionary fiscal actions.

Unit Labor Costs

Unit labor costs, Fig. 11.9, have a countercyclical pattern. In the early phase of an economic recovery, (1982–1931,991–1994, 2001–2003, 2009–2010) unit labor costs decline as output increases and productivity rises. However, later in the economic expansion, unit labor costs rise, 1989–90 for example, as productivity slows, and labor compensation rates rise.

Interest Paid

Interest paid has a procyclical pattern, Fig. 11.10 as interest rates and debt issuance both tend to rise with the economic expansion. Recessions represent a clear break in the pattern as interest rates decline and corporations that can refinance debt at lower interest rates.

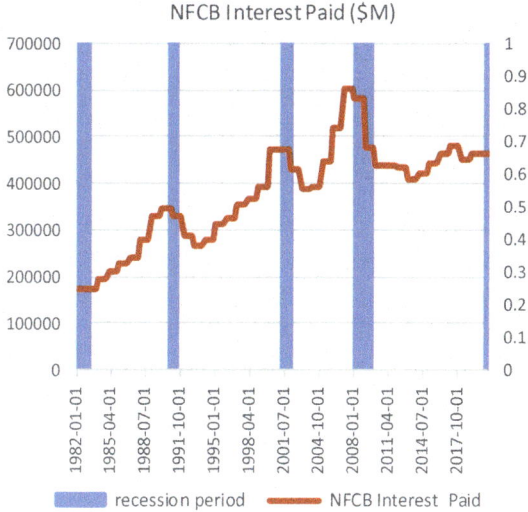

Fig. 11.10 Non-financial corporate interest paid

Expectations, Equity Prices and Earnings

Over time, equity prices should reflect the anticipated future gains in corporate earnings when dividend growth is steady. If, however, expectations are that expected stock prices are projected to rise at a rate that exceeds the rate of growth of earnings and dividends, this disconnect can lead to an equity market correction—earnings fail to validate the optimism of investors as in the dot-com bubble. Here, the utilization of the H–P filter helps identify when market prices are deviating from trend. And while not identifying a bubble, the deviation will call attention to investors to examine deeper the reason, if any, for such deviations.

For equities considered growth stocks, today's prices will not reflect the value of their future dividends as future returns may easily appear in the form of capital gains that may persist for years even without any dividend growth. This then commands equity prices to appreciate to compensate shareholders for falling, or nonexistent, dividend yields.

From 2010 to 2019, several notable technology stocks did appreciate in a manner to obviate the demand by investors for dividends.

Income and Capital Gains

Rising (falling) NYSE/NASDAQ indices are justified by common expectations that income and capital gains (or losses) will be higher (lower) and rising (falling) in the period ahead. Real final sales have a causal link to the NYSE index. In recent years, prospective dividend returns have taken on secondary importance. One possibility is that the rate of equity price appreciation would approach the investor's required rate of return such that expected dividend yields would be negligible. This was true in recent years for many technology equities.

Periods of overvaluation for the equities reflect the expectations of profit growth more than the predicted values from fundamentals. We would expect that equity prices would reflect expected economic growth and future interest rates. Causality is evident, and statistically significant, running from real final sales and high-quality corporate bond rates to equity prices.

Corporate profits reported in the National Income and Product Accounts (NIPA) are distinct from earnings that are the focus of equity markets. NIPA earnings omit income from foreign sources and do not account for capital gains or losses. In addition, NIPA profits leave out dividends from other corporations. For example, periods of inflation reduce the real value of corporate debt and thereby is a gain to the corporation, although not recorded as an improvement in the financial condition of the corporation.[9]

Equity values are linked to the rate of growth earnings, but earnings growth also has some side benefits. In the short run, if investors witness an increase in the growth of earnings, dividend payments would appear more secure. This lowers the perceived risk of an equity investment for any given pace of return.

For informational value, the E/P ratio appears to anticipate changes in the short run of earnings. In turn, equity indices appear to anticipate turns in the economic cycle.[10]

Best Laid Plans: Expectations and Surprises

Equity markets are forward looking. Equity valuations reflect the pace of expected growth, inflation, interest rates, and exchange rates going forward. Yet, the best-laid plans will always face surprises. Since 1982, unanticipated changes in the rate of inflation, often less than expected, and interest rates, also often less than expected, have altered both equity and bond values. In

---

[9] Adjustments to the NIPA data also include adjustments to the value of imputed services and capital stock. For a more comprehensive review see Ellen R. McGrattan and Edward C. Prescott, "Is the Stock Market Overvalued," Federal Reserve Bank of Minneapolis, *Quarterly Review*, 2000 (Fall): 20–40.

[10] See Joe Peek and Eric Rosengren, "The Stock Market and Economic Activity," *New England Economic Review*, 1988 (May/June): 39–50.

turn, economic growth has sometimes exceeded expectations (1980s) and sometimes disappointed (2010–2016).

For investors, there is the ex ante real rate of return which is the difference between the expected return on a financial asset and the expected rate of inflation. In the early 1980s, the expected return on both equities and bonds was low given the experience of the 1970s.

However, the ex post return reflects the actual return given the actual experience of inflation and interest rates. For the 1980s, actual inflation and subsequently interest rates were less than expected. Thereby, real returns on financial assets were greater than expected.

As a result, ex ante and ex post returns on equities and bonds can be quite different illustrated by the decline in financial asset prices in the first half of 2020.[11] Yet by April 2020, a turnaround was in place.[12]

Financial Benchmarks and the Economy: Nominal GDP, Interest Rates, and Equity Valuations

"A tight contest between bonds and equities" June 14, 2019 FT.

For a given household, total financial wealth, FW, is given by three financial assets—money, M, bonds, B, equity, EQ.

$$FW = Cash + P^b B + P^e EQ$$

Where P^b and P^e represent the prices of bonds and equities, respectively

Demand for any asset is a function of wealth, income, and relative returns on bonds, equity, and money. The increase in the relative rate of return on any asset will make that asset more attractive and other assets less attractive. For example, a rise in the pace of inflation relative to expectations lowers the demand for money bonds (cash). A lower price for bonds, relative to expectations, increases the demand for bonds, and equities, diminishing the demand for cash. An increase in the expected rate of return on equities, relative to expectations, raises the demand for equities and diminishes the demand for bonds and cash (the 2018–2019 experience). In addition, investors are more willing to borrow on margin or draw down cash to buy equities.

Increases in expected economic growth and income increase demand for cash and for financial assets that participate in forthcoming economic

---

[11] "Stocks Sink as Coronavirus Cases Mount Outside of Asia," *Wall Street Journal*, February 24, 2020.
[12] U.S. Stocks Log Best Week Since 1974, *Wall Street Journal*, April 9, 2020.

growth—equities, high yield, and high-grade corporate debt. This is the typical scenario at the start of every economic recovery. It leads to higher equity prices and lower corporate bond spreads over Treasuries. In the short run, with the given outstanding stock of equity, the price of equity capital goes up.

With these three markets for financial assets, if two markets are in equilibrium, then the third market is in equilibrium. Equilibrium is achieved when the actual holdings of financial assets equal the desired holdings. This equilibrium condition leads to the recognition that any exogenous change (income, inflation, exchange rates, monetary policy) that impacts one market will alter all three financial asset markets.

"Beneath Bond Market's Surface, Tumbling Real Yields Boost Other Assets," *Wall Street Journal*, **July 21, 2020.**

If not mean reverting, then what factors influence the movement of the P/E ratio over time? NYSE valuations relative to nominal GDP have a more significant volatile pattern than many analysts may first suspect. In addition, the ratio of the NYSE to nominal GDP provides a cyclical pattern that raises some intriguing questions about what and when equity finance might provide a profitable alternative to bond and cash finance to real investment.

For a firm, the option of raising external funds can be an option to borrow short term, from a bank for example, or borrow longer term in the bond market, or go to the equity market. The relative cost of each option determines the choice. There are no simple answers to the capital structure of a firm. For our purposes, however, we recognize some exogenous factors that drive corporate decisions. First, there are taxes. An increase in leverage reduces the tax paid for a taxpaying firm but does raise taxes for investors. For tax years beginning after December 31, 2017, firms need to adhere to the business interest deduction limitation imposed by the Tax Cuts and Jobs Act 0f 2017. The business interest deduction limitation disallows all net business interest expenses more than 30% of the adjusted taxable income of a business.

Risk is a second factor. An increase in corporate debt raises the risk profile of a corporation, discouraging the issuance of debt as firms did in early 2020. Later in 2020, firms employed cash to reduce their debt when economic expectations improved.[13] Third, firms with greater intangible assets as a share of assets are more likely to issue less debt as there as fewer assets available to

---

[13] "Companies Give Up Cash Cushions to Buy Back Debt," *Wall Street Journal*, October 7, 2020.

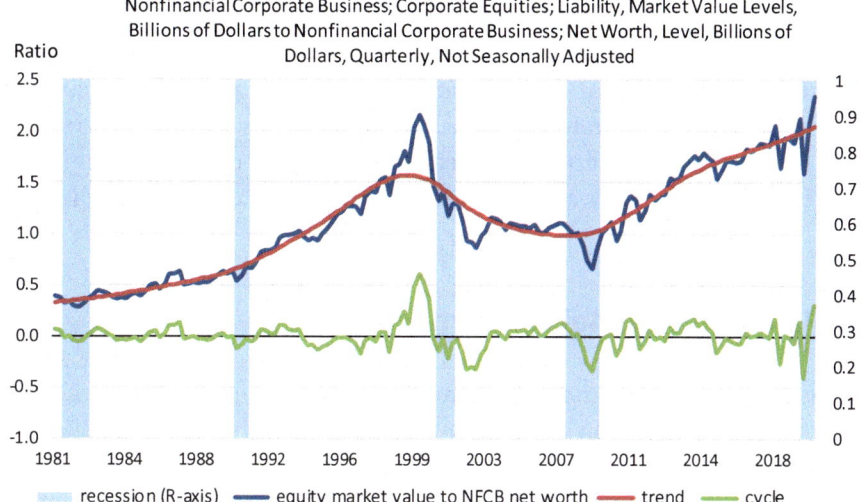

Fig. 11.11 Corporate equity market value as a share of net

liquidate in difficult times. Finally, financial flexibility is important as firms with cash and access to short-term credit can take advantage of opportunities.

Benchmarking Resource Allocation: Altering the Capital Stock of a Company

How do market values influence economic activity? Although not a rule, one guideline for the allocation of capital for a firm is Tobin's Q which we previewed in Chapter 7. The decision to increase capital stock should be made if the market value of a unit of capital exceeds its cost of acquisition. The ratio of the market value to the replacement cost is Tobin's Q (Figure 11.11). Here we examine the market value of equity as a share of corporate net worth.

The firm will increase its capital stock if the discounted value of future marginal revenue capital exceeds the cost of acquiring it. The expected rate of return should exceed its cost of capital. This decision is in the context of an opportunity cost. The return to investment should exceed the cost of capital which could have been used in alternative activities.

In this context, the activities should align with core competencies of the business or the risks would be greater for activities outside the core competency of the management.[14] The cost of capital here reflects the cost of both

---

[14] See Jim Collins discussion of R. J. Reynolds for example in *Good to Great*, New York: Harper Business, 2001 Chapter 3. The Hedgehog Concept.

equity and fixed income and must be forward looking—a reflection of future risks and returns.

Taxes play a role also. The investment tax credit alters the measure of income subject to corporate income taxes and income is reduced by a fraction of its investment expenditures. The effective price per unit of capital is thus reduced while it increases a firm's desired stock of capital, at least in the short run.[15]

Tax Policy and Capital Adjustments

Public policy also alters the allocation of corporate resources to capital stock. Selective taxation or non-taxation of capital is subject to the problems of partial equilibrium analysis which ignores other sector impacts and feedbacks. Taxes, like death, may be certain, but tax policy is not. The incidence of a tax (who the tax falls on) is different from the burden of a tax (who ultimately pays). For example, the incidence of the corporate tax falls on corporations but the burden of the tax impacts individuals. Corporations do not bear taxes.[16]

There are several issues with the taxation of capital beyond the equity and bond issue inherent in the tax deduction of interest. First, a tax with a narrow base incentivizes substitutions and weakens the impact of any tax. Taxing one type of business capital, such as equipment, leads firms to invest more on other capital. Taxes on capital in one state incentivizes a firm to move capital to another state.

In imperfect markets, a tax base may be very elastic in response to tax increases. Capital will then move to another location if possible and the burden of taxation will fall on the relatively immobile economic inputs. Elasticity provides a rough measure of an economic agent's ability to escape the tax.[17]

Public policy tends to focus on short-run revenues and is much less concerned on the longer run impacts on economic performance. Alternatively, there is a false choice when two-period analysis is used. This forces a trade-off between today and tomorrow when most choices have a multi-period set of implications. In part, this reflects the reality that adjusting the capital structure of a firm takes time.

---

[15] Robert E. Hall and Dale Jorgenson, "Tax Policy and Investment Behavior," *American Economic Review* 57, 1967 (June): 391–414.
[16] Harvey S. Rosen, *Public Finance*, McGraw-Hill Irwin, Seventh Edition, 2005, pp. 274–301.
[17] Rosen, op. cit., p. 282.

Recognizing Change in Financial Asset Markets

"Asset prices stretch the banks of resistance," *Financial Times*, **November 20, 2019.**

As for inflation, the Fed raised its benchmark fed funds rate in the first half of 1984 and then again in 2016–2018 concerned with higher inflation, yet realized inflation remained modest leading the Fed to reduce the benchmark funds rate after each tightening period. Fed policy decisions in 2016–2018, although reversed, did have a significant impact on asset prices.[18] As evidenced by the markets response to expected policy and inflation movements, asset price relationships can change. At certain phases of an economic expansion, tighter monetary policy may be perceived as negative for corporate earnings and equity valuations. But if a tighter policy is perceived as obviating future inflation pickups, bond markets may rally.

A seeming inconsistency of bond and equity market prices may be a response to the same set of economic expectations. Equity prices may rise with lower price volatility, lower interest rates, and narrower credit spreads as a sign of economic optimism. Yet, such lower rates could also be a signal of economic pessimism.[19]

Equity market prices and credit spreads reflect economic growth and profit expectations. Meanwhile, bond market prices indicate inflation expectations. As a result, expectations for better economic growth would boost equity valuations while hitting bond prices to the extent better growth would be interpreted as higher future inflation.

Even here, the stage of the economic cycle matters. In the early stages of an economic expansions, a high level of slack in the economy, measured by a high level of unemployment, and the Fed's inflation model indicates little chance of a short-run acceleration of inflation. From our review of corporate profits, we know that profit margins rise in the early phase of an economic recovery and inevitably boosts equity prices.

As an economic cycle matures, however, labor costs rise causing profit margins to often decline thereby weakening equity valuations. Late in an economic expansion, inflation tends to rise prompting the Federal Reserve to raise interest rates causing a further weakening of the valuation of equities and bonds.

---

[18] "Global Bond Sell-Off Rattles Markets," *Financial Times*, January 30, 2018.
[19] "U.S. Government-Bond Yields Fall as Investors Seek Safety from Tech-Stock Slide," *Wall Street Journal*, September 10, 2020,

Evolution of the Cost of Capital Over the Business Cycle

Equity capital is one factor in financing economic growth and yet the cost of equity capital varies over the business cycle. Nominal GDP growth provides a starting point to judge the top-line growth opportunities for business and thereby a measure of incentives to balance against the cost of capital.

Nominal GDP growth supplies evidence of a linear downward trend over time which means nominal GDP growth is not a mean reverting series. Despite this, nominal GDP sets a guide on the revenue earning power of both businesses and workers. This observation stands against the claim that somehow nominal growth and capital returns will come back to some average value over time. Nominal income growth is correlated to nonfinancial profit growth. The peaks in the pace of top-line nominal GDP growth is consistent with peaks in nonfinancial per-tax profits, unadjusted, in profit growth in mid-1987, late 1999, late 2005, and midyear 2014.

The Earnings-Price Ratio: Another Non-Mean Reverting Series

Commentators frequently argue that equity price-earnings ratios are either above or below some average value and that this difference indicates the equity market is under or overvalued.[20] However, mean reverting behavior for a financial time series cannot simply be assumed. An average value can be calculated for any time series, but that does not indicate that the behavior of that series will return to some average value over a given period—if ever.

In fact, the E/P ratio is not mean reverting. There have been significant shifts in the series in October 1987 (downward) and in October 1991 (upward) and then down again in July 2002. In fact, the E/P ratio is not exogenous to the economy but is dependent on the behavior of several economic fundamentals. These include expected nominal growth and interest rate policies, as well as regulatory changes and exogenous shocks that alter the risk and reward calculus. The E/P ratio is not independent of the economic cycle but is instead a product of the many forces of the economic cycle.

While numerous commenters assert that the E/P ratio is above or below some average there is no value to such statements. Rather the E/P ratio reacts

---

[20] For a discussion on this issue by investment practitioners see "Markets Will Gain Despite Looming Risks According to Barron's Roundtable Panelists," *Barron's*, January 11, 2020.

to changes in expected economic growth, expected inflation, interest rates, exchange rates, and possible changes in federal taxation. The E/P ratio is a non-mean reverting series. An E/P ratio above or below some average (calculated over some arbitrary period) does not indicate that the behavior of the E/P time series will return to some hypothetical, but non-existent, average.

Economic Policy, the Cost of Capital, and Economic Growth

Policymakers in federal governments around the world frequently ask the question how can the U.S. economy achieve a faster pace of economic growth? The fundamental dictate is that improved quantity and quality of capital and workers are central to growth.

If the U.S. economy is to upgrade its pace of growth, private firms need to increase both the quantity and quality of capital goods. The nominal price of adding capital is measured by the concept of the user cost of capital, which is subject to the influence of both monetary and fiscal policy.

As illustrated in Fig. 11.12, the real rate of return on benchmark one-year and five-year Treasury notes has drifted down since the Great Recession. These two series have a number of interesting linkages to corporate profits and net worth. The one-year real rate provides insight into profit margins while the five-year real rate signals net worth and yield curve (ten minus

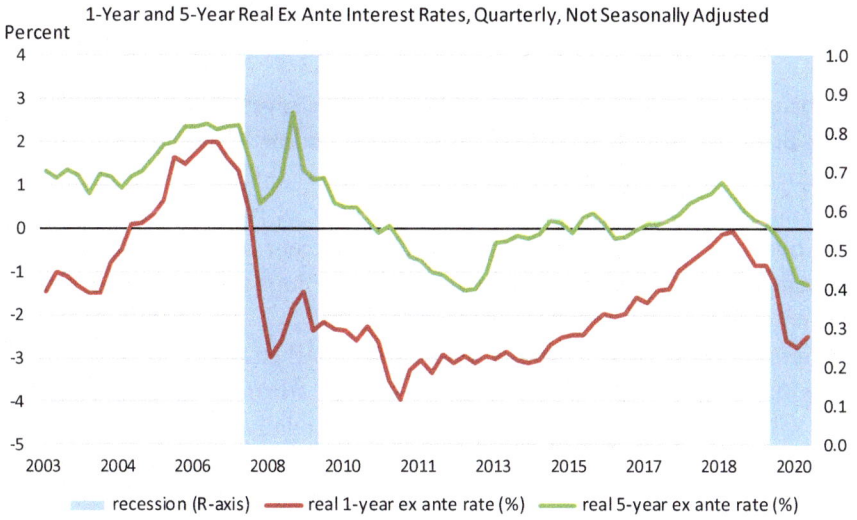

Fig. 11.12 One and five-year ex ante real rates

two-year) movements. The Fed has helped keep nominal interest rates low. But the real interest rate reflects the path of real factors in the economy including demographics, technology, entrepreneurship, and real spending. The real one-year return is calculated as the nominal one-year return less than the University of Michigan's measure of inflation expectations one year ahead. The real five-year return is the nominal five-year return less than break-even inflation rate for the same five-year period.

Nature of the Disequilibrium for the Cost of Capital

Evolution of the Cost and Returns to Capital Over the Economic Cycle

Variability in both the cost and returns to capital over the business cycle creates a matrix of outcomes that renders meaningless the single variable, simple link that some analysts ascribe to market outcomes and economic drivers.

Cost of Capital: Many Routes to the Same Target

The goal is to finance growth no matter the financial environment. Consider the following:

> The month-long government shutdown is forcing some companies to seek alternate routes to go public while the main markets regulator is unable to greenlight IPOs. *Wall Street Journal,* January 21, 2019

Opportunity does not wait. Firms will examine several paths (equity, debt, cash) all in their many forms—banking and shadow banking, domestic and foreign finance, several tranches of debt. This is the great creativity of the financial system. Variability of the relative costs of financial options creates incentives to move financial flows across different asset classes. This is a problem for policymakers. Markets, like water, find a way around political stalemates and inefficient regulations.

There is no simple link between the equity markets and economic growth. Firms can draw upon three main sources of finance—equity, bonds, or cash. Choices of the means to finance reflect relative costs and incentives independent of the pace of economic growth.

Returns to Capital: Variability Over the Cycle, Financial Returns Are not Mean Reverting

Is there value? Such is the essential question for decision makers for both real investment and the financial portfolios. For the investor in the real economy, the pace of business investment, acts as a signal of the expectations of future gains, and varies with the business cycle. Real investment rises with strength in the economy (1994–1999, 2004–2007, 2010 to 2019, with a drop off in 2014–2016). Historically, there was a peak just on the precipice of recession, then a quick drop into economic oblivion.

Markets are interrelated in many complex ways and our analytical approach must reflect that reality. Too many investors set solitary benchmarks, such as the P/E ratio, as the benchmark for casual investment commentary leading to confusion on the part of investors. Such ratios are not mean reverting and these ratios move like a flag in the wind of changing economic forces.

Equity market performance does not stand alone. While, in the short run, performance may give the appearance of a Wile E. Coyote suspension of reality, over time the equity markets must operate in an economic and credit system of linkages. This is not that unusual an event. Equity performance is not a function of just one variable and the economic outlook. In the late 1990s, profit growth decelerated yet equity returns in 1995, 1997, and 1998 did very well. What factors do we need to track expected returns on capital that would support a sustained, intellectually sound, appreciation of equity prices? Let us round up the usual suspects.

Interest Rates, the Dollar and, Yes, the Yield Curve

"Falling Bond Yields Make Equities Hard to Ignore," *Wall Street Journal*, August 13, 2019.

Expected interest rates play a central role. The experience of late 2018 is instructive. When we examine the Consensus Forecast for December 2018, we note that growth was to be slower in 2019 but inflation and interest rates higher. The combination of slower growth with higher inflation and interest rates, not growth alone, provided the impetus for the equity market correction. This was particularly true given the Fed's dot plot and accompanying commentary that the balance sheet reduction was to continue. Some commentators said that the balance sheet does not alter interest rates. This is perhaps true but investors acted as if it did. Belief matters.

"Why a Weaker Dollar Could End This Bull market," *Barron's*, January 28, 2018.

Our trade-weighted dollar plays an interesting role here. The typical commentary asserts that the weakness of the dollar is a stimulant for the economy. One is never sure whether a commentator is citing a weaker nominal or real dollar exchange rate—perhaps that is too much to ask. I digress. Anyway, if the decline in the dollar reflects mounting inflation pressures or a change in the U.S. competitive position, then there is little to be gained for the economy or the financial markets.

Dot plots and the dollar are not enough. The real Fed funds rate rose in 1995 and 2003 and equity performance was above average. What about that pesky yield curve? Certainly in recent months we have heard a lot, perhaps too much, about a flatter, inverted yield curve—however misspecified. A flatter curve would be associated with a less expansionary monetary policy and banking system liquidity. Once again, the yield curve narrowed in 1995 and 1997–1998 and equity market performance was exceptional.

Markets do not stand in isolation. If there is a disequilibrium in the output and equity markets then adjustments must be made in other markets (credit for example) and in investment and business decisions.

Speculation, not Investing, and the Story of the Repetitive Equity Bubble: 1907, 1920s, Nifty-Fifty, Oil, Dot.com, and FANG

Too much finance relative to economic opportunity creates the imbalances we witnessed in Chapter 2 that lead to further adjustments or in the extreme case, to recession and financial revulsion. Why the repetitive appearance of equity bubbles? The very positive capital allocation function is sometimes overshadowed by the proposition that speculation is the name of the game for equities. Speculation is certainly there, for some, but the existence of cognitive biases, such as framing and the recency bias, help explain the behavioral problems in equity pricing.

As is true of pricing and credit cycles, expectations may not match real outcomes thereby providing a dynamic to equity investing and the economy at large.

Shocks on the Upside: Excessive Risk Premiums on the Advent of Structural Change

"What's to come is still unsure," William Shakespeare *Twelfth Night*.

For Canada, the 1970s were a period of large fiscal government deficits, and high unemployment and inflation. A brief recovery in 1994 was followed by an economic slump in 1995–1996. Since that date, the Canadian economy has improved markedly in step with the boom in the United States. In the mid-1990s, Canadian governments began to post annual budgetary surpluses and steadily paid down the national debt. It has turned around its fiscal deficits and posted budget surpluses every fiscal year from 1996 to 2007.

For Ireland, after a bleak period in the 1970s and 1980s, the Celtic Tiger era in the Republic was spurred on by the high technology industries, Apple, and Pharma, that took root in the country in the mid-1990s. Competitive corporation tax rates, an educated English-speaking workforce, access to the single market, and a successful multiyear international marketing campaign by the Ireland Industrial Development Agency were all contributing factors. In the late 1980s, the government made a series of wage agreements with trade unions. Thereafter, wage increases were held at modest levels in exchange for income tax cuts which started to transform the economy from a high tax/low growth model to low tax/high growth.[21]

This enabled Ireland to take advantage of favorable demographics and—over many years—provide opportunities to its educated youth. This reduced emigration and resulted, over time, in net inward migration (previous emigrants returning and immigration from EU). Ireland also benefited relatively more from the fiscal transfers of the European Structural Funds system. After the 2008 crisis, budget control came back into focus. Since then, the Republic of Ireland has seen large economic growth referred to as the "Celtic Phoenix."

For the United States, the era of stagnation in the 1970s, along with a second oil shock, led to an inflation spike. Meeting that spike head on was Fed Chairman Paul Volker who dramatically increased interest rates. Coupled with the fiscal reforms and tax cuts of President Ronald Reagan, the pace of U.S. economic growth rose, and inflation slowed.

Although the attention for many commentators is to focus on the downside, these three examples highlight the upside. Structural shifts in economic policy led to better economic growth and investment returns. For investors, the inflation premiums at the start of the 1980s were very high. Inflation expectations, as measured by the University of Michigan's Consumer Sentiment Survey registered 10.8% in March 1980. Subsequently, inflation came in far below that pace thereby generating higher real returns than expected. Discounting for higher inflation, government and corporate bond yield premiums were also very high. Lower inflation led to significant gains

---

[21] A shift in expectations is critical in the case of Ireland. See Francesco Giavazzi and Marco Pagano, "Can Severe Fiscal Contractions be Expansionary? Tales of Two Small European Countries," *NBER Macroeconomics Annual*, 1990, 5: 75–111.

in corporate and government bond returns in the early 1980s. According to Ibbotson Associates, a leading investment management company,[22] the 5-year holding period returns for long-term corporate bonds was 22.51% from 1982 to 1986. For long-term government bonds, the returns were 21.62%. Ten-year U.S. Treasury rates fell from 14.59% in January 1982 to 7.11% in December 1986.

With lower inflation and interest rates, equity portfolio performance turned around dramatically. The five-year holding period performance from 1977 to 1981 was 8.13% whereas the performance from 1982 to 1986 more than doubled to 19.87%.

From the arena of private finance, we now turn in our next chapter to the challenging evolution of sovereign finance in the post Global Financial Crisis era.

* * *

References

John Y. Campbell and Robert J. Shiller, "Stock Prices, Earnings and Expected Dividends," *Journal of Finance*, 1987, 43 (3) (December). An examination between the complex patterns of stock prices, earnings, and dividends.

Jim Collins, *Good to Great*, New York: Harper Business, 2001 Chapter 3. A discussion of the hedgehog concept and R. J. Reynolds.

Niall Ferguson, *The Ascent of Money*, New York: Penguin Press, 2008. A note on the age of Discovery as an incentive to seek profits and a rate of return on investment.

Victor Fuchs, Alan Krueger and James Poterba, "Why Do Economists Disagree About Policy? The Roles of Beliefs about Parameters and Values," *Mimeo*, Stanford, CA: Stanford University, August 1997. The burden of the corporate income tax falls on the shareholders, workers, and customers of the corporation. How much each pays remains a debate.

Francesco Giavazzi and Marco Pagano, "Can Severe Fiscal Contractions be Expansionary? Tales of Two Small European Countries," *NBER Macroeconomics Annual*, 1990, 5: 75–111. A shift in expectations is critical in the case of Ireland.

Austin Goolsbee, "The Impact and Efficiency of the Corporate Income Tax: Evidence from State Organizational Form Datal," Working paper No. 9141. Cambridge, MA: National Bureau of Economic Research, September 2002. Corporate income taxes are a constant source of debate. This article links taxes to economic growth.

---

[22] Ibbotson Associates, Stocks, Bonds, Bills, and inflation, 2012 Yearbook.

John Steele Gordon, *An Empire of Wealth*, 2004, Harper Collins. Several essays focusing on the growth of the U.S. economy and the financial support behind that growth. One of the twelve must reads.

Robert E. Hall and Dale Jorgenson "Tax policy and Investment Behavior," *American Economic Review*, 1967, 57 (June): 391–414. A focus on the importance of tax policy as an influence on private investment behavior.

Terry A. Marsh and Robert C. Merton, "Dividend Behavior for the Aggregate Stock Market," *Journal of Business*, 1987, 60 (January): 1–40. An examination of linkages between changes in dividends after a sustainable period of earnings.

Ellen R. McGrattan and Edward C. Prescott, "Is the Stock Market Overvalued," Federal Reserve Bank of Minneapolis, *Quarterly Review*, 2000 (Fall): 20–40. Stock market valuation is a perennial headline. In this article, the authors note several adjustments to the NIPA data that include adjustments to the value of imputed services and capital stock.

Joe Peek and Eric Rosengren, "The Stock Market and Economic Activity," *New England Economic Review*, 1988 (May/June): 39–50. A view of the linkage of equity prices and the economy.

Harvey S. Rosen, *Public Finance*, McGraw-Hill Irwin, Seventh Edition, 2005, pp. 274–301. A focus on the elasticity (responsiveness) of real capital to changes in taxation.

Wall Street Journal, Barron's. The stories of present-day adventures and misadventures in equity valuations.

12

Sovereign Finance: When Economic Growth and Sovereign Debt Are a Mismatch

Germany's Weimar Republic is a spectacular example, but not the only one, of the mismatch between the burden of sovereign finance and economic growth. The Weimar Republic was Germany's government from 1919 to 1933, the period after World War I until the rise of Adolph Hitler and Nazi Germany. It was named after the town of Weimar where Germany's new government was formed by a national assembly after Kaiser Wilhelm II abdicated.

Following the end of World War One, the victorious Allies in 1919, led by France and England, imposed a massive reparations bill on Germany as part of the Treaty of Versailles. These reparations made it impossible for Germany to recover given how they impacted its economy.

On the supply side, Germany had lost its merchant marine, its overseas assets and most importantly, its coal-rich territories in the Saar region which were awarded to France. On the demand side, both fiscal and monetary policy were excessive in the size of liquidity/stimulus applied relative to the limited production capacity of the country. The result was soaring hyperinflation between the years 1921 and 1923. Both Germany and the Allies soon faced the reality that future German growth would be inadequate to pay that debt.[1]

---

[1] Equally, it is not clear to what extent Reichsbank chairman Rudolph E.A. von Havenstein was trying to create a crisis, to force the international community to lighten Germany's debts. The result of the hyperinflation was to wipe out German middle-class savings, the worst thing you can do, both politically and economically. Not surprising, the middle class voted for Hitler and the Nazis nine years later.

Into this crisis stepped Charles G. Dawes, an American banker who was charged in 1924 by the Allies to restructure the debt and reduce the size of the reparations. The so-called Dawes Plan reorganized the German central bank and led to the flow of U.S. financial capital into Germany to help restart the economy with German assets as collateral to help it pay reparations. German railways, its National Bank, and many industries were mortgaged as securities to stabilize its currency and back its debt—but even then, the plan was insufficient to meet the demands for debt payments. So, a new plan was put in place named after another American banker, Young, in 1929. The Young Plan lowered even more the reparations payments due. However, the imbalance of the inability to pay, as well as the unwillingness to pay on the part of Germany, reflects that basic imbalance between too much debt and not enough economy. The Weimar Republic was not the first, not the second, major Western European government to fall from the imbalance of spending and revenue.

Charles I, King of England, 1625–1649, and a believer in the divine right of kings, levied taxes in 1634 without the consent of Parliament.[2] Charles had inherited a poor state financial position after the wars conducted by Queen Elizabeth I and King James I. (This war debt inheritance will appear several more times in the year ahead.) Conflicts between Charles and Parliament were continuous. Finally, Charles dismissed Parliament and imposed custom duties and forced loans to pay the crown's debts. Eventually these conflicts erupted into the English Civil War (1642–1651) and Charles was executed in 1649. Clearly, the prerogatives of the King to wage war and spend money were out of line with the ability and willingness of the English people to support such spending.

Monarchs, and elected governments, frequently find themselves in situation where expensive wars cannot be financed by ordinary means. The wars of France's Louis XIV, especially the War of Spanish Succession, imposed a heavy debt burden on the state. As cited earlier, economist John Law emerged at this time with a plan to reduce the national debt with shares of an economic venture in the Mississippi lands of French North America. The

---

[2] Interestingly, the source of this fiscal finance comes down to the inflation indexation of tax burdens that the United States has partially addressed in recent years. The problem was that seventeenth-century inflation had wiped out the yield of traditional taxes such as feudal dues, which were set as fixed nominal amounts. Parliament would not modernize the tax system because it did not want to give the King more power. Taxes were hugely increased after Parliament regained control in 1642 following the English Civil War. Then in 1660, Parliament voted the King an almost-sufficient annual income, but 1660 s wars resulted in the Great Stop of 1672. Problem was solved thereafter by Charles II getting modest subsidies from Louis XIV, but more important, by excises on tobacco and sugar, both of which were growing like crazy in the colonies (sugar being slave-driven, tobacco not so much before 1688; they used indentured British/Irish criminals.).

problem of an imbalance between today's debt and future economic growth to pay for that debt appeared again.

Law had already been imprisoned in England for killing a man but escaped to Amsterdam. The Amsterdam banking system was too conservative to be taken in by him and so he moved on to several Italian states to propose a paper currency system. But it was in France that he made (or found) his mark during the years 1717–1720.

As the economic historian Niall Ferguson wrote: "Why was it in France that Law was given the chance to try his fiscal alchemy? The answer was that France's fiscal problems were especially desperate.[3]"

Law's private bank would issue paper money payable in specie (gold and silver). Paper money was intended to provide the liquidity to revive the French economy. Meanwhile, Law obtained a monopoly of commerce in Louisiana for a period of twenty-five years. Shares in the company were sold. Before long, the currency was debased in terms of the quantity of gold and silver and the monetary printing and reflation roared ahead.

To quote Neill Ferguson again: "Law had no clear idea where to stop.[4]" His incentives were to fuel an asset bubble where he would profit the most. More money was printed. Companies were bought by selling new shares. However, the inability of the Mississippi company to generate the profits implied in the stock offerings raised concerns. Inflation rose. The public wanted their banknotes paid in gold and silver. Law declared bank notes legal tender. Yet, the collapse could not be stopped.[5] The French monarchy's fiscal crisis remained unresolved for Louis XV and Louis XVI until bankruptcy precipitated the French Revolution.[6] Like Charles I of England, Louis XVI's financial failures ended in his execution.

In modern times, the issuance of debt in the short run, in Greece and Italy, more than the ability of the economy in the long run to repay debt generated the same mismatch of revenues and debt payments. In Greece, very low-interest costs allowed the country to run up large structural deficits to finance public sector jobs, pensions, and social benefits such that since 1993

---

[3] Niall Ferguson, *The Ascent of Money*, Penguin Press, 2008, p. 138.
[4] Niall Ferguson, *The Ascent of Money*, Penguin Press, 2008. P. 143.
[5] The Mississippi Bubble did much more damage than the simultaneous South Sea Bubble in England because Law's scam involved paper money while the South Sea Company's bubble was only in equity shares. Middle-class people got Law's banknotes, but generally avoided South Sea speculation. Also, there was a partial bailout of South Sea losers, but none in France; the Regent Phillppe Duke of Orleans who ruled while Louis XV was a child, rejoiced at having lightened the burden of state debts. Again, middle-class savings were wiped out in France; consequently, French kings could not finance their wars against England whereas Britain (with half the population) could finance wars against France, from 1751 through consols, a British security without a maturity date.
[6] Niall Ferguson, *The Ascent of Money*, Penguin Press, p. 154.

the debt to GDP ratio exceeded 100 percent. When the economy, based upon tourism and shipping was hit by the global financial crisis in 2007–2009 the imbalance between debt today and economic growth tomorrow reared its ugly head again. In addition, Greece misreported its budget statistics in 2010 and utilized financial means to hide its borrowing. Prime Minister George Papandreou's deficit of 6% in 2009 grew to 12.7% in 2010. In October, Papandreou announced a deficit of 12% which turned out to be 15%.[7]

In January 2010, the Greek Ministry of Finance published *Stability and Growth Program 2010*.[8] The report listed four main causes of the crisis: poor GDP growth, government debt and deficits, budget compliance, and data credibility. The first two listed say it all—not enough economic growth today to pay for debt issued in the past. The imbalance of debt and income remains the same as expressed by economists Mathew Higgins and Thomas Klitgaard, "*For several years prior to 2010, countries in the euro area periphery engaged in heavy borrowing from foreign private investors, allowing domestic spending to outpace incomes.*[9]"

However, all is not lost. The examples of Ireland and Canada stand in contrast as reviewed in the prior chapter. Finally, there is an important dynamic to the entire process of sovereign finance as identified by economist Ilse Mintz. He identified a two-stage process in the case of the loans provided under the Dawes Plan, which touched off the boom prior to 1924 and then inferior credit after.[10] Loans were made to Germany to help the country repay the reparations while the cash for loans was raised by bonds sold in the United States. Expectations for success were high among the Allies. However, Germany considered the Dawes Plan as temporary. The problem here is that the Dawes Plan was interpreted as a solution to the reparations issue, so the loans were well received at first. Yet, when the solution appeared increasingly

---

[7] Greece was allowed into the European Union (EU) in 1981 far before other countries of similar poverty, so it received huge handouts from EU funds. It thus acquired a "welfarist" mindset and never conducted the economic reforms it needed to, while its living standards soared to around the average of the EU, based on all the free money. Greece also entered the EU using some financial legerdemain which hid significant public debt and so satisfied the Maastricht Criteria (criteria based on economic indicators, that European Union (EU) member states must fulfil to enter the euro zone) through accounting fraud. This process then destabilized the euro, which has a bizarre mechanism of "Target 2" balances whereby members can run perpetual deficits, financed by the Deutsche Bundesbank (the German Central Bank)—over 1 trillion euros during June 2020. Greece's debit balance is only 25 billion euros currently but was much larger than that in 2010–12.

[8] Greek Ministry of Finance "Update of the Hellenic Stability and Growth Programme," January. 15, 2010.

[9] Matthew Higgins and Thomas Klitgaard, "Savings Imbalances and the Euro Area Sovereign debt crisis" Federal Reserve Bank of New York V 17 No 5.

[10] Ilse Mintz, "Deterioration in the Quality of Bonds Issued in the United States, 1920–1930 (New York: National Bureau of Economic Research, 1951).

as a failure to solve the reparations issue, the credits quickly depreciated in value. The gap between expectations and the reality of the outcome is an essential character of many sovereign debt crises. We can see that process in the story of sovereign debt in several emerging market countries during the post-World War II period.

Historical Curiosity or Shot Across the Bow?

"U.S. DefaultWould not Be the First Time" *Wall Street Journal* Nov. 8, 1995.

There are patterns of repayments of sovereign debt that send a warning shot. The inability of a sovereign to repay its debt in the coin of the realm is number one. This is characteristic of advanced and emerging market countries. For the United States, sovereign debt historically was to be paid in gold if demanded by bond holders. This follows the pattern of France for payment in specie. For many emerging markets, the payment was to be made in a foreign currency often the U.S. dollar.

In 1933, President Franklin Roosevelt ended the use of gold in everyday commerce, confiscated the gold, and made payments in paper currency. Effectively this allowed the Federal Reserve to increase the money supply which had been limited by the amount of gold that backed up the currency. In effect, this move allowed the Fed to supply more liquidity to the economy on the real side of the economy but was an effective default and capital loss to owners of public debt. In addition, contracts for payment in gold on demand were abrogated including the Liberty Bond issued by the federal government. Holdings in U.S. banks of gold by foreign entities, including a Swiss Bank, were confiscated and payment was made in gold. The irony was that these contracts and gold holdings were made to avoid debasement. Bond payments, meanwhile, were made in dollars, without a gold link. Gold was revalued from $20 to $35, effectively a 40% percent default.

In essence, the obligations of the U.S. government, as in France years before, were repudiated.

> It is very tempting to a minister to employ such an expedient, as enables him to make a great figure during his administration, without overburdening the people with taxes, or exciting any immediate clamours against himself. ***The practice, therefore, of contracting debt will almost infallibly be abused, in every government.*** It would scarcely be more imprudent to give a prodigal

son a credit in every banker's shop in London, than to impower a statesman to draw bills, in this manner, upon posterity.[11]

* * *

In 1971, President Nixon initiated a second default of the U.S. sovereign debt as part of a policy response to rising inflation. Nixon's economic moves included wage and price controls, an import surcharge to reduce the trade deficit, and the unilateral cancellation of the direct international convertibility of the U.S. dollar to gold. This effectively ended the Bretton Woods system which was based on the concept that balance of payments accounts would be settled in gold at fixed exchange rates. The Bretton Woods system of monetary management established the rules for commercial and financial relations among the United States, Canada, Western European countries, Australia, and Japan after the 1944 Bretton Woods Agreement. It was the first example of a fully negotiated monetary order intended to govern monetary relations among independent states. This balance of payments would be redeemable in gold from the U.S. government. However, un Nixon, U.S. debts were no longer payable in gold and this was effectively a default by the U.S. government that impacted the central banks.[12]

Sovereign debts, when faced with the inability of an economy to pay those debts, will be devalued or defaulted no matter if the debt is issued by the sovereign in its own coin of the realm.

Keynes—Economic Consequences of the Peace[13]

The highly influential British economist John Maynard Keynes was a critic of the Treaty of Versailles because it paid almost no attention whatever to the economic future of Europe. He clearly saw that, as we said earlier, the reparations (debt) imposed today were inconsistent with the ability of the economy to pay the debt tomorrow.

The Treaty included no provisions for the economic rehabilitation of Europe,—nothing to make the defeated Central Powers into good neighbors, nothing to stabilize the new states of Europe, nothing to reclaim Russia.

---

[11] David Hume, Essays, "Moral, Political, Literacy," Essay IX of *Public Credit*. 1777.
[12] This default was less so than in 1933. Everyone knew that Bretton Woods was a makeshift gold standard, and it had been breaking apart since the early 1960s. Unlike in 1933, only central banks could get gold, whose value was fixed at $35. The initial change pushed the official value only to $42. Anyway, there was no default to real people, only central banks.
[13] John Maynard Keynes, *Economic Consequences of the Peace*, MacMillan & CO. London 1919.

Nor did it promote in any way a compact of solidarity among the Allies themselves; no arrangement was reached at Paris for restoring the disordered finances of France and Italy, or to adjust the systems of the Old World and the New World.

The Council of Four (Britain, France, the United States, and Italy) paid no attention to these issues, being preoccupied with other concerns. France's Prime Minister Georges Clemenceau wanted to crush the economic life of his enemy Germany; England's Prime Minister Lloyd George wanted a quick deal that he could bring home that would pass muster for a week, America's President Woodrow Wilson was preoccupied with what was just and right in his view of a more generous peace and post-WWI cooperation (be more specific), and Italy's Prime Minister Vittorio Emanuele Orlando came away disappointed without additional territory. It is an extraordinary fact that the fundamental economic problems of a Europe starving and disintegrating before their eyes was the one area in which it was impossible to arouse the interest of the Four. Reparation was their main excursion into the economic field. They settled it as a problem of politics, and from every point of view except that of the economic future of the nations whose destiny they were charting.

Something Has to Give, Something Will Give

The Warning sign: Issue debt more than the potential of the economy to support those payments.

The English Experience in Fiscal Stimulus: Actions have consequences.

In 1963, Chancellor of the Exchequer Reginald Maudling's initial budget was designed to create a "dash for growth" and to achieve a 4% growth target without inflationary consequences. A year later, in his final budget, the reality of the economic situation was apparent—he proposed increasing taxes and acknowledged that the balance of payments and sterling's exchange rate in the Bretton Woods system were both under severe pressure.[14]

Several years later, Prime Minister Harold Wilson's Chancellor of the Exchequer, James Callaghan, repeatedly said that sterling would not be

---

[14] This problem could have been solved if Prime Minister Winston Churchill had authorized in 1952 called "Operation ROBOT" (an acronym derived from the names of its originators) by which Britain would float the exchange rate and thereby escape the perpetual exchange rate crises of Bretton Woods. Richard Butler (Chancellor of the Exchequer) the Treasury and the Bank of England wanted to do this, but Churchill took the advice of Anthony Eden and Harold Macmillan, members of Churchill's Conservative Party but left-of-center ministers of his cabinet. British history from 1952 to 1979 would have been very different with Operation ROBOT.

devalued. When it was clear to all that it would, Harold Wilson swapped him with Roy Jenkins—Callaghan becoming Home Secretary and Jenkins becoming Chancellor. The devaluation from $2.80 to $2.40 took place in 1967 and bought some time for the economy. In his 1970 budget, Jenkins did alter tax allowances to remove two million people from being taxed when income tax was equivalent to 47.5p in the £, but otherwise he did not adopt any significant expansionary measures.[15] This went down in history as an object lesson that if you do not expand the economy before a general election you lose it.

In 1971–2 Prime Minister Edward Heath's Chancellor, Anthony Barber expanded the fiscal stance and the money supply to deal with growing unemployment, causing the so-called "Barber" boom. This caused a growth in inflation and the policy was consequently reversed: the notorious U-turn. Between 1971 and 1973 Bank of England lending rose from £71 million to £1,332 million. Heath's government also introduced wage and pay freezes to help deal with inflation.

In the experience of several nations (France, Weimar Germany, United States, and the United Kingdom) the fundamental problem is that, over time, debt issuance more than the economy's potential to support those payments will lead to change and in several cases to sovereign default.

In the Short Run All Appears Calm

The U.S. experience since 2009 illustrates the grand assumption that federal spending financed by debt finance appears costless for now—no inflation, lower interest rates, and a stronger currency. But is that true over time?

In the short run, the initial issuance of debt takes place in the context of excess capacity in the economy and financial system along with market and public expectations that are based upon the previous period of experience.

Fiscal and monetary expansion takes place with the expectation that public policy will generate economic growth. Inflation tends to lag the fiscal and monetary stimulus. The central government's credit is taken for granted as good. For the French, Weimar, and British examples, fiscal and monetary stimulus did work in the short run but further printing of paper money altered expectations especially when economic growth failed to show up. Too much money was chasing too few goods. Moreover, the presence of refinancing risk began to appear as interest rates rose and the value of the

---

[15] Jenkins also in 1968 imposed a top rate of tax of 135%, 27 shillings in the pound, which presented a significant disincentive to work and an incentive for tax avoidance.

paper currency began to depreciate. As we had said, printing money based on speculation—the prosperity of Mississippi territories—cannot be sustained.

These results emphasize another basic principle—markets are related. The prices of goods (inflation) is reflected in interest rates (the price of credit), foreign exchange rates, and equity values—the values of stock ownership in the Mississippi Company for example.

Dynamic Process of Stimulus, Change, and Market Interactions

Context matters. In the short run in an economy with excess capacity, a fiscal stimulus, in the context of bond finance, of additional sovereign spending will increase aggregate demand in the economy. A central bank, by engaging in asset purchases, will buy sovereign debt issues at the going prices. Policy thus creates conditions for a horizontal demand curve for sovereign debt at the given nominal interest rate target. The current central bank policy in Japan, the United States, and the European Central Bank is following this approach.

In the short run, inflation remains low as the increase in aggregate demand places little pressure on resource markets (as evidenced by the high levels of unemployment and modest wage increases in both the U.S. and Euro area experiences).

Central banks set nominal interest rates. But business investment and consumer spending respond to the balance between the real interest rate, as a cost of capital, and the expected rate of return on the investment. In the current 2020–21 environment business investment rises and housing demand is very strong.

Initially, the exchange rate value rises as expectations for economic recovery increase as in 2020 with the rise in the U.S. trade-weighted dollar. Expectations for the economic recovery also led to appreciation in equity values in the United States in the first half of 2020 like a reprise of the rise in the value of the Mississippi Company under John Law.

Over time, however, as continued fiscal stimulus is matched by continued bond buying by a central bank, expectations start to turn. The Federal Reserve Bank of New York's Nowcast for the current, 2020, third quarter GDP growth rate was 14.6% on August 7th and by November 6th the forecast for the fourth quarter had dropped to 2.9%. Meanwhile the break-even ten-year inflation rate rose from 0.9% on April 1 to 1.72% as of November.

For resource allocation, below market nominal interest rates, as a policy target of a central bank, will aggravate the misallocation of resources and result in an overinvestment in housing, repeating the pattern set in 2005–2007, and in the American experience of the boom-and-bust period of railroads after the Civil War. Overinvestment was a characteristic of the Mississippi Company as well as for infrastructure in Greece.

The ability to refinance the existing debt, and thereby allowing the government to escape the budget constraint requires that the real growth of the economy exceeds the real rate of interest on the debt. In Diamond's overlapping generations model, the debt of the generation today can be borne by the next generation if the real rate of growth of the economy exceeds the real rate of interest on the debt.[16] This coincides with the observation that so many debt crises and near misses have been associated with a recession in the home country or a global rise of interest rates from abroad.[17]

While nominal interest rates may remain suppressed, the issuance of more debt raises the burden of the debt. Interest expense rises as more debt is being financed, so federal government interest expenses increase relative to economic growth.

From the Congressional Budget Office's Long-Term Budget Outlook

> Deficits. Even after the effects of the 2020 coronavirus pandemic fade, deficits in coming decades are projected to be large by historical standards. In CBO's projections, deficits increase from 5 percent of gross domestic product (GDP) in 2030 to 13 percent by 2050—larger in every year than the average deficit of 3 percent of GDP over the past 50 years.
>
> Debt. By the end of 2020, federal debt held by the public is projected to equal 98 percent of GDP.
>
> The projected budget deficits would boost federal debt to 104 percent of GDP in 2021, to 107 percent of GDP (the highest amount in the nation's history) in 2023, and to 195 percent of GDP by 2050. High and rising federal debt makes the economy more vulnerable to rising interest rates and, depending on how that debt is financed, rising inflation. The growing debt burden also raises borrowing costs, slowing the growth of the economy and national income, and it increases the risk of a fiscal crisis or a gradual decline in the value of Treasury securities.

Interest expense as a percent of GDP rose from 1.6% in 2020 to 6.5% over the period 2041 to 2050. Interest expense contributes to most of the total deficit over the 2030 to 2050 period.

---

[16] Peter A. Diamond, "National Debt in a Neoclassical Growth Model," American Economic Review 55 (December 1965): 1126–1150.

[17] "Emerging economies face rising interest rates as capital flows ebb," Financial Times October 6, 2020.

"Woof! Woof! This Cat Just Won't Bark" by Milton Friedman *Wall Street Journal* **May 16, 1995.**

For the monetary champion Milton Friedman, a cat's failure to bark reflects the failure of elected representatives to fit their talk of restraining spending to their actions. Yet, this is not surprising since policymakers have a bias toward deficits in the conduct of fiscal policy. The benefits of high government spending and low taxes are direct and evident.[18] The costs of higher future taxes, inflation, and low real purchases are indirect and less obvious and are likely to fall on some future generational cohort. In addition, there is usually disagreement among policymakers on how to divide the burden of reducing the deficit and this may delay fiscal reform, as is now evident in the wake of the 2020 U.S. election.[19]

Economists Auerbach, Gale, Orszag, and Potter[20] argue that the federal government will need to make large adjustments to its budget. These adjustments include spending reductions, tax increases, and implicit or explicit reneging on government debt through default or hyperinflation. But adjustments are difficult. Disagreement about how to divide the burden of reducing the deficit can cause a delay in fiscal reform. Each group tries to get the other group to bear a disproportionate share of the burden. There is also the intergenerational problem—taxes paid by future generations to support spending today.

A credit reallocation issue also exists in the short run. For a given supply of credit there remains a crowding out effect—government bonds are financed through mandated bank holdings of government debt which do not allow for private lending through the banking system. However, over the last twenty years there has been a continued increase of shadow banking growth which was not under the regulatory review of authorities. This system often supplies financial credit at certain times that runs counter to the tight credit reigns imposed by regulators. We saw evidence of this in an earlier chapter. The bank loan and deposit ratio fell dramatically in post-2009 as capital requirements were raised and private loans fell as a share of deposits. This reallocation of credit by policymakers can be explicit, as in the South Seas Bubble Act in England, or in the Mississippi Bubble in France.

---

[18] James M. Buchanan and Richard E. Wagner, *Democracy in Deficit: The Political Legacy of Lord Keynes*, Academic Press, New York, 1977.

[19] Alberto Alesina and Allan Drazen, "Why Are Stabilizations Delayed?" American Economic Review 81 (December 1991): 1170–1188.

[20] Alan J. Auerbach, William G. Gale, Peter R. Orszag, and Samra R. Potter, "Budget Blues: The Fiscal Outlook and Options for Reform." In Henry Aaron, James Lindsay, and Pietro Nivola, eds., *Agenda for a Nation*, 109–143. Washington, D.C.: Brookings Institution. 2003.

Policy changes, thereby, become forced change—a crisis happens rather than a smooth transition as witnessed by Greece and Argentina.[21] Possible outcomes include a contraction in fiscal policy, a large decline in aggregate demand, a possible effective default on debt, higher inflation, or a depreciated currency. Argentina has experienced seven currency devaluations in the last twenty years. In November 2020 equity market prices have declined sharply.

The Greek Marathon—of Financial Crisis and Reform

After the global financial crisis 0f 2007–2009, a marathon series of loans were made to Greece in 2010, 2012, and 2015 during negotiations for three economic adjustment programs. Yet, the source of the Greek crisis goes before the global financial crisis. From 1981 to 2006, Greek budget deficits ran above 3% of GDP. Once the euro currency came into place, Greece was able to finance the deficit at low-interest rates as capital flowed into the country.[22] Federal spending in Greece was devoted to military expenditures, public sector jobs, and pensions. The issue is a classical problem—very evident also in the classic period of Rome—stretching the state spending beyond the ability of the economy to support it.[23] The global financial crisis was particularly harsh on tourism and shipping which are two sectors critical to the Greek economy. The solutions applied were the traditional fiscal and monetary nostrums with a heavy dose of economic reforms. On the fiscal front, taxes were raised and spending cut. On the monetary front loans, were provided by the International Monetary Fund (IMF), Eurogroup,[24] and the European Central Bank. A reduction in the private debt owed to banks was also put into place. Between 2009 and 2017, Greek debt to GDP grew from 127 to 179% of GDP.

The price of unsustainable deficits is summed up by economist David Romer.[25]

---

[21] "Argentina, Running Low on Dollars, Faces Fresh Economic Turmoil," October 15, 2020, Wall Street Journal.

[22] Paul Krugman, "European Crisis Realities." *The New York Times* February 25, 2012.

[23] Free bread was a staple of Rome's aid to the populace hence the phrase "bread and circuses" has come to mean the gifts needed to maintain popular support. In true Italian fashion, the bread was supplemented later to include wine and olive oil.

[24] The Eurogroup is term for informal meetings of the finance ministers of the Eurozone—those member states of the European Union (EU) which have adopted the euro as their official currency. The group has 19 members. It exercises political control over the currency and related aspects of the EU's monetary union such as the Stability and Growth Pact.

[25] David Romer, *Advanced Macroeconomics*, McGraw Hill Irwin, third edition, 2006. P. 605.

Forced change is likely to take the form of a crisis rather than a smooth transition… Typically the crisis involves a sharp contraction in fiscal policy, a large decline in aggregate demand, major repercussions in capital and foreign exchange markets, and perhaps default of the government debt.

The implications of fiscal overexpansion and then rectitude are pervasive and impact the markets for goods, credit, equity values, and foreign exchange.

The Sovereign Bond Market—Another Playground in the Credit Market

Commentaries on fiscal policy (taxes, bond issuance, and spending) unfortunately devolve into the pattern of political commentary—lots of opinions, few, if any, facts. We express the demand and supply of government debt as the driving forces of bond prices and yields. As in any serious investigation of any subject, a framework is necessary.

"**Bond Markets no Longer Care Very Much About Deficits.**" *Financial Times* **November 22, 2018.**

A Framework for Analysis

Private sector demand for sovereign debt is a function of expectations of national income, expected real returns (reflecting interest rate and inflation risks), expected exchange rates, and private wealth. Meanwhile, there are significant purchases from the public sector, the Federal Reserve, and other central banks. Finally, there is the mandated holding of U.S. Treasury debt by private banks which is insensitive to interest rates. Other than the exercising of swap agreements, the Fed does not own much non-Treasury sovereign debt.

On the supply side, the supply of sovereign debt is a function of political goals, national income, interest rates and inflation, expected exchange rates, and national wealth.

To illustrate the dynamics of this framework, consider that pattern of euro area sovereign debt in the 2003–2017 period (Fig. 12.1). Political uncertainty in Italy, and then again in Spain, Portugal, and Greece, led the euro to decline relative to the dollar.

But what made Germany different? Germany made a commitment to fiscal conservatism. The expected future path of fiscal policy intimated a limited

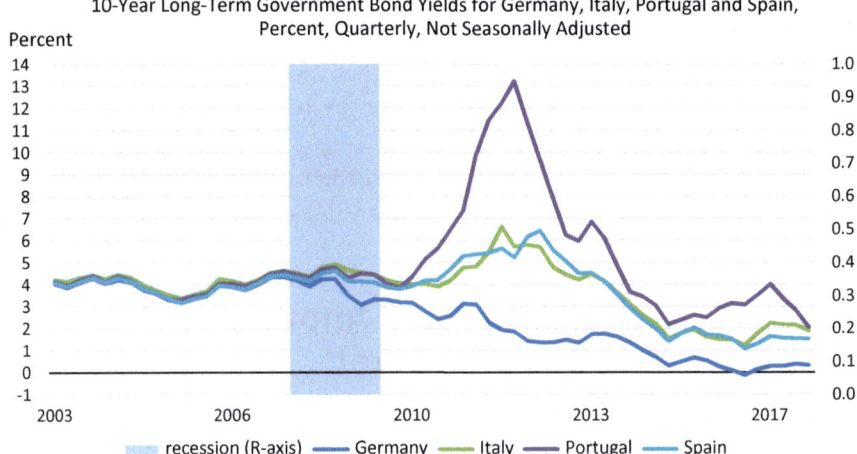

Fig. 12.1 Long-term Euro Government Yields

supply of sovereign debt. For a given demand, a limited supply of German debt meant lower yields. As for the turnaround, consider that Portugal had a budget surplus by 2016 (thereby reducing expectations of future bond supply) while Greece was just cited with a credit upgrade (see "A Greek Economic Revival," *Wall Street Journal* January. 29, 2020) and their yields fell to an all-time low.

USD/Euro Budget Deficits and Growth: The Benefit of Exorbitant Privilege

Fiscal deficits are a function of the tax base and the rate of growth by income. This imparts a countercyclical pattern of rising fiscal deficits when growth slows, and unemployment rates rise. Deficits also respond to rising interest rates which tend to be procyclical.

When we consider our framework for the demand for U.S. sovereign debt, we note the importance of both global private and central bank demand. For private investors, expectations in recent years have been for better relative growth in the United States. They believe there is a greater likelihood of debt repayment and so default risk has declined relative to risks abroad (recall Greece, Portugal, Italy, Spain).

In addition, expected inflation in the United States has not accelerated contrary to many forecasts. In an odd twist, the relatively higher inflation in the United States increased the attraction of U.S. debt since the inflation was also accompanied by expectations of economic growth. In contrast, the lower European inflation and deflation raised concerns about the sustainability of growth. Investors were concerned about the ability of these nations to pay off their debt without a resort to exchange rate depreciation, higher taxes, and higher inflation—the usual nostrums of deficit reduction. Interestingly, Greece had reduced taxes (and regulation) to promote growth and their default premium has subsequently declined.

What We Anticipate Seldom Occurs: But What We Least Expect Generally Happens.—Benjamin Disraeli

Central bank demand has altered the supply and demand calculus in the sovereign debt market and helps explain the pattern of lower yields. Essentially, the sovereign debt market is no longer a free marketplace where supply and demand for sovereign debt reflect the profit incentive of private agents.

The three largest buyers of U.S. sovereign debt are the three central banks—the People's Bank of China, the Bank of Japan, and the Federal Reserve. In addition, increases in capital requirements of banks offset a significant portion of the supply of federal debt as banks will hold a large portion of capital requirements in the form of Treasury debt thus limiting the floating supply of such Treasury debt. All three of these central banks focus on growth and exchange rate stability but not profit-maximization. Central banks also do not mark to market their portfolios (the current market value of an asset compared the asset's value under current market conditions). So sovereign bond price adjustments are partial, delayed, and incomplete in the marketplace.

Moreover, the conduct of a central bank does alter the demand and supply balance in the sovereign debt market. At the start, note that the targets for these three central banks highlight the integration of growth, interest rates, and exchange rate markets that is the core of market pricing.

Given this focus on exchange rates and economic growth, the demand for sovereign debt drives nominal debt returns below what a purely private market would determine. For example, from 2010 to 2018 note the correlation of lower yields and the more than five-fold increase in Federal Reserve Treasury holdings and therefore its balance sheet. Whatever the Fed's motivations for promoting growth at 2%, observe the collateral damage to free-market pricing in the Treasury market.

Although only temporary, Federal Reserve buying of T-bills in recent years, aimed to assure an ample supply of reserves, especially in September 2019 in relation to an uptick in the repo rate. At that time, the Fed was having some difficulty with dealer positions and assessing the appropriate volume of reserve demand. This reinforces the point that Fed purchases alter the ability of the private market to identify a sustainable, risk-free Treasury bill rate to serve as a benchmark for pricing risk-based assets—bank loans, commercial paper, and home mortgage rates.

Central bank behavior has altered the character of the sovereign market relative to its behavior in prior years. It is not surprising that yields have remained consistently lower than many analysts have forecasted since private market fundamentals are only a part, perhaps a small part, of interest rate determination. This behavior is reinforced by new bank regulations that demand the holding of minimum default risk-free (but not interest rate or inflation risk-free assets).[26] Such regulation may not be intended to directly lower interest rates and make government debt easier and less costly to finance. But some private market investors suspect that, in fact, these policies have exactly that effect and have led to the underpricing of risk in the private marketplace.

John BullCan Stand Many Things, but He Cannot Stand Two Per Cent.— Walter Bagehot

With private corporate debt priced off sovereign yields, it is not surprising that corporate debt appears underpriced relative to risk. But when you follow the breadcrumbs, it becomes disingenuous for central bankers to complain about the underpricing of risk in the corporate sector when, the corporate sector's pricing reflects an underpricing of sovereign debt benchmarks.

Far, not so Good

So, what about Benjamin Disraeli? By examining the markets, the issue before us is the mispricing of sovereign debt relative to the pricing in the sovereign marketplace prior to 2008. Unfortunately, the character of the marketplace is simply not the same. Most sovereign debt demand no longer primarily reflects the private market motivations of risk and reward, but instead public sector demands from central banks, as well as the regulatory commands that banks buy sovereign debt as risk-free assets.

From the view of a central bank, there may not appear anything wrong in the attempt to stimulate growth with below market interest rates. However,

---

[26] Once again, reminding we (us) the Federal government has defaulted twice in the twentieth century on its debt.

from the view of a private investor and a financial institution, the pricing of credit is distorted and leads to the misallocation of real and financial capital. Too low administered interest rates misallocate capital. The cost to finance is low relative to the expected rate of return on the investment which results, over time, in too much financial flows to unproductive investments—housing in the 2000s, railroads in the post-Civil War, and direct government interventions such as the Mississippi Bubble and the Darien scheme.[27] Today much of the credit market for student loans or housing is heavily influenced by government policy.

All this causes a fundamental mispricing of credit and a misallocation of real and financial capital in the economy. The longer the mispricing by the central banks continues the greater the squandering of real resources on projects whose real return on capital invested is below the efficient allocation determined in a private market environment.

Are the actions of central banks fighting the tides of slower population and productivity gains to sustain a pace of economic growth above what would be set in a private marketplace and therefore the underpricing of risk and the misallocation of capital? If potential GDP growth is truly below 2% according to the Congressional Budget Office (CBO), then what distortions are to be gained by attempting to achieve a higher pace of growth?

Pricing Federal Debt in a Four Sector Framework

Private sector demand for sovereign debt is a function of expectations of national income, expected real returns (reflecting interest rate and inflation risks), expected exchange rates and the availability of alternative financial returns. Unfortunately, the increased mandate for banks to hold U.S. Treasuries as reserves has distorted the Treasury market pricing since 2009.

On the supply side, we view the supply of sovereign debt as a function of perceived policy desires and any limits that may arise from the cost of finance (interest rates and exchange rate risks).

---

[27] The Darien scheme was a direct intervention by the government of Scotland to invest in Panama in the late 1600s.

Sovereign Debt Finance: The Assumption of Unlimited Demand—Until It is Not!

The supply and demand for sovereign debt reflect the same market forces as other forms of credit with one additional dominant and exogenous factor—political decision making. Moreover, the influence of international markets is even more apparent than in the past.

Sovereign debt is not issued (supply) into an unlimited market (demand) at fixed real interest rates, inflation expectations, and foreign exchange rates. Instead, the issuance of sovereign debt alters market prices in other markets, for example interest rates. Moreover, sovereign debt must compete in the market with corporate debt and equity finance and hence changes the relative rates of return for these assets as well. In recent years, low sovereign interest rates are credited, in part, with rising equity values—TINA, there is no alternative.

The Dynamic Effect: Expectations Altered

Increased sovereign debt supply, moreover, shifts expectations of future debt supply and debt quality and future tax burdens.[28] In this context enters the latest CBO estimates of rising future deficits that alter expectations of future burdens. For CBO, Federal debt held by the public is projected to increase to 98% of GDP in 2020 (compared with 79% in 2019 and 35% in 2007, before the start of the last recession). It could exceed 100% in 2021 and rise to 107% in 2023, the highest in the nation's history.[29] CBO estimates also indicate deficits of $12.9 Trillion over the period from 2021 to 2030 compared to $6.5 Trillion over the period 2021 to 2025.[30]

The increased bond finance, in the context that the deficits will continue and that they will increase over time, sets up a dynamic that opens to door to feedback and repercussion effects. Questions arise as to the ability to finance rising deficits in a period of declining potential growth. This situation would lead to high future interest rates and inflation risks and a lower exchange rate. While the extent of any feedback and repercussion effects may not measure up to the issues of Italy or Greece, and certainly, hopefully, not Argentina, the risk for financial markets will tilt in that direction.[31]

---

[28] Robert Barro, *Macroeconomics*, John Wiley & Sons, 1984 New York, pp. 380- 387.
[29] Congressional Budget Office, "An Update to the Budget Outlook: 2020 to 2030," September 2020.
[30] Op. cit, CBO.
[31] The highest debt/GDP ratios where the debt has subsequently been brought down are 250%, by Britain in 1819 and 1945, after global wars. In 1819, Liverpool brought it down by severe fiscal austerity, without inflation, and with growth accelerating owing to the Industrial Revolution.

The question becomes can this debt be serviced given the expected growth (ability) of the economy to generate the revenues to pay for that debt? Greece and Italy in the years 2010 to 2014 raised questions of their ability to finance that debt given their projected growth rates. They could not without the intervention of the European Union. Other nation's such as Argentina recorded a serious default.

For the United States, today's debt issuance is expected to be paid by future economic growth. Yet here, when deficits are put into the context of an economy's potential growth, the latest CBO estimates present a significant problem. The CBO projects the U.S. economy's potential rate of growth for is 1.6% over the next 30 years in contrast to 2.5% for the period from 1990 to 2019. The debt to GDP ratio will reach 195% by 2050 CBO says.[32]

The CBO says, "There is no set tipping point at which a fiscal crisis becomes likely or imminent." This emphasizes that estimates such as CBO's must be taken in context with interest rates, exchange rates, inflation expectations, and capital flows. As for the latter, the demand for sovereign U.S. Treasury debt has undergone two changes in direction since 2015. Foreign Treasury debt holdings rose in 2018–2019 after declining during the 2016–2018 period. China and Japan remain the major foreign buyers.[33]

The Federal Reserve has pursued a policy of quantitative tightening, thereby reducing its holdings of Treasury debt for a brief period in 2018. The impact on market interest rates and economic expectations was significant. Higher interest rates and lower economic growth expectations signaled that market volatility was high given the position of Treasury deficits. In addition, the modest upward move in rates and the negative economic reaction indicates that the U.S. Treasury market, in the private marketplace, may not be as deep or liquid as historically portrayed. Recent developments have signaled that the fiscal consolidation in the Euro community in the 2010 expansion has given way to increased fiscal deficits.

In 1945, Prime Minister Clement Attlee and his successors imposed an inflationary devaluation of savings on the British middle classes, causing 30 years of relative economic decline. Japan now has a ratio slightly above 250% and they have not demonstrated the ability to bring it down.

[32] "CBO Downgrades Long-Term Projections of Economic Growth" *Wall Street Journal* September 22, 2020.

[33] *U.S. Treasury International Capital Report*, June 28, 2019.

Growth Matters: Rising Interest Rates, Diminished Growth Expectations

Debt finance is conducted in the context of a set of economic expectations—especially the pace of growth. Our focus is the balance, or imbalance, between the amount of the interest paid on debt (a flow) and the growth of the economy (a flow) to meet those interest payments. The debt (stock) to GDP (flow) ratio is misleading. In recent years, growth expectations for European economies have remained low while expectations of U.S. growth have moderated but remain higher than that of the European Union. It was no surprise then that the markets for U.S. debt and equities had difficulty in 2018 dealing with rising Federal Reserve policy rates in an environment of declining growth expectations but was still able to attract capital inflows from abroad.

What is the Character of Economic Factors and Sovereign Debt?

With a simple framework and anticipating feedback and repercussion effects, we can anticipate significant bidirectional causality between major variables. In the basic bond market, the impact of an increase in Treasury finance would be a rise in market rates, ceteris paribus.

Yet, the issuance of federal debt also takes up some of the available loanable funds in the marketplace and diminishes the supply of funds to the private market. Also, bank lending has declined relative to deposits post-2009 regulation and additional bank reserves are tied up in the ownership of Treasury debt rather than being lent to private entities. Estimates of a crowding out effect are not consistent over time and across different study approaches. In one study, for example, economists Eric Engen and R. Glenn Hubbard find that the effect is quite small.[34]

As evident from the Treasury International Capital (TIC) reports, taxes, exchange rates, and foreign capital flows, along with politics, influence the supply of funds coming in from abroad. Feedback and repercussion effects indicate that as any of these factors change in response to increasing federal deficits in an era of declining potential economic growth, then continual adjustments in the financial markets will occur. The precedent of Greece and Italy provides evidence of future effects over time.

---

[34] Eric Engen and R. Glenn Hubbard "Federal Government Debt and Interest Rates," National Bureau of Economic Research Working Paper No. 10681, August 2004.

Changes and Dynamic Character of Sovereign Finance and the Economy

Change is a constant aspect of fiscal policy. The biggest uncertainty is future policy. Lawmakers enact policies different from the ones the CBO assumes as spending restraint and tax policy is altered, sometimes significantly, as federal administrations change. Temporary tax policies are often extended, spending limitations imposed, and then dropped.

Over time, tax policy impacts incentives as well as the longer-run pattern of labor force participation and productivity and thereby future economic growth. Changes in labor force participation and productivity impact potential growth rates for the economy. In addition, age distribution and immigration are important factors.[35] For the CBO, the assumption of interest rates is important to the outlook. One percent higher level of rates has a significant impact on budget deficit estimates. Finally, decisions around the length of the maturity for Treasury debt will impact relative interest rates along the yield curve and the total impact on interest rates.

Debt Monetization

How much does a central bank monetizing and sterilizing the Treasury debt impact interest rates, inflation, and overall economic growth? The issue here revolves around the pace of growth and the level of interest rates. If the real after-tax yield on government bonds is less than the growth rate of real income, except during brief disinflationary periods, then central governments could sustain deficit finance levels over time. Problems arise when real economic growth falls short of expectations and real interest rates so that budget deficits are no longer sustainable. According to economists R.G. Ibbotson and R.A. Sinquefield, the real after-tax yield on government securities has been nowhere near (it has ben much less) the 3.0% per annum average rate of growth of real income over the same years.[36]

Unfortunately, this favorable comparison may fail going forward in a period of lower potential growth and rising deficit finance. However, under certain conditions, the government can issue debt and roll it over indefinitely.[37]

---

[35] Congressional Budget Office, *Long-Term Budget Outlook*, September 2020, pp. 18–23.
[36] R. G. Ibbotson and R.A Sinquefield, "Stocks, Bonds, Bills, and Inflation: The Past and the Future," 1982 edition, Charlottesville, VA., The Financial Analysts Research Foundation, 1982.
[37] Laurence Ball, Douglas Elmendorf, and N. Gregory Mankiw, "The Deficit Gamble," Journal of Money Credit and Banking 30 (November 1998): pp. 699–720.

The Impact of Growth, Interest Rates, and Inflation: A Change in the Pattern

Unfortunately, history has a way of evolving over time. Recent years provide a signal for change. Expectations for growth, interest rates, and inflation will impact the private demand for sovereign debt. But on the supply side, there has been a break in the link between economic growth and deficit finance as seen in Fig. 12.2. Traditionally, deficit finance rises as a percent of GDP as the economy weakens. But that is not the story from the period of 2016 to 2020 as deficits as a percent of GDP increased even while the economy expanded.

Is it possible that deficit finance over the economic cycle has changed as the supply of sovereign debt increases relative to the ability of the economy to support that debt in contrast to the cyclical patterns of the past? Moreover, has the expansion of the Fed's balance sheet since 2010 enabled the economic impact of a rise in the federal deficit to be suppressed as interest rates remained low and inflation subdued?

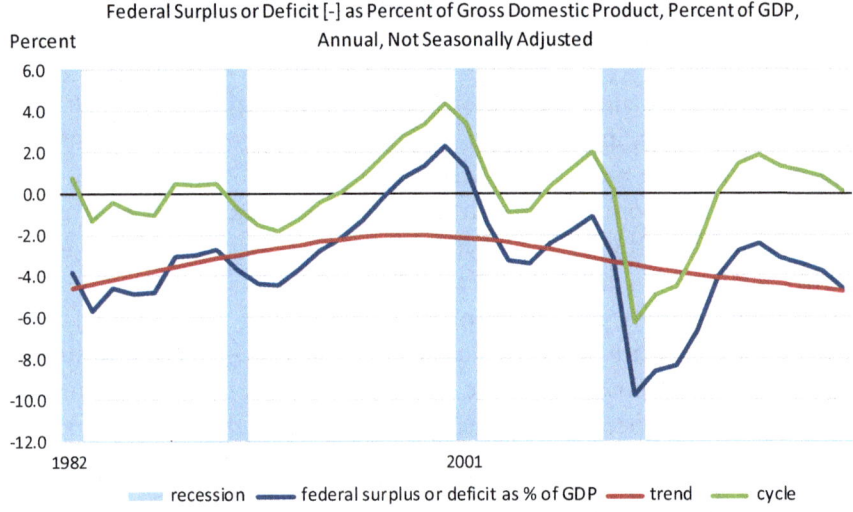

Fig. 12.2 U.S. Federal Budget Surplus/Deficit

Pricing Character of Sovereign Debt

Flatter Sovereign Yield Curve in the 2010 Expansion—Why?

It is not enough to observe that the yield curve has flattened or inverted or steepened. As analysts we must ask why and therefore, we return to our framework—an unhappy combination of private markets and public policy-making. Two graphs, one on the yield curve, one on term and risk premiums provide clues.

As Illustrated in Fig. 12.3, the yield curve, measured as the spread between the 10 year and 2-Year Treasury note yields, declined from 2014 on. Yet the pattern of a flatter yield curve has been in place throughout this expansion. We think of the demand for Treasury debt as a function of expected economic growth, expected inflation, interest rates, the dollar, wealth, and economic policy (specifically central bank policy here and abroad). In addition, there is the feedback loop to growth as well as implications for the allocation of economic resources and society and its influence on potential economic growth.

During the 2010 economic expansion, lower than expected inflation was a dominant private sector driver of the lower yield curve. Lowered inflation outcomes and inflation expectations reduced the term premium for the

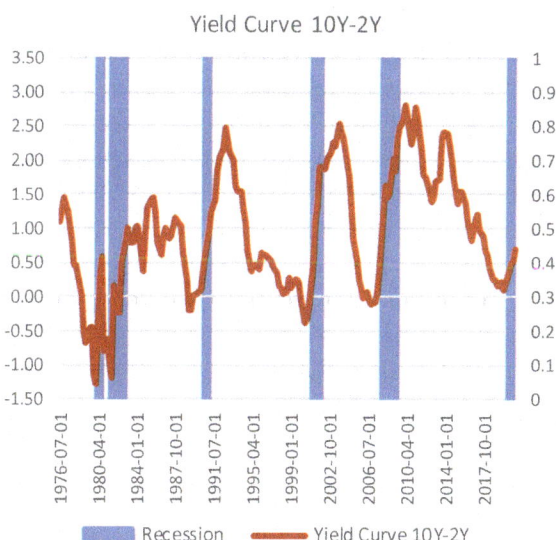

Fig. 12.3 Yield Curve

yield curve. This occurred despite the attempt in 2017–2018 by the Fed to normalize policy by raising the funds rate. This normalization effect on rates added to the pressure to flatten the yield curve as muted increases in measured inflation and inflation expectations reduced the inflation premium in long rates. In addition, the U.S. sovereign debt benefitted from the flight to safety that accompanied the European sovereign debt crisis in the middle of the 2010 expansion.

We can review the breakdown of the yield curve to study its components. Working backward from the existence of the yield curve, what information might be extracted from the pattern of a flatter yield curve? There may be two opposing interpretations. On the negative side, a flatter yield curve may be a signal of slower economic growth ahead.[38] Or a flatter yield curve would indicate to some that the flatter yield curve is not what you would expect if you were concerned about long term, federal deficit finance.[39]

Falling term premiums of U.S. Treasuries were a hallmark of the 2010 expansion. Coupon-bearing Treasury yields rose from their lows, but the term premium remained negative. When thinking about U.S. Treasury yields, it is sometimes useful to break them down into two components: a risk neutral yield (or the expected path of short-term interest rates) and a term premium (what investors demand to compensate them for the uncertainty associated with holding longer-dated Treasuries). Using one leading method for Treasury yield decomposition,[40] the 10-year Treasury breakdowns can be seen in the figure below, Fig. 12.4, which illustrates that the term premium fell for most of the 2010 expansion.

Furthermore, the Fed finished its buying spree just as other major central banks, such as the European Central Bank and the Bank of Japan, ramped up their own asset purchase programs. This spillover effect weighed on the term premium in the United States as investors seeking yield purchased additional U.S. Treasury debt.

We can split the behavior of the five-year Treasury yield curve into a term premium as shown in Fig. 12.4 and a risk neutral yield as the difference between the nominal yield and the term premium. The term premium has a distinct cyclical pattern—the uncertainty of holding longer-term debt peaks at times of recession and then continues to decline throughout the economic

---

[38] One study of the predictive power of the yield is T. Adrian, A. Estrella, and H.S. Shin, "Monetary Cycles, Financial Cycles and the Business Cycle," Federal Reserve Bank of New York Staff Report No. 421, January 2010.
[39] "Flatting Yield Curve Points Calm about US Budget Deficit," *Financial Times* February 26, 2018.
[40] T. Adrian, R K. Crump and E. Moench. (2013). "Pricing the Term Structure with Linear Regressions." Federal Reserve Bank of New York *Staff Report No. 340*. Thanks to my former colleague Azhar Iqbal for the initial work on this point.

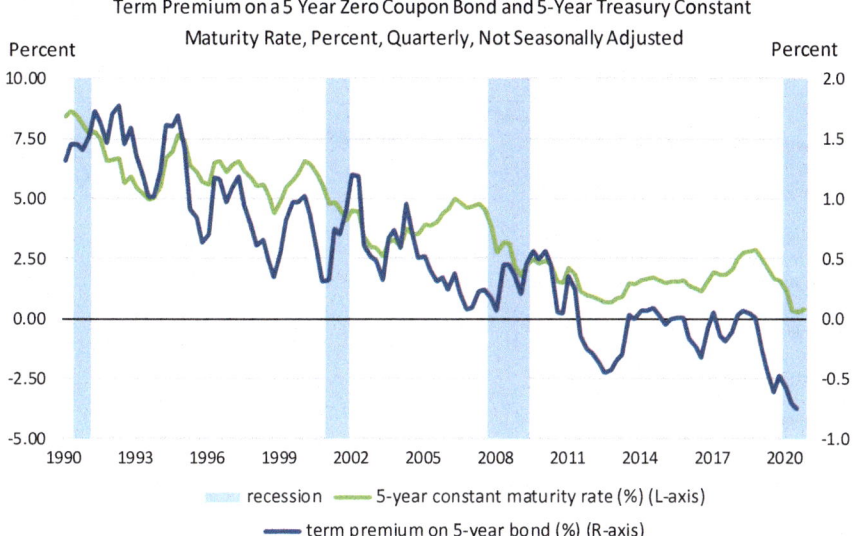

Fig. 12.4 U.S. 5 Year Treasury Rate and Term Premium

expansion. Since the early 1990s the term premium on five-year Treasury debt has continued to decline on a secular basis. Yet, there has also been a cyclical pattern—the uncertainty of holding longer-term debt rises at times of recession and then continues to decline throughout the economic expansion—until 2020. This cyclical pattern was evident in the 2010 to 2019 period even to the point that the term premium drops below zero. Meanwhile, the risk neutral yield (the expected path of short-term rates) rises as monetary policy is expected to return to neutral/stop the easing but again in 2020, there was no expectation that the Fed would raise rates anytime soon. The continued decline in the term premium is consistent with global investors search for yield in the context of less than expected inflation globally and negative policy rates in Europe.

However, there are changes in the wind. First, the five-year break-even inflation rate has risen past the pre-COVID/shutdown peak in 2019 by November 2020 now exceeds the highs of the 2016–2019 period. Second, the issuance of Treasury debt in response to the surge of Federal deficits, Fig. 12.5, presents a sharp change in direction.

Meanwhile, the risk neutral yield (the expected path of short-term rates) rises as monetary policy is expected to return to neutral/stop the easing associated with recessionary periods as indeed the Federal Reserve's action and guidance in late 2016 and throughout 2017 did signal higher short-term rates.

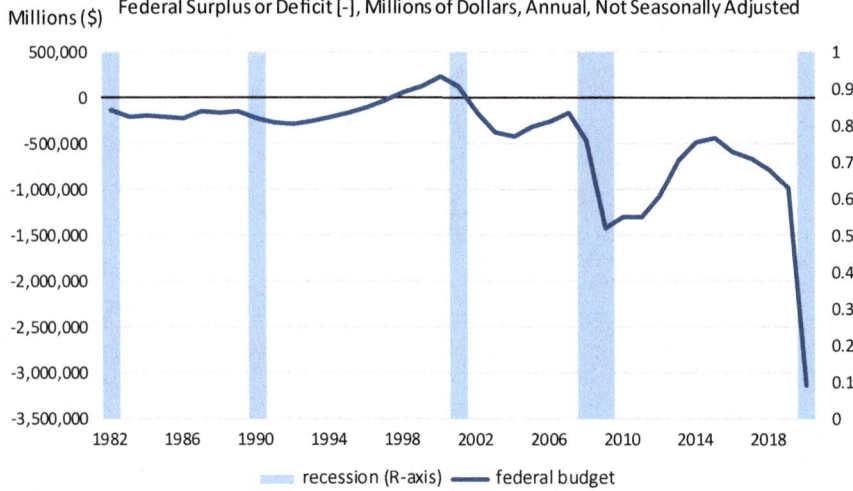

Fig. 12.5 Annual Federal Budget Position Since 1984

From the Figure, the continued decline in the term premium is consistent with global investors search for yield in the context of less than expected inflation globally and negative policy rates in Europe. This search dominates the compensation premium for uncertainty. Also, the steady rise of expected interest rates has faced off with the continued negation of such expectations brought on by reality. Finally, there is the interesting counterfactual question: How much current interest rates could be lower if, in fact, deficit financing placed a lighter burden on the credit markets?

Going forward, rising U.S. Treasury debt issuance is a possible turnaround factor for the term premium. After years of shrinking fiscal deficits and robust private and central bank demand, a few months of higher Treasury coupon auctions and somewhat muted market reactions could lull investors into a false sense of security. With the United States' fiscal outlook grim over the 2020 to 2050 period,[41] as far as the eye can see according to CBO estimates, the robust growth in Treasury demand seen over the past decade will have to continue climbing just as steadily and unabated as U.S. budget deficits continue to grow Fig. 12.5.

---

[41] "The 2020 Long-Term Budget Outlook, Congressional Budget Office," September 2020.

Future Imperfect Uncertainty-Questions from the Road

In 2019 and 2020, the dominant fiscal policy question focused on the future public policy options to deal with the federal debt. In part, this reflects the observation, lost on very few, that deficits have risen as a percent of GDP despite the economic expansion. The rising deficit ratio creates a budget uncertainty as the higher deficit relative to GDP provides less policy flexibility, both fiscal and monetary policy, to act in the post-pandemic future.

Meanwhile, investors also appreciate that a future administration and a compliant legislature could just spend more money. If so, how is such spending financed? Spending drives the fiscal ship of state. Financing the debt and deficit by printing money (we still have a fiat currency, thereby an inflation risk) or taxes (risking a negative impact on incentives) can all be manipulated independently by a future administration. This opens the possibility of the Fed monetizing the debt, thereby raising the risk of an unexpected, even if moderate, rise of inflation. For investors, a regime of low rates and high duration assets can quickly be put under water by even a moderate rise in interest rates.

Coming full circle, taxes could be raised but that reduces the return on work, savings, business investment, and risk-taking. These reductions lower the pace of economic growth and compounding the difficulty of financing the deficit. Certainly, some federal spending serves a good purpose. But it still must be determined where resources are allocated and what is the relationship between the expected rate of return on private investment versus federal spending—the chasm between the efficiency of political and economic allocation of funds.

Private investment is subject to the discipline of the marketplace and successful investment generates a profit. Unfortunately, there is no discipline on the federal government's spending since it is not required, like the states to balance its budget and, in recent years, no pressure to reduce the deficit. Public policy uncertainty leads directly into uncertainty around inflation, interest rates, exchange rates, and the dollar. The backdoor entrance of public policy into the setting of private market prices provides a rich path for price determination in any economic framework.

Yet the prospect of larger deficits as a percent of GDP, as forecasted by the CBO, raises a disconnect with the continuation of the current pattern of low inflation, low-interest rates, and a stronger dollar. How to reconcile the warning signals from deficits and debt and the apparent complacency of financial markets? One path to resolving this conundrum is that the increase in deficit/GDP ratios may suggest a slower pace of future economic growth. Something must give. It may be that slower expected economic growth would explain the lower expectations for inflation and interest rates. Still, foreign capital inflows and mandatory bank purchases of sovereign debt provide the demand for this debt. And it helps lower or moderates any move in Treasury yields overwhelming a strengthening dollar despite the comparative yields and growth expectations for other nations.

History: Germany, Dawes and Young as U.S. Precedent?

History suggests that there is a credibility range for deficits and debt as a share of GDP. This follows the research of others who cite that the problems of deficit finance do not appear below a certain percentage of GDP. Or even above a percentage as the experience of France illustrates. Budget deficits in this nation regularly surpassed Euro area guidelines during 2008–2016. Italian deficits surpassed their 3% ceiling from 2000 to 2016. Perhaps the United States' credibility is even wider given its unique position of issuing both a benchmark currency and a benchmark sovereign debt. Unfortunately, this credibility will be sorely tested if the forecasts of one scenario of a recent CBO report become a reality.[42]

Since the 2010 expansion and prior to the Covid-19 shutdown, the rise in U. S. deficits relative to GDP was associated with a continued period of modest improvements in labor force participation and productivity. These outcomes suggest that potential U.S. GDP growth has moderated along with slower real GDP growth. But this presents a problem for financing a rising burden of entitlement spending in an economy with slower potential and real growth than many policymakers expected when they established these entitlement programs such as Social Security and Medicare/Medicaid.

As for sovereign debt, the experience of Germany in the post-World War I period is instructive since it a prime example of a debt burden that was clearly out of line with the ability of a country to service that debt. At first, Germany made its payments in association with hyperinflation in the early to mid-1920s. The Dawes Plan was put in place to resolve the debt reparations problem by reducing the debt but also by supplying American capital to help Germany make its payments. But this proved to be unworkable. So as mentioned earlier, the Young Plan was put in place in 1930. By this time, the U.S. stock market had crashed, and a global recession was on its way. The lesson? Debt repayments must be in line with a country's ability to pay and

---

[42] "The Precarious global debt picture," Oct. 28, 2120, Financial Times.

grow. This is another example of political objectives inconsistent with the real economy's potential.

Disequilibrium: How Quickly the Outlook Changes

A Sense of Complacency

During the end of 2018, the argument cited in Barron's was that a "few minor tweaks should be sufficient[43]" to deal with the expanding deficits. Yet estimates by CBO were for deficits to rise to 11% of GDP by 2050.

Debt service would rise over time as the weighted average interest rate on U.S. ten-year Treasury debt would increase from 1.3% for 2020–2025 to 4.8 percent by 2050 and debt service would rise from 1.6% in 2020 to 6.5% in the 2041–2050 period.[44] However, we know that the interest burden is a function of several parameters including not only interest rates but also inflation, economic growth, and exchange rates which will influence capital inflows. Then there is always the exogenous wild card of politics which can continue to spike entitlement spending.

Shock: Putting the 1980s Deficit Shock in Perspective

Long before the deficits and debt debates of the Covid-19 shutdown era, there were the debates of the early 1980s. At the time, bond guru Henry Kaufman put the numbers and concepts into a context, a framework, for analysis.[45]

At the time, the conventional notion among economists was that economic growth over time would allow the United States to grow out of the deficits. In addition, reductions in budget deficits will lower interest rates significantly.

However, deficits must be put into context. The impact of deficits on growth and interest rates depends on what stage an economy is in. And interest rates are a function of expected economic growth, expected inflation, exchange rates, and capital inflows. In the post-global financial crises of 2008–2009, interest rates are very much a function of the conduct of monetary policy.

During recessions, fiscal deficits rise but often interest rates decline. This presents a problem for analysts who expected to find a direct link from deficits to interest rates. Instead, the factors of slower growth, central bank easing,

---

[43] "Don't Panic" *Barron's* December 03, 2018.
[44] "The 2020 Long-Term Budget Outlook, Congressional Budget Office," September 2020.
[45] Henry Kaufman, "Deficits and Interest Rates," *Bondweek*, November 28, 1983.

and lower inflation are the driving factors favoring lower interest rates. In addition, in private credit markets, the rising deficits of a recession period are also associated with weakness in private credit demands along with a more accommodative Federal Reserve.

While a dynamic economy such as the United States has an expansionary bias, the upward trend in economic growth would be associated with increasing tax revenues and smaller deficits and thereby lower interest rates, ceteris paribus. However, a prosperous economy tends to germinate expensive federal programs (War on Poverty in the 1960s, Middle East wars in the early 2000s, Obamacare in the mid-2000s) such that federal spending also grows with the economy and deficits are never wiped out by rising prosperity. The counter to these examples was President Bill Clinton's economic policies of trade expansion (NAFTA) and spending reductions which resulted in the first actual budget surpluses since 1969. Government demand for financing during the above periods coincided with rising private demand to fund real economic growth.

The focus on interest rates moves with respect to federal deficits misses the point. The real question, as articulated by Henry Kaufman, was: How much more would interest rates have fallen if the federal budget deficits had been smaller? The impact of federal deficits on interest rates, and the exchange rates as well as the economy, depends on the context of changes in the economy as well as the focus on short-term or long-term impacts of the deficit finance. What happens in the short run may not offer much guidance to change in the long run. In addition, large fiscal deficits were perceived to hamper monetary policy. Federal deficits must be financed and a central bank that conducts policy by short-term interest rates will have an impact on the interest burden of the federal deficits. This was of particular interest post-World War II and led to the Treasury-Fed Accord of March 1951. At that time, the U.S. Treasury and the Federal Reserve reached an agreement to separate government debt management from monetary policy, laying the foundation for the modern Fed. These issues have resurfaced given the increase in Treasury financing post-2009.

Capital Flows: Interest Rates and Treasury Finance

The relationship between interest rate expectations, exchange rates, and Treasury finance during 2017–2019 exemplifies the importance of a framework to understand the movements in market prices.

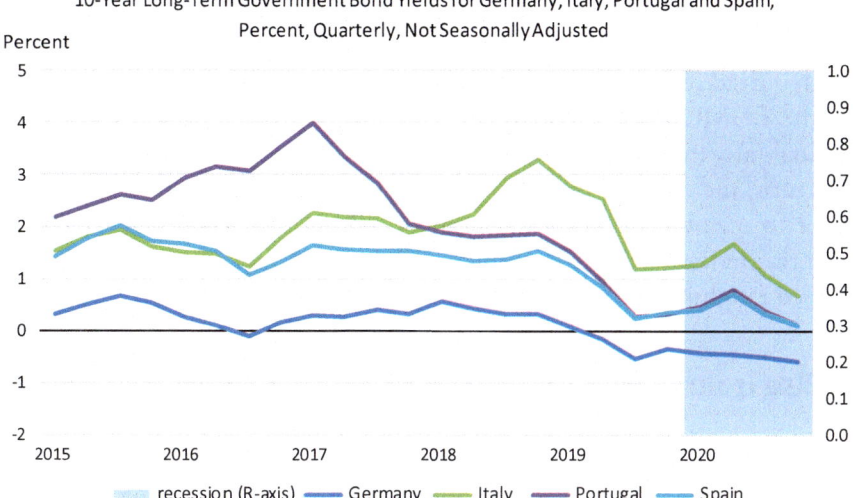

Fig. 12.6 Euro Sovereign Yields 2016 to 2020

Expectations Revisited

Capital flows respond to expectations on relative interest rates and exchange rate dynamics across borders. In addition, we recognize the importance of these capital flows in the global U.S. Treasury market. Expectations, especially for public policy, have played an increasingly important role in market participants' reactions to global events. For example, Italian budget plans violated eurozone spending rules in 2018 and led to a decline in the euro against the dollar.[46] In addition, Italian bond yields rose more than 100 bps (Fig. 12.6) while other Euro yields also rose as a reflection of the political uncertainty in Italy. While it is too soon to determine any effect, these political tensions could have on capital flows, expectations play a role in short-term exchange rate and interest rate dynamics. In the long run, these dynamics affect capital flows.

Changing expectations of central bank actions have also caused volatile swings in foreign exchange rates and interest rates. Rate hikes by the Fed were less supportive of the dollar as the yen appreciated from 116/US dollar in December 2016 to 112.2/U.S. dollar in December 2018. Throughout much of 2017, short-term rate expectations moved in favor of the U.S. dollar, but it declined relative to the yen. In part, perhaps market assessments were that

---

[46] "Italy's Salvini ramps up rhetoric as bonds face new pressure," October 8, 2018 Financial Times.

the Federal Open Market Committee (FOMC) was further along its tightening path relative to other major central banks, and market participants had already priced in future rate hikes to a large extent. Market participants likely saw the FOMC as only having so many rate hikes left before reaching its terminal rate, meaning the potential for rate hike "surprises" is much lower.

In turn, the effect of interest rate expectations on exchange rates has been harder to quantify. As the Fed began to tighten policy in 2015–2016, one could theoretically identify a more direct relationship between the probability of a Fed rate hike and its effect on the dollar.

All Else is not Equal for Capital Flows

The evolving relationship between interest rate expectations, exchange rates, and capital flows has been evident since the 1990s. From the mid-1990s on, the foreign share of the Treasury market steadily grew. Since 2010, the growth of foreign ownership has been accompanied by the rise in ownership by the Federal Reserve. (Fig. 12.7).

As global central banks have engaged in unconventional monetary policy measures, the focus has turned toward perceived policy stances through actions such as quantitative easing, rather than a pure reaction to actual rate hikes. This shift was compounded by unconventional global monetary

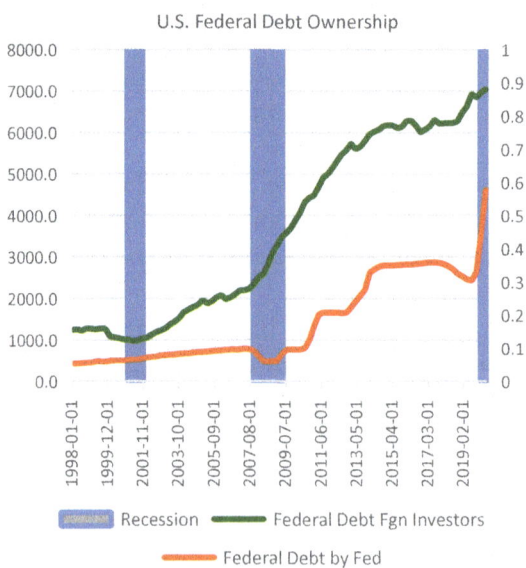

Fig. 12.7 U.S. Federal Debt Held at Federal Reserve and International Holdings

policy and a deteriorating fiscal outlook during one of the longest economic expansions in recent history. These differences influence investors' relative allocation of capital. Decision makers would do well to pay attention to the unique outcomes that stem from differing market expectations. As previously reviewed, such expectations regarding sovereign credit quality were most evident in the Euro debt crisis of the middle of the last decade.

Outlier or Warning Signal? August 2011

Just how sensitive is the U.S. Treasury's position as a benchmark sovereign security? In recent years, rising fiscal deficits have brought into question the position of the U.S. Treasury ten-year benchmark note as the benchmark for pricing both public and sovereign debt. The experience of 2011 indicates that the price sensitivity of interest rates, and the economy, is more sensitive to changing assessments of credit risk than commonly assumed. The default position in 2011 provides some guidance going forward.

Consumer sentiment, as measured by the University of Michigan fell sharply in 2011. When we examine the four market prices, we find that exchange rates, interest rates, and equity valuations all responded as expected. The yen/U.S. dollar evidences a clear break in August (Fig. 12.8) and the relative value of the dollar did indeed decline. During the summer of 2011, the three-month Treasury bill rate spiked as an uncertainty premium for Treasury default entered the market (Fig. 12.9), and equity prices fell sharply. In August 2011, Standard and Poor's downgraded U.S. Treasury debt to AA from AAA. After the downgrade, the ten-year Treasury yield declined

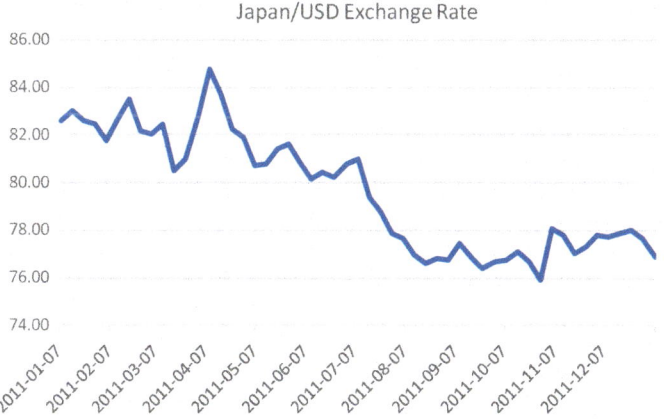

Fig. 12.8 Yen/USD Exchange Rate 2011

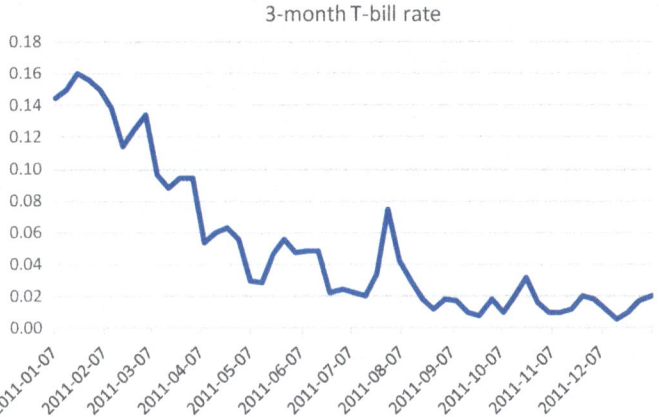

Fig. 12.9 Three-month Treasury bill yield

into October 2011. The trade-weighted dollar rallied in October and equity markets remained in a trading range. Consumer sentiment rebounded the rest of the year.

Yet, concerns about the future position of U.S. Treasury debt remain. In February 2018, the Treasury auction for the two-year, seven-year, and ten-year notes did not go well, and yields rose sharply over the prior auctions.[47] This price action reflected the imbalance of supply and demand at the time. Treasury debt issuance was rising but both the Fed and the Chinese central bank were cutting back—or at least rumored to be cutting back. As the journalist Mary Childs commented—"for now there is no immediate indication of a change in the Treasury debt a benchmark." She goes on: "But there's always the day after tomorrow. At some point, investors could begin to take America's balance sheet a lot more seriously."

One benchmark for a change in the wind that may provide some guidance for decision makers is the five-year break-even inflation rate (Fig. 12.10). There is a sharp dip in the recession periods but already, in 2020, we have seen a bounce back. Is there more to follow?

Financing with a Fiat Currency: The Sovereign Benchmark in History.

As we noted earlier, the three biggest holders of U.S. Treasury debt are the Fed and the central banks of China and Japan. These institutions are not motivated by maximizing profit nor do they mark to market. In a way, the current lower short-term interest rates today do not represent the risk-free benchmark rate framework when years ago this concept was framed within a private market dominated Treasury pricing.

---

[47] Mary Childs, "Treasuries Undergo a Glut Check," Barron's February 24, 2018.

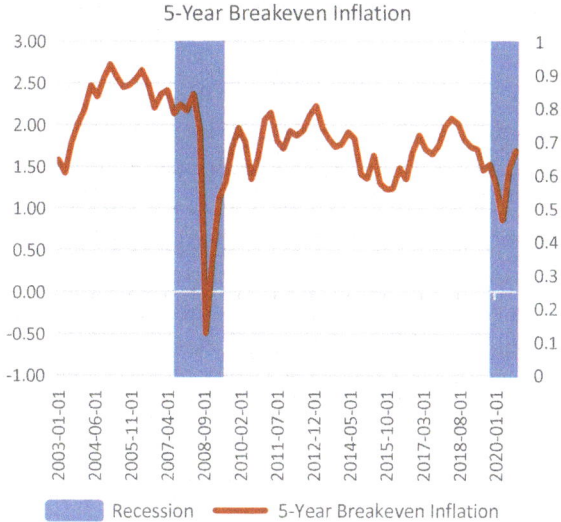

Fig. 12.10 Five-year Breakeven Inflation

The argument that government deficits do not matter for countries—such as the United States that borrow in their own currencies—falls flat when viewed from the history of France with John Law and the United Kingdom after both World War I and World War II. Government debt finance does not operate in isolation. For France, when debt issuance outpaced the ability of the Mississippi enterprise, the devaluation of the currency was rapid, inflation skyrocketed, and the value of Mississippi company shares collapsed. For the United Kingdom, the inability to repay debts led to dropping the gold standard after World War I and devaluations of the pound and rising inflation after World War II. Recall that the United States has already defaulted twice, in the 1930s and the 1970s, as debt due to be paid in gold could not be met. Higher inflation in the 1970s was one way the federal government paid back bondholders with depreciated dollars.

Deficits do matter in an economic framework where market prices are interrelated for credit, goods, equity, and foreign exchange—which is always. Ceteris paribus always matters and the attempt by governments to finance deficits through wage-price controls or interest equalization taxes simply suppresses price movement in the short run but the pressures build, and inflation reasserts itself eventually.

The United States as Net Debtor and the Specter of John Law

Over time, the ability of the sovereign to issue debt has faced limits. For France and John Law, depreciation of the domestic currency finally arrived. For the United Kingdom after World War I, the commitments of empire outran the ability of the economy to generate growth. It remains to be seen if the disequilibrium of U.S. growth and deficit finance will indeed result in significant changes in the markets for credit (rates), inflation, or the exchange rate value of the dollar. Or perhaps, the markets will resolve the imbalances without any longer-run negative outcomes. The outcome remains uncertain.

Finance Via Fiat Money

Without the discipline of a private marketplace for government debt, foreign exchange, or physical goods and services, modern governments can finance fiscal deficits as large as they like for as long as they like with a fiat currency. However, this requires a public confidence in that currency and a very short time horizon.

As poor as the information flow was for France, citizens eventually caught on to the devaluation of the currency, higher goods inflation, and the loss of value of equity in the Mississippi Company. In a modern economy today the information flow is instantaneous and widespread.

As the business historian Niall Ferguson said, "The sovereign debt crisis that is unfolding… it is a fiscal crisis of the western world.[48]"

References

T. Adrian, A. Estrella, and H.S. Shin, "Monetary Cycles, Financial Cycles and the Business Cycle," Federal Reserve Bank of New York Staff Report No. 421, January 2010. A study on the forecasting ability of the yield curve.

T. Adrian, R K. Crump and E. Moench. (2013). "Pricing the Term Structure with Linear Regressions." Federal Reserve Bank of New York *Staff Report No. 340*. A view on pricing the yield curve/term structure of interest rates.

Alberto Alesina, and Allan Drazen, "Why Are Stabilizations Delayed?" American Economic Review 81 (December 1991): 1170–1188. The authors make the case that stabilizations are delayed because of the debate on who bears the burden of the stabilization.

---

[48] Niall Ferguson, *Financial Times* February 10, 2020.

Alan J. Auerbach, William G. Gale, Peter R. Orszag, and Samra R. Potter, "Budget Blues: The Fiscal Outlook and Options for Reform." In Henry Aaron, James Lindsay, and Pietro Nivola, eds., Agenda for a Nation, 109–143. Washington, D.C.: Brookings Institution. 2003.The authors argue that the federal government will need to make large adjustments to its budget. These adjustments include spending reductions, tax increases and implicit or explicit reneging on government debt through default or hyperinflation.

Laurence Ball, Douglas Elmendorf, and N. Gregory Mankiw, "The Deficit Gamble," Journal of Money Credit and Banking 30 (November 1998): pp. 699–720. A view on the fiscal outlook for the U.S. economy.

Robert Barro, *Macroeconomics*, John Wiley & Sons, 1984 New York, pp. 380–387. Barro makes the case that increased sovereign debt supply, moreover, shifts expectations of future debt supply, debt quality and future tax burdens.

James M. Buchanan and Richard E. Wagner, Democracy in Deficit: The Political Legacy of Lord Keynes, Academic Press, New York, 1977. The authors focus on the intergenerational problem. The benefits of high government spending and low taxes are direct and evident. The costs of higher future taxes, inflation and low real purchases are indirect and less obvious and are likely to fall on some future generational cohort.

Congressional Budget Office, "An Update to the Budget Outlook: 2020 to 2030," September 2020

Congressional Budget Office, *Long-Term Budget Outlook*, September 2020. An excellent view of the longer-term trends in the economy and the federal budget.

Peter A. Diamond, "National Debt in a Neoclassical Growth Model," American Economic Review 55 (December 1965): 1126–1150. Diamond's important observation that the debt passed on to future generations can be borne by the next generation if the real rate of growth of the economy exceeds the real rate of interest on the debt.

Eric Engen and R. Glenn Hubbard "Federal Government Debt and Interest Rates," National Bureau of Economic Research Working Paper No. 10681, August 2004. One view that the crowding out effect of government spending is quite small.

Niall Ferguson, The Ascent of Money, Penguin Press, 2008. A review of the career of John Law and sovereign finances of France.

Greek Ministry of Finance "Update of the Hellenic Stability and Growth Programme," January. 15, 2010.

Matthew Higgins and Thomas Klitgaard, "Savings Imbalances and the Euro Area Sovereign debt crisis" Federal Reserve Bank of New York V 17 No 5

David Hume, Essays, "Moral, Political, Literacy", Essay IX of *Public Credit*. 1777. A skeptical view on sovereign credit.

R. G. Ibbotson and R.A Sinquefield, "Stocks, Bonds, Bills, and Inflation: The Past and the Future," 1982 edition. Charlottesville, VA., The Financial Analysts Research Foundation, 1982. An excellent source of information on asset returns over time.

Henry Kaufman, "Deficits and Interest Rates," *Bondweek*, November 28, 1983. One market participant's view.

John Maynard Keynes, *Economic Consequences of the Peace*, MacMillan & CO. London 1919. Keynes' recognition that debt repayments/reparations must be consistent with the ability of the economy to grow to make those payments.

Ilse Mintz, "Deterioration in the Quality of Bonds Issued in the United States, 1920–1930 (New York: National Bureau of Economic Research, 1951). An interesting view on the quality of U.S. debt in the interwar period.

U.S. Treasury International Capital Report, June 28, 2019. An interesting monthly report that follows the patterns of foreign and U.S. international asset purchases.

Conclusion

There is no conclusion. There is no final exam. The processes of economic growth and financial innovation continue. From the time of the founding of the American colonies, incentives for growth and profits required a financial vehicle to create success. This understanding was found in the colonial charters.

The expansion of the American railroad system required, in part, capital inflows from abroad. Later, large enterprises, such as U.S. Steel and railroad mergers, also required a means to combine financial capital to deliver a scale of industrial output to meet the economy's infrastructure. In the post-World War II era, mortgage finance and credit cards were created to enhance the consumer experience.

We are left then with a purposely limited set of principles to guide our analysis for both economic and financial activity. What is important is that these principles are not identified with only one market but how markets act in a modern open economy.

First, market prices are both a signal and an incentive to act. The core market prices for goods (measured by inflation), credit (measured by interest rates), equity (measured by a stock price index), and foreign exchange (measured by the U.S. dollar exchange rate from an American point of view) provide a signal for the expected future path of economic activity and the allocation of capital across economic activities. As an incentive, market prices motivate action on the part of both the supply and demand actors in each market.

Second, there is a matrix of interactions between economic sectors. There are many paths for the interactions; this monograph has focused on four major sectors. Each economic action carries with it an implication of financial activity. Each financial activity carries with it an implication of economic activity. For the successful analyst, it is imperative to pursue recognizing these linkages and interactions and the implications of each as circumstances change.

Third, there are no silos. The most successful strategy meetings I have witnessed have included analysts from the four major sectors reviewed here, as well as numerous other analysts. The outlook for the economy and financial markets reflects the impact of *all* sectors. Too often I have witnessed a strategist, for example an equity strategist, who comments on the equity market without any reference to the activity in the economy or credit markets. Performance in the credit markets depends upon the activity in the economy. The economy reflects that performance in the credit, equity, and foreign exchange markets.

Fourth, movement in the economy and the markets mirrors incentives provided when outcomes differ from expectations. This is most obvious on employment Fridays when the Bureau of Labor Statistics releases its report. Actual job gain is overshadowed in its impact relative to the impact from the discrepancy between consensus expectations and actual outcomes. Central bank policy announcements, movements in leading indicators (such as jobless claims or factory orders), and business sentiment keep an analyst busy recognizing expectations and then analyzing outcomes that differ from expectations, and then, again, the implications of these differences.

Fifth, markets are in constant disequilibrium. A thoughtful analyst realizes this set of disequilibrium impacts since the linkages between markets imply that any market not in equilibrium will cause other markets and their prices to move. The most interesting insights that an analyst can offer are the recognitions of an apparent imbalance of factors in the marketplace. For example, in equity circles this is often cited as over or under valuation. However, how is this valuation determined? In my view, an analyst should identify factors outside the simple price of an equity and these factors are often related to the activities occurring at the time in other markets.

Disequilibrium is also a product of policy actions that set a price that is inconsistent with market forces. This can be seen with wage-price controls, rent controls, exchange rate settings, and financial repression of interest rates. In each case, the imbalance of market forces and public policy price setting often breaks down. The result—an explosion of market prices such as the inflation of the 1970s, the exchange rate shocks after the ERM breakdown and the Treasury-Fed accord of the early 1950s.

Finally, there is the reality of imperfect information. What we see may not be the accurate reflection of reality. Economic data is plagued by seasonality issues and sampling problems. Financial information may not reveal the underlying real fundamentals of a company. Governments also have incentives not to reveal the true nature of public finances—an issue that has repeatedly appeared in the budget and deficit estimates of the European Union.

Not the conclusion you expected. There are no simple, static formulas in a dynamic, always evolving, economy and financial system. An analyst simply must look back at the patterns of cycles and trends, structural breaks, and causality relationships identified in this monograph to recognize that the economy and markets today operate very differently than in the past—especially compared to the pre-1982 inflationary period, and in some markets such as housing, after the 2007–2009 global financial crisis.

Let me close with a quote from one of my favorite analysts:

If a man will begin with certainties, he shall end in doubts; but if he will be content to begin with doubts, he shall end in certainties.
—Francis Bacon, *The Oxford Francis Bacon IV: The Advancement of Learning.*

Index

A

AA Corporate bond rate 173, 348
Accelerator principle 232
Adjustable Rate Mortgages (ARMS) 209, 281
Administered interest/exchange rates 6–8, 10, 11, 13, 18–20, 24, 30, 38, 40, 55, 67, 68, 73–76, 81, 91, 92, 101, 105, 108, 115, 120, 121, 130, 133, 139–142, 148, 153, 157, 159, 169, 170, 175, 178, 210, 270, 307–310, 314, 316, 318, 319, 323, 324, 328, 330, 334, 335, 339, 340, 346, 353, 354, 359, 377, 388, 390, 395, 408, 411, 415, 417, 419–422, 429, 431–435
Age-earnings profile 284
Age of Exploration 371
Allocation of financial capital over time 18, 83, 107, 178, 377
Argentina 1920s 79
Asian Tigers 319
Assets less liabilities 255
Assumption of unlimited demand 420
Asymmetric information 189, 219, 272

B

Bagehot, Walter 147, 270, 418
Balance of payments 38, 106, 314–316, 319, 321, 324, 327–330, 341, 343, 408
Bank credit cycle 197
Bank Willingness to make loans 21, 285, 305
Barber boom 410
Barings Bank 79, 184
Benchmark 10Y UST 66, 67, 75, 92, 111, 113, 116, 120, 144, 157–159, 162–165, 167, 168, 176, 179, 211, 229, 248, 268, 336, 435
Bias
  anchoring bias 11, 31, 36, 56, 57, 63, 79, 110, 112, 176, 229, 245

framing bias 31, 32, 209, 210
normalization of deviance 31, 35, 56, 66, 72, 79, 209
recency bias 31, 36, 56, 63, 70, 110, 208, 229, 275, 276, 398
B of A High yield spread 105, 217, 221, 258, 265, 268
Bond issuance 219, 225, 230, 236, 267, 313, 327, 415
Bonds, supply & demand 98, 220, 221, 225
Brexit 108, 112, 123, 134
Bridge financing 184, 189
British Finance of American railroads 318
Bubble Act 87, 372, 413
Budget constraint 29, 84, 412
Bull, John 147, 234, 418

C

C&I loans, business 69, 186, 197, 199, 205–207
Callaghan, James 126, 409
Canadian dollar/U.S. dollar exchange rate 10, 84, 110, 114, 133, 311, 323, 328, 329, 334, 336, 348, 398
CAPE ratio, cyclically adjusted price-earnings ratio 383
Capital account 315, 342
Central bank buying, Sovereign debt 178, 411, 415–418
Charge-off rates 34, 203, 207, 209, 297
Charge-off rates 207
Charles I 404, 405
China devaluation 2015 136
Chinese yuan 66, 135, 213, 323
Coinage Act of 1873 216
Collateralized debt obligations (CDOs) 7, 249, 278

Commodity prices 8, 13, 24, 58, 67, 72, 73, 100, 101, 103, 105, 119, 139, 142, 145, 318, 341
Congressional Budget Office (CBO) 112, 163, 168, 412, 419–421, 423, 428–431
Consumer credit 5, 34, 35, 205, 209, 278, 281–283, 285, 294–296, 300, 302, 304, 305
Copper 98, 101, 103, 104
Core PCE deflator 38, 90, 97, 154, 155, 173, 175, 253, 262, 271
Corn Laws 341, 342
Corrections 7, 26, 49, 54, 81, 85, 89, 110, 111, 141, 252, 293, 297, 331, 367, 382, 387, 397
Cost of capital 19, 98, 142, 151, 159, 220, 230, 235, 268, 331, 332, 356, 377–379, 384, 385, 391, 394–396, 411
Cost per unit of gross value added of non-financial corporate 350, 351
Cost to finance 7, 228, 235, 419
cotton bonds 247, 339
Credit allocation 12, 37, 145, 147, 150, 153, 156, 157, 160, 162, 169, 177, 210, 211, 213, 308
Credit controls 294, 295
Credit cycles 8, 14, 34, 45, 58, 60, 61, 68, 194, 208, 217, 245, 266, 268, 271, 273, 398
Credit standards 61, 69, 184, 185, 191, 192, 194, 197, 198, 202, 203, 208, 210, 264, 268, 276
Current account 114, 132, 314, 315, 336, 341, 342
Current ratio as current assets/current liabilities 254, 255, 263
Cyclical and secular patterns 151, 188, 195, 221, 259, 380

D

Dash for growth 409
Dawes Plan 404, 406, 430
Debt monetization 423
Debt relative to market value of corporate equities 224
Debt service ratio (DSR) 20, 288, 291–293, 296, 297, 305
Debt to equity ratio 223
Decision making–cognitive biases 35, 64
Delinquency rates 20, 201, 204, 205, 209, 301–303
Demand/supply of credit 143, 144, 150, 151, 158, 179, 186, 190, 191, 194, 198, 199, 201, 202, 210, 221, 236, 279, 285, 413
Disinflation 97, 264, 270
Disruptions 74, 243, 270
Distinguishing trend and cycle in non-financial corporate finance 44, 245
Dividend payments as adding value to IRAs, 401 (k)s 357
Dividend price ratio 380
Dollar as a price 328
Domestic demand 98, 309, 310, 325
Dot.com 39, 53, 68, 78, 79, 87, 89, 115, 143, 159, 283, 398
Due diligence 7, 18, 20, 21, 41, 82, 101, 207, 248, 314, 329, 380, 383
Dutch East India Company 372
Dutch Tulip Bulb bubble 368

E

Earnings per share 382
Earnings-price ratio (E/P ratio) 21, 118, 380, 388, 394, 395
Effective corporate income tax rate 384, 385
Efficient allocation of capital 83, 377, 419

Employment cost index 140, 269, 359
Entrepreneurs 3, 201, 346, 356, 358, 371
Equilibrium and disequilibrium 1, 6, 9, 21–23, 25, 37–39, 42, 49, 55, 66, 73–75, 77, 83–90, 95, 102, 107, 110, 111, 113–115, 121, 122, 128–132, 139–143, 151–154, 156, 160, 169–171, 173, 175–177, 179, 195, 210, 211, 213, 223, 235, 240, 272, 276, 277, 308, 316, 325, 334, 336, 338, 340, 390, 392, 396, 398, 431, 438
Equity market correction 1999 17, 367
Ex-ante 229, 252, 389
Ex ante real rates one-year, five-year 229, 252, 389
Exogenous shock 91, 118, 221, 227, 229, 238, 296, 394
Expectations 6–8, 11, 17, 21, 24, 28, 36, 37, 39–42, 53, 54, 56, 58, 64, 66–69, 70, 72, 75, 76, 78, 81, 86, 87, 89, 91, 98, 104, 108, 111–115, 120, 124, 129, 131, 132, 134, 136, 137, 139, 141, 142, 149–151, 153, 154, 158, 159, 161–168, 170, 172, 173, 176, 197, 199, 201, 206, 208, 211, 213, 217, 218, 220, 221, 225, 226, 228–230, 233, 235, 248, 252, 260, 264, 268, 275, 276, 278, 284, 295, 307, 308, 310, 314, 317, 323–325, 329, 332, 334, 335, 339, 349, 358, 362, 364, 365, 367, 368, 374–376, 380–382, 387–390, 393, 396–399, 406, 407, 410, 411, 415–417, 419–428, 430, 432–435

Expectations versus fundamentals 6, 11, 68, 70, 86, 139, 170, 221, 235, 279, 323, 364, 388
Expected earnings 19, 374
Expected rate of return 7, 159, 228, 279, 371, 389, 391, 411, 419, 429
Export demand 232, 326, 335
Export led growth 319
Exports 19, 74, 106, 114, 128, 129, 153, 159, 221, 247, 309, 310, 313, 315, 316, 321, 325, 327–330, 336, 338, 339, 353, 354, 359
Ex post 359, 389

F

FANG 398
Federal debt held by foreign and international investors 175
Federal debt held by the Federal Reserve 417
Federal Deposit Insurance Corporation (FDIC) 202, 205, 206
Federal Open Market Committee (FOMC) 14, 37, 149, 212, 434
Federal Reserve balance sheet 32, 65, 89, 114, 144, 145, 158, 161, 163–165, 168, 211, 424
Federal Reserve's dual mandate 211, 212
Federal surplus/debt as a percentage of GDP 305, 430
Fiat currency 52, 340, 429, 436, 438
Financial markets as economics fraternal twin 20, 34
Financial obligations ratio 35, 291, 293
Financial repression 179
Financing gap 85, 86, 230, 231, 235, 241, 242, 254, 272

Financing innovation 372
First in-First out (FIFO) 257
Five-year break-even rate 427, 436
FOMC projections 157
Foreign direct investment 325
Four market prices—goods, credit, equity, foreign exchange 6, 64, 66, 67, 435
Future debt burdens 420
Future dividends 382, 387
Future imperfect 252, 429

G

Government intervention 316, 329, 419
Government-Sponsored Enterprises (GSEs) 88, 275
Grand assumption: debt is costless 410
Growth expectations 22, 26, 39, 40, 89, 119, 123, 134, 136, 158, 166, 173, 279, 317, 319, 321, 323, 327, 332, 421, 422, 430
Guidelines versus rules 261, 262, 356, 391
Guidelines versus rules 355

H

High yield 25, 60, 67, 96, 105, 120, 129, 133, 144, 192, 209, 215, 217, 221, 228, 229, 246–249, 258, 265, 267, 268, 328
High yield option adjusted spread 96, 229
Home equity loans on credit (HELOCs) 151, 183, 304
Hope Bank 184
Household balance sheet 2, 276, 277, 279, 280, 283, 292, 293, 299
Household Finance 1980s 273, 296, 305

Household net worth 276, 294, 296, 299, 359
Housing cycle 39, 137
Housing cycles—forces 137

Imperfect capital mobility 342
Imperfect information 177, 178
Imperfect markets 392
Importance of observation of market prices 53
Incentives 18, 38, 40, 62, 82, 88, 131, 139, 148, 156, 193, 203, 210, 217, 219, 225, 229, 230, 234, 243, 244, 257, 261, 262, 271, 272, 275, 276, 317, 318, 331, 339, 345, 347, 356–358, 371, 384, 394, 396, 405, 417, 423, 429
Income and substitution effects 160
Inflation 7, 8, 12–15, 17, 20–23, 25, 26, 33, 35–38, 40, 42, 44, 52, 54–57, 64, 67, 72, 74–76, 82–84, 89–92, 95–97, 99, 100, 112–116, 122, 124, 126–130, 133, 139–141, 143, 145, 148, 151, 152, 154, 157–159, 161–172, 175, 176, 179, 210–212, 218–222, 226, 228, 233, 237, 252, 255, 257–259, 264–266, 268, 271, 272, 277–279, 285, 296, 308–311, 313, 314, 316, 323, 328, 332, 338, 340, 346, 352, 353, 356, 357, 359, 364, 365, 373–376, 379, 380, 388–390, 393, 395–400, 404, 405, 408, 410–421, 423–432, 436–438
Inflation, 1970s 95, 140, 176, 219, 252, 264, 270, 357, 389, 398, 399, 437

Inflation target 44, 57, 90, 112, 129, 145, 153, 179, 265, 313, 332, 364
Innovation as new information 54
Interbank rate, 90-day 127, 311
Interdependence 134, 320, 327
Interest coverage 238, 239, 259, 261, 266, 270
Interest coverage ratio 224, 227, 238, 239, 245, 254, 258, 260, 266
Interest elasticity 152
Interest expense relative to corporate cash flow 21, 224, 254, 255, 258
Internal dynamics of corporate debt, not debt to GDP 252
Interrelated markets 30, 339, 379
Interrelationships between markets 21, 308, 310
Irrational exuberance 53, 71, 88, 89
IS–LM model 309

J

Joint Stock Company 371

K

Keynes—economic consequences of the peace 408

L

Law, John 50–53, 87, 88, 172, 404, 405, 411, 437, 438
Leading indicators of the economy 22–24, 101, 120, 127, 133, 222, 356
Leverage, corporate 21, 223, 224, 236, 237, 254, 258, 259, 263, 264
Life cycle behavior 284

Linkage of economics and finance 20, 35, 241, 251, 262, 308
Linkages between exchange rates 308, 309, 318, 323, 328
Linkages, no silos 14, 20, 135
Liquidity constraints 278
Liquidity preference 151, 165, 309
Loan/deposit ratio 34, 190–193, 413
Loan spreads 73, 143, 191, 192, 209, 268
Loan to value ratio 288
Long-term Government Yields: Europe 400
Louisiana Purchase 184
Louis XIV 50, 52, 404

M

Manufacturing after-tax corporate profits relative to dollar value of 269
Market framework 123
Market price framework as a signal 6
Market value of equity relative to net worth ratio 218, 222, 242, 254, 255, 263, 391
Massachusetts Bay Colony 345
Mean reversion 12, 41, 58, 64, 141, 299
Mean, standard deviation 360
Melt up, melt down 141, 142
Mid-cycle as misleading benchmark 79
Mid-cycle peak 350, 351
Mispricing assets 25, 83, 129
Mississippi Bubble 50, 63, 85, 87, 308, 405, 413, 419
Monetary policy, fiscal policy mix 22, 23, 91, 167, 272, 309, 310, 325, 342, 395
Motivations change: income to capital gains 368
Multi-factor determination 166
Multi sector economy 95

Mundell–Fleming model 309

N

National Association of Securities Dealers Automated Quotations (NASDAQ) 67, 106, 115, 172, 248, 264, 328, 387
Net interest margins 201–204, 206
Net percent of banks reporting stronger demand 99, 150, 189, 199, 287
Net percent of banks tightening standards 199, 281
New car average financing rate 295
New York Stock Exchange (NYSE) 17, 83, 96, 99, 104, 107, 111, 135, 136, 138, 150, 173, 195, 204, 222, 264, 294, 299, 311, 317, 337, 361, 367, 374, 376, 378, 379, 381, 387, 388, 390
Nifty-Fifty 79, 283, 398
No idea where to stop 405
Nominal GDP 4, 14, 17, 18, 53, 59, 83, 238, 239, 259, 264, 346, 347, 359, 360, 374, 376, 389, 390, 394
Noncurrent loan rates 206–208
Nonfinancial corporate business interest paid 271, 350
Non-financial corporate debt 21, 59, 139, 239, 253, 255
Non-financial corporate profits 99, 173, 266, 351
Non-linear profit growth 349, 357
Non-market prices, disequilibrium 143
Non-recursive economy 100, 331
Non-stationarity 92, 116, 127, 171, 200, 223, 232, 279, 281, 283, 297, 299, 349
No price is the right price 142

North American Free Trade Agreement (NAFTA) 14, 322, 353, 374, 376, 432
No single benchmarks 8

O

Over/under valuation 22, 85
Overshooting 53, 54, 88, 111

P

Paid for risk 118
Panic of 1873 216
  1987 Black Monday 340
PCE deflator 14, 38, 44, 57, 90, 92, 96, 97, 99, 116, 117, 140, 162, 164, 166, 195, 211, 222, 259, 268, 310, 315, 328, 337, 338, 359, 364, 373, 375
PCE implicit price deflator 362
Plaza Accord 10, 102, 115, 132, 258, 329, 336, 340
Plymouth Colony 345
Policy determined interest rates 151
Positions in the cycle 55, 269
Pre-tax corporate profits 162, 185, 200, 201, 218, 221, 233, 242, 265, 349, 360, 361, 367
Price/cost of capital 19, 98
Price adjustment 66, 119, 120, 210, 417
Price determination 13, 18, 30, 75, 96, 107, 111, 121, 128, 130, 152, 316, 429
Price determination—policy indetermination 128, 152
Price insensitive buyers 163
Price of credit 147, 150, 151, 156, 159, 169, 187, 192, 328, 411
Price shock—supply side, demand side 114
Pro-cyclical behavior 225, 286

Profitability 112, 150, 151, 175, 192, 201, 238, 307, 353, 358
Profit margins 90, 96, 176, 270, 350–352, 361, 363, 366, 367, 382, 383, 393, 395
Profit per unit of gross value added 366
Profits as reward and incentive 228, 339, 345, 357
Profits earned abroad 353
Profits recession 355, 356

Q

Quick ratio 241, 254, 255

R

Real final sales to domestic purchasers 14, 41, 55, 373
Recession, 1990 58, 85, 171, 185, 193, 206–208, 222, 224, 255, 259, 264, 355, 361, 427
Reparations 52, 330, 331, 403, 404, 406, 408, 409, 430
Repercussion effects 316, 317, 320–322, 327, 420, 422
Retained earnings 232, 238, 258, 359, 382
Risk neutral yield 426, 427

S

Senior Loan Officer Opinion Survey (SLOOS) 21, 34, 150, 189, 197–199, 210, 285, 303
Sense of complacency 431
Shadow banking 186, 195, 202, 208, 209, 246, 396, 413
Shift expectations 11, 399, 420
Shifting preferences 327
Short run versus long run 40, 66, 75, 110, 128, 131, 152, 189, 223, 229, 336, 341, 362, 363,

366, 388, 390, 392, 393, 397, 410, 411, 413, 432
Short-term credit 8, 183, 184, 187, 190, 192, 194, 195, 206, 213, 221, 222, 286, 332, 391
Short-term debt relative to long-term debt 222, 232, 240, 243, 244, 255, 257–259, 263, 264, 271
Short-term debt to total debt ratio 240
Simultaneous equilibrium in all four markets (Walras) 25
South Seas bubble 87, 172, 314, 413
Sovereign debt, supply and demand 327, 411, 415–420, 424
Static stability, positive, neutral, negative 41, 72–76, 78, 86–88, 108, 110, 141, 142
Stationarity 91, 92, 127, 144, 170, 197, 285, 286, 360
Stock-flow comparisons 20, 222, 224, 237, 253–255, 268, 292, 294, 422
Stories as a frame 45
Stronger demand 99, 150, 189, 199, 287
Structural break 8–10, 32, 39, 41–43, 49, 53, 57–59, 64, 73, 75, 91, 92, 102, 110, 116, 127, 130, 131, 148, 149, 151, 154, 157, 170, 171, 176, 186, 190, 193, 197, 200, 212, 221, 224, 235, 237, 248, 271, 281–283, 285, 286, 291, 293, 296, 297, 305, 350, 356, 359, 360, 378, 383
Swiss franc/U.S. dollar exchange rate 322, 339

T

Tax Cuts and Jobs Act of 2017 390
Tax Reform Act of 1986 296
Taylor rule 171

Tensile strength 266
Ten-year high-quality corporate bond rate 230, 388
Ten year to two year yield curve 166, 319
Terming out 246
Term premium 154, 173, 425–428
There is no alternative (TINA) 151, 173, 276, 420
Three-month T-bill rate 139
Three sources of disturbance 325
Tighter auto loan standards 61, 185, 191, 198, 202
Time inconsistency 120, 228, 297, 368
Tobin Q ratio, corporate equity relative to net worth 255, 262
Trade balance 310, 319, 321, 327–329, 360
Trade-weighted dollar 10, 114, 271, 335, 337, 353, 376, 380, 398, 411, 436
Transcontinental Railroad 1, 216, 251
Treasury August 2011 S&P downgrade 119, 435
Treasury International Capital (TIC) reports 421, 422
Treaty of Versailles 403, 408
Trend, cycle 1–3, 39, 42, 54, 55, 76, 80, 83, 86, 88, 100, 121, 123, 192, 194, 215, 222, 240, 245, 248, 266, 268, 287, 361
Trend, cycle, structural break 41, 49, 53, 200, 235, 281, 282, 286, 350

U

Uncertainty of credit allocation in the context of no model for policy or negative rates 12, 37, 145, 147, 150, 153, 156, 157,

160, 162, 169, 210, 211, 213, 308
Unicorn IPOs 358
Unit labor costs 90, 242, 265, 352, 361, 363–367, 383, 386
Unrevised data—market prices 104
U.S. Default 407
Usury ceilings 295

V

Virginia Company 358

W

Weighted average maturity of new car loans 288
Weimar Republic 403, 404
West Texas Intermediate (WTI) 73, 105, 110, 120, 124, 131, 248
Works in theory, works in practice 113

Y

Yen/U.S. dollar exchange rate 10, 120, 129, 134, 162, 175, 319, 336, 435

Printed by Printforce, United Kingdom